Chemistry: Atoms First

Volume 1

Chapters 1–11

ISBN: 978-1-50669-808-3
(Volume 1 of 2)

4750 Venture Drive
Ann Arbor, MI 48108
800-562-2147
www.xanedu.com

Chemistry: Atoms First

SENIOR CONTRIBUTING AUTHORS

EDWARD J. NETH, UNIVERSITY OF CONNECTICUT

PAUL FLOWERS, UNIVERSITY OF NORTH CAROLINA AT PEMBROKE

KLAUS THEOPOLD, UNIVERSITY OF DELAWARE

RICHARD LANGLEY, STEPHEN F. AUSTIN STATE UNIVERSITY

WILLIAM R. ROBINSON, PHD

OpenStax
Rice University
6100 Main Street MS-375
Houston, Texas 77005

To learn more about OpenStax, visit http://openstax.org.
Individual print copies and bulk orders can be purchased through our website.

ISBN-10   1-938168-15-1

ISBN-13   978-1-938168-15-4

Revision   CAF-2016-001(03/17)-LC

OpenStax

OpenStax is a non-profit organization committed to improving student access to quality learning materials. Our free textbooks are developed and peer-reviewed by educators to ensure they are readable, accurate, and meet the scope and sequence requirements of modern college courses. Through our partnerships with companies and foundations committed to reducing costs for students, OpenStax is working to improve access to higher education for all.

OpenStax CNX

The technology platform supporting OpenStax is OpenStax CNX (http://cnx.org), one of the world's first and largest open-education projects. OpenStax CNX provides students with free online and low-cost print editions of the OpenStax library and provides instructors with tools to customize the content so that they can have the perfect book for their course.

Rice University

OpenStax and OpenStax CNX are initiatives of Rice University. As a leading research university with a distinctive commitment to undergraduate education, Rice University aspires to path-breaking research, unsurpassed teaching, and contributions to the betterment of our world. It seeks to fulfill this mission by cultivating a diverse community of learning and discovery that produces leaders across the spectrum of human endeavor.

Foundation Support

OpenStax is grateful for the tremendous support of our sponsors. Without their strong engagement, the goal of free access to high-quality textbooks would remain just a dream.

Laura and John Arnold Foundation (LJAF) actively seeks opportunities to invest in organizations and thought leaders that have a sincere interest in implementing fundamental changes that not only yield immediate gains, but also repair broken systems for future generations. LJAF currently focuses its strategic investments on education, criminal justice, research integrity, and public accountability.

The William and Flora Hewlett Foundation has been making grants since 1967 to help solve social and environmental problems at home and around the world. The Foundation concentrates its resources on activities in education, the environment, global development and population, performing arts, and philanthropy, and makes grants to support disadvantaged communities in the San Francisco Bay Area.

Guided by the belief that every life has equal value, the Bill & Melinda Gates Foundation works to help all people lead healthy, productive lives. In developing countries, it focuses on improving people's health with vaccines and other life-saving tools and giving them the chance to lift themselves out of hunger and extreme poverty. In the United States, it seeks to significantly improve education so that all young people have the opportunity to reach their full potential. Based in Seattle, Washington, the foundation is led by CEO Jeff Raikes and Co-chair William H. Gates Sr., under the direction of Bill and Melinda Gates and Warren Buffett.

The Maxfield Foundation supports projects with potential for high impact in science, education, sustainability, and other areas of social importance.

Our mission at the Twenty Million Minds Foundation is to grow access and success by eliminating unnecessary hurdles to affordability. We support the creation, sharing, and proliferation of more effective, more affordable educational content by leveraging disruptive technologies, open educational resources, and new models for collaboration between for-profit, nonprofit, and public entities.

Table of Contents

Preface

Welcome to *Chemistry: Atoms First*, an OpenStax resource. This textbook was written to increase student access to high-quality learning materials, maintaining the highest standards of academic rigor at little or no cost.

About OpenStax

OpenStax is a nonprofit based at Rice University, and it's our mission to improve student access to education. Our first openly licensed college textbook was published in 2012 and our initiative has since scaled to over 20 books used by hundreds of thousands of students across the globe. Our adaptive learning technology, designed to improve learning outcomes through personalized educational paths, is currently being piloted for K–12 and college. The OpenStax mission is made possible through the generous support of philanthropic foundations. Through these partnerships and with the help of additional low-cost resources from our OpenStax Partners, OpenStax is breaking down the most common barriers to learning and empowering students and instructors to succeed.

About OpenStax's Resources

Customization

Chemistry: Atoms First is licensed under the Creative Commons Attribution 4.0 International (CC BY) license, which means you can distribute, remix, and build upon the content, as long as you credit OpenStax for the original creation. Because our books are openly licensed, you are free to use the entire book or pick and choose the sections that are most relevant to the needs of your course. Feel free to remix the content by assigning your students select chapters and sections in your syllabus in the order that you prefer. You can even provide a direct link in your syllabus to the sections in the web view of your book.

Errata

All OpenStax textbooks undergo a rigorous review process. However, like any professional-grade textbook, errors sometimes occur. Since our books are web-based, we can make updates periodically when deemed pedagogically necessary. If you have a correction to suggest, submit it through the link on your book page on openstax.org. All errata suggestions are reviewed by subject matter experts. OpenStax is committed to remaining transparent about all updates, so you will also find a list of past errata changes on your book page on openstax.org.

Format

You can access this textbook for free in web view or PDF through openstax.org, and in low-cost print.

About *Chemistry: Atoms First*

This text is an atoms-first adaptation of OpenStax *Chemistry*. The intention of "atoms-first" involves a few basic principles: first, it introduces atomic and molecular structure much earlier than the traditional approach, and it threads these themes through subsequent chapters. This approach may be chosen as a way to delay the introduction of material such as stoichiometry that students traditionally find abstract and difficult, thereby allowing students time to acclimate their study skills to chemistry. Additionally, it gives students a basis for understanding the application of quantitative principles to the chemistry that underlies the entire course. It also aims to center the study of chemistry on the atomic foundation that many will expand upon in a later course covering organic chemistry, easing that transition when the time arrives.

Coverage and Scope

In *Chemistry: Atoms First* , we strive to make chemistry, as a discipline, interesting and accessible to students. With this objective in mind, the content of this textbook has been developed and arranged to provide a logical progression from fundamental to more advanced concepts of chemical science. All of the material included in a traditional general chemistry course is here. It has been reorganized in an atoms-first approach and, where necessary, new material has been added to allow for continuity and to improve the flow of topics. The text can be used for a traditional two-semester introduction to chemistry or for a three-semester introduction, an approach becoming more common at many institutions. The goal is to provide a progressive, graduated introduction to chemistry that focuses on the fundamentally atom-focused nature of the subject. Topics are introduced within the context of familiar experiences whenever possible, treated with an appropriate rigor to satisfy the intellect of the learner, and reinforced in subsequent discussions of related content. The organization and pedagogical features were developed and vetted with feedback from chemistry educators dedicated to the project.

Chapter 1: Essential Ideas

Chapter 2: Atoms, Molecules, and Ions

Chapter 3: Electronic Structure and Periodic Properties of Elements

Chapter 4: Chemical Bonding and Molecular Geometry

Chapter 5: Advanced Theories of Bonding

Chapter 6: Composition of Substances and Solutions

Chapter 7: Stoichiometry of Chemical Reactions

Chapter 8: Gases

Chapter 9: Thermochemistry

Chapter 10: Liquids and Solids

Chapter 11: Solutions and Colloids

Chapter 12: Thermodynamics

Chapter 13: Fundamental Equilibrium Concepts

Chapter 14: Acid-Base Equilibria

Chapter 15: Equilibria of Other Reaction Classes

Chapter 16: Electrochemistry

Chapter 17: Kinetics

Chapter 18: Representative Metals, Metalloids, and Nonmetals

Chapter 19: Transition Metals and Coordination Chemistry

Chapter 20: Nuclear Chemistry

Chapter 21: Organic Chemistry

Partnership with University of Connecticut and UConn Undergraduate Student Government

Chemistry: Atoms First is a peer-reviewed, openly licensed introductory textbook produced through a collaborative publishing partnership between OpenStax and the University of Connecticut and UConn Undergraduate Student Government Association.

Pedagogical Foundation

Throughout *Chemistry: Atoms First*, you will find features that draw the students into scientific inquiry by taking selected topics a step further. Students and educators alike will appreciate discussions in these feature boxes.

Chemistry in Everyday Life ties chemistry concepts to everyday issues and real-world applications of science that students encounter in their lives. Topics include cell phones, solar thermal energy power plants, plastics recycling, and measuring blood pressure.

How Sciences Interconnect feature boxes discuss chemistry in context of its interconnectedness with other scientific disciplines. Topics include neurotransmitters, greenhouse gases and climate change, and proteins and enzymes.

Portrait of a Chemist features present a short bio and an introduction to the work of prominent figures from history and present day so that students can see the "face" of contributors in this field as well as science in action.

Comprehensive Art Program

Our art program is designed to enhance students' understanding of concepts through clear, effective illustrations, diagrams, and photographs.

(a)　　　　　(b)　　　　　(c)　　　　　(d)　　　　　(e)

A very small number of α particles are significantly deflected

A few α particles are slightly deflected

Most α particles pass straight through foil

Beam of α particles

Radium source of α particles

Luminescent screen to detect scattered α particles

Thin gold foil

HCl(g)

H₂O(l)

HCl(g) → HCl(aq)

(a)

Cl⁻(aq)

H₂O(l)

H₃O⁺(aq)

HCl(aq) + H₂O(l) → H₃O⁺(aq) + Cl⁻(aq)

(b)

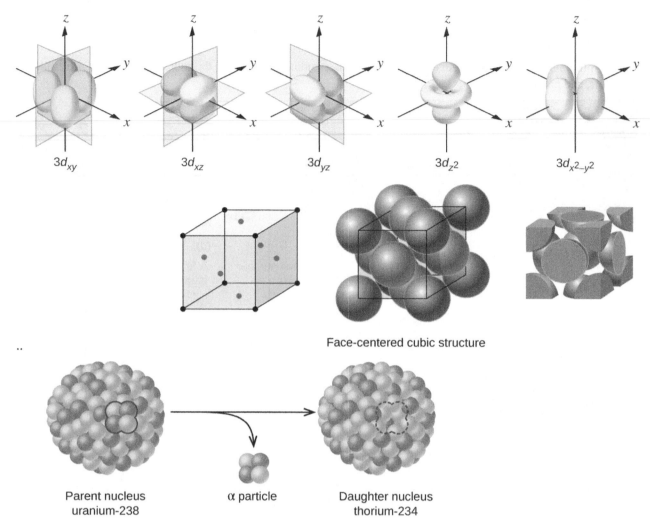

$3d_{xy}$ $3d_{xz}$ $3d_{yz}$ $3d_{z^2}$ $3d_{x^2-y^2}$

Face-centered cubic structure

Parent nucleus
uranium-238

α particle

Daughter nucleus
thorium-234

Interactives That Engage

Chemistry: Atoms First incorporates links to relevant interactive exercises and animations that help bring topics to life through our **Link to Learning** feature. Examples include:

    PhET simulations

    IUPAC data and interactives

    TED talks

Assessments That Reinforce Key Concepts

In-chapter **Examples** walk students through problems by posing a question, stepping out a solution, and then asking students to practice the skill with a "Check Your Learning" component. The book also includes assessments at the end of each chapter so students can apply what they've learned through practice problems.

Additional Resources
Student and Instructor Resources

We've compiled additional resources for both students and instructors, including Getting Started Guides, PowerPoint slides, and an instructor answer guide. Instructor resources require a verified instructor account, which can be requested on your openstax.org log-in. Take advantage of these resources to supplement your OpenStax book.

Partner Resources

OpenStax partners are our allies in the mission to make high-quality learning materials affordable and accessible to students and instructors everywhere. Their tools integrate seamlessly with our OpenStax titles at a low cost. To access the partner resources for your text, visit your book page on openstax.org.

About the University of Connecticut

The University of Connecticut is one of the top public research universities in the nation, with more than 30,000 students pursuing answers to critical questions in labs, lecture halls, and the community. Knowledge exploration throughout the University's network of campuses is united by a culture of innovation. An unprecedented commitment from the state of Connecticut ensures UConn attracts internationally renowned faculty and the world's brightest students. A tradition of coaching winning athletes makes UConn a standout in Division 1 sports and fuels our academic spirit. As a vibrant, progressive leader, UConn fosters a diverse and dynamic culture that meets the challenges of a changing global society.

About Our Team
Senior Contributing Authors

Paul Flowers, University of North Carolina–Pembroke
Dr. Paul Flowers earned a BS in Chemistry from St. Andrews Presbyterian College in 1983 and a PhD in Analytical Chemistry from the University of Tennessee in 1988. After a one-year postdoctoral appointment at Los Alamos National Laboratory, he joined the University of North Carolina–Pembroke in the fall of 1989. Dr. Flowers teaches courses in general and analytical chemistry, and conducts experimental research involving the development of new devices and methods for microscale chemical analysis.

Klaus Theopold, University of Delaware
Dr. Klaus Theopold (born in Berlin, Germany) received his Vordiplom from the Universität Hamburg in 1977. He then decided to pursue his graduate studies in the United States, where he received his PhD in inorganic chemistry from UC Berkeley in 1982. After a year of postdoctoral research at MIT, he joined the faculty at Cornell University. In 1990, he moved to the University of Delaware, where he is a Professor in the Department of Chemistry and Biochemistry and serves as an Associate Director of the University's Center for Catalytic Science and Technology. Dr. Theopold regularly teaches graduate courses in inorganic and organometallic chemistry as well as General Chemistry.

Richard Langley, Stephen F. Austin State University
Dr. Richard Langley earned BS degrees in Chemistry and Mineralogy from Miami University of Ohio in the early 1970s and went on to receive his PhD in Chemistry from the University of Nebraska in 1977. After a postdoctoral fellowship at the Arizona State University Center for Solid State Studies, Dr. Langley taught in the University of Wisconsin system and participated in research at Argonne National Laboratory. Moving to Stephen F. Austin State University in 1982, Dr. Langley today serves as Professor of Chemistry. His areas of specialization are solid state chemistry, synthetic inorganic chemistry, fluorine chemistry, and chemical education.

Edward J. Neth, University of Connecticut (*Chemistry: Atoms First*)
Dr. Edward J. Neth earned his BS in Chemistry (minor in Politics) at Fairfield University in 1985 and his MS (1988) and PhD (1995; Inorganic/Materials Chemistry) at the University of Connecticut. He joined the University of Connecticut in 2004 as a lecturer and currently teaches general and inorganic chemistry; his background includes having worked as a network engineer in both corporate and university settings, and he has served as Director of Academic Computing at New Haven University. He currently teaches a three-semester, introductory chemistry sequence at UConn and is involved with training and coordinating teaching assistants.

William R. Robinson, PhD

Contributing Authors

Mark Blaser, Shasta College

Simon Bott, University of Houston
Donald Carpenetti, Craven Community College
Andrew Eklund, Alfred University
Emad El-Giar, University of Louisiana at Monroe
Don Frantz, Wilfrid Laurier University
Paul Hooker, Westminster College
Jennifer Look, Mercer University
George Kaminski, Worcester Polytechnic Institute
Carol Martinez, Central New Mexico Community College
Troy Milliken, Jackson State University
Vicki Moravec, Trine University
Jason Powell, Ferrum College
Thomas Sorensen, University of Wisconsin–Milwaukee
Allison Soult, University of Kentucky

Reviewers

Casey Akin, College Station Independent School District
Lara AL-Hariri, University of Massachusetts–Amherst
Sahar Atwa, University of Louisiana at Monroe
Todd Austell, University of North Carolina–Chapel Hill
Bobby Bailey, University of Maryland–University College
Robert Baker, Trinity College
Jeffrey Bartz, Kalamazoo College
Greg Baxley, Cuesta College
Ashley Beasley Green, National Institute of Standards and Technology
Patricia Bianconi, University of Massachusetts
Lisa Blank, Lyme Central School District
Daniel Branan, Colorado Community College System
Dorian Canelas, Duke University
Emmanuel Chang, York College
Carolyn Collins, College of Southern Nevada
Colleen Craig, University of Washington
Yasmine Daniels, Montgomery College–Germantown
Patricia Dockham, Grand Rapids Community College
Erick Fuoco, Richard J. Daley College
Andrea Geyer, University of Saint Francis
Daniel Goebbert, University of Alabama
John Goodwin, Coastal Carolina University
Stephanie Gould, Austin College
Patrick Holt, Bellarmine University
Kevin Kolack, Queensborough Community College
Amy Kovach, Roberts Wesleyan College
Judit Kovacs Beagle, University of Dayton
Krzysztof Kuczera, University of Kansas
Marcus Lay, University of Georgia
Pamela Lord, University of Saint Francis
Oleg Maksimov, Excelsior College
John Matson, Virginia Tech
Katrina Miranda, University of Arizona
Douglas Mulford, Emory University
Mark Ott, Jackson College

Adrienne Oxley, Columbia College

Richard Pennington, Georgia Gwinnett College

Rodney Powell, Coastal Carolina Community College

Jeanita Pritchett, Montgomery College–Rockville

Aheda Saber, University of Illinois at Chicago

Raymond Sadeghi, University of Texas at San Antonio

Nirmala Shankar, Rutgers University

Jonathan Smith, Temple University

Bryan Spiegelberg, Rider University

Ron Sternfels, Roane State Community College

Cynthia Strong, Cornell College

Kris Varazo, Francis Marion University

Victor Vilchiz, Virginia State University

Alex Waterson, Vanderbilt University

Juchao Yan, Eastern New Mexico University

Mustafa Yatin, Salem State University

Kazushige Yokoyama, State University of New York at Geneseo

Curtis Zaleski, Shippensburg University

Wei Zhang, University of Colorado–Boulder

Chapter 1

Essential Ideas

Figure 1.1 Chemical substances and processes are essential for our existence, providing sustenance, keeping us clean and healthy, fabricating electronic devices, enabling transportation, and much more. (credit "left": modification of work by "vxla"/Flickr; credit "left middle": modification of work by "the Italian voice"/Flickr; credit "right middle": modification of work by Jason Trim; credit "right": modification of work by "gosheshe"/Flickr)

Chapter Outline

1.1 Chemistry in Context

1.2 Phases and Classification of Matter

1.3 Physical and Chemical Properties

1.4 Measurements

1.5 Measurement Uncertainty, Accuracy, and Precision

1.6 Mathematical Treatment of Measurement Results

Introduction

Your alarm goes off and, after hitting "snooze" once or twice, you pry yourself out of bed. You make a cup of coffee to help you get going, and then you shower, get dressed, eat breakfast, and check your phone for messages. On your way to school, you stop to fill your car's gas tank, almost making you late for the first day of chemistry class. As you find a seat in the classroom, you read the question projected on the screen: "Welcome to class! Why should we study chemistry?"

Do you have an answer? You may be studying chemistry because it fulfills an academic requirement, but if you consider your daily activities, you might find chemistry interesting for other reasons. Most everything you do and encounter during your day involves chemistry. Making coffee, cooking eggs, and toasting bread involve chemistry. The products you use—like soap and shampoo, the fabrics you wear, the electronics that keep you connected to your world, the gasoline that propels your car—all of these and more involve chemical substances and processes. Whether you are aware or not, chemistry is part of your everyday world. In this course, you will learn many of the essential principles underlying the chemistry of modern-day life.

1.1 Chemistry in Context

By the end of this module, you will be able to:

- Outline the historical development of chemistry
- Provide examples of the importance of chemistry in everyday life
- Describe the scientific method
- Differentiate among hypotheses, theories, and laws
- Provide examples illustrating macroscopic, microscopic, and symbolic domains

Throughout human history, people have tried to convert matter into more useful forms. Our Stone Age ancestors chipped pieces of flint into useful tools and carved wood into statues and toys. These endeavors involved changing the shape of a substance without changing the substance itself. But as our knowledge increased, humans began to change the composition of the substances as well—clay was converted into pottery, hides were cured to make garments, copper ores were transformed into copper tools and weapons, and grain was made into bread.

Humans began to practice chemistry when they learned to control fire and use it to cook, make pottery, and smelt metals. Subsequently, they began to separate and use specific components of matter. A variety of drugs such as aloe, myrrh, and opium were isolated from plants. Dyes, such as indigo and Tyrian purple, were extracted from plant and animal matter. Metals were combined to form alloys—for example, copper and tin were mixed together to make bronze—and more elaborate smelting techniques produced iron. Alkalis were extracted from ashes, and soaps were prepared by combining these alkalis with fats. Alcohol was produced by fermentation and purified by distillation.

Attempts to understand the behavior of matter extend back for more than 2500 years. As early as the sixth century BC, Greek philosophers discussed a system in which water was the basis of all things. You may have heard of the Greek postulate that matter consists of four elements: earth, air, fire, and water. Subsequently, an amalgamation of chemical technologies and philosophical speculations were spread from Egypt, China, and the eastern Mediterranean by alchemists, who endeavored to transform "base metals" such as lead into "noble metals" like gold, and to create elixirs to cure disease and extend life (Figure 1.2).

Figure 1.2 This portrayal shows an alchemist's workshop circa 1580. Although alchemy made some useful contributions to how to manipulate matter, it was not scientific by modern standards. (credit: Chemical Heritage Foundation)

From alchemy came the historical progressions that led to modern chemistry: the isolation of drugs from natural sources, metallurgy, and the dye industry. Today, chemistry continues to deepen our understanding and improve our ability to harness and control the behavior of matter. This effort has been so successful that many people do not realize either the central position of chemistry among the sciences or the importance and universality of chemistry in daily life.

Chemistry: The Central Science

Chemistry is sometimes referred to as "the central science" due to its interconnectedness with a vast array of other STEM disciplines (STEM stands for areas of study in the science, technology, engineering, and math fields). Chemistry and the language of chemists play vital roles in biology, medicine, materials science, forensics, environmental science, and many other fields (Figure 1.3). The basic principles of physics are essential for understanding many aspects of chemistry, and there is extensive overlap between many subdisciplines within the two fields, such as chemical physics and nuclear chemistry. Mathematics, computer science, and information theory provide important tools that help us calculate, interpret, describe, and generally make sense of the chemical world. Biology and chemistry converge in biochemistry, which is crucial to understanding the many complex factors and processes that keep living organisms (such as us) alive. Chemical engineering, materials science, and nanotechnology combine chemical principles and empirical findings to produce useful substances, ranging from gasoline to fabrics to electronics. Agriculture, food science, veterinary science, and brewing and wine making help provide sustenance in the form of food and drink to the world's population. Medicine, pharmacology, biotechnology, and botany identify and produce substances that help keep us healthy. Environmental science, geology, oceanography, and atmospheric science incorporate many chemical ideas to help us better understand and protect our physical world. Chemical ideas are used to help understand the universe in astronomy and cosmology.

Figure 1.3 Knowledge of chemistry is central to understanding a wide range of scientific disciplines. This diagram shows just some of the interrelationships between chemistry and other fields.

What are some changes in matter that are essential to daily life? Digesting and assimilating food, synthesizing polymers that are used to make clothing, containers, cookware, and credit cards, and refining crude oil into gasoline and other products are just a few examples. As you proceed through this course, you will discover many different examples of changes in the composition and structure of matter, how to classify these changes and how they occurred, their causes, the changes in energy that accompany them, and the principles and laws involved. As you learn about these things, you will be learning **chemistry**, the study of the composition, properties, and interactions of matter. The practice of chemistry is not limited to chemistry books or laboratories: It happens whenever someone is involved in changes in matter or in conditions that may lead to such changes.

The Scientific Method

Chemistry is a science based on observation and experimentation. Doing chemistry involves attempting to answer questions and explain observations in terms of the laws and theories of chemistry, using procedures that are accepted by the scientific community. There is no single route to answering a question or explaining an observation, but there is an aspect common to every approach: Each uses knowledge based on experiments that can be reproduced to verify the results. Some routes involve a **hypothesis**, a tentative explanation of observations that acts as a guide for gathering and checking information. We test a hypothesis by experimentation, calculation, and/or comparison with the experiments of others and then refine it as needed.

Some hypotheses are attempts to explain the behavior that is summarized in laws. The **laws** of science summarize a vast number of experimental observations, and describe or predict some facet of the natural world. If such a hypothesis turns out to be capable of explaining a large body of experimental data, it can reach the status of a theory. Scientific **theories** are well-substantiated, comprehensive, testable explanations of particular aspects of nature. Theories are accepted because they provide satisfactory explanations, but they can be modified if new data become available. The path of discovery that leads from question and observation to law or hypothesis to theory, combined with experimental verification of the hypothesis and any necessary modification of the theory, is called the **scientific method** (Figure 1.4).

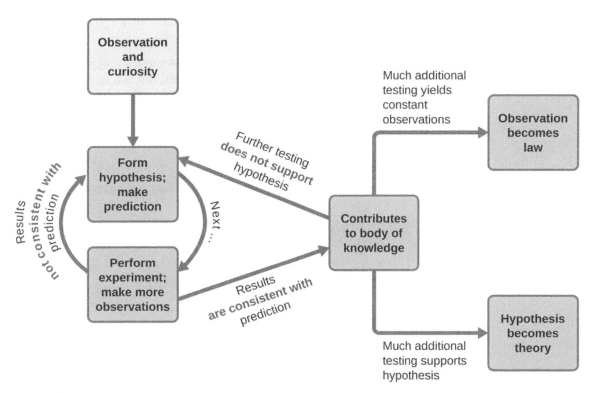

Figure 1.4 The scientific method follows a process similar to the one shown in this diagram. All the key components are shown, in roughly the right order. Scientific progress is seldom neat and clean: It requires open inquiry and the reworking of questions and ideas in response to findings.

The Domains of Chemistry

Chemists study and describe the behavior of matter and energy in three different domains: macroscopic, microscopic, and symbolic. These domains provide different ways of considering and describing chemical behavior.

Macro is a Greek word that means "large." The **macroscopic domain** is familiar to us: It is the realm of everyday things that are large enough to be sensed directly by human sight or touch. In daily life, this includes the food you eat and the breeze you feel on your face. The macroscopic domain includes everyday and laboratory chemistry, where we observe and measure physical and chemical properties, or changes such as density, solubility, and flammability.

The **microscopic domain** of chemistry is almost always visited in the imagination. *Micro* also comes from Greek and means "small." Some aspects of the microscopic domains are visible through a microscope, such as a magnified image of graphite or bacteria. Viruses, for instance, are too small to be seen with the naked eye, but when we're suffering from a cold, we're reminded of how real they are.

However, most of the subjects in the microscopic domain of chemistry—such as atoms and molecules—are too small to be seen even with standard microscopes and often must be pictured in the mind. Other components of the microscopic domain include ions and electrons, protons and neutrons, and chemical bonds, each of which is far too small to see. This domain includes the individual metal atoms in a wire, the ions that compose a salt crystal, the changes in individual molecules that result in a color change, the conversion of nutrient molecules into tissue and energy, and the evolution of heat as bonds that hold atoms together are created.

The **symbolic domain** contains the specialized language used to represent components of the macroscopic and microscopic domains. Chemical symbols (such as those used in the periodic table), chemical formulas, and chemical equations are part of the symbolic domain, as are graphs and drawings. We can also consider calculations as part of the symbolic domain. These symbols play an important role in chemistry because they help interpret the behavior of the macroscopic domain in terms of the components of the microscopic domain. One of the challenges for students learning chemistry is recognizing that the same symbols can represent different things in the macroscopic and microscopic domains, and one of the features that makes chemistry fascinating is the use of a domain that must be imagined to explain behavior in a domain that can be observed.

A helpful way to understand the three domains is via the essential and ubiquitous substance of water. That water is a liquid at moderate temperatures, will freeze to form a solid at lower temperatures, and boil to form a gas at higher temperatures (Figure 1.5) are macroscopic observations. But some properties of water fall into the microscopic domain—what we cannot observe with the naked eye. The description of water as comprised of two hydrogen atoms and one oxygen atom, and the explanation of freezing and boiling in terms of attractions between these molecules, is within the microscopic arena. The formula H_2O, which can describe water at either the macroscopic or microscopic levels, is an example of the symbolic domain. The abbreviations (g) for gas, (s) for solid, and (l) for liquid are also symbolic.

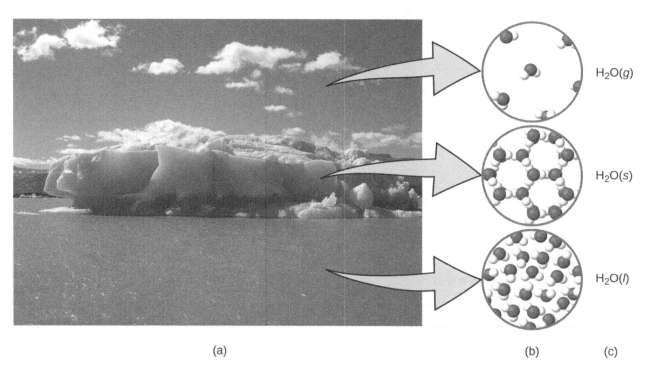

(a)   (b)   (c)

Figure 1.5 (a) Moisture in the air, icebergs, and the ocean represent water in the macroscopic domain. (b) At the molecular level (microscopic domain), gas molecules are far apart and disorganized, solid water molecules are close together and organized, and liquid molecules are close together and disorganized. (c) The formula H_2O symbolizes water, and (g), (s), and (l) symbolize its phases. Note that clouds are actually comprised of either very small liquid water droplets or solid water crystals; gaseous water in our atmosphere is not visible to the naked eye, although it may be sensed as humidity. (credit a: modification of work by "Gorkaazk"/Wikimedia Commons)

1.2 Phases and Classification of Matter

By the end of this section, you will be able to:

- Describe the basic properties of each physical state of matter: solid, liquid, and gas
- Define and give examples of atoms and molecules
- Classify matter as an element, compound, homogeneous mixture, or heterogeneous mixture with regard to its physical state and composition
- Distinguish between mass and weight
- Apply the law of conservation of matter

Matter is defined as anything that occupies space and has mass, and it is all around us. Solids and liquids are more obviously matter: We can see that they take up space, and their weight tells us that they have mass. Gases are also matter; if gases did not take up space, a balloon would stay collapsed rather than inflate when filled with gas.

Solids, liquids, and gases are the three states of matter commonly found on earth (Figure 1.6). A **solid** is rigid and possesses a definite shape. A **liquid** flows and takes the shape of a container, except that it forms a flat or slightly curved upper surface when acted upon by gravity. (In zero gravity, liquids assume a spherical shape.) Both liquid and solid samples have volumes that are very nearly independent of pressure. A **gas** takes both the shape and volume of its container.

Solid

Has fixed shape and volume

Liquid

Takes shape of container
Forms horizontal surface
Has fixed volume

Gas

Expands to fill container

Figure 1.6   The three most common states or phases of matter are solid, liquid, and gas.

A fourth state of matter, plasma, occurs naturally in the interiors of stars. A **plasma** is a gaseous state of matter that contains appreciable numbers of electrically charged particles (Figure 1.7). The presence of these charged particles imparts unique properties to plasmas that justify their classification as a state of matter distinct from gases. In addition to stars, plasmas are found in some other high-temperature environments (both natural and man-made), such as lightning strikes, certain television screens, and specialized analytical instruments used to detect trace amounts of metals.

Figure 1.7   A plasma torch can be used to cut metal. (credit: "Hypertherm"/Wikimedia Commons)

Link to Learning

In a tiny cell in a plasma television, the plasma emits ultraviolet light, which in turn causes the display at that location to appear a specific color. The composite of these tiny dots of color makes up the image that you see. Watch this **video (http://openstaxcollege.org/l/16plasma)** to learn more about plasma and the places you encounter it.

Some samples of matter appear to have properties of solids, liquids, and/or gases at the same time. This can occur when the sample is composed of many small pieces. For example, we can pour sand as if it were a liquid because it is composed of many small grains of solid sand. Matter can also have properties of more than one state when it is a mixture, such as with clouds. Clouds appear to behave somewhat like gases, but they are actually mixtures of air (gas) and tiny particles of water (liquid or solid).

The **mass** of an object is a measure of the amount of matter in it. One way to measure an object's mass is to measure the force it takes to accelerate the object. It takes much more force to accelerate a car than a bicycle because the car has much more mass. A more common way to determine the mass of an object is to use a balance to compare its mass with a standard mass.

Although weight is related to mass, it is not the same thing. **Weight** refers to the force that gravity exerts on an object. This force is directly proportional to the mass of the object. The weight of an object changes as the force of gravity changes, but its mass does not. An astronaut's mass does not change just because she goes to the moon. But her weight on the moon is only one-sixth her earth-bound weight because the moon's gravity is only one-sixth that of the earth's. She may feel "weightless" during her trip when she experiences negligible external forces (gravitational or any other), although she is, of course, never "massless."

The **law of conservation of matter** summarizes many scientific observations about matter: It states that *there is no detectable change in the total quantity of matter present when matter converts from one type to another (a chemical change) or changes among solid, liquid, or gaseous states (a physical change).* Brewing beer and the operation of batteries provide examples of the conservation of matter (**Figure 1.8**). During the brewing of beer, the ingredients (water, yeast, grains, malt, hops, and sugar) are converted into beer (water, alcohol, carbonation, and flavoring substances) with no actual loss of substance. This is most clearly seen during the bottling process, when glucose turns into ethanol and carbon dioxide, and the total mass of the substances does not change. This can also be seen in a lead-acid car battery: The original substances (lead, lead oxide, and sulfuric acid), which are capable of producing electricity, are changed into other substances (lead sulfate and water) that do not produce electricity, with no change in the actual amount of matter.

Figure 1.8 (a) The mass of beer precursor materials is the same as the mass of beer produced: Sugar has become alcohol and carbonation. (b) The mass of the lead, lead oxide plates, and sulfuric acid that goes into the production of electricity is exactly equal to the mass of lead sulfate and water that is formed.

Although this conservation law holds true for all conversions of matter, convincing examples are few and far between because, outside of the controlled conditions in a laboratory, we seldom collect all of the material that is produced during a particular conversion. For example, when you eat, digest, and assimilate food, all of the matter in the original food is preserved. But because some of the matter is incorporated into your body, and much is excreted as various types of waste, it is challenging to verify by measurement.

Atoms and Molecules

An **atom** is the smallest particle of an element that has the properties of that element and can enter into a chemical combination. Consider the element gold, for example. Imagine cutting a gold nugget in half, then cutting one of the halves in half, and repeating this process until a piece of gold remained that was so small that it could not be cut in half (regardless of how tiny your knife may be). This minimally sized piece of gold is an atom (from the Greek *atomos*, meaning "indivisible") (**Figure 1.9**). This atom would no longer be gold if it were divided any further.

(a)   (b)

Figure 1.9   (a) This photograph shows a gold nugget. (b) A scanning-tunneling microscope (STM) can generate views of the surfaces of solids, such as this image of a gold crystal. Each sphere represents one gold atom. (credit a: modification of work by United States Geological Survey; credit b: modification of work by "Erwinrossen"/Wikimedia Commons)

The first suggestion that matter is composed of atoms is attributed to the Greek philosophers Leucippus and Democritus, who developed their ideas in the 5th century BCE. However, it was not until the early nineteenth century that John Dalton (1766–1844), a British schoolteacher with a keen interest in science, supported this hypothesis with quantitative measurements. Since that time, repeated experiments have confirmed many aspects of this hypothesis, and it has become one of the central theories of chemistry. Other aspects of Dalton's atomic theory are still used but with minor revisions (details of Dalton's theory are provided in the chapter on atoms and molecules).

An atom is so small that its size is difficult to imagine. One of the smallest things we can see with our unaided eye is a single thread of a spider web: These strands are about 1/10,000 of a centimeter (0.0001 cm) in diameter. Although the cross-section of one strand is almost impossible to see without a microscope, it is huge on an atomic scale. A single carbon atom in the web has a diameter of about 0.000000015 centimeter, and it would take about 7000 carbon atoms to span the diameter of the strand. To put this in perspective, if a carbon atom were the size of a dime, the cross-section of one strand would be larger than a football field, which would require about 150 million carbon atom "dimes" to cover it. (Figure 1.10) shows increasingly close microscopic and atomic-level views of ordinary cotton.

(a)   (b)   (c)   (d)   (e)

Figure 1.10   These images provide an increasingly closer view: (a) a cotton boll, (b) a single cotton fiber viewed under an optical microscope (magnified 40 times), (c) an image of a cotton fiber obtained with an electron microscope (much higher magnification than with the optical microscope); and (d and e) atomic-level models of the fiber (spheres of different colors represent atoms of different elements). (credit c: modification of work by "Featheredtar"/Wikimedia Commons)

An atom is so light that its mass is also difficult to imagine. A billion lead atoms (1,000,000,000 atoms) weigh about 3×10^{-13} grams, a mass that is far too light to be weighed on even the world's most sensitive balances. It would require over 300,000,000,000,000 lead atoms (300 trillion, or 3×10^{14}) to be weighed, and they would weigh only 0.0000001 gram.

It is rare to find collections of individual atoms. Only a few elements, such as the gases helium, neon, and argon, consist of a collection of individual atoms that move about independently of one another. Other elements, such as the gases hydrogen, nitrogen, oxygen, and chlorine, are composed of units that consist of pairs of atoms (Figure 1.11). One form of the element phosphorus consists of units composed of four phosphorus atoms. The element sulfur exists in various forms, one of which consists of units composed of eight sulfur atoms. These units are called molecules. A **molecule** consists of two or more atoms joined by strong forces called chemical bonds. The atoms in a molecule move around as a unit, much like the cans of soda in a six-pack or a bunch of keys joined together on a single key ring. A molecule may consist of two or more identical atoms, as in the molecules found in the elements hydrogen, oxygen, and sulfur, or it may consist of two or more different atoms, as in the molecules found in water. Each water molecule is a unit that contains two hydrogen atoms and one oxygen atom. Each glucose molecule is a unit that contains 6 carbon atoms, 12 hydrogen atoms, and 6 oxygen atoms. Like atoms, molecules are incredibly small and light. If an ordinary glass of water were enlarged to the size of the earth, the water molecules inside it would be about the size of golf balls.

Figure 1.11   The elements hydrogen, oxygen, phosphorus, and sulfur form molecules consisting of two or more atoms of the same element. The compounds water, carbon dioxide, and glucose consist of combinations of atoms of different elements.

Classifying Matter

We can classify matter into several categories. Two broad categories are mixtures and pure substances. A **pure substance** has a constant composition. All specimens of a pure substance have exactly the same makeup and properties. Any sample of sucrose (table sugar) consists of 42.1% carbon, 6.5% hydrogen, and 51.4% oxygen by mass. Any sample of sucrose also has the same physical properties, such as melting point, color, and sweetness, regardless of the source from which it is isolated.

We can divide pure substances into two classes: elements and compounds. Pure substances that cannot be broken down into simpler substances by chemical changes are called **elements**. Iron, silver, gold, aluminum, sulfur, oxygen, and copper are familiar examples of the more than 100 known elements, of which about 90 occur naturally on the earth, and two dozen or so have been created in laboratories.

Pure substances that can be broken down by chemical changes are called **compounds**. This breakdown may produce either elements or other compounds, or both. Mercury(II) oxide, an orange, crystalline solid, can be broken down by heat into the elements mercury and oxygen (Figure 1.12). When heated in the absence of air, the compound sucrose is broken down into the element carbon and the compound water. (The initial stage of this process, when the sugar is turning brown, is known as caramelization—this is what imparts the characteristic sweet and nutty flavor to caramel apples, caramelized onions, and caramel). Silver(I) chloride is a white solid that can be broken down into its elements, silver and chlorine, by absorption of light. This property is the basis for the use of this compound in photographic films and photochromic eyeglasses (those with lenses that darken when exposed to light).

(a)

(b)

(c)

Figure 1.12 (a)The compound mercury(II) oxide, (b)when heated, (c) decomposes into silvery droplets of liquid mercury and invisible oxygen gas. (credit: modification of work by Paul Flowers)

Link to Learning

Many compounds break down when heated. This site (http://openstaxcollege.org/l/16mercury) shows the breakdown of mercury oxide, HgO. You can also view an example of the photochemical decomposition of silver chloride (http://openstaxcollege.org/l/16silvchloride) (AgCl), the basis of early photography.

The properties of combined elements are different from those in the free, or uncombined, state. For example, white crystalline sugar (sucrose) is a compound resulting from the chemical combination of the element carbon, which is a black solid in one of its uncombined forms, and the two elements hydrogen and oxygen, which are colorless gases when uncombined. Free sodium, an element that is a soft, shiny, metallic solid, and free chlorine, an element that is a yellow-green gas, combine to form sodium chloride (table salt), a compound that is a white, crystalline solid.

A **mixture** is composed of two or more types of matter that can be present in varying amounts and can be separated by physical changes, such as evaporation (you will learn more about this later). A mixture with a composition that varies from point to point is called a **heterogeneous mixture**. Italian dressing is an example of a heterogeneous mixture (Figure 1.13). Its composition can vary because we can make it from varying amounts of oil, vinegar, and herbs. It is not the same from point to point throughout the mixture—one drop may be mostly vinegar, whereas a different drop may be mostly oil or herbs because the oil and vinegar separate and the herbs settle. Other examples of heterogeneous mixtures are chocolate chip cookies (we can see the separate bits of chocolate, nuts, and cookie dough) and granite (we can see the quartz, mica, feldspar, and more).

A **homogeneous mixture**, also called a **solution**, exhibits a uniform composition and appears visually the same throughout. An example of a solution is a sports drink, consisting of water, sugar, coloring, flavoring, and electrolytes mixed together uniformly (Figure 1.13). Each drop of a sports drink tastes the same because each drop contains the same amounts of water, sugar, and other components. Note that the composition of a sports drink can vary—it could be made with somewhat more or less sugar, flavoring, or other components, and still be a sports drink. Other examples of homogeneous mixtures include air, maple syrup, gasoline, and a solution of salt in water.

(a)   (b)

Figure 1.13   (a) Oil and vinegar salad dressing is a heterogeneous mixture because its composition is not uniform throughout. (b) A commercial sports drink is a homogeneous mixture because its composition is uniform throughout. (credit a "left": modification of work by John Mayer; credit a "right": modification of work by Umberto Salvagnin; credit b "left: modification of work by Jeff Bedford)

Although there are just over 100 elements, tens of millions of chemical compounds result from different combinations of these elements. Each compound has a specific composition and possesses definite chemical and physical properties by which we can distinguish it from all other compounds. And, of course, there are innumerable ways to combine elements and compounds to form different mixtures. A summary of how to distinguish between the various major classifications of matter is shown in (Figure 1.14).

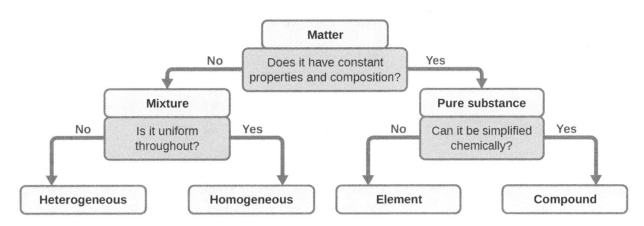

Figure 1.14   Depending on its properties, a given substance can be classified as a homogeneous mixture, a heterogeneous mixture, a compound, or an element.

Eleven elements make up about 99% of the earth's crust and atmosphere (Table 1.1). Oxygen constitutes nearly one-half and silicon about one-quarter of the total quantity of these elements. A majority of elements on earth are found in chemical combinations with other elements; about one-quarter of the elements are also found in the free state.

Elemental Composition of Earth

Element	Symbol	Percent Mass	Element	Symbol	Percent Mass
oxygen	O	49.20	chlorine	Cl	0.19
silicon	Si	25.67	phosphorus	P	0.11
aluminum	Al	7.50	manganese	Mn	0.09

Table 1.1

Elemental Composition of Earth

Element	Symbol	Percent Mass	Element	Symbol	Percent Mass
iron	Fe	4.71	carbon	C	0.08
calcium	Ca	3.39	sulfur	S	0.06
sodium	Na	2.63	barium	Ba	0.04
potassium	K	2.40	nitrogen	N	0.03
magnesium	Mg	1.93	fluorine	F	0.03
hydrogen	H	0.87	strontium	Sr	0.02
titanium	Ti	0.58	all others	-	0.47

Table 1.1

Chemistry in Everyday Life

Decomposition of Water / Production of Hydrogen

Water consists of the elements hydrogen and oxygen combined in a 2 to 1 ratio. Water can be broken down into hydrogen and oxygen gases by the addition of energy. One way to do this is with a battery or power supply, as shown in (Figure 1.15).

Figure 1.15 The decomposition of water is shown at the macroscopic, microscopic, and symbolic levels. The battery provides an electric current (microscopic) that decomposes water. At the macroscopic level, the liquid separates into the gases hydrogen (on the left) and oxygen (on the right). Symbolically, this change is presented by showing how liquid H_2O separates into H_2 and O_2 gases.

The breakdown of water involves a rearrangement of the atoms in water molecules into different molecules, each composed of two hydrogen atoms and two oxygen atoms, respectively. Two water molecules form one oxygen molecule and two hydrogen molecules. The representation for what occurs, $2H_2O(l) \longrightarrow 2H_2(g) + O_2(g)$, will be explored in more depth in later chapters.

The two gases produced have distinctly different properties. Oxygen is not flammable but is required for combustion of a fuel, and hydrogen is highly flammable and a potent energy source. How might this knowledge be applied in our world? One application involves research into more fuel-efficient transportation. Fuel-cell vehicles (FCV) run on hydrogen instead of gasoline (Figure 1.16). They are more efficient than vehicles with internal combustion engines, are nonpolluting, and reduce greenhouse gas emissions, making us less dependent on fossil fuels. FCVs are not yet economically viable, however, and current hydrogen production depends on natural gas. If we can develop a process to economically decompose water, or produce hydrogen in another environmentally sound way, FCVs may be the way of the future.

Figure 1.16 A fuel cell generates electrical energy from hydrogen and oxygen via an electrochemical process and produces only water as the waste product.

Chemistry in Everyday Life

Chemistry of Cell Phones

Imagine how different your life would be without cell phones (Figure 1.17) and other smart devices. Cell phones are made from numerous chemical substances, which are extracted, refined, purified, and assembled using an extensive and in-depth understanding of chemical principles. About 30% of the elements that are found in nature are found within a typical smart phone. The case/body/frame consists of a combination of sturdy, durable polymers comprised primarily of carbon, hydrogen, oxygen, and nitrogen [acrylonitrile butadiene styrene (ABS) and polycarbonate thermoplastics], and light, strong, structural metals, such as aluminum, magnesium, and iron. The display screen is made from a specially toughened glass (silica glass strengthened by the addition of aluminum, sodium, and potassium) and coated with a material to make it conductive (such as indium tin oxide). The circuit board uses a semiconductor material (usually silicon); commonly used metals like copper, tin, silver, and gold; and more unfamiliar elements such as yttrium, praseodymium, and gadolinium. The battery relies upon lithium ions and a variety of other materials, including iron, cobalt, copper, polyethylene oxide, and polyacrylonitrile.

Figure 1.17 Almost one-third of naturally occurring elements are used to make a cell phone. (credit: modification of work by John Taylor)

1.3 Physical and Chemical Properties

By the end of this section, you will be able to:

- Identify properties of and changes in matter as physical or chemical
- Identify properties of matter as extensive or intensive

The characteristics that enable us to distinguish one substance from another are called properties. A **physical property** is a characteristic of matter that is not associated with a change in its chemical composition. Familiar examples of physical properties include density, color, hardness, melting and boiling points, and electrical conductivity. We can observe some physical properties, such as density and color, without changing the physical state of the matter observed. Other physical properties, such as the melting temperature of iron or the freezing temperature of water, can only be observed as matter undergoes a physical change. A **physical change** is a change in the state or properties of matter without any accompanying change in its chemical composition (the identities of the substances contained in the matter). We observe a physical change when wax melts, when sugar dissolves in coffee, and when steam condenses into liquid water (Figure 1.18). Other examples of physical changes include magnetizing and demagnetizing metals (as is done with common antitheft security tags) and grinding solids into powders (which can sometimes yield noticeable changes in color). In each of these examples, there is a change in the physical state, form, or properties of the substance, but no change in its chemical composition.

(a)   (b)

Figure 1.18 (a) Wax undergoes a physical change when solid wax is heated and forms liquid wax. (b) Steam condensing inside a cooking pot is a physical change, as water vapor is changed into liquid water. (credit a: modification of work by "95jb14"/Wikimedia Commons; credit b: modification of work by "mjneuby"/Flickr)

The change of one type of matter into another type (or the inability to change) is a **chemical property**. Examples of chemical properties include flammability, toxicity, acidity, reactivity (many types), and heat of combustion. Iron, for example, combines with oxygen in the presence of water to form rust; chromium does not oxidize (Figure 1.19). Nitroglycerin is very dangerous because it explodes easily; neon poses almost no hazard because it is very unreactive.

(a)   (b)

Figure 1.19 (a) One of the chemical properties of iron is that it rusts; (b) one of the chemical properties of chromium is that it does not. (credit a: modification of work by Tony Hisgett; credit b: modification of work by "Atoma"/Wikimedia Commons)

To identify a chemical property, we look for a chemical change. A **chemical change** always produces one or more types of matter that differ from the matter present before the change. The formation of rust is a chemical change because rust is a different kind of matter than the iron, oxygen, and water present before the rust formed. The explosion of nitroglycerin is a chemical change because the gases produced are very different kinds of matter from the original substance. Other examples of chemical changes include reactions that are performed in a lab (such as copper reacting with nitric acid), all forms of combustion (burning), and food being cooked, digested, or rotting (Figure 1.20).

Figure 1.20   (a) Copper and nitric acid undergo a chemical change to form copper nitrate and brown, gaseous nitrogen dioxide. (b) During the combustion of a match, cellulose in the match and oxygen from the air undergo a chemical change to form carbon dioxide and water vapor. (c) Cooking red meat causes a number of chemical changes, including the oxidation of iron in myoglobin that results in the familiar red-to-brown color change. (d) A banana turning brown is a chemical change as new, darker (and less tasty) substances form. (credit b: modification of work by Jeff Turner; credit c: modification of work by Gloria Cabada-Leman; credit d: modification of work by Roberto Verzo)

Properties of matter fall into one of two categories. If the property depends on the amount of matter present, it is an **extensive property**. The mass and volume of a substance are examples of extensive properties; for instance, a gallon of milk has a larger mass and volume than a cup of milk. The value of an extensive property is directly proportional to the amount of matter in question. If the property of a sample of matter does not depend on the amount of matter present, it is an **intensive property**. Temperature is an example of an intensive property. If the gallon and cup of milk are each at 20 °C (room temperature), when they are combined, the temperature remains at 20 °C. As another example, consider the distinct but related properties of heat and temperature. A drop of hot cooking oil spattered on your arm causes brief, minor discomfort, whereas a pot of hot oil yields severe burns. Both the drop and the pot of oil are at the same temperature (an intensive property), but the pot clearly contains much more heat (extensive property).

Chemistry in Everyday Life

Hazard Diamond

You may have seen the symbol shown in Figure 1.21 on containers of chemicals in a laboratory or workplace. Sometimes called a "fire diamond" or "hazard diamond," this chemical hazard diamond provides valuable information that briefly summarizes the various dangers of which to be aware when working with a particular substance.

4 Deadly
3 Extreme danger
2 Hazardous
1 Slightly hazardous
0 Normal material

Health hazard

Flash points:
4 Below 73 °F
3 Below 100 °F
2 Above 100 °F not exceeding 200 °F
1 Above 200 °F
0 Will not burn

Fire hazard

Reactivity
4 May detonate
3 Shock and heat may detonate
2 Violent chemical change
1 Unstable if heated
0 Stable

Specific hazard
OX   Oxidizer
ACID Acid
ALK   Alkali
COR   Corrosive
W   Use no water
☢   Radioactive

Figure 1.21   The National Fire Protection Agency (NFPA) hazard diamond summarizes the major hazards of a chemical substance.

The National Fire Protection Agency (NFPA) 704 Hazard Identification System was developed by NFPA to provide safety information about certain substances. The system details flammability, reactivity, health, and other hazards. Within the overall diamond symbol, the top (red) diamond specifies the level of fire hazard (temperature range for flash point). The blue (left) diamond indicates the level of health hazard. The yellow (right) diamond describes reactivity hazards, such as how readily the substance will undergo detonation or a violent chemical change. The white (bottom) diamond points out special hazards, such as if it is an oxidizer (which allows the substance to burn in the absence of air/oxygen), undergoes an unusual or dangerous reaction with water, is corrosive, acidic, alkaline, a biological hazard, radioactive, and so on. Each hazard is rated on a scale from 0 to 4, with 0 being no hazard and 4 being extremely hazardous.

While many elements differ dramatically in their chemical and physical properties, some elements have similar properties. We can identify sets of elements that exhibit common behaviors. For example, many elements conduct heat and electricity well, whereas others are poor conductors. These properties can be used to sort the elements into three classes: metals (elements that conduct well), nonmetals (elements that conduct poorly), and metalloids (elements that have properties of both metals and nonmetals).

The periodic table is a table of elements that places elements with similar properties close together (**Figure 1.22**). You will learn more about the periodic table as you continue your study of chemistry.

Figure 1.22 The periodic table shows how elements may be grouped according to certain similar properties. Note the background color denotes whether an element is a metal, metalloid, or nonmetal, whereas the element symbol color indicates whether it is a solid, liquid, or gas.

1.4 Measurements

By the end of this section, you will be able to:

- Explain the process of measurement
- Identify the three basic parts of a quantity
- Describe the properties and units of length, mass, volume, density, temperature, and time
- Perform basic unit calculations and conversions in the metric and other unit systems

Measurements provide the macroscopic information that is the basis of most of the hypotheses, theories, and laws that describe the behavior of matter and energy in both the macroscopic and microscopic domains of chemistry. Every measurement provides three kinds of information: the size or magnitude of the measurement (a number); a standard of comparison for the measurement (a unit); and an indication of the uncertainty of the measurement. While the number and unit are explicitly represented when a quantity is written, the uncertainty is an aspect of the measurement result that is more implicitly represented and will be discussed later.

The number in the measurement can be represented in different ways, including decimal form and scientific notation.

(Scientific notation is also known as exponential notation; a review of this topic can be found in Appendix B.) For example, the maximum takeoff weight of a Boeing 777-200ER airliner is 298,000 kilograms, which can also be written as 2.98×10^5 kg. The mass of the average mosquito is about 0.0000025 kilograms, which can be written as 2.5×10^{-6} kg.

Units, such as liters, pounds, and centimeters, are standards of comparison for measurements. When we buy a 2-liter bottle of a soft drink, we expect that the volume of the drink was measured, so it is two times larger than the volume that everyone agrees to be 1 liter. The meat used to prepare a 0.25-pound hamburger is measured so it weighs one-fourth as much as 1 pound. Without units, a number can be meaningless, confusing, or possibly life threatening. Suppose a doctor prescribes phenobarbital to control a patient's seizures and states a dosage of "100" without specifying units. Not only will this be confusing to the medical professional giving the dose, but the consequences can be dire: 100 mg given three times per day can be effective as an anticonvulsant, but a single dose of 100 g is more than 10 times the lethal amount.

We usually report the results of scientific measurements in SI units, an updated version of the metric system, using the units listed in Table 1.2. Other units can be derived from these base units. The standards for these units are fixed by international agreement, and they are called the **International System of Units** or **SI Units** (from the French, *Le Système International d'Unités*). SI units have been used by the United States National Institute of Standards and Technology (NIST) since 1964.

Base Units of the SI System

Property Measured	Name of Unit	Symbol of Unit
length	meter	m
mass	kilogram	kg
time	second	s
temperature	kelvin	K
electric current	ampere	A
amount of substance	mole	mol
luminous intensity	candela	cd

Table 1.2

Sometimes we use units that are fractions or multiples of a base unit. Ice cream is sold in quarts (a familiar, non-SI base unit), pints (0.5 quart), or gallons (4 quarts). We also use fractions or multiples of units in the SI system, but these fractions or multiples are always powers of 10. Fractional or multiple SI units are named using a prefix and the name of the base unit. For example, a length of 1000 meters is also called a kilometer because the prefix *kilo* means "one thousand," which in scientific notation is 10^3 (1 kilometer = 1000 m = 10^3 m). The prefixes used and the powers to which 10 are raised are listed in Table 1.3.

Common Unit Prefixes

Prefix	Symbol	Factor	Example
femto	f	10^{-15}	1 femtosecond (fs) = 1×10^{-15} s (0.000000000000001 s)
pico	p	10^{-12}	1 picometer (pm) = 1×10^{-12} m (0.000000000001 m)
nano	n	10^{-9}	4 nanograms (ng) = 4×10^{-9} g (0.000000004 g)

Table 1.3

Common Unit Prefixes

Prefix	Symbol	Factor	Example
micro	μ	10^{-6}	1 microliter (μL) = 1 × 10^{-6} L (0.000001 L)
milli	m	10^{-3}	2 millimoles (mmol) = 2 × 10^{-3} mol (0.002 mol)
centi	c	10^{-2}	7 centimeters (cm) = 7 × 10^{-2} m (0.07 m)
deci	d	10^{-1}	1 deciliter (dL) = 1 × 10^{-1} L (0.1 L)
kilo	k	10^{3}	1 kilometer (km) = 1 × 10^{3} m (1000 m)
mega	M	10^{6}	3 megahertz (MHz) = 3 × 10^{6} Hz (3,000,000 Hz)
giga	G	10^{9}	8 gigayears (Gyr) = 8 × 10^{9} yr (8,000,000,000 Gyr)
tera	T	10^{12}	5 terawatts (TW) = 5 × 10^{12} W (5,000,000,000,000 W)

Table 1.3

Link to Learning

Need a refresher or more practice with scientific notation? Visit this site (http://openstaxcollege.org/l/16notation) to go over the basics of scientific notation.

SI Base Units

The initial units of the metric system, which eventually evolved into the SI system, were established in France during the French Revolution. The original standards for the meter and the kilogram were adopted there in 1799 and eventually by other countries. This section introduces four of the SI base units commonly used in chemistry. Other SI units will be introduced in subsequent chapters.

Length

The standard unit of **length** in both the SI and original metric systems is the **meter (m)**. A meter was originally specified as 1/10,000,000 of the distance from the North Pole to the equator. It is now defined as the distance light in a vacuum travels in 1/299,792,458 of a second. A meter is about 3 inches longer than a yard (**Figure 1.23**); one meter is about 39.37 inches or 1.094 yards. Longer distances are often reported in kilometers (1 km = 1000 m = 10^{3} m), whereas shorter distances can be reported in centimeters (1 cm = 0.01 m = 10^{-2} m) or millimeters (1 mm = 0.001 m = 10^{-3} m).

Figure 1.23 The relative lengths of 1 m, 1 yd, 1 cm, and 1 in. are shown (not actual size), as well as comparisons of 2.54 cm and 1 in., and of 1 m and 1.094 yd.

Mass

The standard unit of mass in the SI system is the **kilogram (kg)**. A kilogram was originally defined as the mass of a liter of water (a cube of water with an edge length of exactly 0.1 meter). It is now defined by a certain cylinder of platinum-iridium alloy, which is kept in France (**Figure 1.24**). Any object with the same mass as this cylinder is said to have a mass of 1 kilogram. One kilogram is about 2.2 pounds. The gram (g) is exactly equal to 1/1000 of the mass of the kilogram (10^{-3} kg).

Figure 1.24 This replica prototype kilogram is housed at the National Institute of Standards and Technology (NIST) in Maryland. (credit: National Institutes of Standards and Technology)

Temperature

Temperature is an intensive property. The SI unit of temperature is the **kelvin (K)**. The IUPAC convention is to use kelvin (all lowercase) for the word, K (uppercase) for the unit symbol, and neither the word "degree" nor the degree symbol (°). The degree **Celsius (°C)** is also allowed in the SI system, with both the word "degree" and the degree symbol used for Celsius measurements. Celsius degrees are the same magnitude as those of kelvin, but the two scales place their zeros in different places. Water freezes at 273.15 K (0 °C) and boils at 373.15 K (100 °C) by definition, and normal human body temperature is approximately 310 K (37 °C). The conversion between these two units and the Fahrenheit scale will be discussed later in this chapter.

Time

The SI base unit of time is the **second (s)**. Small and large time intervals can be expressed with the appropriate prefixes; for example, 3 microseconds = 0.000003 s = 3×10^{-6} and 5 megaseconds = 5,000,000 s = 5×10^{6} s. Alternatively, hours, days, and years can be used.

Derived SI Units

We can derive many units from the seven SI base units. For example, we can use the base unit of length to define a unit of volume, and the base units of mass and length to define a unit of density.

Volume

Volume is the measure of the amount of space occupied by an object. The standard SI unit of volume is defined by the base unit of length (**Figure 1.25**). The standard volume is a **cubic meter (m^3)**, a cube with an edge length of exactly one meter. To dispense a cubic meter of water, we could build a cubic box with edge lengths of exactly one meter. This box would hold a cubic meter of water or any other substance.

A more commonly used unit of volume is derived from the decimeter (0.1 m, or 10 cm). A cube with edge lengths of exactly one decimeter contains a volume of one cubic decimeter (dm^3). A **liter (L)** is the more common name for the cubic decimeter. One liter is about 1.06 quarts.

A **cubic centimeter (cm^3)** is the volume of a cube with an edge length of exactly one centimeter. The abbreviation **cc** (for **c**ubic **c**entimeter) is often used by health professionals. A cubic centimeter is also called a **milliliter (mL)** and is 1/1000 of a liter.

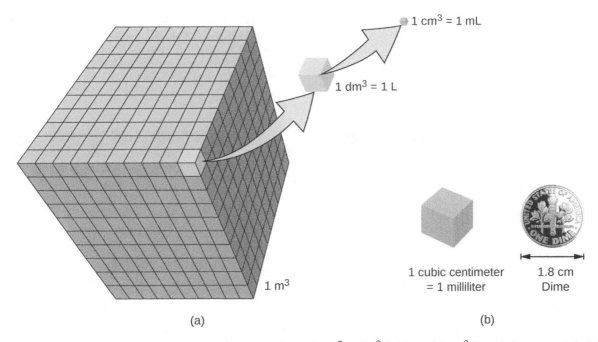

Figure 1.25 (a) The relative volumes are shown for cubes of 1 m^3, 1 dm^3 (1 L), and 1 cm^3 (1 mL) (not to scale). (b) The diameter of a dime is compared relative to the edge length of a 1-cm^3 (1-mL) cube.

Density

We use the mass and volume of a substance to determine its density. Thus, the units of density are defined by the base units of mass and length.

The **density** of a substance is the ratio of the mass of a sample of the substance to its volume. The SI unit for density is the kilogram per cubic meter (kg/m^3). For many situations, however, this as an inconvenient unit, and we often use grams per cubic centimeter (g/cm^3) for the densities of solids and liquids, and grams per liter (g/L) for gases. Although there are exceptions, most liquids and solids have densities that range from about 0.7 g/cm^3 (the density of gasoline) to 19 g/cm^3 (the density of gold). The density of air is about 1.2 g/L. Table 1.4 shows the densities of some common substances.

Densities of Common Substances

Solids	Liquids	Gases (at 25 °C and 1 atm)
ice (at 0 °C) 0.92 g/cm^3	water 1.0 g/cm^3	dry air 1.20 g/L
oak (wood) 0.60–0.90 g/cm^3	ethanol 0.79 g/cm^3	oxygen 1.31 g/L
iron 7.9 g/cm^3	acetone 0.79 g/cm^3	nitrogen 1.14 g/L
copper 9.0 g/cm^3	glycerin 1.26 g/cm^3	carbon dioxide 1.80 g/L
lead 11.3 g/cm^3	olive oil 0.92 g/cm^3	helium 0.16 g/L
silver 10.5 g/cm^3	gasoline 0.70–0.77 g/cm^3	neon 0.83 g/L
gold 19.3 g/cm^3	mercury 13.6 g/cm^3	radon 9.1 g/L

Table 1.4

While there are many ways to determine the density of an object, perhaps the most straightforward method involves separately finding the mass and volume of the object, and then dividing the mass of the sample by its volume. In the following example, the mass is found directly by weighing, but the volume is found indirectly through length measurements.

$$\text{density} = \frac{\text{mass}}{\text{volume}}$$

Example 1.1

Calculation of Density

Gold—in bricks, bars, and coins—has been a form of currency for centuries. In order to swindle people into paying for a brick of gold without actually investing in a brick of gold, people have considered filling the centers of hollow gold bricks with lead to fool buyers into thinking that the entire brick is gold. It does not work: Lead is a dense substance, but its density is not as great as that of gold, 19.3 g/cm^3. What is the density of lead if a cube of lead has an edge length of 2.00 cm and a mass of 90.7 g?

Solution

The density of a substance can be calculated by dividing its mass by its volume. The volume of a cube is calculated by cubing the edge length.

$$\text{volume of lead cube} = 2.00 \text{ cm} \times 2.00 \text{ cm} \times 2.00 \text{ cm} = 8.00 \text{ cm}^3$$

$$\text{density} = \frac{\text{mass}}{\text{volume}} = \frac{90.7 \text{ g}}{8.00 \text{ cm}^3} = \frac{11.3 \text{ g}}{1.00 \text{ cm}^3} = 11.3 \text{ g/cm}^3$$

(We will discuss the reason for rounding to the first decimal place in the next section.)

Check Your Learning

(a) To three decimal places, what is the volume of a cube (cm^3) with an edge length of 0.843 cm?

(b) If the cube in part (a) is copper and has a mass of 5.34 g, what is the density of copper to two decimal places?

Answer: (a) 0.599 cm^3; (b) 8.91 g/cm^3

Link to Learning

To learn more about the relationship between mass, volume, and density, use this **interactive simulator (http://openstaxcollege.org/l/16phetmasvolden)** to explore the density of different materials, like wood, ice, brick, and aluminum.

Example 1.2

Using Displacement of Water to Determine Density

This **PhET simulation (http://openstaxcollege.org/l/16phetmasvolden)** illustrates another way to determine density, using displacement of water. Determine the density of the red and yellow blocks.

Solution

When you open the density simulation and select Same Mass, you can choose from several 5.00-kg colored blocks that you can drop into a tank containing 100.00 L water. The yellow block floats (it is less dense than water), and the water level rises to 105.00 L. While floating, the yellow block displaces 5.00 L water, an amount equal to the weight of the block. The red block sinks (it is more dense than water, which has density = 1.00 kg/L), and the water level rises to 101.25 L.

The red block therefore displaces 1.25 L water, an amount equal to the volume of the block. The density of the red block is:

$$\text{density} = \frac{\text{mass}}{\text{volume}} = \frac{5.00 \text{ kg}}{1.25 \text{ L}} = 4.00 \text{ kg/L}$$

Note that since the yellow block is not completely submerged, you cannot determine its density from this information. But if you hold the yellow block on the bottom of the tank, the water level rises to 110.00 L, which means that it now displaces 10.00 L water, and its density can be found:

$$\text{density} = \frac{\text{mass}}{\text{volume}} = \frac{5.00 \text{ kg}}{10.00 \text{ L}} = 0.500 \text{ kg/L}$$

Check Your Learning

Remove all of the blocks from the water and add the green block to the tank of water, placing it approximately in the middle of the tank. Determine the density of the green block.

Answer: 2.00 kg/L

1.5 Measurement Uncertainty, Accuracy, and Precision

By the end of this section, you will be able to:

- Define accuracy and precision
- Distinguish exact and uncertain numbers
- Correctly represent uncertainty in quantities using significant figures
- Apply proper rounding rules to computed quantities

Counting is the only type of measurement that is free from uncertainty, provided the number of objects being counted does not change while the counting process is underway. The result of such a counting measurement is an example of an **exact number**. If we count eggs in a carton, we know *exactly* how many eggs the carton contains. The numbers of defined quantities are also exact. By definition, 1 foot is exactly 12 inches, 1 inch is exactly 2.54 centimeters, and 1 gram is exactly 0.001 kilogram. Quantities derived from measurements other than counting, however, are uncertain to varying extents due to practical limitations of the measurement process used.

Significant Figures in Measurement

The numbers of measured quantities, unlike defined or directly counted quantities, are not exact. To measure the volume of liquid in a graduated cylinder, you should make a reading at the bottom of the meniscus, the lowest point on the curved surface of the liquid.

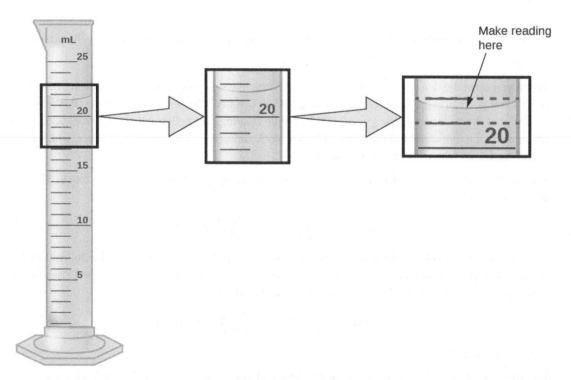

Figure 1.26 To measure the volume of liquid in this graduated cylinder, you must mentally subdivide the distance between the 21 and 22 mL marks into tenths of a milliliter, and then make a reading (estimate) at the bottom of the meniscus.

Refer to the illustration in Figure 1.26. The bottom of the meniscus in this case clearly lies between the 21 and 22 markings, meaning the liquid volume is *certainly* greater than 21 mL but less than 22 mL. The meniscus appears to be a bit closer to the 22-mL mark than to the 21-mL mark, and so a reasonable estimate of the liquid's volume would be 21.6 mL. In the number 21.6, then, the digits 2 and 1 are certain, but the 6 is an estimate. Some people might estimate the meniscus position to be equally distant from each of the markings and estimate the tenth-place digit as 5, while others may think it to be even closer to the 22-mL mark and estimate this digit to be 7. Note that it would be pointless to attempt to estimate a digit for the hundredths place, given that the tenths-place digit is uncertain. In general, numerical scales such as the one on this graduated cylinder will permit measurements to one-tenth of the smallest scale division. The scale in this case has 1-mL divisions, and so volumes may be measured to the nearest 0.1 mL.

This concept holds true for all measurements, even if you do not actively make an estimate. If you place a quarter on a standard electronic balance, you may obtain a reading of 6.72 g. The digits 6 and 7 are certain, and the 2 indicates that the mass of the quarter is likely between 6.71 and 6.73 grams. The quarter weighs *about* 6.72 grams, with a nominal uncertainty in the measurement of ± 0.01 gram. If we weigh the quarter on a more sensitive balance, we may find that its mass is 6.723 g. This means its mass lies between 6.722 and 6.724 grams, an uncertainty of 0.001 gram. Every measurement has some **uncertainty**, which depends on the device used (and the user's ability). All of the digits in a measurement, including the uncertain last digit, are called **significant figures** or **significant digits**. Note that zero may be a measured value; for example, if you stand on a scale that shows weight to the nearest pound and it shows "120," then the 1 (hundreds), 2 (tens) and 0 (ones) are all significant (measured) values.

Whenever you make a measurement properly, all the digits in the result are significant. But what if you were analyzing a reported value and trying to determine what is significant and what is not? Well, for starters, all nonzero digits are significant, and it is only zeros that require some thought. We will use the terms "leading," "trailing," and "captive" for the zeros and will consider how to deal with them.

Starting with the first nonzero digit on the left, count this digit and all remaining digits to the right. This is the number of significant figures in the measurement unless the last digit is a trailing zero lying to the left of the decimal point.

Captive zeros result from measurement and are therefore always significant. Leading zeros, however, are never significant—they merely tell us where the decimal point is located.

The leading zeros in this example are not significant. We could use exponential notation (as described in Appendix B) and express the number as 8.32407×10^{-3}; then the number 8.32407 contains all of the significant figures, and 10^{-3} locates the decimal point.

The number of significant figures is uncertain in a number that ends with a zero to the left of the decimal point location. The zeros in the measurement 1,300 grams could be significant or they could simply indicate where the decimal point is located. The ambiguity can be resolved with the use of exponential notation: 1.3×10^3 (two significant figures), 1.30×10^3 (three significant figures, if the tens place was measured), or 1.300×10^3 (four significant figures, if the ones place was also measured). In cases where only the decimal-formatted number is available, it is prudent to assume that all trailing zeros are not significant.

When determining significant figures, be sure to pay attention to reported values and think about the measurement and significant figures in terms of what is reasonable or likely when evaluating whether the value makes sense. For example, the official January 2014 census reported the resident population of the US as 317,297,725. Do you think the US population was correctly determined to the reported nine significant figures, that is, to the exact number of people? People are constantly being born, dying, or moving into or out of the country, and assumptions are made to account for the large number of people who are not actually counted. Because of these uncertainties, it might be more reasonable to expect that we know the population to within perhaps a million or so, in which case the population should be reported as 3.17×10^8 people.

Significant Figures in Calculations

A second important principle of uncertainty is that results calculated from a measurement are at least as uncertain as the measurement itself. We must take the uncertainty in our measurements into account to avoid misrepresenting the uncertainty in calculated results. One way to do this is to report the result of a calculation with the correct number of significant figures, which is determined by the following three rules for **rounding** numbers:

1. When we add or subtract numbers, we should round the result to the same number of decimal places as the number with the least number of decimal places (the least precise value in terms of addition and subtraction).

2. When we multiply or divide numbers, we should round the result to the same number of digits as the number with the least number of significant figures (the least precise value in terms of multiplication and division).

3. If the digit to be dropped (the one immediately to the right of the digit to be retained) is less than 5, we "round down" and leave the retained digit unchanged; if it is more than 5, we "round up" and increase the retained digit by 1; if the dropped digit *is* 5, we round up or down, whichever yields an even value for the retained digit. (The last part of this rule may strike you as a bit odd, but it's based on reliable statistics and is aimed at avoiding any bias when dropping the digit "5," since it is equally close to both possible values of the retained digit.)

The following examples illustrate the application of this rule in rounding a few different numbers to three significant figures:

- 0.028675 rounds "up" to 0.0287 (the dropped digit, 7, is greater than 5)

- 18.3384 rounds "down" to 18.3 (the dropped digit, 3, is less than 5)

- 6.8752 rounds "up" to 6.88 (the dropped digit is 5, and the retained digit is even)

- 92.85 rounds "down" to 92.8 (the dropped digit is 5, and the retained digit is even)

Let's work through these rules with a few examples.

Example 1.3

Rounding Numbers

Round the following to the indicated number of significant figures:

(a) 31.57 (to two significant figures)

(b) 8.1649 (to three significant figures)

(c) 0.051065 (to four significant figures)

(d) 0.90275 (to four significant figures)

Solution

(a) 31.57 rounds "up" to 32 (the dropped digit is 5, and the retained digit is even)

(b) 8.1649 rounds "down" to 8.16 (the dropped digit, 4, is less than 5)

(c) 0.051065 rounds "down" to 0.05106 (the dropped digit is 5, and the retained digit is even)

(d) 0.90275 rounds "up" to 0.9028 (the dropped digit is 5, and the retained digit is even)

Check Your Learning

Round the following to the indicated number of significant figures:

(a) 0.424 (to two significant figures)

(b) 0.0038661 (to three significant figures)

(c) 421.25 (to four significant figures)

(d) 28,683.5 (to five significant figures)

Answer: (a) 0.42; (b) 0.00387; (c) 421.2; (d) 28,684

Example 1.4

Addition and Subtraction with Significant Figures

Rule: When we add or subtract numbers, we should round the result to the same number of decimal places as the number with the least number of decimal places (i.e., the least precise value in terms of addition and subtraction).

(a) Add 1.0023 g and 4.383 g.

(b) Subtract 421.23 g from 486 g.

Solution

(a)
$$\begin{array}{r} 1.0023 \text{ g} \\ + 4.383 \text{ g} \\ \hline 5.3853 \text{ g} \end{array}$$

Answer is 5.385 g (round to the thousandths place; three decimal places)

(b)
$$\begin{array}{r} 486 \text{ g} \\ -421.23 \text{ g} \\ \hline 64.77 \text{ g} \end{array}$$

Answer is 65 g (round to the ones place; no decimal places)

$$
\begin{array}{r}
1.002\,3 \leftarrow \text{Ten thousandths place}\\
+\ 4.383 \leftarrow \text{Thousandths place: least precise}\\
\hline
5.385\,5
\end{array}
$$

Round to thousandths

(a)

$$
\begin{array}{r}
486\quad\ \text{g}\\
-\ 421.23\ \text{g}\\
\hline
64.77\ \text{g} \longrightarrow \text{Answer is 65 g}
\end{array}
$$

Round to ones

(b)

Check Your Learning

(a) Add 2.334 mL and 0.31 mL.

(b) Subtract 55.8752 m from 56.533 m.

Answer: (a) 2.64 mL; (b) 0.658 m

Example 1.5

Multiplication and Division with Significant Figures

Rule: When we multiply or divide numbers, we should round the result to the same number of digits as the number with the least number of significant figures (the least precise value in terms of multiplication and division).

(a) Multiply 0.6238 cm by 6.6 cm.

(b) Divide 421.23 g by 486 mL.

Solution

(a) $0.6238\ \text{cm} \times 6.6\ \text{cm} = 4.11708\ \text{cm}^2 \longrightarrow$ result is $4.1\ \text{cm}^2$ (round to two significant figures)

four significant figures $\times$ two significant figures $\longrightarrow$ two significant figures answer

(b) $\dfrac{421.23\ \text{g}}{486\ \text{mL}} = 0.86728...\ \text{g/mL} \longrightarrow$ result is 0.867 g/mL (round to three significant figures)

$\dfrac{\text{five significant figures}}{\text{three significant figures}} \longrightarrow$ three significant figures answer

Check Your Learning

(a) Multiply 2.334 cm and 0.320 cm.

(b) Divide 55.8752 m by 56.53 s.

Answer: (a) 0.747 cm^2 (b) 0.9884 m/s

In the midst of all these technicalities, it is important to keep in mind the reason why we use significant figures and rounding rules—to correctly represent the certainty of the values we report and to ensure that a calculated result is not represented as being more certain than the least certain value used in the calculation.

Example 1.6

Calculation with Significant Figures

One common bathtub is 13.44 dm long, 5.920 dm wide, and 2.54 dm deep. Assume that the tub is rectangular and calculate its approximate volume in liters.

Solution

$$V = l \times w \times d$$
$$= 13.44 \text{ dm} \times 5.920 \text{ dm} \times 2.54 \text{ dm}$$
$$= 202.09459... \text{ dm}^3 \text{ (value from calculator)}$$
$$= 202 \text{ dm}^3 \text{, or 202 L (answer rounded to three significant figures)}$$

Check Your Learning

What is the density of a liquid with a mass of 31.1415 g and a volume of 30.13 cm³?

Answer: 1.034 g/mL

Example 1.7

Experimental Determination of Density Using Water Displacement

A piece of rebar is weighed and then submerged in a graduated cylinder partially filled with water, with results as shown.

Rebar mass
= 69.658 g

"Final" volume
= 22.4 mL

"Initial" volume
= 13.5 mL

(a) Use these values to determine the density of this piece of rebar.

(b) Rebar is mostly iron. Does your result in (a) support this statement? How?

Solution

The volume of the piece of rebar is equal to the volume of the water displaced:

$$\text{volume} = 22.4 \text{ mL} - 13.5 \text{ mL} = 8.9 \text{ mL} = 8.9 \text{ cm}^3$$

(rounded to the nearest 0.1 mL, per the rule for addition and subtraction)

The density is the mass-to-volume ratio:

$$\text{density} = \frac{\text{mass}}{\text{volume}} = \frac{69.658 \text{ g}}{8.9 \text{ cm}^3} = 7.8 \text{ g/cm}^3$$

(rounded to two significant figures, per the rule for multiplication and division)

From Table 1.4, the density of iron is 7.9 g/cm^3, very close to that of rebar, which lends some support to the fact that rebar is mostly iron.

Check Your Learning

An irregularly shaped piece of a shiny yellowish material is weighed and then submerged in a graduated cylinder, with results as shown.

Mass
= 51.842 g

"Final" volume
= 19.8 mL

"Initial" volume
= 17.1 mL

(a) Use these values to determine the density of this material.

(b) Do you have any reasonable guesses as to the identity of this material? Explain your reasoning.

Answer: (a) 19 g/cm^3; (b) It is likely gold; the right appearance for gold and very close to the density given for gold in Table 1.4.

Accuracy and Precision

Scientists typically make repeated measurements of a quantity to ensure the quality of their findings and to know both the **precision** and the **accuracy** of their results. Measurements are said to be precise if they yield very similar results when repeated in the same manner. A measurement is considered accurate if it yields a result that is very close to the true or accepted value. Precise values agree with each other; accurate values agree with a true value. These characterizations can be extended to other contexts, such as the results of an archery competition (Figure 1.27).

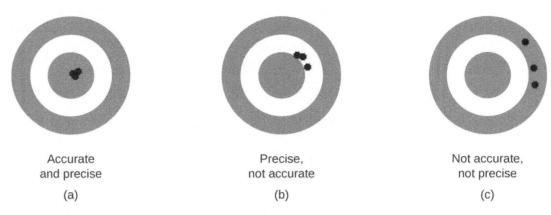

Accurate
and precise
(a)

Precise,
not accurate
(b)

Not accurate,
not precise
(c)

Figure 1.27 (a) These arrows are close to both the bull's eye and one another, so they are both accurate and precise. (b) These arrows are close to one another but not on target, so they are precise but not accurate. (c) These arrows are neither on target nor close to one another, so they are neither accurate nor precise.

Suppose a quality control chemist at a pharmaceutical company is tasked with checking the accuracy and precision of three different machines that are meant to dispense 10 ounces (296 mL) of cough syrup into storage bottles. She proceeds to use each machine to fill five bottles and then carefully determines the actual volume dispensed, obtaining the results tabulated in Table 1.5.

Volume (mL) of Cough Medicine Delivered by 10-oz (296 mL) Dispensers

Dispenser #1	Dispenser #2	Dispenser #3
283.3	298.3	296.1
284.1	294.2	295.9
283.9	296.0	296.1
284.0	297.8	296.0
284.1	293.9	296.1

Table 1.5

Considering these results, she will report that dispenser #1 is precise (values all close to one another, within a few tenths of a milliliter) but not accurate (none of the values are close to the target value of 296 mL, each being more than 10 mL too low). Results for dispenser #2 represent improved accuracy (each volume is less than 3 mL away from 296 mL) but worse precision (volumes vary by more than 4 mL). Finally, she can report that dispenser #3 is working well, dispensing cough syrup both accurately (all volumes within 0.1 mL of the target volume) and precisely (volumes differing from each other by no more than 0.2 mL).

1.6 Mathematical Treatment of Measurement Results

By the end of this section, you will be able to:

- Explain the dimensional analysis (factor label) approach to mathematical calculations involving quantities
- Use dimensional analysis to carry out unit conversions for a given property and computations involving two or more properties

It is often the case that a quantity of interest may not be easy (or even possible) to measure directly but instead must be calculated from other directly measured properties and appropriate mathematical relationships. For example, consider measuring the average speed of an athlete running sprints. This is typically accomplished by measuring the *time* required for the athlete to run from the starting line to the finish line, and the *distance* between these two lines, and then computing *speed* from the equation that relates these three properties:

$$\text{speed} = \frac{\text{distance}}{\text{time}}$$

An Olympic-quality sprinter can run 100 m in approximately 10 s, corresponding to an average speed of

$$\frac{100 \text{ m}}{10 \text{ s}} = 10 \text{ m/s}$$

Note that this simple arithmetic involves dividing the numbers of each measured quantity to yield the number of the computed quantity (100/10 = 10) *and likewise* dividing the units of each measured quantity to yield the unit of the computed quantity (m/s = m/s). Now, consider using this same relation to predict the time required for a person running at this speed to travel a distance of 25 m. The same relation between the three properties is used, but in this case, the two quantities provided are a speed (10 m/s) and a distance (25 m). To yield the sought property, time, the equation must be rearranged appropriately:

$$\text{time} = \frac{\text{distance}}{\text{speed}}$$

The time can then be computed as:

$$\frac{25 \text{ m}}{10 \text{ m/s}} = 2.5 \text{ s}$$

Again, arithmetic on the numbers (25/10 = 2.5) was accompanied by the same arithmetic on the units (m/m/s = s) to yield the number and unit of the result, 2.5 s. Note that, just as for numbers, when a unit is divided by an identical unit (in this case, m/m), the result is "1"—or, as commonly phrased, the units "cancel."

These calculations are examples of a versatile mathematical approach known as **dimensional analysis** (or the **factor-label method**). Dimensional analysis is based on this premise: *the units of quantities must be subjected to the same mathematical operations as their associated numbers.* This method can be applied to computations ranging from simple unit conversions to more complex, multi-step calculations involving several different quantities.

Conversion Factors and Dimensional Analysis

A ratio of two equivalent quantities expressed with different measurement units can be used as a **unit conversion factor**. For example, the lengths of 2.54 cm and 1 in. are equivalent (by definition), and so a unit conversion factor may be derived from the ratio,

$$\frac{2.54 \text{ cm}}{1 \text{ in.}} (2.54 \text{ cm} = 1 \text{ in.}) \text{ or } 2.54 \frac{\text{cm}}{\text{in.}}$$

Several other commonly used conversion factors are given in Table 1.6.

Common Conversion Factors

Length	Volume	Mass
1 m = 1.0936 yd	1 L = 1.0567 qt	1 kg = 2.2046 lb
1 in. = 2.54 cm (exact)	1 qt = 0.94635 L	1 lb = 453.59 g
1 km = 0.62137 mi	1 ft^3 = 28.317 L	1 (avoirdupois) oz = 28.349 g
1 mi = 1609.3 m	1 tbsp = 14.787 mL	1 (troy) oz = 31.103 g

Table 1.6

When we multiply a quantity (such as distance given in inches) by an appropriate unit conversion factor, we convert the quantity to an equivalent value with different units (such as distance in centimeters). For example, a basketball player's vertical jump of 34 inches can be converted to centimeters by:

$$34 \text{ in.} \times \frac{2.54 \text{ cm}}{1 \text{ in.}} = 86 \text{ cm}$$

Since this simple arithmetic involves *quantities*, the premise of dimensional analysis requires that we multiply both *numbers and units*. The numbers of these two quantities are multiplied to yield the number of the product quantity, 86, whereas the units are multiplied to yield $\frac{\text{in.} \times \text{cm}}{\text{in.}}$. Just as for numbers, a ratio of identical units is also numerically equal to one, $\frac{\text{in.}}{\text{in.}} = 1$, and the unit product thus simplifies to *cm*. (When identical units divide to yield a factor of 1, they are said to "cancel.") Using dimensional analysis, we can determine that a unit conversion factor has been set up correctly by checking to confirm that the original unit will cancel, and the result will contain the sought (converted) unit.

Example 1.8

Using a Unit Conversion Factor

The mass of a competition frisbee is 125 g. Convert its mass to ounces using the unit conversion factor derived from the relationship 1 oz = 28.349 g (Table 1.6).

Solution

If we have the conversion factor, we can determine the mass in kilograms using an equation similar the one used for converting length from inches to centimeters.

$$x \text{ oz} = 125 \text{ g} \times \text{unit conversion factor}$$

We write the unit conversion factor in its two forms:

$$\frac{1 \text{ oz}}{28.349 \text{ g}} \text{ and } \frac{28.349 \text{ g}}{1 \text{ oz}}$$

The correct unit conversion factor is the ratio that cancels the units of grams and leaves ounces.

$$
\begin{aligned}
x \text{ oz} &= 125 \text{ g} \times \frac{1 \text{ oz}}{28.349 \text{ g}} \\
&= \left(\frac{125}{28.349}\right) \text{oz} \\
&= 4.41 \text{ oz (three significant figures)}
\end{aligned}
$$

Check Your Learning

Convert a volume of 9.345 qt to liters.

Answer: 8.844 L

Beyond simple unit conversions, the factor-label method can be used to solve more complex problems involving computations. Regardless of the details, the basic approach is the same—all the *factors* involved in the calculation must be appropriately oriented to insure that their *labels* (units) will appropriately cancel and/or combine to yield the desired unit in the result. This is why it is referred to as the factor-label method. As your study of chemistry continues, you will encounter many opportunities to apply this approach.

Example 1.9

Computing Quantities from Measurement Results and Known Mathematical Relations

What is the density of common antifreeze in units of g/mL? A 4.00-qt sample of the antifreeze weighs 9.26 lb.

Solution

Since $\text{density} = \frac{\text{mass}}{\text{volume}}$, we need to divide the mass in grams by the volume in milliliters. In general: the number of units of B = the number of units of A $\times$ unit conversion factor. The necessary conversion factors are given in Table 1.6: 1 lb = 453.59 g; 1 L = 1.0567 qt; 1 L = 1,000 mL. We can convert mass from pounds to grams in one step:

$$9.26 \text{ lb} \times \frac{453.59 \text{ g}}{1 \text{ lb}} = 4.20 \times 10^3 \text{ g}$$

We need to use two steps to convert volume from quarts to milliliters.

> **Step 1.** *Convert quarts to liters.*
> $$4.00 \text{ qt} \times \frac{1 \text{ L}}{1.0567 \text{ qt}} = 3.78 \text{ L}$$

> **Step 2.** *Convert liters to milliliters.*
> $$3.78 \text{ L} \times \frac{1000 \text{ mL}}{1 \text{ L}} = 3.78 \times 10^3 \text{ mL}$$

Then,

$$\text{density} = \frac{4.20 \times 10^3 \text{ g}}{3.78 \times 10^3 \text{ mL}} = 1.11 \text{ g/mL}$$

Alternatively, the calculation could be set up in a way that uses three unit conversion factors sequentially as follows:

$$\frac{9.26 \text{ lb}}{4.00 \text{ qt}} \times \frac{453.59 \text{ g}}{1 \text{ lb}} \times \frac{1.0567 \text{ qt}}{1 \text{ L}} \times \frac{1 \text{ L}}{1000 \text{ mL}} = 1.11 \text{ g/mL}$$

Check Your Learning

What is the volume in liters of 1.000 oz, given that 1 L = 1.0567 qt and 1 qt = 32 oz (exactly)?

Answer: 2.956×10^{-2} L

Example 1.10

Computing Quantities from Measurement Results and Known Mathematical Relations

While being driven from Philadelphia to Atlanta, a distance of about 1250 km, a 2014 Lamborghini Aventador Roadster uses 213 L gasoline.

(a) What (average) fuel economy, in miles per gallon, did the Roadster get during this trip?

(b) If gasoline costs $3.80 per gallon, what was the fuel cost for this trip?

Solution

(a) We first convert distance from kilometers to miles:

$$1250 \text{ km} \times \frac{0.62137 \text{ mi}}{1 \text{ km}} = 777 \text{ mi}$$

and then convert volume from liters to gallons:

$$213 \text{ L} \times \frac{1.0567 \text{ qt}}{1 \text{ L}} \times \frac{1 \text{ gal}}{4 \text{ qt}} = 56.3 \text{ gal}$$

Then,

$$\text{(average) mileage} = \frac{777 \text{ mi}}{56.3 \text{ gal}} = 13.8 \text{ miles/gallon} = 13.8 \text{ mpg}$$

Alternatively, the calculation could be set up in a way that uses all the conversion factors sequentially, as follows:

$$\frac{1250 \text{ km}}{213 \text{ L}} \times \frac{0.62137 \text{ mi}}{1 \text{ km}} \times \frac{1 \text{ L}}{1.0567 \text{ qt}} \times \frac{4 \text{ qt}}{1 \text{ gal}} = 13.8 \text{ mpg}$$

(b) Using the previously calculated volume in gallons, we find:

$$56.3 \text{ gal} \times \frac{\$3.80}{1 \text{ gal}} = \$214$$

Check Your Learning

A Toyota Prius Hybrid uses 59.7 L gasoline to drive from San Francisco to Seattle, a distance of 1300 km (two significant digits).

(a) What (average) fuel economy, in miles per gallon, did the Prius get during this trip?

(b) If gasoline costs $3.90 per gallon, what was the fuel cost for this trip?

Answer: (a) 51 mpg; (b) $62

Conversion of Temperature Units

We use the word temperature to refer to the hotness or coldness of a substance. One way we measure a change in temperature is to use the fact that most substances expand when their temperature increases and contract when their temperature decreases. The mercury or alcohol in a common glass thermometer changes its volume as the temperature changes. Because the volume of the liquid changes more than the volume of the glass, we can see the liquid expand when it gets warmer and contract when it gets cooler.

To mark a scale on a thermometer, we need a set of reference values: Two of the most commonly used are the freezing and boiling temperatures of water at a specified atmospheric pressure. On the Celsius scale, 0 °C is defined as the freezing temperature of water and 100 °C as the boiling temperature of water. The space between the two temperatures is divided into 100 equal intervals, which we call degrees. On the **Fahrenheit** scale, the freezing point of water is defined as 32 °F and the boiling temperature as 212 °F. The space between these two points on a Fahrenheit thermometer is divided into 180 equal parts (degrees).

Defining the Celsius and Fahrenheit temperature scales as described in the previous paragraph results in a slightly more complex relationship between temperature values on these two scales than for different units of measure for other properties. Most measurement units for a given property are directly proportional to one another ($y = mx$). Using familiar length units as one example:

$$\text{length in feet} = \left(\frac{1 \text{ ft}}{12 \text{ in.}}\right) \times \text{length in inches}$$

where y = length in feet, x = length in inches, and the proportionality constant, m, is the conversion factor. The Celsius and Fahrenheit temperature scales, however, do not share a common zero point, and so the relationship between these two scales is a linear one rather than a proportional one ($y = mx + b$). Consequently, converting a temperature from one of these scales into the other requires more than simple multiplication by a conversion factor, m, it also must take into account differences in the scales' zero points (b).

The linear equation relating Celsius and Fahrenheit temperatures is easily derived from the two temperatures used to define each scale. Representing the Celsius temperature as x and the Fahrenheit temperature as y, the slope, m, is computed to be:

$$m = \frac{\Delta y}{\Delta x} = \frac{212\ °\text{F} - 32\ °\text{F}}{100\ °\text{C} - 0\ °\text{C}} = \frac{180\ °\text{F}}{100\ °\text{C}} = \frac{9\ °\text{F}}{5\ °\text{C}}$$

The y-intercept of the equation, b, is then calculated using either of the equivalent temperature pairs, (100 °C, 212 °F) or (0 °C, 32 °F), as:

$$b = y - mx = 32\ °\text{F} - \frac{9\ °\text{F}}{5\ °\text{C}} \times 0\ °\text{C} = 32\ °\text{F}$$

The equation relating the temperature scales is then:

$$T_{°\text{F}} = \left(\frac{9\ °\text{F}}{5\ °\text{C}} \times T_{°\text{C}}\right) + 32\ °\text{C}$$

An abbreviated form of this equation that omits the measurement units is:

$$T_{°\text{F}} = \frac{9}{5} \times T_{°\text{C}} + 32$$

Rearrangement of this equation yields the form useful for converting from Fahrenheit to Celsius:

$$T_{°\text{C}} = \frac{5}{9}(T_{°\text{F}} - 32)$$

As mentioned earlier in this chapter, the SI unit of temperature is the kelvin (K). Unlike the Celsius and Fahrenheit scales, the kelvin scale is an absolute temperature scale in which 0 (zero) K corresponds to the lowest temperature that can theoretically be achieved. The early 19th-century discovery of the relationship between a gas's volume and temperature suggested that the volume of a gas would be zero at −273.15 °C. In 1848, British physicist William Thompson, who later adopted the title of Lord Kelvin, proposed an absolute temperature scale based on this concept (further treatment of this topic is provided in this text's chapter on gases).

The freezing temperature of water on this scale is 273.15 K and its boiling temperature 373.15 K. Notice the numerical difference in these two reference temperatures is 100, the same as for the Celsius scale, and so the linear relation between these two temperature scales will exhibit a slope of $1\ \frac{\text{K}}{°\text{C}}$. Following the same approach, the equations for converting between the kelvin and Celsius temperature scales are derived to be:

$$T_\text{K} = T_{°\text{C}} + 273.15$$
$$T_{°\text{C}} = T_\text{K} - 273.15$$

The 273.15 in these equations has been determined experimentally, so it is not exact. **Figure 1.28** shows the relationship among the three temperature scales. Recall that we do not use the degree sign with temperatures on the kelvin scale.

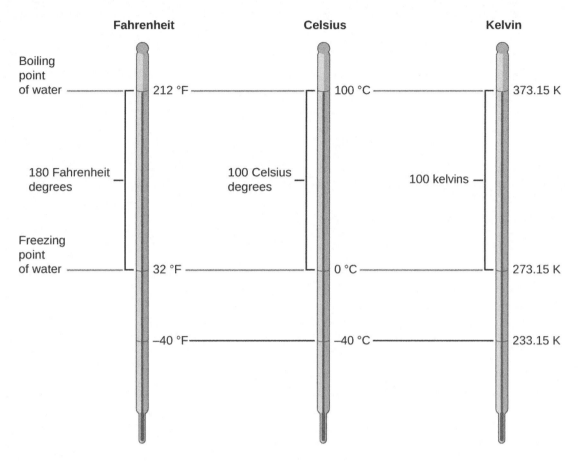

Figure 1.28 The Fahrenheit, Celsius, and kelvin temperature scales are compared.

Although the kelvin (absolute) temperature scale is the official SI temperature scale, Celsius is commonly used in many scientific contexts and is the scale of choice for nonscience contexts in almost all areas of the world. Very few countries (the U.S. and its territories, the Bahamas, Belize, Cayman Islands, and Palau) still use Fahrenheit for weather, medicine, and cooking.

Example 1.11

Conversion from Celsius

Normal body temperature has been commonly accepted as 37.0 °C (although it varies depending on time of day and method of measurement, as well as among individuals). What is this temperature on the kelvin scale and on the Fahrenheit scale?

Solution

$$\text{K} = {}^\circ\text{C} + 273.15 = 37.0 + 273.2 = 310.2 \text{ K}$$
$${}^\circ\text{F} = \frac{9}{5}{}^\circ\text{C} + 32.0 = \left(\frac{9}{5} \times 37.0\right) + 32.0 = 66.6 + 32.0 = 98.6 \ {}^\circ\text{F}$$

Check Your Learning

Convert 80.92 °C to K and °F.

Answer: 354.07 K, 177.7 °F

Example 1.12

Conversion from Fahrenheit

Baking a ready-made pizza calls for an oven temperature of 450 °F. If you are in Europe, and your oven thermometer uses the Celsius scale, what is the setting? What is the kelvin temperature?

Solution

$$°C = \frac{5}{9}(°F - 32) = \frac{5}{9}(450 - 32) = \frac{5}{9} \times 418 = 232\ °C \longrightarrow \text{set oven to } 230\ °C \qquad \text{(two significant figures)}$$

$$K = °C + 273.15 = 230 + 273 = 503\ K \longrightarrow 5.0 \times 10^2\ K \qquad \text{(two significant figures)}$$

Check Your Learning

Convert 50 °F to °C and K.

Answer: 10 °C, 280 K

Key Terms

accuracy how closely a measurement aligns with a correct value

atom smallest particle of an element that can enter into a chemical combination

Celsius (°C) unit of temperature; water freezes at 0 °C and boils at 100 °C on this scale

chemical change change producing a different kind of matter from the original kind of matter

chemical property behavior that is related to the change of one kind of matter into another kind of matter

chemistry study of the composition, properties, and interactions of matter

compound pure substance that can be decomposed into two or more elements

cubic centimeter (cm^3 or cc) volume of a cube with an edge length of exactly 1 cm

cubic meter (m^3) SI unit of volume

density ratio of mass to volume for a substance or object

dimensional analysis (also, factor-label method) versatile mathematical approach that can be applied to computations ranging from simple unit conversions to more complex, multi-step calculations involving several different quantities

element substance that is composed of a single type of atom; a substance that cannot be decomposed by a chemical change

exact number number derived by counting or by definition

extensive property property of a substance that depends on the amount of the substance

Fahrenheit unit of temperature; water freezes at 32 °F and boils at 212 °F on this scale

gas state in which matter has neither definite volume nor shape

heterogeneous mixture combination of substances with a composition that varies from point to point

homogeneous mixture (also, solution) combination of substances with a composition that is uniform throughout

hypothesis tentative explanation of observations that acts as a guide for gathering and checking information

intensive property property of a substance that is independent of the amount of the substance

kelvin (K) SI unit of temperature; 273.15 K = 0 °C

kilogram (kg) standard SI unit of mass; 1 kg = approximately 2.2 pounds

law statement that summarizes a vast number of experimental observations, and describes or predicts some aspect of the natural world

law of conservation of matter when matter converts from one type to another or changes form, there is no detectable change in the total amount of matter present

length measure of one dimension of an object

liquid state of matter that has a definite volume but indefinite shape

liter (L) (also, cubic decimeter) unit of volume; 1 L = 1,000 cm^3

macroscopic domain realm of everyday things that are large enough to sense directly by human sight and touch

mass fundamental property indicating amount of matter

matter anything that occupies space and has mass

meter (m) standard metric and SI unit of length; 1 m = approximately 1.094 yards

microscopic domain realm of things that are much too small to be sensed directly

milliliter (mL) 1/1,000 of a liter; equal to 1 cm^3

mixture matter that can be separated into its components by physical means

molecule bonded collection of two or more atoms of the same or different elements

physical change change in the state or properties of matter that does not involve a change in its chemical composition

physical property characteristic of matter that is not associated with any change in its chemical composition

plasma gaseous state of matter containing a large number of electrically charged atoms and/or molecules

precision how closely a measurement matches the same measurement when repeated

pure substance homogeneous substance that has a constant composition

rounding procedure used to ensure that calculated results properly reflect the uncertainty in the measurements used in the calculation

scientific method path of discovery that leads from question and observation to law or hypothesis to theory, combined with experimental verification of the hypothesis and any necessary modification of the theory

second (s) SI unit of time

SI units (International System of Units) standards fixed by international agreement in the International System of Units (*Le Système International d'Unités*)

significant figures (also, significant digits) all of the measured digits in a determination, including the uncertain last digit

solid state of matter that is rigid, has a definite shape, and has a fairly constant volume

symbolic domain specialized language used to represent components of the macroscopic and microscopic domains, such as chemical symbols, chemical formulas, chemical equations, graphs, drawings, and calculations

theory well-substantiated, comprehensive, testable explanation of a particular aspect of nature

uncertainty estimate of amount by which measurement differs from true value

unit standard of comparison for measurements

unit conversion factor ratio of equivalent quantities expressed with different units; used to convert from one unit to a different unit

volume amount of space occupied by an object

weight force that gravity exerts on an object

Key Equations

- $density = \dfrac{mass}{volume}$

- $T_{°C} = \dfrac{5}{9} \times T_{°F} - 32$

- $T_{°F} = \dfrac{9}{5} \times T_{°C} + 32$

- $T_K = °C + 273.15$

- $T_{°C} = K - 273.15$

Summary

1.1 Chemistry in Context

Chemistry deals with the composition, structure, and properties of matter, and the ways by which various forms of matter may be interconverted. Thus, it occupies a central place in the study and practice of science and technology. Chemists use the scientific method to perform experiments, pose hypotheses, and formulate laws and develop theories, so that they can better understand the behavior of the natural world. To do so, they operate in the macroscopic, microscopic, and symbolic domains. Chemists measure, analyze, purify, and synthesize a wide variety of substances that are important to our lives.

1.2 Phases and Classification of Matter

Matter is anything that occupies space and has mass. The basic building block of matter is the atom, the smallest unit of an element that can enter into combinations with atoms of the same or other elements. In many substances, atoms are combined into molecules. On earth, matter commonly exists in three states: solids, of fixed shape and volume; liquids, of variable shape but fixed volume; and gases, of variable shape and volume. Under high-temperature conditions, matter also can exist as a plasma. Most matter is a mixture: It is composed of two or more types of matter that can be present in varying amounts and can be separated by physical means. Heterogeneous mixtures vary in composition from point to point; homogeneous mixtures have the same composition from point to point. Pure substances consist of only one type of matter. A pure substance can be an element, which consists of only one type of atom and cannot be broken down by a chemical change, or a compound, which consists of two or more types of atoms.

1.3 Physical and Chemical Properties

All substances have distinct physical and chemical properties, and may undergo physical or chemical changes. Physical properties, such as hardness and boiling point, and physical changes, such as melting or freezing, do not involve a change in the composition of matter. Chemical properties, such flammability and acidity, and chemical changes, such as rusting, involve production of matter that differs from that present beforehand.

Measurable properties fall into one of two categories. Extensive properties depend on the amount of matter present, for example, the mass of gold. Intensive properties do not depend on the amount of matter present, for example, the density of gold. Heat is an example of an extensive property, and temperature is an example of an intensive property.

1.4 Measurements

Measurements provide quantitative information that is critical in studying and practicing chemistry. Each measurement has an amount, a unit for comparison, and an uncertainty. Measurements can be represented in either decimal or scientific notation. Scientists primarily use the SI (International System) or metric systems. We use base SI units such as meters, seconds, and kilograms, as well as derived units, such as liters (for volume) and g/cm^3 (for density). In many cases, we find it convenient to use unit prefixes that yield fractional and multiple units, such as microseconds (10^{-6} seconds) and megahertz (10^6 hertz), respectively.

1.5 Measurement Uncertainty, Accuracy, and Precision

Quantities can be exact or measured. Measured quantities have an associated uncertainty that is represented by the number of significant figures in the measurement. The uncertainty of a calculated value depends on the uncertainties in the values used in the calculation and is reflected in how the value is rounded. Measured values can be accurate (close to the true value) and/or precise (showing little variation when measured repeatedly).

1.6 Mathematical Treatment of Measurement Results

Measurements are made using a variety of units. It is often useful or necessary to convert a measured quantity from one unit into another. These conversions are accomplished using unit conversion factors, which are derived by simple applications of a mathematical approach called the factor-label method or dimensional analysis. This strategy is also employed to calculate sought quantities using measured quantities and appropriate mathematical relations.

Exercises

1.1 Chemistry in Context

1. Explain how you could experimentally determine whether the outside temperature is higher or lower than 0 °C (32 °F) without using a thermometer.

2. Identify each of the following statements as being most similar to a hypothesis, a law, or a theory. Explain your reasoning.

(a) Falling barometric pressure precedes the onset of bad weather.

(b) All life on earth has evolved from a common, primitive organism through the process of natural selection.

(c) My truck's gas mileage has dropped significantly, probably because it's due for a tune-up.

3. Identify each of the following statements as being most similar to a hypothesis, a law, or a theory. Explain your reasoning.

(a) The pressure of a sample of gas is directly proportional to the temperature of the gas.

(b) Matter consists of tiny particles that can combine in specific ratios to form substances with specific properties.

(c) At a higher temperature, solids (such as salt or sugar) will dissolve better in water.

4. Identify each of the underlined items as a part of either the macroscopic domain, the microscopic domain, or the symbolic domain of chemistry. For any in the symbolic domain, indicate whether they are symbols for a macroscopic or a microscopic feature.

(a) The mass of a lead pipe is 14 lb.

(b) The mass of a certain chlorine atom is 35 amu.

(c) A bottle with a label that reads Al contains aluminum metal.

(d) Al is the symbol for an aluminum atom.

5. Identify each of the underlined items as a part of either the macroscopic domain, the microscopic domain, or the symbolic domain of chemistry. For those in the symbolic domain, indicate whether they are symbols for a macroscopic or a microscopic feature.

(a) A certain molecule contains one H atom and one Cl atom.

(b) Copper wire has a density of about 8 g/cm^3.

(c) The bottle contains 15 grams of Ni powder.

(d) A sulfur molecule is composed of eight sulfur atoms.

6. According to one theory, the pressure of a gas increases as its volume decreases because the molecules in the gas have to move a shorter distance to hit the walls of the container. Does this theory follow a macroscopic or microscopic description of chemical behavior? Explain your answer.

7.   The amount of heat required to melt 2 lbs of ice is twice the amount of heat required to melt 1 lb of ice. Is this observation a macroscopic or microscopic description of chemical behavior? Explain your answer.

1.2 Phases and Classification of Matter

8.   Why do we use an object's mass, rather than its weight, to indicate the amount of matter it contains?

9.   What properties distinguish solids from liquids? Liquids from gases? Solids from gases?

10.   How does a heterogeneous mixture differ from a homogeneous mixture? How are they similar?

11.   How does a homogeneous mixture differ from a pure substance? How are they similar?

12.   How does an element differ from a compound? How are they similar?

13.   How do molecules of elements and molecules of compounds differ? In what ways are they similar?

14.   How does an atom differ from a molecule? In what ways are they similar?

15.   Many of the items you purchase are mixtures of pure compounds. Select three of these commercial products and prepare a list of the ingredients that are pure compounds.

16.   Classify each of the following as an element, a compound, or a mixture:

(a) copper

(b) water

(c) nitrogen

(d) sulfur

(e) air

(f) sucrose

(g) a substance composed of molecules each of which contains two iodine atoms

(h) gasoline

17.   Classify each of the following as an element, a compound, or a mixture:

(a) iron

(b) oxygen

(c) mercury oxide

(d) pancake syrup

(e) carbon dioxide

(f) a substance composed of molecules each of which contains one hydrogen atom and one chlorine atom

(g) baking soda

(h) baking powder

18.   A sulfur atom and a sulfur molecule are not identical. What is the difference?

19.   How are the molecules in oxygen gas, the molecules in hydrogen gas, and water molecules similar? How do they differ?

20.   We refer to astronauts in space as weightless, but not without mass. Why?

21.   As we drive an automobile, we don't think about the chemicals consumed and produced. Prepare a list of the principal chemicals consumed and produced during the operation of an automobile.

22.   Matter is everywhere around us. Make a list by name of fifteen different kinds of matter that you encounter every day. Your list should include (and label at least one example of each) the following: a solid, a liquid, a gas, an element, a compound, a homogenous mixture, a heterogeneous mixture, and a pure substance.

23. When elemental iron corrodes it combines with oxygen in the air to ultimately form red brown iron(III) oxide which we call rust. (a) If a shiny iron nail with an initial mass of 23.2 g is weighed after being coated in a layer of rust, would you expect the mass to have increased, decreased, or remained the same? Explain. (b) If the mass of the iron nail increases to 24.1 g, what mass of oxygen combined with the iron?

24. As stated in the text, convincing examples that demonstrate the law of conservation of matter outside of the laboratory are few and far between. Indicate whether the mass would increase, decrease, or stay the same for the following scenarios where chemical reactions take place:

(a) Exactly one pound of bread dough is placed in a baking tin. The dough is cooked in an oven at 350 °F releasing a wonderful aroma of freshly baked bread during the cooking process. Is the mass of the baked loaf less than, greater than, or the same as the one pound of original dough? Explain.

(b) When magnesium burns in air a white flaky ash of magnesium oxide is produced. Is the mass of magnesium oxide less than, greater than, or the same as the original piece of magnesium? Explain.

(c) Antoine Lavoisier, the French scientist credited with first stating the law of conservation of matter, heated a mixture of tin and air in a sealed flask to produce tin oxide. Did the mass of the sealed flask and contents decrease, increase, or remain the same after the heating?

25. Yeast converts glucose to ethanol and carbon dioxide during anaerobic fermentation as depicted in the simple chemical equation here:

glucose $\longrightarrow$ ethanol + carbon dioxide

(a) If 200.0 g of glucose is fully converted, what will be the total mass of ethanol and carbon dioxide produced?

(b) If the fermentation is carried out in an open container, would you expect the mass of the container and contents after fermentation to be less than, greater than, or the same as the mass of the container and contents before fermentation? Explain.

(c) If 97.7 g of carbon dioxide is produced, what mass of ethanol is produced?

1.3 Physical and Chemical Properties

26. Classify the six underlined properties in the following paragraph as chemical or physical:

Fluorine is a pale yellow <u>gas</u> that <u>reacts with most substances</u>. The free element <u>melts at −220 °C</u> and <u>boils at −188 °C</u>. Finely divided <u>metals burn in fluorine</u> with a bright flame. <u>Nineteen grams of fluorine will react with 1.0 gram of hydrogen</u>.

27. Classify each of the following changes as physical or chemical:

(a) condensation of steam

(b) burning of gasoline

(c) souring of milk

(d) dissolving of sugar in water

(e) melting of gold

28. Classify each of the following changes as physical or chemical:

(a) coal burning

(b) ice melting

(c) mixing chocolate syrup with milk

(d) explosion of a firecracker

(e) magnetizing of a screwdriver

29. The volume of a sample of oxygen gas changed from 10 mL to 11 mL as the temperature changed. Is this a chemical or physical change?

30. A 2.0-liter volume of hydrogen gas combined with 1.0 liter of oxygen gas to produce 2.0 liters of water vapor. Does oxygen undergo a chemical or physical change?

31. Explain the difference between extensive properties and intensive properties.

32. Identify the following properties as either extensive or intensive.

(a) volume

(b) temperature

(c) humidity

(d) heat

(e) boiling point

33. The density (d) of a substance is an intensive property that is defined as the ratio of its mass (m) to its volume (V). $\text{density} = \frac{\text{mass}}{\text{volume}}$ $d = \frac{m}{V}$

Considering that mass and volume are both extensive properties, explain why their ratio, density, is intensive.

1.4 Measurements

34. Is one liter about an ounce, a pint, a quart, or a gallon?

35. Is a meter about an inch, a foot, a yard, or a mile?

36. Indicate the SI base units or derived units that are appropriate for the following measurements:

(a) the length of a marathon race (26 miles 385 yards)

(b) the mass of an automobile

(c) the volume of a swimming pool

(d) the speed of an airplane

(e) the density of gold

(f) the area of a football field

(g) the maximum temperature at the South Pole on April 1, 1913

37. Indicate the SI base units or derived units that are appropriate for the following measurements:

(a) the mass of the moon

(b) the distance from Dallas to Oklahoma City

(c) the speed of sound

(d) the density of air

(e) the temperature at which alcohol boils

(f) the area of the state of Delaware

(g) the volume of a flu shot or a measles vaccination

38. Give the name and symbol of the prefixes used with SI units to indicate multiplication by the following exact quantities.

(a) 10^3

(b) 10^{-2}

(c) 0.1

(d) 10^{-3}

(e) 1,000,000

(f) 0.000001

39. Give the name of the prefix and the quantity indicated by the following symbols that are used with SI base units.

(a) c

(b) d

(c) G

(d) k

(e) m

(f) n

(g) p

(h) T

40. A large piece of jewelry has a mass of 132.6 g. A graduated cylinder initially contains 48.6 mL water. When the jewelry is submerged in the graduated cylinder, the total volume increases to 61.2 mL.

(a) Determine the density of this piece of jewelry.

(b) Assuming that the jewelry is made from only one substance, what substance is it likely to be? Explain.

41. Visit this **PhET density simulation (http://openstaxcollege.org/l/16phetmasvolden)** and select the Same Volume Blocks.

(a) What are the mass, volume, and density of the yellow block?

(b) What are the mass, volume and density of the red block?

(c) List the block colors in order from smallest to largest mass.

(d) List the block colors in order from lowest to highest density.

(e) How are mass and density related for blocks of the same volume?

42. Visit this **PhET density simulation (http://openstaxcollege.org/l/16phetmasvolden)** and select Custom Blocks and then My Block.

(a) Enter mass and volume values for the block such that the mass in kg is *less than* the volume in L. What does the block do? Why? Is this always the case when mass < volume?

(b) Enter mass and volume values for the block such that the mass in kg is *more than* the volume in L. What does the block do? Why? Is this always the case when mass > volume?

(c) How would (a) and (b) be different if the liquid in the tank were ethanol instead of water?

(d) How would (a) and (b) be different if the liquid in the tank were mercury instead of water?

43. Visit this **PhET density simulation (http://openstaxcollege.org/l/16phetmasvolden)** and select Mystery Blocks.

(a) Pick one of the Mystery Blocks and determine its mass, volume, density, and its likely identity.

(b) Pick a different Mystery Block and determine its mass, volume, density, and its likely identity.

(c) Order the Mystery Blocks from least dense to most dense. Explain.

1.5 Measurement Uncertainty, Accuracy, and Precision

44. Express each of the following numbers in scientific notation with correct significant figures:

(a) 711.0

(b) 0.239

(c) 90743

(d) 134.2

(e) 0.05499

(f) 10000.0

(g) 0.000000738592

45. Express each of the following numbers in exponential notation with correct significant figures:

(a) 704

(b) 0.03344

(c) 547.9

(d) 22086

(e) 1000.00

(f) 0.0000000651

(g) 0.007157

46. Indicate whether each of the following can be determined exactly or must be measured with some degree of uncertainty:

(a) the number of eggs in a basket

(b) the mass of a dozen eggs

(c) the number of gallons of gasoline necessary to fill an automobile gas tank

(d) the number of cm in 2 m

(e) the mass of a textbook

(f) the time required to drive from San Francisco to Kansas City at an average speed of 53 mi/h

47. Indicate whether each of the following can be determined exactly or must be measured with some degree of uncertainty:

(a) the number of seconds in an hour

(b) the number of pages in this book

(c) the number of grams in your weight

(d) the number of grams in 3 kilograms

(e) the volume of water you drink in one day

(f) the distance from San Francisco to Kansas City

48. How many significant figures are contained in each of the following measurements?

(a) 38.7 g

(b) 2×10^{18} m

(c) 3,486,002 kg

(d) 9.74150×10^{-4} J

(e) 0.0613 cm^3

(f) 17.0 kg

(g) 0.01400 g/mL

49. How many significant figures are contained in each of the following measurements?

(a) 53 cm

(b) 2.05×10^8 m

(c) 86,002 J

(d) 9.740×10^4 m/s

(e) 10.0613 m^3

(f) 0.17 g/mL

(g) 0.88400 s

50. The following quantities were reported on the labels of commercial products. Determine the number of significant figures in each.

(a) 0.0055 g active ingredients

(b) 12 tablets

(c) 3% hydrogen peroxide

(d) 5.5 ounces

(e) 473 mL

(f) 1.75% bismuth

(g) 0.001% phosphoric acid

(h) 99.80% inert ingredients

51. Round off each of the following numbers to two significant figures:

(a) 0.436

(b) 9.000

(c) 27.2

(d) 135

(e) 1.497×10^{-3}

(f) 0.445

52. Round off each of the following numbers to two significant figures:

(a) 517

(b) 86.3

(c) 6.382×10^3

(d) 5.0008

(e) 22.497

(f) 0.885

53. Perform the following calculations and report each answer with the correct number of significant figures.

(a) 628×342

(b) $(5.63 \times 10^2) \times (7.4 \times 10^3)$

(c) $\dfrac{28.0}{13.483}$

(d) 8119×0.000023

(e) $14.98 + 27{,}340 + 84.7593$

(f) $42.7 + 0.259$

54. Perform the following calculations and report each answer with the correct number of significant figures.

(a) 62.8×34

(b) $0.147 + 0.0066 + 0.012$

(c) $38 \times 95 \times 1.792$

(d) $15 - 0.15 - 0.6155$

(e) $8.78 \times \left(\dfrac{0.0500}{0.478}\right)$

(f) $140 + 7.68 + 0.014$

(g) $28.7 - 0.0483$

(h) $\dfrac{(88.5 - 87.57)}{45.13}$

55. Consider the results of the archery contest shown in this figure.

(a) Which archer is most precise?

(b) Which archer is most accurate?

(c) Who is both least precise and least accurate?

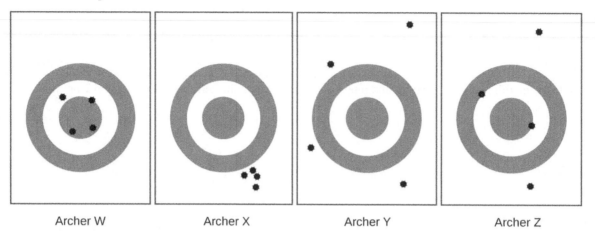

| Archer W | Archer X | Archer Y | Archer Z |

56. Classify the following sets of measurements as accurate, precise, both, or neither.

(a) Checking for consistency in the weight of chocolate chip cookies: 17.27 g, 13.05 g, 19.46 g, 16.92 g

(b) Testing the volume of a batch of 25-mL pipettes: 27.02 mL, 26.99 mL, 26.97 mL, 27.01 mL

(c) Determining the purity of gold: 99.9999%, 99.9998%, 99.9998%, 99.9999%

1.6 Mathematical Treatment of Measurement Results

57. Write conversion factors (as ratios) for the number of:

(a) yards in 1 meter

(b) liters in 1 liquid quart

(c) pounds in 1 kilogram

58. Write conversion factors (as ratios) for the number of:

(a) kilometers in 1 mile

(b) liters in 1 cubic foot

(c) grams in 1 ounce

59. The label on a soft drink bottle gives the volume in two units: 2.0 L and 67.6 fl oz. Use this information to derive a conversion factor between the English and metric units. How many significant figures can you justify in your conversion factor?

60. The label on a box of cereal gives the mass of cereal in two units: 978 grams and 34.5 oz. Use this information to find a conversion factor between the English and metric units. How many significant figures can you justify in your conversion factor?

61. Soccer is played with a round ball having a circumference between 27 and 28 in. and a weight between 14 and 16 oz. What are these specifications in units of centimeters and grams?

62. A woman's basketball has a circumference between 28.5 and 29.0 inches and a maximum weight of 20 ounces (two significant figures). What are these specifications in units of centimeters and grams?

63. How many milliliters of a soft drink are contained in a 12.0-oz can?

64. A barrel of oil is exactly 42 gal. How many liters of oil are in a barrel?

65. The diameter of a red blood cell is about 3×10^{-4} in. What is its diameter in centimeters?

66. The distance between the centers of the two oxygen atoms in an oxygen molecule is 1.21×10^{-8} cm. What is this distance in inches?

67. Is a 197-lb weight lifter light enough to compete in a class limited to those weighing 90 kg or less?

68. A very good 197-lb weight lifter lifted 192 kg in a move called the clean and jerk. What was the mass of the weight lifted in pounds?

69. Many medical laboratory tests are run using 5.0 μL blood serum. What is this volume in milliliters?

70. If an aspirin tablet contains 325 mg aspirin, how many grams of aspirin does it contain?

71. Use scientific (exponential) notation to express the following quantities in terms of the SI base units in Table 1.3:

(a) 0.13 g

(b) 232 Gg

(c) 5.23 pm

(d) 86.3 mg

(e) 37.6 cm

(f) 54 μm

(g) 1 Ts

(h) 27 ps

(i) 0.15 mK

72. Complete the following conversions between SI units.

(a) 612 g = _____ mg

(b) 8.160 m = _____ cm

(c) 3779 μg = _____ g

(d) 781 mL = _____ L

(e) 4.18 kg = _____ g

(f) 27.8 m = _____ km

(g) 0.13 mL = _____ L

(h) 1738 km = _____ m

(i) 1.9 Gg = _____ g

73. Gasoline is sold by the liter in many countries. How many liters are required to fill a 12.0-gal gas tank?

74. Milk is sold by the liter in many countries. What is the volume of exactly 1/2 gal of milk in liters?

75. A long ton is defined as exactly 2240 lb. What is this mass in kilograms?

76. Make the conversion indicated in each of the following:

(a) the men's world record long jump, 29 ft 4¼ in., to meters

(b) the greatest depth of the ocean, about 6.5 mi, to kilometers

(c) the area of the state of Oregon, 96,981 mi^2, to square kilometers

(d) the volume of 1 gill (exactly 4 oz) to milliliters

(e) the estimated volume of the oceans, 330,000,000 mi^3, to cubic kilometers.

(f) the mass of a 3525-lb car to kilograms

(g) the mass of a 2.3-oz egg to grams

77. Make the conversion indicated in each of the following:

(a) the length of a soccer field, 120 m (three significant figures), to feet

(b) the height of Mt. Kilimanjaro, at 19,565 ft the highest mountain in Africa, to kilometers

(c) the area of an 8.5 × 11-inch sheet of paper in cm^2

(d) the displacement volume of an automobile engine, 161 $in.^3$, to liters

(e) the estimated mass of the atmosphere, 5.6×10^{15} tons, to kilograms

(f) the mass of a bushel of rye, 32.0 lb, to kilograms

(g) the mass of a 5.00-grain aspirin tablet to milligrams (1 grain = 0.00229 oz)

78. Many chemistry conferences have held a 50-Trillion Angstrom Run (two significant figures). How long is this run in kilometers and in miles? (1 Å = 1×10^{-10} m)

79. A chemist's 50-Trillion Angstrom Run (see **Exercise 1.78**) would be an archeologist's 10,900 cubit run. How long is one cubit in meters and in feet? (1 Å = 1×10^{-8} cm)

80. The gas tank of a certain luxury automobile holds 22.3 gallons according to the owner's manual. If the density of gasoline is 0.8206 g/mL, determine the mass in kilograms and pounds of the fuel in a full tank.

81. As an instructor is preparing for an experiment, he requires 225 g phosphoric acid. The only container readily available is a 150-mL Erlenmeyer flask. Is it large enough to contain the acid, whose density is 1.83 g/mL?

82. To prepare for a laboratory period, a student lab assistant needs 125 g of a compound. A bottle containing 1/4 lb is available. Did the student have enough of the compound?

83. A chemistry student is 159 cm tall and weighs 45.8 kg. What is her height in inches and weight in pounds?

84. In a recent Grand Prix, the winner completed the race with an average speed of 229.8 km/h. What was his speed in miles per hour, meters per second, and feet per second?

85. Solve these problems about lumber dimensions.

(a) To describe to a European how houses are constructed in the US, the dimensions of "two-by-four" lumber must be converted into metric units. The thickness × width × length dimensions are 1.50 in. × 3.50 in. × 8.00 ft in the US. What are the dimensions in cm × cm × m?

(b) This lumber can be used as vertical studs, which are typically placed 16.0 in. apart. What is that distance in centimeters?

86. The mercury content of a stream was believed to be above the minimum considered safe—1 part per billion (ppb) by weight. An analysis indicated that the concentration was 0.68 parts per billion. What quantity of mercury in grams was present in 15.0 L of the water, the density of which is 0.998 g/ml? (1 ppb Hg = $\frac{1 \text{ ng Hg}}{1 \text{ g water}}$)

87. Calculate the density of aluminum if 27.6 cm^3 has a mass of 74.6 g.

88. Osmium is one of the densest elements known. What is its density if 2.72 g has a volume of 0.121 cm^3?

89. Calculate these masses.

(a) What is the mass of 6.00 cm^3 of mercury, density = 13.5939 g/cm^3?

(b) What is the mass of 25.0 mL octane, density = 0.702 g/cm^3?

90. Calculate these masses.

(a) What is the mass of 4.00 cm^3 of sodium, density = 0.97 g/cm^3 ?

(b) What is the mass of 125 mL gaseous chlorine, density = 3.16 g/L?

91. Calculate these volumes.

(a) What is the volume of 25 g iodine, density = 4.93 g/cm^3?

(b) What is the volume of 3.28 g gaseous hydrogen, density = 0.089 g/L?

92. Calculate these volumes.

(a) What is the volume of 11.3 g graphite, density = 2.25 g/cm^3?

(b) What is the volume of 39.657 g bromine, density = 2.928 g/cm^3?

93. Convert the boiling temperature of gold, 2966 °C, into degrees Fahrenheit and kelvin.

94. Convert the temperature of scalding water, 54 °C, into degrees Fahrenheit and kelvin.

95. Convert the temperature of the coldest area in a freezer, −10 °F, to degrees Celsius and kelvin.

96. Convert the temperature of dry ice, −77 °C, into degrees Fahrenheit and kelvin.

97. Convert the boiling temperature of liquid ammonia, −28.1 °F, into degrees Celsius and kelvin.

98. The label on a pressurized can of spray disinfectant warns against heating the can above 130 °F. What are the corresponding temperatures on the Celsius and kelvin temperature scales?

99. The weather in Europe was unusually warm during the summer of 1995. The TV news reported temperatures as high as 45 °C. What was the temperature on the Fahrenheit scale?

Chapter 2

Atoms, Molecules, and Ions

Figure 2.1 Analysis of molecules in an exhaled breath can provide valuable information, leading to early diagnosis of diseases or detection of environmental exposure to harmful substances. (credit: modification of work by Paul Flowers)

Chapter Outline

2.1 Early Ideas in Atomic Theory

2.2 Evolution of Atomic Theory

2.3 Atomic Structure and Symbolism

2.4 Chemical Formulas

Introduction

Your overall health and susceptibility to disease depends upon the complex interaction between your genetic makeup and environmental exposure, with the outcome difficult to predict. Early detection of biomarkers, substances that indicate an organism's disease or physiological state, could allow diagnosis and treatment before a condition becomes serious or irreversible. Recent studies have shown that your exhaled breath can contain molecules that may be biomarkers for recent exposure to environmental contaminants or for pathological conditions ranging from asthma to lung cancer. Scientists are working to develop biomarker "fingerprints" that could be used to diagnose a specific disease based on the amounts and identities of certain molecules in a patient's exhaled breath. An essential concept underlying this goal is that of a molecule's identity, which is determined by the numbers and types of atoms it contains, and how they are bonded together. This chapter will describe some of the fundamental chemical principles related to the composition of matter, including those central to the concept of molecular identity.

This chapter will lay the foundation for our study of the language of chemistry. The concepts of this foundation include the atomic theory, the composition and mass of an atom, the variability of the composition of isotopes, ion formation, chemical bonds in ionic and covalent compounds, the types of chemical reactions, and the naming of compounds.

2.1 Early Ideas in Atomic Theory

By the end of this section, you will be able to:

- State the postulates of Dalton's atomic theory
- Use postulates of Dalton's atomic theory to explain the laws of definite and multiple proportions

The language used in chemistry is seen and heard in many disciplines, ranging from medicine to engineering to forensics to art. The language of chemistry includes its own vocabulary as well as its own form of shorthand. Chemical symbols are used to represent atoms and elements. Chemical formulas depict molecules as well as the composition of compounds. Chemical equations provide information about the quality and quantity of the changes associated with chemical reactions.

Atomic Theory through the Nineteenth Century

The earliest recorded discussion of the basic structure of matter comes from ancient Greek philosophers, the scientists of their day. In the fifth century BC, Leucippus and Democritus argued that all matter was composed of small, finite particles that they called *atomos*, a term derived from the Greek word for "indivisible." They thought of atoms as moving particles that differed in shape and size, and which could join together. Later, Aristotle and others came to the conclusion that matter consisted of various combinations of the four "elements"—fire, earth, air, and water—and could be infinitely divided. Interestingly, these philosophers thought about atoms and "elements" as philosophical concepts, but apparently never considered performing experiments to test their ideas.

The Aristotelian view of the composition of matter held sway for over two thousand years, until English schoolteacher John Dalton helped to revolutionize chemistry with his hypothesis that the behavior of matter could be explained using an atomic theory. First published in 1807, many of Dalton's hypotheses about the microscopic features of matter are still valid in modern atomic theory. Here are the postulates of **Dalton's atomic theory**.

1. Matter is composed of exceedingly small particles called atoms. An atom is the smallest unit of an element that can participate in a chemical change.

2. An element consists of only one type of atom, which has a mass that is characteristic of the element and is the same for all atoms of that element (**Figure 2.2**). A macroscopic sample of an element contains an incredibly large number of atoms, all of which have identical chemical properties.

Figure 2.2   A pre-1982 copper penny (left) contains approximately 3×10^{22} copper atoms (several dozen are represented as brown spheres at the right), each of which has the same chemical properties. (credit: modification of work by "slgckgc"/Flickr)

3. Atoms of one element differ in properties from atoms of all other elements.

4. A compound consists of atoms of two or more elements combined in a small, whole-number ratio. In a given compound, the numbers of atoms of each of its elements are always present in the same ratio (**Figure 2.3**).

Copper(II) oxide

Figure 2.3 Copper(II) oxide, a powdery, black compound, results from the combination of two types of atoms—copper (brown spheres) and oxygen (red spheres)—in a 1:1 ratio. (credit: modification of work by "Chemicalinterest"/Wikimedia Commons)

5. Atoms are neither created nor destroyed during a chemical change, but are instead rearranged to yield substances that are different from those present before the change (**Figure 2.4**).

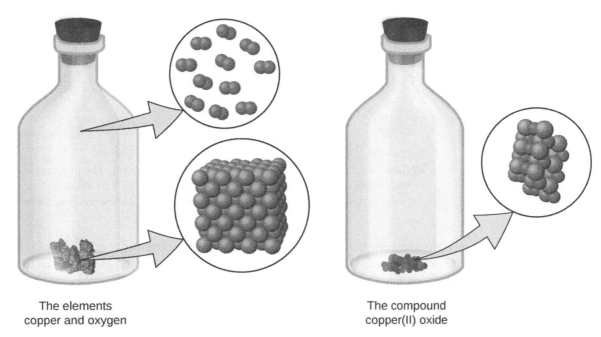

The elements
copper and oxygen

The compound
copper(II) oxide

Figure 2.4 When the elements copper (a shiny, red-brown solid, shown here as brown spheres) and oxygen (a clear and colorless gas, shown here as red spheres) react, their atoms rearrange to form a compound containing copper and oxygen (a powdery, black solid). (credit copper: modification of work by http://images-of-elements.com/copper.php)

Dalton's atomic theory provides a microscopic explanation of the many macroscopic properties of matter that you've learned about. For example, if an element such as copper consists of only one kind of atom, then it cannot be broken down into simpler substances, that is, into substances composed of fewer types of atoms. And if atoms are neither created nor destroyed during a chemical change, then the total mass of matter present when matter changes from one type to another will remain constant (the law of conservation of matter).

Example 2.1

Testing Dalton's Atomic Theory

In the following drawing, the green spheres represent atoms of a certain element. The purple spheres represent atoms of another element. If the spheres touch, they are part of a single unit of a compound. Does the following chemical change represented by these symbols violate any of the ideas of Dalton's atomic theory? If so, which one?

Starting materials   Products of the change

Solution

The starting materials consist of two green spheres and two purple spheres. The products consist of only one green sphere and one purple sphere. This violates Dalton's postulate that atoms are neither created nor destroyed during a chemical change, but are merely redistributed. (In this case, atoms appear to have been destroyed.)

Check Your Learning

In the following drawing, the green spheres represent atoms of a certain element. The purple spheres represent atoms of another element. If the spheres touch, they are part of a single unit of a compound. Does the following chemical change represented by these symbols violate any of the ideas of Dalton's atomic theory? If so, which one?

Starting materials   Products of the change

Answer: The starting materials consist of four green spheres and two purple spheres. The products consist of four green spheres and two purple spheres. This does not violate any of Dalton's postulates: Atoms are neither created nor destroyed, but are redistributed in small, whole-number ratios.

Dalton knew of the experiments of French chemist Joseph Proust, who demonstrated that *all samples of a pure compound contain the same elements in the same proportion by mass*. This statement is known as the **law of definite proportions** or the **law of constant composition**. The suggestion that the numbers of atoms of the elements in a given compound always exist in the same ratio is consistent with these observations. For example, when different samples of isooctane (a component of gasoline and one of the standards used in the octane rating system) are analyzed, they are found to have a carbon-to-hydrogen mass ratio of 5.33:1, as shown in Table 2.1.

Constant Composition of Isooctane

Sample	Carbon	Hydrogen	Mass Ratio	
A	14.82 g	2.78 g	$\dfrac{14.82 \text{ g carbon}}{2.78 \text{ g hydrogen}}$	$= \dfrac{5.33 \text{ g carbon}}{1.00 \text{ g hydrogen}}$
B	22.33 g	4.19 g	$\dfrac{22.33 \text{ g carbon}}{4.19 \text{ g hydrogen}}$	$= \dfrac{5.33 \text{ g carbon}}{1.00 \text{ g hydrogen}}$
C	19.40 g	3.64 g	$\dfrac{19.40 \text{ g carbon}}{3.63 \text{ g hydrogen}}$	$= \dfrac{5.33 \text{ g carbon}}{1.00 \text{ g hydrogen}}$

Table 2.1

It is worth noting that although all samples of a particular compound have the same mass ratio, the converse is not true in general. That is, samples that have the same mass ratio are not necessarily the same substance. For example, there are many compounds other than isooctane that also have a carbon-to-hydrogen mass ratio of 5.33:1.00.

Dalton also used data from Proust, as well as results from his own experiments, to formulate another interesting law. The **law of multiple proportions** states that *when two elements react to form more than one compound, a fixed mass of one element will react with masses of the other element in a ratio of small, whole numbers.* For example, copper and chlorine can form a green, crystalline solid with a mass ratio of 0.558 g chlorine to 1 g copper, as well as a brown crystalline solid with a mass ratio of 1.116 g chlorine to 1 g copper. These ratios by themselves may not seem particularly interesting or informative; however, if we take a ratio of these ratios, we obtain a useful and possibly surprising result: a small, whole-number ratio.

$$\frac{\dfrac{1.116 \text{ g Cl}}{1 \text{ g Cu}}}{\dfrac{0.558 \text{ g Cl}}{1 \text{ g Cu}}} = \frac{2}{1}$$

This 2-to-1 ratio means that the brown compound has twice the amount of chlorine per amount of copper as the green compound.

This can be explained by atomic theory if the copper-to-chlorine ratio in the brown compound is 1 copper atom to 2 chlorine atoms, and the ratio in the green compound is 1 copper atom to 1 chlorine atom. The ratio of chlorine atoms (and thus the ratio of their masses) is therefore 2 to 1 (**Figure 2.5**).

Figure 2.5 Compared to the copper chlorine compound in (a), where copper is represented by brown spheres and chlorine by green spheres, the copper chlorine compound in (b) has twice as many chlorine atoms per copper atom. (credit a: modification of work by "Benjah-bmm27"/Wikimedia Commons; credit b: modification of work by "Walkerma"/Wikimedia Commons)

Example 2.2

Laws of Definite and Multiple Proportions

A sample of compound A (a clear, colorless gas) is analyzed and found to contain 4.27 g carbon and 5.69 g oxygen. A sample of compound B (also a clear, colorless gas) is analyzed and found to contain 5.19 g carbon and 13.84 g oxygen. Are these data an example of the law of definite proportions, the law of multiple proportions, or neither? What do these data tell you about substances A and B?

Solution

In compound A, the mass ratio of carbon to oxygen is:

$$\frac{1.33 \text{ g O}}{1 \text{ g C}}$$

In compound B, the mass ratio of carbon to oxygen is:

$$\frac{2.67 \text{ g O}}{1 \text{ g C}}$$

The ratio of these ratios is:

$$\frac{\frac{1.33 \text{ g O}}{1 \text{ g C}}}{\frac{2.67 \text{ g O}}{1 \text{ g C}}} = \frac{1}{2}$$

This supports the law of multiple proportions. This means that A and B are different compounds, with A having one-half as much carbon per amount of oxygen (or twice as much oxygen per amount of carbon) as B. A possible pair of compounds that would fit this relationship would be A = CO_2 and B = CO.

Check Your Learning

A sample of compound X (a clear, colorless, combustible liquid with a noticeable odor) is analyzed and found to contain 14.13 g carbon and 2.96 g hydrogen. A sample of compound Y (a clear, colorless, combustible liquid with a noticeable odor that is slightly different from X's odor) is analyzed and found to contain 19.91 g carbon and 3.34 g hydrogen. Are these data an example of the law of definite proportions, the law of multiple proportions, or neither? What do these data tell you about substances X and Y?

Answer: In compound X, the mass ratio of carbon to hydrogen is $\frac{14.13 \text{ g C}}{2.96 \text{ g H}}$. In compound Y, the mass ratio of carbon to oxygen is $\frac{19.91 \text{ g C}}{3.34 \text{ g H}}$. The ratio of these ratios is

$\frac{\frac{14.13 \text{ g C}}{2.96 \text{ g H}}}{\frac{19.91 \text{ g C}}{3.34 \text{ g H}}} = \frac{4.77 \text{ g C/g H}}{5.96 \text{ g C/g H}} = 0.800 = \frac{4}{5}$. This small, whole-number ratio supports the law of multiple

proportions. This means that X and Y are different compounds.

2.2 Evolution of Atomic Theory

By the end of this section, you will be able to:

- Outline milestones in the development of modern atomic theory
- Summarize and interpret the results of the experiments of Thomson, Millikan, and Rutherford
- Describe the three subatomic particles that compose atoms
- Define isotopes and give examples for several elements

In the two centuries since Dalton developed his ideas, scientists have made significant progress in furthering our understanding of atomic theory. Much of this came from the results of several seminal experiments that revealed the details of the internal structure of atoms. Here, we will discuss some of those key developments, with an emphasis on application of the scientific method, as well as understanding how the experimental evidence was analyzed. While the historical persons and dates behind these experiments can be quite interesting, it is most important to understand the concepts resulting from their work.

Atomic Theory after the Nineteenth Century

If matter were composed of atoms, what were atoms composed of? Were they the smallest particles, or was there something smaller? In the late 1800s, a number of scientists interested in questions like these investigated the electrical discharges that could be produced in low-pressure gases, with the most significant discovery made by English physicist J. J. Thomson using a cathode ray tube. This apparatus consisted of a sealed glass tube from which almost all the air had been removed; the tube contained two metal electrodes. When high voltage was applied across the electrodes, a visible beam called a cathode ray appeared between them. This beam was deflected toward the positive charge and away from the negative charge, and was produced in the same way with identical properties when different metals were used for the electrodes. In similar experiments, the ray was simultaneously deflected by an applied magnetic field, and measurements of the extent of deflection and the magnetic field strength allowed Thomson to calculate the charge-to-mass ratio of the cathode ray particles. The results of these measurements indicated that these particles were much lighter than atoms (Figure 2.6).

Figure 2.6   (a) J. J. Thomson produced a visible beam in a cathode ray tube. (b) This is an early cathode ray tube, invented in 1897 by Ferdinand Braun. (c) In the cathode ray, the beam (shown in yellow) comes from the cathode and is accelerated past the anode toward a fluorescent scale at the end of the tube. Simultaneous deflections by applied electric and magnetic fields permitted Thomson to calculate the mass-to-charge ratio of the particles composing the cathode ray. (credit a: modification of work by Nobel Foundation; credit b: modification of work by Eugen Nesper; credit c: modification of work by "Kurzon"/Wikimedia Commons)

Based on his observations, here is what Thomson proposed and why: The particles are attracted by positive (+) charges and repelled by negative (−) charges, so they must be negatively charged (like charges repel and unlike charges attract); they are less massive than atoms and indistinguishable, regardless of the source material, so they must be fundamental, subatomic constituents of all atoms. Although controversial at the time, Thomson's idea was gradually accepted, and his cathode ray particle is what we now call an **electron**, a negatively charged, subatomic particle with a mass more than one thousand-times less that of an atom. The term "electron" was coined in 1891 by Irish physicist George Stoney, from "*electr*ic i*on*."

In 1909, more information about the electron was uncovered by American physicist Robert A. Millikan via his "oil drop" experiments. Millikan created microscopic oil droplets, which could be electrically charged by friction as they formed or by using X-rays. These droplets initially fell due to gravity, but their downward progress could be slowed or even reversed by an electric field lower in the apparatus. By adjusting the electric field strength and making careful measurements and appropriate calculations, Millikan was able to determine the charge on individual drops (**Figure 2.7**).

Oil drop	Charge in coulombs (C)
A	4.8×10^{-19} C
B	3.2×10^{-19} C
C	6.4×10^{-19} C
D	1.6×10^{-19} C
E	4.8×10^{-19} C

Figure 2.7 Millikan's experiment measured the charge of individual oil drops. The tabulated data are examples of a few possible values.

Looking at the charge data that Millikan gathered, you may have recognized that the charge of an oil droplet is always a multiple of a specific charge, 1.6×10^{-19} C. Millikan concluded that this value must therefore be a fundamental charge—the charge of a single electron—with his measured charges due to an excess of one electron (1 times 1.6×10^{-19} C), two electrons (2 times 1.6×10^{-19} C), three electrons (3 times 1.6×10^{-19} C), and so on, on a given oil droplet. Since the charge of an electron was now known due to Millikan's research, and the charge-to-mass ratio was already known due to Thomson's research (1.759×10^{11} C/kg), it only required a simple calculation to determine the mass of the electron as well.

$$\text{Mass of electron} = 1.602 \times 10^{-19} \text{ C} \times \frac{1 \text{ kg}}{1.759 \times 10^{11} \text{ C}} = 9.107 \times 10^{-31} \text{ kg}$$

Scientists had now established that the atom was not indivisible as Dalton had believed, and due to the work of Thomson, Millikan, and others, the charge and mass of the negative, subatomic particles—the electrons—were known. However, the positively charged part of an atom was not yet well understood. In 1904, Thomson proposed the "plum pudding" model of atoms, which described a positively charged mass with an equal amount of negative charge in the form of electrons embedded in it, since all atoms are electrically neutral. A competing model had been proposed in 1903 by Hantaro Nagaoka, who postulated a Saturn-like atom, consisting of a positively charged sphere surrounded by a halo of electrons (Figure 2.8).

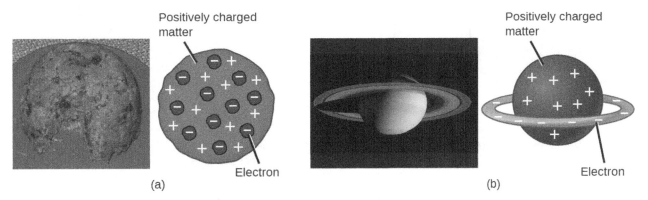

Figure 2.8 (a) Thomson suggested that atoms resembled plum pudding, an English dessert consisting of moist cake with embedded raisins ("plums"). (b) Nagaoka proposed that atoms resembled the planet Saturn, with a ring of electrons surrounding a positive "planet." (credit a: modification of work by "Man vyi"/Wikimedia Commons; credit b: modification of work by "NASA"/Wikimedia Commons)

The next major development in understanding the atom came from Ernest Rutherford, a physicist from New Zealand who largely spent his scientific career in Canada and England. He performed a series of experiments using a beam of high-speed, positively charged **alpha particles (α particles)** that were produced by the radioactive decay of radium; α particles consist of two protons and two neutrons (you will learn more about radioactive decay in the chapter on nuclear chemistry). Rutherford and his colleagues Hans Geiger (later famous for the Geiger counter) and Ernest Marsden aimed a beam of α particles, the source of which was embedded in a lead block to absorb most of the radiation, at a very thin piece of gold foil and examined the resultant scattering of the α particles using a luminescent screen that glowed briefly where hit by an α particle.

What did they discover? Most particles passed right through the foil without being deflected at all. However, some were diverted slightly, and a very small number were deflected almost straight back toward the source (Figure 2.9). Rutherford described finding these results: "It was quite the most incredible event that has ever happened to me in my life. It was almost as incredible as if you fired a 15-inch shell at a piece of tissue paper and it came back and hit you"[1] (p. 68).

---

1. Ernest Rutherford, "The Development of the Theory of Atomic Structure," ed. J. A. Ratcliffe, in *Background to Modern Science*, eds. Joseph Needham and Walter Pagel, (Cambridge, UK: Cambridge University Press, 1938), 61–74. Accessed September 22, 2014, https://ia600508.us.archive.org/3/items/backgroundtomode032734mbp/backgroundtomode032734mbp.pdf.

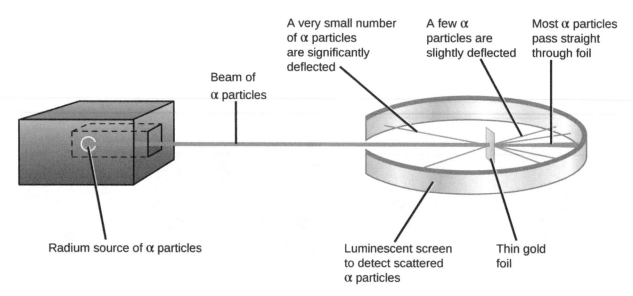

Figure 2.9 Geiger and Rutherford fired α particles at a piece of gold foil and detected where those particles went, as shown in this schematic diagram of their experiment. Most of the particles passed straight through the foil, but a few were deflected slightly and a very small number were significantly deflected.

Here is what Rutherford deduced: Because most of the fast-moving α particles passed through the gold atoms undeflected, they must have traveled through essentially empty space inside the atom. Alpha particles are positively charged, so deflections arose when they encountered another positive charge (like charges repel each other). Since like charges repel one another, the few positively charged α particles that changed paths abruptly must have hit, or closely approached, another body that also had a highly concentrated, positive charge. Since the deflections occurred a small fraction of the time, this charge only occupied a small amount of the space in the gold foil. Analyzing a series of such experiments in detail, Rutherford drew two conclusions:

1. The volume occupied by an atom must consist of a large amount of empty space.

2. A small, relatively heavy, positively charged body, the **nucleus**, must be at the center of each atom.

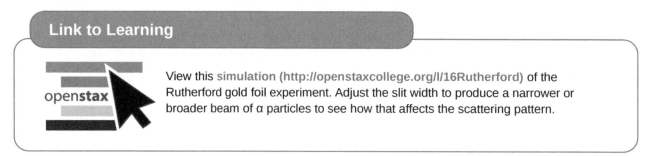

Link to Learning

View this simulation (http://openstaxcollege.org/l/16Rutherford) of the Rutherford gold foil experiment. Adjust the slit width to produce a narrower or broader beam of α particles to see how that affects the scattering pattern.

This analysis led Rutherford to propose a model in which an atom consists of a very small, positively charged nucleus, in which most of the mass of the atom is concentrated, surrounded by the negatively charged electrons, so that the atom is electrically neutral (**Figure 2.10**). After many more experiments, Rutherford also discovered that the nuclei of other elements contain the hydrogen nucleus as a "building block," and he named this more fundamental particle the **proton**, the positively charged, subatomic particle found in the nucleus. With one addition, which you will learn next, this nuclear model of the atom, proposed over a century ago, is still used today.

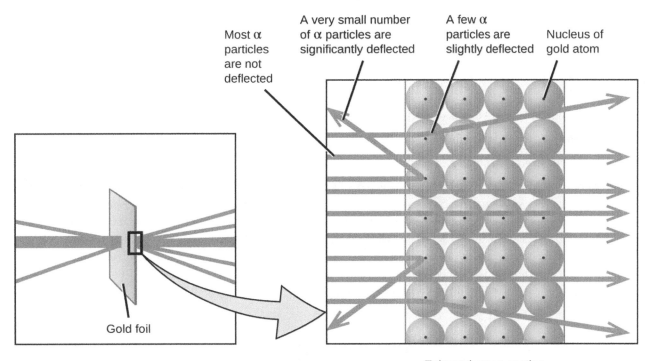

Enlarged cross-section

Figure 2.10 The α particles are deflected only when they collide with or pass close to the much heavier, positively charged gold nucleus. Because the nucleus is very small compared to the size of an atom, very few α particles are deflected. Most pass through the relatively large region occupied by electrons, which are too light to deflect the rapidly moving particles.

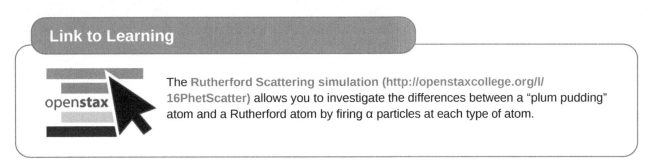

Link to Learning

The **Rutherford Scattering simulation (http://openstaxcollege.org/l/ 16PhetScatter)** allows you to investigate the differences between a "plum pudding" atom and a Rutherford atom by firing α particles at each type of atom.

Another important finding was the discovery of isotopes. During the early 1900s, scientists identified several substances that appeared to be new elements, isolating them from radioactive ores. For example, a "new element" produced by the radioactive decay of thorium was initially given the name mesothorium. However, a more detailed analysis showed that mesothorium was chemically identical to radium (another decay product), despite having a different atomic mass. This result, along with similar findings for other elements, led the English chemist Frederick Soddy to realize that an element could have types of atoms with different masses that were chemically indistinguishable. These different types are called **isotopes**—atoms of the same element that differ in mass. Soddy was awarded the Nobel Prize in Chemistry in 1921 for this discovery.

One puzzle remained: The nucleus was known to contain almost all of the mass of an atom, with the number of protons only providing half, or less, of that mass. Different proposals were made to explain what constituted the remaining mass, including the existence of neutral particles in the nucleus. As you might expect, detecting uncharged particles is very challenging, and it was not until 1932 that James Chadwick found evidence of **neutrons**, uncharged, subatomic particles with a mass approximately the same as that of protons. The existence of the neutron also explained isotopes: They differ in mass because they have different numbers of neutrons, but they are chemically identical because they have the same number of protons. This will be explained in more detail later.

2.3 Atomic Structure and Symbolism

By the end of this section, you will be able to:

- Write and interpret symbols that depict the atomic number, mass number, and charge of an atom or ion
- Define the atomic mass unit and average atomic mass
- Calculate average atomic mass and isotopic abundance

The development of modern atomic theory revealed much about the inner structure of atoms. It was learned that an atom contains a very small nucleus composed of positively charged protons and uncharged neutrons, surrounded by a much larger volume of space containing negatively charged electrons. The nucleus contains the majority of an atom's mass because protons and neutrons are much heavier than electrons, whereas electrons occupy almost all of an atom's volume. The diameter of an atom is on the order of 10^{-10} m, whereas the diameter of the nucleus is roughly 10^{-15} m—about 100,000 times smaller. For a perspective about their relative sizes, consider this: If the nucleus were the size of a blueberry, the atom would be about the size of a football stadium (Figure 2.11).

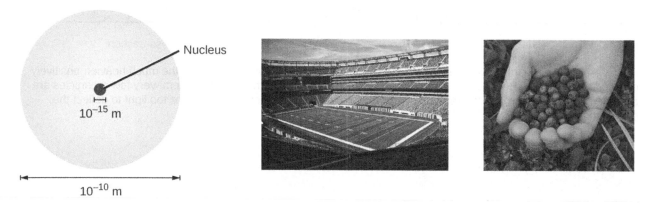

Figure 2.11 If an atom could be expanded to the size of a football stadium, the nucleus would be the size of a single blueberry. (credit middle: modification of work by "babyknight"/Wikimedia Commons; credit right: modification of work by Paxson Woelber)

Atoms—and the protons, neutrons, and electrons that compose them—are extremely small. For example, a carbon atom weighs less than 2×10^{-23} g, and an electron has a charge of less than 2×10^{-19} C (coulomb). When describing the properties of tiny objects such as atoms, we use appropriately small units of measure, such as the **atomic mass unit (amu)** and the **fundamental unit of charge (e)**. The amu was originally defined based on hydrogen, the lightest element, then later in terms of oxygen. Since 1961, it has been defined with regard to the most abundant isotope of carbon, atoms of which are assigned masses of exactly 12 amu. (This isotope is known as "carbon-12" as will be discussed later in this module.) Thus, one amu is exactly $\frac{1}{12}$ of the mass of one carbon-12 atom: 1 amu = 1.6605×10^{-24} g. (The **Dalton (Da)** and the **unified atomic mass unit (u)** are alternative units that are equivalent to the amu.) The fundamental unit of charge (also called the elementary charge) equals the magnitude of the charge of an electron (e) with e = 1.602×10^{-19} C.

A proton has a mass of 1.0073 amu and a charge of 1+. A neutron is a slightly heavier particle with a mass 1.0087 amu and a charge of zero; as its name suggests, it is neutral. The electron has a charge of 1− and is a much lighter particle with a mass of about 0.00055 amu (it would take about 1800 electrons to equal the mass of one proton. The properties of these fundamental particles are summarized in Table 2.2. (An observant student might notice that the sum of an atom's subatomic particles does not equal the atom's actual mass: The total mass of six protons, six neutrons, and six electrons is 12.0993 amu, slightly larger than 12.00 amu. This "missing" mass is known as the mass defect, and you will learn about it in the chapter on nuclear chemistry.)

Properties of Subatomic Particles

Name	Location	Charge (C)	Unit Charge	Mass (amu)	Mass (g)
electron	outside nucleus	-1.602×10^{-19}	1–	0.00055	0.00091×10^{-24}
proton	nucleus	1.602×10^{-19}	1+	1.00727	1.67262×10^{-24}
neutron	nucleus	0	0	1.00866	1.67493×10^{-24}

Table 2.2

The number of protons in the nucleus of an atom is its **atomic number (Z)**. This is the defining trait of an element: Its value determines the identity of the atom. For example, any atom that contains six protons is the element carbon and has the atomic number 6, regardless of how many neutrons or electrons it may have. A neutral atom must contain the same number of positive and negative charges, so the number of protons equals the number of electrons. Therefore, the atomic number also indicates the number of electrons in an atom. The total number of protons and neutrons in an atom is called its **mass number (A)**. The number of neutrons is therefore the difference between the mass number and the atomic number: A – Z = number of neutrons.

$$\text{atomic number (Z)} \quad = \quad \text{number of protons}$$
$$\text{mass number (A)} \quad = \quad \text{number of protons} + \text{number of neutrons}$$
$$A - Z \quad = \quad \text{number of neutrons}$$

Atoms are electrically neutral if they contain the same number of positively charged protons and negatively charged electrons. When the numbers of these subatomic particles are *not* equal, the atom is electrically charged and is called an **ion**. The charge of an atom is defined as follows:

Atomic charge = number of protons − number of electrons

As will be discussed in more detail, atoms (and molecules) typically acquire charge by gaining or losing electrons. An atom that gains one or more electrons will exhibit a negative charge and is called an **anion**. Positively charged atoms called **cations** are formed when an atom loses one or more electrons. For example, a neutral sodium atom (Z = 11) has 11 electrons. If this atom loses one electron, it will become a cation with a 1+ charge (11 − 10 = 1+). A neutral oxygen atom (Z = 8) has eight electrons, and if it gains two electrons it will become an anion with a 2− charge (8 − 10 = 2−).

Example 2.3

Composition of an Atom

Iodine is an essential trace element in our diet; it is needed to produce thyroid hormone. Insufficient iodine in the diet can lead to the development of a goiter, an enlargement of the thyroid gland (Figure 2.12).

(a)   (b)

Figure 2.12   (a) Insufficient iodine in the diet can cause an enlargement of the thyroid gland called a goiter. (b) The addition of small amounts of iodine to salt, which prevents the formation of goiters, has helped eliminate this concern in the US where salt consumption is high. (credit a: modification of work by "Almazi"/Wikimedia Commons; credit b: modification of work by Mike Mozart)

The addition of small amounts of iodine to table salt (iodized salt) has essentially eliminated this health concern in the United States, but as much as 40% of the world's population is still at risk of iodine deficiency. The iodine atoms are added as anions, and each has a 1− charge and a mass number of 127. Determine the numbers of protons, neutrons, and electrons in one of these iodine anions.

Solution

The atomic number of iodine (53) tells us that a neutral iodine atom contains 53 protons in its nucleus and 53 electrons outside its nucleus. Because the sum of the numbers of protons and neutrons equals the mass number, 127, the number of neutrons is 74 (127 − 53 = 74). Since the iodine is added as a 1− anion, the number of electrons is 54 [53 − (1−) = 54].

Check Your Learning

An ion of platinum has a mass number of 195 and contains 74 electrons. How many protons and neutrons does it contain, and what is its charge?

Answer: 78 protons; 117 neutrons; charge is 4+

Chemical Symbols

A **chemical symbol** is an abbreviation that we use to indicate an element or an atom of an element. For example, the symbol for mercury is Hg (**Figure 2.13**). We use the same symbol to indicate one atom of mercury (microscopic domain) or to label a container of many atoms of the element mercury (macroscopic domain).

Figure 2.13   The symbol Hg represents the element mercury regardless of the amount; it could represent one atom of mercury or a large amount of mercury.

The symbols for several common elements and their atoms are listed in Table 2.3. Some symbols are derived from the common name of the element; others are abbreviations of the name in another language. Most symbols have one or two letters, but three-letter symbols have been used to describe some elements that have atomic numbers greater than 112. To avoid confusion with other notations, only the first letter of a symbol is capitalized. For example, Co is the symbol for the element cobalt, but CO is the notation for the compound carbon monoxide, which contains atoms of the elements carbon (C) and oxygen (O). All known elements and their symbols are in the periodic table in Figure 3.380 (also found in image).

Some Common Elements and Their Symbols

Element	Symbol	Element	Symbol
aluminum	Al	iron	Fe (from *ferrum*)
bromine	Br	lead	Pb (from *plumbum*)
calcium	Ca	magnesium	Mg
carbon	C	mercury	Hg (from *hydrargyrum*)
chlorine	Cl	nitrogen	N
chromium	Cr	oxygen	O
cobalt	Co	potassium	K (from *kalium*)
copper	Cu (from *cuprum*)	silicon	Si
fluorine	F	silver	Ag (from *argentum*)
gold	Au (from *aurum*)	sodium	Na (from *natrium*)
helium	He	sulfur	S
hydrogen	H	tin	Sn (from *stannum*)
iodine	I	zinc	Zn

Table 2.3

Traditionally, the discoverer (or discoverers) of a new element names the element. However, until the name is recognized by the International Union of Pure and Applied Chemistry (IUPAC), the recommended name of the new element is based on the Latin word(s) for its atomic number. For example, element 106 was called unnilhexium (Unh), element 107 was called unnilseptium (Uns), and element 108 was called unniloctium (Uno) for several years. These elements are now named after scientists (or occasionally locations); for example, element 106 is now known as *seaborgium* (Sg) in honor of Glenn Seaborg, a Nobel Prize winner who was active in the discovery of several heavy elements.

Link to Learning

Visit this site (http://openstaxcollege.org/l/16IUPAC) to learn more about IUPAC, the International Union of Pure and Applied Chemistry, and explore its periodic table.

Isotopes

The symbol for a specific isotope of any element is written by placing the mass number as a superscript to the left of the element symbol (**Figure 2.14**). The atomic number is sometimes written as a subscript preceding the symbol, but since this number defines the element's identity, as does its symbol, it is often omitted. For example, magnesium exists as a mixture of three isotopes, each with an atomic number of 12 and with mass numbers of 24, 25, and 26, respectively. These isotopes can be identified as ^{24}Mg, ^{25}Mg, and ^{26}Mg. These isotope symbols are read as "element, mass number" and can be symbolized consistent with this reading. For instance, ^{24}Mg is read as "magnesium 24," and can be written as "magnesium-24" or "Mg-24." ^{25}Mg is read as "magnesium 25," and can be written as "magnesium-25" or "Mg-25." All magnesium atoms have 12 protons in their nucleus. They differ only because a ^{24}Mg atom has 12 neutrons in its nucleus, a ^{25}Mg atom has 13 neutrons, and a ^{26}Mg has 14 neutrons.

Mass number ——— 4   2+ —— Charge   24   2+

$$\text{He} \qquad\qquad \text{Mg}$$

Atomic number —— 2   12
(often omitted)

Figure 2.14 The symbol for an atom indicates the element via its usual two-letter symbol, the mass number as a left superscript, the atomic number as a left subscript (sometimes omitted), and the charge as a right superscript.

Information about the naturally occurring isotopes of elements with atomic numbers 1 through 10 is given in **Table 2.4**. Note that in addition to standard names and symbols, the isotopes of hydrogen are often referred to using common names and accompanying symbols. Hydrogen-2, symbolized ^{2}H, is also called deuterium and sometimes symbolized D. Hydrogen-3, symbolized ^{3}H, is also called tritium and sometimes symbolized T.

Nuclear Compositions of Atoms of the Very Light Elements

Element	Symbol	Atomic Number	Number of Protons	Number of Neutrons	Mass (amu)	% Natural Abundance
hydrogen	$^1_1$H (protium)	1	1	0	1.0078	99.989

Table 2.4

Nuclear Compositions of Atoms of the Very Light Elements

Element	Symbol	Atomic Number	Number of Protons	Number of Neutrons	Mass (amu)	% Natural Abundance
	$_1^2$H (deuterium)	1	1	1	2.0141	0.0115
	$_1^3$H (tritium)	1	1	2	3.01605	— (trace)
helium	$_2^3$He	2	2	1	3.01603	0.00013
	$_2^4$He	2	2	2	4.0026	100
lithium	$_3^6$Li	3	3	3	6.0151	7.59
	$_3^7$Li	3	3	4	7.0160	92.41
beryllium	$_4^9$Be	4	4	5	9.0122	100
boron	$_5^{10}$B	5	5	5	10.0129	19.9
	$_5^{11}$B	5	5	6	11.0093	80.1
carbon	$_6^{12}$C	6	6	6	12.0000	98.89
	$_6^{13}$C	6	6	7	13.0034	1.11
	$_6^{14}$C	6	6	8	14.0032	— (trace)
nitrogen	$_7^{14}$N	7	7	7	14.0031	99.63
	$_7^{15}$N	7	7	8	15.0001	0.37
oxygen	$_8^{16}$O	8	8	8	15.9949	99.757
	$_8^{17}$O	8	8	9	16.9991	0.038
	$_8^{18}$O	8	8	10	17.9992	0.205
fluorine	$_9^{19}$F	9	9	10	18.9984	100
neon	$_{10}^{20}$Ne	10	10	10	19.9924	90.48
	$_{10}^{21}$Ne	10	10	11	20.9938	0.27
	$_{10}^{22}$Ne	10	10	12	21.9914	9.25

Table 2.4

Link to Learning

Use this **Build an Atom simulator (http://openstaxcollege.org/l/ 16PhetAtomBld)** to build atoms of the first 10 elements, see which isotopes exist, check nuclear stability, and gain experience with isotope symbols.

Atomic Mass

Because each proton and each neutron contribute approximately one amu to the mass of an atom, and each electron contributes far less, the **atomic mass** of a single atom is approximately equal to its mass number (a whole number). However, the average masses of atoms of most elements are not whole numbers because most elements exist naturally as mixtures of two or more isotopes.

The mass of an element shown in a periodic table or listed in a table of atomic masses is a weighted, average mass of all the isotopes present in a naturally occurring sample of that element. This is equal to the sum of each individual isotope's mass multiplied by its fractional abundance.

$$\text{average mass} = \sum_i (\text{fractional abundance} \times \text{isotopic mass})_i$$

For example, the element boron is composed of two isotopes: About 19.9% of all boron atoms are ^{10}B with a mass of 10.0129 amu, and the remaining 80.1% are ^{11}B with a mass of 11.0093 amu. The average atomic mass for boron is calculated to be:

$$\begin{aligned}\text{boron average mass} &= (0.199 \times 10.0129 \text{ amu}) + (0.801 \times 11.0093 \text{ amu}) \\ &= 1.99 \text{ amu} + 8.82 \text{ amu} \\ &= 10.81 \text{ amu}\end{aligned}$$

It is important to understand that no single boron atom weighs exactly 10.8 amu; 10.8 amu is the average mass of all boron atoms, and individual boron atoms weigh either approximately 10 amu or 11 amu.

Example 2.4

Calculation of Average Atomic Mass

A meteorite found in central Indiana contains traces of the noble gas neon picked up from the solar wind during the meteorite's trip through the solar system. Analysis of a sample of the gas showed that it consisted of 91.84% ^{20}Ne (mass 19.9924 amu), 0.47% ^{21}Ne (mass 20.9940 amu), and 7.69% ^{22}Ne (mass 21.9914 amu). What is the average mass of the neon in the solar wind?

Solution

$$\begin{aligned}\text{average mass} &= (0.9184 \times 19.9924 \text{ amu}) + (0.0047 \times 20.9940 \text{ amu}) + (0.0769 \times 21.9914 \text{ amu}) \\ &= (18.36 + 0.099 + 1.69) \text{ amu} \\ &= 20.15 \text{ amu}\end{aligned}$$

The average mass of a neon atom in the solar wind is 20.15 amu. (The average mass of a terrestrial neon atom is 20.1796 amu. This result demonstrates that we may find slight differences in the natural abundance of isotopes, depending on their origin.)

Check Your Learning

A sample of magnesium is found to contain 78.70% of ^{24}Mg atoms (mass 23.98 amu), 10.13% of ^{25}Mg atoms (mass 24.99 amu), and 11.17% of ^{26}Mg atoms (mass 25.98 amu). Calculate the average mass of a Mg atom.

Answer: 24.31 amu

We can also do variations of this type of calculation, as shown in the next example.

Example 2.5

Calculation of Percent Abundance

Naturally occurring chlorine consists of ^{35}Cl (mass 34.96885 amu) and ^{37}Cl (mass 36.96590 amu), with an average mass of 35.453 amu. What is the percent composition of Cl in terms of these two isotopes?

Solution

The average mass of chlorine is the fraction that is ^{35}Cl times the mass of ^{35}Cl plus the fraction that is ^{37}Cl times the mass of ^{37}Cl.

$$\text{average mass} = (\text{fraction of } ^{35}\text{Cl} \times \text{mass of } ^{35}\text{Cl}) + (\text{fraction of } ^{37}\text{Cl} \times \text{mass of } ^{37}\text{Cl})$$

If we let x represent the fraction that is ^{35}Cl, then the fraction that is ^{37}Cl is represented by $1.00 - x$.

(The fraction that is ^{35}Cl + the fraction that is ^{37}Cl must add up to 1, so the fraction of ^{37}Cl must equal 1.00 − the fraction of ^{35}Cl.)

Substituting this into the average mass equation, we have:

$$
\begin{aligned}
35.453 \text{ amu} &= (x \times 34.96885 \text{ amu}) + [(1.00 - x) \times 36.96590 \text{ amu}] \\
35.453 &= 34.96885x + 36.96590 - 36.96590x \\
1.99705x &= 1.513 \\
x &= \frac{1.513}{1.99705} = 0.7576
\end{aligned}
$$

So solving yields: $x = 0.7576$, which means that $1.00 - 0.7576 = 0.2424$. Therefore, chlorine consists of 75.76% ^{35}Cl and 24.24% ^{37}Cl.

Check Your Learning

Naturally occurring copper consists of ^{63}Cu (mass 62.9296 amu) and ^{65}Cu (mass 64.9278 amu), with an average mass of 63.546 amu. What is the percent composition of Cu in terms of these two isotopes?

Answer: 69.15% Cu-63 and 30.85% Cu-65

Link to Learning

Visit this site (http://openstaxcollege.org/l/16PhetAtomMass) to make mixtures of the main isotopes of the first 18 elements, gain experience with average atomic mass, and check naturally occurring isotope ratios using the Isotopes and Atomic Mass simulation.

The occurrence and natural abundances of isotopes can be experimentally determined using an instrument called a mass spectrometer. Mass spectrometry (MS) is widely used in chemistry, forensics, medicine, environmental science, and many other fields to analyze and help identify the substances in a sample of material. In a typical mass spectrometer (Figure 2.15), the sample is vaporized and exposed to a high-energy electron beam that causes the sample's atoms (or molecules) to become electrically charged, typically by losing one or more electrons. These cations then pass through a (variable) electric or magnetic field that deflects each cation's path to an extent that depends on both its mass and charge (similar to how the path of a large steel ball bearing rolling past a magnet is deflected to a lesser extent that that of a small steel BB). The ions are detected, and a plot of the relative number of ions generated versus their mass-to-charge ratios (a *mass spectrum*) is made. The height of each vertical feature or peak in a mass spectrum is proportional to the fraction of cations with the specified mass-to-charge ratio. Since its initial use during the development of modern atomic theory, MS has evolved to become a powerful tool for chemical analysis in a wide range of applications.

Figure 2.15   Analysis of zirconium in a mass spectrometer produces a mass spectrum with peaks showing the different isotopes of Zr.

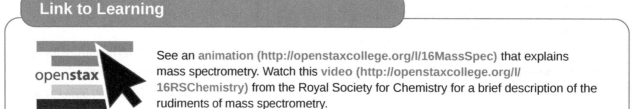

Link to Learning

See an animation (http://openstaxcollege.org/l/16MassSpec) that explains mass spectrometry. Watch this video (http://openstaxcollege.org/l/16RSChemistry) from the Royal Society for Chemistry for a brief description of the rudiments of mass spectrometry.

2.4 Chemical Formulas

By the end of this section, you will be able to:

- Symbolize the composition of molecules using molecular formulas and empirical formulas
- Represent the bonding arrangement of atoms within molecules using structural formulas
- Define the amount unit mole and the related quantity Avogadro's number
- Explain the relation between mass, moles, and numbers of atoms or molecules and perform calculations deriving these quantities from one another

Molecular and Empirical Formulas

A **molecular formula** is a representation of a molecule that uses chemical symbols to indicate the types of atoms followed by subscripts to show the number of atoms of each type in the molecule. (A subscript is used only when more than one atom of a given type is present.) Molecular formulas are also used as abbreviations for the names of compounds.

The **structural formula** for a compound gives the same information as its molecular formula (the types and numbers of atoms in the molecule) but also shows how the atoms are connected in the molecule. The structural formula for methane contains symbols for one C atom and four H atoms, indicating the number of atoms in the molecule (**Figure 2.16**). The lines represent bonds that hold the atoms together. (A chemical bond is an attraction between atoms or ions that holds them together in a molecule or a crystal.) We will discuss chemical bonds and see how to predict the arrangement of atoms in a molecule later. For now, simply know that the lines are an indication of how the atoms are connected in a molecule. A ball-and-stick model shows the geometric arrangement of the atoms with atomic sizes not to scale, and a space-filling model shows the relative sizes of the atoms.

Figure 2.16   A methane molecule can be represented as (a) a molecular formula, (b) a structural formula, (c) a ball-and-stick model, and (d) a space-filling model. Carbon and hydrogen atoms are represented by black and white spheres, respectively.

Although many elements consist of discrete, individual atoms, some exist as molecules made up of two or more atoms of the element chemically bonded together. For example, most samples of the elements hydrogen, oxygen, and nitrogen are composed of molecules that contain two atoms each (called diatomic molecules) and thus have the molecular formulas H_2, O_2, and N_2, respectively. Other elements commonly found as diatomic molecules are fluorine (F_2), chlorine (Cl_2), bromine (Br_2), and iodine (I_2). The most common form of the element sulfur is composed of molecules that consist of eight atoms of sulfur; its molecular formula is S_8 (**Figure 2.17**).

Figure 2.17   A molecule of sulfur is composed of eight sulfur atoms and is therefore written as S_8. It can be represented as (a) a structural formula, (b) a ball-and-stick model, and (c) a space-filling model. Sulfur atoms are represented by yellow spheres.

It is important to note that a subscript following a symbol and a number in front of a symbol do not represent the same thing; for example, H_2 and 2H represent distinctly different species. H_2 is a molecular formula; it represents a diatomic molecule of hydrogen, consisting of two atoms of the element that are chemically bonded together. The expression 2H, on the other hand, indicates two separate hydrogen atoms that are not combined as a unit. The expression $2H_2$ represents two molecules of diatomic hydrogen (**Figure 2.18**).

Figure 2.18 The symbols H, 2H, H_2, and $2H_2$ represent very different entities.

Compounds are formed when two or more elements chemically combine, resulting in the formation of bonds. For example, hydrogen and oxygen can react to form water, and sodium and chlorine can react to form table salt. We sometimes describe the composition of these compounds with an **empirical formula**, which indicates the types of atoms present and *the simplest whole-number ratio of the number of atoms (or ions) in the compound*. For example, titanium dioxide (used as pigment in white paint and in the thick, white, blocking type of sunscreen) has an empirical formula of TiO_2. This identifies the elements titanium (Ti) and oxygen (O) as the constituents of titanium dioxide, and indicates the presence of twice as many atoms of the element oxygen as atoms of the element titanium (**Figure 2.19**).

Figure 2.19 (a) The white compound titanium dioxide provides effective protection from the sun. (b) A crystal of titanium dioxide, TiO_2, contains titanium and oxygen in a ratio of 1 to 2. The titanium atoms are gray and the oxygen atoms are red. (credit a: modification of work by "osseous"/Flickr)

As discussed previously, we can describe a compound with a molecular formula, in which the subscripts indicate the *actual numbers of atoms* of each element in a molecule of the compound. In many cases, the molecular formula of a substance is derived from experimental determination of both its empirical formula and its molecular mass (the sum of atomic masses for all atoms composing the molecule). For example, it can be determined experimentally that benzene contains two elements, carbon (C) and hydrogen (H), and that for every carbon atom in benzene, there is one hydrogen atom. Thus, the empirical formula is CH. An experimental determination of the molecular mass reveals that a molecule of benzene contains six carbon atoms and six hydrogen atoms, so the molecular formula for benzene is C_6H_6 (**Figure 2.20**).

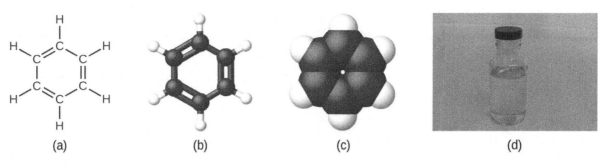

Figure 2.20 Benzene, C_6H_6, is produced during oil refining and has many industrial uses. A benzene molecule can be represented as (a) a structural formula, (b) a ball-and-stick model, and (c) a space-filling model. (d) Benzene is a clear liquid. (credit d: modification of work by Sahar Atwa)

If we know a compound's formula, we can easily determine the empirical formula. (This is somewhat of an academic exercise; the reverse chronology is generally followed in actual practice.) For example, the molecular formula for acetic acid, the component that gives vinegar its sharp taste, is $C_2H_4O_2$. This formula indicates that a molecule of acetic acid (**Figure 2.21**) contains two carbon atoms, four hydrogen atoms, and two oxygen atoms. The ratio of atoms is 2:4:2. Dividing by the lowest common denominator (2) gives the simplest, whole-number ratio of atoms, 1:2:1, so the empirical formula is CH_2O. Note that a molecular formula is always a whole-number multiple of an empirical formula.

Figure 2.21 (a) Vinegar contains acetic acid, $C_2H_4O_2$, which has an empirical formula of CH_2O. It can be represented as (b) a structural formula and (c) as a ball-and-stick model. (credit a: modification of work by "HomeSpot HQ"/Flickr)

Example 2.6

Empirical and Molecular Formulas

Molecules of glucose (blood sugar) contain 6 carbon atoms, 12 hydrogen atoms, and 6 oxygen atoms. What are the molecular and empirical formulas of glucose?

Solution

The molecular formula is $C_6H_{12}O_6$ because one molecule actually contains 6 C, 12 H, and 6 O atoms. The simplest whole-number ratio of C to H to O atoms in glucose is 1:2:1, so the empirical formula is CH_2O.

Check Your Learning

A molecule of metaldehyde (a pesticide used for snails and slugs) contains 8 carbon atoms, 16 hydrogen atoms, and 4 oxygen atoms. What are the molecular and empirical formulas of metaldehyde?

Answer: Molecular formula, $C_8H_{16}O_4$; empirical formula, C_2H_4O

Link to Learning

You can explore molecule building (http://openstaxcollege.org/l/16molbuilding) using an online simulation.

Portrait of a Chemist

Lee Cronin

What is it that chemists do? According to Lee Cronin (Figure 2.22), chemists make very complicated molecules by "chopping up" small molecules and "reverse engineering" them. He wonders if we could "make a really cool universal chemistry set" by what he calls "app-ing" chemistry. Could we "app" chemistry?

In a 2012 TED talk, Lee describes one fascinating possibility: combining a collection of chemical "inks" with a 3D printer capable of fabricating a reaction apparatus (tiny test tubes, beakers, and the like) to fashion a "universal toolkit of chemistry." This toolkit could be used to create custom-tailored drugs to fight a new superbug or to "print" medicine personally configured to your genetic makeup, environment, and health situation. Says Cronin, "What Apple did for music, I'd like to do for the discovery and distribution of prescription drugs."[2] View his full talk (http://openstaxcollege.org/l/16LeeCronin) at the TED website.

---

2. Lee Cronin, "Print Your Own Medicine," Talk presented at TED Global 2012, Edinburgh, Scotland, June 2012.

Figure 2.22 Chemist Lee Cronin has been named one of the UK's 10 most inspirational scientists. The youngest chair at the University of Glasgow, Lee runs a large research group, collaborates with many scientists worldwide, has published over 250 papers in top scientific journals, and has given more than 150 invited talks. His research focuses on complex chemical systems and their potential to transform technology, but also branches into nanoscience, solar fuels, synthetic biology, and even artificial life and evolution. (credit: image courtesy of Lee Cronin)

It is important to be aware that it may be possible for the same atoms to be arranged in different ways: Compounds with the same molecular formula may have different atom-to-atom bonding and therefore different structures. For example, could there be another compound with the same formula as acetic acid, $C_2H_4O_2$? And if so, what would be the structure of its molecules?

If you predict that another compound with the formula $C_2H_4O_2$ could exist, then you demonstrated good chemical insight and are correct. Two C atoms, four H atoms, and two O atoms can also be arranged to form a methyl formate, which is used in manufacturing, as an insecticide, and for quick-drying finishes. Methyl formate molecules have one of the oxygen atoms between the two carbon atoms, differing from the arrangement in acetic acid molecules. Acetic acid and methyl formate are examples of **isomers**—compounds with the same chemical formula but different molecular structures (Figure 2.23). Note that this small difference in the arrangement of the atoms has a major effect on their respective chemical properties. You would certainly not want to use a solution of methyl formate as a substitute for a solution of acetic acid (vinegar) when you make salad dressing.

Acetic acid
$C_2H_4O_2$

(a)

Methyl formate
$C_2H_4O_2$

(b)

Figure 2.23 Molecules of (a) acetic acid and methyl formate (b) are structural isomers; they have the same formula ($C_2H_4O_2$) but different structures (and therefore different chemical properties).

Many types of isomers exist (**Figure 2.24**). Acetic acid and methyl formate are **structural isomers**, compounds in which the molecules differ in how the atoms are connected to each other. There are also various types of **spatial isomers**, in which the relative orientations of the atoms in space can be different. For example, the compound carvone (found in caraway seeds, spearmint, and mandarin orange peels) consists of two isomers that are mirror images of each other. S-(+)-carvone smells like caraway, and R-(−)-carvone smells like spearmint.

(+)-Carvone
$C_{10}H_{14}O$

(−)-Carvone
$C_{10}H_{14}O$

Figure 2.24 Molecules of carvone are spatial isomers; they only differ in the relative orientations of the atoms in space. (credit bottom left: modification of work by "Miansari66"/Wikimedia Commons; credit bottom right: modification of work by Forest & Kim Starr)

The Mole

The identity of a substance is defined not only by the types of atoms or ions it contains, but by the quantity of each type of atom or ion. For example, water, H_2O, and hydrogen peroxide, H_2O_2, are alike in that their respective molecules are composed of hydrogen and oxygen atoms. However, because a hydrogen peroxide molecule contains two oxygen atoms, as opposed to the water molecule, which has only one, the two substances exhibit very different properties. Today, we possess sophisticated instruments that allow the direct measurement of these defining microscopic traits; however, the same traits were originally derived from the measurement of macroscopic properties (the masses and volumes of bulk quantities of matter) using relatively simple tools (balances and volumetric glassware). This experimental approach required the introduction of a new unit for amount of substances, the *mole*, which remains indispensable in modern chemical science.

The mole is an amount unit similar to familiar units like pair, dozen, gross, etc. It provides a specific measure of *the number* of atoms or molecules in a bulk sample of matter. A **mole** is defined as the amount of substance containing the same number of discrete entities (such as atoms, molecules, and ions) as the number of atoms in a sample of pure ^{12}C weighing exactly 12 g. One Latin connotation for the word "mole" is "large mass" or "bulk," which is consistent with its use as the name for this unit. The mole provides a link between an easily measured macroscopic property, bulk mass, and an extremely important fundamental property, number of atoms, molecules, and so forth.

The number of entities composing a mole has been experimentally determined to be $6.02214179 \times 10^{23}$, a fundamental constant named **Avogadro's number (N_A)** or the Avogadro constant in honor of Italian scientist Amedeo Avogadro. This constant is properly reported with an explicit unit of "per mole," a conveniently rounded version being 6.022×10^{23}/mol.

Consistent with its definition as an amount unit, 1 mole of any element contains the same number of atoms as 1 mole of any other element. The masses of 1 mole of different elements, however, are different, since the masses of the individual atoms are drastically different. The **molar mass** of an element (or compound) is the mass in grams of 1 mole of that substance, a property expressed in units of grams per mole (g/mol) (see Figure 2.25).

Figure 2.25 Each sample contains 6.022×10^{23} atoms —1.00 mol of atoms. From left to right (top row): 65.4 g zinc, 12.0 g carbon, 24.3 g magnesium, and 63.5 g copper. From left to right (bottom row): 32.1 g sulfur, 28.1 g silicon, 207 g lead, and 118.7 g tin. (credit: modification of work by Mark Ott)

Because the definitions of both the mole and the atomic mass unit are based on the same reference substance, ^{12}C, the molar mass of any substance is numerically equivalent to its atomic or formula weight in amu. Per the amu definition, a single ^{12}C atom weighs 12 amu (its atomic mass is 12 amu). According to the definition of the mole, 12 g of ^{12}C contains 1 mole of ^{12}C atoms (its molar mass is 12 g/mol). This relationship holds for all elements, since their atomic masses are measured relative to that of the amu-reference substance, ^{12}C. Extending this principle, the molar mass of a compound in grams is likewise numerically equivalent to its formula mass in amu (**Figure 2.26**).

Figure 2.26 Each sample contains 6.02×10^{23} molecules or formula units—1.00 mol of the compound or element. Clock-wise from the upper left: 130.2 g of $C_8H_{17}OH$ (1-octanol, formula mass 130.2 amu), 454.4 g of HgI_2 (mercury(II) iodide, formula mass 454.4 amu), 32.0 g of CH_3OH (methanol, formula mass 32.0 amu) and 256.5 g of S_8 (sulfur, formula mass 256.5 amu). (credit: Sahar Atwa)

Element	Average Atomic Mass (amu)	Molar Mass (g/mol)	Atoms/Mole
C	12.01	12.01	6.022×10^{23}
H	1.008	1.008	6.022×10^{23}
O	16.00	16.00	6.022×10^{23}
Na	22.99	22.99	6.022×10^{23}
Cl	35.45	33.45	6.022×10^{23}

While atomic mass and molar mass are numerically equivalent, keep in mind that they are vastly different in terms of scale, as represented by the vast difference in the magnitudes of their respective units (amu versus g). To appreciate the enormity of the mole, consider a small drop of water weighing about 0.03 g (see **Figure 2.27**). Although this represents just a tiny fraction of 1 mole of water (~18 g), it contains more water molecules than can be clearly imagined. If the molecules were distributed equally among the roughly seven billion people on earth, each person would receive more than 100 billion molecules.

Figure 2.27   The number of molecules in a single droplet of water is roughly 100 billion times greater than the number of people on earth. (credit: "tanakawho"/Wikimedia commons)

Link to Learning

The mole is used in chemistry to represent 6.022×10^{23} of something, but it can be difficult to conceptualize such a large number. Watch this video (http://openstaxcollege.org/l/16molevideo) and then complete the "Think" questions that follow. Explore more about the mole by reviewing the information under "Dig Deeper."

The relationships between formula mass, the mole, and Avogadro's number can be applied to compute various quantities that describe the composition of substances and compounds. For example, if we know the mass and chemical composition of a substance, we can determine the number of moles and calculate number of atoms or molecules in the sample. Likewise, if we know the number of moles of a substance, we can derive the number of atoms or molecules and calculate the substance's mass.

Example 2.7

Deriving Moles from Grams for an Element

According to nutritional guidelines from the US Department of Agriculture, the estimated average requirement for dietary potassium is 4.7 g. What is the estimated average requirement of potassium in moles?

Solution

The mass of K is provided, and the corresponding amount of K in moles is requested. Referring to the periodic table, the atomic mass of K is 39.10 amu, and so its molar mass is 39.10 g/mol. The given mass of K (4.7 g) is a bit more than one-tenth the molar mass (39.10 g), so a reasonable "ballpark" estimate of the number of moles would be slightly greater than 0.1 mol.

The molar amount of a substance may be calculated by dividing its mass (g) by its molar mass (g/mol):

The factor-label method supports this mathematical approach since the unit "g" cancels and the answer has units of "mol:"

$$4.7 \; \cancel{g} \; K \left(\frac{\text{mol K}}{39.10 \; \cancel{g}} \right) = 0.12 \; \text{mol K}$$

The calculated magnitude (0.12 mol K) is consistent with our ballpark expectation, since it is a bit greater than 0.1 mol.

Check Your Learning

Beryllium is a light metal used to fabricate transparent X-ray windows for medical imaging instruments. How many moles of Be are in a thin-foil window weighing 3.24 g?

Answer: 0.360 mol

Example 2.8

Deriving Grams from Moles for an Element

A liter of air contains 9.2×10^{-4} mol argon. What is the mass of Ar in a liter of air?

Solution

The molar amount of Ar is provided and must be used to derive the corresponding mass in grams. Since the amount of Ar is less than 1 mole, the mass will be less than the mass of 1 mole of Ar, approximately 40 g. The molar amount in question is approximately one-one thousandth ($\sim 10^{-3}$) of a mole, and so the corresponding mass should be roughly one-one thousandth of the molar mass (~ 0.04 g):

In this case, logic dictates (and the factor-label method supports) multiplying the provided amount (mol) by the molar mass (g/mol):

$$9.2 \times 10^{-4} \text{ mol Ar} \left(\frac{39.95 \text{ g}}{\text{mol Ar}} \right) = 0.037 \text{ g Ar}$$

The result is in agreement with our expectations, around 0.04 g Ar.

Check Your Learning

What is the mass of 2.561 mol of gold?

Answer: 504.4 g

Example 2.9

Deriving Number of Atoms from Mass for an Element

Copper is commonly used to fabricate electrical wire (**Figure 2.28**). How many copper atoms are in 5.00 g of copper wire?

Figure 2.28 Copper wire is composed of many, many atoms of Cu. (credit: Emilian Robert Vicol)

Solution

The number of Cu atoms in the wire may be conveniently derived from its mass by a two-step computation: first calculating the molar amount of Cu, and then using Avogadro's number (N_A) to convert this molar amount to number of Cu atoms:

Considering that the provided sample mass (5.00 g) is a little less than one-tenth the mass of 1 mole of Cu (~64 g), a reasonable estimate for the number of atoms in the sample would be on the order of one-tenth N_A, or approximately 10^{22} Cu atoms. Carrying out the two-step computation yields:

$$5.00 \ \cancel{\text{g}} \ \text{Cu} \left(\frac{\cancel{\text{mol}} \ \text{Cu}}{63.55 \ \cancel{\text{g}}} \right) \left(\frac{6.022 \times 10^{23} \ \text{atoms}}{\cancel{\text{mol}}} \right) = 4.74 \times 10^{22} \ \text{atoms of copper}$$

The factor-label method yields the desired cancellation of units, and the computed result is on the order of 10^{22} as expected.

Check Your Learning

A prospector panning for gold in a river collects 15.00 g of pure gold. How many Au atoms are in this quantity of gold?

Answer: 4.586×10^{22} Au atoms

Example 2.10

Deriving Moles from Grams for a Compound

Our bodies synthesize protein from amino acids. One of these amino acids is glycine, which has the molecular formula $C_2H_5O_2N$. How many moles of glycine molecules are contained in 28.35 g of glycine?

Solution

We can derive the number of moles of a compound from its mass following the same procedure we used for an element in Example 2.7:

The molar mass of glycine is required for this calculation, and it is computed in the same fashion as its molecular mass. One mole of glycine, $C_2H_5O_2N$, contains 2 moles of carbon, 5 moles of hydrogen, 2 moles of oxygen, and 1 mole of nitrogen:

Element	Quantity (mol element/ mol compound)		Molar mass (g/mol element)		Subtotal (g/mol compound)	
C	2	×	12.01	=	24.02	
H	5	×	1.008	=	5.040	
O	2	×	16.00	=	32.00	
N	1	×	14.007	=	14.007	
Molecular mass (g/mol compound)					75.07	

The provided mass of glycine (~28 g) is a bit more than one-third the molar mass (~75 g/mol), so we would expect the computed result to be a bit greater than one-third of a mole (~0.33 mol). Dividing the compound's mass by its molar mass yields:

$$28.35 \ \cancel{\text{g}} \ \text{glycine} \left(\frac{\text{mol glycine}}{75.07 \ \cancel{\text{g}}} \right) = 0.378 \ \text{mol glycine}$$

This result is consistent with our rough estimate.

Check Your Learning

How many moles of sucrose, $C_{12}H_{22}O_{11}$, are in a 25-g sample of sucrose?

Answer: 0.073 mol

Example 2.11

Deriving Grams from Moles for a Compound

Vitamin C is a covalent compound with the molecular formula $C_6H_8O_6$. The recommended daily dietary allowance of vitamin C for children aged 4–8 years is 1.42×10^{-4} mol. What is the mass of this allowance in grams?

Solution

As for elements, the mass of a compound can be derived from its molar amount as shown:

The molar mass for this compound is computed to be 176.124 g/mol. The given number of moles is a very small fraction of a mole ($\sim 10^{-4}$ or one-ten thousandth); therefore, we would expect the corresponding mass to be about one-ten thousandth of the molar mass (~ 0.02 g). Performing the calculation, we get:

$$1.42 \times 10^{-4} \text{ mol vitamin C} \left(\frac{176.124 \text{ g}}{\text{mol vitamin C}} \right) = 0.0250 \text{ g vitamin C}$$

This is consistent with the anticipated result.

Check Your Learning

What is the mass of 0.443 mol of hydrazine, N_2H_4?

Answer: 14.2 g

Example 2.12

Deriving the Number of Atoms and Molecules from the Mass of a Compound

A packet of an artificial sweetener contains 40.0 mg of saccharin ($C_7H_5NO_3S$), which has the structural formula:

Given that saccharin has a molar mass of 183.18 g/mol, how many saccharin molecules are in a 40.0-mg (0.0400-g) sample of saccharin? How many carbon atoms are in the same sample?

Solution

The number of molecules in a given mass of compound is computed by first deriving the number of moles, as demonstrated in Example 2.10, and then multiplying by Avogadro's number:

Using the provided mass and molar mass for saccharin yields:

$$0.0400 \; \cancel{g} \; C_7H_5NO_3S \left(\frac{\cancel{mol} \; C_7H_5NO_3S}{183.18 \; \cancel{g} \; C_7H_5NO_3S} \right) \left(\frac{6.022 \times 10^{23} \; C_7H_5NO_3S \; \text{molecules}}{1 \; \cancel{mol} \; C_7H_5NO_3S} \right)$$

$$= 1.31 \times 10^{20} \; C_7H_5NO_3S \; \text{molecules}$$

The compound's formula shows that each molecule contains seven carbon atoms, and so the number of C atoms in the provided sample is:

$$1.31 \times 10^{20} \; C_7H_5NO_3S \; \text{molecules} \left(\frac{7 \; C \; \text{atoms}}{1 \; C_7H_5NO_3S \; \text{molecule}} \right) = 9.20 \times 10^{21} \; C \; \text{atoms}$$

Check Your Learning

How many C_4H_{10} molecules are contained in 9.213 g of this compound? How many hydrogen atoms?

Answer: 9.545×10^{22} molecules C_4H_{10}; 9.545×10^{23} atoms H

How Sciences Interconnect

Counting Neurotransmitter Molecules in the Brain

The brain is the control center of the central nervous system (Figure 2.29). It sends and receives signals to and from muscles and other internal organs to monitor and control their functions; it processes stimuli detected by sensory organs to guide interactions with the external world; and it houses the complex physiological processes that give rise to our intellect and emotions. The broad field of neuroscience spans all aspects of the structure and function of the central nervous system, including research on the anatomy and physiology of the brain. Great progress has been made in brain research over the past few decades, and the BRAIN Initiative, a federal initiative announced in 2013, aims to accelerate and capitalize on these advances through the concerted efforts of various industrial, academic, and government agencies (more details available at www.whitehouse.gov/share/brain-initiative).

(a)   (b)

Figure 2.29   (a) A typical human brain weighs about 1.5 kg and occupies a volume of roughly 1.1 L. (b) Information is transmitted in brain tissue and throughout the central nervous system by specialized cells called neurons (micrograph shows cells at 1600× magnification).

Specialized cells called neurons transmit information between different parts of the central nervous system by way of electrical and chemical signals. Chemical signaling occurs at the interface between different neurons when one of the cells releases molecules (called neurotransmitters) that diffuse across the small gap between the cells (called the synapse) and bind to the surface of the other cell. These neurotransmitter molecules are stored in small intracellular structures called vesicles that fuse to the cell wall and then break open to release their contents when the neuron is appropriately stimulated. This process is called exocytosis (see Figure 2.30). One neurotransmitter that has been very extensively studied is dopamine, $C_8H_{11}NO_2$. Dopamine is involved in various neurological processes that impact a wide variety of human behaviors. Dysfunctions in the dopamine systems of the brain underlie serious neurological diseases such as Parkinson's and schizophrenia.

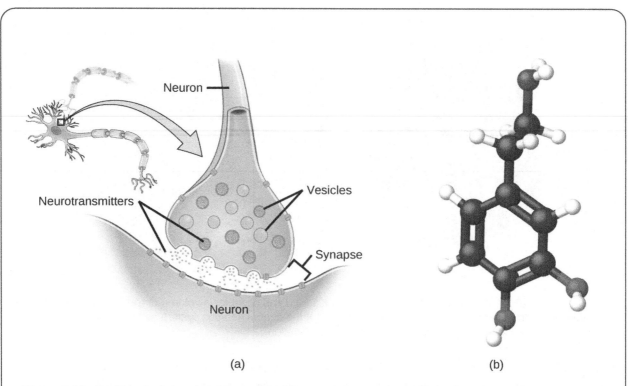

(a)   (b)

Figure 2.30   (a) Chemical signals are transmitted from neurons to other cells by the release of neurotransmitter molecules into the small gaps (synapses) between the cells. (b) Dopamine, $C_8H_{11}NO_2$, is a neurotransmitter involved in a number of neurological processes.

One important aspect of the complex processes related to dopamine signaling is the number of neurotransmitter molecules released during exocytosis. Since this number is a central factor in determining neurological response (and subsequent human thought and action), it is important to know how this number changes with certain controlled stimulations, such as the administration of drugs. It is also important to understand the mechanism responsible for any changes in the number of neurotransmitter molecules released—for example, some dysfunction in exocytosis, a change in the number of vesicles in the neuron, or a change in the number of neurotransmitter molecules in each vesicle.

Significant progress has been made recently in directly measuring the number of dopamine molecules stored in individual vesicles and the amount actually released when the vesicle undergoes exocytosis. Using miniaturized probes that can selectively detect dopamine molecules in very small amounts, scientists have determined that the vesicles of a certain type of mouse brain neuron contain an average of 30,000 dopamine molecules per vesicle (about 5×10^{-20} mol or 50 zmol). Analysis of these neurons from mice subjected to various drug therapies shows significant changes in the average number of dopamine molecules contained in individual vesicles, increasing or decreasing by up to three-fold, depending on the specific drug used. These studies also indicate that not all of the dopamine in a given vesicle is released during exocytosis, suggesting that it may be possible to regulate the fraction released using pharmaceutical therapies.[3]

3.   Omiatek, Donna M., Amanda J. Bressler, Ann-Sofie Cans, Anne M. Andrews, Michael L. Heien, and Andrew G. Ewing. "The Real Catecholamine Content of Secretory Vesicles in the CNS Revealed by Electrochemical Cytometry." *Scientific Report* 3 (2013): 1447, accessed January 14, 2015, doi:10.1038/srep01447.

Key Terms

alpha particle (α particle) positively charged particle consisting of two protons and two neutrons

anion negatively charged atom or molecule (contains more electrons than protons)

atomic mass average mass of atoms of an element, expressed in amu

atomic mass unit (amu) (also, unified atomic mass unit, u, or Dalton, Da) unit of mass equal to $\frac{1}{12}$ of the mass of a ^{12}C atom

atomic number (Z) number of protons in the nucleus of an atom

cation positively charged atom or molecule (contains fewer electrons than protons)

chemical symbol one-, two-, or three-letter abbreviation used to represent an element or its atoms

Dalton (Da) alternative unit equivalent to the atomic mass unit

Dalton's atomic theory set of postulates that established the fundamental properties of atoms

electron negatively charged, subatomic particle of relatively low mass located outside the nucleus

empirical formula formula showing the composition of a compound given as the simplest whole-number ratio of atoms

fundamental unit of charge (also called the elementary charge) equals the magnitude of the charge of an electron (e) with $e = 1.602 \times 10^{-19}$ C

ion electrically charged atom or molecule (contains unequal numbers of protons and electrons)

isomers compounds with the same chemical formula but different structures

isotopes atoms that contain the same number of protons but different numbers of neutrons

law of constant composition (also, law of definite proportions) all samples of a pure compound contain the same elements in the same proportions by mass

law of definite proportions (also, law of constant composition) all samples of a pure compound contain the same elements in the same proportions by mass

law of multiple proportions when two elements react to form more than one compound, a fixed mass of one element will react with masses of the other element in a ratio of small whole numbers

mass number (A) sum of the numbers of neutrons and protons in the nucleus of an atom

molecular formula formula indicating the composition of a molecule of a compound and giving the actual number of atoms of each element in a molecule of the compound.

neutron uncharged, subatomic particle located in the nucleus

nucleus massive, positively charged center of an atom made up of protons and neutrons

proton positively charged, subatomic particle located in the nucleus

spatial isomers compounds in which the relative orientations of the atoms in space differ

structural formula shows the atoms in a molecule and how they are connected

structural isomer one of two substances that have the same molecular formula but different physical and chemical properties because their atoms are bonded differently

unified atomic mass unit (u) alternative unit equivalent to the atomic mass unit

Key Equations

- average mass $= \sum_{i} (\text{fractional abundance} \times \text{isotopic mass})_i$

Summary

2.1 Early Ideas in Atomic Theory

The ancient Greeks proposed that matter consists of extremely small particles called atoms. Dalton postulated that each element has a characteristic type of atom that differs in properties from atoms of all other elements, and that atoms of different elements can combine in fixed, small, whole-number ratios to form compounds. Samples of a particular compound all have the same elemental proportions by mass. When two elements form different compounds, a given mass of one element will combine with masses of the other element in a small, whole-number ratio. During any chemical change, atoms are neither created nor destroyed.

2.2 Evolution of Atomic Theory

Although no one has actually seen the inside of an atom, experiments have demonstrated much about atomic structure. Thomson's cathode ray tube showed that atoms contain small, negatively charged particles called electrons. Millikan discovered that there is a fundamental electric charge—the charge of an electron. Rutherford's gold foil experiment showed that atoms have a small, dense, positively charged nucleus; the positively charged particles within the nucleus are called protons. Chadwick discovered that the nucleus also contains neutral particles called neutrons. Soddy demonstrated that atoms of the same element can differ in mass; these are called isotopes.

2.3 Atomic Structure and Symbolism

An atom consists of a small, positively charged nucleus surrounded by electrons. The nucleus contains protons and neutrons; its diameter is about 100,000 times smaller than that of the atom. The mass of one atom is usually expressed in atomic mass units (amu), which is referred to as the atomic mass. An amu is defined as exactly $\frac{1}{12}$ of the mass of a carbon-12 atom and is equal to 1.6605×10^{-24} g.

Protons are relatively heavy particles with a charge of 1+ and a mass of 1.0073 amu. Neutrons are relatively heavy particles with no charge and a mass of 1.0087 amu. Electrons are light particles with a charge of 1− and a mass of 0.00055 amu. The number of protons in the nucleus is called the atomic number (Z) and is the property that defines an atom's elemental identity. The sum of the numbers of protons and neutrons in the nucleus is called the mass number and, expressed in amu, is approximately equal to the mass of the atom. An atom is neutral when it contains equal numbers of electrons and protons.

Isotopes of an element are atoms with the same atomic number but different mass numbers; isotopes of an element, therefore, differ from each other only in the number of neutrons within the nucleus. When a naturally occurring element is composed of several isotopes, the atomic mass of the element represents the average of the masses of the isotopes involved. A chemical symbol identifies the atoms in a substance using symbols, which are one-, two-, or three-letter abbreviations for the atoms.

2.4 Chemical Formulas

A molecular formula uses chemical symbols and subscripts to indicate the exact numbers of different atoms in a molecule or compound. An empirical formula gives the simplest, whole-number ratio of atoms in a compound. A structural formula indicates the bonding arrangement of the atoms in the molecule. Ball-and-stick and space-filling models show the geometric arrangement of atoms in a molecule. Isomers are compounds with the same molecular formula but different arrangements of atoms. A convenient amount unit for expressing very large numbers of atoms or molecules is the mole. Experimental measurements have determined the number of entities composing 1 mole of substance to be 6.022×10^{23}, a quantity called Avogadro's number. The mass in grams of 1 mole of substance is its molar mass.

Exercises

2.1 Early Ideas in Atomic Theory

1. In the following drawing, the green spheres represent atoms of a certain element. The purple spheres represent atoms of another element. If the spheres of different elements touch, they are part of a single unit of a compound. The following chemical change represented by these spheres may violate one of the ideas of Dalton's atomic theory. Which one?

Starting materials   Products of the change

2. Which postulate of Dalton's theory is consistent with the following observation concerning the weights of reactants and products? When 100 grams of solid calcium carbonate is heated, 44 grams of carbon dioxide and 56 grams of calcium oxide are produced.

3. Identify the postulate of Dalton's theory that is violated by the following observations: 59.95% of one sample of titanium dioxide is titanium; 60.10% of a different sample of titanium dioxide is titanium.

4. Samples of compound X, Y, and Z are analyzed, with results shown here.

Compound	Description	Mass of Carbon	Mass of Hydrogen
X	clear, colorless, liquid with strong odor	1.776 g	0.148 g
Y	clear, colorless, liquid with strong odor	1.974 g	0.329 g
Z	clear, colorless, liquid with strong odor	7.812 g	0.651 g

Do these data provide example(s) of the law of definite proportions, the law of multiple proportions, neither, or both? What do these data tell you about compounds X, Y, and Z?

2.2 Evolution of Atomic Theory

5. The existence of isotopes violates one of the original ideas of Dalton's atomic theory. Which one?

6. How are electrons and protons similar? How are they different?

7. How are protons and neutrons similar? How are they different?

8. Predict and test the behavior of α particles fired at a "plum pudding" model atom.

(a) Predict the paths taken by α particles that are fired at atoms with a Thomson's plum pudding model structure. Explain why you expect the α particles to take these paths.

(b) If α particles of higher energy than those in (a) are fired at plum pudding atoms, predict how their paths will differ from the lower-energy α particle paths. Explain your reasoning.

(c) Now test your predictions from (a) and (b). Open the **Rutherford Scattering simulation (http://openstaxcollege.org/l/16PhetScatter)** and select the "Plum Pudding Atom" tab. Set "Alpha Particles Energy" to "min," and select "show traces." Click on the gun to start firing α particles. Does this match your prediction from (a)? If not, explain why the actual path would be that shown in the simulation. Hit the pause button, or "Reset All." Set "Alpha Particles Energy" to "max," and start firing α particles. Does this match your prediction from (b)? If not, explain the effect of increased energy on the actual paths as shown in the simulation.

9. Predict and test the behavior of α particles fired at a Rutherford atom model.

(a) Predict the paths taken by α particles that are fired at atoms with a Rutherford atom model structure. Explain why you expect the α particles to take these paths.

(b) If α particles of higher energy than those in (a) are fired at Rutherford atoms, predict how their paths will differ from the lower-energy α particle paths. Explain your reasoning.

(c) Predict how the paths taken by the α particles will differ if they are fired at Rutherford atoms of elements other than gold. What factor do you expect to cause this difference in paths, and why?

(d) Now test your predictions from (a), (b), and (c). Open the **Rutherford Scattering simulation (http://openstaxcollege.org/l/16PhetScatter)** and select the "Rutherford Atom" tab. Due to the scale of the simulation, it is best to start with a small nucleus, so select "20" for both protons and neutrons, "min" for energy, show traces, and then start firing α particles. Does this match your prediction from (a)? If not, explain why the actual path would be that shown in the simulation. Pause or reset, set energy to "max," and start firing α particles. Does this match your prediction from (b)? If not, explain the effect of increased energy on the actual path as shown in the simulation. Pause or reset, select "40" for both protons and neutrons, "min" for energy, show traces, and fire away. Does this match your prediction from (c)? If not, explain why the actual path would be that shown in the simulation. Repeat this with larger numbers of protons and neutrons. What generalization can you make regarding the type of atom and effect on the path of α particles? Be clear and specific.

2.3 Atomic Structure and Symbolism

10. In what way are isotopes of a given element always different? In what way(s) are they always the same?

11. Write the symbol for each of the following ions:

(a) the ion with a 1+ charge, atomic number 55, and mass number 133

(b) the ion with 54 electrons, 53 protons, and 74 neutrons

(c) the ion with atomic number 15, mass number 31, and a 3− charge

(d) the ion with 24 electrons, 30 neutrons, and a 3+ charge

12. Write the symbol for each of the following ions:

(a) the ion with a 3+ charge, 28 electrons, and a mass number of 71

(b) the ion with 36 electrons, 35 protons, and 45 neutrons

(c) the ion with 86 electrons, 142 neutrons, and a 4+ charge

(d) the ion with a 2+ charge, atomic number 38, and mass number 87

13. Open the **Build an Atom simulation (http://openstaxcollege.org/l/16PhetAtomBld)** and click on the Atom icon.

(a) Pick any one of the first 10 elements that you would like to build and state its symbol.

(b) Drag protons, neutrons, and electrons onto the atom template to make an atom of your element.
State the numbers of protons, neutrons, and electrons in your atom, as well as the net charge and mass number.

(c) Click on "Net Charge" and "Mass Number," check your answers to (b), and correct, if needed.

(d) Predict whether your atom will be stable or unstable. State your reasoning.

(e) Check the "Stable/Unstable" box. Was your answer to (d) correct? If not, first predict what you can do to make a stable atom of your element, and then do it and see if it works. Explain your reasoning.

14. Open the **Build an Atom simulation (http://openstaxcollege.org/l/16PhetAtomBld)**

(a) Drag protons, neutrons, and electrons onto the atom template to make a neutral atom of Oxygen-16 and give the isotope symbol for this atom.

(b) Now add two more electrons to make an ion and give the symbol for the ion you have created.

15. Open the **Build an Atom simulation (http://openstaxcollege.org/l/16PhetAtomBld)**

(a) Drag protons, neutrons, and electrons onto the atom template to make a neutral atom of Lithium-6 and give the isotope symbol for this atom.

(b) Now remove one electron to make an ion and give the symbol for the ion you have created.

16. Determine the number of protons, neutrons, and electrons in the following isotopes that are used in medical diagnoses:

(a) atomic number 9, mass number 18, charge of 1−

(b) atomic number 43, mass number 99, charge of 7+

(c) atomic number 53, atomic mass number 131, charge of 1−

(d) atomic number 81, atomic mass number 201, charge of 1+

(e) Name the elements in parts (a), (b), (c), and (d).

17. The following are properties of isotopes of two elements that are essential in our diet. Determine the number of protons, neutrons and electrons in each and name them.

(a) atomic number 26, mass number 58, charge of 2+

(b) atomic number 53, mass number 127, charge of 1−

18. Give the number of protons, electrons, and neutrons in neutral atoms of each of the following isotopes:

(a) $_{5}^{10}\text{B}$

(b) $_{80}^{199}\text{Hg}$

(c) $_{29}^{63}\text{Cu}$

(d) $_{6}^{13}\text{C}$

(e) $_{34}^{77}\text{Se}$

19. Give the number of protons, electrons, and neutrons in neutral atoms of each of the following isotopes:

(a) $_{3}^{7}\text{Li}$

(b) $_{52}^{125}\text{Te}$

(c) $_{47}^{109}\text{Ag}$

(d) $_{7}^{15}\text{N}$

(e) $_{15}^{31}\text{P}$

20. Click on the **site (http://openstaxcollege.org/l/16PhetAtomMass)** and select the "Mix Isotopes" tab, hide the "Percent Composition" and "Average Atomic Mass" boxes, and then select the element boron.

(a) Write the symbols of the isotopes of boron that are shown as naturally occurring in significant amounts.

(b) Predict the relative amounts (percentages) of these boron isotopes found in nature. Explain the reasoning behind your choice.

(c) Add isotopes to the black box to make a mixture that matches your prediction in (b). You may drag isotopes from their bins or click on "More" and then move the sliders to the appropriate amounts.

(d) Reveal the "Percent Composition" and "Average Atomic Mass" boxes. How well does your mixture match with your prediction? If necessary, adjust the isotope amounts to match your prediction.

(e) Select "Nature's" mix of isotopes and compare it to your prediction. How well does your prediction compare with the naturally occurring mixture? Explain. If necessary, adjust your amounts to make them match "Nature's" amounts as closely as possible.

21. Repeat Exercise 2.20 using an element that has three naturally occurring isotopes.

22. An element has the following natural abundances and isotopic masses: 90.92% abundance with 19.99 amu, 0.26% abundance with 20.99 amu, and 8.82% abundance with 21.99 amu. Calculate the average atomic mass of this element.

23. Average atomic masses listed by IUPAC are based on a study of experimental results. Bromine has two isotopes ^{79}Br and ^{81}Br, whose masses (78.9183 and 80.9163 amu) and abundances (50.69% and 49.31%) were determined in earlier experiments. Calculate the average atomic mass of bromine based on these experiments.

24. Variations in average atomic mass may be observed for elements obtained from different sources. Lithium provides an example of this. The isotopic composition of lithium from naturally occurring minerals is 7.5% ^{6}Li and 92.5% ^{7}Li, which have masses of 6.01512 amu and 7.01600 amu, respectively. A commercial source of lithium, recycled from a military source, was 3.75% ^{6}Li (and the rest ^{7}Li). Calculate the average atomic mass values for each of these two sources.

25. The average atomic masses of some elements may vary, depending upon the sources of their ores. Naturally occurring boron consists of two isotopes with accurately known masses (^{10}B, 10.0129 amu and ^{11}B, 11.0931 amu). The actual atomic mass of boron can vary from 10.807 to 10.819, depending on whether the mineral source is from Turkey or the United States. Calculate the percent abundances leading to the two values of the average atomic masses of boron from these two countries.

26. The $^{18}O{:}^{16}O$ abundance ratio in some meteorites is greater than that used to calculate the average atomic mass of oxygen on earth. Is the average mass of an oxygen atom in these meteorites greater than, less than, or equal to that of a terrestrial oxygen atom?

2.4 Chemical Formulas

27. Explain why the symbol for an atom of the element oxygen and the formula for a molecule of oxygen differ.

28. Explain why the symbol for the element sulfur and the formula for a molecule of sulfur differ.

29. Write the molecular and empirical formulas of the following compounds:

(a)

$$O=C=O$$

(b)

$$H-C\equiv C-H$$

(c)

(d)

30. Write the molecular and empirical formulas of the following compounds:

(a)

(b)

(c)

(d)

31. Determine the empirical formulas for the following compounds:

(a) caffeine, $C_8H_{10}N_4O_2$

(b) fructose, $C_{12}H_{22}O_{11}$

(c) hydrogen peroxide, H_2O_2

(d) glucose, $C_6H_{12}O_6$

(e) ascorbic acid (vitamin C), $C_6H_8O_6$

32. Determine the empirical formulas for the following compounds:

(a) acetic acid, $C_2H_4O_2$

(b) citric acid, $C_6H_8O_7$

(c) hydrazine, N_2H_4

(d) nicotine, $C_{10}H_{14}N_2$

(e) butane, C_4H_{10}

33. Write the empirical formulas for the following compounds:

(a)

```
    H   O
    |   ||
H — C — C — O — H
    |
    H
```

(b)

```
    H   O       H   H
    |   ||      |   |
H — C — C — O — C — C — H
    |           |   |
    H           H   H
```

34. Open the **Build a Molecule simulation (http://openstaxcollege.org/l/16molbuilding)** and select the "Larger Molecules" tab. Select an appropriate atoms "Kit" to build a molecule with two carbon and six hydrogen atoms. Drag atoms into the space above the "Kit" to make a molecule. A name will appear when you have made an actual molecule that exists (even if it is not the one you want). You can use the scissors tool to separate atoms if you would like to change the connections. Click on "3D" to see the molecule, and look at both the space-filling and ball-and-stick possibilities.

(a) Draw the structural formula of this molecule and state its name.

(b) Can you arrange these atoms in any way to make a different compound?

35. Use the **Build a Molecule simulation (http://openstaxcollege.org/l/16molbuilding)** to repeat **Exercise 2.34**, but build a molecule with two carbons, six hydrogens, and one oxygen.

(a) Draw the structural formula of this molecule and state its name.

(b) Can you arrange these atoms to make a different molecule? If so, draw its structural formula and state its name.

(c) How are the molecules drawn in (a) and (b) the same? How do they differ? What are they called (the type of relationship between these molecules, not their names).

36. Use the **Build a Molecule simulation (http://openstaxcollege.org/l/16molbuilding)** to repeat **Exercise 2.34**, but build a molecule with three carbons, seven hydrogens, and one chlorine.

(a) Draw the structural formula of this molecule and state its name.

(b) Can you arrange these atoms to make a different molecule? If so, draw its structural formula and state its name.

(c) How are the molecules drawn in (a) and (b) the same? How do they differ? What are they called (the type of relationship between these molecules, not their names)?

37. Write a sentence that describes how to determine the number of moles of a compound in a known mass of the compound if we know its molecular formula.

38. Compare 1 mole of H_2, 1 mole of O_2, and 1 mole of F_2.

(a) Which has the largest number of molecules? Explain why.

(b) Which has the greatest mass? Explain why.

39. Which contains the greatest mass of oxygen: 0.75 mol of ethanol (C_2H_5OH), 0.60 mol of formic acid (HCO_2H), or 1.0 mol of water (H_2O)? Explain why.

40. Which contains the greatest number of moles of oxygen atoms: 1 mol of ethanol (C_2H_5OH), 1 mol of formic acid (HCO_2H), or 1 mol of water (H_2O)? Explain why.

41. How are the molecular mass and the molar mass of a compound similar and how are they different?

42. Calculate the molar mass of each of the following compounds:

(a) hydrogen fluoride, HF

(b) ammonia, NH_3

(c) nitric acid, HNO_3

(d) silver sulfate, Ag_2SO_4

(e) boric acid, $B(OH)_3$

43. Calculate the molar mass of each of the following:

(a) S_8

(b) C_5H_{12}

(c) $Sc_2(SO_4)_3$

(d) CH_3COCH_3 (acetone)

(e) $C_6H_{12}O_6$ (glucose)

44. Calculate the empirical or molecular formula mass and the molar mass of each of the following minerals:

(a) limestone, $CaCO_3$

(b) halite, NaCl

(c) beryl, $Be_3Al_2Si_6O_{18}$

(d) malachite, $Cu_2(OH)_2CO_3$

(e) turquoise, $CuAl_6(PO_4)_4(OH)_8(H_2O)_4$

45. Calculate the molar mass of each of the following:

(a) the anesthetic halothane, $C_2HBrClF_3$

(b) the herbicide paraquat, $C_{12}H_{14}N_2Cl_2$

(c) caffeine, $C_8H_{10}N_4O_2$

(d) urea, $CO(NH_2)_2$

(e) a typical soap, $C_{17}H_{35}CO_2Na$

46. Determine the number of moles of compound and the number of moles of each type of atom in each of the following:

(a) 25.0 g of propylene, C_3H_6

(b) 3.06×10^{-3} g of the amino acid glycine, $C_2H_5NO_2$

(c) 25 lb of the herbicide Treflan, $C_{13}H_{16}N_2O_4F$ (1 lb = 454 g)

(d) 0.125 kg of the insecticide Paris Green, $Cu_4(AsO_3)_2(CH_3CO_2)_2$

(e) 325 mg of aspirin, $C_6H_4(CO_2H)(CO_2CH_3)$

47. Determine the mass of each of the following:

(a) 0.0146 mol KOH

(b) 10.2 mol ethane, C_2H_6

(c) 1.6×10^{-3} mol Na_2SO_4

(d) 6.854×10^3 mol glucose, $C_6H_{12}O_6$

(e) 2.86 mol $Co(NH_3)_6Cl_3$

48. Determine the number of moles of the compound and determine the number of moles of each type of atom in each of the following:

(a) 2.12 g of potassium bromide, KBr

(b) 0.1488 g of phosphoric acid, H_3PO_4

(c) 23 kg of calcium carbonate, $CaCO_3$

(d) 78.452 g of aluminum sulfate, $Al_2(SO_4)_3$

(e) 0.1250 mg of caffeine, $C_8H_{10}N_4O_2$

49. Determine the mass of each of the following:

(a) 2.345 mol LiCl

(b) 0.0872 mol acetylene, C_2H_2

(c) 3.3×10^{-2} mol Na_2CO_3

(d) 1.23×10^3 mol fructose, $C_6H_{12}O_6$

(e) 0.5758 mol $FeSO_4(H_2O)_7$

50. The approximate minimum daily dietary requirement of the amino acid leucine, $C_6H_{13}NO_2$, is 1.1 g. What is this requirement in moles?

51. Determine the mass in grams of each of the following:

(a) 0.600 mol of oxygen atoms

(b) 0.600 mol of oxygen molecules, O_2

(c) 0.600 mol of ozone molecules, O_3

52. A 55-kg woman has 7.5×10^{-3} mol of hemoglobin (molar mass = 64,456 g/mol) in her blood. How many hemoglobin molecules is this? What is this quantity in grams?

53. Determine the number of atoms and the mass of zirconium, silicon, and oxygen found in 0.3384 mol of zircon, $ZrSiO_4$, a semiprecious stone.

54. Determine which of the following contains the greatest mass of hydrogen: 1 mol of CH_4, 0.6 mol of C_6H_6, or 0.4 mol of C_3H_8.

55. Determine which of the following contains the greatest mass of aluminum: 122 g of $AlPO_4$, 266 g of Al_2Cl_6, or 225 g of Al_2S_3.

56. Diamond is one form of elemental carbon. An engagement ring contains a diamond weighing 1.25 carats (1 carat = 200 mg). How many atoms are present in the diamond?

57. The Cullinan diamond was the largest natural diamond ever found (January 25, 1905). It weighed 3104 carats (1 carat = 200 mg). How many carbon atoms were present in the stone?

58. One 55-gram serving of a particular cereal supplies 270 mg of sodium, 11% of the recommended daily allowance. How many moles and atoms of sodium are in the recommended daily allowance?

59. A certain nut crunch cereal contains 11.0 grams of sugar (sucrose, $C_{12}H_{22}O_{11}$) per serving size of 60.0 grams. How many servings of this cereal must be eaten to consume 0.0278 moles of sugar?

60. A tube of toothpaste contains 0.76 g of sodium monofluorophosphate (Na_2PO_3F) in 100 mL.

(a) What mass of fluorine atoms in mg was present?

(b) How many fluorine atoms were present?

61. Which of the following represents the least number of molecules?

(a) 20.0 g of H_2O (18.02 g/mol)

(b) 77.0 g of CH_4 (16.06 g/mol)

(c) 68.0 g of CaH_2 (42.09 g/mol)

(d) 100.0 g of N_2O (44.02 g/mol)

(e) 84.0 g of HF (20.01 g/mol)

Chapter 3

Electronic Structure and Periodic Properties of Elements

Figure 3.1   The Crab Nebula consists of remnants of a supernova (the explosion of a star). NASA's Hubble Space Telescope produced this composite image. Measurements of the emitted light wavelengths enabled astronomers to identify the elements in the nebula, determining that it contains specific ions including S^+ (green filaments) and O^{2+} (red filaments). (credit: modification of work by NASA and ESA)

Chapter Outline

Introduction

In 1054, Chinese astronomers recorded the appearance of a "guest star" in the sky, visible even during the day, which then disappeared slowly over the next two years. The sudden appearance was due to a supernova explosion, which was much brighter than the original star. Even though this supernova was observed almost a millennium ago, the remaining Crab Nebula (**Figure 3.1**) continues to release energy today. It emits not only visible light but also infrared light, X-rays, and other forms of electromagnetic radiation. The nebula emits both continuous spectra (the blue-white glow) and atomic emission spectra (the colored filaments). In this chapter, we will discuss light and other forms of electromagnetic radiation and how they are related to the electronic structure of atoms. We will also see how this radiation can be used to identify elements, even from thousands of light years away.

3.1 Electromagnetic Energy

By the end of this section, you will be able to:

- Explain the basic behavior of waves, including travelling waves and standing waves
- Describe the wave nature of light
- Use appropriate equations to calculate related light-wave properties such as period, frequency, wavelength, and energy
- Distinguish between line and continuous emission spectra
- Describe the particle nature of light

The nature of light has been a subject of inquiry since antiquity. In the seventeenth century, Isaac Newton performed experiments with lenses and prisms and was able to demonstrate that white light consists of the individual colors of the rainbow combined together. Newton explained his optics findings in terms of a "corpuscular" view of light, in which light was composed of streams of extremely tiny particles travelling at high speeds according to Newton's laws of motion. Others in the seventeenth century, such as Christiaan Huygens, had shown that optical phenomena such as reflection and refraction could be equally well explained in terms of light as waves travelling at high speed through a medium called "luminiferous aether" that was thought to permeate all space. Early in the nineteenth century, Thomas Young demonstrated that light passing through narrow, closely spaced slits produced interference patterns that could not be explained in terms of Newtonian particles but could be easily explained in terms of waves. Later in the nineteenth century, after James Clerk Maxwell developed his theory of **electromagnetic radiation** and showed that light was the visible part of a vast spectrum of electromagnetic waves, the particle view of light became thoroughly discredited. By the end of the nineteenth century, scientists viewed the physical universe as roughly comprising two separate domains: matter composed of particles moving according to Newton's laws of motion, and electromagnetic radiation consisting of waves governed by Maxwell's equations. Today, these domains are referred to as classical mechanics and classical electrodynamics (or classical electromagnetism). Although there were a few physical phenomena that could not be explained within this framework, scientists at that time were so confident of the overall soundness of this framework that they viewed these aberrations as puzzling paradoxes that would ultimately be resolved somehow within this framework. As we shall see, these paradoxes led to a contemporary framework that intimately connects particles and waves at a fundamental level called wave-particle duality, which has superseded the classical view.

Visible light and other forms of electromagnetic radiation play important roles in chemistry, since they can be used to infer the energies of electrons within atoms and molecules. Much of modern technology is based on electromagnetic radiation. For example, radio waves from a mobile phone, X-rays used by dentists, the energy used to cook food in your microwave, the radiant heat from red-hot objects, and the light from your television screen are forms of electromagnetic radiation that all exhibit wavelike behavior.

Waves

A **wave** is an oscillation or periodic movement that can transport energy from one point in space to another. Common examples of waves are all around us. Shaking the end of a rope transfers energy from your hand to the other end of the rope, dropping a pebble into a pond causes waves to ripple outward along the water's surface, and the expansion of air that accompanies a lightning strike generates sound waves (thunder) that can travel outward for several miles. In each of these cases, kinetic energy is transferred through matter (the rope, water, or air) while the matter remains essentially in place. An insightful example of a wave occurs in sports stadiums when fans in a narrow region of seats rise simultaneously and stand with their arms raised up for a few seconds before sitting down again while the fans in neighboring sections likewise stand up and sit down in sequence. While this wave can quickly encircle a large stadium in a few seconds, none of the fans actually travel with the wave-they all stay in or above their seats.

Waves need not be restricted to travel through matter. As Maxwell showed, electromagnetic waves consist of an electric field oscillating in step with a perpendicular magnetic field, both of which are perpendicular to the direction of travel. These waves can travel through a vacuum at a constant speed of 2.998×10^8 m/s, the speed of light (denoted by c).

All waves, including forms of electromagnetic radiation, are characterized by, a **wavelength** (denoted by λ, the lowercase Greek letter lambda), a **frequency** (denoted by v, the lowercase Greek letter nu), and an **amplitude**. As can be seen in Figure 3.2, the wavelength is the distance between two consecutive peaks or troughs in a wave (measured in meters in the SI system). Electromagnetic waves have wavelengths that fall within an enormous range-wavelengths of kilometers (10^3 m) to picometers (10^{-12} m) have been observed. The frequency is the number of wave cycles that pass a specified point in space in a specified amount of time (in the SI system, this is measured in seconds). A cycle corresponds to one complete wavelength. The unit for frequency, expressed as cycles per second [s^{-1}], is the **hertz (Hz)**. Common multiples of this unit are megahertz, (1 MHz = 1×10^6 Hz) and gigahertz (1 GHz = 1×10^9 Hz). The amplitude corresponds to the magnitude of the wave's displacement and so, in Figure 3.2, this corresponds to one-half the height between the peaks and troughs. The amplitude is related to the intensity of the wave, which for light is the brightness, and for sound is the loudness.

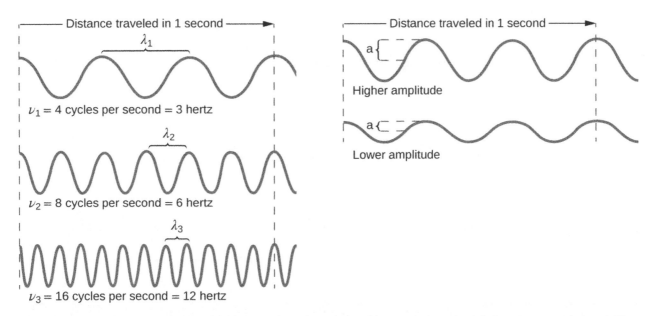

Figure 3.2 One-dimensional sinusoidal waves show the relationship among wavelength, frequency, and speed. The wave with the shortest wavelength has the highest frequency. Amplitude is one-half the height of the wave from peak to trough.

The product of a wave's wavelength (λ) and its frequency (v), λv, is the speed of the wave. Thus, for electromagnetic radiation in a vacuum:

$$c = 2.998 \times 10^8 \, \text{ms}^{-1} = \lambda v$$

Wavelength and frequency are inversely proportional: As the wavelength increases, the frequency decreases. The inverse proportionality is illustrated in Figure 3.3. This figure also shows the **electromagnetic spectrum**, the range of all types of electromagnetic radiation. Each of the various colors of visible light has specific frequencies and wavelengths associated with them, and you can see that visible light makes up only a small portion of the electromagnetic spectrum. Because the technologies developed to work in various parts of the electromagnetic spectrum are different, for reasons of convenience and historical legacies, different units are typically used for different parts of the spectrum. For example, radio waves are usually specified as frequencies (typically in units of MHz), while the visible region is usually specified in wavelengths (typically in units of nm or angstroms).

Figure 3.3 Portions of the electromagnetic spectrum are shown in order of decreasing frequency and increasing wavelength. Examples of some applications for various wavelengths include positron emission tomography (PET) scans, X-ray imaging, remote controls, wireless Internet, cellular telephones, and radios. (credit "Cosmic ray": modification of work by NASA; credit "PET scan": modification of work by the National Institute of Health; credit "X-ray": modification of work by Dr. Jochen Lengerke; credit "Dental curing": modification of work by the Department of the Navy; credit "Night vision": modification of work by the Department of the Army; credit "Remote": modification of work by Emilian Robert Vicol; credit "Cell phone": modification of work by Brett Jordan; credit "Microwave oven": modification of work by Billy Mabray; credit "Ultrasound": modification of work by Jane Whitney; credit "AM radio": modification of work by Dave Clausen)

Example 3.1

Determining the Frequency and Wavelength of Radiation

A sodium streetlight gives off yellow light that has a wavelength of 589 nm (1 nm = 1 × 10^{-9} m). What is the frequency of this light?

Solution

We can rearrange the equation $c = \lambda \nu$ to solve for the frequency:

$$\nu = \frac{c}{\lambda}$$

Since c is expressed in meters per second, we must also convert 589 nm to meters.

$$\nu = \left(\frac{2.998 \times 10^8 \, \text{m·s}^{-1}}{589 \, \text{nm}} \right) \left(\frac{1 \times 10^9 \, \text{nm}}{1 \, \text{m}} \right) = 5.09 \times 10^{14} \, \text{s}^{-1}$$

Check Your Learning

One of the frequencies used to transmit and receive cellular telephone signals in the United States is 850

MHz. What is the wavelength in meters of these radio waves?

Answer: 0.353 m = 35.3 cm

Chemistry in Everyday Life

Wireless Communication

Figure 3.4 Radio and cell towers are typically used to transmit long-wavelength electromagnetic radiation. Increasingly, cell towers are designed to blend in with the landscape, as with the Tucson, Arizona, cell tower (right) disguised as a palm tree. (credit left: modification of work by Sir Mildred Pierce; credit middle: modification of work by M.O. Stevens)

Many valuable technologies operate in the radio (3 kHz-300 GHz) frequency region of the electromagnetic spectrum. At the low frequency (low energy, long wavelength) end of this region are AM (amplitude modulation) radio signals (540-2830 kHz) that can travel long distances. FM (frequency modulation) radio signals are used at higher frequencies (87.5-108.0 MHz). In AM radio, the information is transmitted by varying the amplitude of the wave (Figure 3.5). In FM radio, by contrast, the amplitude is constant and the instantaneous frequency varies.

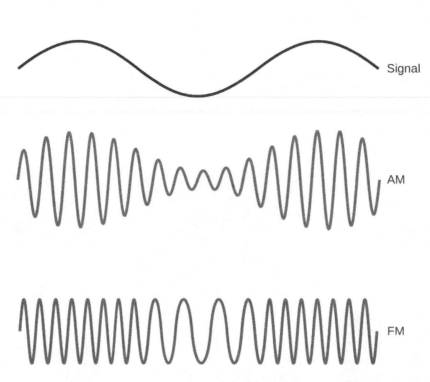

Figure 3.5 This schematic depicts how amplitude modulation (AM) and frequency modulation (FM) can be used to transmit a radio wave.

Other technologies also operate in the radio-wave portion of the electromagnetic spectrum. For example, 4G cellular telephone signals are approximately 880 MHz, while Global Positioning System (GPS) signals operate at 1.228 and 1.575 GHz, local area wireless technology (Wi-Fi) networks operate at 2.4 to 5 GHz, and highway toll sensors operate at 5.8 GHz. The frequencies associated with these applications are convenient because such waves tend not to be absorbed much by common building materials.

One particularly characteristic phenomenon of waves results when two or more waves come into contact: They interfere with each other. **Figure 3.6** shows the **interference patterns** that arise when light passes through narrow slits closely spaced about a wavelength apart. The fringe patterns produced depend on the wavelength, with the fringes being more closely spaced for shorter wavelength light passing through a given set of slits. When the light passes through the two slits, each slit effectively acts as a new source, resulting in two closely spaced waves coming into contact at the detector (the camera in this case). The dark regions in **Figure 3.6** correspond to regions where the peaks for the wave from one slit happen to coincide with the troughs for the wave from the other slit (destructive interference), while the brightest regions correspond to the regions where the peaks for the two waves (or their two troughs) happen to coincide (constructive interference). Likewise, when two stones are tossed close together into a pond, interference patterns are visible in the interactions between the waves produced by the stones. Such interference patterns cannot be explained by particles moving according to the laws of classical mechanics.

Figure 3.6   Interference fringe patterns are shown for light passing through two closely spaced, narrow slits. The spacing of the fringes depends on the wavelength, with the fringes being more closely spaced for the shorter-wavelength blue light. (credit: PASCO)

Portrait of a Chemist

Dorothy Hodgkin

Because the wavelengths of X-rays (10-10,000 picometers [pm]) are comparable to the size of atoms, X-rays can be used to determine the structure of molecules. When a beam of X-rays is passed through molecules packed together in a crystal, the X-rays collide with the electrons and scatter. Constructive and destructive interference of these scattered X-rays creates a specific diffraction pattern. Calculating backward from this pattern, the positions of each of the atoms in the molecule can be determined very precisely. One of the pioneers who helped create this technology was Dorothy Crowfoot Hodgkin.

She was born in Cairo, Egypt, in 1910, where her British parents were studying archeology. Even as a young girl, she was fascinated with minerals and crystals. When she was a student at Oxford University, she began researching how X-ray crystallography could be used to determine the structure of biomolecules. She invented new techniques that allowed her and her students to determine the structures of vitamin B_{12}, penicillin, and many other important molecules. Diabetes, a disease that affects 382 million people worldwide, involves the hormone insulin. Hodgkin began studying the structure of insulin in 1934, but it required several decades of advances in the field before she finally reported the structure in 1969. Understanding the structure has led to better understanding of the disease and treatment options.

Not all waves are travelling waves. **Standing waves** (also known as **stationary waves**) remain constrained within some region of space. As we shall see, standing waves play an important role in our understanding of the electronic structure of atoms and molecules. The simplest example of a standing wave is a one-dimensional wave associated with a vibrating string that is held fixed at its two end points. Figure 3.7 shows the four lowest-energy standing waves (the fundamental wave and the lowest three harmonics) for a vibrating string at a particular amplitude. Although the string's motion lies mostly within a plane, the wave itself is considered to be one dimensional, since it lies along the length of the string. The motion of string segments in a direction perpendicular to the string length generates the waves and so the amplitude of the waves is visible as the maximum displacement of the curves seen in Figure 3.7. The key observation from the figure is *that only those waves having an integer number, n, of half-wavelengths between the end points can form*. A system with fixed end points such as this restricts the number and type of the possible waveforms. This is an example of **quantization**, in which only discrete values from a more general set of continuous values of some property are observed. Another important observation is that the harmonic waves (those waves displaying more than one-half wavelength) all have one or more points between the two end points that are not in motion. These special points are **nodes**. The energies of the standing waves with a given amplitude in a vibrating string increase with the number of half-wavelengths n. Since the number of nodes is $n - 1$, the energy can also be said to depend on the number of nodes, generally increasing as the number of nodes increases.

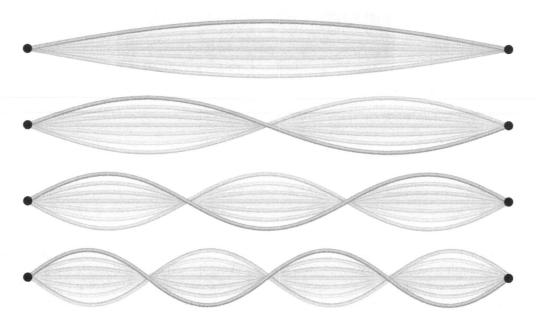

Figure 3.7 A vibrating string shows some one-dimensional standing waves. Since the two end points of the string are held fixed, only waves having an integer number of half-wavelengths can form. The points on the string between the end points that are not moving are called the nodes.

An example of two-dimensional standing waves is shown in Figure 3.8, which shows the vibrational patterns on a flat surface. Although the vibrational amplitudes cannot be seen like they could in the vibrating string, the nodes have been made visible by sprinkling the drum surface with a powder that collects on the areas of the surface that have minimal displacement. For one-dimensional standing waves, the nodes were points on the line, but for two-dimensional standing waves, the nodes are lines on the surface (for three-dimensional standing waves, the nodes are two-dimensional surfaces within the three-dimensional volume). Because of the circular symmetry of the drum surface, its boundary conditions (the drum surface being tightly constrained to the circumference of the drum) result in two types of nodes: radial nodes that sweep out all angles at constant radii and, thus, are seen as circles about the center, and angular nodes that sweep out all radii at constant angles and, thus, are seen as lines passing through the center. The upper left image in Figure 3.8 shows two radial nodes, while the image in the lower right shows the vibrational pattern associated with three radial nodes and two angular nodes.

Figure 3.8 Two-dimensional standing waves can be visualized on a vibrating surface. The surface has been sprinkled with a powder that collects near the nodal lines. There are two types of nodes visible: radial nodes (circles) and angular nodes (radii).

Link to Learning

You can watch the formation of various radial nodes here (http://openstaxcollege.org/l/16radnodes) as singer Imogen Heap projects her voice across a kettle drum.

Blackbody Radiation and the Ultraviolet Catastrophe

The last few decades of the nineteenth century witnessed intense research activity in commercializing newly discovered electric lighting. This required obtaining a better understanding of the distributions of light emitted from various sources being considered. Artificial lighting is usually designed to mimic natural sunlight within the limitations of the underlying technology. Such lighting consists of a range of broadly distributed frequencies that form a **continuous spectrum**. Figure 3.9 shows the wavelength distribution for sunlight. The most intense radiation is in the visible region, with the intensity dropping off rapidly for shorter wavelength ultraviolet (UV) light, and more slowly for longer wavelength infrared (IR) light.

Figure 3.9 The spectral distribution (light intensity vs. wavelength) of sunlight reaches the Earth's atmosphere as UV light, visible light, and IR light. The unabsorbed sunlight at the top of the atmosphere has a distribution that approximately matches the theoretical distribution of a blackbody at 5250 °C, represented by the blue curve. (credit: modification of work by American Society for Testing and Materials (ASTM) Terrestrial Reference Spectra for Photovoltaic Performance Evaluation)

In Figure 3.9, the solar distribution is compared to a representative distribution, called a blackbody spectrum, that corresponds to a temperature of 5250 °C. The blackbody spectrum matches the solar spectrum quite well. A **blackbody** is a convenient, ideal emitter that approximates the behavior of many materials when heated. It is "ideal" in the same sense that an ideal gas is a convenient, simple representation of real gases that works well, provided that the pressure is not too high nor the temperature too low. A good approximation of a blackbody that can be used to observe blackbody radiation is a metal oven that can be heated to very high temperatures. The oven has a small hole allowing for the light being emitted within the oven to be observed with a spectrometer so that the wavelengths and their intensities can be measured. Figure 3.10 shows the resulting curves for some representative temperatures. Each distribution depends only on a single parameter: the temperature. The maxima in the blackbody curves, λ_{max}, shift to shorter wavelengths as the temperature increases, reflecting the observation that metals being heated to high temperatures begin to glow a darker red that becomes brighter as the temperature increases, eventually becoming white hot at very high temperatures as the intensities of all of the visible wavelengths become appreciable. This common observation was at the heart of the first paradox that showed the fundamental limitations of classical physics that we will examine.

Physicists derived mathematical expressions for the blackbody curves using well-accepted concepts from the theories of classical mechanics and classical electromagnetism. The theoretical expressions as functions of temperature fit the observed experimental blackbody curves well at longer wavelengths, but showed significant discrepancies at shorter wavelengths. Not only did the theoretical curves not show a peak, they absurdly showed the intensity becoming infinitely large as the wavelength became smaller, which would imply that everyday objects at room temperature should be emitting large amounts of UV light. This became known as the "ultraviolet catastrophe" because no one could find any problems with the theoretical treatment that could lead to such unrealistic short-wavelength behavior. Finally, around 1900, Max Planck derived a theoretical expression for blackbody radiation that fit the experimental observations exactly (within experimental error). Planck developed his theoretical treatment by extending the earlier work that had been based on the premise that the atoms composing the oven vibrated at increasing frequencies (or decreasing wavelengths) as the temperature increased, with these vibrations being the source of the emitted electromagnetic radiation. But where the earlier treatments had allowed the vibrating atoms to have any energy values obtained from a continuous set of energies (perfectly reasonable, according to classical physics), Planck found that by restricting the vibrational energies to discrete values for each frequency, he could derive an expression for blackbody radiation that correctly had the intensity dropping rapidly for the short wavelengths in the UV region.

$$E = nh\upsilon, \; n = 1, \; 2, \; 3, \; \ldots$$

The quantity h is a constant now known as Planck's constant, in his honor. Although Planck was pleased he had resolved the blackbody radiation paradox, he was disturbed that to do so, he needed to assume the vibrating atoms required quantized energies, which he was unable to explain. The value of Planck's constant is very small, 6.626 $\times \; 10^{-34}$ joule seconds (J s), which helps explain why energy quantization had not been observed previously in macroscopic phenomena.

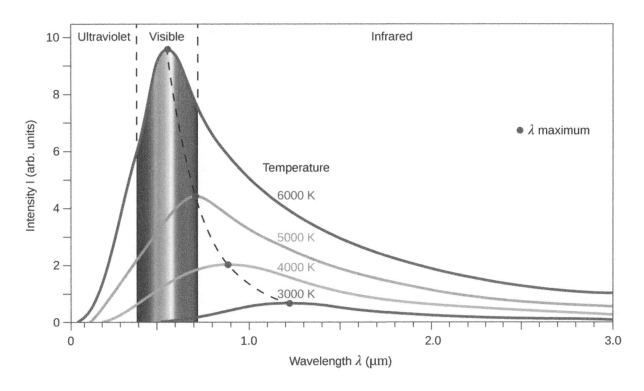

Figure 3.10 Blackbody spectral distribution curves are shown for some representative temperatures.

The Photoelectric Effect

The next paradox in the classical theory to be resolved concerned the photoelectric effect (**Figure 3.11**). It had been observed that electrons could be ejected from the clean surface of a metal when light having a frequency greater than some threshold frequency was shone on it. Surprisingly, the kinetic energy of the ejected electrons did not depend on the brightness of the light, but increased with increasing frequency of the light. Since the electrons in the metal had a certain amount of binding energy keeping them there, the incident light needed to have more energy to free the electrons. According to classical wave theory, a wave's energy depends on its intensity (which depends on its amplitude), not its frequency. One part of these observations was that the number of electrons ejected within in a given time period was seen to increase as the brightness increased. In 1905, Albert Einstein was able to resolve the paradox by incorporating Planck's quantization findings into the discredited particle view of light (Einstein actually won his Nobel prize for this work, and not for his theories of relativity for which he is most famous).

Einstein argued that the quantized energies that Planck had postulated in his treatment of blackbody radiation could be applied to the light in the photoelectric effect so that the light striking the metal surface should not be viewed as a wave, but instead as a stream of particles (later called **photons**) whose energy depended on their frequency, according to Planck's formula, $E = h\nu$ (or, in terms of wavelength using $c = \nu\lambda$, $E = \frac{hc}{\lambda}$). Electrons were ejected when hit by photons having sufficient energy (a frequency greater than the threshold). The greater the frequency, the greater the kinetic energy imparted to the escaping electrons by the collisions. Processes that increase the energy of an atom involve the absorption of light and are called **endothermic**. Processes that decrease the energy involve emission of light and are called **exothermic**. Einstein also argued that the light intensity did not depend on the amplitude of the incoming wave, but instead corresponded to the number of photons striking the surface within a given time period. This explains why the number of ejected electrons increased with increasing brightness, since the greater the number of incoming photons, the greater the likelihood that they would collide with some of the electrons.

With Einstein's findings, the nature of light took on a new air of mystery. Although many light phenomena could be explained either in terms of waves or particles, certain phenomena, such as the interference patterns obtained when light passed through a double slit, were completely contrary to a particle view of light, while other phenomena, such as the photoelectric effect, were completely contrary to a wave view of light. Somehow, at a deep fundamental level still not fully understood, light is both wavelike and particle-like. This is known as **wave-particle duality**.

Figure 3.11 Photons with low frequencies do not have enough energy to cause electrons to be ejected via the photoelectric effect. For any frequency of light above the threshold frequency, the kinetic energy of ejected electron will be proportional to the energy of the incoming photon.

Example 3.2

Calculating the Energy of Radiation

When we see light from a neon sign, we are observing radiation from excited neon atoms. If this radiation has a wavelength of 640 nm, what is the energy of the photon being emitted?

Solution

We use the part of Planck's equation that includes the wavelength, λ, and convert units of nanometers to meters so that the units of λ and c are the same.

$$E = \frac{hc}{\lambda}$$

$$E = \frac{(6.626 \times 10^{-34}\,\text{J·s})(2.998 \times 10^{8}\,\text{m·s}^{-1})}{(640\,\text{nm})\left(\frac{1\,\text{m}}{10^{9}\,\text{nm}}\right)}$$

$$E = 3.10 \times 10^{-19}\,\text{J}$$

Check Your Learning

The microwaves in an oven are of a specific frequency that will heat the water molecules contained in food. (This is why most plastics and glass do not become hot in a microwave oven-they do not contain water molecules.) This frequency is about 3×10^{9} Hz. What is the energy of one photon in these microwaves?

Answer: 2×10^{-24} J

Link to Learning

Use this simulation program (http://openstaxcollege.org/l/16photelec) to experiment with the photoelectric effect to see how intensity, frequency, type of metal, and other factors influence the ejected photons.

Example 3.3

Photoelectric Effect

Identify which of the following statements are false and, where necessary, change the italicized word or phrase to make them true, consistent with Einstein's explanation of the photoelectric effect.

(a) Increasing the brightness of incoming light *increases* the kinetic energy of the ejected electrons.

(b) Increasing the *wavelength* of incoming light increases the kinetic energy of the ejected electrons.

(c) Increasing the brightness of incoming light *increases* the number of ejected electrons.

(d) Increasing the *frequency* of incoming light can increase the number of ejected electrons.

Solution

(a) False. Increasing the brightness of incoming light *has no effect* on the kinetic energy of the ejected electrons. Only energy, not the number or amplitude, of the photons influences the kinetic energy of the electrons.

(b) False. Increasing the *frequency* of incoming light increases the kinetic energy of the ejected electrons. Frequency is proportional to energy and inversely proportional to wavelength. Frequencies above the threshold value transfer the excess energy into the kinetic energy of the electrons.

(c) True. Because the number of collisions with photons increases with brighter light, the number of ejected electrons increases.

(d) True with regard to the threshold energy binding the electrons to the metal. Below this threshold, electrons are not emitted and above it they are. Once over the threshold value, further increasing the frequency does not increase the number of ejected electrons

Check Your Learning

Calculate the threshold energy in kJ/mol of electrons in aluminum, given that the lowest frequency photon for which the photoelectric effect is observed is 9.87×10^{14} Hz.

Answer: 3.94×10^5 kJ/mol

Line Spectra

Another paradox within the classical electromagnetic theory that scientists in the late nineteenth century struggled with concerned the light emitted from atoms and molecules. When solids, liquids, or condensed gases are heated sufficiently, they radiate some of the excess energy as light. Photons produced in this manner have a range of energies, and thereby produce a continuous spectrum in which an unbroken series of wavelengths is present. Most of the light generated from stars (including our sun) is produced in this fashion. You can see all the visible wavelengths of light present in sunlight by using a prism to separate them. As can be seen in Figure 3.9, sunlight also contains UV light (shorter wavelengths) and IR light (longer wavelengths) that can be detected using instruments but that are invisible to the human eye. Incandescent (glowing) solids such as tungsten filaments in incandescent lights also give off light that contains all wavelengths of visible light. These continuous spectra can often be approximated by blackbody radiation curves at some appropriate temperature, such as those shown in Figure 3.10.

In contrast to continuous spectra, light can also occur as discrete or **line spectra** having very narrow line widths interspersed throughout the spectral regions such as those shown in Figure 3.13. Exciting a gas at low partial pressure using an electrical current, or heating it, will produce line spectra. Fluorescent light bulbs and neon signs operate in this way (Figure 3.12). Each element displays its own characteristic set of lines, as do molecules, although their spectra are generally much more complicated.

Figure 3.12 Neon signs operate by exciting a gas at low partial pressure using an electrical current. This sign shows the elaborate artistic effects that can be achieved. (credit: Dave Shaver)

Each emission line consists of a single wavelength of light, which implies that the light emitted by a gas consists of a set of discrete energies. For example, when an electric discharge passes through a tube containing hydrogen gas at low pressure, the H_2 molecules are broken apart into separate H atoms and we see a blue-pink color. Passing the light through a prism produces a line spectrum, indicating that this light is composed of photons of four visible wavelengths, as shown in Figure 3.13.

Figure 3.13 Compare the two types of emission spectra: continuous spectrum of white light (top) and the line spectra of the light from excited sodium, hydrogen, calcium, and mercury atoms.

The origin of discrete spectra in atoms and molecules was extremely puzzling to scientists in the late nineteenth century, since according to classical electromagnetic theory, only continuous spectra should be observed. Even more puzzling, in 1885, Johann Balmer was able to derive an empirical equation that related the four visible wavelengths of light emitted by hydrogen atoms to whole integers. That equation is the following one, in which k is a constant:

$$\frac{1}{\lambda} = k\left(\frac{1}{4} - \frac{1}{n^2}\right), \ n = 3, \ 4, \ 5, \ 6$$

Other discrete lines for the hydrogen atom were found in the UV and IR regions. Johannes Rydberg generalized Balmer's work and developed an empirical formula that predicted all of hydrogen's emission lines, not just those restricted to the visible range, where, n_1 and n_2 are integers, $n_1 < n_2$, and R_∞ is the Rydberg constant (1.097 × 10^7 m^{-1}).

$$\frac{1}{\lambda} = R_\infty\left(\frac{1}{n_1^2} - \frac{1}{n_2^2}\right)$$

Even in the late nineteenth century, spectroscopy was a very precise science, and so the wavelengths of hydrogen were measured to very high accuracy, which implied that the Rydberg constant could be determined very precisely as well. That such a simple formula as the Rydberg formula could account for such precise measurements seemed astounding at the time, but it was the eventual explanation for emission spectra by Neils Bohr in 1913 that ultimately convinced scientists to abandon classical physics and spurred the development of modern quantum mechanics.

3.2 The Bohr Model

By the end of this section, you will be able to:

- Describe the Bohr model of the hydrogen atom
- Use the Rydberg equation to calculate energies of light emitted or absorbed by hydrogen atoms

Following the work of Ernest Rutherford and his colleagues in the early twentieth century, the picture of atoms consisting of tiny dense nuclei surrounded by lighter and even tinier electrons continually moving about the nucleus was well established. This picture was called the planetary model, since it pictured the atom as a miniature "solar system" with the electrons orbiting the nucleus like planets orbiting the sun. The simplest atom is hydrogen, consisting of a single proton as the nucleus about which a single electron moves. The electrostatic force attracting the electron to the proton depends only on the distance between the two particles. The electrostatic force has the same form as the gravitational force between two mass particles except that the electrostatic force depends on the magnitudes of the charges on the particles (+1 for the proton and −1 for the electron) instead of the magnitudes of the particle masses that govern the gravitational force. Since forces can be derived from potentials, it is convenient to work with potentials instead, since they are forms of energy. The electrostatic potential is also called the Coulomb potential. Because the electrostatic potential has the same form as the gravitational potential, according to classical mechanics, the equations of motion should be similar, with the electron moving around the nucleus in circular or elliptical orbits (hence the label "planetary" model of the atom). Potentials of the form $V(r)$ that depend only on the radial distance r are known as central potentials. Central potentials have spherical symmetry, and so rather than specifying the position of the electron in the usual Cartesian coordinates (x, y, z), it is more convenient to use polar spherical coordinates centered at the nucleus, consisting of a linear coordinate r and two angular coordinates, usually specified by the Greek letters theta (θ) and phi (Φ). These coordinates are similar to the ones used in GPS devices and most smart phones that track positions on our (nearly) spherical earth, with the two angular coordinates specified by the latitude and longitude, and the linear coordinate specified by sea-level elevation. Because of the spherical symmetry of central potentials, the energy and angular momentum of the classical hydrogen atom are constants, and the orbits are constrained to lie in a plane like the planets orbiting the sun. This classical mechanics description of the atom is incomplete, however, since an electron moving in an elliptical orbit would be accelerating (by changing direction) and, according to classical electromagnetism, it should continuously emit electromagnetic radiation. This loss in orbital energy should result in the electron's orbit getting continually smaller until it spirals into the nucleus, implying that atoms are inherently unstable.

In 1913, Niels Bohr attempted to resolve the atomic paradox by ignoring classical electromagnetism's prediction that the orbiting electron in hydrogen would continuously emit light. Instead, he incorporated into the classical mechanics description of the atom Planck's ideas of quantization and Einstein's finding that light consists of photons whose energy is proportional to their frequency. Bohr assumed that the electron orbiting the nucleus would not normally emit any radiation (the stationary state hypothesis), but it would emit or absorb a photon if it moved to a different orbit. The energy absorbed or emitted would reflect differences in the orbital energies according to this equation:

$$| \Delta E | \ = \ | E_{\text{f}} - E_{\text{i}} | \ = h\nu = \frac{hc}{\lambda}$$

In this equation, h is Planck's constant and E_i and E_f are the initial and final orbital energies, respectively. The absolute value of the energy difference is used, since frequencies and wavelengths are always positive. Instead of allowing for continuous values for the angular momentum, energy, and orbit radius, Bohr assumed that only discrete values for these could occur (actually, quantizing any one of these would imply that the other two are also quantized). Bohr's expression for the quantized energies is:

$$E_n = -\frac{k}{n^2}, \ n = 1, \ 2, \ 3, \ \ldots$$

In this expression, k is a constant comprising fundamental constants such as the electron mass and charge and Planck's constant. Inserting the expression for the orbit energies into the equation for ΔE gives

$$\Delta E = k\left(\frac{1}{n_1^2} - \frac{1}{n_2^2}\right) = \frac{hc}{\lambda}$$

or

$$\frac{1}{\lambda} = \frac{k}{hc}\left(\frac{1}{n_1^2} - \frac{1}{n_2^2}\right)$$

which is identical to the Rydberg equation for $R_\infty = \frac{k}{hc}$. When Bohr calculated his theoretical value for the Rydberg constant, R_∞, and compared it with the experimentally accepted value, he got excellent agreement. Since the Rydberg constant was one of the most precisely measured constants at that time, this level of agreement was astonishing and meant that **Bohr's model** was taken seriously, despite the many assumptions that Bohr needed to derive it.

The lowest few energy levels are shown in **Figure 3.14**. One of the fundamental laws of physics is that matter is most stable with the lowest possible energy. Thus, the electron in a hydrogen atom usually moves in the $n = 1$ orbit, the orbit in which it has the lowest energy. When the electron is in this lowest energy orbit, the atom is said to be in its **ground electronic state** (or simply ground state). If the atom receives energy from an outside source, it is possible for the electron to move to an orbit with a higher n value and the atom is now in an **excited electronic state** (or simply an excited state) with a higher energy. When an electron transitions from an excited state (higher energy orbit) to a less excited state, or ground state, the difference in energy is emitted as a photon. Similarly, if a photon is absorbed by an atom, the energy of the photon moves an electron from a lower energy orbit up to a more excited one. We can relate the energy of electrons in atoms to what we learned previously about energy. The law of conservation of energy says that we can neither create nor destroy energy. Thus, if a certain amount of external energy is required to excite an electron from one energy level to another, that same amount of energy will be liberated when the electron returns to its initial state (**Figure 3.15**). In effect, an atom can "store" energy by using it to promote an electron to a state with a higher energy and release it when the electron returns to a lower state. The energy can be released as one quantum of energy, as the electron returns to its ground state (say, from $n = 5$ to $n = 1$), or it can be released as two or more smaller quanta as the electron falls to an intermediate state, then to the ground state (say, from $n = 5$ to $n = 4$, emitting one quantum, then to $n = 1$, emitting a second quantum).

Since Bohr's model involved only a single electron, it could also be applied to the single electron ions He^+, Li^{2+}, Be^{3+}, and so forth, which differ from hydrogen only in their nuclear charges, and so one-electron atoms and ions are collectively referred to as hydrogen-like atoms. The energy expression for hydrogen-like atoms is a generalization of the hydrogen atom energy, in which Z is the nuclear charge (+1 for hydrogen, +2 for He, +3 for Li, and so on) and k has a value of 2.179×10^{-18} J.

$$E_n = -\frac{kZ^2}{n^2}$$

The sizes of the circular orbits for hydrogen-like atoms are given in terms of their radii by the following expression, in which α_0 is a constant called the Bohr radius, with a value of 5.292×10^{-11} m:

$$r = \frac{n^2}{Z}a_0$$

The equation also shows us that as the electron's energy increases (as n increases), the electron is found at greater distances from the nucleus. This is implied by the inverse dependence on r in the Coulomb potential, since, as the electron moves away from the nucleus, the electrostatic attraction between it and the nucleus decreases, and it is held less tightly in the atom. Note that as n gets larger and the orbits get larger, their energies get closer to zero, and so the limits $n \longrightarrow \infty$ $n \longrightarrow \infty$, and $r \longrightarrow \infty$ $r \longrightarrow \infty$ imply that $E = 0$ corresponds to the ionization limit where the electron is completely removed from the nucleus. Thus, for hydrogen in the ground state $n = 1$, the ionization energy would be:

$$\Delta E = E_{n \longrightarrow \infty} - E_1 = 0 + k = k$$

With three extremely puzzling paradoxes now solved (blackbody radiation, the photoelectric effect, and the hydrogen atom), and all involving Planck's constant in a fundamental manner, it became clear to most physicists at that time that the classical theories that worked so well in the macroscopic world were fundamentally flawed and could not be extended down into the microscopic domain of atoms and molecules. Unfortunately, despite Bohr's remarkable achievement in deriving a theoretical expression for the Rydberg constant, he was unable to extend his theory to the next simplest atom, He, which only has two electrons. Bohr's model was severely flawed, since it was still based on the classical mechanics notion of precise orbits, a concept that was later found to be untenable in the microscopic domain, when a proper model of quantum mechanics was developed to supersede classical mechanics.

Figure 3.14   Quantum numbers and energy levels in a hydrogen atom. The more negative the calculated value, the lower the energy.

Example 3.4

Calculating the Energy of an Electron in a Bohr Orbit

Early researchers were very excited when they were able to predict the energy of an electron at a particular distance from the nucleus in a hydrogen atom. If a spark promotes the electron in a hydrogen atom into an orbit with $n = 3$, what is the calculated energy, in joules, of the electron?

Solution

The energy of the electron is given by this equation:

$$E = \frac{-kZ^2}{n^2}$$

The atomic number, Z, of hydrogen is 1; $k = 2.179 \times 10^{-18}$ J; and the electron is characterized by an n value of 3. Thus,

$$E = \frac{-(2.179 \times 10^{-18}\ \text{J}) \times (1)^2}{(3)^2} = -2.421 \times 10^{-19}\ \text{J}$$

Check Your Learning

The electron in Figure 3.15 is promoted even further to an orbit with $n = 6$. What is its new energy?

Answer: -6.053×10^{-20} J

Figure 3.15 The horizontal lines show the relative energy of orbits in the Bohr model of the hydrogen atom, and the vertical arrows depict the energy of photons absorbed (left) or emitted (right) as electrons move between these orbits.

Example 3.5

Calculating the Energy and Wavelength of Electron Transitions in a One–electron (Bohr) System

What is the energy (in joules) and the wavelength (in meters) of the line in the spectrum of hydrogen that represents the movement of an electron from Bohr orbit with $n = 4$ to the orbit with $n = 6$? In what part of the electromagnetic spectrum do we find this radiation?

Solution

In this case, the electron starts out with $n = 4$, so $n_1 = 4$. It comes to rest in the $n = 6$ orbit, so $n_2 = 6$. The difference in energy between the two states is given by this expression:

$$\Delta E = E_1 - E_2 = 2.179 \times 10^{-18}\left(\frac{1}{n_1^2} - \frac{1}{n_2^2}\right)$$

$$\Delta E = 2.179 \times 10^{-18}\left(\frac{1}{4^2} - \frac{1}{6^2}\right)\text{J}$$

$$\Delta E = 2.179 \times 10^{-18}\left(\frac{1}{16} - \frac{1}{36}\right)\text{J}$$

$$\Delta E = 7.566 \times 10^{-20}\text{ J}$$

This energy difference is positive, indicating a photon enters the system (is absorbed) to excite the electron from the $n = 4$ orbit up to the $n = 6$ orbit. The wavelength of a photon with this energy is found by the expression $E = \frac{hc}{\lambda}$. Rearrangement gives:

$$\lambda = \frac{hc}{E}$$

$$= \left(6.626 \times 10^{-34} \text{ J·s}\right) \times \frac{2.998 \times 10^8 \text{ m·s}^{-1}}{7.566 \times 10^{-20} \text{ J}}$$

$$= 2.626 \times 10^{-6} \text{ m}$$

From Figure 3.3, we can see that this wavelength is found in the infrared portion of the electromagnetic spectrum.

Check Your Learning

What is the energy in joules and the wavelength in meters of the photon produced when an electron falls from the $n = 5$ to the $n = 3$ level in a He^+ ion ($Z = 2$ for He^+)?

Answer: 6.198×10^{-19} J; 3.205×10^{-7} m

Bohr's model of the hydrogen atom provides insight into the behavior of matter at the microscopic level, but it is does not account for electron–electron interactions in atoms with more than one electron. It does introduce several important features of all models used to describe the distribution of electrons in an atom. These features include the following:

- The energies of electrons (energy levels) in an atom are quantized, described by **quantum numbers**: integer numbers having only specific allowed value and used to characterize the arrangement of electrons in an atom.

- An electron's energy increases with increasing distance from the nucleus.

- The discrete energies (lines) in the spectra of the elements result from quantized electronic energies.

Of these features, the most important is the postulate of quantized energy levels for an electron in an atom. As a consequence, the model laid the foundation for the quantum mechanical model of the atom. Bohr won a Nobel Prize in Physics for his contributions to our understanding of the structure of atoms and how that is related to line spectra emissions.

3.3 Development of Quantum Theory

By the end of this section, you will be able to:

- Extend the concept of wave–particle duality that was observed in electromagnetic radiation to matter as well

- Understand the general idea of the quantum mechanical description of electrons in an atom, and that it uses the notion of three-dimensional wave functions, or orbitals, that define the distribution of probability to find an electron in a particular part of space

- List and describe traits of the four quantum numbers that form the basis for completely specifying the state of an electron in an atom

Bohr's model explained the experimental data for the hydrogen atom and was widely accepted, but it also raised many questions. Why did electrons orbit at only fixed distances defined by a single quantum number $n = 1, 2, 3$, and so on, but never in between? Why did the model work so well describing hydrogen and one-electron ions, but could not correctly predict the emission spectrum for helium or any larger atoms? To answer these questions, scientists needed to completely revise the way they thought about matter.

Behavior in the Microscopic World

We know how matter behaves in the macroscopic world—objects that are large enough to be seen by the naked eye follow the rules of classical physics. A billiard ball moving on a table will behave like a particle: It will continue in a straight line unless it collides with another ball or the table cushion, or is acted on by some other force (such as friction). The ball has a well-defined position and velocity (or a well-defined momentum, $p = mv$, defined by mass m and velocity v) at any given moment. In other words, the ball is moving in a classical trajectory. This is the typical behavior of a classical object.

When waves interact with each other, they show interference patterns that are not displayed by macroscopic particles such as the billiard ball. For example, interacting waves on the surface of water can produce interference patters similar to those shown on **Figure 3.16**. This is a case of wave behavior on the macroscopic scale, and it is clear that particles and waves are very different phenomena in the macroscopic realm.

Figure 3.16 An interference pattern on the water surface is formed by interacting waves. The waves are caused by reflection of water from the rocks. (credit: modification of work by Sukanto Debnath)

As technological improvements allowed scientists to probe the microscopic world in greater detail, it became increasingly clear by the 1920s that very small pieces of matter follow a different set of rules from those we observe for large objects. The unquestionable separation of waves and particles was no longer the case for the microscopic world.

One of the first people to pay attention to the special behavior of the microscopic world was Louis de Broglie. He asked the question: If electromagnetic radiation can have particle-like character, can electrons and other submicroscopic particles exhibit wavelike character? In his 1925 doctoral dissertation, de Broglie extended the wave–particle duality of light that Einstein used to resolve the photoelectric-effect paradox to material particles. He predicted that a particle with mass m and velocity v (that is, with linear momentum p) should also exhibit the behavior of a wave with a wavelength value λ, given by this expression in which h is the familiar Planck's constant:

$$\lambda = \frac{h}{mv} = \frac{h}{p}$$

This is called the *de Broglie wavelength*. Unlike the other values of λ discussed in this chapter, the de Broglie wavelength is a characteristic of particles and other bodies, not electromagnetic radiation (note that this equation involves velocity [v, m/s], not frequency [v, Hz]. Although these two symbols are identical, they mean very different things). Where Bohr had postulated the electron as being a particle orbiting the nucleus in quantized orbits, de Broglie argued that Bohr's assumption of quantization can be explained if the electron is considered not as a particle, but rather as a circular standing wave such that only an integer number of wavelengths could fit exactly within the orbit (**Figure 3.17**).

Figure 3.17 If an electron is viewed as a wave circling around the nucleus, an integer number of wavelengths must fit into the orbit for this standing wave behavior to be possible.

For a circular orbit of radius r, the circumference is $2\pi r$, and so de Broglie's condition is:

$$2\pi r = n\lambda, \ n = 1, \ 2, \ 3, \ \ldots$$

Since the de Broglie expression relates the wavelength to the momentum and, hence, velocity, this implies:

$$2\pi r = n\lambda = \frac{nh}{p} = \frac{nh}{mv} = \frac{nhr}{mvr} = \frac{nhr}{L}$$

This expression can be rearranged to give Bohr's formula for the quantization of the angular momentum:

$$L = \frac{nh}{2\pi} = n\hbar$$

Classical angular momentum L for a circular motion is equal to the product of the radius of the circle and the momentum of the moving particle p.

$$L = rp = rmv \text{ (for a circular motion)}$$

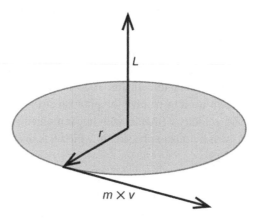

Figure 3.18 The diagram shows angular momentum for a circular motion.

Shortly after de Broglie proposed the wave nature of matter, two scientists at Bell Laboratories, C. J. Davisson and L. H. Germer, demonstrated experimentally that electrons can exhibit wavelike behavior by showing an interference pattern for electrons travelling through a regular atomic pattern in a crystal. The regularly spaced atomic layers served as slits, as used in other interference experiments. Since the spacing between the layers serving as slits needs to be similar in size to the wavelength of the tested wave for an interference pattern to form, Davisson and Germer used a crystalline nickel target for their "slits," since the spacing of the atoms within the lattice was approximately the same as the de Broglie wavelengths of the electrons that they used. **Figure 3.19** shows an interference pattern. It is strikingly similar to the interference patterns for light shown in **m51037 (http://cnx.org/content/m51037/ latest/#CNX_Chem_06_01_LiteInterf)** . The wave–particle duality of matter can be seen in **Figure 3.19** by observing what happens if electron collisions are recorded over a long period of time. Initially, when only a few electrons have been recorded, they show clear particle-like behavior, having arrived in small localized packets that appear to be random. As more and more electrons arrived and were recorded, a clear interference pattern that is the hallmark of wavelike behavior emerged. Thus, it appears that while electrons are small localized particles, their motion does not follow the equations of motion implied by classical mechanics, but instead it is governed by some type of a wave equation that governs a probability distribution even for a single electron's motion. Thus the wave–particle duality first observed with photons is actually a fundamental behavior intrinsic to all quantum particles.

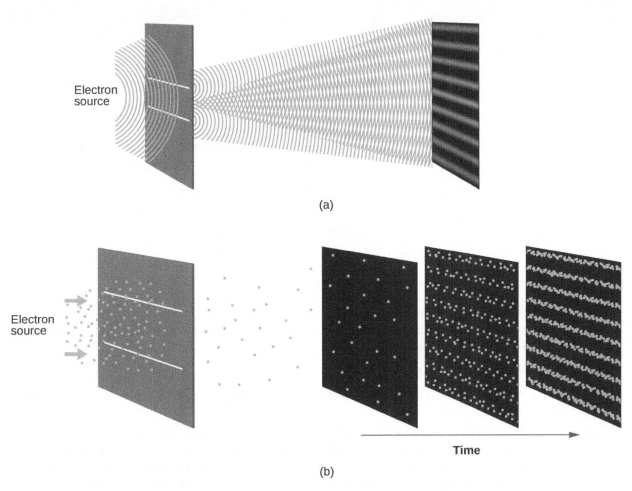

Figure 3.19 (a) The interference pattern for electrons passing through very closely spaced slits demonstrates that quantum particles such as electrons can exhibit wavelike behavior. (b) The experimental results illustrated here demonstrate the wave–particle duality in electrons. The electrons pass through very closely spaced slits, forming an interference pattern, with increasing numbers of electrons being recorded from the left image to the right. With only a few electrons recorded, it is clear that the electrons arrive as individual localized "particles," but in a seemingly random pattern. As more electrons arrive, a wavelike interference pattern begins to emerge. Note that the probability of the final electron location is still governed by the wave-type distribution, even for a single electron, but it can be observed more easily if many electron collisions have been recorded.

Link to Learning

View the Dr. Quantum – Double Slit Experiment cartoon (http://openstaxcollege.org/l/16duality) for an easy-to-understand description of wave–particle duality and the associated experiments.

Example 3.6

Calculating the Wavelength of a Particle

If an electron travels at a velocity of 1.000×10^7 m s^{-1} and has a mass of 9.109×10^{-28} g, what is its wavelength?

Solution

We can use de Broglie's equation to solve this problem, but we first must do a unit conversion of Planck's constant. You learned earlier that $1 \text{ J} = 1 \text{ kg m}^2/\text{s}^2$. Thus, we can write $h = 6.626 \times 10^{-34}$ J s as 6.626×10^{-34} kg m^2/s.

$$\lambda = \frac{h}{mv}$$

$$= \frac{6.626 \times 10^{-34} \text{ kg m}^2/\text{s}}{\left(9.109 \times 10^{-31} \text{ kg}\right)\left(1.000 \times 10^7 \text{ m/s}\right)}$$

$$= 7.274 \times 10^{-11} \text{ m}$$

This is a small value, but it is significantly larger than the size of an electron in the classical (particle) view. This size is the same order of magnitude as the size of an atom. This means that electron wavelike behavior is going to be noticeable in an atom.

Check Your Learning

Calculate the wavelength of a softball with a mass of 100 g traveling at a velocity of 35 m s^{-1}, assuming that it can be modeled as a single particle.

Answer: 1.9×10^{-34} m. We never think of a thrown softball having a wavelength, since this wavelength is so small it is impossible for our senses or any known instrument to detect (strictly speaking, the wavelength of a real baseball would correspond to the wavelengths of its constituent atoms and molecules, which, while much larger than this value, would still be microscopically tiny). The de Broglie wavelength is only appreciable for matter that has a very small mass and/or a very high velocity.

Werner Heisenberg considered the limits of how accurately we can measure properties of an electron or other microscopic particles. He determined that there is a fundamental limit to how accurately one can measure both a particle's position and its momentum simultaneously. The more accurately we measure the momentum of a particle, the less accurately we can determine its position at that time, and vice versa. This is summed up in what we now call the **Heisenberg uncertainty principle**: *It is fundamentally impossible to determine simultaneously and exactly both the momentum and the position of a particle.* For a particle of mass m moving with velocity v_x in the x direction (or equivalently with momentum p_x), the product of the uncertainty in the position, Δx, and the uncertainty in the momentum, Δp_x, must be greater than or equal to $\frac{\hbar}{2}$ (recall that $\hbar = \frac{h}{2\pi}$, the value of Planck's constant divided by 2π).

$$\Delta x \times \Delta p_x = (\Delta x)(m\Delta v) \geq \frac{\hbar}{2}$$

This equation allows us to calculate the limit to how precisely we can know both the simultaneous position of an object and its momentum. For example, if we improve our measurement of an electron's position so that the uncertainty in the position (Δx) has a value of, say, 1 pm (10^{-12} m, about 1% of the diameter of a hydrogen atom), then our determination of its momentum must have an uncertainty with a value of at least

$$\left[\Delta p = m\Delta v = \frac{h}{(2\Delta x)}\right] = \frac{\left(1.055 \times 10^{-34}\ \text{kg m}^2/\text{s}\right)}{\left(2 \times 1 \times 10^{-12}\ \text{m}\right)} = 5 \times 10^{-23}\ \text{kg m/s}.$$

The value of $\hbar$ is not large, so the uncertainty in the position or momentum of a macroscopic object like a baseball is too insignificant to observe. However, the mass of a microscopic object such as an electron is small enough that the uncertainty can be large and significant.

It should be noted that Heisenberg's uncertainty principle is not just limited to uncertainties in position and momentum, but it also links other dynamical variables. For example, when an atom absorbs a photon and makes a transition from one energy state to another, the uncertainty in the energy and the uncertainty in the time required for the transition are similarly related, as $\Delta E\ \Delta t \geq \frac{\hbar}{2}$. As will be discussed later, even the vector components of angular momentum cannot all be specified exactly simultaneously.

Heisenberg's principle imposes ultimate limits on what is knowable in science. The uncertainty principle can be shown to be a consequence of wave–particle duality, which lies at the heart of what distinguishes modern quantum theory from classical mechanics. Recall that the equations of motion obtained from classical mechanics are trajectories where, at any given instant in time, both the position and the momentum of a particle can be determined exactly. Heisenberg's uncertainty principle implies that such a view is untenable in the microscopic domain and that there are fundamental limitations governing the motion of quantum particles. This does not mean that microscopic particles do not move in trajectories, it is just that measurements of trajectories are limited in their precision. In the realm of quantum mechanics, measurements introduce changes into the system that is being observed.

Link to Learning

Read this article (http://openstaxcollege.org/l/16uncertainty) that describes a recent macroscopic demonstration of the uncertainty principle applied to microscopic objects.

The Quantum–Mechanical Model of an Atom

Shortly after de Broglie published his ideas that the electron in a hydrogen atom could be better thought of as being a circular standing wave instead of a particle moving in quantized circular orbits, as Bohr had argued, Erwin Schrödinger extended de Broglie's work by incorporating the de Broglie relation into a wave equation, deriving what is today known as the Schrödinger equation. When Schrödinger applied his equation to hydrogen-like atoms, he was able to reproduce Bohr's expression for the energy and, thus, the Rydberg formula governing hydrogen spectra, and he did so without having to invoke Bohr's assumptions of stationary states and quantized orbits, angular momenta, and energies; quantization in Schrödinger's theory was a natural consequence of the underlying mathematics of the wave equation. Like de Broglie, Schrödinger initially viewed the electron in hydrogen as being a physical wave instead of a particle, but where de Broglie thought of the electron in terms of circular stationary waves, Schrödinger properly thought in terms of three-dimensional stationary waves, or **wavefunctions**, represented by the Greek letter psi, ψ. A few years later, Max Born proposed an interpretation of the wavefunction ψ that is still accepted today: Electrons are still particles, and so the waves represented by ψ are not physical waves but, instead, are complex probability amplitudes. The square of the magnitude of a wavefunction $|\psi|^2$ describes the probability of the quantum particle being present near a certain location in space. This means that wavefunctions can be used to determine the distribution of the electron's density with respect to the nucleus in an atom. In the most general form, the Schrödinger equation can be written as:

$$\hat{H}\psi = E\psi$$

$\hat{H}$ is the Hamiltonian operator, a set of mathematical operations representing the total energy of the quantum particle (such as an electron in an atom), ψ is the wavefunction of this particle that can be used to find the special distribution of the probability of finding the particle, and E is the actual value of the total energy of the particle.

Schrödinger's work, as well as that of Heisenberg and many other scientists following in their footsteps, is generally referred to as **quantum mechanics**.

Link to Learning

You may also have heard of Schrödinger because of his famous thought experiment. This story (http://openstaxcollege.org/l/16superpos) explains the concepts of superposition and entanglement as related to a cat in a box with poison.

Understanding Quantum Theory of Electrons in Atoms

The goal of this section is to understand the electron orbitals (location of electrons in atoms), their different energies, and other properties. The use of quantum theory provides the best understanding to these topics. This knowledge is a precursor to chemical bonding.

As was described previously, electrons in atoms can exist only on discrete energy levels but not between them. It is said that the energy of an electron in an atom is quantized, that is, it can be equal only to certain specific values and can jump from one energy level to another but not transition smoothly or stay between these levels.

The energy levels are labeled with an n value, where $n = 1, 2, 3, \ldots$. Generally speaking, the energy of an electron in an atom is greater for greater values of n. This number, n, is referred to as the principal quantum number. The **principal quantum number** defines the location of the energy level. It is essentially the same concept as the n in the Bohr atom description. Another name for the principal quantum number is the shell number. The **shells** of an atom can be thought of concentric circles radiating out from the nucleus. The electrons that belong to a specific shell are most likely to be found within the corresponding circular area. The further we proceed from the nucleus, the higher the shell number, and so the higher the energy level (**Figure 3.20**). The positively charged protons in the nucleus stabilize the electronic orbitals by electrostatic attraction between the positive charges of the protons and the negative charges of the electrons. So the further away the electron is from the nucleus, the greater the energy it has.

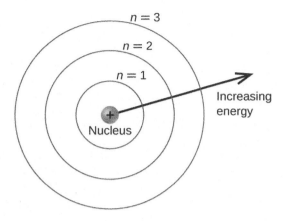

Figure 3.20 Different shells are numbered by principal quantum numbers.

This quantum mechanical model for where electrons reside in an atom can be used to look at electronic transitions, the events when an electron moves from one energy level to another. If the transition is to a higher energy level, energy is absorbed, and the energy change has a positive value. To obtain the amount of energy necessary for the transition to a higher energy level, a photon is absorbed by the atom. A transition to a lower energy level involves a release of energy, and the energy change is negative. This process is accompanied by emission of a photon by the atom. The following equation summarizes these relationships and is based on the hydrogen atom:

$$\Delta E = E_{\text{final}} - E_{\text{initial}}$$

$$= -2.18 \times 10^{-18} \left(\frac{1}{n_{\text{f}}^2} - \frac{1}{n_{\text{i}}^2} \right) \text{J}$$

The values n_{f} and n_{i} are the final and initial energy states of the electron. m51039 (http://cnx.org/content/ m51039/latest/#fs-idp30549440) in the previous section of the chapter demonstrates calculations of such energy changes.

The principal quantum number is one of three quantum numbers used to characterize an orbital. An **atomic orbital**, which is distinct from an *orbit*, is a general region in an atom within which an electron is most probable to reside. The quantum mechanical model specifies the probability of finding an electron in the three-dimensional space around the nucleus and is based on solutions of the Schrödinger equation. In addition, the principal quantum number defines the energy of an electron in a hydrogen or hydrogen-like atom or an ion (an atom or an ion with only one electron) and the general region in which discrete energy levels of electrons in a multi-electron atoms and ions are located.

Another quantum number is *l*, the **angular momentum quantum number**. It is an integer that defines the shape of the orbital, and takes on the values, $l = 0, 1, 2, \ldots, n - 1$. This means that an orbital with $n = 1$ can have only one value of *l*, $l = 0$, whereas $n = 2$ permits $l = 0$ and $l = 1$, and so on. The principal quantum number defines the general size and energy of the orbital. The *l* value specifies the shape of the orbital. Orbitals with the same value of *l* form a **subshell**. In addition, the greater the angular momentum quantum number, the greater is the angular momentum of an electron at this orbital.

Orbitals with $l = 0$ are called *s* **orbitals** (or the *s* subshells). The value $l = 1$ corresponds to the *p* orbitals. For a given *n*, *p* **orbitals** constitute a *p* subshell (e.g., *3p* if $n = 3$). The orbitals with $l = 2$ are called the *d* **orbitals**, followed by the *f-*, *g-, and h*-orbitals for $l = 3, 4, 5$, and there are higher values we will not consider.

There are certain distances from the nucleus at which the probability density of finding an electron located at a particular orbital is zero. In other words, the value of the wavefunction ψ is zero at this distance for this orbital. Such a value of radius *r* is called a radial node. The number of radial nodes in an orbital is $n - l - 1$.

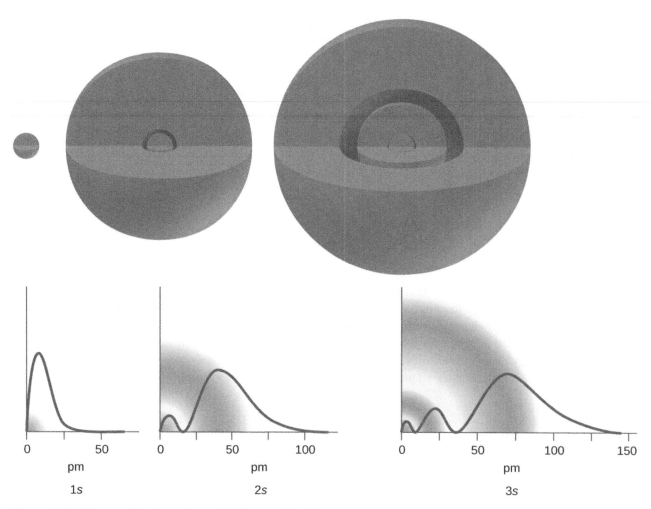

Figure 3.21   The graphs show the probability (y axis) of finding an electron for the $1s$, $2s$, $3s$ orbitals as a function of distance from the nucleus.

Consider the examples in **Figure 3.21**. The orbitals depicted are of the s type, thus $l = 0$ for all of them. It can be seen from the graphs of the probability densities that there are $1 - 0 - 1 = 0$ places where the density is zero (nodes) for $1s$ ($n = 1$), $2 - 0 - 1 = 1$ node for $2s$, and $3 - 0 - 1 = 2$ nodes for the $3s$ orbitals.

The s subshell electron density distribution is spherical and the p subshell has a dumbbell shape. The d and f **orbitals** are more complex. These shapes represent the three-dimensional regions within which the electron is likely to be found.

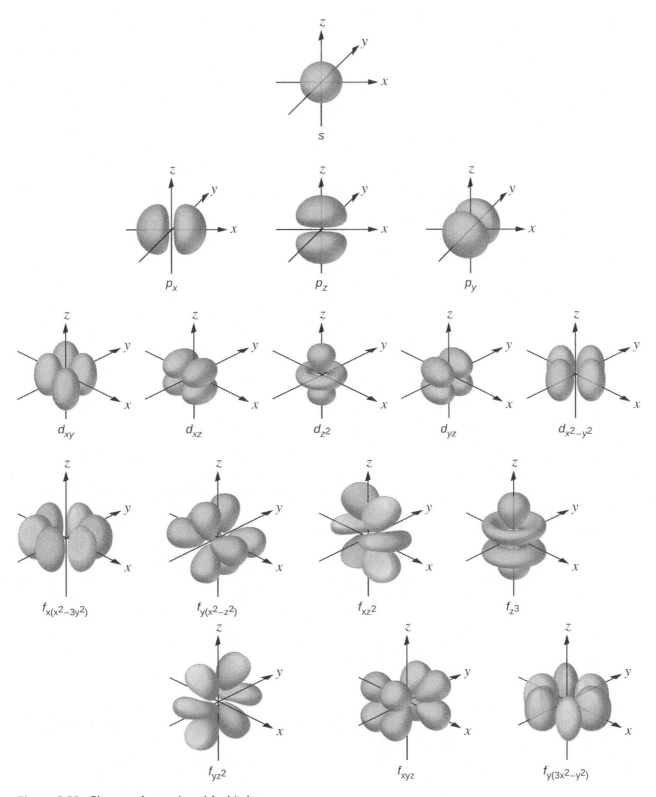

Figure 3.22 Shapes of *s*, *p*, *d*, and *f* orbitals.

If an electron has an angular momentum ($l \neq 0$), then this vector can point in different directions. In addition, the *z* component of the angular momentum can have more than one value. This means that if a magnetic field is applied in the *z* direction, orbitals with different values of the *z* component of the angular momentum will have different energies resulting from interacting with the field. The **magnetic quantum number**, called m_l, specifies the z component of the angular momentum for a particular orbital. For example, for an s orbital, $l = 0$, and the only value of m_l is zero. For p orbitals, $l = 1$, and m_l can be equal to $-1, 0,$ or $+1$. Generally speaking, m_l can be equal to $-l, -(l - 1), ..., -1, 0, +1,$ $..., (l - 1), l$. The total number of possible orbitals with the same value of l (a subshell) is $2l + 1$. Thus, there is one s-orbital for $ml = 0$, there are three p-orbitals for $ml = 1$, five d-orbitals for $ml = 2$, seven f-orbitals for $ml = 3$, and so forth. The principal quantum number defines the general value of the electronic energy. The angular momentum quantum number determines the shape of the orbital. And the magnetic quantum number specifies orientation of the orbital in space, as can be seen in Figure 3.22.

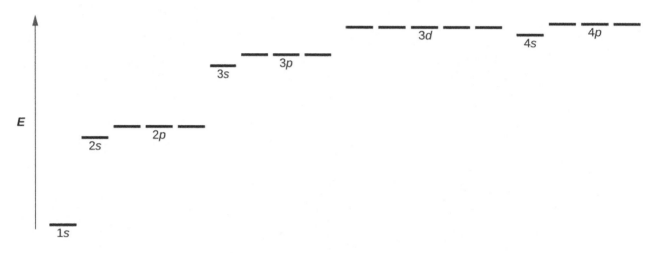

Figure 3.23 The chart shows the energies of electron orbitals in a multi-electron atom.

Figure 3.23 illustrates the energy levels for various orbitals. The number before the orbital name (such as $2s$, $3p$, and so forth) stands for the principal quantum number, n. The letter in the orbital name defines the subshell with a specific angular momentum quantum number $l = 0$ for s orbitals, 1 for p orbitals, 2 for d orbitals. Finally, there are more than one possible orbitals for $l \geq 1$, each corresponding to a specific value of m_l. In the case of a hydrogen atom or a one-electron ion (such as He^+, Li^{2+}, and so on), energies of all the orbitals with the same n are the same. This is called a degeneracy, and the energy levels for the same principal quantum number, n, are called degenerate energy levels. However, in atoms with more than one electron, this degeneracy is eliminated by the electron–electron interactions, and orbitals that belong to different subshells have different energies, as shown on Figure 3.23. Orbitals within the same subshell (for example ns, np, nd, nf, such as $2p$, $3s$) are still degenerate and have the same energy.

While the three quantum numbers discussed in the previous paragraphs work well for describing electron orbitals, some experiments showed that they were not sufficient to explain all observed results. It was demonstrated in the 1920s that when hydrogen-line spectra are examined at extremely high resolution, some lines are actually not single peaks but, rather, pairs of closely spaced lines. This is the so-called fine structure of the spectrum, and it implies that there are additional small differences in energies of electrons even when they are located in the same orbital. These observations led Samuel Goudsmit and George Uhlenbeck to propose that electrons have a fourth quantum number. They called this the **spin quantum number**, or m_s.

The other three quantum numbers, n, l, and m_l, are properties of specific atomic orbitals that also define in what part of the space an electron is most likely to be located. Orbitals are a result of solving the Schrödinger equation for electrons in atoms. The electron spin is a different kind of property. It is a completely quantum phenomenon with no analogues in the classical realm. In addition, it cannot be derived from solving the Schrödinger equation and is not related to the normal spatial coordinates (such as the Cartesian x, y, and z). Electron spin describes an intrinsic electron "rotation" or "spinning." Each electron acts as a tiny magnet or a tiny rotating object with an angular momentum, even though this rotation cannot be observed in terms of the spatial coordinates.

The magnitude of the overall electron spin can only have one value, and an electron can only "spin" in one of two quantized states. One is termed the α state, with the z component of the spin being in the positive direction of the z axis. This corresponds to the spin quantum number $m_s = \frac{1}{2}$. The other is called the β state, with the z component of the spin being negative and $m_s = -\frac{1}{2}$. Any electron, regardless of the atomic orbital it is located in, can only have one of those two values of the spin quantum number. The energies of electrons having $m_s = -\frac{1}{2}$ and $m_s = \frac{1}{2}$ are different if an external magnetic field is applied.

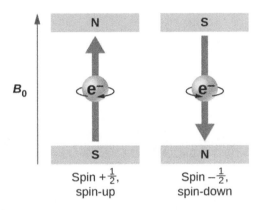

Figure 3.24 Electrons with spin values $\pm\frac{1}{2}$ in an external magnetic field.

Figure 3.24 illustrates this phenomenon. An electron acts like a tiny magnet. Its moment is directed up (in the positive direction of the z axis) for the $\frac{1}{2}$ spin quantum number and down (in the negative z direction) for the spin quantum number of $-\frac{1}{2}$. A magnet has a lower energy if its magnetic moment is aligned with the external magnetic field (the left electron on Figure 3.24) and a higher energy for the magnetic moment being opposite to the applied field. This is why an electron with $m_s = \frac{1}{2}$ has a slightly lower energy in an external field in the positive z direction, and an electron with $m_s = -\frac{1}{2}$ has a slightly higher energy in the same field. This is true even for an electron occupying the same orbital in an atom. A spectral line corresponding to a transition for electrons from the same orbital but with different spin quantum numbers has two possible values of energy; thus, the line in the spectrum will show a fine structure splitting.

The Pauli Exclusion Principle

An electron in an atom is completely described by four quantum numbers: n, l, m_l, and m_s. The first three quantum numbers define the orbital and the fourth quantum number describes the intrinsic electron property called spin. An Austrian physicist Wolfgang Pauli formulated a general principle that gives the last piece of information that we need to understand the general behavior of electrons in atoms. The **Pauli exclusion principle** can be formulated as follows: No two electrons in the same atom can have exactly the same set of all the four quantum numbers. What this means is that electrons can share the same orbital (the same set of the quantum numbers n, l, and m_l), but only if their spin quantum numbers m_s have different values. Since the spin quantum number can only have two values $\left(\pm\frac{1}{2}\right)$, no more than two electrons can occupy the same orbital (and if two electrons are located in the same orbital, they must have opposite spins). Therefore, any atomic orbital can be populated by only zero, one, or two electrons.

The properties and meaning of the quantum numbers of electrons in atoms are briefly summarized in Table 3.1.

Quantum Numbers, Their Properties, and Significance

Name	Symbol	Allowed values	Physical meaning
principal quantum number	n	1, 2, 3, 4, ...	shell, the general region for the value of energy for an electron on the orbital
angular momentum or azimuthal quantum number	l	$0 \leq l \leq n - 1$	subshell, the shape of the orbital
magnetic quantum number	m_l	$-l \leq m_l \leq l$	orientation of the orbital
spin quantum number	m_s	$\frac{1}{2}, -\frac{1}{2}$	direction of the intrinsic quantum "spinning" of the electron

Table 3.1

Example 3.7

Working with Shells and Subshells

Indicate the number of subshells, the number of orbitals in each subshell, and the values of l and m_l for the orbitals in the $n = 4$ shell of an atom.

Solution

For $n = 4$, l can have values of 0, 1, 2, and 3. Thus, s, p, d, and f subshells are found in the $n = 4$ shell of an atom. For $l = 0$ (the s subshell), m_l can only be 0. Thus, there is only one $4s$ orbital. For $l = 1$ (p-type orbitals), m can have values of $-1, 0, +1$, so we find three $4p$ orbitals. For $l = 2$ (d-type orbitals), m_l can have values of $-2, -1, 0, +1, +2$, so we have five $4d$ orbitals. When $l = 3$ (f-type orbitals), m_l can have values of $-3, -2, -1, 0, +1, +2, +3$, and we can have seven $4f$ orbitals. Thus, we find a total of 16 orbitals in the $n = 4$ shell of an atom.

Check Your Learning

Identify the subshell in which electrons with the following quantum numbers are found: (a) $n = 3$, $l = 1$; (b) $n = 5$, $l = 3$; (c) $n = 2$, $l = 0$.

Answer: (a) $3p$ (b) $5f$ (c) $2s$

Example 3.8

Maximum Number of Electrons

Calculate the maximum number of electrons that can occupy a shell with (a) $n = 2$, (b) $n = 5$, and (c) n as a variable. Note you are only looking at the orbitals with the specified n value, not those at lower energies.

Solution

(a) When $n = 2$, there are four orbitals (a single $2s$ orbital, and three orbitals labeled $2p$). These four orbitals can contain eight electrons.

(b) When $n = 5$, there are five subshells of orbitals that we need to sum:

1 orbital labeled $5s$
3 orbitals labeled $5p$
5 orbitals labeled $5d$
7 orbitals labeled $5f$

$+9$ orbitals labeled $5g$
_____
25 orbitals total

Again, each orbital holds two electrons, so 50 electrons can fit in this shell.

(c) The number of orbitals in any shell n will equal n^2. There can be up to two electrons in each orbital, so the maximum number of electrons will be $2 \times n^2$

Check Your Learning

If a shell contains a maximum of 32 electrons, what is the principal quantum number, n?

Answer: $n = 4$

Example 3.9

Working with Quantum Numbers

Complete the following table for atomic orbitals:

Orbital	n	l	m_l degeneracy	Radial nodes (no.)
4f				
	4	1		
	7		7	3
5d				

Solution

The table can be completed using the following rules:

- The orbital designation is nl, where $l = 0, 1, 2, 3, 4, 5, \ldots$ is mapped to the letter sequence s, p, d, f, g, h, …,

- The m_l degeneracy is the number of orbitals within an l subshell, and so is $2l + 1$ (there is one s orbital, three p orbitals, five d orbitals, seven f orbitals, and so forth).

- The number of radial nodes is equal to $n - l - 1$.

Orbital	n	l	m_l degeneracy	Radial nodes (no.)
4f	4	3	7	0
4p	4	1	3	2
7f	7	3	7	3
5d	5	2	5	2

Check Your Learning

How many orbitals have $l = 2$ and $n = 3$?

Answer: The five degenerate $3d$ orbitals

3.4 Electronic Structure of Atoms (Electron Configurations)

By the end of this section, you will be able to:

- Derive the predicted ground-state electron configurations of atoms

- Identify and explain exceptions to predicted electron configurations for atoms and ions

- Relate electron configurations to element classifications in the periodic table

Having introduced the basics of atomic structure and quantum mechanics, we can use our understanding of quantum numbers to determine how atomic orbitals relate to one another. This allows us to determine which orbitals are occupied by electrons in each atom. The specific arrangement of electrons in orbitals of an atom determines many of the chemical properties of that atom.

Orbital Energies and Atomic Structure

The energy of atomic orbitals increases as the principal quantum number, n, increases. In any atom with two or more electrons, the repulsion between the electrons makes energies of subshells with different values of l differ so that the energy of the orbitals increases within a shell in the order $s < p < d < f$. **Figure 3.25** depicts how these two trends in increasing energy relate. The $1s$ orbital at the bottom of the diagram is the orbital with electrons of lowest energy. The energy increases as we move up to the $2s$ and then $2p$, $3s$, and $3p$ orbitals, showing that the increasing n value has more influence on energy than the increasing l value for small atoms. However, this pattern does not hold for larger atoms. The $3d$ orbital is higher in energy than the $4s$ orbital. Such overlaps continue to occur frequently as we move up the chart.

Figure 3.25 Generalized energy-level diagram for atomic orbitals in an atom with two or more electrons (not to scale).

Electrons in successive atoms on the periodic table tend to fill low-energy orbitals first. Thus, many students find it confusing that, for example, the $5p$ orbitals fill immediately after the $4d$, and immediately before the $6s$. The filling order is based on observed experimental results, and has been confirmed by theoretical calculations. As the principal quantum number, n, increases, the size of the orbital increases and the electrons spend more time farther from the nucleus. Thus, the attraction to the nucleus is weaker and the energy associated with the orbital is higher (less stabilized). But this is not the only effect we have to take into account. Within each shell, as the value of l increases, the electrons are less penetrating (meaning there is less electron density found close to the nucleus), in the order $s > p > d > f$. Electrons that are closer to the nucleus slightly repel electrons that are farther out, offsetting the more dominant electron–nucleus attractions slightly (recall that all electrons have -1 charges, but nuclei have $+Z$ charges). This phenomenon is called shielding and will be discussed in more detail in the next section. Electrons in orbitals that experience more shielding are less stabilized and thus higher in energy. For small orbitals ($1s$ through $3p$), the increase in energy due to n is more significant than the increase due to l; however, for larger orbitals the two trends are comparable and cannot be simply predicted. We will discuss methods for remembering the observed order.

The arrangement of electrons in the orbitals of an atom is called the **electron configuration** of the atom. We describe an electron configuration with a symbol that contains three pieces of information (Figure 3.26):

1. The number of the principal quantum shell, n,

2. The letter that designates the orbital type (the subshell, l), and

3. A superscript number that designates the number of electrons in that particular subshell.

For example, the notation $2p^4$ (read "two–p–four") indicates four electrons in a p subshell ($l = 1$) with a principal quantum number (n) of 2. The notation $3d^8$ (read "three–d–eight") indicates eight electrons in the d subshell (i.e., $l = 2$) of the principal shell for which $n = 3$.

Figure 3.26 The diagram of an electron configuration specifies the subshell (*n* and *l* value, with letter symbol) and superscript number of electrons.

The Aufbau Principle

To determine the electron configuration for any particular atom, we can "build" the structures in the order of atomic numbers. Beginning with hydrogen, and continuing across the periods of the periodic table, we add one proton at a time to the nucleus and one electron to the proper subshell until we have described the electron configurations of all the elements. This procedure is called the **Aufbau principle**, from the German word *Aufbau* ("to build up"). Each added electron occupies the subshell of lowest energy available (in the order shown in Figure 3.25), subject to the limitations imposed by the allowed quantum numbers according to the Pauli exclusion principle. Electrons enter higher-energy subshells only after lower-energy subshells have been filled to capacity. Figure 3.27 illustrates the traditional way to remember the filling order for atomic orbitals. Since the arrangement of the periodic table is based on the electron configurations, Figure 3.28 provides an alternative method for determining the electron configuration. The filling order simply begins at hydrogen and includes each subshell as you proceed in increasing *Z* order. For example, after filling the 3*p* block up to Ar, we see the orbital will be 4s (K, Ca), followed by the 3*d* orbitals.

Figure 3.27 The arrow leads through each subshell in the appropriate filling order for electron configurations. This chart is straightforward to construct. Simply make a column for all the *s* orbitals with each *n* shell on a separate row. Repeat for *p*, *d*, and *f*. Be sure to only include orbitals allowed by the quantum numbers (no 1*p* or 2*d*, and so forth). Finally, draw diagonal lines from top to bottom as shown.

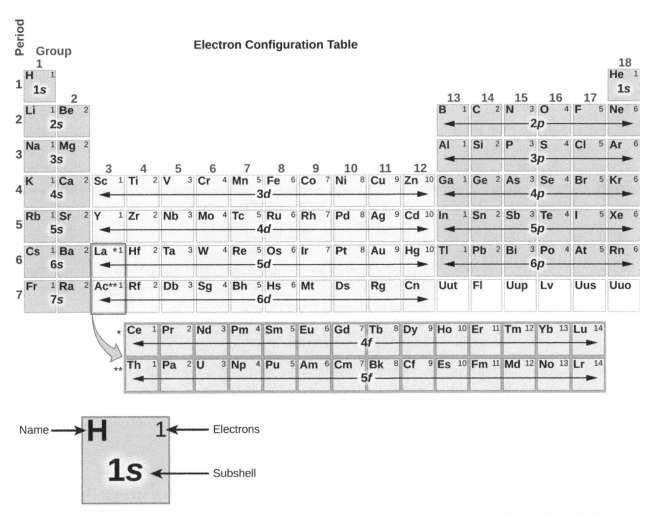

Figure 3.28 This periodic table shows the electron configuration for each subshell. By "building up" from hydrogen, this table can be used to determine the electron configuration for any atom on the periodic table.

We will now construct the ground-state electron configuration and orbital diagram for a selection of atoms in the first and second periods of the periodic table. **Orbital diagrams** are pictorial representations of the electron configuration, showing the individual orbitals and the pairing arrangement of electrons. We start with a single hydrogen atom (atomic number 1), which consists of one proton and one electron. Referring to **Figure 3.27** or **Figure 3.28**, we would expect to find the electron in the 1s orbital. By convention, the $m_s = +\frac{1}{2}$ value is usually filled first. The electron configuration and the orbital diagram are:

$$\text{H} \qquad 1s^1 \qquad \boxed{\uparrow}$$
$$\qquad\qquad\qquad 1s$$

Following hydrogen is the noble gas helium, which has an atomic number of 2. The helium atom contains two protons and two electrons. The first electron has the same four quantum numbers as the hydrogen atom electron ($n = 1$, $l = 0$, $m_l = 0$, $m_s = +\frac{1}{2}$). The second electron also goes into the 1s orbital and fills that orbital. The second electron has the same n, l, and m_l quantum numbers, but must have the opposite spin quantum number, $m_s = -\frac{1}{2}$. This is in accord with the Pauli exclusion principle: No two electrons in the same atom can have the same set of four quantum numbers. For orbital diagrams, this means two arrows go in each box (representing two electrons in each orbital) and the arrows must point in opposite directions (representing paired spins). The electron configuration and orbital diagram of helium are:

$$\text{He} \quad 1s^2 \quad \boxed{\uparrow\downarrow}$$
$$1s$$

The $n = 1$ shell is completely filled in a helium atom.

The next atom is the alkali metal lithium with an atomic number of 3. The first two electrons in lithium fill the $1s$ orbital and have the same sets of four quantum numbers as the two electrons in helium. The remaining electron must occupy the orbital of next lowest energy, the $2s$ orbital (**Figure 3.27** or **Figure 3.28**). Thus, the electron configuration and orbital diagram of lithium are:

$$\text{Li} \quad 1s^2 2s^1 \quad \boxed{\uparrow\downarrow} \ \boxed{\uparrow}$$
$$1s \qquad 2s$$

An atom of the alkaline earth metal beryllium, with an atomic number of 4, contains four protons in the nucleus and four electrons surrounding the nucleus. The fourth electron fills the remaining space in the $2s$ orbital.

$$\text{Be} \quad 1s^2 2s^2 \quad \boxed{\uparrow\downarrow} \ \boxed{\uparrow\downarrow}$$
$$1s \qquad 2s$$

An atom of boron (atomic number 5) contains five electrons. The $n = 1$ shell is filled with two electrons and three electrons will occupy the $n = 2$ shell. Because any s subshell can contain only two electrons, the fifth electron must occupy the next energy level, which will be a $2p$ orbital. There are three degenerate $2p$ orbitals ($m_l = -1, 0, +1$) and the electron can occupy any one of these p orbitals. When drawing orbital diagrams, we include empty boxes to depict any empty orbitals in the same subshell that we are filling.

$$\text{B} \quad 1s^2 2s^2 2p^1 \quad \boxed{\uparrow\downarrow} \ \boxed{\uparrow\downarrow} \ \boxed{\uparrow}\ \boxed{\ }\ \boxed{\ }$$
$$1s \qquad 2s \qquad 2p$$

Carbon (atomic number 6) has six electrons. Four of them fill the $1s$ and $2s$ orbitals. The remaining two electrons occupy the $2p$ subshell. We now have a choice of filling one of the $2p$ orbitals and pairing the electrons or of leaving the electrons unpaired in two different, but degenerate, p orbitals. The orbitals are filled as described by **Hund's rule**: the lowest-energy configuration for an atom with electrons within a set of degenerate orbitals is that having the maximum number of unpaired electrons. Thus, the two electrons in the carbon $2p$ orbitals have identical n, l, and m_s quantum numbers and differ in their m_l quantum number (in accord with the Pauli exclusion principle). The electron configuration and orbital diagram for carbon are:

$$\text{C} \quad 1s^2 2s^2 2p^2 \quad \boxed{\uparrow\downarrow} \ \boxed{\uparrow\downarrow} \ \boxed{\uparrow}\ \boxed{\uparrow}\ \boxed{\ }$$
$$1s \qquad 2s \qquad 2p$$

Nitrogen (atomic number 7) fills the $1s$ and $2s$ subshells and has one electron in each of the three $2p$ orbitals, in accordance with Hund's rule. These three electrons have unpaired spins. Oxygen (atomic number 8) has a pair of electrons in any one of the $2p$ orbitals (the electrons have opposite spins) and a single electron in each of the other two. Fluorine (atomic number 9) has only one $2p$ orbital containing an unpaired electron. All of the electrons in the noble gas neon (atomic number 10) are paired, and all of the orbitals in the $n = 1$ and the $n = 2$ shells are filled. The electron configurations and orbital diagrams of these four elements are:

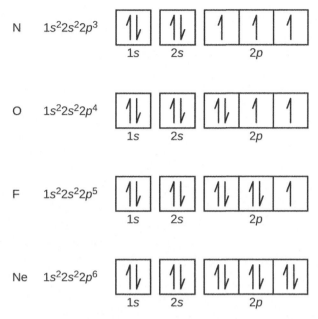

The alkali metal sodium (atomic number 11) has one more electron than the neon atom. This electron must go into the lowest-energy subshell available, the $3s$ orbital, giving a $1s^2 2s^2 2p^6 3s^1$ configuration. The electrons occupying the outermost shell orbital(s) (highest value of n) are called **valence electrons**, and those occupying the inner shell orbitals are called **core electrons** (Figure 3.29). Since the core electron shells correspond to noble gas electron configurations, we can abbreviate electron configurations by writing the noble gas that matches the core electron configuration, along with the valence electrons in a condensed format. For our sodium example, the symbol [Ne] represents core electrons, ($1s^2 2s^2 2p^6$) and our abbreviated or condensed configuration is $[Ne]3s^1$.

Figure 3.29   A core-abbreviated electron configuration (right) replaces the core electrons with the noble gas symbol whose configuration matches the core electron configuration of the other element.

Similarly, the abbreviated configuration of lithium can be represented as $[He]2s^1$, where [He] represents the configuration of the helium atom, which is identical to that of the filled inner shell of lithium. Writing the configurations in this way emphasizes the similarity of the configurations of lithium and sodium. Both atoms, which are in the alkali metal family, have only one electron in a valence s subshell outside a filled set of inner shells.

$$\text{Li: } [He]2s^1$$
$$\text{Na: } [Ne]3s^1$$

The alkaline earth metal magnesium (atomic number 12), with its 12 electrons in a $[Ne]3s^2$ configuration, is analogous to its family member beryllium, $[He]2s^2$. Both atoms have a filled s subshell outside their filled inner shells. Aluminum (atomic number 13), with 13 electrons and the electron configuration $[Ne]3s^2 3p^1$, is analogous to its family member boron, $[He]2s^2 2p^1$.

The electron configurations of silicon (14 electrons), phosphorus (15 electrons), sulfur (16 electrons), chlorine (17 electrons), and argon (18 electrons) are analogous in the electron configurations of their outer shells to their corresponding family members carbon, nitrogen, oxygen, fluorine, and neon, respectively, except that the principal quantum number of the outer shell of the heavier elements has increased by one to $n = 3$. Figure 3.30 shows the lowest energy, or ground-state, electron configuration for these elements as well as that for atoms of each of the known elements.

Figure 3.30 This version of the periodic table shows the outer-shell electron configuration of each element. Note that down each group, the configuration is often similar.

When we come to the next element in the periodic table, the alkali metal potassium (atomic number 19), we might expect that we would begin to add electrons to the $3d$ subshell. However, all available chemical and physical evidence indicates that potassium is like lithium and sodium, and that the next electron is not added to the $3d$ level but is, instead, added to the $4s$ level (**Figure 3.30**). As discussed previously, the $3d$ orbital with no radial nodes is higher in energy because it is less penetrating and more shielded from the nucleus than the $4s$, which has three radial nodes. Thus, potassium has an electron configuration of $[Ar]4s^1$. Hence, potassium corresponds to Li and Na in its valence shell configuration. The next electron is added to complete the $4s$ subshell and calcium has an electron configuration of $[Ar]4s^2$. This gives calcium an outer-shell electron configuration corresponding to that of beryllium and magnesium.

Beginning with the transition metal scandium (atomic number 21), additional electrons are added successively to the $3d$ subshell. This subshell is filled to its capacity with 10 electrons (remember that for $l = 2$ [d orbitals], there are $2l + 1 = 5$ values of m_l, meaning that there are five d orbitals that have a combined capacity of 10 electrons). The $4p$ subshell fills next. Note that for three series of elements, scandium (Sc) through copper (Cu), yttrium (Y) through silver (Ag), and lutetium (Lu) through gold (Au), a total of 10 d electrons are successively added to the $(n-1)$ shell next to the n shell to bring that $(n-1)$ shell from 8 to 18 electrons. For two series, lanthanum (La) through lutetium (Lu) and actinium (Ac) through lawrencium (Lr), 14 f electrons ($l = 3$, $2l + 1 = 7$ m_l values; thus, seven orbitals with a combined capacity of 14 electrons) are successively added to the $(n-2)$ shell to bring that shell from 18 electrons to a total of 32 electrons.

Example 3.10

Quantum Numbers and Electron Configurations

What is the electron configuration and orbital diagram for a phosphorus atom? What are the four quantum numbers for the last electron added?

Solution

The atomic number of phosphorus is 15. Thus, a phosphorus atom contains 15 electrons. The order of filling of the energy levels is 1s, 2s, 2p, 3s, 3p, 4s, . . . The 15 electrons of the phosphorus atom will fill up to the 3p orbital, which will contain three electrons:

P $1s^2 2s^2 2p^6 3s^2 3p^3$

The last electron added is a 3p electron. Therefore, $n = 3$ and, for a p-type orbital, $l = 1$. The m_l value could be −1, 0, or +1. The three p orbitals are degenerate, so any of these m_l values is correct. For unpaired electrons, convention assigns the value of $+\frac{1}{2}$ for the spin quantum number; thus, $m_s = +\frac{1}{2}$.

Check Your Learning

Identify the atoms from the electron configurations given:

(a) [Ar]$4s^2 3d^5$

(b) [Kr]$5s^2 4d^{10} 5p^6$

Answer: (a) Mn (b) Xe

The periodic table can be a powerful tool in predicting the electron configuration of an element. However, we do find exceptions to the order of filling of orbitals that are shown in Figure 3.27 or Figure 3.28. For instance, the electron configurations (shown in Figure 3.30) of the transition metals chromium (Cr; atomic number 24) and copper (Cu; atomic number 29), among others, are not those we would expect. In general, such exceptions involve subshells with very similar energy, and small effects can lead to changes in the order of filling.

In the case of Cr and Cu, we find that half-filled and completely filled subshells apparently represent conditions of preferred stability. This stability is such that an electron shifts from the 4s into the 3d orbital to gain the extra stability of a half-filled 3d subshell (in Cr) or a filled 3d subshell (in Cu). Other exceptions also occur. For example, niobium (Nb, atomic number 41) is predicted to have the electron configuration [Kr]$5s^2 4d^3$. Experimentally, we observe that its ground-state electron configuration is actually [Kr]$5s^1 4d^4$. We can rationalize this observation by saying that the electron–electron repulsions experienced by pairing the electrons in the 5s orbital are larger than the gap in energy between the 5s and 4d orbitals. There is no simple method to predict the exceptions for atoms where the magnitude of the repulsions between electrons is greater than the small differences in energy between subshells.

Electron Configurations and the Periodic Table

As described earlier, the periodic table arranges atoms based on increasing atomic number so that elements with the same chemical properties recur periodically. When their electron configurations are added to the table (Figure 3.30), we also see a periodic recurrence of similar electron configurations in the outer shells of these elements. Because they are in the outer shells of an atom, valence electrons play the most important role in chemical reactions. The outer electrons have the highest energy of the electrons in an atom and are more easily lost or shared than the core electrons. Valence electrons are also the determining factor in some physical properties of the elements.

Elements in any one group (or column) have the same number of valence electrons; the alkali metals lithium and sodium each have only one valence electron, the alkaline earth metals beryllium and magnesium each have two, and the halogens fluorine and chlorine each have seven valence electrons. The similarity in chemical properties among elements of the same group occurs because they have the same number of valence electrons. It is the loss, gain, or sharing of valence electrons that defines how elements react.

It is important to remember that the periodic table was developed on the basis of the chemical behavior of the elements, well before any idea of their atomic structure was available. Now we can understand why the periodic table has the arrangement it has—the arrangement puts elements whose atoms have the same number of valence electrons in the same group. This arrangement is emphasized in Figure 3.30, which shows in periodic-table form the electron configuration of the last subshell to be filled by the Aufbau principle. The colored sections of Figure 3.30 show the three categories of elements classified by the orbitals being filled: main group, transition, and inner transition elements. These classifications determine which orbitals are counted in the **valence shell**, or highest energy level orbitals of an atom.

1. **Main group elements** (sometimes called **representative elements**) are those in which the last electron added enters an s or a p orbital in the outermost shell, shown in blue and red in Figure 3.30. This category includes all the nonmetallic elements, as well as many metals and the intermediate semimetallic elements. The valence electrons for main group elements are those with the highest n level. For example, gallium (Ga, atomic number 31) has the electron configuration $[Ar]\underline{4s^2}3d^{10}\underline{4p^1}$, which contains three valence electrons (underlined). The completely filled d orbitals count as core, not valence, electrons.

2. **Transition elements or transition metals**. These are metallic elements in which the last electron added enters a d orbital. The valence electrons (those added after the last noble gas configuration) in these elements include the ns and $(n-1)$ d electrons. The official IUPAC definition of transition elements specifies those with partially filled d orbitals. Thus, the elements with completely filled orbitals (Zn, Cd, Hg, as well as Cu, Ag, and Au in Figure 3.30) are not technically transition elements. However, the term is frequently used to refer to the entire d block (colored yellow in Figure 3.30), and we will adopt this usage in this textbook.

3. **Inner transition elements** are metallic elements in which the last electron added occupies an f orbital. They are shown in green in Figure 3.30. The valence shells of the inner transition elements consist of the $(n-2)f$, the $(n-1)d$, and the ns subshells. There are two inner transition series:

   a. The lanthanide series: lanthanide (La) through lutetium (Lu)

   b. The actinide series: actinide (Ac) through lawrencium (Lr)

Lanthanum and actinium, because of their similarities to the other members of the series, are included and used to name the series, even though they are transition metals with no f electrons.

Electron Configurations of Ions

We have seen that ions are formed when atoms gain or lose electrons. A cation (positively charged ion) forms when one or more electrons are removed from a parent atom. For main group elements, the electrons that were added last are the first electrons removed. For transition metals and inner transition metals, however, electrons in the s orbital are easier to remove than the d or f electrons, and so the highest ns electrons are lost, and then the $(n-1)d$ or $(n-2)f$ electrons are removed. An anion (negatively charged ion) forms when one or more electrons are added to a parent atom. The added electrons fill in the order predicted by the Aufbau principle.

Example 3.11

Predicting Electron Configurations of Ions

What is the electron configuration and orbital diagram of:

(a) Na^+

(b) P^{3-}

(c) Al^{2+}

(d) Fe^{2+}

(e) Sm^{3+}

Solution

First, write out the electron configuration for each parent atom. We have chosen to show the full, unabbreviated configurations to provide more practice for students who want it, but listing the core-abbreviated electron configurations is also acceptable.

Next, determine whether an electron is gained or lost. Remember electrons are negatively charged, so ions with a positive charge have *lost* an electron. For main group elements, the last orbital gains or loses the electron. For transition metals, the last s orbital loses an electron before the d orbitals.

(a) Na: $1s^2 2s^2 2p^6 3s^1$. Sodium cation loses one electron, so Na^+: $1s^2 2s^2 2p^6 3s^1 = Na^+$: $1s^2 2s^2 2p^6$.

(b) P: $1s^2 2s^2 2p^6 3s^2 3p^3$. Phosphorus trianion gains three electrons, so P^{3-}: $1s^2 2s^2 2p^6 3s^2 3p^6$.

(c) Al: $1s^2 2s^2 2p^6 3s^2 3p^1$. Aluminum dication loses two electrons Al^{2+}: $1s^2 2s^2 2p^6 3s^2 3p^1 =$ Al^{2+}: $1s^2 2s^2 2p^6 3s^1$.

(d) Fe: $1s^2 2s^2 2p^6 3s^2 3p^6 4s^2 3d^6$. Iron(II) loses two electrons and, since it is a transition metal, they are removed from the $4s$ orbital Fe^{2+}: $1s^2 2s^2 2p^6 3s^2 3p^6 4s^2 3d^6 = 1s^2 2s^2 2p^6 3s^2 3p^6 3d^6$.

(e). Sm: $1s^2 2s^2 2p^6 3s^2 3p^6 4s^2 3d^{10} 4p^6 5s^2 4d^{10} 5p^6 6s^2 4f^6$. Samarium trication loses three electrons. The first two will be lost from the $6s$ orbital, and the final one is removed from the $4f$ orbital. Sm^{3+}: $1s^2 2s^2 2p^6 3s^2 3p^6 4s^2 3d^{10} 4p^6 5s^2 4d^{10} 5p^6 6s^2 4f^6 = 1s^2 2s^2 2p^6 3s^2 3p^6 4s^2 3d^{10} 4p^6 5s^2 4d^{10} 5p^6 4f^5$.

Check Your Learning

Which ion with a +2 charge has the electron configuration $1s^2 2s^2 2p^6 3s^2 3p^6 3d^{10} 4s^2 4p^6 4d^5$? Which ion with a +3 charge has this configuration?

Answer: Tc^{2+}, Ru^{3+}

3.5 Periodic Variations in Element Properties

By the end of this section, you will be able to:

- Describe and explain the observed trends in atomic size, ionization energy, and electron affinity of the elements

The elements in groups (vertical columns) of the periodic table exhibit similar chemical behavior. This similarity occurs because the members of a group have the same number and distribution of electrons in their valence shells. However, there are also other patterns in chemical properties on the periodic table. For example, as we move down a group, the metallic character of the atoms increases. Oxygen, at the top of group 16 (6A), is a colorless gas; in the middle of the group, selenium is a semiconducting solid; and, toward the bottom, polonium is a silver-grey solid that conducts electricity.

As we go across a period from left to right, we add a proton to the nucleus and an electron to the valence shell with each successive element. As we go down the elements in a group, the number of electrons in the valence shell remains constant, but the principal quantum number increases by one each time. An understanding of the electronic structure of the elements allows us to examine some of the properties that govern their chemical behavior. These properties vary periodically as the electronic structure of the elements changes. They are (1) size (radius) of atoms and ions, (2) ionization energies, and (3) electron affinities.

Variation in Covalent Radius

The quantum mechanical picture makes it difficult to establish a definite size of an atom. However, there are several practical ways to define the radius of atoms and, thus, to determine their relative sizes that give roughly similar values. We will use the **covalent radius** (Figure 3.31), which is defined as one-half the distance between the nuclei of two identical atoms when they are joined by a covalent bond (this measurement is possible because atoms within molecules still retain much of their atomic identity). We know that as we scan down a group, the principal quantum number, n, increases by one for each element. Thus, the electrons are being added to a region of space that is increasingly distant from the nucleus. Consequently, the size of the atom (and its covalent radius) must increase as we increase the distance of the outermost electrons from the nucleus. This trend is illustrated for the covalent radii of the halogens in Table 3.2 and Figure 3.31. The trends for the entire periodic table can be seen in Figure 3.31.

Covalent Radii of the Halogen Group Elements

Atom	Covalent radius (pm)	Nuclear charge
F	64	+9
Cl	99	+17
Br	114	+35
I	133	+53
At	148	+85

Table 3.2

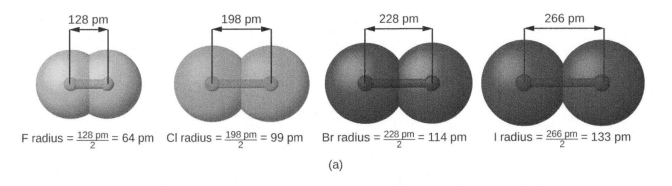

F radius = $\frac{128\ pm}{2}$ = 64 pm   Cl radius = $\frac{198\ pm}{2}$ = 99 pm   Br radius = $\frac{228\ pm}{2}$ = 114 pm   I radius = $\frac{266\ pm}{2}$ = 133 pm

(a)

(b)

Figure 3.31 (a) The radius of an atom is defined as one-half the distance between the nuclei in a molecule consisting of two identical atoms joined by a covalent bond. The atomic radius for the halogens increases down the group as n increases. (b) Covalent radii of the elements are shown to scale. The general trend is that radii increase down a group and decrease across a period.

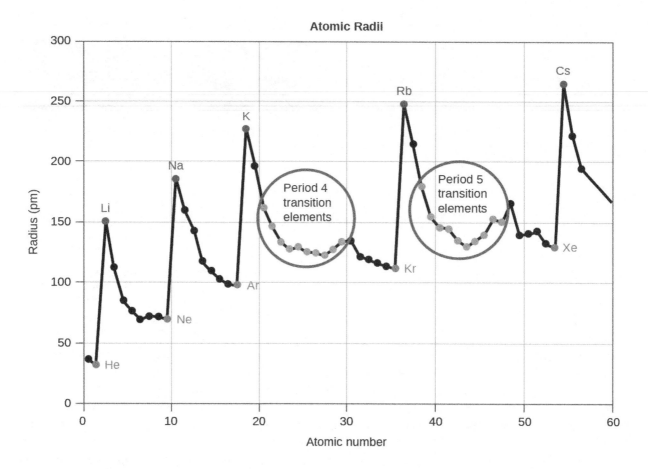

Figure 3.32 Within each period, the trend in atomic radius decreases as Z increases; for example, from K to Kr. Within each group (e.g., the alkali metals shown in purple), the trend is that atomic radius increases as Z increases.

As shown in **Figure 3.32**, as we move across a period from left to right, we generally find that each element has a smaller covalent radius than the element preceding it. This might seem counterintuitive because it implies that atoms with more electrons have a smaller atomic radius. This can be explained with the concept of **effective nuclear charge, Z_{eff}**. This is the pull exerted on a specific electron by the nucleus, taking into account any electron–electron repulsions. For hydrogen, there is only one electron and so the nuclear charge (Z) and the effective nuclear charge (Z_{eff}) are equal. For all other atoms, the inner electrons partially *shield* the outer electrons from the pull of the nucleus, and thus:

$$Z_{eff} = Z - shielding$$

Shielding is determined by the probability of another electron being between the electron of interest and the nucleus, as well as by the electron–electron repulsions the electron of interest encounters. Core electrons are adept at shielding, while electrons in the same valence shell do not block the nuclear attraction experienced by each other as efficiently. Thus, each time we move from one element to the next across a period, Z increases by one, but the shielding increases only slightly. Thus, Z_{eff} increases as we move from left to right across a period. The stronger pull (higher effective nuclear charge) experienced by electrons on the right side of the periodic table draws them closer to the nucleus, making the covalent radii smaller.

Thus, as we would expect, the outermost or valence electrons are easiest to remove because they have the highest energies, are shielded more, and are farthest from the nucleus. As a general rule, when the representative elements form cations, they do so by the loss of the *ns* or *np* electrons that were added last in the Aufbau process. The transition elements, on the other hand, lose the *ns* electrons before they begin to lose the $(n - 1)d$ electrons, even though the *ns* electrons are added first, according to the Aufbau principle.

Example 3.12

Sorting Atomic Radii

Predict the order of increasing covalent radius for Ge, Fl, Br, Kr.

Solution

Radius increases as we move down a group, so Ge < Fl (Note: Fl is the symbol for flerovium, element 114, NOT fluorine). Radius decreases as we move across a period, so Kr < Br < Ge. Putting the trends together, we obtain Kr < Br < Ge < Fl.

Check Your Learning

Give an example of an atom whose size is smaller than fluorine.

Answer: Ne or He

Variation in Ionic Radii

Ionic radius is the measure used to describe the size of an ion. A cation always has fewer electrons and the same number of protons as the parent atom; it is smaller than the atom from which it is derived (**Figure 3.33**). For example, the covalent radius of an aluminum atom ($1s^2 2s^2 2p^6 3s^2 3p^1$) is 118 pm, whereas the ionic radius of an Al^{3+} ($1s^2 2s^2 2p^6$) is 68 pm. As electrons are removed from the outer valence shell, the remaining core electrons occupying smaller shells experience a greater effective nuclear charge Z_{eff} (as discussed) and are drawn even closer to the nucleus.

Figure 3.33 The radius for a cation is smaller than the parent atom (Al), due to the lost electrons; the radius for an anion is larger than the parent (S), due to the gained electrons.

Cations with larger charges are smaller than cations with smaller charges (e.g., V^{2+} has an ionic radius of 79 pm, while that of V^{3+} is 64 pm). Proceeding down the groups of the periodic table, we find that cations of successive elements with the same charge generally have larger radii, corresponding to an increase in the principal quantum number, n.

An anion (negative ion) is formed by the addition of one or more electrons to the valence shell of an atom. This results in a greater repulsion among the electrons and a decrease in Z_{eff} per electron. Both effects (the increased number of electrons and the decreased Z_{eff}) cause the radius of an anion to be larger than that of the parent atom (**Figure 3.33**). For example, a sulfur atom ($[Ne]3s^2 3p^4$) has a covalent radius of 104 pm, whereas the ionic radius of the sulfide anion ($[Ne]3s^2 3p^6$) is 170 pm. For consecutive elements proceeding down any group, anions have larger principal quantum numbers and, thus, larger radii.

Atoms and ions that have the same electron configuration are said to be **isoelectronic**. Examples of isoelectronic species are N^{3-}, O^{2-}, F^-, Ne, Na^+, Mg^{2+}, and Al^{3+} ($1s^2 2s^2 2p^6$). Another isoelectronic series is P^{3-}, S^{2-}, Cl^-, Ar, K^+, Ca^{2+}, and Sc^{3+} ($[Ne]3s^2 3p^6$). For atoms or ions that are isoelectronic, the number of protons determines the size. The greater the nuclear charge, the smaller the radius in a series of isoelectronic ions and atoms.

Variation in Ionization Energies

The amount of energy required to remove the most loosely bound electron from a gaseous atom in its ground state is called its first **ionization energy** (IE_1). The first ionization energy for an element, X, is the energy required to form a cation with +1 charge:

$$X(g) \longrightarrow X^+(g) + e^- \qquad IE_1$$

The energy required to remove the second most loosely bound electron is called the second ionization energy (IE$_2$).

$$X^+(g) \longrightarrow X^{2+}(g) + e^- \qquad IE_2$$

The energy required to remove the third electron is the third ionization energy, and so on. Energy is always required to remove electrons from atoms or ions, so ionization processes are endothermic and IE values are always positive. For larger atoms, the most loosely bound electron is located farther from the nucleus and so is easier to remove. Thus, as size (atomic radius) increases, the ionization energy should decrease. Relating this logic to what we have just learned about radii, we would expect first ionization energies to decrease down a group and to increase across a period.

Figure 3.34 graphs the relationship between the first ionization energy and the atomic number of several elements. The values of first ionization energy for the elements are given in Figure 3.35. Within a period, the IE$_1$ generally increases with increasing Z. Down a group, the IE$_1$ value generally decreases with increasing Z. There are some systematic deviations from this trend, however. Note that the ionization energy of boron (atomic number 5) is less than that of beryllium (atomic number 4) even though the nuclear charge of boron is greater by one proton. This can be explained because the energy of the subshells increases as l increases, due to penetration and shielding (as discussed previously in this chapter). Within any one shell, the s electrons are lower in energy than the p electrons. This means that an s electron is harder to remove from an atom than a p electron in the same shell. The electron removed during the ionization of beryllium ([He]$2s^2$) is an s electron, whereas the electron removed during the ionization of boron ([He]$2s^2 2p^1$) is a p electron; this results in a lower first ionization energy for boron, even though its nuclear charge is greater by one proton. Thus, we see a small deviation from the predicted trend occurring each time a new subshell begins.

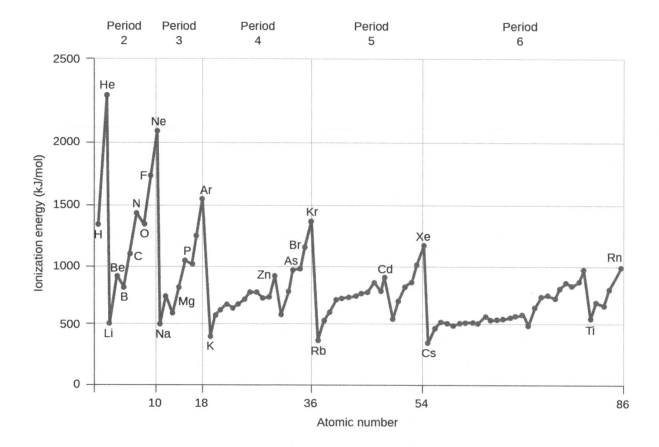

Figure 3.34   The first ionization energy of the elements in the first five periods are plotted against their atomic number.

Figure 3.35 This version of the periodic table shows the first ionization energy of (IE_1), in kJ/mol, of selected elements.

Another deviation occurs as orbitals become more than one-half filled. The first ionization energy for oxygen is slightly less than that for nitrogen, despite the trend in increasing IE_1 values across a period. Looking at the orbital diagram of oxygen, we can see that removing one electron will eliminate the electron–electron repulsion caused by pairing the electrons in the $2p$ orbital and will result in a half-filled orbital (which is energetically favorable). Analogous changes occur in succeeding periods (note the dip for sulfur after phosphorus in **Figure 3.35**).

$$\text{O} \quad 1s^2 2s^2 2p^4$$

Removing an electron from a cation is more difficult than removing an electron from a neutral atom because of the greater electrostatic attraction to the cation. Likewise, removing an electron from a cation with a higher positive charge is more difficult than removing an electron from an ion with a lower charge. Thus, successive ionization energies for one element always increase. As seen in **Table 3.3**, there is a large increase in the ionization energies (color change) for each element. This jump corresponds to removal of the core electrons, which are harder to remove than the valence electrons. For example, Sc and Ga both have three valence electrons, so the rapid increase in ionization energy occurs after the third ionization.

Successive Ionization Energies for Selected Elements (kJ/mol)

Element	IE_1	IE_2	IE_3	IE_4	IE_5	IE_6	IE_7
K	418.8	3051.8	4419.6	5876.9	7975.5	9590.6	11343
Ca	589.8	1145.4	4912.4	6490.6	8153.0	10495.7	12272.9
Sc	633.1	1235.0	2388.7	7090.6	8842.9	10679.0	13315.0
Ga	578.8	1979.4	2964.6	6180	8298.7	10873.9	13594.8
Ge	762.2	1537.5	3302.1	4410.6	9021.4	Not available	Not available

Table 3.3

Successive Ionization Energies for Selected Elements (kJ/mol)

Element	IE$_1$	IE$_2$	IE$_3$	IE$_4$	IE$_5$	IE$_6$	IE$_7$
As	944.5	1793.6	2735.5	4836.8	6042.9	12311.5	Not available

Table 3.3

Example 3.13

Ranking Ionization Energies

Predict the order of increasing energy for the following processes: IE$_1$ for Al, IE$_1$ for Tl, IE$_2$ for Na, IE$_3$ for Al.

Solution

Removing the $6p^1$ electron from Tl is easier than removing the $3p^1$ electron from Al because the higher n orbital is farther from the nucleus, so IE$_1$(Tl) < IE$_1$(Al). Ionizing the third electron from Al $(Al^{2+} \longrightarrow Al^{3+} + e^-)$ requires more energy because the cation Al^{2+} exerts a stronger pull on the electron than the neutral Al atom, so IE$_1$(Al) < IE$_3$(Al). The second ionization energy for sodium removes a core electron, which is a much higher energy process than removing valence electrons. Putting this all together, we obtain: IE$_1$(Tl) < IE$_1$(Al) < IE$_3$(Al) < IE$_2$(Na).

Check Your Learning

Which has the lowest value for IE$_1$: O, Po, Pb, or Ba?

Answer: Ba

Variation in Electron Affinities

The **electron affinity** [EA] is the energy change for the process of adding an electron to a gaseous atom to form an anion (negative ion).

$$X(g) + e^- \longrightarrow X^-(g) \qquad EA_1$$

This process can be either endothermic or exothermic, depending on the element. The EA of some of the elements is given in Figure 3.36. You can see that many of these elements have negative values of EA, which means that energy is released when the gaseous atom accepts an electron. However, for some elements, energy is required for the atom to become negatively charged and the value of their EA is positive. Just as with ionization energy, subsequent EA values are associated with forming ions with more charge. The second EA is the energy associated with adding an electron to an anion to form a –2 ion, and so on.

As we might predict, it becomes easier to add an electron across a series of atoms as the effective nuclear charge of the atoms increases. We find, as we go from left to right across a period, EAs tend to become more negative. The exceptions found among the elements of group 2 (2A), group 15 (5A), and group 18 (8A) can be understood based on the electronic structure of these groups. The noble gases, group 18 (8A), have a completely filled shell and the incoming electron must be added to a higher n level, which is more difficult to do. Group 2 (2A) has a filled ns subshell, and so the next electron added goes into the higher energy np, so, again, the observed EA value is not as the trend would predict. Finally, group 15 (5A) has a half-filled np subshell and the next electron must be paired with an existing np electron. In all of these cases, the initial relative stability of the electron configuration disrupts the trend in EA.

We also might expect the atom at the top of each group to have the largest EA; their first ionization potentials suggest that these atoms have the largest effective nuclear charges. However, as we move down a group, we see that the second element in the group most often has the greatest EA. The reduction of the EA of the first member can be attributed to the small size of the $n = 2$ shell and the resulting large electron–electron repulsions. For example, chlorine, with an EA value of –348 kJ/mol, has the highest value of any element in the periodic table. The EA of fluorine is –322 kJ/mol. When we add an electron to a fluorine atom to form a fluoride anion (F^-), we add an electron to the $n = 2$ shell. The electron is attracted to the nucleus, but there is also significant repulsion from the other electrons already present in this small valence shell. The chlorine atom has the same electron configuration in the valence shell, but because the entering electron is going into the $n = 3$ shell, it occupies a considerably larger region of space and the electron–electron repulsions are reduced. The entering electron does not experience as much repulsion and the chlorine atom accepts an additional electron more readily.

Electron Affinity Values for Selected Elements (kJ/mol)

Period \ Group	1	2	3	4	5	6	7	8	9	10	11	12	13	14	15	16	17	18
1	H –72																	He +20*
2	Li –60	Be +240*											B –23	C –123	N 0	O –141	F –322	Ne –30
3	Na –53	Mg +230*											Al –44	Si –120	P –74	S –20	Cl –348	Ar +35*
4	K –48	Ca +150*	Sc	Ti	V	Cr	Mn	Fe	Co	Ni	Cu	Zn	Ga –40*	Ge –115	As –7	Se –195	Br –324	Kr +40*
5	Rb –46	Sr +160*	Y	Zr	Nb	Mo	Tc	Ru	Rh	Pd	Ag	Cd	In –40*	Sn –121	Sb –101	Te –190	I –295	Xe +40*
6	Cs –45	Ba +50*	La	Hf	Ta	W	Re	Os	Ir	Pt	Au	Hg	Tl –50	Pb –101	Bi –101	Po –170	At –270*	Rn +40*
7	Fr	Ra																

* Calculated value

Figure 3.36 This version of the periodic table displays the electron affinity values (in kJ/mol) for selected elements.

The properties discussed in this section (size of atoms and ions, effective nuclear charge, ionization energies, and electron affinities) are central to understanding chemical reactivity. For example, because fluorine has an energetically favorable EA and a large energy barrier to ionization (IE), it is much easier to form fluorine anions than cations. Metallic properties including conductivity and malleability (the ability to be formed into sheets) depend on having electrons that can be removed easily. Thus, metallic character increases as we move down a group and decreases across a period in the same trend observed for atomic size because it is easier to remove an electron that is farther away from the nucleus.

3.6 The Periodic Table

By the end of this section, you will be able to:

- State the periodic law and explain the organization of elements in the periodic table
- Predict the general properties of elements based on their location within the periodic table
- Identify metals, nonmetals, and metalloids by their properties and/or location on the periodic table

As early chemists worked to purify ores and discovered more elements, they realized that various elements could be grouped together by their similar chemical behaviors. One such grouping includes lithium (Li), sodium (Na), and potassium (K): These elements all are shiny, conduct heat and electricity well, and have similar chemical properties. A second grouping includes calcium (Ca), strontium (Sr), and barium (Ba), which also are shiny, good conductors of heat and electricity, and have chemical properties in common. However, the specific properties of these two groupings are notably different from each other. For example: Li, Na, and K are much more reactive than are Ca, Sr, and Ba; Li, Na, and K form compounds with oxygen in a ratio of two of their atoms to one oxygen atom, whereas Ca, Sr, and Ba form compounds with one of their atoms to one oxygen atom. Fluorine (F), chlorine (Cl), bromine (Br), and iodine (I) also exhibit similar properties to each other, but these properties are drastically different from those of any of the elements above.

Dimitri Mendeleev in Russia (1869) and Lothar Meyer in Germany (1870) independently recognized that there was a periodic relationship among the properties of the elements known at that time. Both published tables with the elements arranged according to increasing atomic mass. But Mendeleev went one step further than Meyer: He used his table to predict the existence of elements that would have the properties similar to aluminum and silicon, but were yet unknown. The discoveries of gallium (1875) and germanium (1886) provided great support for Mendeleev's work. Although Mendeleev and Meyer had a long dispute over priority, Mendeleev's contributions to the development of the periodic table are now more widely recognized (Figure 3.37).

Reihen	Gruppo I. — R^2O	Gruppo II. — RO	Gruppo III. — R^2O^3	Gruppo IV. RH^4 RO^2	Gruppo V. RH^3 R^2O^5	Gruppo VI. RH^2 RO^3	Gruppo VII. RH R^2O^7	Gruppo VIII. — RO^4
1	H=1							
2	Li=7	Be=9,4	B=11	C=12	N=14	O=16	F=19	
3	Na=23	Mg=24	Al=27,8	Si=28	P=31	S=32	Cl=35,5	
4	K=39	Ca=40	—=44	Ti=48	V=51	Cr=52	Mn=55	Fe=56, Co=59, Ni=59, Cu=63.
5	(Cu=63)	Zn=65	—=68	—=72	As=75	Se=78	Br=80	
6	Rb=85	Sr=87	?Yt=88	Zr=90	Nb=94	Mo=96	—=100	Ru=104, Rh=104, Pd=106, Ag=108.
7	(Ag=108)	Cd=112	In=113	Sn=118	Sb=122	Te=125	J=127	
8	Cs=133	Ba=137	?Di=138	?Ce=140	—	—	—	— — — —
9	(—)		—	—	—	—	—	
10	—	—	?Er=178	?La=180	Ta=182	W=184	—	Os=195, Ir=197, Pt=198, Au=199.
11	(Au=199)	Hg=200	Tl=204	Pb=207	Bi=208	—	—	
12	—	—	—	Th=231	—	U=240	—	— — — —

(a)   (b)

Figure 3.37   (a) Dimitri Mendeleev is widely credited with creating (b) the first periodic table of the elements. (credit a: modification of work by Serge Lachinov; credit b: modification of work by "Den fjättrade ankan"/Wikimedia Commons)

By the twentieth century, it became apparent that the periodic relationship involved atomic numbers rather than atomic masses. The modern statement of this relationship, the **periodic law**, is as follows: *the properties of the elements are periodic functions of their atomic numbers*. A modern **periodic table** arranges the elements in increasing order of their atomic numbers and groups atoms with similar properties in the same vertical column (Figure 3.38). Each box represents an element and contains its atomic number, symbol, average atomic mass, and (sometimes) name. The elements are arranged in seven horizontal rows, called **periods** or **series**, and 18 vertical columns, called **groups**. Groups are labeled at the top of each column. In the United States, the labels traditionally were numerals with capital letters. However, IUPAC recommends that the numbers 1 through 18 be used, and these labels are more common. For the table to fit on a single page, parts of two of the rows, a total of 14 columns, are usually written below the main body of the table.

Figure 3.38 Elements in the periodic table are organized according to their properties.

Many elements differ dramatically in their chemical and physical properties, but some elements are similar in their behaviors. For example, many elements appear shiny, are malleable (able to be deformed without breaking) and ductile (can be drawn into wires), and conduct heat and electricity well. Other elements are not shiny, malleable, or ductile, and are poor conductors of heat and electricity. We can sort the elements into large classes with common properties: **metals** (elements that are shiny, malleable, good conductors of heat and electricity—shaded yellow); **nonmetals** (elements that appear dull, poor conductors of heat and electricity—shaded green); and **metalloids** (elements that conduct heat and electricity moderately well, and possess some properties of metals and some properties of nonmetals—shaded purple).

The elements can also be classified into the **main-group elements** (or **representative elements**) in the columns labeled 1, 2, and 13–18; the **transition metals** in the columns labeled 3–12; and **inner transition metals** in the two rows at the bottom of the table (the top-row elements are called **lanthanides** and the bottom-row elements are **actinides**; **Figure 3.39**). The elements can be subdivided further by more specific properties, such as the composition of the compounds they form. For example, the elements in group 1 (the first column) form compounds that consist of one atom of the element and one atom of hydrogen. These elements (except hydrogen) are known as **alkali metals**, and they all have similar chemical properties. The elements in group 2 (the second column) form compounds consisting of one atom of the element and two atoms of hydrogen: These are called **alkaline earth metals**, with similar properties among members of that group. Other groups with specific names are the **pnictogens** (group 15), **chalcogens** (group 16), **halogens** (group 17), and the **noble gases** (group 18, also known as **inert gases**). The groups can also be referred to by the first element of the group: For example, the chalcogens can be called the oxygen group or oxygen family. Hydrogen is a unique, nonmetallic element with properties similar to both group 1 and group 7 elements. For that reason, hydrogen may be shown at the top of both groups, or by itself.

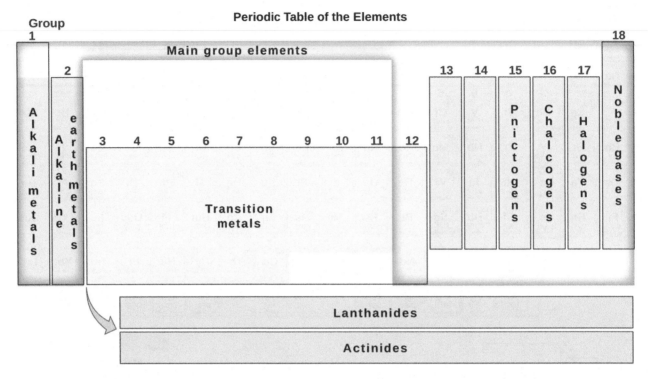

Figure 3.39 The periodic table organizes elements with similar properties into groups.

Link to Learning

Click on this link (http://openstaxcollege.org/l/16Periodic) for an interactive periodic table, which you can use to explore the properties of the elements (includes podcasts and videos of each element). You may also want to try this one (http://openstaxcollege.org/l/16Periodic2) that shows photos of all the elements.

Example 3.14

Naming Groups of Elements

Atoms of each of the following elements are essential for life. Give the group name for the following elements:

(a) chlorine

(b) calcium

(c) sodium

(d) sulfur

Solution

The family names are as follows:

(a) halogen

(b) alkaline earth metal

(c) alkali metal

(d) chalcogen

Check Your Learning

Give the group name for each of the following elements:

(a) krypton

(b) selenium

(c) barium

(d) lithium

Answer: (a) noble gas; (b) chalcogen; (c) alkaline earth metal; (d) alkali metal

In studying the periodic table, you might have noticed something about the atomic masses of some of the elements. Element 43 (technetium), element 61 (promethium), and most of the elements with atomic number 84 (polonium) and higher have their atomic mass given in square brackets. This is done for elements that consist entirely of unstable, radioactive isotopes (you will learn more about radioactivity in the nuclear chemistry chapter). An average atomic weight cannot be determined for these elements because their radioisotopes may vary significantly in relative abundance, depending on the source, or may not even exist in nature. The number in square brackets is the atomic mass number (and approximate atomic mass) of the most stable isotope of that element.

3.7 Molecular and Ionic Compounds

By the end of this section, you will be able to:

- Define ionic and molecular (covalent) compounds
- Predict the type of compound formed from elements based on their location within the periodic table
- Determine formulas for simple ionic compounds

In ordinary chemical reactions, the nucleus of each atom (and thus the identity of the element) remains unchanged. Electrons, however, can be added to atoms by transfer from other atoms, lost by transfer to other atoms, or shared with other atoms. The transfer and sharing of electrons among atoms govern the chemistry of the elements. During the formation of some compounds, atoms gain or lose electrons, and form electrically charged particles called ions (Figure 3.40).

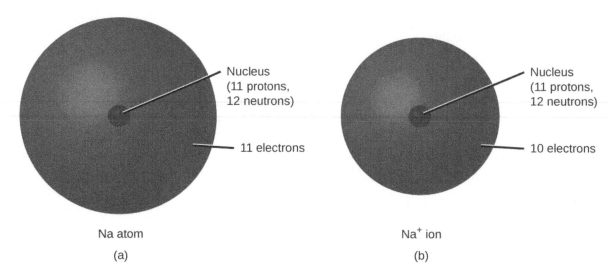

Figure 3.40 (a) A sodium atom (Na) has equal numbers of protons and electrons (11) and is uncharged. (b) A sodium cation (Na^+) has lost an electron, so it has one more proton (11) than electrons (10), giving it an overall positive charge, signified by a superscripted plus sign.

You can use the periodic table to predict whether an atom will form an anion or a cation, and you can often predict the charge of the resulting ion. Atoms of many main-group metals lose enough electrons to leave them with the same number of electrons as an atom of the preceding noble gas. To illustrate, an atom of an alkali metal (group 1) loses one electron and forms a cation with a 1+ charge; an alkaline earth metal (group 2) loses two electrons and forms a cation with a 2+ charge, and so on. For example, a neutral calcium atom, with 20 protons and 20 electrons, readily loses two electrons. This results in a cation with 20 protons, 18 electrons, and a 2+ charge. It has the same number of electrons as atoms of the preceding noble gas, argon, and is symbolized Ca^{2+}. The name of a metal ion is the same as the name of the metal atom from which it forms, so Ca^{2+} is called a calcium ion.

When atoms of nonmetal elements form ions, they generally gain enough electrons to give them the same number of electrons as an atom of the next noble gas in the periodic table. Atoms of group 17 gain one electron and form anions with a 1− charge; atoms of group 16 gain two electrons and form ions with a 2− charge, and so on. For example, the neutral bromine atom, with 35 protons and 35 electrons, can gain one electron to provide it with 36 electrons. This results in an anion with 35 protons, 36 electrons, and a 1− charge. It has the same number of electrons as atoms of the next noble gas, krypton, and is symbolized Br^-. (A discussion of the theory supporting the favored status of noble gas electron numbers reflected in these predictive rules for ion formation is provided in a later chapter of this text.)

Note the usefulness of the periodic table in predicting likely ion formation and charge (**Figure 3.41**). Moving from the far left to the right on the periodic table, main-group elements tend to form cations with a charge equal to the group number. That is, group 1 elements form 1+ ions; group 2 elements form 2+ ions, and so on. Moving from the far right to the left on the periodic table, elements often form anions with a negative charge equal to the number of groups moved left from the noble gases. For example, group 17 elements (one group left of the noble gases) form 1− ions; group 16 elements (two groups left) form 2− ions, and so on. This trend can be used as a guide in many cases, but its predictive value decreases when moving toward the center of the periodic table. In fact, transition metals and some other metals often exhibit variable charges that are not predictable by their location in the table. For example, copper can form ions with a 1+ or 2+ charge, and iron can form ions with a 2+ or 3+ charge.

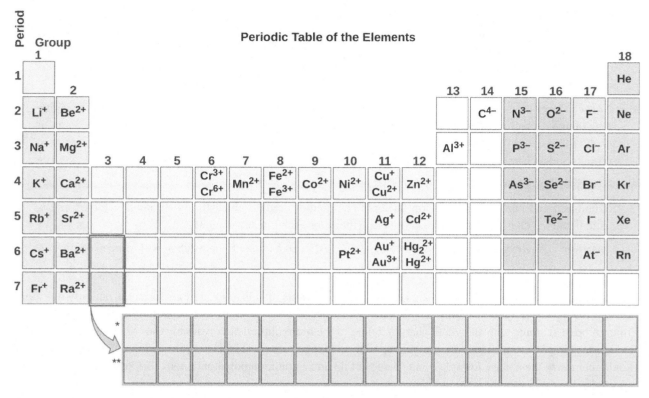

Figure 3.41 Some elements exhibit a regular pattern of ionic charge when they form ions.

Example 3.15

Composition of Ions

An ion found in some compounds used as antiperspirants contains 13 protons and 10 electrons. What is its symbol?

Solution

Because the number of protons remains unchanged when an atom forms an ion, the atomic number of the element must be 13. Knowing this lets us use the periodic table to identify the element as Al (aluminum). The Al atom has lost three electrons and thus has three more positive charges (13) than it has electrons (10). This is the aluminum cation, Al^{3+}.

Check Your Learning

Give the symbol and name for the ion with 34 protons and 36 electrons.

Answer: Se^{2-}, the selenide ion

Example 3.16

Formation of Ions

Magnesium and nitrogen react to form an ionic compound. Predict which forms an anion, which forms a cation, and the charges of each ion. Write the symbol for each ion and name them.

Solution

Magnesium's position in the periodic table (group 2) tells us that it is a metal. Metals form positive ions (cations). A magnesium atom must lose two electrons to have the same number electrons as an atom of the previous noble gas, neon. Thus, a magnesium atom will form a cation with two fewer electrons than protons and a charge of 2+. The symbol for the ion is Mg^{2+}, and it is called a magnesium ion.

Nitrogen's position in the periodic table (group 15) reveals that it is a nonmetal. Nonmetals form negative ions (anions). A nitrogen atom must gain three electrons to have the same number of electrons as an atom of the following noble gas, neon. Thus, a nitrogen atom will form an anion with three more electrons than protons and a charge of 3−. The symbol for the ion is N^{3-}, and it is called a nitride ion.

Check Your Learning

Aluminum and carbon react to form an ionic compound. Predict which forms an anion, which forms a cation, and the charges of each ion. Write the symbol for each ion and name them.

Answer: Al will form a cation with a charge of 3+: Al^{3+}, an aluminum ion. Carbon will form an anion with a charge of 4−: C^{4-}, a carbide ion.

The ions that we have discussed so far are called **monatomic ions**, that is, they are ions formed from only one atom. We also find many **polyatomic ions**. These ions, which act as discrete units, are electrically charged molecules (a group of bonded atoms with an overall charge). Some of the more important polyatomic ions are listed in Table 3.4. **Oxyanions** are polyatomic ions that contain one or more oxygen atoms. At this point in your study of chemistry, you should memorize the names, formulas, and charges of the most common polyatomic ions. Because you will use them repeatedly, they will soon become familiar.

Common Polyatomic Ions

Name	Formula	Related Acid	Formula
ammonium	NH_4^+		
hydronium	H_3O^+		
oxide	O^{2-}		
peroxide	O_2^{2-}		
hydroxide	OH^-		
acetate	CH_3COO^-	acetic acid	CH_3COOH
cyanide	CN^-	hydrocyanic acid	HCN
azide	N_3^-	hydrazoic acid	HN_3
carbonate	CO_3^{2-}	carbonic acid	H_2CO_3
bicarbonate	HCO_3^-		
nitrate	NO_3^-	nitric acid	HNO_3
nitrite	NO_2^-	nitrous acid	HNO_2
sulfate	SO_4^{2-}	sulfiric acid	H_2SO_4

Table 3.4

Common Polyatomic Ions

Name	Formula	Related Acid	Formula
hydrogen sulfate	$HSO_4{}^-$		
sulfite	$SO_3{}^{2-}$	sulfurous acid	H_2SO_3
hydrogen sulfite	$HSO_3{}^-$		
phosphate	$PO_4{}^{3-}$	phosphoric acid	H_3PO_4
hydrogen phosphate	$HPO_4{}^{2-}$		
dihydrogen phosphate	$H_2PO_4{}^-$		
perchlorate	$ClO_4{}^-$	perchloric acid	$HClO_4$
chlorate	$ClO_3{}^-$	chloric acid	$HClO_3$
chlorite	$ClO_2{}^-$	chlorous acid	$HClO_2$
hypochlorite	ClO^-	hypochlorous acid	$HClO$
chromate	$CrO_4{}^{2-}$	chromic acid	$H_2Cr_2O_4$
dichromate	$Cr_2O_7{}^{2-}$	dichromic acid	$H_2Cr_2O_7$
permanganate	$MnO_4{}^-$	permanganic acid	$HMnO_4$

Table 3.4

Note that there is a system for naming some polyatomic ions; -*ate* and -*ite* are suffixes designating polyatomic ions containing more or fewer oxygen atoms. *Per-* (short for "hyper") and *hypo-* (meaning "under") are prefixes meaning more oxygen atoms than -*ate* and fewer oxygen atoms than -*ite*, respectively. For example, perchlorate is $ClO_4{}^-$, chlorate is $ClO_3{}^-$, chlorite is $ClO_2{}^-$ and hypochlorite is ClO^-. Unfortunately, the number of oxygen atoms corresponding to a given suffix or prefix is not consistent; for example, nitrate is $NO_3{}^-$ while sulfate is $SO_4{}^{2-}$. This will be covered in more detail later in the module on nomenclature.

The nature of the attractive forces that hold atoms or ions together within a compound is the basis for classifying chemical bonding. When electrons are transferred and ions form, **ionic bonds** result. Ionic bonds are electrostatic forces of attraction, that is, the attractive forces experienced between objects of opposite electrical charge (in this case, cations and anions). When electrons are "shared" and molecules form, **covalent bonds** result. Covalent bonds are the attractive forces between the positively charged nuclei of the bonded atoms and one or more pairs of electrons that are located between the atoms. Compounds are classified as ionic or molecular (covalent) on the basis of the bonds present in them.

Ionic Compounds

When an element composed of atoms that readily lose electrons (a metal) reacts with an element composed of atoms that readily gain electrons (a nonmetal), a transfer of electrons usually occurs, producing ions. The compound formed by this transfer is stabilized by the electrostatic attractions (ionic bonds) between the ions of opposite charge present in the compound. For example, when each sodium atom in a sample of sodium metal (group 1) gives up one electron to form a sodium cation, Na^+, and each chlorine atom in a sample of chlorine gas (group 17) accepts one electron to form a chloride anion, Cl^-, the resulting compound, NaCl, is composed of sodium ions and chloride ions in the ratio of one Na^+ ion for each Cl^- ion. Similarly, each calcium atom (group 2) can give up two electrons and transfer one to each of two chlorine atoms to form $CaCl_2$, which is composed of Ca^{2+} and Cl^- ions in the ratio of one Ca^{2+} ion to two Cl^- ions.

A compound that contains ions and is held together by ionic bonds is called an **ionic compound**. The periodic table can help us recognize many of the compounds that are ionic: When a metal is combined with one or more nonmetals, the compound is usually ionic. This guideline works well for predicting ionic compound formation for most of the compounds typically encountered in an introductory chemistry course. However, it is not always true (for example, aluminum chloride, $AlCl_3$, is not ionic).

You can often recognize ionic compounds because of their properties. Ionic compounds are solids that typically melt at high temperatures and boil at even higher temperatures. For example, sodium chloride melts at 801 °C and boils at 1413 °C. (As a comparison, the molecular compound water melts at 0 °C and boils at 100 °C.) In solid form, an ionic compound is not electrically conductive because its ions are unable to flow ("electricity" is the flow of charged particles). When molten, however, it can conduct electricity because its ions are able to move freely through the liquid (Figure 3.42).

Figure 3.42 Sodium chloride melts at 801 °C and conducts electricity when molten. (credit: modification of work by Mark Blaser and Matt Evans)

Link to Learning

Watch this video (http://openstaxcollege.org/l/16moltensalt) to see a mixture of salts melt and conduct electricity.

In every ionic compound, the total number of positive charges of the cations equals the total number of negative charges of the anions. Thus, ionic compounds are electrically neutral overall, even though they contain positive and negative ions. We can use this observation to help us write the formula of an ionic compound. The formula of an ionic compound must have a ratio of ions such that the numbers of positive and negative charges are equal.

Example 3.17

Predicting the Formula of an Ionic Compound

The gemstone sapphire (Figure 3.43) is mostly a compound of aluminum and oxygen that contains aluminum cations, Al^{3+}, and oxygen anions, O^{2-}. What is the formula of this compound?

Figure 3.43   Although pure aluminum oxide is colorless, trace amounts of iron and titanium give blue sapphire its characteristic color. (credit: modification of work by Stanislav Doronenko)

Solution

Because the ionic compound must be electrically neutral, it must have the same number of positive and negative charges. Two aluminum ions, each with a charge of 3+, would give us six positive charges, and three oxide ions, each with a charge of 2−, would give us six negative charges. The formula would be Al_2O_3.

Check Your Learning

Predict the formula of the ionic compound formed between the sodium cation, Na^+, and the sulfide anion, S^{2-}.

Answer: Na_2S

Many ionic compounds contain polyatomic ions (Table 3.4) as the cation, the anion, or both. As with simple ionic compounds, these compounds must also be electrically neutral, so their formulas can be predicted by treating the polyatomic ions as discrete units. We use parentheses in a formula to indicate a group of atoms that behave as a unit. For example, the formula for calcium phosphate, one of the minerals in our bones, is $Ca_3(PO_4)_2$. This formula indicates that there are three calcium ions (Ca^{2+}) for every two phosphate $(PO_4{}^{3-})$ groups. The $PO_4{}^{3-}$ groups are discrete units, each consisting of one phosphorus atom and four oxygen atoms, and having an overall charge of 3−. The compound is electrically neutral, and its formula shows a total count of three Ca, two P, and eight O atoms.

Example 3.18

Predicting the Formula of a Compound with a Polyatomic Anion

Baking powder contains calcium dihydrogen phosphate, an ionic compound composed of the ions Ca^{2+} and $H_2PO_4{}^-$. What is the formula of this compound?

Solution

The positive and negative charges must balance, and this ionic compound must be electrically neutral. Thus, we must have two negative charges to balance the 2+ charge of the calcium ion. This requires a ratio of one Ca^{2+} ion to two $H_2PO_4{}^-$ ions. We designate this by enclosing the formula for the dihydrogen phosphate ion in parentheses and adding a subscript 2. The formula is $Ca(H_2PO_4)_2$.

Check Your Learning

Predict the formula of the ionic compound formed between the lithium ion and the peroxide ion, $O_2{}^{2-}$ (Hint: Use the periodic table to predict the sign and the charge on the lithium ion.)

Answer: Li_2O_2

Because an ionic compound is not made up of single, discrete molecules, it may not be properly symbolized using a *molecular* formula. Instead, ionic compounds must be symbolized by a formula indicating the *relative numbers* of its constituent ions. For compounds containing only monatomic ions (such as NaCl) and for many compounds containing polyatomic ions (such as $CaSO_4$), these formulas are just the empirical formulas introduced earlier. However, the formulas for some ionic compounds containing polyatomic ions are not empirical formulas. For example, the ionic compound sodium oxalate is comprised of Na^+ and $C_2O_4{}^{2-}$ ions combined in a 2:1 ratio, and its formula is written as $Na_2C_2O_4$. The subscripts in this formula are not the smallest-possible whole numbers, as each can be divided by 2 to yield the empirical formula, $NaCO_2$. This is not the accepted formula for sodium oxalate, however, as it does not accurately represent the compound's polyatomic anion, $C_2O_4{}^{2-}$.

Molecular Compounds

Many compounds do not contain ions but instead consist solely of discrete, neutral molecules. These **molecular compounds** (covalent compounds) result when atoms share, rather than transfer (gain or lose), electrons. Covalent bonding is an important and extensive concept in chemistry, and it will be treated in considerable detail in a later chapter of this text. We can often identify molecular compounds on the basis of their physical properties. Under normal conditions, molecular compounds often exist as gases, low-boiling liquids, and low-melting solids, although many important exceptions exist.

Whereas ionic compounds are usually formed when a metal and a nonmetal combine, covalent compounds are usually formed by a combination of nonmetals. Thus, the periodic table can help us recognize many of the compounds that are covalent. While we can use the positions of a compound's elements in the periodic table to predict whether it is ionic or covalent at this point in our study of chemistry, you should be aware that this is a very simplistic approach that does not account for a number of interesting exceptions. Shades of gray exist between ionic and molecular compounds, and you'll learn more about those later.

Example 3.19

Predicting the Type of Bonding in Compounds

Predict whether the following compounds are ionic or molecular:

(a) KI, the compound used as a source of iodine in table salt

(b) H_2O_2, the bleach and disinfectant hydrogen peroxide

(c) $CHCl_3$, the anesthetic chloroform

(d) Li_2CO_3, a source of lithium in antidepressants

Solution

(a) Potassium (group 1) is a metal, and iodine (group 17) is a nonmetal; KI is predicted to be ionic.

(b) Hydrogen (group 1) is a nonmetal, and oxygen (group 16) is a nonmetal; H_2O_2 is predicted to be molecular.

(c) Carbon (group 14) is a nonmetal, hydrogen (group 1) is a nonmetal, and chlorine (group 17) is a nonmetal; $CHCl_3$ is predicted to be molecular.

(d) Lithium (group 1) is a metal, and carbonate is a polyatomic ion; Li_2CO_3 is predicted to be ionic.

Check Your Learning

Using the periodic table, predict whether the following compounds are ionic or covalent:

(a) SO_2

(b) CaF_2

(c) N_2H_4

(d) $Al_2(SO_4)_3$

Answer: (a) molecular; (b) ionic; (c) molecular; (d) ionic

Key Terms

actinide inner transition metal in the bottom of the bottom two rows of the periodic table

alkali metal element in group 1

alkaline earth metal element in group 2

amplitude extent of the displacement caused by a wave (for sinusoidal waves, it is one-half the difference from the peak height to the trough depth, and the intensity is proportional to the square of the amplitude)

angular momentum quantum number (*l*) quantum number distinguishing the different shapes of orbitals; it is also a measure of the orbital angular momentum

atomic orbital mathematical function that describes the behavior of an electron in an atom (also called the wavefunction), it can be used to find the probability of locating an electron in a specific region around the nucleus, as well as other dynamical variables

Aufbau principle procedure in which the electron configuration of the elements is determined by "building" them in order of atomic numbers, adding one proton to the nucleus and one electron to the proper subshell at a time

blackbody idealized perfect absorber of all incident electromagnetic radiation; such bodies emit electromagnetic radiation in characteristic continuous spectra called blackbody radiation

Bohr's model of the hydrogen atom structural model in which an electron moves around the nucleus only in circular orbits, each with a specific allowed radius; the orbiting electron does not normally emit electromagnetic radiation, but does so when changing from one orbit to another.

chalcogen element in group 16

continuous spectrum electromagnetic radiation given off in an unbroken series of wavelengths (e.g., white light from the sun)

core electron electron in an atom that occupies the orbitals of the inner shells

covalent bond attractive force between the nuclei of a molecule's atoms and pairs of electrons between the atoms

covalent compound (also, molecular compound) composed of molecules formed by atoms of two or more different elements

covalent radius one-half the distance between the nuclei of two identical atoms when they are joined by a covalent bond

***d* orbital** region of space with high electron density that is either four lobed or contains a dumbbell and torus shape; describes orbitals with $l = 2$. An electron in this orbital is called a *d* electron

effective nuclear charge charge that leads to the Coulomb force exerted by the nucleus on an electron, calculated as the nuclear charge minus shielding

electromagnetic radiation energy transmitted by waves that have an electric-field component and a magnetic-field component

electromagnetic spectrum range of energies that electromagnetic radiation can comprise, including radio, microwaves, infrared, visible, ultraviolet, X-rays, and gamma rays; since electromagnetic radiation energy is proportional to the frequency and inversely proportional to the wavelength, the spectrum can also be specified by ranges of frequencies or wavelengths

electron affinity energy required to add an electron to a gaseous atom to form an anion

electron configuration electronic structure of an atom in its ground state given as a listing of the orbitals occupied by the electrons

electron density a measure of the probability of locating an electron in a particular region of space, it is equal to the squared absolute value of the wave function ψ

endothermic processes that increase the energy of an atom and involve the absorption of light

excited state state having an energy greater than the ground-state energy

exothermic processes that decrease the energy of an atom and involve the emission of light

_f_ orbital multilobed region of space with high electron density, describes orbitals with $l = 3$. An electron in this orbital is called an _f_ electron

frequency (_v_) number of wave cycles (peaks or troughs) that pass a specified point in space per unit time

ground state state in which the electrons in an atom, ion, or molecule have the lowest energy possible

group vertical column of the periodic table

halogen element in group 17

Heisenberg uncertainty principle rule stating that it is impossible to exactly determine both certain conjugate dynamical properties such as the momentum and the position of a particle at the same time. The uncertainty principle is a consequence of quantum particles exhibiting wave–particle duality

hertz (Hz) the unit of frequency, which is the number of cycles per second, s^{-1}

Hund's rule every orbital in a subshell is singly occupied with one electron before any one orbital is doubly occupied, and all electrons in singly occupied orbitals have the same spin

inert gas (also, noble gas) element in group 18

inner transition metal (also, lanthanide or actinide) element in the bottom two rows; if in the first row, also called lanthanide, or if in the second row, also called actinide

intensity property of wave-propagated energy related to the amplitude of the wave, such as brightness of light or loudness of sound

interference pattern pattern typically consisting of alternating bright and dark fringes; it results from constructive and destructive interference of waves

ionic bond electrostatic forces of attraction between the oppositely charged ions of an ionic compound

ionic compound compound composed of cations and anions combined in ratios, yielding an electrically neutral substance

ionization energy energy required to remove an electron from a gaseous atom or ion. The associated number (e.g., second ionization energy) corresponds to the charge of the ion produced (X^{2+})

isoelectronic group of ions or atoms that have identical electron configurations

lanthanide inner transition metal in the top of the bottom two rows of the periodic table

line spectrum electromagnetic radiation emitted at discrete wavelengths by a specific atom (or atoms) in an excited state

magnetic quantum number (m_l) quantum number signifying the orientation of an atomic orbital around the nucleus; orbitals having different values of m_l but the same subshell value of l have the same energy (are degenerate), but this degeneracy can be removed by application of an external magnetic field

main-group element (also, representative element) element in columns 1, 2, and 12–18

metal element that is shiny, malleable, good conductor of heat and electricity

metalloid element that conducts heat and electricity moderately well, and possesses some properties of metals and some properties of nonmetals

molecular compound (also, covalent compound) composed of molecules formed by atoms of two or more different elements

monatomic ion ion composed of a single atom

noble gas (also, inert gas) element in group 18

node any point of a standing wave with zero amplitude

nonmetal element that appears dull, poor conductor of heat and electricity

orbital diagram pictorial representation of the electron configuration showing each orbital as a box and each electron as an arrow

oxyanion polyatomic anion composed of a central atom bonded to oxygen atoms

p orbital dumbbell-shaped region of space with high electron density, describes orbitals with $l = 1$. An electron in this orbital is called a p electron

Pauli exclusion principle specifies that no two electrons in an atom can have the same value for all four quantum numbers

period (also, series) horizontal row of the periodic table

periodic law properties of the elements are periodic function of their atomic numbers.

periodic table table of the elements that places elements with similar chemical properties close together

photon smallest possible packet of electromagnetic radiation, a particle of light

pnictogen element in group 15

polyatomic ion ion composed of more than one atom

principal quantum number (n) quantum number specifying the shell an electron occupies in an atom

quantization occurring only in specific discrete values, not continuous

quantum mechanics field of study that includes quantization of energy, wave-particle duality, and the Heisenberg uncertainty principle to describe matter

quantum number integer number having only specific allowed values and used to characterize the arrangement of electrons in an atom

representative element (also, main-group element) element in columns 1, 2, and 12–18

s orbital spherical region of space with high electron density, describes orbitals with $l = 0$. An electron in this orbital is called an s electron

series (also, period) horizontal row of the period table

shell set of orbitals with the same principal quantum number, n

spin quantum number (m_s) number specifying the electron spin direction, either $+\frac{1}{2}$ or $-\frac{1}{2}$

standing wave (also, stationary wave) localized wave phenomenon characterized by discrete wavelengths determined by the boundary conditions used to generate the waves; standing waves are inherently quantized

subshell set of orbitals in an atom with the same values of n and l

transition metal element in columns 3–11

valence electrons electrons in the outermost or valence shell (highest value of n) of a ground-state atom; determine how an element reacts

valence shell outermost shell of electrons in a ground-state atom; for main group elements, the orbitals with the highest n level (s and p subshells) are in the valence shell, while for transition metals, the highest energy s and d subshells make up the valence shell and for inner transition elements, the highest s, d, and f subshells are included

wave oscillation that can transport energy from one point to another in space

wave-particle duality term used to describe the fact that elementary particles including matter exhibit properties of both particles (including localized position, momentum) and waves (including nonlocalization, wavelength, frequency)

wavefunction (ψ) mathematical description of an atomic orbital that describes the shape of the orbital; it can be used to calculate the probability of finding the electron at any given location in the orbital, as well as dynamical variables such as the energy and the angular momentum

wavelength (λ) distance between two consecutive peaks or troughs in a wave

Key Equations

- $c = \lambda v$

- $E = hv = \dfrac{hc}{\lambda}, \quad$ where $h = 6.626 \times 10^{-34}$ J s

- $\dfrac{1}{\lambda} = R_\infty \left(\dfrac{1}{n_1^2} - \dfrac{1}{n_2^2} \right)$

- $E_n = -\dfrac{kZ^2}{n^2}, \quad n = 1, \ 2, \ 3, \ \dots$

- $\Delta E = kZ^2 \left(\dfrac{1}{n_1^2} - \dfrac{1}{n_2^2} \right)$

- $r = \dfrac{n^2}{Z} a_0$

Summary

3.1 Electromagnetic Energy

Light and other forms of electromagnetic radiation move through a vacuum with a constant speed, c, of 2.998×10^8 m s^{-1}. This radiation shows wavelike behavior, which can be characterized by a frequency, v, and a wavelength, λ, such that $c = \lambda v$. Light is an example of a travelling wave. Other important wave phenomena include standing waves, periodic oscillations, and vibrations. Standing waves exhibit quantization, since their wavelengths are limited to discrete integer multiples of some characteristic lengths. Electromagnetic radiation that passes through two closely spaced narrow slits having dimensions roughly similar to the wavelength will show an interference pattern that is a result of constructive and destructive interference of the waves. Electromagnetic radiation also demonstrates properties of particles called photons. The energy of a photon is related to the frequency (or alternatively, the wavelength) of the radiation as $E = hv$ (or $E = \dfrac{hc}{\lambda}$), where h is Planck's constant. That light demonstrates both wavelike and particle-like behavior is known as wave-particle duality. All forms of electromagnetic radiation share these properties, although various forms including X-rays, visible light, microwaves, and radio waves interact differently with matter and have very different practical applications. Electromagnetic radiation can be generated by exciting matter to higher energies, such as by heating it. The emitted light can be either continuous (incandescent sources like the sun) or discrete (from specific types of excited atoms). Continuous spectra often have distributions that can be approximated as blackbody radiation at some appropriate temperature. The line spectrum of hydrogen can be obtained by passing the light from an electrified tube of hydrogen gas through a prism. This line spectrum was simple enough that an empirical formula called the Rydberg formula could be derived from the spectrum. Three historically important paradoxes from the late 19th and early 20th centuries that could not be explained within the existing framework of classical mechanics and classical electromagnetism were the blackbody problem, the photoelectric effect, and the discrete spectra of atoms. The resolution of these paradoxes ultimately led to quantum theories that superseded the classical theories.

3.2 The Bohr Model

Bohr incorporated Planck's and Einstein's quantization ideas into a model of the hydrogen atom that resolved the paradox of atom stability and discrete spectra. The Bohr model of the hydrogen atom explains the connection between the quantization of photons and the quantized emission from atoms. Bohr described the hydrogen atom in terms of an electron moving in a circular orbit about a nucleus. He postulated that the electron was restricted to certain orbits characterized by discrete energies. Transitions between these allowed orbits result in the absorption or emission of photons. When an electron moves from a higher-energy orbit to a more stable one, energy is emitted in the form of a photon. To move an electron from a stable orbit to a more excited one, a photon of energy must be absorbed. Using the Bohr model, we can calculate the energy of an electron and the radius of its orbit in any one-electron system.

3.3 Development of Quantum Theory

Macroscopic objects act as particles. Microscopic objects (such as electrons) have properties of both a particle and a wave. Their exact trajectories cannot be determined. The quantum mechanical model of atoms describes the three-dimensional position of the electron in a *probabilistic* manner according to a mathematical function called a wavefunction, often denoted as ψ. Atomic wavefunctions are also called orbitals. The squared magnitude of the wavefunction describes the distribution of the probability of finding the electron in a particular region in space. Therefore, atomic orbitals describe the areas in an atom where electrons are most likely to be found.

An atomic orbital is characterized by three quantum numbers. The principal quantum number, n, can be any positive integer. The general region for value of energy of the orbital and the average distance of an electron from the nucleus are related to n. Orbitals having the same value of n are said to be in the same shell. The angular momentum quantum number, l, can have any integer value from 0 to $n - 1$. This quantum number describes the shape or type of the orbital. Orbitals with the same principal quantum number and the same l value belong to the same subshell. The magnetic quantum number, m_l, with $2l + 1$ values ranging from $-l$ to $+l$, describes the orientation of the orbital in space. In addition, each electron has a spin quantum number, m_s, that can be equal to $\pm \frac{1}{2}$. No two electrons in the same atom can have the same set of values for all the four quantum numbers.

3.4 Electronic Structure of Atoms (Electron Configurations)

The relative energy of the subshells determine the order in which atomic orbitals are filled ($1s$, $2s$, $2p$, $3s$, $3p$, $4s$, $3d$, $4p$, and so on). Electron configurations and orbital diagrams can be determined by applying the Pauli exclusion principle (no two electrons can have the same set of four quantum numbers) and Hund's rule (whenever possible, electrons retain unpaired spins in degenerate orbitals).

Electrons in the outermost orbitals, called valence electrons, are responsible for most of the chemical behavior of elements. In the periodic table, elements with analogous valence electron configurations usually occur within the same group. There are some exceptions to the predicted filling order, particularly when half-filled or completely filled orbitals can be formed. The periodic table can be divided into three categories based on the orbital in which the last electron to be added is placed: main group elements (s and p orbitals), transition elements (d orbitals), and inner transition elements (f orbitals).

3.5 Periodic Variations in Element Properties

Electron configurations allow us to understand many periodic trends. Covalent radius increases as we move down a group because the n level (orbital size) increases. Covalent radius mostly decreases as we move left to right across a period because the effective nuclear charge experienced by the electrons increases, and the electrons are pulled in tighter to the nucleus. Anionic radii are larger than the parent atom, while cationic radii are smaller, because the number of valence electrons has changed while the nuclear charge has remained constant. Ionization energy (the energy associated with forming a cation) decreases down a group and mostly increases across a period because it is easier to remove an electron from a larger, higher energy orbital. Electron affinity (the energy associated with forming an anion) is more favorable (exothermic) when electrons are placed into lower energy orbitals, closer to the nucleus. Therefore, electron affinity becomes increasingly negative as we move left to right across the periodic table and decreases as we move down a group. For both IE and electron affinity data, there are exceptions to the trends when dealing with completely filled or half-filled subshells.

3.6 The Periodic Table

The discovery of the periodic recurrence of similar properties among the elements led to the formulation of the periodic table, in which the elements are arranged in order of increasing atomic number in rows known as periods and columns known as groups. Elements in the same group of the periodic table have similar chemical properties. Elements can be classified as metals, metalloids, and nonmetals, or as a main-group elements, transition metals, and inner transition metals. Groups are numbered 1–18 from left to right. The elements in group 1 are known as the alkali metals; those in group 2 are the alkaline earth metals; those in 15 are the pnictogens; those in 16 are the chalcogens; those in 17 are the halogens; and those in 18 are the noble gases.

3.7 Molecular and Ionic Compounds

Metals (particularly those in groups 1 and 2) tend to lose the number of electrons that would leave them with the same number of electrons as in the preceding noble gas in the periodic table. By this means, a positively charged ion is formed. Similarly, nonmetals (especially those in groups 16 and 17, and, to a lesser extent, those in Group 15) can gain the number of electrons needed to provide atoms with the same number of electrons as in the next noble gas in the periodic table. Thus, nonmetals tend to form negative ions. Positively charged ions are called cations, and negatively charged ions are called anions. Ions can be either monatomic (containing only one atom) or polyatomic (containing more than one atom).

Compounds that contain ions are called ionic compounds. Ionic compounds generally form from metals and nonmetals. Compounds that do not contain ions, but instead consist of atoms bonded tightly together in molecules (uncharged groups of atoms that behave as a single unit), are called covalent compounds. Covalent compounds usually form from two nonmetals.

Exercises

3.1 Electromagnetic Energy

1. The light produced by a red neon sign is due to the emission of light by excited neon atoms. Qualitatively describe the spectrum produced by passing light from a neon lamp through a prism.

2. An FM radio station found at 103.1 on the FM dial broadcasts at a frequency of $1.031 \times 10^8 \text{ s}^{-1}$ (103.1 MHz). What is the wavelength of these radio waves in meters?

3. FM-95, an FM radio station, broadcasts at a frequency of $9.51 \times 10^7 \text{ s}^{-1}$ (95.1 MHz). What is the wavelength of these radio waves in meters?

4. A bright violet line occurs at 435.8 nm in the emission spectrum of mercury vapor. What amount of energy, in joules, must be released by an electron in a mercury atom to produce a photon of this light?

5. Light with a wavelength of 614.5 nm looks orange. What is the energy, in joules, per photon of this orange light? What is the energy in eV ($1 \text{ eV} = 1.602 \times 10^{-19} \text{ J}$)?

6. Heated lithium atoms emit photons of light with an energy of $2.961 \times 10^{-19} \text{ J}$. Calculate the frequency and wavelength of one of these photons. What is the total energy in 1 mole of these photons? What is the color of the emitted light?

7. A photon of light produced by a surgical laser has an energy of $3.027 \times 10^{-19} \text{ J}$. Calculate the frequency and wavelength of the photon. What is the total energy in 1 mole of photons? What is the color of the emitted light?

8. When rubidium ions are heated to a high temperature, two lines are observed in its line spectrum at wavelengths (a) $7.9 \times 10^{-7} \text{ m}$ and (b) $4.2 \times 10^{-7} \text{ m}$. What are the frequencies of the two lines? What color do we see when we heat a rubidium compound?

9. The emission spectrum of cesium contains two lines whose frequencies are (a) $3.45 \times 10^{14} \text{ Hz}$ and (b) $6.53 \times 10^{14} \text{ Hz}$. What are the wavelengths and energies per photon of the two lines? What color are the lines?

10. Photons of infrared radiation are responsible for much of the warmth we feel when holding our hands before a fire. These photons will also warm other objects. How many infrared photons with a wavelength of $1.5 \times 10^{-6} \text{ m}$ must be absorbed by the water to warm a cup of water (175 g) from 25.0 °C to 40 °C?

11. One of the radiographic devices used in a dentist's office emits an X-ray of wavelength $2.090 \times 10^{-11} \text{ m}$. What is the energy, in joules, and frequency of this X-ray?

12. The eyes of certain reptiles pass a single visual signal to the brain when the visual receptors are struck by photons of a wavelength of 850 nm. If a total energy of $3.15 \times 10^{-14} \text{ J}$ is required to trip the signal, what is the minimum number of photons that must strike the receptor?

13. RGB color television and computer displays use cathode ray tubes that produce colors by mixing red, green, and blue light. If we look at the screen with a magnifying glass, we can see individual dots turn on and off as the colors change. Using a spectrum of visible light, determine the approximate wavelength of each of these colors. What is the frequency and energy of a photon of each of these colors?

14. Answer the following questions about a Blu-ray laser:

(a) The laser on a Blu-ray player has a wavelength of 405 nm. In what region of the electromagnetic spectrum is this radiation? What is its frequency?

(b) A Blu-ray laser has a power of 5 milliwatts (1 watt = $1 \, J \, s^{-1}$). How many photons of light are produced by the laser in 1 hour?

(c) The ideal resolution of a player using a laser (such as a Blu-ray player), which determines how close together data can be stored on a compact disk, is determined using the following formula: Resolution = $0.60(\lambda/NA)$, where λ is the wavelength of the laser and NA is the numerical aperture. Numerical aperture is a measure of the size of the spot of light on the disk; the larger the NA, the smaller the spot. In a typical Blu-ray system, NA = 0.95. If the 405-nm laser is used in a Blu-ray player, what is the closest that information can be stored on a Blu-ray disk?

(d) The data density of a Blu-ray disk using a 405-nm laser is 1.5×10^7 bits mm^{-2}. Disks have an outside diameter of 120 mm and a hole of 15-mm diameter. How many data bits can be contained on the disk? If a Blu-ray disk can hold 9,400,000 pages of text, how many data bits are needed for a typed page? (Hint: Determine the area of the disk that is available to hold data. The area inside a circle is given by $A = \pi r^2$, where the radius r is one-half of the diameter.)

15. What is the threshold frequency for sodium metal if a photon with frequency $6.66 \times 10^{14} \, s^{-1}$ ejects an electron with 7.74×10^{-20} J kinetic energy? Will the photoelectric effect be observed if sodium is exposed to orange light?

3.2 The Bohr Model

16. Why is the electron in a Bohr hydrogen atom bound less tightly when it has a quantum number of 3 than when it has a quantum number of 1?

17. What does it mean to say that the energy of the electrons in an atom is quantized?

18. Using the Bohr model, determine the energy, in joules, necessary to ionize a ground-state hydrogen atom. Show your calculations.

19. The electron volt (eV) is a convenient unit of energy for expressing atomic-scale energies. It is the amount of energy that an electron gains when subjected to a potential of 1 volt; 1 eV = 1.602×10^{-19} J. Using the Bohr model, determine the energy, in electron volts, of the photon produced when an electron in a hydrogen atom moves from the orbit with $n = 5$ to the orbit with $n = 2$. Show your calculations.

20. Using the Bohr model, determine the lowest possible energy, in joules, for the electron in the Li^{2+} ion.

21. Using the Bohr model, determine the lowest possible energy for the electron in the He^+ ion.

22. Using the Bohr model, determine the energy of an electron with $n = 6$ in a hydrogen atom.

23. Using the Bohr model, determine the energy of an electron with $n = 8$ in a hydrogen atom.

24. How far from the nucleus in angstroms (1 angstrom = 1×10^{-10} m) is the electron in a hydrogen atom if it has an energy of -8.72×10^{-20} J?

25. What is the radius, in angstroms, of the orbital of an electron with $n = 8$ in a hydrogen atom?

26. Using the Bohr model, determine the energy in joules of the photon produced when an electron in a He^+ ion moves from the orbit with $n = 5$ to the orbit with $n = 2$.

27. Using the Bohr model, determine the energy in joules of the photon produced when an electron in a Li^{2+} ion moves from the orbit with $n = 2$ to the orbit with $n = 1$.

28. Consider a large number of hydrogen atoms with electrons randomly distributed in the $n = 1, 2, 3,$ and 4 orbits.

(a) How many different wavelengths of light are emitted by these atoms as the electrons fall into lower-energy orbitals?

(b) Calculate the lowest and highest energies of light produced by the transitions described in part (a).

(c) Calculate the frequencies and wavelengths of the light produced by the transitions described in part (b).

29. How are the Bohr model and the Rutherford model of the atom similar? How are they different?

30. The spectra of hydrogen and of calcium are shown in **Figure 3.13**. What causes the lines in these spectra? Why are the colors of the lines different? Suggest a reason for the observation that the spectrum of calcium is more complicated than the spectrum of hydrogen.

3.3 Development of Quantum Theory

31. How are the Bohr model and the quantum mechanical model of the hydrogen atom similar? How are they different?

32. What are the allowed values for each of the four quantum numbers: n, l, m_l, and m_s?

33. Describe the properties of an electron associated with each of the following four quantum numbers: n, l, m_l, and m_s.

34. Answer the following questions:

(a) Without using quantum numbers, describe the differences between the shells, subshells, and orbitals of an atom.

(b) How do the quantum numbers of the shells, subshells, and orbitals of an atom differ?

35. Identify the subshell in which electrons with the following quantum numbers are found:

(a) $n = 2$, $l = 1$

(b) $n = 4$, $l = 2$

(c) $n = 6$, $l = 0$

36. Which of the subshells described in the previous question contain degenerate orbitals? How many degenerate orbitals are in each?

37. Identify the subshell in which electrons with the following quantum numbers are found:

(a) $n = 3$, $l = 2$

(b) $n = 1$, $l = 0$

(c) $n = 4$, $l = 3$

38. Which of the subshells described in the previous question contain degenerate orbitals? How many degenerate orbitals are in each?

39. Sketch the boundary surface of a $d_{x^2-y^2}$ and a p_y orbital. Be sure to show and label the axes.

40. Sketch the p_x and d_{xz} orbitals. Be sure to show and label the coordinates.

41. Consider the orbitals shown here in outline.

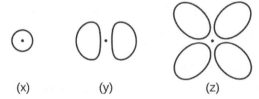

(x)   (y)   (z)

(a) What is the maximum number of electrons contained in an orbital of type (x)? Of type (y)? Of type (z)?

(b) How many orbitals of type (x) are found in a shell with $n = 2$? How many of type (y)? How many of type (z)?

(c) Write a set of quantum numbers for an electron in an orbital of type (x) in a shell with $n = 4$. Of an orbital of type (y) in a shell with $n = 2$. Of an orbital of type (z) in a shell with $n = 3$.

(d) What is the smallest possible n value for an orbital of type (x)? Of type (y)? Of type (z)?

(e) What are the possible l and m_l values for an orbital of type (x)? Of type (y)? Of type (z)?

42. State the Heisenberg uncertainty principle. Describe briefly what the principle implies.

43. How many electrons could be held in the second shell of an atom if the spin quantum number m_s could have three values instead of just two? (Hint: Consider the Pauli exclusion principle.)

44. Which of the following equations describe particle-like behavior? Which describe wavelike behavior? Do any involve both types of behavior? Describe the reasons for your choices.

(a) $c = \lambda v$

(b) $E = \dfrac{mv^2}{2}$

(c) $r = \dfrac{n^2 a_0}{Z}$

(d) $E = hv$

(e) $\lambda = \dfrac{h}{mv}$

45. Write a set of quantum numbers for each of the electrons with an n of 4 in a Se atom.

3.4 Electronic Structure of Atoms (Electron Configurations)

46. Read the labels of several commercial products and identify monatomic ions of at least four transition elements contained in the products. Write the complete electron configurations of these cations.

47. Read the labels of several commercial products and identify monatomic ions of at least six main group elements contained in the products. Write the complete electron configurations of these cations and anions.

48. Using complete subshell notation (not abbreviations, $1s^2 2s^2 2p^6$, and so forth), predict the electron configuration of each of the following atoms:

(a) C

(b) P

(c) V

(d) Sb

(e) Sm

49. Using complete subshell notation ($1s^2 2s^2 2p^6$, and so forth), predict the electron configuration of each of the following atoms:

(a) N

(b) Si

(c) Fe

(d) Te

(e) Tb

50. Is $1s^2 2s^2 2p^6$ the symbol for a macroscopic property or a microscopic property of an element? Explain your answer.

51. What additional information do we need to answer the question "Which ion has the electron configuration $1s^2 2s^2 2p^6 3s^2 3p^6$"?

52. Draw the orbital diagram for the valence shell of each of the following atoms:

(a) C

(b) P

(c) V

(d) Sb

(e) Ru

53. Use an orbital diagram to describe the electron configuration of the valence shell of each of the following atoms:

(a) N

(b) Si

(c) Fe

(d) Te

(e) Mo

54. Using complete subshell notation ($1s^2 2s^2 2p^6$, and so forth), predict the electron configurations of the following ions.

(a) N^{3-}

(b) Ca^{2+}

(c) S^-

(d) Cs^{2+}

(e) Cr^{2+}

(f) Gd^{3+}

55. Which atom has the electron configuration $1s^2 2s^2 2p^6 3s^2 3p^6 4s^2 3d^{10} 4p^6 5s^2 4d^2$?

56. Which atom has the electron configuration $1s^2 2s^2 2p^6 3s^2 3p^6 3d^7 4s^2$?

57. Which ion with a +1 charge has the electron configuration $1s^2 2s^2 2p^6 3s^2 3p^6 3d^{10} 4s^2 4p^6$? Which ion with a –2 charge has this configuration?

58. Which of the following atoms contains only three valence electrons: Li, B, N, F, Ne?

59. Which of the following has two unpaired electrons?

(a) Mg

(b) Si

(c) S

(d) Both Mg and S

(e) Both Si and S.

60. Which atom would be expected to have a half-filled $6p$ subshell?

61. Which atom would be expected to have a half-filled $4s$ subshell?

62. In one area of Australia, the cattle did not thrive despite the presence of suitable forage. An investigation showed the cause to be the absence of sufficient cobalt in the soil. Cobalt forms cations in two oxidation states, Co^{2+} and Co^{3+}. Write the electron structure of the two cations.

63. Thallium was used as a poison in the Agatha Christie mystery story "The Pale Horse." Thallium has two possible cationic forms, +1 and +3. The +1 compounds are the more stable. Write the electron structure of the +1 cation of thallium.

64. Write the electron configurations for the following atoms or ions:

(a) B^{3+}

(b) O^-

(c) Cl^{3+}

(d) Ca^{2+}

(e) Ti

65. Cobalt–60 and iodine–131 are radioactive isotopes commonly used in nuclear medicine. How many protons, neutrons, and electrons are in atoms of these isotopes? Write the complete electron configuration for each isotope.

66. Write a set of quantum numbers for each of the electrons with an n of 3 in a Sc atom.

3.5 Periodic Variations in Element Properties

67. Based on their positions in the periodic table, predict which has the smallest atomic radius: Mg, Sr, Si, Cl, I.

68. Based on their positions in the periodic table, predict which has the largest atomic radius: Li, Rb, N, F, I.

69. Based on their positions in the periodic table, predict which has the largest first ionization energy: Mg, Ba, B, O, Te.

70. Based on their positions in the periodic table, predict which has the smallest first ionization energy: Li, Cs, N, F, I.

71. Based on their positions in the periodic table, rank the following atoms in order of increasing first ionization energy: F, Li, N, Rb

72. Based on their positions in the periodic table, rank the following atoms or compounds in order of increasing first ionization energy: Mg, O, S, Si

73. Atoms of which group in the periodic table have a valence shell electron configuration of ns^2np^3?

74. Atoms of which group in the periodic table have a valence shell electron configuration of ns^2?

75. Based on their positions in the periodic table, list the following atoms in order of increasing radius: Mg, Ca, Rb, Cs.

76. Based on their positions in the periodic table, list the following atoms in order of increasing radius: Sr, Ca, Si, Cl.

77. Based on their positions in the periodic table, list the following ions in order of increasing radius: K^+, Ca^{2+}, Al^{3+}, Si^{4+}.

78. List the following ions in order of increasing radius: Li^+, Mg^{2+}, Br^-, Te^{2-}.

79. Which atom and/or ion is (are) isoelectronic with Br^+: Se^{2+}, Se, As^-, Kr, Ga^{3+}, Cl^-?

80. Which of the following atoms and ions is (are) isoelectronic with S^{2+}: Si^{4+}, Cl^{3+}, Ar, As^{3+}, Si, Al^{3+}?

81. Compare both the numbers of protons and electrons present in each to rank the following ions in order of increasing radius: As^{3-}, Br^-, K^+, Mg^{2+}.

82. Of the five elements Al, Cl, I, Na, Rb, which has the most exothermic reaction? (E represents an atom.) What name is given to the energy for the reaction? Hint: note the process depicted does *not* correspond to electron affinity

$$E^+(g) + e^- \longrightarrow E(g)$$

83. Of the five elements Sn, Si, Sb, O, Te, which has the most endothermic reaction? (E represents an atom.) What name is given to the energy for the reaction?

$$E(g) \longrightarrow E^+(g) + e^-$$

84. The ionic radii of the ions S^{2-}, Cl^-, and K^+ are 184, 181, 138 pm respectively. Explain why these ions have different sizes even though they contain the same number of electrons.

85. Which main group atom would be expected to have the lowest second ionization energy?

86. Explain why Al is a member of group 13 rather than group 3?

3.6 The Periodic Table

87. Using the periodic table, classify each of the following elements as a metal or a nonmetal, and then further classify each as a main-group (representative) element, transition metal, or inner transition metal:

(a) uranium

(b) bromine

(c) strontium

(d) neon

(e) gold

(f) americium

(g) rhodium

(h) sulfur

(i) carbon

(j) potassium

88. Using the periodic table, classify each of the following elements as a metal or a nonmetal, and then further classify each as a main-group (representative) element, transition metal, or inner transition metal:

(a) cobalt

(b) europium

(c) iodine

(d) indium

(e) lithium

(f) oxygen

(h) cadmium

(i) terbium

(j) rhenium

89. Using the periodic table, identify the lightest member of each of the following groups:

(a) noble gases

(b) alkaline earth metals

(c) alkali metals

(d) chalcogens

90. Using the periodic table, identify the heaviest member of each of the following groups:

(a) alkali metals

(b) chalcogens

(c) noble gases

(d) alkaline earth metals

91. Use the periodic table to give the name and symbol for each of the following elements:

(a) the noble gas in the same period as germanium

(b) the alkaline earth metal in the same period as selenium

(c) the halogen in the same period as lithium

(d) the chalcogen in the same period as cadmium

92. Use the periodic table to give the name and symbol for each of the following elements:

(a) the halogen in the same period as the alkali metal with 11 protons

(b) the alkaline earth metal in the same period with the neutral noble gas with 18 electrons

(c) the noble gas in the same row as an isotope with 30 neutrons and 25 protons

(d) the noble gas in the same period as gold

93. Write a symbol for each of the following neutral isotopes. Include the atomic number and mass number for each.

(a) the alkali metal with 11 protons and a mass number of 23

(b) the noble gas element with 75 neutrons in its nucleus and 54 electrons in the neutral atom

(c) the isotope with 33 protons and 40 neutrons in its nucleus

(d) the alkaline earth metal with 88 electrons and 138 neutrons

94. Write a symbol for each of the following neutral isotopes. Include the atomic number and mass number for each.

(a) the chalcogen with a mass number of 125

(b) the halogen whose longest-lived isotope is radioactive

(c) the noble gas, used in lighting, with 10 electrons and 10 neutrons

(d) the lightest alkali metal with three neutrons

3.7 Molecular and Ionic Compounds

95. Using the periodic table, predict whether the following chlorides are ionic or covalent: KCl, NCl_3, ICl, $MgCl_2$, PCl_5, and CCl_4.

96. Using the periodic table, predict whether the following chlorides are ionic or covalent: $SiCl_4$, PCl_3, $CaCl_2$, $CsCl$, $CuCl_2$, and $CrCl_3$.

97. For each of the following compounds, state whether it is ionic or covalent. If it is ionic, write the symbols for the ions involved:

(a) NF_3

(b) BaO,

(c) $(NH_4)_2CO_3$

(d) $Sr(H_2PO_4)_2$

(e) IBr

(f) Na_2O

98. For each of the following compounds, state whether it is ionic or covalent, and if it is ionic, write the symbols for the ions involved:

(a) $KClO_4$

(b) $MgC_2H_3O_2$

(c) H_2S

(d) Ag_2S

(e) N_2Cl_4

(f) $Co(NO_3)_2$

99. For each of the following pairs of ions, write the symbol for the formula of the compound they will form:

(a) Ca^{2+}, S^{2-}

(b) NH_4^+, SO_4^{2-}

(c) Al^{3+}, Br^-

(d) Na^+, HPO_4^{2-}

(e) Mg^{2+}, PO_4^{3-}

100. For each of the following pairs of ions, write the symbol for the formula of the compound they will form:

(a) K^+, O^{2-}

(b) NH_4^+, PO_4^{3-}

(c) Al^{3+}, O^{2-}

(d) Na^+, CO_3^{2-}

(e) Ba^{2+}, PO_4^{3-}

Chapter 4

Chemical Bonding and Molecular Geometry

Figure 4.1 Nicknamed "buckyballs," buckminsterfullerene molecules (C_{60}) contain only carbon atoms. Here they are shown in a ball-and-stick model (left). These molecules have single and double carbon-carbon bonds arranged to form a geometric framework of hexagons and pentagons, similar to the pattern on a soccer ball (center). This unconventional molecular structure is named after architect R. Buckminster Fuller, whose innovative designs combined simple geometric shapes to create large, strong structures such as this weather radar dome near Tucson, Arizona (right). (credit middle: modification of work by "Petey21"/Wikimedia Commons; credit right: modification of work by Bill Morrow)

Chapter Outline

Introduction

It has long been known that pure carbon occurs in different forms (allotropes) including graphite and diamonds. But it was not until 1985 that a new form of carbon was recognized: buckminsterfullerene, commonly known as a "buckyball." This molecule was named after the architect and inventor R. Buckminster Fuller (1895–1983), whose signature architectural design was the geodesic dome, characterized by a lattice shell structure supporting a spherical surface. Experimental evidence revealed the formula, C_{60}, and then scientists determined how 60 carbon atoms could form one symmetric, stable molecule. They were guided by bonding theory—the topic of this chapter—which explains how individual atoms connect to form more complex structures.

4.1 Ionic Bonding

By the end of this section, you will be able to:

- Explain the formation of cations, anions, and ionic compounds
- Predict the charge of common metallic and nonmetallic elements, and write their electron configurations

As you have learned, ions are atoms or molecules bearing an electrical charge. A cation (a positive ion) forms when a neutral atom loses one or more electrons from its valence shell, and an anion (a negative ion) forms when a neutral atom gains one or more electrons in its valence shell.

Compounds composed of ions are called ionic compounds (or salts), and their constituent ions are held together by **ionic bonds**: electrostatic forces of attraction between oppositely charged cations and anions. The properties of ionic compounds shed some light on the nature of ionic bonds. Ionic solids exhibit a crystalline structure and tend to be rigid and brittle; they also tend to have high melting and boiling points, which suggests that ionic bonds are very strong. Ionic solids are also poor conductors of electricity for the same reason—the strength of ionic bonds prevents ions from moving freely in the solid state. Most ionic solids, however, dissolve readily in water. Once dissolved or melted, ionic compounds are excellent conductors of electricity and heat because the ions can move about freely.

Neutral atoms and their associated ions have very different physical and chemical properties. Sodium *atoms* form sodium metal, a soft, silvery-white metal that burns vigorously in air and reacts explosively with water. Chlorine *atoms* form chlorine gas, Cl_2, a yellow-green gas that is extremely corrosive to most metals and very poisonous to animals and plants. The vigorous reaction between the elements sodium and chlorine forms the white, crystalline compound sodium chloride, common table salt, which contains sodium *cations* and chloride *anions* (**Figure 4.2**). The compound composed of these ions exhibits properties entirely different from the properties of the elements sodium and chlorine. Chlorine is poisonous, but sodium chloride is essential to life; sodium atoms react vigorously with water, but sodium chloride simply dissolves in water.

(a)   (b)   (c)

Figure 4.2   (a) Sodium is a soft metal that must be stored in mineral oil to prevent reaction with air or water. (b) Chlorine is a pale yellow-green gas. (c) When combined, they form white crystals of sodium chloride (table salt). (credit a: modification of work by "Jurii"/Wikimedia Commons)

The Formation of Ionic Compounds

Binary ionic compounds are composed of just two elements: a metal (which forms the cations) and a nonmetal (which forms the anions). For example, NaCl is a binary ionic compound. We can think about the formation of such compounds in terms of the periodic properties of the elements. Many metallic elements have relatively low ionization potentials and lose electrons easily. These elements lie to the left in a period or near the bottom of a group on the periodic table. Nonmetal atoms have relatively high electron affinities and thus readily gain electrons lost by metal atoms, thereby filling their valence shells. Nonmetallic elements are found in the upper-right corner of the periodic table.

As all substances must be electrically neutral, the total number of positive charges on the cations of an ionic compound must equal the total number of negative charges on its anions. The formula of an ionic compound represents the simplest ratio of the numbers of ions necessary to give identical numbers of positive and negative charges. For example, the formula for aluminum oxide, Al_2O_3, indicates that this ionic compound contains two aluminum cations, Al^{3+}, for every three oxide anions, O^{2-} [thus, $(2 \times +3) + (3 \times -2) = 0$].

It is important to note, however, that the formula for an ionic compound does *not* represent the physical arrangement of its ions. It is incorrect to refer to a sodium chloride (NaCl) "molecule" because there is not a single ionic bond, per se, between any specific pair of sodium and chloride ions. The attractive forces between ions are isotropic—the same in all directions—meaning that any particular ion is equally attracted to all of the nearby ions of opposite charge. This results in the ions arranging themselves into a tightly bound, three-dimensional lattice structure. Sodium chloride, for example, consists of a regular arrangement of equal numbers of Na^+ cations and Cl^- anions (**Figure 4.3**).

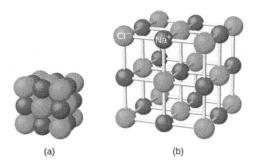

(a)   (b)

Figure 4.3 The atoms in sodium chloride (common table salt) are arranged to (a) maximize opposite charges interacting. The smaller spheres represent sodium ions, the larger ones represent chloride ions. In the expanded view (b), the geometry can be seen more clearly. Note that each ion is "bonded" to all of the surrounding ions—six in this case.

The strong electrostatic attraction between Na^+ and Cl^- ions holds them tightly together in solid NaCl. It requires 769 kJ of energy to dissociate one mole of solid NaCl into separate gaseous Na^+ and Cl^- ions:

$$NaCl(s) \longrightarrow Na^+(g) + Cl^-(g) \qquad \Delta H = 769 \text{ kJ}$$

Electronic Structures of Cations

When forming a cation, an atom of a main group element tends to lose all of its valence electrons, thus assuming the electronic structure of the noble gas that precedes it in the periodic table. For groups 1 (the alkali metals) and 2 (the alkaline earth metals), the group numbers are equal to the numbers of valence shell electrons and, consequently, to the charges of the cations formed from atoms of these elements when all valence shell electrons are removed. For example, calcium is a group 2 element whose neutral atoms have 20 electrons and a ground state electron configuration of $1s^2 2s^2 2p^6 3s^2 3p^6 4s^2$. When a Ca atom loses both of its valence electrons, the result is a cation with 18 electrons, a 2+ charge, and an electron configuration of $1s^2 2s^2 2p^6 3s^2 3p^6$. The Ca^{2+} ion is therefore isoelectronic with the noble gas Ar.

For groups 12–17, the group numbers exceed the number of valence electrons by 10 (accounting for the possibility of full *d* subshells in atoms of elements in the fourth and greater periods). Thus, the charge of a cation formed by the loss of all valence electrons is equal to the group number minus 10. For example, aluminum (in group 13) forms 3+ ions (Al^{3+}).

Exceptions to the expected behavior involve elements toward the bottom of the groups. In addition to the expected ions Tl^{3+}, Sn^{4+}, Pb^{4+}, and Bi^{5+}, a partial loss of these atoms' valence shell electrons can also lead to the formation of Tl^+, Sn^{2+}, Pb^{2+}, and Bi^{3+} ions. The formation of these 1+, 2+, and 3+ cations is ascribed to the **inert pair effect**, which reflects the relatively low energy of the valence *s*-electron pair for atoms of the heavy elements of groups 13, 14, and 15. Mercury (group 12) also exhibits an unexpected behavior: it forms a diatomic ion, Hg_2^{2+} (an ion formed from two mercury atoms, with an Hg-Hg bond), in addition to the expected monatomic ion Hg^{2+} (formed from only one mercury atom).

Transition and inner transition metal elements behave differently than main group elements. Most transition metal cations have 2+ or 3+ charges that result from the loss of their outermost s electron(s) first, sometimes followed by the loss of one or two d electrons from the next-to-outermost shell. For example, iron ($1s^2 2s^2 2p^6 3s^2 3p^6 3d^6 4s^2$) forms the ion Fe^{2+} ($1s^2 2s^2 2p^6 3s^2 3p^6 3d^6$) by the loss of the $4s$ electron and the ion Fe^{3+} ($1s^2 2s^2 2p^6 3s^2 3p^6 3d^5$) by the loss of the $4s$ electron and one of the $3d$ electrons. Although the d orbitals of the transition elements are—according to the Aufbau principle—the last to fill when building up electron configurations, the outermost s electrons are the first to be lost when these atoms ionize. When the inner transition metals form ions, they usually have a 3+ charge, resulting from the loss of their outermost s electrons and a d or f electron.

Example 4.1

Determining the Electronic Structures of Cations

There are at least 14 elements categorized as "essential trace elements" for the human body. They are called "essential" because they are required for healthy bodily functions, "trace" because they are required only in small amounts, and "elements" in spite of the fact that they are really ions. Two of these essential trace elements, chromium and zinc, are required as Cr^{3+} and Zn^{2+}. Write the electron configurations of these cations.

Solution

First, write the electron configuration for the neutral atoms:

Zn: $[Ar]3d^{10}4s^2$

Cr: $[Ar]3d^5 4s^1$

Next, remove electrons from the highest energy orbital. For the transition metals, electrons are removed from the s orbital first and then from the d orbital. For the p-block elements, electrons are removed from the p orbitals and then from the s orbital. Zinc is a member of group 12, so it should have a charge of 2+, and thus loses only the two electrons in its s orbital. Chromium is a transition element and should lose its s electrons and then its d electrons when forming a cation. Thus, we find the following electron configurations of the ions:

Zn^{2+}: $[Ar]3d^{10}$

Cr^{3+}: $[Ar]3d^3$

Check Your Learning

Potassium and magnesium are required in our diet. Write the electron configurations of the ions expected from these elements.

Answer: K^+: $[Ar]$, Mg^{2+}: $[Ne]$

Electronic Structures of Anions

Most monatomic anions form when a neutral nonmetal atom gains enough electrons to completely fill its outer s and p orbitals, thereby reaching the electron configuration of the next noble gas. Thus, it is simple to determine the charge on such a negative ion: The charge is equal to the number of electrons that must be gained to fill the s and p orbitals of the parent atom. Oxygen, for example, has the electron configuration $1s^2 2s^2 2p^4$, whereas the oxygen anion has the electron configuration of the noble gas neon (Ne), $1s^2 2s^2 2p^6$. The two additional electrons required to fill the valence orbitals give the oxide ion the charge of 2– (O^{2-}).

Example 4.2

Determining the Electronic Structure of Anions

Selenium and iodine are two essential trace elements that form anions. Write the electron configurations of the anions.

Solution

Se^{2-}: $[Ar]3d^{10}4s^24p^6$

I^-: $[Kr]4d^{10}5s^25p^6$

Check Your Learning

Write the electron configurations of a phosphorus atom and its negative ion. Give the charge on the anion.

Answer: P: $[Ne]3s^23p^3$; P^{3-}: $[Ne]3s^23p^6$

4.2 Covalent Bonding

By the end of this section, you will be able to:

- Describe the formation of covalent bonds

- Define electronegativity and assess the polarity of covalent bonds

In ionic compounds, electrons are transferred between atoms of different elements to form ions. But this is not the only way that compounds can be formed. Atoms can also make chemical bonds by sharing electrons equally between each other. Such bonds are called **covalent bonds**. Covalent bonds are formed between two atoms when both have similar tendencies to attract electrons to themselves (i.e., when both atoms have identical or fairly similar ionization energies and electron affinities). For example, two hydrogen atoms bond covalently to form an H_2 molecule; each hydrogen atom in the H_2 molecule has two electrons stabilizing it, giving each atom the same number of valence electrons as the noble gas He.

Compounds that contain covalent bonds exhibit different physical properties than ionic compounds. Because the attraction between molecules, which are electrically neutral, is weaker than that between electrically charged ions, covalent compounds generally have much lower melting and boiling points than ionic compounds. In fact, many covalent compounds are liquids or gases at room temperature, and, in their solid states, they are typically much softer than ionic solids. Furthermore, whereas ionic compounds are good conductors of electricity when dissolved in water, most covalent compounds are insoluble in water; since they are electrically neutral, they are poor conductors of electricity in any state.

Formation of Covalent Bonds

Nonmetal atoms frequently form covalent bonds with other nonmetal atoms. For example, the hydrogen molecule, H_2, contains a covalent bond between its two hydrogen atoms. Figure 4.4 illustrates why this bond is formed. Starting on the far right, we have two separate hydrogen atoms with a particular potential energy, indicated by the red line. Along the x-axis is the distance between the two atoms. As the two atoms approach each other (moving left along the x-axis), their valence orbitals ($1s$) begin to overlap. The single electrons on each hydrogen atom then interact with both atomic nuclei, occupying the space around both atoms. The strong attraction of each shared electron to both nuclei stabilizes the system, and the potential energy decreases as the bond distance decreases. If the atoms continue to approach each other, the positive charges in the two nuclei begin to repel each other, and the potential energy increases. The **bond length** is determined by the distance at which the lowest potential energy is achieved.

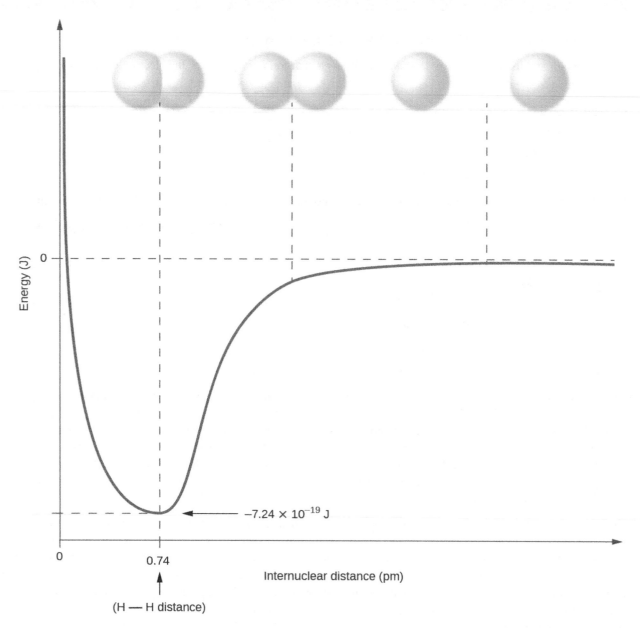

Figure 4.4 The potential energy of two separate hydrogen atoms (right) decreases as they approach each other, and the single electrons on each atom are shared to form a covalent bond. The bond length is the internuclear distance at which the lowest potential energy is achieved.

Pure vs. Polar Covalent Bonds

If the atoms that form a covalent bond are identical, as in H_2, Cl_2, and other diatomic molecules, then the electrons in the bond must be shared equally. We refer to this as a **pure covalent bond**. Electrons shared in pure covalent bonds have an equal probability of being near each nucleus.

In the case of Cl_2, each atom starts off with seven valence electrons, and each Cl shares one electron with the other, forming one covalent bond:

$$Cl + Cl \longrightarrow Cl_2$$

The total number of electrons around each individual atom consists of six nonbonding electrons and two shared (i.e., bonding) electrons for eight total electrons, matching the number of valence electrons in the noble gas argon. Since the bonding atoms are identical, Cl_2 also features a pure covalent bond.

When the atoms linked by a covalent bond are different, the bonding electrons are shared, but no longer equally. Instead, the bonding electrons are more attracted to one atom than the other, giving rise to a shift of electron density toward that atom. This unequal distribution of electrons is known as a **polar covalent bond**, characterized by a partial positive charge on one atom and a partial negative charge on the other. The atom that attracts the electrons more strongly acquires the partial negative charge and vice versa. For example, the electrons in the H–Cl bond of a hydrogen chloride molecule spend more time near the chlorine atom than near the hydrogen atom. Thus, in an HCl molecule, the chlorine atom carries a partial negative charge and the hydrogen atom has a partial positive charge. Figure 4.5 shows the distribution of electrons in the H–Cl bond. Note that the shaded area around Cl is much larger than it is around H. Compare this to Figure 4.4, which shows the even distribution of electrons in the H_2 nonpolar bond.

We sometimes designate the positive and negative atoms in a polar covalent bond using a lowercase Greek letter "delta," δ, with a plus sign or minus sign to indicate whether the atom has a partial positive charge (δ+) or a partial negative charge (δ–). This symbolism is shown for the H–Cl molecule in Figure 4.5.

(a) (b)

Figure 4.5 (a) The distribution of electron density in the HCl molecule is uneven. The electron density is greater around the chlorine nucleus. The small, black dots indicate the location of the hydrogen and chlorine nuclei in the molecule. (b) Symbols δ+ and δ– indicate the polarity of the H–Cl bond.

Electronegativity

Whether a bond is nonpolar or polar covalent is determined by a property of the bonding atoms called **electronegativity**. Electronegativity is a measure of the tendency of an atom to attract electrons (or electron density) towards itself. It determines how the shared electrons are distributed between the two atoms in a bond. The more strongly an atom attracts the electrons in its bonds, the larger its electronegativity. Electrons in a polar covalent bond are shifted toward the more electronegative atom; thus, the more electronegative atom is the one with the partial negative charge. The greater the difference in electronegativity, the more polarized the electron distribution and the larger the partial charges of the atoms.

Figure 4.6 shows the electronegativity values of the elements as proposed by one of the most famous chemists of the twentieth century: Linus Pauling (Figure 4.7). In general, electronegativity increases from left to right across a period in the periodic table and decreases down a group. Thus, the nonmetals, which lie in the upper right, tend to have the highest electronegativities, with fluorine the most electronegative element of all (EN = 4.0). Metals tend to be less electronegative elements, and the group 1 metals have the lowest electronegativities. Note that noble gases are excluded from this figure because these atoms usually do not share electrons with others atoms since they have a full valence shell. (While noble gas compounds such as XeO_2 do exist, they can only be formed under extreme conditions, and thus they do not fit neatly into the general model of electronegativity.)

Figure 4.6 The electronegativity values derived by Pauling follow predictable periodic trends with the higher electronegativities toward the upper right of the periodic table.

Electronegativity versus Electron Affinity

We must be careful not to confuse electronegativity and electron affinity. The electron affinity of an element is a measurable physical quantity, namely, the energy released or absorbed when an isolated gas-phase atom acquires an electron, measured in kJ/mol. Electronegativity, on the other hand, describes how tightly an atom attracts electrons in a bond. It is a dimensionless quantity that is calculated, not measured. Pauling derived the first electronegativity values by comparing the amounts of energy required to break different types of bonds. He chose an arbitrary relative scale ranging from 0 to 4.

Portrait of a Chemist

Linus Pauling

Linus Pauling, shown in Figure 4.7, is the only person to have received two unshared (individual) Nobel Prizes: one for chemistry in 1954 for his work on the nature of chemical bonds and one for peace in 1962 for his opposition to weapons of mass destruction. He developed many of the theories and concepts that are foundational to our current understanding of chemistry, including electronegativity and resonance structures.

Figure 4.7 Linus Pauling (1901–1994) made many important contributions to the field of chemistry. He was also a prominent activist, publicizing issues related to health and nuclear weapons.

Pauling also contributed to many other fields besides chemistry. His research on sickle cell anemia revealed the cause of the disease—the presence of a genetically inherited abnormal protein in the blood—and paved the way for the field of molecular genetics. His work was also pivotal in curbing the testing of nuclear weapons; he proved that radioactive fallout from nuclear testing posed a public health risk.

Electronegativity and Bond Type

The absolute value of the difference in electronegativity (ΔEN) of two bonded atoms provides a rough measure of the polarity to be expected in the bond and, thus, the bond type. When the difference is very small or zero, the bond is covalent and nonpolar. When it is large, the bond is polar covalent or ionic. The absolute values of the electronegativity differences between the atoms in the bonds H–H, H–Cl, and Na–Cl are 0 (nonpolar), 0.9 (polar covalent), and 2.1 (ionic), respectively. The degree to which electrons are shared between atoms varies from completely equal (pure covalent bonding) to not at all (ionic bonding). **Figure 4.8** shows the relationship between electronegativity difference and bond type.

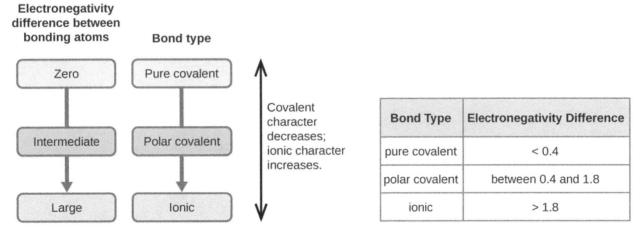

Bond Type	Electronegativity Difference
pure covalent	< 0.4
polar covalent	between 0.4 and 1.8
ionic	> 1.8

Figure 4.8 As the electronegativity difference increases between two atoms, the bond becomes more ionic.

A rough approximation of the electronegativity differences associated with covalent, polar covalent, and ionic bonds is shown in **Figure 4.8**. This table is just a general guide, however, with many exceptions. For example, the H and

F atoms in HF have an electronegativity difference of 1.9, and the N and H atoms in NH_3 a difference of 0.9, yet both of these compounds form bonds that are considered polar covalent. Likewise, the Na and Cl atoms in NaCl have an electronegativity difference of 2.1, and the Mn and I atoms in MnI_2 have a difference of 1.0, yet both of these substances form ionic compounds.

The best guide to the covalent or ionic character of a bond is to consider the types of atoms involved and their relative positions in the periodic table. Bonds between two nonmetals are generally covalent; bonding between a metal and a nonmetal is often ionic.

Some compounds contain both covalent and ionic bonds. The atoms in polyatomic ions, such as OH^-, NO_3^-, and NH_4^+, are held together by polar covalent bonds. However, these polyatomic ions form ionic compounds by combining with ions of opposite charge. For example, potassium nitrate, KNO_3, contains the K^+ cation and the polyatomic NO_3^- anion. Thus, bonding in potassium nitrate is ionic, resulting from the electrostatic attraction between the ions K^+ and NO_3^-, as well as covalent between the nitrogen and oxygen atoms in NO_3^-.

Example 4.3

Electronegativity and Bond Polarity

Bond polarities play an important role in determining the structure of proteins. Using the electronegativity values in Figure 4.6, arrange the following covalent bonds—all commonly found in amino acids—in order of increasing polarity. Then designate the positive and negative atoms using the symbols δ+ and δ–:

C–H, C–N, C–O, N–H, O–H, S–H

Solution

The polarity of these bonds increases as the absolute value of the electronegativity difference increases. The atom with the δ– designation is the more electronegative of the two. Table 4.1 shows these bonds in order of increasing polarity.

Bond Polarity and Electronegativity Difference

Bond	ΔEN	Polarity
C–H	0.4	$\overset{\delta-}{C}-\overset{\delta+}{H}$
S–H	0.4	$\overset{\delta-}{S}-\overset{\delta+}{H}$
C–N	0.5	$\overset{\delta+}{C}-\overset{\delta-}{N}$
N–H	0.9	$\overset{\delta-}{N}-\overset{\delta+}{H}$
C–O	1.0	$\overset{\delta+}{C}-\overset{\delta-}{O}$
O–H	1.4	$\overset{\delta-}{O}-\overset{\delta+}{H}$

Table 4.1

Check Your Learning

Silicones are polymeric compounds containing, among others, the following types of covalent bonds: Si–O, Si–C, C–H, and C–C. Using the electronegativity values in Figure 4.6, arrange the bonds in order of increasing polarity and designate the positive and negative atoms using the symbols $\delta+$ and $\delta-$.

Answer:

Bond	Electronegativity Difference	Polarity
C–C	0.0	nonpolar
C–H	0.4	$\overset{\delta-}{C}-\overset{\delta+}{H}$
Si–C	0.7	$\overset{\delta+}{Si}-\overset{\delta-}{C}$
Si–O	1.7	$\overset{\delta+}{Si}-\overset{\delta-}{O}$

4.3 Chemical Nomenclature

By the end of this module, you will be able to:

- Derive names for common types of inorganic compounds using a systematic approach

Nomenclature, a collection of rules for naming things, is important in science and in many other situations. This module describes an approach that is used to name simple ionic and molecular compounds, such as NaCl, $CaCO_3$, and N_2O_4. The simplest of these are **binary compounds**, those containing only two elements, but we will also consider how to name ionic compounds containing polyatomic ions, and one specific, very important class of compounds known as acids (subsequent chapters in this text will focus on these compounds in great detail). We will limit our attention here to inorganic compounds, compounds that are composed principally of elements other than carbon, and will follow the nomenclature guidelines proposed by IUPAC. The rules for organic compounds, in which carbon is the principle element, will be treated in a later chapter on organic chemistry.

Ionic Compounds

To name an inorganic compound, we need to consider the answers to several questions. First, is the compound ionic or molecular? If the compound is ionic, does the metal form ions of only one type (fixed charge) or more than one type (variable charge)? Are the ions monatomic or polyatomic? If the compound is molecular, does it contain hydrogen? If so, does it also contain oxygen? From the answers we derive, we place the compound in an appropriate category and then name it accordingly.

Compounds Containing Only Monatomic Ions

The name of a binary compound containing monatomic ions consists of the name of the cation (the name of the metal) followed by the name of the anion (the name of the nonmetallic element with its ending replaced by the suffix –*ide*). Some examples are given in Table 4.2.

Names of Some Ionic Compounds

NaCl, sodium chloride	Na_2O, sodium oxide
KBr, potassium bromide	CdS, cadmium sulfide
CaI_2, calcium iodide	Mg_3N_2, magnesium nitride
CsF, cesium fluoride	Ca_3P_2, calcium phosphide
LiCl, lithium chloride	Al_4C_3, aluminum carbide

Table 4.2

Compounds Containing Polyatomic Ions

Compounds containing polyatomic ions are named similarly to those containing only monatomic ions, except there is no need to change to an –*ide* ending, since the suffix is already present in the name of the anion. Examples are shown in Table 4.3.

Names of Some Polyatomic Ionic Compounds

$KC_2H_3O_2$, potassium acetate	$(NH_4)Cl$, ammonium chloride
$NaHCO_3$, sodium bicarbonate	$CaSO_4$, calcium sulfate
$Al_2(CO_3)_3$, aluminum carbonate	$Mg_3(PO_4)_2$, magnesium phosphate

Table 4.3

Chemistry in Everyday Life

Ionic Compounds in Your Cabinets

Every day you encounter and use a large number of ionic compounds. Some of these compounds, where they are found, and what they are used for are listed in Table 4.4. Look at the label or ingredients list on the various products that you use during the next few days, and see if you run into any of those in this table, or find other ionic compounds that you could now name or write as a formula.

Everyday Ionic Compounds

Ionic Compound	Use
NaCl, sodium chloride	ordinary table salt
KI, potassium iodide	added to "iodized" salt for thyroid health
NaF, sodium fluoride	ingredient in toothpaste
$NaHCO_3$, sodium bicarbonate	baking soda; used in cooking (and as antacid)
Na_2CO_3, sodium carbonate	washing soda; used in cleaning agents
NaOCl, sodium hypochlorite	active ingredient in household bleach
$CaCO_3$ calcium carbonate	ingredient in antacids

Everyday Ionic Compounds

Ionic Compound	Use
$Mg(OH)_2$, magnesium hydroxide	ingredient in antacids
$Al(OH)_3$, aluminum hydroxide	ingredient in antacids
NaOH, sodium hydroxide	lye; used as drain cleaner
K_3PO_4, potassium phosphate	food additive (many purposes)
$MgSO_4$, magnesium sulfate	added to purified water
Na_2HPO_4, sodium hydrogen phosphate	anti-caking agent; used in powdered products
Na_2SO_3, sodium sulfite	preservative

Table 4.4

Compounds Containing a Metal Ion with a Variable Charge

Most of the transition metals can form two or more cations with different charges. Compounds of these metals with nonmetals are named with the same method as compounds in the first category, except the charge of the metal ion is specified by a Roman numeral in parentheses after the name of the metal. The charge of the metal ion is determined from the formula of the compound and the charge of the anion. For example, consider binary ionic compounds of iron and chlorine. Iron typically exhibits a charge of either 2+ or 3+ (see Figure 3.41), and the two corresponding compound formulas are $FeCl_2$ and $FeCl_3$. The simplest name, "iron chloride," will, in this case, be ambiguous, as it does not distinguish between these two compounds. In cases like this, the charge of the metal ion is included as a Roman numeral in parentheses immediately following the metal name. These two compounds are then unambiguously named iron(II) chloride and iron(III) chloride, respectively. Other examples are provided in Table 4.5.

Names of Some Transition Metal Ionic Compounds

Transition Metal Ionic Compound	Name
$FeCl_3$	iron(III) chloride
Hg_2O	mercury(I) oxide
HgO	mercury(II) oxide
$Cu_3(PO_4)_2$	copper(II) phosphate

Table 4.5

Out-of-date nomenclature used the suffixes *–ic* and *–ous* to designate metals with higher and lower charges, respectively: Iron(III) chloride, $FeCl_3$, was previously called ferric chloride, and iron(II) chloride, $FeCl_2$, was known as ferrous chloride. Though this naming convention has been largely abandoned by the scientific community, it remains in use by some segments of industry. For example, you may see the words *stannous fluoride* on a tube of toothpaste. This represents the formula SnF_2, which is more properly named tin(II) fluoride. The other fluoride of tin is SnF_4, which was previously called stannic fluoride but is now named tin(IV) fluoride.

Example 4.4

Naming Ionic Compounds

Name the following ionic compounds, which contain a metal that can have more than one ionic charge:

(a) Fe_2S_3

(b) CuSe

(c) GaN

(d) $CrCl_3$

(e) $Ti_2(SO_4)_3$

Solution

The anions in these compounds have a fixed negative charge (S^{2-}, Se^{2-}, N^{3-}, Cl^-, and $SO_4{}^{2-}$), and the compounds must be neutral. Because the total number of positive charges in each compound must equal the total number of negative charges, the positive ions must be Fe^{3+}, Cu^{2+}, Ga^{3+}, Cr^{3+}, and Ti^{3+}. These charges are used in the names of the metal ions:

(a) iron(III) sulfide

(b) copper(II) selenide

(c) gallium(III) nitride

(d) chromium(III) chloride

(e) titanium(III) sulfate

Check Your Learning

Write the formulas of the following ionic compounds:

(a) chromium(III) phosphide

(b) mercury(II) sulfide

(c) manganese(II) phosphate

(d) copper(I) oxide

(e) chromium(VI) fluoride

Answer: (a) CrP; (b) HgS; (c) $Mn_3(PO_4)_2$; (d) Cu_2O; (e) CrF_6

Chemistry in Everyday Life

Erin Brokovich and Chromium Contamination

In the early 1990s, legal file clerk Erin Brockovich (Figure 4.9) discovered a high rate of serious illnesses in the small town of Hinckley, California. Her investigation eventually linked the illnesses to groundwater contaminated by Cr(VI) used by Pacific Gas & Electric (PG&E) to fight corrosion in a nearby natural gas pipeline. As dramatized in the film *Erin Brokovich* (for which Julia Roberts won an Oscar), Erin and lawyer Edward Masry sued PG&E for contaminating the water near Hinckley in 1993. The settlement they won in 1996—$333 million—was the largest amount ever awarded for a direct-action lawsuit in the US at that time.

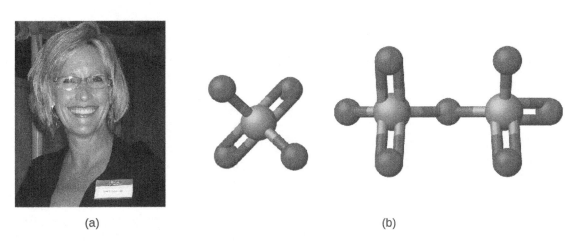

(a)   (b)

Figure 4.9 (a) Erin Brockovich found that Cr(VI), used by PG&E, had contaminated the Hinckley, California, water supply. (b) The Cr(VI) ion is often present in water as the polyatomic ions chromate, $CrO_4{}^{2-}$ (left), and dichromate, $Cr_2O_7{}^{2-}$ (right).

Chromium compounds are widely used in industry, such as for chrome plating, in dye-making, as preservatives, and to prevent corrosion in cooling tower water, as occurred near Hinckley. In the environment, chromium exists primarily in either the Cr(III) or Cr(VI) forms. Cr(III), an ingredient of many vitamin and nutritional supplements, forms compounds that are not very soluble in water, and it has low toxicity. But Cr(VI) is much more toxic and forms compounds that are reasonably soluble in water. Exposure to small amounts of Cr(VI) can lead to damage of the respiratory, gastrointestinal, and immune systems, as well as the kidneys, liver, blood, and skin.

Despite cleanup efforts, Cr(VI) groundwater contamination remains a problem in Hinckley and other locations across the globe. A 2010 study by the Environmental Working Group found that of 35 US cities tested, 31 had higher levels of Cr(VI) in their tap water than the public health goal of 0.02 parts per billion set by the California Environmental Protection Agency.

Molecular (Covalent) Compounds

The bonding characteristics of inorganic molecular compounds are different from ionic compounds, and they are named using a different system as well. The charges of cations and anions dictate their ratios in ionic compounds, so specifying the names of the ions provides sufficient information to determine chemical formulas. However, because covalent bonding allows for significant variation in the combination ratios of the atoms in a molecule, the names for molecular compounds must explicitly identify these ratios.

Compounds Composed of Two Elements

When two nonmetallic elements form a molecular compound, several combination ratios are often possible. For example, carbon and oxygen can form the compounds CO and CO_2. Since these are different substances with different properties, they cannot both have the same name (they cannot both be called carbon oxide). To deal with this situation, we use a naming method that is somewhat similar to that used for ionic compounds, but with added prefixes to specify the numbers of atoms of each element. The name of the more metallic element (the one farther to the left and/or bottom of the periodic table) is first, followed by the name of the more nonmetallic element (the one farther to the right and/or top) with its ending changed to the suffix –ide. The numbers of atoms of each element are designated by the Greek prefixes shown in Table 4.6.

Nomenclature Prefixes

Number	Prefix		Number	Prefix
1 (sometimes omitted)	mono-		6	hexa-
2	di-		7	hepta-
3	tri-		8	octa-
4	tetra-		9	nona-
5	penta-		10	deca-

Table 4.6

When only one atom of the first element is present, the prefix *mono-* is usually deleted from that part. Thus, CO is named carbon monoxide, and CO_2 is called carbon dioxide. When two vowels are adjacent, the *a* in the Greek prefix is usually dropped. Some other examples are shown in Table 4.7.

Names of Some Molecular Compounds Composed of Two Elements

Compound	Name		Compound	Name
SO_2	sulfur dioxide		BCl_3	boron trichloride
SO_3	sulfur trioxide		SF_6	sulfur hexafluoride
NO_2	nitrogen dioxide		PF_5	phosphorus pentafluoride
N_2O_4	dinitrogen tetroxide		P_4O_{10}	tetraphosphorus decaoxide
N_2O_5	dinitrogen pentoxide		IF_7	iodine heptafluoride

Table 4.7

There are a few common names that you will encounter as you continue your study of chemistry. For example, although NO is often called nitric oxide, its proper name is nitrogen monoxide. Similarly, N_2O is known as nitrous oxide even though our rules would specify the name dinitrogen monoxide. (And H_2O is usually called water, not dihydrogen monoxide.) You should commit to memory the common names of compounds as you encounter them.

Example 4.5

Naming Covalent Compounds

Name the following covalent compounds:

(a) SF_6

(b) N_2O_3

(c) Cl_2O_7

(d) P_4O_6

Solution

Because these compounds consist solely of nonmetals, we use prefixes to designate the number of atoms of each element:

(a) sulfur hexafluoride

(b) dinitrogen trioxide

(c) dichlorine heptoxide

(d) tetraphosphorus hexoxide

Check Your Learning

Write the formulas for the following compounds:

(a) phosphorus pentachloride

(b) dinitrogen monoxide

(c) iodine heptafluoride

(d) carbon tetrachloride

Answer: (a) PCl_5; (b) N_2O; (c) IF_7; (d) CCl_4

Link to Learning

The following website (http://openstaxcollege.org/l/16chemcompname) provides practice with naming chemical compounds and writing chemical formulas. You can choose binary, polyatomic, and variable charge ionic compounds, as well as molecular compounds.

Binary Acids

Some compounds containing hydrogen are members of an important class of substances known as acids. The chemistry of these compounds is explored in more detail in later chapters of this text, but for now, it will suffice to note that many acids release hydrogen ions, H^+, when dissolved in water. To denote this distinct chemical property, a mixture of water with an acid is given a name derived from the compound's name. If the compound is a **binary acid** (comprised of hydrogen and one other nonmetallic element):

1. The word "hydrogen" is changed to the prefix *hydro-*

2. The other nonmetallic element name is modified by adding the suffix *-ic*

3. The word "acid" is added as a second word

For example, when the gas HCl (hydrogen chloride) is dissolved in water, the solution is called *hydrochloric acid*. Several other examples of this nomenclature are shown in Table 4.8.

Names of Some Simple Acids

Name of Gas	Name of Acid
HF(g), hydrogen fluoride	HF(aq), hydrofluoric acid
HCl(g), hydrogen chloride	HCl(aq), hydrochloric acid
HBr(g), hydrogen bromide	HBr(aq), hydrobromic acid
HI(g), hydrogen iodide	HI(aq), hydroiodic acid
H_2S(g), hydrogen sulfide	H_2S(aq), hydrosulfuric acid

Table 4.8

Oxyacids

Many compounds containing three or more elements (such as organic compounds or coordination compounds) are subject to specialized nomenclature rules that you will learn later. However, we will briefly discuss the important compounds known as **oxyacids**, compounds that contain hydrogen, oxygen, and at least one other element, and are bonded in such a way as to impart acidic properties to the compound (you will learn the details of this in a later chapter). Typical oxyacids consist of hydrogen combined with a polyatomic, oxygen-containing ion. To name oxyacids:

1. Omit "hydrogen"

2. Start with the root name of the anion

3. Replace –*ate* with –*ic*, or –*ite* with –*ous*

4. Add "acid"

For example, consider H_2CO_3 (which you might be tempted to call "hydrogen carbonate"). To name this correctly, "hydrogen" is omitted; the –*ate* of carbonate is replace with –*ic*; and acid is added—so its name is carbonic acid. Other examples are given in Table 4.9. There are some exceptions to the general naming method (e.g., H_2SO_4 is called sulfuric acid, not sulfic acid, and H_2SO_3 is sulfurous, not sulfous, acid).

Names of Common Oxyacids

Formula	Anion Name	Acid Name
$HC_2H_3O_2$	acetate	acetic acid
HNO_3	nitrate	nitric acid
HNO_2	nitrite	nitrous acid
$HClO_4$	perchlorate	perchloric acid
H_2CO_3	carbonate	carbonic acid
H_2SO_4	sulfate	sulfuric acid
H_2SO_3	sulfite	sulfurous acid
H_3PO_4	phosphate	phosphoric acid

Table 4.9

4.4 Lewis Symbols and Structures

By the end of this section, you will be able to:

- Write Lewis symbols for neutral atoms and ions
- Draw Lewis structures depicting the bonding in simple molecules

Thus far in this chapter, we have discussed the various types of bonds that form between atoms and/or ions. In all cases, these bonds involve the sharing or transfer of valence shell electrons between atoms. In this section, we will explore the typical method for depicting valence shell electrons and chemical bonds, namely Lewis symbols and Lewis structures.

Lewis Symbols

We use Lewis symbols to describe valence electron configurations of atoms and monatomic ions. A **Lewis symbol** consists of an elemental symbol surrounded by one dot for each of its valence electrons:

$$\cdot Ca \cdot$$

Figure 4.10 shows the Lewis symbols for the elements of the third period of the periodic table.

Atoms	Electronic Configuration	Lewis Symbol
sodium	$[Ne]3s^1$	Na $\cdot$
magnesium	$[Ne]3s^2$	$\cdot$ Mg $\cdot$
aluminum	$[Ne]3s^23p^1$	$\cdot \overset{\bullet}{Al} \cdot$
silicon	$[Ne]3s^23p^2$	$\cdot \overset{\bullet}{\underset{\bullet}{Si}} \cdot$
phosphorus	$[Ne]3s^23p^3$	$\cdot \overset{\bullet\bullet}{\underset{\bullet}{P}} \cdot$
sulfur	$[Ne]3s^23p^4$	$: \overset{\bullet\bullet}{\underset{\bullet}{S}} \cdot$
chlorine	$[Ne]3s^23p^5$	$: \overset{\bullet\bullet}{\underset{\bullet\bullet}{Cl}} \cdot$
argon	$[Ne]3s^23p^6$	$: \overset{\bullet\bullet}{\underset{\bullet\bullet}{Ar}} :$

Figure 4.10 Lewis symbols illustrating the number of valence electrons for each element in the third period of the periodic table.

Lewis symbols can also be used to illustrate the formation of cations from atoms, as shown here for sodium and calcium:

Na $\cdot \longrightarrow$ Na$^+$ + e$^-$ $\qquad$ $\cdot$Ca$\cdot \longrightarrow$ Ca^{2+} + 2e$^-$

sodium $\qquad$ sodium $\qquad$ calcium $\qquad$ calcium
atom $\qquad$ cation $\qquad$ atom $\qquad$ cation

Likewise, they can be used to show the formation of anions from atoms, as shown here for chlorine and sulfur:

$: \overset{\bullet\bullet}{\underset{\bullet\bullet}{Cl}} \cdot$ + e$^-$ $\longrightarrow$ $: \overset{\bullet\bullet}{\underset{\bullet\bullet}{Cl}} :^-$ $\qquad$ $: \overset{\bullet\bullet}{\underset{\bullet}{S}} \cdot$ + 2e$^-$ $\longrightarrow$ $: \overset{\bullet\bullet}{\underset{\bullet\bullet}{S}} :^{2-}$

chlorine $\qquad$ chlorine $\qquad$ sulfur $\qquad$ sulfide
atom $\qquad$ anion $\qquad$ atom $\qquad$ anion

Figure 4.11 demonstrates the use of Lewis symbols to show the transfer of electrons during the formation of ionic compounds.

Metal		Nonmetal		Ionic Compound
Na ·	+	$:\overset{..}{\underset{..}{Cl}}·$	$\longrightarrow$	$Na^+\left[:\overset{..}{\underset{..}{Cl}}:\right]^-$
sodium atom		chlorine atom		sodium chloride (sodium ion and chloride ion)
·Mg·	+	$:\overset{..}{\underset{.}{O}}·$	$\longrightarrow$	$Mg^{2+}\left[:\overset{..}{\underset{..}{O}}:\right]^{2-}$
magnesium atom		oxygen atom		magnesium oxide (magnesium ion and oxide ion)
·Ca·	+	$2:\overset{..}{\underset{..}{F}}·$	$\longrightarrow$	$Ca^{2+}\left[:\overset{..}{\underset{..}{F}}:\right]^-_2$
calcium atom		fluorine atoms		calcium fluoride (calcium ion and two fluoride ions)

Figure 4.11 Cations are formed when atoms lose electrons, represented by fewer Lewis dots, whereas anions are formed by atoms gaining electrons. The total number of electrons does not change.

Lewis Structures

We also use Lewis symbols to indicate the formation of covalent bonds, which are shown in **Lewis structures**, drawings that describe the bonding in molecules and polyatomic ions. For example, when two chlorine atoms form a chlorine molecule, they share one pair of electrons:

$$:\overset{..}{\underset{..}{Cl}}·+·\overset{..}{\underset{..}{Cl}}: \longrightarrow :\overset{..}{\underset{..}{Cl}}:\overset{..}{\underset{..}{Cl}}:$$

chlorine   chlorine
atoms   molecule

The Lewis structure indicates that each Cl atom has three pairs of electrons that are not used in bonding (called **lone pairs**) and one shared pair of electrons (written between the atoms). A dash (or line) is sometimes used to indicate a shared pair of electrons:

$$H—H \qquad :\overset{..}{\underset{..}{Cl}}—\overset{..}{\underset{..}{Cl}}:$$

A single shared pair of electrons is called a **single bond**. Each Cl atom interacts with eight valence electrons: the six in the lone pairs and the two in the single bond.

The Octet Rule

The other halogen molecules (F_2, Br_2, I_2, and At_2) form bonds like those in the chlorine molecule: one single bond between atoms and three lone pairs of electrons per atom. This allows each halogen atom to have a noble gas electron configuration. The tendency of main group atoms to form enough bonds to obtain eight valence electrons is known as the **octet rule**.

The number of bonds that an atom can form can often be predicted from the number of electrons needed to reach an octet (eight valence electrons); this is especially true of the nonmetals of the second period of the periodic table (C, N, O, and F). For example, each atom of a group 14 element has four electrons in its outermost shell and therefore requires four more electrons to reach an octet. These four electrons can be gained by forming four covalent bonds, as illustrated here for carbon in CCl_4 (carbon tetrachloride) and silicon in SiH_4 (silane). Because hydrogen only needs two electrons to fill its valence shell, it is an exception to the octet rule. The transition elements and inner transition elements also do not follow the octet rule:

carbon tetrachloride   silane

Group 15 elements such as nitrogen have five valence electrons in the atomic Lewis symbol: one lone pair and three unpaired electrons. To obtain an octet, these atoms form three covalent bonds, as in NH_3 (ammonia). Oxygen and other atoms in group 16 obtain an octet by forming two covalent bonds:

ammonia   Water   hydrogen
                                fluoride

Double and Triple Bonds

As previously mentioned, when a pair of atoms shares one pair of electrons, we call this a single bond. However, a pair of atoms may need to share more than one pair of electrons in order to achieve the requisite octet. A **double bond** forms when two pairs of electrons are shared between a pair of atoms, as between the carbon and oxygen atoms in CH_2O (formaldehyde) and between the two carbon atoms in C_2H_4 (ethylene):

formaldehyde   ethylene

A **triple bond** forms when three electron pairs are shared by a pair of atoms, as in carbon monoxide (CO) and the cyanide ion (CN^-):

carbon monoxide   cyanide ion

Writing Lewis Structures with the Octet Rule

For very simple molecules and molecular ions, we can write the Lewis structures by merely pairing up the unpaired electrons on the constituent atoms. See these examples:

For more complicated molecules and molecular ions, it is helpful to follow the step-by-step procedure outlined here:

1. Determine the total number of valence (outer shell) electrons. For cations, subtract one electron for each

positive charge. For anions, add one electron for each negative charge.

2. Draw a skeleton structure of the molecule or ion, arranging the atoms around a central atom. (Generally, the least electronegative element should be placed in the center.) Connect each atom to the central atom with a single bond (one electron pair).

3. Distribute the remaining electrons as lone pairs on the terminal atoms (except hydrogen), completing an octet around each atom.

4. Place all remaining electrons on the central atom.

5. Rearrange the electrons of the outer atoms to make multiple bonds with the central atom in order to obtain octets wherever possible.

Let us determine the Lewis structures of SiH_4, CHO_2^-, NO^+, and OF_2 as examples in following this procedure:

1. Determine the total number of valence (outer shell) electrons in the molecule or ion.

    - For a molecule, we add the number of valence electrons on each atom in the molecule:

      SiH_4

      Si: 4 valence electrons/atom $\times$ 1 atom = 4

      $\underline{+ \text{ H: 1 valence electron/atom} \times 4 \text{ atoms} = 4}$

      = 8 valence electrons

    - For a *negative ion*, such as CHO_2^-, we add the number of valence electrons on the atoms to the number of negative charges on the ion (one electron is gained for each single negative charge):

      CHO_2^-

      C: 4 valence electrons/atom $\times$ 1 atom = 4
      H: 1 valence electron/atom $\times$ 1 atom = 1
      O: 6 valence electrons/atom $\times$ 2 atoms = 12

      $\underline{+ \hspace{3cm} \text{1 additional electron} = 1}$

      = 18 valence electrons

    - For a *positive ion*, such as NO^+, we add the number of valence electrons on the atoms in the ion and then subtract the number of positive charges on the ion (one electron is lost for each single positive charge) from the total number of valence electrons:

      NO^+

      N: 5 valence electrons/atom $\times$ 1 atom = 5
      O: 6 valence electron/atom $\times$ 1 atom = 6
      $\underline{+ \text{ } -1 \text{ electron (positive charge)} \hspace{1cm} = -1}$

      = 10 valence electrons

    - Since OF_2 is a neutral molecule, we simply add the number of valence electrons:

      OF_2

      O: 6 valence electrons/atom $\times$ 1 atom = 6
      $\underline{+ \text{ F: 7 valence electrons/atom} \times 2 \text{ atoms} = 14}$

      = 20 valence electrons

2. Draw a skeleton structure of the molecule or ion, arranging the atoms around a central atom and connecting each atom to the central atom with a single (one electron pair) bond. (Note that we denote ions with brackets around the structure, indicating the charge outside the brackets:)

$$
\begin{array}{ccccc}
& & & & \\
\text{H} & & \left[\begin{array}{c} \text{O} \\ \| \\ \text{C} \\ \diagup \;\; \diagdown \\ \text{H} \qquad \text{O} \end{array}\right]^{-} & \big[\text{N}{-}\text{O}\big]^{+} & \text{F}{-}\text{O}{-}\text{F}
\end{array}
$$

$$\text{H}{-}\text{Si}{-}\text{H}$$

When several arrangements of atoms are possible, as for $CHO_2{}^-$, we must use experimental evidence to choose the correct one. In general, the less electronegative elements are more likely to be central atoms. In $CHO_2{}^-$, the less electronegative carbon atom occupies the central position with the oxygen and hydrogen atoms surrounding it. Other examples include P in $POCl_3$, S in SO_2, and Cl in $ClO_4{}^-$. An exception is that hydrogen is almost never a central atom. As the most electronegative element, fluorine also cannot be a central atom.

3. Distribute the remaining electrons as lone pairs on the terminal atoms (except hydrogen) to complete their valence shells with an octet of electrons.

   • There are no remaining electrons on SiH_4, so it is unchanged:

4. Place all remaining electrons on the central atom.

   • For SiH_4, $CHO_2{}^-$, and NO^+, there are no remaining electrons; we already placed all of the electrons determined in Step 1.

   • For OF_2, we had 16 electrons remaining in Step 3, and we placed 12, leaving 4 to be placed on the central atom:

$$:\!\ddot{\text{F}}\!-\!\ddot{\text{O}}\!-\!\ddot{\text{F}}\!:$$

5. Rearrange the electrons of the outer atoms to make multiple bonds with the central atom in order to obtain octets wherever possible.

   • SiH_4: Si already has an octet, so nothing needs to be done.

   • $CHO_2{}^-$: We have distributed the valence electrons as lone pairs on the oxygen atoms, but the carbon atom lacks an octet:

   • NO^+: For this ion, we added eight valence electrons, but neither atom has an octet. We cannot add any more electrons since we have already used the total that we found in Step 1, so we must move electrons to form a multiple bond:

$$\big[:\!\ddot{\text{N}}{-}\ddot{\text{O}}\!:\big]^{+} \quad \text{gives} \quad \big[:\!\ddot{\text{N}}{=}\ddot{\text{O}}\!:\big]^{+}$$

   This still does not produce an octet, so we must move another pair, forming a triple bond:

$$\big[:\!\text{N}{\equiv}\text{O}\!:\big]^{+}$$

   • In OF_2, each atom has an octet as drawn, so nothing changes.

Example 4.6

Writing Lewis Structures

NASA's Cassini-Huygens mission detected a large cloud of toxic hydrogen cyanide (HCN) on Titan, one of Saturn's moons. Titan also contains ethane (H_3CCH_3), acetylene (HCCH), and ammonia (NH_3). What are the Lewis structures of these molecules?

Solution

Step 1. *Calculate the number of valence electrons.*
HCN: $(1 \times 1) + (4 \times 1) + (5 \times 1) = 10$
H_3CCH_3: $(1 \times 3) + (2 \times 4) + (1 \times 3) = 14$
HCCH: $(1 \times 1) + (2 \times 4) + (1 \times 1) = 10$
NH_3: $(5 \times 1) + (3 \times 1) = 8$

Step 2. *Draw a skeleton and connect the atoms with single bonds.* Remember that H is never a central atom:

Step 3. *Where needed, distribute electrons to the terminal atoms:*

HCN: six electrons placed on N
H_3CCH_3: no electrons remain
HCCH: no terminal atoms capable of accepting electrons
NH_3: no terminal atoms capable of accepting electrons

Step 4. *Where needed, place remaining electrons on the central atom:*

HCN: no electrons remain
H_3CCH_3: no electrons remain
HCCH: four electrons placed on carbon
NH_3: two electrons placed on nitrogen

Step 5. *Where needed, rearrange electrons to form multiple bonds in order to obtain an octet on each atom:*
HCN: form two more C–N bonds
H_3CCH_3: all atoms have the correct number of electrons
HCCH: form a triple bond between the two carbon atoms
NH_3: all atoms have the correct number of electrons

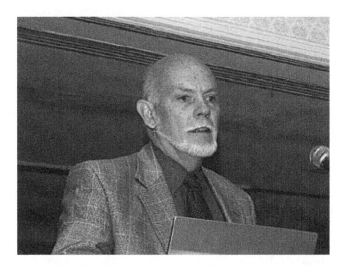

Check Your Learning

Both carbon monoxide, CO, and carbon dioxide, CO_2, are products of the combustion of fossil fuels. Both of these gases also cause problems: CO is toxic and CO_2 has been implicated in global climate change. What are the Lewis structures of these two molecules?

Answer:

$$:C\!\equiv\!O\!: \qquad :\ddot{O}\!=\!C\!=\!\ddot{O}\!:$$

How Sciences Interconnect

Fullerene Chemistry

Carbon soot has been known to man since prehistoric times, but it was not until fairly recently that the molecular structure of the main component of soot was discovered. In 1996, the Nobel Prize in Chemistry was awarded to Richard Smalley (Figure 4.12), Robert Curl, and Harold Kroto for their work in discovering a new form of carbon, the C_{60} buckminsterfullerene molecule (Figure 4.1). An entire class of compounds, including spheres and tubes of various shapes, were discovered based on C_{60}. This type of molecule, called a fullerene, shows promise in a variety of applications. Because of their size and shape, fullerenes can encapsulate other molecules, so they have shown potential in various applications from hydrogen storage to targeted drug delivery systems. They also possess unique electronic and optical properties that have been put to good use in solar powered devices and chemical sensors.

Figure 4.12 Richard Smalley (1943–2005), a professor of physics, chemistry, and astronomy at Rice University, was one of the leading advocates for fullerene chemistry. Upon his death in 2005, the US Senate honored him as the "Father of Nanotechnology." (credit: United States Department of Energy)

Exceptions to the Octet Rule

Many covalent molecules have central atoms that do not have eight electrons in their Lewis structures. These molecules fall into three categories:

- Odd-electron molecules have an odd number of valence electrons, and therefore have an unpaired electron.

- Electron-deficient molecules have a central atom that has fewer electrons than needed for a noble gas configuration.

- Hypervalent molecules have a central atom that has more electrons than needed for a noble gas configuration.

Odd-electron Molecules

We call molecules that contain an odd number of electrons **free radicals**. Nitric oxide, NO, is an example of an odd-electron molecule; it is produced in internal combustion engines when oxygen and nitrogen react at high temperatures.

To draw the Lewis structure for an odd-electron molecule like NO, we follow the same five steps we would for other molecules, but with a few minor changes:

1. *Determine the total number of valence (outer shell) electrons.* The sum of the valence electrons is 5 (from N) + 6 (from O) = 11. The odd number immediately tells us that we have a free radical, so we know that not every atom can have eight electrons in its valence shell.

2. *Draw a skeleton structure of the molecule.* We can easily draw a skeleton with an N–O single bond:
   N–O

3. *Distribute the remaining electrons as lone pairs on the terminal atoms.* In this case, there is no central atom, so we distribute the electrons around both atoms. We give eight electrons to the more electronegative atom in these situations; thus oxygen has the filled valence shell:

$$:\overset{\displaystyle .}{N}—\overset{\displaystyle ..}{\underset{\displaystyle ..}{O}}:$$

4. *Place all remaining electrons on the central atom.* Since there are no remaining electrons, this step does not apply.

5. *Rearrange the electrons to make multiple bonds with the central atom in order to obtain octets wherever possible.* We know that an odd-electron molecule cannot have an octet for every atom, but we want to get each atom as close to an octet as possible. In this case, nitrogen has only five electrons around it. To move closer to an octet for nitrogen, we take one of the lone pairs from oxygen and use it to form a NO double bond. (We cannot take another lone pair of electrons on oxygen and form a triple bond because nitrogen would then have nine electrons:)

$$:\overset{\displaystyle .}{N}\!=\!\overset{\displaystyle ..}{O}:$$

Electron-deficient Molecules

We will also encounter a few molecules that contain central atoms that do not have a filled valence shell. Generally, these are molecules with central atoms from groups 2 and 12, outer atoms that are hydrogen, or other atoms that do not form multiple bonds. For example, in the Lewis structures of beryllium dihydride, BeH_2, and boron trifluoride, BF_3, the beryllium and boron atoms each have only four and six electrons, respectively. It is possible to draw a structure with a double bond between a boron atom and a fluorine atom in BF_3, satisfying the octet rule, but experimental evidence indicates the bond lengths are closer to that expected for B–F single bonds. This suggests the best Lewis structure has three B–F single bonds and an electron deficient boron. The reactivity of the compound is also consistent with an electron deficient boron. However, the B–F bonds are slightly shorter than what is actually expected for B–F single bonds, indicating that some double bond character is found in the actual molecule.

$$H—Be—H$$

An atom like the boron atom in BF_3, which does not have eight electrons, is very reactive. It readily combines with a molecule containing an atom with a lone pair of electrons. For example, NH_3 reacts with BF_3 because the lone pair on nitrogen can be shared with the boron atom:

Hypervalent Molecules

Elements in the second period of the periodic table ($n = 2$) can accommodate only eight electrons in their valence shell orbitals because they have only four valence orbitals (one $2s$ and three $2p$ orbitals). Elements in the third and higher periods ($n \geq 3$) have more than four valence orbitals and can share more than four pairs of electrons with other atoms because they have empty d orbitals in the same shell. Molecules formed from these elements are sometimes called **hypervalent molecules**. Figure 4.13 shows the Lewis structures for two hypervalent molecules, PCl_5 and SF_6.

Figure 4.13   In PCl_5, the central atom phosphorus shares five pairs of electrons. In SF_6, sulfur shares six pairs of electrons.

In some hypervalent molecules, such as IF_5 and XeF_4, some of the electrons in the outer shell of the central atom are lone pairs:

When we write the Lewis structures for these molecules, we find that we have electrons left over after filling the valence shells of the outer atoms with eight electrons. These additional electrons must be assigned to the central atom.

Example 4.7

Writing Lewis Structures: Octet Rule Violations

Xenon is a noble gas, but it forms a number of stable compounds. We examined XeF_4 earlier. What are the Lewis structures of XeF_2 and XeF_6?

Solution

We can draw the Lewis structure of any covalent molecule by following the six steps discussed earlier. In this case, we can condense the last few steps, since not all of them apply.

Step 1. *Calculate the number of valence electrons:*

XeF_2: $8 + (2 \times 7) = 22$

XeF_6: $8 + (6 \times 7) = 50$

Step 2. *Draw a skeleton joining the atoms by single bonds.* Xenon will be the central atom because fluorine cannot be a central atom:

F—Xe—F

Step 3. *Distribute the remaining electrons.*

XeF_2: We place three lone pairs of electrons around each F atom, accounting for 12 electrons and giving each F atom 8 electrons. Thus, six electrons (three lone pairs) remain. These lone pairs must be placed on the Xe atom. This is acceptable because Xe atoms have empty valence shell d orbitals and can accommodate more than eight electrons. The Lewis structure of XeF_2 shows two bonding pairs and three lone pairs of electrons around the Xe atom:

XeF_6: We place three lone pairs of electrons around each F atom, accounting for 36 electrons. Two electrons remain, and this lone pair is placed on the Xe atom:

Check Your Learning

The halogens form a class of compounds called the interhalogens, in which halogen atoms covalently bond to each other. Write the Lewis structures for the interhalogens $BrCl_3$ and $ICl_4{}^-$.

Answer:

4.5 Formal Charges and Resonance

By the end of this section, you will be able to:

- Compute formal charges for atoms in any Lewis structure
- Use formal charges to identify the most reasonable Lewis structure for a given molecule
- Explain the concept of resonance and draw Lewis structures representing resonance forms for a given molecule

In the previous section, we discussed how to write Lewis structures for molecules and polyatomic ions. As we have seen, however, in some cases, there is seemingly more than one valid structure for a molecule. We can use the concept of formal charges to help us predict the most appropriate Lewis structure when more than one is reasonable.

Calculating Formal Charge

The **formal charge** of an atom in a molecule is the *hypothetical* charge the atom would have if we could redistribute the electrons in the bonds evenly between the atoms. Another way of saying this is that formal charge results when we take the number of valence electrons of a neutral atom, subtract the nonbonding electrons, and then subtract the number of bonds connected to that atom in the Lewis structure.

Thus, we calculate formal charge as follows:

$$\text{formal charge} = \text{\# valence shell electrons (free atom)} - \text{\# lone pair electrons} - \frac{1}{2}\text{\# bonding electrons}$$

We can double-check formal charge calculations by determining the sum of the formal charges for the whole structure. The sum of the formal charges of all atoms in a molecule must be zero; the sum of the formal charges in an ion should equal the charge of the ion.

We must remember that the formal charge calculated for an atom is not the *actual* charge of the atom in the molecule. Formal charge is only a useful bookkeeping procedure; it does not indicate the presence of actual charges.

Example 4.8

Calculating Formal Charge from Lewis Structures

Assign formal charges to each atom in the interhalogen ion $ICl_4{}^-$.

Solution

  Step 1. *We divide the bonding electron pairs equally for all I–Cl bonds:*

  Step 2. *We assign lone pairs of electrons to their atoms.* Each Cl atom now has seven electrons assigned to it, and the I atom has eight.

  Step 3. *Subtract this number from the number of valence electrons for the neutral atom:*

  I: $7 - 8 = -1$

  Cl: $7 - 7 = 0$

  The sum of the formal charges of all the atoms equals –1, which is identical to the charge of the ion (–1).

Check Your Learning

Calculate the formal charge for each atom in the carbon monoxide molecule:

$$:C\equiv O:$$

Answer: C –1, O +1

Example 4.9

Calculating Formal Charge from Lewis Structures

Assign formal charges to each atom in the interhalogen molecule $BrCl_3$.

Solution

  Step 1. *Assign one of the electrons in each Br–Cl bond to the Br atom and one to the Cl atom in that bond:*

$$:\overset{..}{\underset{..}{Cl}}-\overset{..}{\underset{|}{Br}}-\overset{..}{\underset{..}{Cl}}:$$
$$:\overset{..}{\underset{..}{Cl}}:$$

Step 2. *Assign the lone pairs to their atom.* Now each Cl atom has seven electrons and the Br atom has seven electrons.

Step 3. *Subtract this number from the number of valence electrons for the neutral atom.* This gives the formal charge:

Br: 7 − 7 = 0

Cl: 7 − 7 = 0

All atoms in $BrCl_3$ have a formal charge of zero, and the sum of the formal charges totals zero, as it must in a neutral molecule.

Check Your Learning

Determine the formal charge for each atom in NCl_3.

Answer: N: 0; all three Cl atoms: 0

$$:\overset{..}{\underset{..}{Cl}}-\overset{..}{\underset{|}{N}}-\overset{..}{\underset{..}{Cl}}:$$
$$:\overset{..}{\underset{..}{Cl}}:$$

Using Formal Charge to Predict Molecular Structure

The arrangement of atoms in a molecule or ion is called its **molecular structure**. In many cases, following the steps for writing Lewis structures may lead to more than one possible molecular structure—different multiple bond and lone-pair electron placements or different arrangements of atoms, for instance. A few guidelines involving formal charge can be helpful in deciding which of the possible structures is most likely for a particular molecule or ion:

1. A molecular structure in which all formal charges are zero is preferable to one in which some formal charges are not zero.

2. If the Lewis structure must have nonzero formal charges, the arrangement with the smallest nonzero formal charges is preferable.

3. Lewis structures are preferable when adjacent formal charges are zero or of the opposite sign.

4. When we must choose among several Lewis structures with similar distributions of formal charges, the structure with the negative formal charges on the more electronegative atoms is preferable.

To see how these guidelines apply, let us consider some possible structures for carbon dioxide, CO_2. We know from our previous discussion that the less electronegative atom typically occupies the central position, but formal charges allow us to understand *why* this occurs. We can draw three possibilities for the structure: carbon in the center and double bonds, carbon in the center with a single and triple bond, and oxygen in the center with double bonds:

$$\overset{..}{\underset{..}{O}}=C=\overset{..}{\underset{..}{O}} \qquad :O\equiv C-\overset{..}{\underset{..}{O}}: \qquad \overset{..}{\underset{..}{O}}=O=\overset{..}{\underset{..}{C}}\qquad \text{Structure}$$

$$\;\;0\;\;\;\;0\;\;\;\;0 \qquad\qquad +1\;\;\;0\;\;\;-1 \qquad\qquad 0\;\;\;+2\;\;\;-2 \qquad \text{Formal charge}$$

Comparing the three formal charges, we can definitively identify the structure on the left as preferable because it has only formal charges of zero (Guideline 1).

As another example, the thiocyanate ion, an ion formed from a carbon atom, a nitrogen atom, and a sulfur atom, could have three different molecular structures: CNS^-, NCS^-, or CSN^-. The formal charges present in each of these molecular structures can help us pick the most likely arrangement of atoms. Possible Lewis structures and the formal charges for each of the three possible structures for the thiocyanate ion are shown here:

Structure $\quad \left[:\ddot{N}=C=\ddot{S}:\right]^{-} \quad \left[:\ddot{C}=N=\ddot{S}:\right]^{-} \quad \left[:\ddot{C}=S=\ddot{N}:\right]^{-}$

Formal charge $\quad -1 \quad 0 \quad 0 \qquad -2 \quad +1 \quad 0 \qquad -2 \quad +2 \quad -1$

Note that the sum of the formal charges in each case is equal to the charge of the ion (–1). However, the first arrangement of atoms is preferred because it has the lowest number of atoms with nonzero formal charges (Guideline 2). Also, it places the least electronegative atom in the center, and the negative charge on the more electronegative element (Guideline 4).

Example 4.10

Using Formal Charge to Determine Molecular Structure

Nitrous oxide, N_2O, commonly known as laughing gas, is used as an anesthetic in minor surgeries, such as the routine extraction of wisdom teeth. Which is the likely structure for nitrous oxide?

$$\ddot{N}=N=\ddot{O} \quad \text{or} \quad \ddot{N}=O=\ddot{N}$$

Solution

Determining formal charge yields the following:

$$:\ddot{N}=N=\ddot{O}: \qquad :\ddot{N}=O=\ddot{N}:$$
$$\;\;-1 \quad +1 \quad 0 \qquad\;\; -1 \quad +2 \quad -1$$

The structure with a terminal oxygen atom best satisfies the criteria for the most stable distribution of formal charge:

$$:\ddot{N}=N=\ddot{O}:$$

The number of atoms with formal charges are minimized (Guideline 2), and there is no formal charge larger than one (Guideline 2). This is again consistent with the preference for having the less electronegative atom in the central position.

Check Your Learning

Which is the most likely molecular structure for the nitrite $(NO_2{}^{-})$ ion?

$$\left[:\ddot{N}=\ddot{O}-\ddot{O}:\right]^{-} \quad \text{or} \quad \left[:\ddot{O}=\ddot{N}-\ddot{O}:\right]^{-}$$

Answer: ONO^{-}

Resonance

You may have noticed that the nitrite anion in Example 4.10 can have two possible structures with the atoms in the same positions. The electrons involved in the N–O double bond, however, are in different positions:

$$\left[:\ddot{O}-\ddot{N}=\ddot{O}\right]^{-} \quad \left[\ddot{O}=\ddot{N}-\ddot{O}:\right]^{-}$$

If nitrite ions do indeed contain a single and a double bond, we would expect for the two bond lengths to be different. A double bond between two atoms is shorter (and stronger) than a single bond between the same two atoms. Experiments show, however, that both N–O bonds in $NO_2{}^{-}$ have the same strength and length, and are identical in all other properties.

It is not possible to write a single Lewis structure for $NO_2{}^{-}$ in which nitrogen has an octet and both bonds are equivalent. Instead, we use the concept of **resonance**: if two or more Lewis structures with the same arrangement of atoms can be written for a molecule or ion, the actual distribution of electrons is an *average* of that shown by the various Lewis structures. The actual distribution of electrons in each of the nitrogen-oxygen bonds in NO_2^- is the average of a double bond and a single bond. We call the individual Lewis structures **resonance forms**. The actual electronic structure of the molecule (the average of the resonance forms) is called a **resonance hybrid** of the individual resonance forms. A double-headed arrow between Lewis structures indicates that they are resonance forms. Thus, the electronic structure of the NO_2^- ion is shown as:

$$\left[\ddot{\underset{..}{O}} {-}\ddot{N}{-}\ddot{\underset{..}{O}} \right]^- \longleftrightarrow \left[\ddot{\underset{..}{O}} {-}\ddot{N}{-}\ddot{\underset{..}{O}} \right]^-$$

We should remember that a molecule described as a resonance hybrid *never* possesses an electronic structure described by either resonance form. It does not fluctuate between resonance forms; rather, the actual electronic structure is *always* the average of that shown by all resonance forms. George Wheland, one of the pioneers of resonance theory, used a historical analogy to describe the relationship between resonance forms and resonance hybrids. A medieval traveler, having never before seen a rhinoceros, described it as a hybrid of a dragon and a unicorn because it had many properties in common with both. Just as a rhinoceros is neither a dragon sometimes nor a unicorn at other times, a resonance hybrid is neither of its resonance forms at any given time. Like a rhinoceros, it is a real entity that experimental evidence has shown to exist. It has some characteristics in common with its resonance forms, but the resonance forms themselves are convenient, imaginary images (like the unicorn and the dragon).

The carbonate anion, CO_3^{2-}, provides a second example of resonance:

$$\left[\ddot{O} {\underset{\ddot{O}}{\overset{|}{C}}} {\ddot{O}} \right]^{2-} \longleftrightarrow \left[\ddot{O} {\underset{O}{\overset{|}{C}}} {\ddot{O}} \right]^{2-} \longleftrightarrow \left[\ddot{O} {\underset{\ddot{O}}{\overset{||}{C}}} {\ddot{O}} \right]^{2-}$$

One oxygen atom must have a double bond to carbon to complete the octet on the central atom. All oxygen atoms, however, are equivalent, and the double bond could form from any one of the three atoms. This gives rise to three resonance forms of the carbonate ion. Because we can write three identical resonance structures, we know that the actual arrangement of electrons in the carbonate ion is the average of the three structures. Again, experiments show that all three C–O bonds are exactly the same.

Link to Learning

The online Lewis Structure Make (http://openstaxcollege.org/l/16LewisMake) includes many examples to practice drawing resonance structures.

4.6 Molecular Structure and Polarity

By the end of this section, you will be able to:

- Predict the structures of small molecules using valence shell electron pair repulsion (VSEPR) theory
- Explain the concepts of polar covalent bonds and molecular polarity
- Assess the polarity of a molecule based on its bonding and structure

Thus far, we have used two-dimensional Lewis structures to represent molecules. However, molecular structure is actually three-dimensional, and it is important to be able to describe molecular bonds in terms of their distances, angles, and relative arrangements in space (Figure 4.14). A **bond angle** is the angle between any two bonds that include a common atom, usually measured in degrees. A **bond distance** (or bond length) is the distance between the nuclei of two bonded atoms along the straight line joining the nuclei. Bond distances are measured in Ångstroms (1 Å = 10^{-10} m) or picometers (1 pm = 10^{-12} m, 100 pm = 1 Å).

Figure 4.14 Bond distances (lengths) and angles are shown for the formaldehyde molecule, H_2CO.

VSEPR Theory

Valence shell electron-pair repulsion theory (VSEPR theory) enables us to predict the molecular structure, including approximate bond angles around a central atom, of a molecule from an examination of the number of bonds and lone electron pairs in its Lewis structure. The VSEPR model assumes that electron pairs in the valence shell of a central atom will adopt an arrangement that minimizes repulsions between these electron pairs by maximizing the distance between them. The electrons in the valence shell of a central atom form either bonding pairs of electrons, located primarily between bonded atoms, or lone pairs. The electrostatic repulsion of these electrons is reduced when the various regions of high electron density assume positions as far from each other as possible.

VSEPR theory predicts the arrangement of electron pairs around each central atom and, usually, the correct arrangement of atoms in a molecule. We should understand, however, that the theory only considers electron-pair repulsions. Other interactions, such as nuclear-nuclear repulsions and nuclear-electron attractions, are also involved in the final arrangement that atoms adopt in a particular molecular structure.

As a simple example of VSEPR theory, let us predict the structure of a gaseous BeF_2 molecule. The Lewis structure of BeF_2 (Figure 4.15) shows only two electron pairs around the central beryllium atom. With two bonds and no lone pairs of electrons on the central atom, the bonds are as far apart as possible, and the electrostatic repulsion between these regions of high electron density is reduced to a minimum when they are on opposite sides of the central atom. The bond angle is 180° (Figure 4.15).

180°

:F—Be—F:

Figure 4.15 The BeF_2 molecule adopts a linear structure in which the two bonds are as far apart as possible, on opposite sides of the Be atom.

Figure 4.16 illustrates this and other electron-pair geometries that minimize the repulsions among regions of high electron density (bonds and/or lone pairs). Two regions of electron density around a central atom in a molecule form a **linear** geometry; three regions form a **trigonal planar** geometry; four regions form a **tetrahedral** geometry; five regions form a **trigonal bipyramidal** geometry; and six regions form an **octahedral** geometry.

Number of regions	Two regions of high electron density (bonds and/or unshared pairs)	Three regions of high electron density (bonds and/or unshared pairs)	Four regions of high electron density (bonds and/or unshared pairs)	Five regions of high electron density (bonds and/or unshared pairs)	Six regions of high electron density (bonds and/or unshared pairs)
Spatial arrangement	180°	120°	109.5°	90° 120°	90° 90°
Line-dash-wedge notation	H—Be—H	H–B(–H)–H	H–C(–H)(–H)–H	F–P(F)(F)(F)–F	F–S(F)(F)(F)(F)–F
Electron pair geometry	Linear; 180° angle	Trigonal planar; all angles 120°	Tetrahedral; all angles 109.5°	Trigonal bipyramidal; angles of 90° or 120° An attached atom may be equatorial (in the plane of the triangle) or axial (above or below the plane of the triangle).	Octahedral; all angles 90° or 180°

Figure 4.16 The basic electron-pair geometries predicted by VSEPR theory maximize the space around any region of electron density (bonds or lone pairs).

Electron-pair Geometry versus Molecular Structure

It is important to note that electron-pair geometry around a central atom is *not* the same thing as its molecular structure. The electron-pair geometries shown in Figure 4.16 describe all regions where electrons are located, bonds as well as lone pairs. Molecular structure describes the location of the *atoms*, not the electrons.

We differentiate between these two situations by naming the geometry that includes *all* electron pairs the **electron-pair geometry**. The structure that includes only the placement of the atoms in the molecule is called the **molecular structure**. The electron-pair geometries will be the same as the molecular structures when there are no lone electron pairs around the central atom, but they will be different when there are lone pairs present on the central atom.

For example, the methane molecule, CH_4, which is the major component of natural gas, has four bonding pairs of electrons around the central carbon atom; the electron-pair geometry is tetrahedral, as is the molecular structure (Figure 4.17). On the other hand, the ammonia molecule, NH_3, also has four electron pairs associated with the nitrogen atom, and thus has a tetrahedral electron-pair geometry. One of these regions, however, is a lone pair, which is not included in the molecular structure, and this lone pair influences the shape of the molecule (Figure 4.18).

Figure 4.17 The molecular structure of the methane molecule, CH_4, is shown with a tetrahedral arrangement of the hydrogen atoms. VSEPR structures like this one are often drawn using the wedge and dash notation, in which solid lines represent bonds in the plane of the page, solid wedges represent bonds coming up out of the plane, and dashed lines represent bonds going down into the plane.

Figure 4.18 (a) The electron-pair geometry for the ammonia molecule is tetrahedral with one lone pair and three single bonds. (b) The trigonal pyramidal molecular structure is determined from the electron-pair geometry. (c) The actual bond angles deviate slightly from the idealized angles because the lone pair takes up a larger region of space than do the single bonds, causing the HNH angle to be slightly smaller than 109.5°.

As seen in **Figure 4.18**, small distortions from the ideal angles in **Figure 4.16** can result from differences in repulsion between various regions of electron density. VSEPR theory predicts these distortions by establishing an order of repulsions and an order of the amount of space occupied by different kinds of electron pairs. The order of electron-pair repulsions from greatest to least repulsion is:

$$\text{lone pair-lone pair} > \text{lone pair-bonding pair} > \text{bonding pair-bonding pair}$$

This order of repulsions determines the amount of space occupied by different regions of electrons. A lone pair of electrons occupies a larger region of space than the electrons in a triple bond; in turn, electrons in a triple bond occupy more space than those in a double bond, and so on. The order of sizes from largest to smallest is:

$$\text{lone pair} > \text{triple bond} > \text{double bond} > \text{single bond}$$

Consider formaldehyde, H_2CO, which is used as a preservative for biological and anatomical specimens (**Figure 4.14**). This molecule has regions of high electron density that consist of two single bonds and one double bond. The basic geometry is trigonal planar with 120° bond angles, but we see that the double bond causes slightly larger angles (121°), and the angle between the single bonds is slightly smaller (118°).

In the ammonia molecule, the three hydrogen atoms attached to the central nitrogen are not arranged in a flat, trigonal planar molecular structure, but rather in a three-dimensional trigonal pyramid (**Figure 4.18**) with the nitrogen atom at the apex and the three hydrogen atoms forming the base. The ideal bond angles in a trigonal pyramid are based on the tetrahedral electron pair geometry. Again, there are slight deviations from the ideal because lone pairs occupy larger regions of space than do bonding electrons. The H–N–H bond angles in NH_3 are slightly smaller than the 109.5° angle in a regular tetrahedron (**Figure 4.16**) because the lone pair-bonding pair repulsion is greater than the bonding pair-bonding pair repulsion (**Figure 4.18**). **Figure 4.19** illustrates the ideal molecular structures, which are predicted based on the electron-pair geometries for various combinations of lone pairs and bonding pairs.

Number of electron pairs	Electron pair geometries: 0 lone pair	1 lone pair	2 lone pairs	3 lone pairs	4 lone pairs
2	**180°** X—E—X **Linear**				
3	X E X **120°** **Trigonal planar**	X E X **<120°** **Bent or angular**			
4	X E X **109°** **Tetrahedral**	X E X **<109°** **Trigonal pyramid**	X E X **<<109°** **Bent or angular**		
5	X E X **90°** **120°** **Trigonal bipyramid**	**<90°** X **<120°** E **Sawhorse or seesaw**	X **<90°** E X **T-shape**	X **180°** E **Linear**	
6	X E X **90°** **Octahedral**	X **<90°** E X **Square pyramid**	X E X **90°** **Square planar**	X E X X **<90°** **T-shape**	X **180°** E X **Linear**

Figure 4.19 The molecular structures are identical to the electron-pair geometries when there are no lone pairs present (first column). For a particular number of electron pairs (row), the molecular structures for one or more lone pairs are determined based on modifications of the corresponding electron-pair geometry.

According to VSEPR theory, the terminal atom locations (Xs in Figure 4.19) are equivalent within the linear, trigonal planar, and tetrahedral electron-pair geometries (the first three rows of the table). It does not matter which X is replaced with a lone pair because the molecules can be rotated to convert positions. For trigonal bipyramidal electron-pair geometries, however, there are two distinct X positions, as shown in Figure 4.20: an **axial position** (if we hold a model of a trigonal bipyramid by the two axial positions, we have an axis around which we can rotate the model) and an **equatorial position** (three positions form an equator around the middle of the molecule). As shown in Figure 4.19, the axial position is surrounded by bond angles of 90°, whereas the equatorial position has more space available because of the 120° bond angles. In a trigonal bipyramidal electron-pair geometry, lone pairs always occupy equatorial positions because these more spacious positions can more easily accommodate the larger lone pairs.

Theoretically, we can come up with three possible arrangements for the three bonds and two lone pairs for the ClF_3 molecule (Figure 4.20). The stable structure is the one that puts the lone pairs in equatorial locations, giving a T-shaped molecular structure.

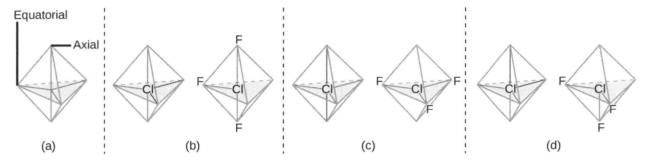

(a)   (b)   (c)   (d)

Figure 4.20 (a) In a trigonal bipyramid, the two axial positions are located directly across from one another, whereas the three equatorial positions are located in a triangular arrangement. (b–d) The two lone pairs (red lines) in ClF_3 have several possible arrangements, but the T-shaped molecular structure (b) is the one actually observed, consistent with the larger lone pairs both occupying equatorial positions.

When a central atom has two lone electron pairs and four bonding regions, we have an octahedral electron-pair geometry. The two lone pairs are on opposite sides of the octahedron (180° apart), giving a square planar molecular structure that minimizes lone pair-lone pair repulsions (**Figure 4.19**).

Predicting Electron Pair Geometry and Molecular Structure

The following procedure uses VSEPR theory to determine the electron pair geometries and the molecular structures:

1. Write the Lewis structure of the molecule or polyatomic ion.

2. Count the number of regions of electron density (lone pairs and bonds) around the central atom. A single, double, or triple bond counts as one region of electron density.

3. Identify the electron-pair geometry based on the number of regions of electron density: linear, trigonal planar, tetrahedral, trigonal bipyramidal, or octahedral (**Figure 4.19**, first column).

4. Use the number of lone pairs to determine the molecular structure (**Figure 4.19**). If more than one arrangement of lone pairs and chemical bonds is possible, choose the one that will minimize repulsions, remembering that lone pairs occupy more space than multiple bonds, which occupy more space than single bonds. In trigonal bipyramidal arrangements, repulsion is minimized when every lone pair is in an equatorial position. In an octahedral arrangement with two lone pairs, repulsion is minimized when the lone pairs are on opposite sides of the central atom.

The following examples illustrate the use of VSEPR theory to predict the molecular structure of molecules or ions that have no lone pairs of electrons. In this case, the molecular structure is identical to the electron pair geometry.

Example 4.11

Predicting Electron-pair Geometry and Molecular Structure: CO_2 and BCl_3

Predict the electron-pair geometry and molecular structure for each of the following:

(a) carbon dioxide, CO_2, a molecule produced by the combustion of fossil fuels

(b) boron trichloride, BCl_3, an important industrial chemical

Solution

(a) We write the Lewis structure of CO_2 as:

$$\ddot{O}=C=\ddot{O}$$

This shows us two regions of high electron density around the carbon atom—each double bond counts as one region, and there are no lone pairs on the carbon atom. Using VSEPR theory, we predict that the two regions of electron density arrange themselves on opposite sides of the central atom with a bond angle of 180°. The electron-pair geometry and molecular structure are identical, and CO_2 molecules are linear.

(b) We write the Lewis structure of BCl_3 as:

$$:\ddot{C}l:$$
$$|$$
$$:\ddot{C}l-B-\ddot{C}l:$$

Thus we see that BCl_3 contains three bonds, and there are no lone pairs of electrons on boron. The arrangement of three regions of high electron density gives a trigonal planar electron-pair geometry. The B–Cl bonds lie in a plane with 120° angles between them. BCl_3 also has a trigonal planar molecular structure (Figure 4.21).

Figure 4.21

The electron-pair geometry and molecular structure of BCl_3 are both trigonal planar. Note that the VSEPR geometry indicates the correct bond angles (120°), unlike the Lewis structure shown above.

Check Your Learning

Carbonate, $CO_3{}^{2-}$, is a common polyatomic ion found in various materials from eggshells to antacids. What are the electron-pair geometry and molecular structure of this polyatomic ion?

Answer: The electron-pair geometry is trigonal planar and the molecular structure is trigonal planar. Due to resonance, all three C–O bonds are identical. Whether they are single, double, or an average of the two, each bond counts as one region of electron density.

Example 4.12

Predicting Electron-pair Geometry and Molecular Structure: Ammonium

Two of the top 50 chemicals produced in the United States, ammonium nitrate and ammonium sulfate, both used as fertilizers, contain the ammonium ion. Predict the electron-pair geometry and molecular structure of the $NH_4{}^+$ cation.

Solution

We write the Lewis structure of $NH_4{}^+$ as:

$$\left[\begin{array}{c} H \\ | \\ H-N-H \\ | \\ H \end{array}\right]^+$$

We can see that $NH_4{}^+$ contains four bonds from the nitrogen atom to hydrogen atoms and no lone pairs.

We expect the four regions of high electron density to arrange themselves so that they point to the corners of a tetrahedron with the central nitrogen atom in the middle (Figure 4.19). Therefore, the electron pair geometry of NH_4^+ is tetrahedral, and the molecular structure is also tetrahedral (Figure 4.22).

$$\left[\begin{array}{c} H \\ | \\ H \overset{\displaystyle N}{\diagup} \!\!\!\!\!\! \diagdown H \\ | \\ H \end{array} \right]^+$$

Figure 4.22 The ammonium ion displays a tetrahedral electron-pair geometry as well as a tetrahedral molecular structure.

Check Your Learning

Identify a molecule with trigonal bipyramidal molecular structure.

Answer: Any molecule with five electron pairs around the central atoms including no lone pairs will be trigonal bipyramidal. PF_5 is a common example.

The next several examples illustrate the effect of lone pairs of electrons on molecular structure.

Example 4.13

Predicting Electron-pair Geometry and Molecular Structure: Lone Pairs on the Central Atom

Predict the electron-pair geometry and molecular structure of a water molecule.

Solution

The Lewis structure of H_2O indicates that there are four regions of high electron density around the oxygen atom: two lone pairs and two chemical bonds:

$$\begin{array}{c} H \\ | \\ H - \underset{\displaystyle \cdot\cdot}{O} \!\!: \end{array}$$

We predict that these four regions are arranged in a tetrahedral fashion (Figure 4.23), as indicated in Figure 4.19. Thus, the electron-pair geometry is tetrahedral and the molecular structure is bent with an angle slightly less than 109.5°. In fact, the bond angle is 104.5°.

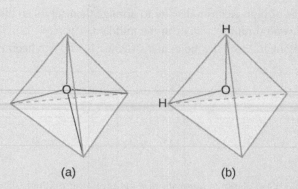

Figure 4.23 (a) H_2O has four regions of electron density around the central atom, so it has a tetrahedral electron-pair geometry. (b) Two of the electron regions are lone pairs, so the molecular structure is bent.

Check Your Learning

The hydronium ion, H_3O^+, forms when acids are dissolved in water. Predict the electron-pair geometry and molecular structure of this cation.

Answer: electron pair geometry: tetrahedral; molecular structure: trigonal pyramidal

Example 4.14

Predicting Electron-pair Geometry and Molecular Structure: SF$_4$

Sulfur tetrafluoride, SF_4, is extremely valuable for the preparation of fluorine-containing compounds used as herbicides (i.e., SF_4 is used as a fluorinating agent). Predict the electron-pair geometry and molecular structure of a SF_4 molecule.

Solution

The Lewis structure of SF_4 indicates five regions of electron density around the sulfur atom: one lone pair and four bonding pairs:

We expect these five regions to adopt a trigonal bipyramidal electron-pair geometry. To minimize lone pair repulsions, the lone pair occupies one of the equatorial positions. The molecular structure (Figure 4.24) is that of a seesaw (Figure 4.19).

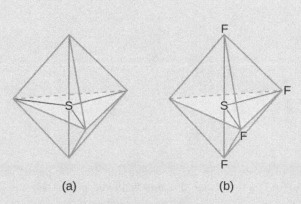

(a)   (b)

Figure 4.24   (a) SF4 has a trigonal bipyramidal arrangement of the five regions of electron density. (b) One of the regions is a lone pair, which results in a seesaw-shaped molecular structure.

Check Your Learning

Predict the electron pair geometry and molecular structure for molecules of XeF_2.

Answer: The electron-pair geometry is trigonal bipyramidal. The molecular structure is linear.

Example 4.15

Predicting Electron-pair Geometry and Molecular Structure: XeF_4

Of all the noble gases, xenon is the most reactive, frequently reacting with elements such as oxygen and fluorine. Predict the electron-pair geometry and molecular structure of the XeF_4 molecule.

Solution

The Lewis structure of XeF_4 indicates six regions of high electron density around the xenon atom: two lone pairs and four bonds:

$$:\!F\!-\!Xe\!-\!F\!:$$

These six regions adopt an octahedral arrangement (Figure 4.19), which is the electron-pair geometry. To minimize repulsions, the lone pairs should be on opposite sides of the central atom (Figure 4.25). The five atoms are all in the same plane and have a square planar molecular structure.

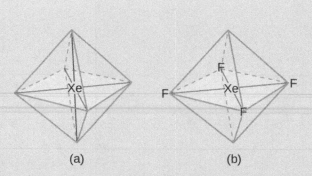

Figure 4.25 (a) XeF_4 adopts an octahedral arrangement with two lone pairs (red lines) and four bonds in the electron-pair geometry. (b) The molecular structure is square planar with the lone pairs directly across from one another.

Check Your Learning

In a certain molecule, the central atom has three lone pairs and two bonds. What will the electron pair geometry and molecular structure be?

Answer: electron pair geometry: trigonal bipyramidal; molecular structure: linear

Molecular Structure for Multicenter Molecules

When a molecule or polyatomic ion has only one central atom, the molecular structure completely describes the shape of the molecule. Larger molecules do not have a single central atom, but are connected by a chain of interior atoms that each possess a "local" geometry. The way these local structures are oriented with respect to each other also influences the molecular shape, but such considerations are largely beyond the scope of this introductory discussion. For our purposes, we will only focus on determining the local structures.

Example 4.16

Predicting Structure in Multicenter Molecules

The Lewis structure for the simplest amino acid, glycine, $H_2NCH_2CO_2H$, is shown here. Predict the local geometry for the nitrogen atom, the two carbon atoms, and the oxygen atom with a hydrogen atom attached:

Solution

Consider each central atom independently. The electron-pair geometries:

- nitrogen—four regions of electron density; tetrahedral
- carbon (CH_2)—four regions of electron density; tetrahedral
- carbon (CO_2)—three regions of electron density; trigonal planar

- oxygen ($\underline{O}$H)—four regions of electron density; tetrahedral

The local structures:

- nitrogen—three bonds, one lone pair; trigonal pyramidal
- carbon ($\underline{C}$H$_2$)—four bonds, no lone pairs; tetrahedral
- carbon ($\underline{C}$O$_2$)—three bonds (double bond counts as one bond), no lone pairs; trigonal planar
- oxygen ($\underline{O}$H)—two bonds, two lone pairs; bent (109°)

Check Your Learning

Another amino acid is alanine, which has the Lewis structure shown here. Predict the electron-pair geometry and local structure of the nitrogen atom, the three carbon atoms, and the oxygen atom with hydrogen attached:

Answer: electron-pair geometries: nitrogen—tetrahedral; carbon ($\underline{C}$H)—tetrahedral; carbon ($\underline{C}$H$_3$)—tetrahedral; carbon ($\underline{C}$O$_2$)—trigonal planar; oxygen ($\underline{O}$H)—tetrahedral; local structures: nitrogen—trigonal pyramidal; carbon ($\underline{C}$H)—tetrahedral; carbon ($\underline{C}$H$_3$)—tetrahedral; carbon ($\underline{C}$O$_2$)—trigonal planar; oxygen ($\underline{O}$H)—bent (109°)

Link to Learning

The molecular shape simulator (http://openstaxcollege.org/l/16MolecShape) lets you build various molecules and practice naming their electron-pair geometries and molecular structures.

Example 4.17

Molecular Simulation

Using molecular shape simulator (http://openstaxcollege.org/l/16MolecShape) allows us to control whether bond angles and/or lone pairs are displayed by checking or unchecking the boxes under "Options" on the right. We can also use the "Name" checkboxes at bottom-left to display or hide the electron pair geometry (called "electron geometry" in the simulator) and/or molecular structure (called "molecular shape" in the simulator).

Build the molecule HCN in the simulator based on the following Lewis structure:

$$H–C \equiv N$$

Click on each bond type or lone pair at right to add that group to the central atom. Once you have the complete molecule, rotate it to examine the predicted molecular structure. What molecular structure is this?

Solution

The molecular structure is linear.

Molecular Polarity and Dipole Moment

As discussed previously, polar covalent bonds connect two atoms with differing electronegativities, leaving one atom with a partial positive charge (δ+) and the other atom with a partial negative charge (δ−), as the electrons are pulled toward the more electronegative atom. This separation of charge gives rise to a **bond dipole moment**. The magnitude of a bond dipole moment is represented by the Greek letter mu (μ) and is given by the formula shown here, where Q is the magnitude of the partial charges (determined by the electronegativity difference) and r is the distance between the charges:

$$\mu = Qr$$

This bond moment can be represented as a **vector**, a quantity having both direction and magnitude (**Figure 4.26**). Dipole vectors are shown as arrows pointing along the bond from the less electronegative atom toward the more electronegative atom. A small plus sign is drawn on the less electronegative end to indicate the partially positive end of the bond. The length of the arrow is proportional to the magnitude of the electronegativity difference between the two atoms.

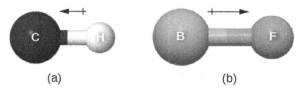

(a)   (b)

Figure 4.26   (a) There is a small difference in electronegativity between C and H, represented as a short vector. (b) The electronegativity difference between B and F is much larger, so the vector representing the bond moment is much longer.

A whole molecule may also have a separation of charge, depending on its molecular structure and the polarity of each of its bonds. If such a charge separation exists, the molecule is said to be a **polar molecule** (or dipole); otherwise the molecule is said to be nonpolar. The **dipole moment** measures the extent of net charge separation in the molecule as a whole. We determine the dipole moment by adding the bond moments in three-dimensional space, taking into account the molecular structure.

For diatomic molecules, there is only one bond, so its bond dipole moment determines the molecular polarity. Homonuclear diatomic molecules such as Br_2 and N_2 have no difference in electronegativity, so their dipole moment is zero. For heteronuclear molecules such as CO, there is a small dipole moment. For HF, there is a larger dipole moment because there is a larger difference in electronegativity.

When a molecule contains more than one bond, the geometry must be taken into account. If the bonds in a molecule are arranged such that their bond moments cancel (vector sum equals zero), then the molecule is nonpolar. This is the situation in CO_2 (**Figure 4.27**). Each of the bonds is polar, but the molecule as a whole is nonpolar. From the Lewis structure, and using VSEPR theory, we determine that the CO_2 molecule is linear with polar C=O bonds on opposite sides of the carbon atom. The bond moments cancel because they are pointed in opposite directions. In the case of the water molecule (**Figure 4.27**), the Lewis structure again shows that there are two bonds to a central atom, and the electronegativity difference again shows that each of these bonds has a nonzero bond moment. In this case, however, the molecular structure is bent because of the lone pairs on O, and the two bond moments do not cancel. Therefore, water does have a net dipole moment and is a polar molecule (dipole).

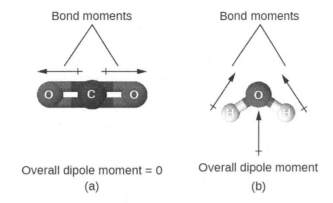

Figure 4.27 The overall dipole moment of a molecule depends on the individual bond dipole moments and how they are arranged. (a) Each CO bond has a bond dipole moment, but they point in opposite directions so that the net CO_2 molecule is nonpolar. (b) In contrast, water is polar because the OH bond moments do not cancel out.

The OCS molecule has a structure similar to CO_2, but a sulfur atom has replaced one of the oxygen atoms. To determine if this molecule is polar, we draw the molecular structure. VSEPR theory predicts a linear molecule:

The C-O bond is considerably polar. Although C and S have very similar electronegativity values, S is slightly more electronegative than C, and so the C-S bond is just slightly polar. Because oxygen is more electronegative than sulfur, the oxygen end of the molecule is the negative end.

Chloromethane, CH_3Cl, is another example of a polar molecule. Although the polar C–Cl and C–H bonds are arranged in a tetrahedral geometry, the C–Cl bonds have a larger bond moment than the C–H bond, and the bond moments do not completely cancel each other. All of the dipoles have an upward component in the orientation shown, since carbon is more electronegative than hydrogen and less electronegative than chlorine:

When we examine the highly symmetrical molecules BF_3 (trigonal planar), CH_4 (tetrahedral), PF_5 (trigonal bipyramidal), and SF_6 (octahedral), in which all the polar bonds are identical, the molecules are nonpolar. The bonds in these molecules are arranged such that their dipoles cancel. However, just because a molecule contains identical bonds does not mean that the dipoles will always cancel. Many molecules that have identical bonds and lone pairs on the central atoms have bond dipoles that do not cancel. Examples include H_2S and NH_3. A hydrogen atom is at the positive end and a nitrogen or sulfur atom is at the negative end of the polar bonds in these molecules:

To summarize, to be polar, a molecule must:

1. Contain at least one polar covalent bond.

2. Have a molecular structure such that the sum of the vectors of each bond dipole moment does not cancel.

Properties of Polar Molecules

Polar molecules tend to align when placed in an electric field with the positive end of the molecule oriented toward the negative plate and the negative end toward the positive plate (Figure 4.28). We can use an electrically charged object to attract polar molecules, but nonpolar molecules are not attracted. Also, polar solvents are better at dissolving polar substances, and nonpolar solvents are better at dissolving nonpolar substances.

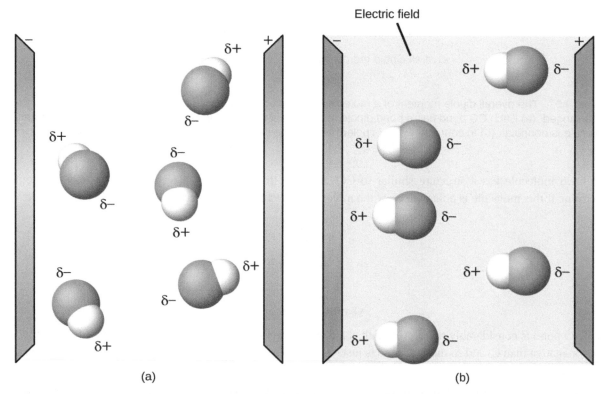

(a)   (b)

Figure 4.28   (a) Molecules are always randomly distributed in the liquid state in the absence of an electric field. (b) When an electric field is applied, polar molecules like HF will align to the dipoles with the field direction.

Link to Learning

The molecule polarity simulation (http://openstaxcollege.org/l/16MolecPolarity) provides many ways to explore dipole moments of bonds and molecules.

Example 4.18

Polarity Simulations

Open the molecule polarity simulation (http://openstaxcollege.org/l/16MolecPolarity) and select the "Three Atoms" tab at the top. This should display a molecule ABC with three electronegativity adjustors. You can display or hide the bond moments, molecular dipoles, and partial charges at the right. Turning on the Electric Field will show whether the molecule moves when exposed to a field, similar to Figure 4.28.

Use the electronegativity controls to determine how the molecular dipole will look for the starting bent molecule if:

(a) A and C are very electronegative and B is in the middle of the range.

(b) A is very electronegative, and B and C are not.

Solution

(a) Molecular dipole moment points immediately between A and C.

(b) Molecular dipole moment points along the A–B bond, toward A.

Check Your Learning

Determine the partial charges that will give the largest possible bond dipoles.

Answer: The largest bond moments will occur with the largest partial charges. The two solutions above represent how unevenly the electrons are shared in the bond. The bond moments will be maximized when the electronegativity difference is greatest. The controls for A and C should be set to one extreme, and B should be set to the opposite extreme. Although the magnitude of the bond moment will not change based on whether B is the most electronegative or the least, the direction of the bond moment will.

Key Terms

axial position location in a trigonal bipyramidal geometry in which there is another atom at a 180° angle and the equatorial positions are at a 90° angle

binary acid compound that contains hydrogen and one other element, bonded in a way that imparts acidic properties to the compound (ability to release H^+ ions when dissolved in water)

binary compound compound containing two different elements.

bond angle angle between any two covalent bonds that share a common atom

bond dipole moment separation of charge in a bond that depends on the difference in electronegativity and the bond distance represented by partial charges or a vector

bond distance (also, bond length) distance between the nuclei of two bonded atoms

bond length distance between the nuclei of two bonded atoms at which the lowest potential energy is achieved

covalent bond bond formed when electrons are shared between atoms

dipole moment property of a molecule that describes the separation of charge determined by the sum of the individual bond moments based on the molecular structure

double bond covalent bond in which two pairs of electrons are shared between two atoms

electron-pair geometry arrangement around a central atom of all regions of electron density (bonds, lone pairs, or unpaired electrons)

electronegativity tendency of an atom to attract electrons in a bond to itself

equatorial position one of the three positions in a trigonal bipyramidal geometry with 120° angles between them; the axial positions are located at a 90° angle

formal charge charge that would result on an atom by taking the number of valence electrons on the neutral atom and subtracting the nonbonding electrons and the number of bonds (one-half of the bonding electrons)

free radical molecule that contains an odd number of electrons

hypervalent molecule molecule containing at least one main group element that has more than eight electrons in its valence shell

inert pair effect tendency of heavy atoms to form ions in which their valence *s* electrons are not lost

ionic bond strong electrostatic force of attraction between cations and anions in an ionic compound

Lewis structure diagram showing lone pairs and bonding pairs of electrons in a molecule or an ion

Lewis symbol symbol for an element or monatomic ion that uses a dot to represent each valence electron in the element or ion

linear shape in which two outside groups are placed on opposite sides of a central atom

lone pair two (a pair of) valence electrons that are not used to form a covalent bond

molecular structure arrangement of atoms in a molecule or ion

molecular structure structure that includes only the placement of the atoms in the molecule

nomenclature system of rules for naming objects of interest

octahedral shape in which six outside groups are placed around a central atom such that a three-dimensional shape is generated with four groups forming a square and the other two forming the apex of two pyramids, one above and one below the square plane

octet rule guideline that states main group atoms will form structures in which eight valence electrons interact with each nucleus, counting bonding electrons as interacting with both atoms connected by the bond

oxyacid compound that contains hydrogen, oxygen, and one other element, bonded in a way that imparts acidic properties to the compound (ability to release H^+ ions when dissolved in water)

polar covalent bond covalent bond between atoms of different electronegativities; a covalent bond with a positive end and a negative end

polar molecule (also, dipole) molecule with an overall dipole moment

pure covalent bond (also, nonpolar covalent bond) covalent bond between atoms of identical electronegativities

resonance situation in which one Lewis structure is insufficient to describe the bonding in a molecule and the average of multiple structures is observed

resonance forms two or more Lewis structures that have the same arrangement of atoms but different arrangements of electrons

resonance hybrid average of the resonance forms shown by the individual Lewis structures

single bond bond in which a single pair of electrons is shared between two atoms

tetrahedral shape in which four outside groups are placed around a central atom such that a three-dimensional shape is generated with four corners and 109.5° angles between each pair and the central atom

trigonal bipyramidal shape in which five outside groups are placed around a central atom such that three form a flat triangle with 120° angles between each pair and the central atom, and the other two form the apex of two pyramids, one above and one below the triangular plane

trigonal planar shape in which three outside groups are placed in a flat triangle around a central atom with 120° angles between each pair and the central atom

triple bond bond in which three pairs of electrons are shared between two atoms

valence shell electron-pair repulsion theory (VSEPR) theory used to predict the bond angles in a molecule based on positioning regions of high electron density as far apart as possible to minimize electrostatic repulsion

vector quantity having magnitude and direction

Key Equations

- formal charge $= $ # valence shell electrons (free atom) $-$ # one pair electrons $- \frac{1}{2}$ # bonding electrons

Summary

4.1 Ionic Bonding

Atoms gain or lose electrons to form ions with particularly stable electron configurations. The charges of cations formed by the representative metals may be determined readily because, with few exceptions, the electronic structures of these ions have either a noble gas configuration or a completely filled electron shell. The charges of anions formed by the nonmetals may also be readily determined because these ions form when nonmetal atoms gain enough electrons to fill their valence shells.

4.2 Covalent Bonding

Covalent bonds form when electrons are shared between atoms and are attracted by the nuclei of both atoms. In pure covalent bonds, the electrons are shared equally. In polar covalent bonds, the electrons are shared unequally, as one atom exerts a stronger force of attraction on the electrons than the other. The ability of an atom to attract a pair of electrons in a chemical bond is called its electronegativity. The difference in electronegativity between two atoms determines how polar a bond will be. In a diatomic molecule with two identical atoms, there is no difference in electronegativity, so the bond is nonpolar or pure covalent. When the electronegativity difference is very large, as is the case between metals and nonmetals, the bonding is characterized as ionic.

4.3 Chemical Nomenclature

Chemists use nomenclature rules to clearly name compounds. Ionic and molecular compounds are named using somewhat-different methods. Binary ionic compounds typically consist of a metal and a nonmetal. The name of the metal is written first, followed by the name of the nonmetal with its ending changed to –ide. For example, K_2O is called potassium oxide. If the metal can form ions with different charges, a Roman numeral in parentheses follows the name of the metal to specify its charge. Thus, $FeCl_2$ is iron(II) chloride and $FeCl_3$ is iron(III) chloride. Some compounds contain polyatomic ions; the names of common polyatomic ions should be memorized. Molecular compounds can form compounds with different ratios of their elements, so prefixes are used to specify the numbers of atoms of each element in a molecule of the compound. Examples include SF_6, sulfur hexafluoride, and N_2O_4, dinitrogen tetroxide. Acids are an important class of compounds containing hydrogen and having special nomenclature rules. Binary acids are named using the prefix hydro-, changing the –ide suffix to –ic, and adding "acid;" HCl is hydrochloric acid. Oxyacids are named by changing the ending of the anion to –ic, and adding "acid;" H_2CO_3 is carbonic acid.

4.4 Lewis Symbols and Structures

Valence electronic structures can be visualized by drawing Lewis symbols (for atoms and monatomic ions) and Lewis structures (for molecules and polyatomic ions). Lone pairs, unpaired electrons, and single, double, or triple bonds are used to indicate where the valence electrons are located around each atom in a Lewis structure. Most structures—especially those containing second row elements—obey the octet rule, in which every atom (except H) is surrounded by eight electrons. Exceptions to the octet rule occur for odd-electron molecules (free radicals), electron-deficient molecules, and hypervalent molecules.

4.5 Formal Charges and Resonance

In a Lewis structure, formal charges can be assigned to each atom by treating each bond as if one-half of the electrons are assigned to each atom. These hypothetical formal charges are a guide to determining the most appropriate Lewis structure. A structure in which the formal charges are as close to zero as possible is preferred. Resonance occurs in cases where two or more Lewis structures with identical arrangements of atoms but different distributions of electrons can be written. The actual distribution of electrons (the resonance hybrid) is an average of the distribution indicated by the individual Lewis structures (the resonance forms).

4.6 Molecular Structure and Polarity

VSEPR theory predicts the three-dimensional arrangement of atoms in a molecule. It states that valence electrons will assume an electron-pair geometry that minimizes repulsions between areas of high electron density (bonds and/or lone pairs). Molecular structure, which refers only to the placement of atoms in a molecule and not the electrons, is equivalent to electron-pair geometry only when there are no lone electron pairs around the central atom. A dipole moment measures a separation of charge. For one bond, the bond dipole moment is determined by the difference in electronegativity between the two atoms. For a molecule, the overall dipole moment is determined by both the individual bond moments and how these dipoles are arranged in the molecular structure. Polar molecules (those with an appreciable dipole moment) interact with electric fields, whereas nonpolar molecules do not.

Exercises

4.1 Ionic Bonding

1. Does a cation gain protons to form a positive charge or does it lose electrons?

2. Iron(III) sulfate [$Fe_2(SO_4)_3$] is composed of Fe^{3+} and $SO_4{}^{2-}$ ions. Explain why a sample of iron(III) sulfate is uncharged.

3. Which of the following atoms would be expected to form negative ions in binary ionic compounds and which would be expected to form positive ions: P, I, Mg, Cl, In, Cs, O, Pb, Co?

4. Which of the following atoms would be expected to form negative ions in binary ionic compounds and which would be expected to form positive ions: Br, Ca, Na, N, F, Al, Sn, S, Cd?

5. Predict the charge on the monatomic ions formed from the following atoms in binary ionic compounds:

(a) P

(b) Mg

(c) Al

(d) O

(e) Cl

(f) Cs

6. Predict the charge on the monatomic ions formed from the following atoms in binary ionic compounds:

(a) I

(b) Sr

(c) K

(d) N

(e) S

(f) In

7. Write the electron configuration for each of the following ions:

(a) As^{3-}

(b) I^-

(c) Be^{2+}

(d) Cd^{2+}

(e) O^{2-}

(f) Ga^{3+}

(g) Li^+

(h) N^{3-}

(i) Sn^{2+}

(j) Co^{2+}

(k) Fe^{2+}

(l) As^{3+}

8. Write the electron configuration for the monatomic ions formed from the following elements (which form the greatest concentration of monatomic ions in seawater):

(a) Cl

(b) Na

(c) Mg

(d) Ca

(e) K

(f) Br

(g) Sr

(h) F

9. Write out the full electron configuration for each of the following atoms and for the monatomic ion found in binary ionic compounds containing the element:

(a) Al

(b) Br

(c) Sr

(d) Li

(e) As

(f) S

10. From the labels of several commercial products, prepare a list of six ionic compounds in the products. For each compound, write the formula. (You may need to look up some formulas in a suitable reference.)

4.2 Covalent Bonding

11. Why is it incorrect to speak of a molecule of solid NaCl?

12. What information can you use to predict whether a bond between two atoms is covalent or ionic?

13. Predict which of the following compounds are ionic and which are covalent, based on the location of their constituent atoms in the periodic table:

(a) Cl_2CO

(b) MnO

(c) NCl_3

(d) $CoBr_2$

(e) K_2S

(f) CO

(g) CaF_2

(h) HI

(i) CaO

(j) IBr

(k) CO_2

14. Explain the difference between a nonpolar covalent bond, a polar covalent bond, and an ionic bond.

15. From its position in the periodic table, determine which atom in each pair is more electronegative:

(a) Br or Cl

(b) N or O

(c) S or O

(d) P or S

(e) Si or N

(f) Ba or P

(g) N or K

16. From its position in the periodic table, determine which atom in each pair is more electronegative:

(a) N or P

(b) N or Ge

(c) S or F

(d) Cl or S

(e) H or C

(f) Se or P

(g) C or Si

17. From their positions in the periodic table, arrange the atoms in each of the following series in order of increasing electronegativity:

(a) C, F, H, N, O

(b) Br, Cl, F, H, I

(c) F, H, O, P, S

(d) Al, H, Na, O, P

(e) Ba, H, N, O, As

18. From their positions in the periodic table, arrange the atoms in each of the following series in order of increasing electronegativity:

(a) As, H, N, P, Sb

(b) Cl, H, P, S, Si

(c) Br, Cl, Ge, H, Sr

(d) Ca, H, K, N, Si

(e) Cl, Cs, Ge, H, Sr

19. Which atoms can bond to sulfur so as to produce a positive partial charge on the sulfur atom?

20. Which is the most polar bond?

(a) C–C

(b) C–H

(c) N–H

(d) O–H

(e) Se–H

21. Identify the more polar bond in each of the following pairs of bonds:

(a) HF or HCl

(b) NO or CO

(c) SH or OH

(d) PCl or SCl

(e) CH or NH

(f) SO or PO

(g) CN or NN

22. Which of the following molecules or ions contain polar bonds?

(a) O_3

(b) S_8

(c) O_2^{2-}

(d) NO_3^-

(e) CO_2

(f) H_2S

(g) BH_4^-

4.3 Chemical Nomenclature

23. Name the following compounds:

(a) CsCl

(b) BaO

(c) K_2S

(d) $BeCl_2$

(e) HBr

(f) AlF_3

24. Name the following compounds:

(a) NaF

(b) Rb_2O

(c) BCl_3

(d) H_2Se

(e) P_4O_6

(f) ICl_3

25. Write the formulas of the following compounds:

(a) rubidium bromide

(b) magnesium selenide

(c) sodium oxide

(d) calcium chloride

(e) hydrogen fluoride

(f) gallium phosphide

(g) aluminum bromide

(h) ammonium sulfate

26. Write the formulas of the following compounds:

(a) lithium carbonate

(b) sodium perchlorate

(c) barium hydroxide

(d) ammonium carbonate

(e) sulfuric acid

(f) calcium acetate

(g) magnesium phosphate

(h) sodium sulfite

27. Write the formulas of the following compounds:

(a) chlorine dioxide

(b) dinitrogen tetraoxide

(c) potassium phosphide

(d) silver(I) sulfide

(e) aluminum nitride

(f) silicon dioxide

28. Write the formulas of the following compounds:

(a) barium chloride

(b) magnesium nitride

(c) sulfur dioxide

(d) nitrogen trichloride

(e) dinitrogen trioxide

(f) tin(IV) chloride

29. Each of the following compounds contains a metal that can exhibit more than one ionic charge. Name these compounds:

(a) Cr_2O_3

(b) $FeCl_2$

(c) CrO_3

(d) $TiCl_4$

(e) CoO

(f) MoS_2

30. Each of the following compounds contains a metal that can exhibit more than one ionic charge. Name these compounds:

(a) $NiCO_3$

(b) MoO_3

(c) $Co(NO_3)_2$

(d) V_2O_5

(e) MnO_2

(f) Fe_2O_3

31. The following ionic compounds are found in common household products. Write the formulas for each compound:

(a) potassium phosphate

(b) copper(II) sulfate

(c) calcium chloride

(d) titanium dioxide

(e) ammonium nitrate

(f) sodium bisulfate (the common name for sodium hydrogen sulfate)

32. The following ionic compounds are found in common household products. Name each of the compounds:

(a) $Ca(H_2PO_4)_2$

(b) $FeSO_4$

(c) $CaCO_3$

(d) MgO

(e) $NaNO_2$

(f) KI

33. What are the IUPAC names of the following compounds?

(a) manganese dioxide

(b) mercurous chloride (Hg_2Cl_2)

(c) ferric nitrate [$Fe(NO_3)_3$]

(d) titanium tetrachloride

(e) cupric bromide ($CuBr_2$)

4.4 Lewis Symbols and Structures

34. Write the Lewis symbols for each of the following ions:

(a) As^{3-}

(b) I^-

(c) Be^{2+}

(d) O^{2-}

(e) Ga^{3+}

(f) Li^+

(g) N^{3-}

35. Many monatomic ions are found in seawater, including the ions formed from the following list of elements. Write the Lewis symbols for the monatomic ions formed from the following elements:

(a) Cl

(b) Na

(c) Mg

(d) Ca

(e) K

(f) Br

(g) Sr

(h) F

36. Write the Lewis symbols of the ions in each of the following ionic compounds and the Lewis symbols of the atom from which they are formed:

(a) MgS

(b) Al_2O_3

(c) $GaCl_3$

(d) K_2O

(e) Li_3N

(f) KF

37. In the Lewis structures listed here, M and X represent various elements in the third period of the periodic table. Write the formula of each compound using the chemical symbols of each element:

(a)

$$\left[M^{2+}\right]\left[:\!\overset{\cdot\cdot}{\underset{\cdot\cdot}{X}}\!:\right]^{2-}$$

(b)

$$\left[M^{3+}\right]\left[:\!\overset{\cdot\cdot}{\underset{\cdot\cdot}{X}}\!:\right]^{-}_{3}$$

(c)

$$\left[M^{+}\right]_{2}\left[:\!\overset{\cdot\cdot}{\underset{\cdot\cdot}{X}}\!:\right]^{2-}$$

(d)

$$\left[M^{3+}\right]_{2}\left[:\!\overset{\cdot\cdot}{\underset{\cdot\cdot}{X}}\!:\right]^{2-}_{3}$$

38. Write the Lewis structure for the diatomic molecule P_2, an unstable form of phosphorus found in high-temperature phosphorus vapor.

39. Write Lewis structures for the following:

(a) H_2

(b) HBr

(c) PCl_3

(d) SF_2

(e) H_2CCH_2

(f) HNNH

(g) H_2CNH

(h) NO^-

(i) N_2

(j) CO

(k) CN^-

40. Write Lewis structures for the following:

(a) O_2

(b) H_2CO

(c) AsF_3

(d) ClNO

(e) $SiCl_4$

(f) H_3O^+

(g) $NH_4{}^+$

(h) $BF_4{}^-$

(i) HCCH

(j) ClCN

(k) $C_2{}^{2+}$

41. Write Lewis structures for the following:

(a) ClF_3

(b) PCl_5

(c) BF_3

(d) $PF_6{}^-$

42. Write Lewis structures for the following:

(a) SeF_6

(b) XeF_4

(c) $SeCl_3{}^+$

(d) Cl_2BBCl_2 (contains a B–B bond)

43. Write Lewis structures for:

(a) $PO_4{}^{3-}$

(b) $ICl_4{}^-$

(c) $SO_3{}^{2-}$

(d) HONO

44. Correct the following statement: "The bonds in solid $PbCl_2$ are ionic; the bond in a HCl molecule is covalent. Thus, all of the valence electrons in $PbCl_2$ are located on the Cl^- ions, and all of the valence electrons in a HCl molecule are shared between the H and Cl atoms."

45. Write Lewis structures for the following molecules or ions:

(a) SbH_3

(b) XeF_2

(c) Se_8 (a cyclic molecule with a ring of eight Se atoms)

46. Methanol, H_3COH, is used as the fuel in some race cars. Ethanol, C_2H_5OH, is used extensively as motor fuel in Brazil. Both methanol and ethanol produce CO_2 and H_2O when they burn. Write the chemical equations for these combustion reactions using Lewis structures instead of chemical formulas.

47. Many planets in our solar system contain organic chemicals including methane (CH_4) and traces of ethylene (C_2H_4), ethane (C_2H_6), propyne (H_3CCCH), and diacetylene (HCCCCH). Write the Lewis structures for each of these molecules.

48. Carbon tetrachloride was formerly used in fire extinguishers for electrical fires. It is no longer used for this purpose because of the formation of the toxic gas phosgene, Cl_2CO. Write the Lewis structures for carbon tetrachloride and phosgene.

49. Identify the atoms that correspond to each of the following electron configurations. Then, write the Lewis symbol for the common ion formed from each atom:

(a) $1s^2 2s^2 2p^5$

(b) $1s^2 2s^2 2p^6 3s^2$

(c) $1s^2 2s^2 2p^6 3s^2 3p^6 4s^2 3d^{10}$

(d) $1s^2 2s^2 2p^6 3s^2 3p^6 4s^2 3d^{10} 4p^4$

(e) $1s^2 2s^2 2p^6 3s^2 3p^6 4s^2 3d^{10} 4p^1$

50. The arrangement of atoms in several biologically important molecules is given here. Complete the Lewis structures of these molecules by adding multiple bonds and lone pairs. Do not add any more atoms.

(a) the amino acid serine:

(b) urea:

(c) pyruvic acid:

(d) uracil:

(e) carbonic acid:

51. A compound with a molar mass of about 28 g/mol contains 85.7% carbon and 14.3% hydrogen by mass. Write the Lewis structure for a molecule of the compound.

52. A compound with a molar mass of about 42 g/mol contains 85.7% carbon and 14.3% hydrogen by mass. Write the Lewis structure for a molecule of the compound.

53. Two arrangements of atoms are possible for a compound with a molar mass of about 45 g/mol that contains 52.2% C, 13.1% H, and 34.7% O by mass. Write the Lewis structures for the two molecules.

54. How are single, double, and triple bonds similar? How do they differ?

4.5 Formal Charges and Resonance

55. Write resonance forms that describe the distribution of electrons in each of these molecules or ions.

(a) selenium dioxide, OSeO

(b) nitrate ion, NO_3^-

(c) nitric acid, HNO_3 (N is bonded to an OH group and two O atoms)

(d) benzene, C_6H_6:

(e) the formate ion:

56. Write resonance forms that describe the distribution of electrons in each of these molecules or ions.

(a) sulfur dioxide, SO_2

(b) carbonate ion, CO_3^{2-}

(c) hydrogen carbonate ion, HCO_3^- (C is bonded to an OH group and two O atoms)

(d) pyridine:

(e) the allyl ion:

57. Write the resonance forms of ozone, O_3, the component of the upper atmosphere that protects the Earth from ultraviolet radiation.

58. Sodium nitrite, which has been used to preserve bacon and other meats, is an ionic compound. Write the resonance forms of the nitrite ion, NO_2^-.

59. In terms of the bonds present, explain why acetic acid, CH_3CO_2H, contains two distinct types of carbon-oxygen bonds, whereas the acetate ion, formed by loss of a hydrogen ion from acetic acid, only contains one type of carbon-oxygen bond. The skeleton structures of these species are shown:

60. Write the Lewis structures for the following, and include resonance structures where appropriate. Indicate which has the strongest carbon-oxygen bond.

(a) CO_2

(b) CO

61. Toothpastes containing sodium hydrogen carbonate (sodium bicarbonate) and hydrogen peroxide are widely used. Write Lewis structures for the hydrogen carbonate ion and hydrogen peroxide molecule, with resonance forms where appropriate.

62. Determine the formal charge of each element in the following:

(a) HCl

(b) CF_4

(c) PCl_3

(d) PF_5

63. Determine the formal charge of each element in the following:

(a) H_3O^+

(b) $SO_4{}^{2-}$

(c) NH_3

(d) $O_2{}^{2-}$

(e) H_2O_2

64. Calculate the formal charge of chlorine in the molecules Cl_2, $BeCl_2$, and ClF_5.

65. Calculate the formal charge of each element in the following compounds and ions:

(a) F_2CO

(b) NO^-

(c) $BF_4{}^-$

(d) $SnCl_3{}^-$

(e) H_2CCH_2

(f) ClF_3

(g) SeF_6

(h) $PO_4{}^{3-}$

66. Draw all possible resonance structures for each of these compounds. Determine the formal charge on each atom in each of the resonance structures:

(a) O_3

(b) SO_2

(c) $NO_2{}^-$

(d) $NO_3{}^-$

67. Based on formal charge considerations, which of the following would likely be the correct arrangement of atoms in nitrosyl chloride: ClNO or ClON?

68. Based on formal charge considerations, which of the following would likely be the correct arrangement of atoms in hypochlorous acid: HOCl or OClH?

69. Based on formal charge considerations, which of the following would likely be the correct arrangement of atoms in sulfur dioxide: OSO or SOO?

70. Draw the structure of hydroxylamine, H_3NO, and assign formal charges; look up the structure. Is the actual structure consistent with the formal charges?

71. Iodine forms a series of fluorides (listed here). Write Lewis structures for each of the four compounds and determine the formal charge of the iodine atom in each molecule:

(a) IF

(b) IF_3

(c) IF_5

(d) IF_7

72. Write the Lewis structure and chemical formula of the compound with a molar mass of about 70 g/mol that contains 19.7% nitrogen and 80.3% fluorine by mass, and determine the formal charge of the atoms in this compound.

73. Which of the following structures would we expect for nitrous acid? Determine the formal charges:

74. Sulfuric acid is the industrial chemical produced in greatest quantity worldwide. About 90 billion pounds are produced each year in the United States alone. Write the Lewis structure for sulfuric acid, H_2SO_4, which has two oxygen atoms and two OH groups bonded to the sulfur.

4.6 Molecular Structure and Polarity

75. Explain why the HOH molecule is bent, whereas the HBeH molecule is linear.

76. What feature of a Lewis structure can be used to tell if a molecule's (or ion's) electron-pair geometry and molecular structure will be identical?

77. Explain the difference between electron-pair geometry and molecular structure.

78. Why is the H–N–H angle in NH_3 smaller than the H–C–H bond angle in CH_4? Why is the H–N–H angle in $NH_4{}^+$ identical to the H–C–H bond angle in CH_4?

79. Explain how a molecule that contains polar bonds can be nonpolar.

80. As a general rule, MX_n molecules (where M represents a central atom and X represents terminal atoms; n = 2 – 5) are polar if there is one or more lone pairs of electrons on M. NH_3 (M = N, X = H, n = 3) is an example. There are two molecular structures with lone pairs that are exceptions to this rule. What are they?

81. Predict the electron pair geometry and the molecular structure of each of the following molecules or ions:

(a) SF_6

(b) PCl_5

(c) BeH_2

(d) CH_3^+

82. Identify the electron pair geometry and the molecular structure of each of the following molecules or ions:

(a) IF_6^+

(b) CF_4

(c) BF_3

(d) SiF_5^-

(e) $BeCl_2$

83. What are the electron-pair geometry and the molecular structure of each of the following molecules or ions?

(a) ClF_5

(b) ClO_2^-

(c) $TeCl_4^{2-}$

(d) PCl_3

(e) SeF_4

(f) PH_2^-

84. Predict the electron pair geometry and the molecular structure of each of the following ions:

(a) H_3O^+

(b) PCl_4^-

(c) $SnCl_3^-$

(d) $BrCl_4^-$

(e) ICl_3

(f) XeF_4

(g) SF_2

85. Identify the electron pair geometry and the molecular structure of each of the following molecules:

(a) ClNO (N is the central atom)

(b) CS_2

(c) Cl_2CO (C is the central atom)

(d) Cl_2SO (S is the central atom)

(e) SO_2F_2 (S is the central atom)

(f) XeO_2F_2 (Xe is the central atom)

(g) $ClOF_2^+$ (Cl is the central atom)

86. Predict the electron pair geometry and the molecular structure of each of the following:

(a) IOF_5 (I is the central atom)

(b) $POCl_3$ (P is the central atom)

(c) Cl_2SeO (Se is the central atom)

(d) $ClSO^+$ (S is the central atom)

(e) F_2SO (S is the central atom)

(f) NO_2^-

(g) SiO_4^{4-}

87. Which of the following molecules and ions contain polar bonds? Which of these molecules and ions have dipole moments?

(a) ClF_5

(b) ClO_2^-

(c) $TeCl_4^{2-}$

(d) PCl_3

(e) SeF_4

(f) PH_2^-

(g) XeF_2

88. Which of these molecules and ions contain polar bonds? Which of these molecules and ions have dipole moments?

(a) H_3O^+

(b) PCl_4^-

(c) $SnCl_3^-$

(d) $BrCl_4^-$

(e) ICl_3

(f) XeF_4

(g) SF_2

89. Which of the following molecules have dipole moments?

(a) CS_2

(b) SeS_2

(c) CCl_2F_2

(d) PCl_3 (P is the central atom)

(e) $ClNO$ (N is the central atom)

90. Identify the molecules with a dipole moment:

(a) SF_4

(b) CF_4

(c) Cl_2CCBr_2

(d) CH_3Cl

(e) H_2CO

91. The molecule XF_3 has a dipole moment. Is X boron or phosphorus?

92. The molecule XCl_2 has a dipole moment. Is X beryllium or sulfur?

93. Is the Cl_2BBCl_2 molecule polar or nonpolar?

94. There are three possible structures for PCl_2F_3 with phosphorus as the central atom. Draw them and discuss how measurements of dipole moments could help distinguish among them.

95. Describe the molecular structure around the indicated atom or atoms:

(a) the sulfur atom in sulfuric acid, H_2SO_4 [$(HO)_2SO_2$]

(b) the chlorine atom in chloric acid, $HClO_3$ [$HOClO_2$]

(c) the oxygen atom in hydrogen peroxide, HOOH

(d) the nitrogen atom in nitric acid, HNO_3 [$HONO_2$]

(e) the oxygen atom in the OH group in nitric acid, HNO_3 [$HONO_2$]

(f) the central oxygen atom in the ozone molecule, O_3

(g) each of the carbon atoms in propyne, CH_3CCH

(h) the carbon atom in Freon, CCl_2F_2

(i) each of the carbon atoms in allene, H_2CCCH_2

96. Draw the Lewis structures and predict the shape of each compound or ion:

(a) CO_2

(b) $NO_2{}^-$

(c) SO_3

(d) $SO_3{}^{2-}$

97. A molecule with the formula AB_2, in which A and B represent different atoms, could have one of three different shapes. Sketch and name the three different shapes that this molecule might have. Give an example of a molecule or ion for each shape.

98. A molecule with the formula AB_3, in which A and B represent different atoms, could have one of three different shapes. Sketch and name the three different shapes that this molecule might have. Give an example of a molecule or ion that has each shape.

99. Draw the Lewis electron dot structures for these molecules, including resonance structures where appropriate:

(a) $CS_3{}^{2-}$

(b) CS_2

(c) CS

(d) predict the molecular shapes for $CS_3{}^{2-}$ and CS_2 and explain how you arrived at your predictions

100. What is the molecular structure of the stable form of FNO_2? (N is the central atom.)

101. A compound with a molar mass of about 42 g/mol contains 85.7% carbon and 14.3% hydrogen. What is its molecular structure?

102. Use the simulation (http://openstaxcollege.org/l/16MolecPolarity) to perform the following exercises for a two-atom molecule:

(a) Adjust the electronegativity value so the bond dipole is pointing toward B. Then determine what the electronegativity values must be to switch the dipole so that it points toward A.

(b) With a partial positive charge on A, turn on the electric field and describe what happens.

(c) With a small partial negative charge on A, turn on the electric field and describe what happens.

(d) Reset all, and then with a large partial negative charge on A, turn on the electric field and describe what happens.

103. Use the simulation (http://openstaxcollege.org/l/16MolecPolarity) to perform the following exercises for a real molecule. You may need to rotate the molecules in three dimensions to see certain dipoles.

(a) Sketch the bond dipoles and molecular dipole (if any) for O_3. Explain your observations.

(b) Look at the bond dipoles for NH_3. Use these dipoles to predict whether N or H is more electronegative.

(c) Predict whether there should be a molecular dipole for NH_3 and, if so, in which direction it will point. Check the molecular dipole box to test your hypothesis.

104. Use the Molecule Shape simulator (http://openstaxcollege.org/l/16MolecShape) to build a molecule. Starting with the central atom, click on the double bond to add one double bond. Then add one single bond and one lone pair. Rotate the molecule to observe the complete geometry. Name the electron group geometry and molecular structure and predict the bond angle. Then click the check boxes at the bottom and right of the simulator to check your answers.

105. Use the Molecule Shape simulator (http://openstaxcollege.org/l/16MolecShape) to explore real molecules. On the Real Molecules tab, select H_2O. Switch between the "real" and "model" modes. Explain the difference observed.

106. Use the Molecule Shape simulator (http://openstaxcollege.org/l/16MolecShape) to explore real molecules. On the Real Molecules tab, select "model" mode and S_2O. What is the model bond angle? Explain whether the "real" bond angle should be larger or smaller than the ideal model angle.

Chapter 5

Advanced Theories of Bonding

Figure 5.1 Oxygen molecules orient randomly most of the time, as shown in the top magnified view. However, when we pour liquid oxygen through a magnet, the molecules line up with the magnetic field, and the attraction allows them to stay suspended between the poles of the magnet where the magnetic field is strongest. Other diatomic molecules (like N_2) flow past the magnet. The detailed explanation of bonding described in this chapter allows us to understand this phenomenon. (credit: modification of work by Jefferson Lab)

Chapter Outline

5.1 Valence Bond Theory

5.2 Hybrid Atomic Orbitals

5.3 Multiple Bonds

5.4 Molecular Orbital Theory

Introduction

We have examined the basic ideas of bonding, showing that atoms share electrons to form molecules with stable Lewis structures and that we can predict the shapes of those molecules by valence shell electron pair repulsion (VSEPR) theory. These ideas provide an important starting point for understanding chemical bonding. But these models sometimes fall short in their abilities to predict the behavior of real substances. How can we reconcile the geometries of s, p, and d atomic orbitals with molecular shapes that show angles like 120° and 109.5°? Furthermore, we know that electrons and magnetic behavior are related through electromagnetic fields. Both N_2 and O_2 have fairly similar Lewis structures that contain lone pairs of electrons.

$$:N{\equiv}N: \qquad :\overset{\cdot\cdot}{O}{=}\overset{\cdot\cdot}{O}:$$

Yet oxygen demonstrates very different magnetic behavior than nitrogen. We can pour liquid nitrogen through a magnetic field with no visible interactions, while liquid oxygen (shown in **Figure 5.1**) is attracted to the magnet and floats in the magnetic field. We need to understand the additional concepts of valence bond theory, orbital hybridization, and molecular orbital theory to understand these observations.

5.1 Valence Bond Theory

By the end of this section, you will be able to:

- Describe the formation of covalent bonds in terms of atomic orbital overlap
- Define and give examples of σ and π bonds

As we know, a scientific theory is a strongly supported explanation for observed natural laws or large bodies of experimental data. For a theory to be accepted, it must explain experimental data and be able to predict behavior. For example, VSEPR theory has gained widespread acceptance because it predicts three-dimensional molecular shapes that are consistent with experimental data collected for thousands of different molecules. However, VSEPR theory does not provide an explanation of chemical bonding.

Atomic Orbital Overlap

There are successful theories that describe the electronic structure of atoms. We can use quantum mechanics to predict the specific regions around an atom where electrons are likely to be located: A spherical shape for an *s* orbital, a dumbbell shape for a *p* orbital, and so forth. However, these predictions only describe the orbitals around free atoms. When atoms bond to form molecules, atomic orbitals are not sufficient to describe the regions where electrons will be located in the molecule. A more complete understanding of electron distributions requires a model that can account for the electronic structure of molecules. One popular theory holds that a covalent bond forms when a pair of electrons is shared by two atoms and is simultaneously attracted by the nuclei of both atoms. In the following sections, we will discuss how such bonds are described by valence bond theory and hybridization.

Valence bond theory describes a covalent bond as the overlap of half-filled atomic orbitals (each containing a single electron) that yield a pair of electrons shared between the two bonded atoms. We say that orbitals on two different atoms **overlap** when a portion of one orbital and a portion of a second orbital occupy the same region of space. According to valence bond theory, a covalent bond results when two conditions are met: (1) an orbital on one atom overlaps an orbital on a second atom and (2) the single electrons in each orbital combine to form an electron pair. The mutual attraction between this negatively charged electron pair and the two atoms' positively charged nuclei serves to physically link the two atoms through a force we define as a covalent bond. The strength of a covalent bond depends on the extent of overlap of the orbitals involved. Orbitals that overlap extensively form bonds that are stronger than those that have less overlap.

The energy of the system depends on how much the orbitals overlap. Figure 5.2 illustrates how the sum of the energies of two hydrogen atoms (the colored curve) changes as they approach each other. When the atoms are far apart there is no overlap, and by convention we set the sum of the energies at zero. As the atoms move together, their orbitals begin to overlap. Each electron begins to feel the attraction of the nucleus in the other atom. In addition, the electrons begin to repel each other, as do the nuclei. While the atoms are still widely separated, the attractions are slightly stronger than the repulsions, and the energy of the system decreases. (A bond begins to form.) As the atoms move closer together, the overlap increases, so the attraction of the nuclei for the electrons continues to increase (as do the repulsions among electrons and between the nuclei). At some specific distance between the atoms, which varies depending on the atoms involved, the energy reaches its lowest (most stable) value. This optimum distance between the two bonded nuclei is the bond distance between the two atoms. The bond is stable because at this point, the attractive and repulsive forces combine to create the lowest possible energy configuration. If the distance between the nuclei were to decrease further, the repulsions between nuclei and the repulsions as electrons are confined in closer proximity to each other would become stronger than the attractive forces. The energy of the system would then rise (making the system destabilized), as shown at the far left of Figure 5.2.

Figure 5.2   (a) The interaction of two hydrogen atoms changes as a function of distance. (b) The energy of the system changes as the atoms interact. The lowest (most stable) energy occurs at a distance of 74 pm, which is the bond length observed for the H_2 molecule.

In addition to the distance between two orbitals, the orientation of orbitals also affects their overlap (other than for two *s* orbitals, which are spherically symmetric). Greater overlap is possible when orbitals are oriented such that they overlap on a direct line between the two nuclei. **Figure 5.3** illustrates this for two *p* orbitals from different atoms; the overlap is greater when the orbitals overlap end to end rather than at an angle.

(a)   (b)

Figure 5.3   (a) The overlap of two *p* orbitals is greatest when the orbitals are directed end to end. (b) Any other arrangement results in less overlap. The dots indicate the locations of the nuclei.

The overlap of two *s* orbitals (as in H_2), the overlap of an *s* orbital and a *p* orbital (as in HCl), and the end-to-end overlap of two *p* orbitals (as in Cl_2) all produce **sigma bonds (σ bonds)**, as illustrated in **Figure 5.4**. A σ bond is a covalent bond in which the electron density is concentrated in the region along the internuclear axis; that is, a line between the nuclei would pass through the center of the overlap region. Single bonds in Lewis structures are described as σ bonds in valence bond theory.

(a)   (b)   (c)

Figure 5.4 Sigma (σ) bonds form from the overlap of the following: (a) two *s* orbitals, (b) an *s* orbital and a *p* orbital, and (c) two *p* orbitals. The dots indicate the locations of the nuclei.

A **pi bond (π bond)** is a type of covalent bond that results from the side-by-side overlap of two *p* orbitals, as illustrated in **Figure 5.5**. In a π bond, the regions of orbital overlap lie on opposite sides of the internuclear axis. Along the axis itself, there is a **node**, that is, a plane with no probability of finding an electron.

Figure 5.5 Pi (π) bonds form from the side-by-side overlap of two *p* orbitals. The dots indicate the location of the nuclei.

While all single bonds are σ bonds, multiple bonds consist of both σ and π bonds. As the Lewis structures in suggest, O_2 contains a double bond, and N_2 contains a triple bond. The double bond consists of one σ bond and one π bond, and the triple bond consists of one σ bond and two π bonds. Between any two atoms, the first bond formed will always be a σ bond, but there can only be one σ bond in any one location. In any multiple bond, there will be one σ bond, and the remaining one or two bonds will be π bonds. These bonds are described in more detail later in this chapter.

H—Cl: :O=O: :N≡N:

One σ bond   One σ bond   One σ bond
No π bonds   One π bond   Two π bonds

Example 5.1

Counting σ and π Bonds

Butadiene, C_6H_6, is used to make synthetic rubber. Identify the number of σ and π bonds contained in this molecule.

Solution

There are six σ C–H bonds and one σ C–C bond, for a total of seven from the single bonds. There are two double bonds that each have a π bond in addition to the σ bond. This gives a total nine σ and two π bonds overall.

Check Your Learning

Identify each illustration as depicting a σ or π bond:

(a) side-by-side overlap of a 4p and a 2p orbital

(b) end-to-end overlap of a 4p and 4p orbital

(c) end-to-end overlap of a 4p and a 2p orbital

(a)   (b)   (c)

Answer: (a) is a π bond with a node along the axis connecting the nuclei while (b) and (c) are σ bonds that overlap along the axis.

Dipole Moments and Ionic Character

Now that we have seen the importance of understanding the connection between the location of electrons in atoms and the properties of elements, we can expand our understanding of the connection between atoms. This will be an introduction to more advanced aspects of the chemical bond, which is the very heart of chemistry itself. With the sole exception of the noble gases, atoms by themselves do not possess the most stable possible electron configuration. That is where the concept of chemical bonding comes into its own: atoms can attain a stable configuration by exchanging electrons with another atom, resulting in the formation of ions.

Ions, in turn, can associate by charge – simple Coulombic attraction – resulting in the formation of compounds we call ionic compounds. We will look at the ionic nature of bonds first, from a simple positive-negative attraction standpoint. Just as important is that some atoms bond by sharing rather than exchanging electrons; the sharing of electrons gives rise to the covalent bond. To add just one more dimension, some chemical species are neither completely ionic nor completely covalent; these species possess a permanent dipole, and are classified as polar.

In your introductory physics course, you will likely discuss the concept of Coulombic interactions in much more rigorous detail than we will do here. We are interested primarily in the differences in properties between species that arise from their relative covalent, ionic, or polar nature – not in a rigorous model of those properties. We are concerned with the connection between potential energy and force and the relative separation (or lack of separation) between charges. We begin by defining the electric or Coulomb force as the product of the charges divided by the square of the distance between those charges:

$$F = \frac{Q_1 Q_2}{d^2}$$

Here, Q is taken to be the fundamental constant of electron charge: one electron has a charge of 1.60218×10^{-19} C . (We will work exclusively in the SI system, so distances will be measured in meters (m)).

And as you may recall, energy is force times distance, so

$$E = \frac{Q_1 Q_2}{d}$$

To illustrate the trend in attractive force, we will consider first the attractive force between two ions of single charge separated by a distance of $2d$:

$$F = \frac{(1)(-1)}{(2d)^2} = -\frac{1}{4d^2}$$

And then the attractive force between two ions of double charge separated by a distance d:

$$F = \frac{(2)(-2)}{(d)^2} = -\frac{4}{d^2}$$

The force of attraction increases with the charge and decreases with increased distance. If all matter were composed of ions that would be the end of the story, but it clearly is not. There are molecules for which the charge – either positive or negative – is permanently concentrated more on one atom than the other. Notice we say atom, because these compounds are not composed of ions but rather of atoms sharing electrons through covalent bonds.

Bond Dipole Moments

The concept of a bond dipole moment allows us to examine the partial separation of charge between atoms. It is a simple model when applied to diatomic molecules, which will be more than sufficient for our purposes. The dipole moment of a bond is defined as the charge times the distance – charge once again being measured in multiples of the charge on an electron, or coulombs. The distance will always be in meters. Because we are considering very small charges and distances, and because it is the relative separation of charge rather than the actual value for it that we are interested in, we will introduce a new unit called the Debye, named after the physical chemist Peter Debye:

$$1 \text{ Debye (D)} = 3.336 \times 10^{-30} \text{ C-m} \qquad \mu = Q \times d$$

The usefulness of the Debye unit will be shown by example:
For HCl, the bond dipole moment is known to be 1.08 D
For HI, the bond dipole moment is known to be 0.44 D

Comparing the two, we can see that HI is less polar than HCl, which is what we would expect based on electronegativity values.

We have now made a transition between the concept of an ionic compound and a partially ionic one. Of course, the partially ionic compound must also by definition be partially covalent.

Partial Ionic Character

The concept of the bond dipole moment helps bridge the concepts of ionic and covalent bonding. Because there is a separation of charge that is less complete than it is in an ionic bond, we can refer to polar bonds as being partially ionic in nature. In contrast to sodium chloride, hydrogen chloride shows partial charges (indicated with a delta notation) on the hydrogen and chlorine. As you would expect from the electronegativity values, hydrogen carries a partial positive charge, while chlorine carries a partial negative charge. Where do these charges come from?

It is easy to come up with the partial charges by comparing the actual dipole moments (which can be obtained experimentally, using spectroscopy) with the dipole expected in the limiting case (that is, if we were to consider the molecule ionic). The actual dipole moment is 1.03 D.

Example 5.2

Finding the Partial Ionic Character

What are the partial charges of an HCl molecule, whose bond length is 0.127 nm?

Solution

The bond dipole moment is $\left(1.60218 \times 10^{19} \text{ C}\right)\left(0.127 \times 10^{-9} \text{ m}\right)$ or $2.03 \times 10^{-29} \text{ C-m}$. Converted to D, this is $\left(2.03 \times 10^{-29} \text{ C-m}\right)\left(\dfrac{1 \text{ Debye}}{3.336 \times 10^{-30} \text{ C-m}}\right)$ or 6.09 D. Were HCl completely ionic, this would be its molecular dipole moment. To get the partial ionic character, we divide This means the bond is about 17% ionic – or, put another way, the positive charge in H is +0.17 and the partial negative charge on chlorine, –0.17.

Check Your Learning

Repeat the calculation for HI, which has a dipole moment of 0.42 D and a bond length of 0.161 nm.

Answer: Calculated 7.73, percent 5.43

What does the result suggest about the relative polarity of the HI bond vs. that of the HCl bond? Does the calculated dipole and percent ionic character reconcile with the difference in electronegativity between Cl and I?

The electron configuration of an atom or ion is key to understanding the chemical behavior of an element. The atoms that make up the element combine in various ways, ranging from the mostly ionic (NaCl) to the partially ionic (HCl) to what we will call purely covalent. At the most fundamental level, all chemical bonds involve electrons, and a significant percentage of chemical and physical properties can be explained by considering the location and separation of charge in a species. By understanding the structure of matter at the atomic level, we can begin to build an understanding of the behavior of matter at both the microscopic and macroscopic levels.

An understanding of dipoles and partial ionic character is fundamental to understanding the interactions between particles, which we will examine in the chapter on liquids and solids. These intermolecular forces become important in the liquid and solid states of matter.

5.2 Hybrid Atomic Orbitals

By the end of this section, you will be able to:

- Explain the concept of atomic orbital hybridization
- Determine the hybrid orbitals associated with various molecular geometries

Thinking in terms of overlapping atomic orbitals is one way for us to explain how chemical bonds form in diatomic molecules. However, to understand how molecules with more than two atoms form stable bonds, we require a more detailed model. As an example, let us consider the water molecule, in which we have one oxygen atom bonding to two hydrogen atoms. Oxygen has the electron configuration $1s^2 2s^2 2p^4$, with two unpaired electrons (one in each of the two $2p$ orbitals). Valence bond theory would predict that the two O–H bonds form from the overlap of these two $2p$ orbitals with the $1s$ orbitals of the hydrogen atoms. If this were the case, the bond angle would be 90°, as shown in **Figure 5.6**, because p orbitals are perpendicular to each other. Experimental evidence shows that the bond angle is 104.5°, not 90°. The prediction of the valence bond theory model does not match the real-world observations of a water molecule; a different model is needed.

Figure 5.6 The hypothetical overlap of two of the $2p$ orbitals on an oxygen atom (red) with the $1s$ orbitals of two hydrogen atoms (blue) would produce a bond angle of 90°. This is not consistent with experimental evidence.[1]

Quantum-mechanical calculations suggest why the observed bond angles in H_2O differ from those predicted by the overlap of the $1s$ orbital of the hydrogen atoms with the $2p$ orbitals of the oxygen atom. The mathematical expression known as the wave function, ψ, contains information about each orbital and the wavelike properties of electrons in an isolated atom. When atoms are bound together in a molecule, the wave functions combine to produce new mathematical descriptions that have different shapes. This process of combining the wave functions for atomic orbitals is called **hybridization** and is mathematically accomplished by the *linear combination of atomic orbitals*, LCAO, (a technique that we will encounter again later). The new orbitals that result are called **hybrid orbitals**. The valence orbitals in an *isolated* oxygen atom are a $2s$ orbital and three $2p$ orbitals. The valence orbitals in an

---

1. Note that orbitals may sometimes be drawn in an elongated "balloon" shape rather than in a more realistic "plump" shape in order to make the geometry easier to visualize.

oxygen atom in a water molecule differ; they consist of four equivalent hybrid orbitals that point approximately toward the corners of a tetrahedron (Figure 5.7). Consequently, the overlap of the O and H orbitals should result in a tetrahedral bond angle (109.5°). The observed angle of 104.5° is experimental evidence for which quantum-mechanical calculations give a useful explanation: Valence bond theory must include a hybridization component to give accurate predictions.

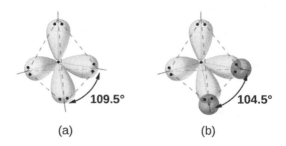

Figure 5.7 (a) A water molecule has four regions of electron density, so VSEPR theory predicts a tetrahedral arrangement of hybrid orbitals. (b) Two of the hybrid orbitals on oxygen contain lone pairs, and the other two overlap with the $1s$ orbitals of hydrogen atoms to form the O–H bonds in H_2O. This description is more consistent with the experimental structure.

The following ideas are important in understanding hybridization:

1. Hybrid orbitals do not exist in isolated atoms. They are formed only in covalently bonded atoms.

2. Hybrid orbitals have shapes and orientations that are very different from those of the atomic orbitals in isolated atoms.

3. A set of hybrid orbitals is generated by combining atomic orbitals. The number of hybrid orbitals in a set is equal to the number of atomic orbitals that were combined to produce the set.

4. All orbitals in a set of hybrid orbitals are equivalent in shape and energy.

5. The type of hybrid orbitals formed in a bonded atom depends on its electron-pair geometry as predicted by the VSEPR theory.

6. Hybrid orbitals overlap to form σ bonds. Unhybridized orbitals overlap to form π bonds.

In the following sections, we shall discuss the common types of hybrid orbitals.

sp Hybridization

The beryllium atom in a gaseous $BeCl_2$ molecule is an example of a central atom with no lone pairs of electrons in a linear arrangement of three atoms. There are two regions of valence electron density in the $BeCl_2$ molecule that correspond to the two covalent Be–Cl bonds. To accommodate these two electron domains, two of the Be atom's four valence orbitals will mix to yield two hybrid orbitals. This hybridization process involves mixing of the valence *s* orbital with one of the valence *p* orbitals to yield two equivalent *sp* **hybrid orbitals** that are oriented in a linear geometry (Figure 5.8). In this figure, the set of *sp* orbitals appears similar in shape to the original *p* orbital, but there is an important difference. The number of atomic orbitals combined always equals the number of hybrid orbitals formed. The *p* orbital is one orbital that can hold up to two electrons. The *sp* set is two equivalent orbitals that point 180° from each other. The two electrons that were originally in the *s* orbital are now distributed to the two *sp* orbitals, which are half filled. In gaseous $BeCl_2$, these half-filled hybrid orbitals will overlap with orbitals from the chlorine atoms to form two identical σ bonds.

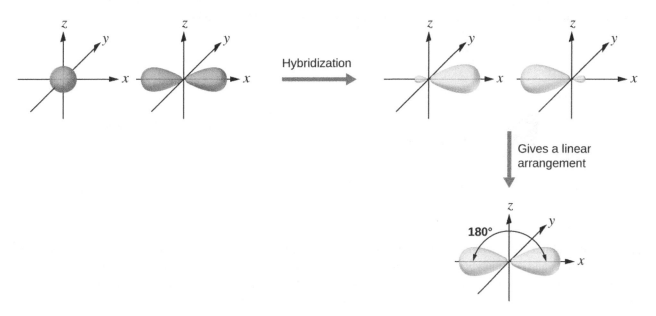

Figure 5.8 Hybridization of an *s* orbital (blue) and a *p* orbital (red) of the same atom produces two *sp* hybrid orbitals (yellow). Each hybrid orbital is oriented primarily in just one direction. Note that each *sp* orbital contains one lobe that is significantly larger than the other. The set of two *sp* orbitals are oriented at 180°, which is consistent with the geometry for two domains.

We illustrate the electronic differences in an isolated Be atom and in the bonded Be atom in the orbital energy-level diagram in **Figure 5.9**. These diagrams represent each orbital by a horizontal line (indicating its energy) and each electron by an arrow. Energy increases toward the top of the diagram. We use one upward arrow to indicate one electron in an orbital and two arrows (up and down) to indicate two electrons of opposite spin.

Figure 5.9 This orbital energy-level diagram shows the *sp* hybridized orbitals on Be in the linear BeCl$_2$ molecule. Each of the two *sp* hybrid orbitals holds one electron and is thus half filled and available for bonding via overlap with a Cl 3*p* orbital.

When atomic orbitals hybridize, the valence electrons occupy the newly created orbitals. The Be atom had two valence electrons, so each of the *sp* orbitals gets one of these electrons. Each of these electrons pairs up with the unpaired electron on a chlorine atom when a hybrid orbital and a chlorine orbital overlap during the formation of the Be–Cl bonds.

Any central atom surrounded by just two regions of valence electron density in a molecule will exhibit *sp* hybridization. Other examples include the mercury atom in the linear $HgCl_2$ molecule, the zinc atom in $Zn(CH_3)_2$, which contains a linear C–Zn–C arrangement, and the carbon atoms in HCCH and CO_2.

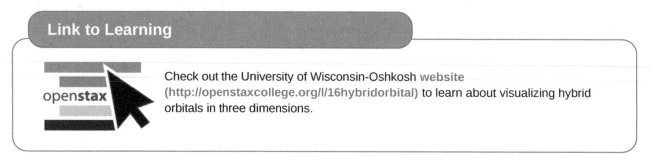

Link to Learning

Check out the University of Wisconsin-Oshkosh website (http://openstaxcollege.org/l/16hybridorbital) to learn about visualizing hybrid orbitals in three dimensions.

sp^2 Hybridization

The valence orbitals of a central atom surrounded by three regions of electron density consist of a set of three sp^2 **hybrid orbitals** and one unhybridized p orbital. This arrangement results from sp^2 hybridization, the mixing of one s orbital and two p orbitals to produce three identical hybrid orbitals oriented in a trigonal planar geometry (**Figure 5.10**).

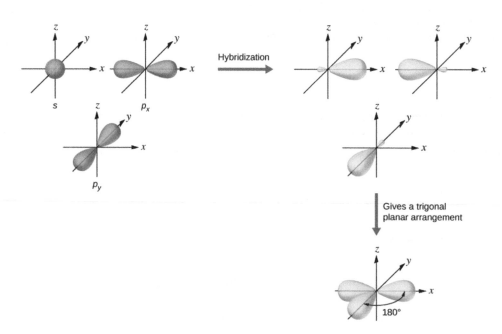

Figure 5.10 The hybridization of an s orbital (blue) and two p orbitals (red) produces three equivalent sp^2 hybridized orbitals (yellow) oriented at 120° with respect to each other. The remaining unhybridized p orbital is not shown here, but is located along the z axis.

Although quantum mechanics yields the "plump" orbital lobes as depicted in **Figure 5.10**, sometimes for clarity these orbitals are drawn thinner and without the minor lobes, as in **Figure 5.11**, to avoid obscuring other features of a given illustration. We will use these "thinner" representations whenever the true view is too crowded to easily visualize.

Figure 5.11 This alternate way of drawing the trigonal planar sp^2 hybrid orbitals is sometimes used in more crowded figures.

The observed structure of the borane molecule, BH_3, suggests sp^2 hybridization for boron in this compound. The molecule is trigonal planar, and the boron atom is involved in three bonds to hydrogen atoms (**Figure 5.12**). We can illustrate the comparison of orbitals and electron distribution in an isolated boron atom and in the bonded atom in BH_3 as shown in the orbital energy level diagram in **Figure 5.13**. We redistribute the three valence electrons of the boron atom in the three sp^2 hybrid orbitals, and each boron electron pairs with a hydrogen electron when B–H bonds form.

Figure 5.12 BH_3 is an electron-deficient molecule with a trigonal planar structure.

Figure 5.13 In an isolated B atom, there are one 2s and three 2p valence orbitals. When boron is in a molecule with three regions of electron density, three of the orbitals hybridize and create a set of three sp^2 orbitals and one unhybridized 2p orbital. The three half-filled hybrid orbitals each overlap with an orbital from a hydrogen atom to form three σ bonds in BH_3.

Any central atom surrounded by three regions of electron density will exhibit sp^2 hybridization. This includes molecules with a lone pair on the central atom, such as ClNO (**Figure 5.14**), or molecules with two single bonds and a double bond connected to the central atom, as in formaldehyde, CH_2O, and ethene, H_2CCH_2.

Figure 5.14 The central atom(s) in each of the structures shown contain three regions of electron density and are sp^2 hybridized. As we know from the discussion of VSEPR theory, a region of electron density contains all of the electrons that point in one direction. A lone pair, an unpaired electron, a single bond, or a multiple bond would each count as one region of electron density.

sp^3 Hybridization

The valence orbitals of an atom surrounded by a tetrahedral arrangement of bonding pairs and lone pairs consist of a set of four sp^3 **hybrid orbitals**. The hybrids result from the mixing of one s orbital and all three p orbitals that produces four identical sp^3 hybrid orbitals (**Figure 5.15**). Each of these hybrid orbitals points toward a different corner of a tetrahedron.

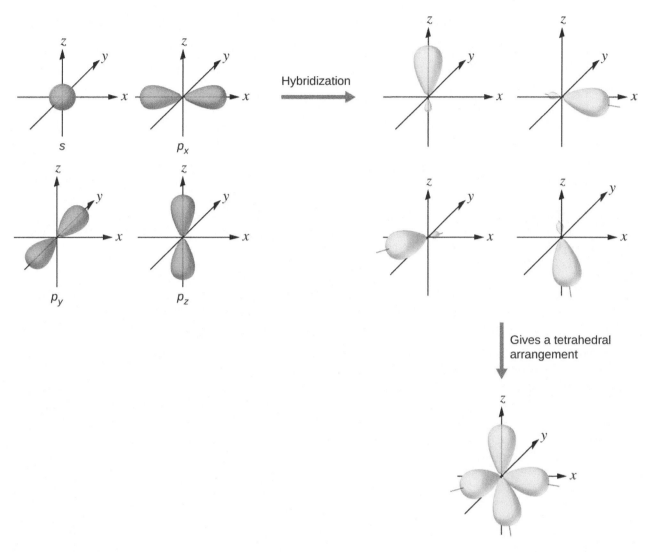

Figure 5.15 The hybridization of an *s* orbital (blue) and three *p* orbitals (red) produces four equivalent sp^3 hybridized orbitals (yellow) oriented at 109.5° with respect to each other.

A molecule of methane, CH_4, consists of a carbon atom surrounded by four hydrogen atoms at the corners of a tetrahedron. The carbon atom in methane exhibits sp^3 hybridization. We illustrate the orbitals and electron distribution in an isolated carbon atom and in the bonded atom in CH_4 in **Figure 5.16**. The four valence electrons of the carbon atom are distributed equally in the hybrid orbitals, and each carbon electron pairs with a hydrogen electron when the C–H bonds form.

Figure 5.16 The four valence atomic orbitals from an isolated carbon atom all hybridize when the carbon bonds in a molecule like CH_4 with four regions of electron density. This creates four equivalent sp^3 hybridized orbitals. Overlap of each of the hybrid orbitals with a hydrogen orbital creates a C–H σ bond.

In a methane molecule, the $1s$ orbital of each of the four hydrogen atoms overlaps with one of the four sp^3 orbitals of the carbon atom to form a sigma (σ) bond. This results in the formation of four strong, equivalent covalent bonds between the carbon atom and each of the hydrogen atoms to produce the methane molecule, CH_4.

The structure of ethane, C_2H_6, is similar to that of methane in that each carbon in ethane has four neighboring atoms arranged at the corners of a tetrahedron—three hydrogen atoms and one carbon atom (**Figure 5.17**). However, in ethane an sp^3 orbital of one carbon atom overlaps end to end with an sp^3 orbital of a second carbon atom to form a σ bond between the two carbon atoms. Each of the remaining sp^3 hybrid orbitals overlaps with an s orbital of a hydrogen atom to form carbon–hydrogen σ bonds. The structure and overall outline of the bonding orbitals of ethane are shown in **Figure 5.17**. The orientation of the two CH_3 groups is not fixed relative to each other. Experimental evidence shows that rotation around σ bonds occurs easily.

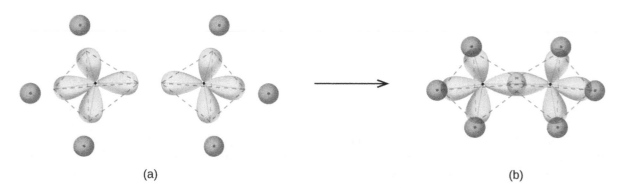

(a)   (b)

Figure 5.17 (a) In the ethane molecule, C_2H_6, each carbon has four sp^3 orbitals. (b) These four orbitals overlap to form seven σ bonds.

An sp^3 hybrid orbital can also hold a lone pair of electrons. For example, the nitrogen atom in ammonia is surrounded by three bonding pairs and a lone pair of electrons directed to the four corners of a tetrahedron. The nitrogen atom is sp^3 hybridized with one hybrid orbital occupied by the lone pair.

The molecular structure of water is consistent with a tetrahedral arrangement of two lone pairs and two bonding pairs of electrons. Thus we say that the oxygen atom is sp^3 hybridized, with two of the hybrid orbitals occupied by lone pairs and two by bonding pairs. Since lone pairs occupy more space than bonding pairs, structures that contain lone pairs have bond angles slightly distorted from the ideal. Perfect tetrahedra have angles of 109.5°, but the observed angles in ammonia (107.3°) and water (104.5°) are slightly smaller. Other examples of sp^3 hybridization include CCl_4,

PCl$_3$, and NCl$_3$.

sp^{3}d and sp^{3}d^2 Hybridization

To describe the five bonding orbitals in a trigonal bipyramidal arrangement, we must use five of the valence shell atomic orbitals (the s orbital, the three p orbitals, and one of the d orbitals), which gives five **sp^{3}d hybrid orbitals**. With an octahedral arrangement of six hybrid orbitals, we must use six valence shell atomic orbitals (the s orbital, the three p orbitals, and two of the d orbitals in its valence shell), which gives six **sp^{3}d^2 hybrid orbitals**. These hybridizations are only possible for atoms that have d orbitals in their valence subshells (that is, not those in the first or second period).

In a molecule of phosphorus pentachloride, PCl$_5$, there are five P–Cl bonds (thus five pairs of valence electrons around the phosphorus atom) directed toward the corners of a trigonal bipyramid. We use the 3s orbital, the three 3p orbitals, and one of the 3d orbitals to form the set of five sp^{3}d hybrid orbitals (**Figure 5.19**) that are involved in the P–Cl bonds. Other atoms that exhibit sp^{3}d hybridization include the sulfur atom in SF$_4$ and the chlorine atoms in ClF$_3$ and in ClF$_4$$^+$. (The electrons on fluorine atoms are omitted for clarity.)

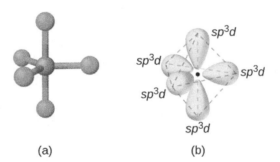

Figure 5.18 The three compounds pictured exhibit sp^{3}d hybridization in the central atom and a trigonal bipyramid form. SF$_4$ and ClF$_4$$^+$ have one lone pair of electrons on the central atom, and ClF$_3$ has two lone pairs giving it the T-shape shown.

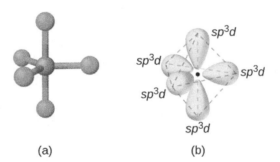

Figure 5.19 (a) The five regions of electron density around phosphorus in PCl$_5$ require five hybrid sp^{3}d orbitals. (b) These orbitals combine to form a trigonal bipyramidal structure with each large lobe of the hybrid orbital pointing at a vertex. As before, there are also small lobes pointing in the opposite direction for each orbital (not shown for clarity).

The sulfur atom in sulfur hexafluoride, SF$_6$, exhibits sp^{3}d^2 hybridization. A molecule of sulfur hexafluoride has six bonding pairs of electrons connecting six fluorine atoms to a single sulfur atom. There are no lone pairs of electrons on the central atom. To bond six fluorine atoms, the 3s orbital, the three 3p orbitals, and two of the 3d orbitals form six equivalent sp^{3}d^2 hybrid orbitals, each directed toward a different corner of an octahedron. Other atoms that exhibit sp^{3}d^2 hybridization include the phosphorus atom in PCl$_6$$^-$, the iodine atom in the interhalogens IF$_6$$^+$, IF$_5$, ICl$_4$$^-$, IF$_4$$^-$ and the xenon atom in XeF$_4$.

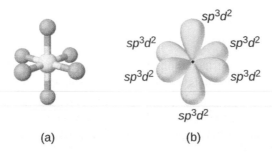

Figure 5.20 (a) Sulfur hexafluoride, SF_6, has an octahedral structure that requires sp^3d^2 hybridization. (b) The six sp^3d^2 orbitals form an octahedral structure around sulfur. Again, the minor lobe of each orbital is not shown for clarity.

Assignment of Hybrid Orbitals to Central Atoms

The hybridization of an atom is determined based on the number of regions of electron density that surround it. The geometrical arrangements characteristic of the various sets of hybrid orbitals are shown in **Figure 5.21**. These arrangements are identical to those of the electron-pair geometries predicted by VSEPR theory. VSEPR theory predicts the shapes of molecules, and hybrid orbital theory provides an explanation for how those shapes are formed. To find the hybridization of a central atom, we can use the following guidelines:

1. Determine the Lewis structure of the molecule.

2. Determine the number of regions of electron density around an atom using VSEPR theory, in which single bonds, multiple bonds, radicals, and lone pairs each count as one region.

3. Assign the set of hybridized orbitals from **Figure 5.21** that corresponds to this geometry.

Regions of Electron Density	Arrangement		Hybridization
2		linear	sp
3		trigonal planar	sp^2
4		tetrahedral	sp^3
5		trigonal bipyramidal	sp^3d
6		octahedral	sp^3d^2

Figure 5.21 The shapes of hybridized orbital sets are consistent with the electron-pair geometries. For example, an atom surrounded by three regions of electron density is sp^2 hybridized, and the three sp^2 orbitals are arranged in a trigonal planar fashion.

It is important to remember that hybridization was devised to rationalize experimentally observed molecular geometries. The model works well for molecules containing small central atoms, in which the valence electron pairs are close together in space. However, for larger central atoms, the valence-shell electron pairs are farther from the nucleus, and there are fewer repulsions. Their compounds exhibit structures that are often not consistent with VSEPR theory, and hybridized orbitals are not necessary to explain the observed data. For example, we have discussed the H–O–H bond angle in H_2O, 104.5°, which is more consistent with sp^3 hybrid orbitals (109.5°) on the central atom than with $2p$ orbitals (90°). Sulfur is in the same group as oxygen, and H_2S has a similar Lewis structure. However, it has a much smaller bond angle (92.1°), which indicates much less hybridization on sulfur than oxygen. Continuing down the group, tellurium is even larger than sulfur, and for H_2Te, the observed bond angle (90°) is consistent with overlap of the $5p$ orbitals, without invoking hybridization. We invoke hybridization where it is necessary to explain the observed structures.

Example 5.3

Assigning Hybridization

Ammonium sulfate is important as a fertilizer. What is the hybridization of the sulfur atom in the sulfate ion, $SO_4{}^{2-}$?

Solution

The Lewis structure of sulfate shows there are four regions of electron density. The hybridization is sp^3.

Check Your Learning

What is the hybridization of the selenium atom in SeF_4?

Answer: The selenium atom is sp^3d hybridized.

Example 5.4

Assigning Hybridization

Urea, $NH_2C(O)NH_2$, is sometimes used as a source of nitrogen in fertilizers. What is the hybridization of each nitrogen and carbon atom in urea?

Solution

The Lewis structure of urea is

$$
\begin{array}{c}
\ddot{\overset{\displaystyle ..}{O}} \\
\| \\
H\!-\!\ddot{N}\!-\!C\!-\!\ddot{N}\!-\!H \\
| \qquad\quad | \\
H \qquad\quad H
\end{array}
$$

The nitrogen atoms are surrounded by four regions of electron density, which arrange themselves in a tetrahedral electron-pair geometry. The hybridization in a tetrahedral arrangement is sp^3 (Figure 5.21). This is the hybridization of the nitrogen atoms in urea.

The carbon atom is surrounded by three regions of electron density, positioned in a trigonal planar arrangement. The hybridization in a trigonal planar electron pair geometry is sp^2 (Figure 5.21), which is the hybridization of the carbon atom in urea.

Check Your Learning

Acetic acid, $H_3CC(O)OH$, is the molecule that gives vinegar its odor and sour taste. What is the hybridization of the two carbon atoms in acetic acid?

$$
\begin{array}{c}
:\!\ddot{O}\!: \\
\| \\
H \quad\; C \\
\backslash \quad / \quad \backslash \\
\quad C \qquad \ddot{O}\!: \\
H^{\prime\prime} \quad \backslash \qquad | \\
H \qquad H
\end{array}
$$

Answer: $H_3\underline{C}$, sp^3; $\underline{C}(O)OH$, sp^2

5.3 Multiple Bonds

By the end of this section, you will be able to:

- Describe multiple covalent bonding in terms of atomic orbital overlap
- Relate the concept of resonance to π-bonding and electron delocalization

The hybrid orbital model appears to account well for the geometry of molecules involving single covalent bonds. Is it also capable of describing molecules containing double and triple bonds? We have already discussed that multiple bonds consist of σ and π bonds. Next we can consider how we visualize these components and how they relate to hybrid orbitals. The Lewis structure of ethene, C_2H_4, shows us that each carbon atom is surrounded by one other carbon atom and two hydrogen atoms.

$$
\begin{array}{c}
H \qquad\qquad H \\
\backslash \qquad\qquad / \\
C \!=\! C \\
/ \qquad\qquad \backslash \\
H \qquad\qquad H
\end{array}
$$

The three bonding regions form a trigonal planar electron-pair geometry. Thus we expect the σ bonds from each carbon atom are formed using a set of sp^2 hybrid orbitals that result from hybridization of two of the $2p$ orbitals and the $2s$ orbital (Figure 5.22). These orbitals form the C–H single bonds and the σ bond in the $C = C$ double bond (Figure 5.23). The π bond in the $C = C$ double bond results from the overlap of the third (remaining) $2p$ orbital on each carbon atom that is not involved in hybridization. This unhybridized p orbital (lobes shown in red and blue in Figure 5.23) is perpendicular to the plane of the sp^2 hybrid orbitals. Thus the unhybridized $2p$ orbitals overlap in a side-by-side fashion, above and below the internuclear axis (Figure 5.23) and form a π bond.

Figure 5.22 In ethene, each carbon atom is sp^2 hybridized, and the sp^2 orbitals and the p orbital are singly occupied. The hybrid orbitals overlap to form σ bonds, while the p orbitals on each carbon atom overlap to form a π bond.

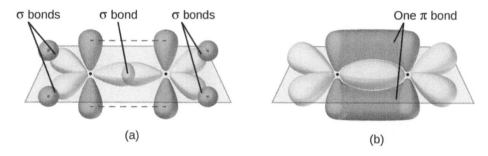

Figure 5.23 In the ethene molecule, C_2H_4, there are (a) five σ bonds. One C–C σ bond results from overlap of sp^2 hybrid orbitals on the carbon atom with one sp^2 hybrid orbital on the other carbon atom. Four C–H bonds result from the overlap between the C atoms' sp^2 orbitals with s orbitals on the hydrogen atoms. (b) The π bond is formed by the side-by-side overlap of the two unhybridized p orbitals in the two carbon atoms. The two lobes of the π bond are above and below the plane of the σ system.

In an ethene molecule, the four hydrogen atoms and the two carbon atoms are all in the same plane. If the two planes of sp^2 hybrid orbitals tilted relative to each other, the p orbitals would not be oriented to overlap efficiently to create the π bond. The planar configuration for the ethene molecule occurs because it is the most stable bonding arrangement. This is a significant difference between σ and π bonds; rotation around single (σ) bonds occurs easily because the end-to-end orbital overlap does not depend on the relative orientation of the orbitals on each atom in the bond. In other words, rotation around the internuclear axis does not change the extent to which the σ bonding orbitals overlap because the bonding electron density is symmetric about the axis. Rotation about the internuclear axis is much more difficult for multiple bonds; however, this would drastically alter the off-axis overlap of the π bonding orbitals, essentially breaking the π bond.

In molecules with sp hybrid orbitals, two unhybridized p orbitals remain on the atom (**Figure 5.24**). We find this situation in acetylene, $H-C{\equiv}C-H$, which is a linear molecule. The sp hybrid orbitals of the two carbon atoms overlap end to end to form a σ bond between the carbon atoms (**Figure 5.25**). The remaining sp orbitals form σ bonds with hydrogen atoms. The two unhybridized p orbitals per carbon are positioned such that they overlap side by side and, hence, form two π bonds. The two carbon atoms of acetylene are thus bound together by one σ bond and two π bonds, giving a triple bond.

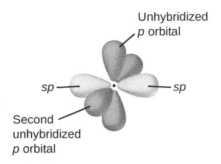

Figure 5.24 Diagram of the two linear *sp* hybrid orbitals of a carbon atom, which lie in a straight line, and the two unhybridized *p* orbitals at perpendicular angles.

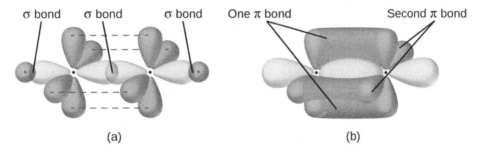

Figure 5.25 (a) In the acetylene molecule, C_2H_2, there are two C–H σ bonds and a $C \equiv C$ triple bond involving one C–C σ bond and two C–C π bonds. The dashed lines, each connecting two lobes, indicate the side-by-side overlap of the four unhybridized *p* orbitals. (b) This shows the overall outline of the bonds in C_2H_2. The two lobes of each of the π bonds are positioned across from each other around the line of the C–C σ bond.

Hybridization involves only σ bonds, lone pairs of electrons, and single unpaired electrons (radicals). Structures that account for these features describe the correct hybridization of the atoms. However, many structures also include resonance forms. Remember that resonance forms occur when various arrangements of π bonds are possible. Since the arrangement of π bonds involves only the unhybridized orbitals, resonance does not influence the assignment of hybridization.

For example, molecule benzene has two resonance forms (**Figure 5.26**). We can use either of these forms to determine that each of the carbon atoms is bonded to three other atoms with no lone pairs, so the correct hybridization is sp^2. The electrons in the unhybridized *p* orbitals form π bonds. Neither resonance structure completely describes the electrons in the π bonds. They are not located in one position or the other, but in reality are delocalized throughout the ring. Valence bond theory does not easily address delocalization. Bonding in molecules with resonance forms is better described by molecular orbital theory. (See the next module.)

Figure 5.26 Each carbon atom in benzene, C_6H_6, is sp^2 hybridized, independently of which resonance form is considered. The electrons in the π bonds are not located in one set of p orbitals or the other, but rather delocalized throughout the molecule.

Example 5.5

Assignment of Hybridization Involving Resonance

Some acid rain results from the reaction of sulfur dioxide with atmospheric water vapor, followed by the formation of sulfuric acid. Sulfur dioxide, SO_2, is a major component of volcanic gases as well as a product of the combustion of sulfur-containing coal. What is the hybridization of the S atom in SO_2?

Solution

The resonance structures of SO_2 are

The sulfur atom is surrounded by two bonds and one lone pair of electrons in either resonance structure. Therefore, the electron-pair geometry is trigonal planar, and the hybridization of the sulfur atom is sp^2.

Check Your Learning

Another acid in acid rain is nitric acid, HNO_3, which is produced by the reaction of nitrogen dioxide, NO_2, with atmospheric water vapor. What is the hybridization of the nitrogen atom in NO_2? (Note: the lone electron on nitrogen occupies a hybridized orbital just as a lone pair would.)

Answer: sp^2

5.4 Molecular Orbital Theory

By the end of this section, you will be able to:

- Outline the basic quantum-mechanical approach to deriving molecular orbitals from atomic orbitals
- Describe traits of bonding and antibonding molecular orbitals
- Calculate bond orders based on molecular electron configurations
- Write molecular electron configurations for first- and second-row diatomic molecules
- Relate these electron configurations to the molecules' stabilities and magnetic properties

For almost every covalent molecule that exists, we can now draw the Lewis structure, predict the electron-pair geometry, predict the molecular geometry, and come close to predicting bond angles. However, one of the most important molecules we know, the oxygen molecule O_2, presents a problem with respect to its Lewis structure. We would write the following Lewis structure for O_2:

$$:\ddot{O}{=}\ddot{O}:$$

This electronic structure adheres to all the rules governing Lewis theory. There is an O=O double bond, and each oxygen atom has eight electrons around it. However, this picture is at odds with the magnetic behavior of oxygen. By itself, O_2 is not magnetic, but it is attracted to magnetic fields. Thus, when we pour liquid oxygen past a strong magnet, it collects between the poles of the magnet and defies gravity, as in **Figure 5.1**. Such attraction to a magnetic field is called **paramagnetism**, and it arises in molecules that have unpaired electrons. And yet, the Lewis structure of O_2 indicates that all electrons are paired. How do we account for this discrepancy?

Magnetic susceptibility measures the force experienced by a substance in a magnetic field. When we compare the weight of a sample to the weight measured in a magnetic field (**Figure 5.27**), paramagnetic samples that are attracted to the magnet will appear heavier because of the force exerted by the magnetic field. We can calculate the number of unpaired electrons based on the increase in weight.

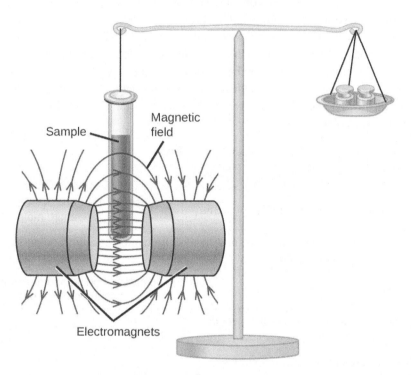

Figure 5.27 A Gouy balance compares the mass of a sample in the presence of a magnetic field with the mass with the electromagnet turned off to determine the number of unpaired electrons in a sample.

Experiments show that each O_2 molecule has two unpaired electrons. The Lewis-structure model does not predict the presence of these two unpaired electrons. Unlike oxygen, the apparent weight of most molecules decreases slightly in the presence of an inhomogeneous magnetic field. Materials in which all of the electrons are paired are **diamagnetic** and weakly repel a magnetic field. Paramagnetic and diamagnetic materials do not act as permanent magnets. Only in the presence of an applied magnetic field do they demonstrate attraction or repulsion.

Molecular orbital theory (MO theory) provides an explanation of chemical bonding that accounts for the paramagnetism of the oxygen molecule. It also explains the bonding in a number of other molecules, such as violations of the octet rule and more molecules with more complicated bonding (beyond the scope of this text) that are difficult to describe with Lewis structures. Additionally, it provides a model for describing the energies of electrons in a molecule and the probable location of these electrons. Unlike valence bond theory, which uses hybrid orbitals that are assigned to one specific atom, MO theory uses the combination of atomic orbitals to yield molecular orbitals that are *delocalized* over the entire molecule rather than being localized on its constituent atoms. MO theory also helps us understand why some substances are electrical conductors, others are semiconductors, and still others are insulators. Table 5.1 summarizes the main points of the two complementary bonding theories. Both theories provide different, useful ways of describing molecular structure.

Comparison of Bonding Theories

Valence Bond Theory	Molecular Orbital Theory
considers bonds as localized between one pair of atoms	considers electrons delocalized throughout the entire molecule
creates bonds from overlap of atomic orbitals (s, p, d...) and hybrid orbitals (sp, sp^2, sp^3...)	combines atomic orbitals to form molecular orbitals (σ, σ^*, π, π^*)
forms σ or π bonds	creates bonding and antibonding interactions based on which orbitals are filled
predicts molecular shape based on the number of regions of electron density	predicts the arrangement of electrons in molecules
needs multiple structures to describe resonance	

Table 5.1

Molecular orbital theory describes the distribution of electrons in molecules in much the same way that the distribution of electrons in atoms is described using atomic orbitals. Using quantum mechanics, the behavior of an electron in a molecule is still described by a wave function, Ψ, analogous to the behavior in an atom. Just like electrons around isolated atoms, electrons around atoms in molecules are limited to discrete (quantized) energies. The region of space in which a valence electron in a molecule is likely to be found is called a **molecular orbital** (Ψ^2). Like an atomic orbital, a molecular orbital is full when it contains two electrons with opposite spin.

We will consider the molecular orbitals in molecules composed of two identical atoms (H_2 or Cl_2, for example). Such molecules are called **homonuclear diatomic molecules**. In these diatomic molecules, several types of molecular orbitals occur.

The mathematical process of combining atomic orbitals to generate molecular orbitals is called the **linear combination of atomic orbitals (LCAO)**. The wave function describes the wavelike properties of an electron. Molecular orbitals are combinations of atomic orbital wave functions. Combining waves can lead to constructive interference, in which peaks line up with peaks, or destructive interference, in which peaks line up with troughs

(Figure 5.28). In orbitals, the waves are three dimensional, and they combine with in-phase waves producing regions with a higher probability of electron density and out-of-phase waves producing nodes, or regions of no electron density.

(a)   (b)

Figure 5.28   (a) When in-phase waves combine, constructive interference produces a wave with greater amplitude. (b) When out-of-phase waves combine, destructive interference produces a wave with less (or no) amplitude.

There are two types of molecular orbitals that can form from the overlap of two atomic *s* orbitals on adjacent atoms. The two types are illustrated in **Figure 5.29**. The in-phase combination produces a lower energy σ_s **molecular orbital** (read as "sigma-s") in which most of the electron density is directly between the nuclei. The out-of-phase addition (which can also be thought of as subtracting the wave functions) produces a higher energy **molecular orbital** (read as "sigma-s-star") molecular orbital in which there is a node between the nuclei. The asterisk signifies that the orbital is an antibonding orbital. Electrons in a σ_s orbital are attracted by both nuclei at the same time and are more stable (of lower energy) than they would be in the isolated atoms. Adding electrons to these orbitals creates a force that holds the two nuclei together, so we call these orbitals **bonding orbitals**. Electrons in the σ_s^* orbitals are located well away from the region between the two nuclei. The attractive force between the nuclei and these electrons pulls the two nuclei apart. Hence, these orbitals are called **antibonding orbitals**. Electrons fill the lower-energy bonding orbital before the higher-energy antibonding orbital, just as they fill lower-energy atomic orbitals before they fill higher-energy atomic orbitals.

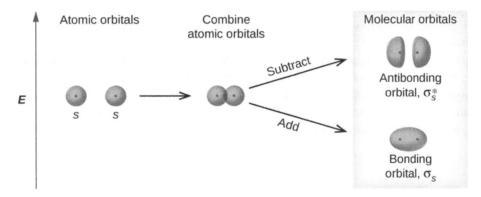

Figure 5.29   Sigma (σ) and sigma-star (σ^*) molecular orbitals are formed by the combination of two *s* atomic orbitals. The plus (+) signs indicate the locations of nuclei.

In *p* orbitals, the wave function gives rise to two lobes with opposite phases, analogous to how a two-dimensional wave has both parts above and below the average. We indicate the phases by shading the orbital lobes different colors. When orbital lobes of the same phase overlap, constructive wave interference increases the electron density. When regions of opposite phase overlap, the destructive wave interference decreases electron density and creates nodes. When *p* orbitals overlap end to end, they create σ and σ* orbitals (Figure 5.30). If two atoms are located along the *x*-axis in a Cartesian coordinate system, the two p_x orbitals overlap end to end and form σ_{px} (bonding) and σ_{px}^* (antibonding) (read as "sigma-p-x" and "sigma-p-x star," respectively). Just as with *s*-orbital overlap, the asterisk indicates the orbital with a node between the nuclei, which is a higher-energy, antibonding orbital.

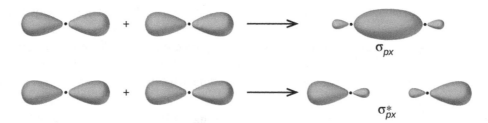

Figure 5.30   Combining wave functions of two *p* atomic orbitals along the internuclear axis creates two molecular orbitals, σ_p and σ_p^*.

The side-by-side overlap of two *p* orbitals gives rise to a **pi (π) bonding molecular orbital** and a **π* antibonding molecular orbital**, as shown in Figure 5.31. In valence bond theory, we describe π bonds as containing a nodal plane containing the internuclear axis and perpendicular to the lobes of the *p* orbitals, with electron density on either side of the node. In molecular orbital theory, we describe the π orbital by this same shape, and a π bond exists when this orbital contains electrons. Electrons in this orbital interact with both nuclei and help hold the two atoms together, making it a bonding orbital. For the out-of-phase combination, there are two nodal planes created, one along the internuclear axis and a perpendicular one between the nuclei.

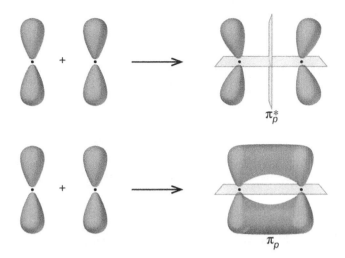

Figure 5.31 Side-by-side overlap of each two *p* orbitals results in the formation of two π molecular orbitals. Combining the out-of-phase orbitals results in an antibonding molecular orbital with two nodes. One contains the internuclear axis, and one is perpendicular to the axis. Combining the in-phase orbitals results in a bonding orbital. There is a node (blue) containing the internuclear axis with the two lobes of the orbital located above and below this node.

In the molecular orbitals of diatomic molecules, each atom also has two sets of *p* orbitals oriented side by side (p_y and p_z), so these four atomic orbitals combine pairwise to create two π orbitals and two π* orbitals. The π_{py} and π^*_{py} orbitals are oriented at right angles to the π_{pz} and π^*_{pz} orbitals. Except for their orientation, the π_{py} and π_{pz} orbitals are identical and have the same energy; they are **degenerate orbitals**. The π^*_{py} and π^*_{pz} antibonding orbitals are also degenerate and identical except for their orientation. A total of six molecular orbitals results from the combination of the six atomic *p* orbitals in two atoms: σ_{px} and σ^*_{px}, π_{py} and π^*_{py}, π_{pz} and π^*_{pz}.

Example 5.6

Molecular Orbitals

Predict what type (if any) of molecular orbital would result from adding the wave functions so each pair of orbitals shown overlap. The orbitals are all similar in energy.

$3p_x$ and $3p_x$

(a)

$3p_x$ and $3p_y$

(b)

$3p_y$ and $3p_y$

(c)

Solution

(a) is an in-phase combination, resulting in a σ_{3p} orbital

(b) will not result in a new orbital because the in-phase component (bottom) and out-of-phase component (top) cancel out. Only orbitals with the correct alignment can combine.

(c) is an out-of-phase combination, resulting in a π^*_{3p} orbital.

Check Your Learning

Label the molecular orbital shown as σ or π, bonding or antibonding and indicate where the node occurs.

Answer: The orbital is located along the internuclear axis, so it is a σ orbital. There is a node bisecting the internuclear axis, so it is an antibonding orbital.

Portrait of a Chemist

Walter Kohn: Nobel Laureate

Walter Kohn (Figure 5.32) is a theoretical physicist who studies the electronic structure of solids. His work combines the principles of quantum mechanics with advanced mathematical techniques. This technique, called density functional theory, makes it possible to compute properties of molecular orbitals, including their shape and energies. Kohn and mathematician John Pople were awarded the Nobel Prize in Chemistry in 1998 for their contributions to our understanding of electronic structure. Kohn also made significant contributions to the physics of semiconductors.

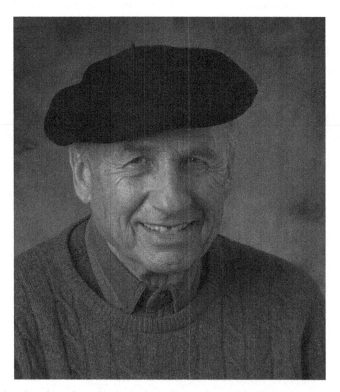

Figure 5.32   Walter Kohn developed methods to describe molecular orbitals. (credit: image courtesy of Walter Kohn)

Kohn's biography has been remarkable outside the realm of physical chemistry as well. He was born in Austria, and during World War II he was part of the Kindertransport program that rescued 10,000 children from the Nazi regime. His summer jobs included discovering gold deposits in Canada and helping Polaroid explain how its instant film worked. Although he is now an emeritus professor, he is still actively working on projects involving global warming and renewable energy.

How Sciences Interconnect

Computational Chemistry in Drug Design

While the descriptions of bonding described in this chapter involve many theoretical concepts, they also have many practical, real-world applications. For example, drug design is an important field that uses our understanding of chemical bonding to develop pharmaceuticals. This interdisciplinary area of study uses biology (understanding diseases and how they operate) to identify specific targets, such as a binding site that is involved in a disease pathway. By modeling the structures of the binding site and potential drugs, computational chemists can predict which structures can fit together and how effectively they will bind (see Figure 5.33). Thousands of potential candidates can be narrowed down to a few of the most promising candidates. These candidate molecules are then carefully tested to determine side effects, how effectively they can be transported through the body, and other factors. Dozens of important new pharmaceuticals have been discovered with the aid of computational chemistry, and new research projects are underway.

Figure 5.33   The molecule shown, HIV-1 protease, is an important target for pharmaceutical research. By designing molecules that bind to this protein, scientists are able to drastically inhibit the progress of the disease.

Molecular Orbital Energy Diagrams

The relative energy levels of atomic and molecular orbitals are typically shown in a **molecular orbital diagram** (Figure 5.34). For a diatomic molecule, the atomic orbitals of one atom are shown on the left, and those of the other atom are shown on the right. Each horizontal line represents one orbital that can hold two electrons. The molecular orbitals formed by the combination of the atomic orbitals are shown in the center. Dashed lines show which of the atomic orbitals combine to form the molecular orbitals. For each pair of atomic orbitals that combine, one lower-energy (bonding) molecular orbital and one higher-energy (antibonding) orbital result. Thus we can see that combining the six $2p$ atomic orbitals results in three bonding orbitals (one σ and two π) and three antibonding orbitals (one σ^* and two π^*).

We predict the distribution of electrons in these molecular orbitals by filling the orbitals in the same way that we fill atomic orbitals, by the Aufbau principle. Lower-energy orbitals fill first, electrons spread out among degenerate orbitals before pairing, and each orbital can hold a maximum of two electrons with opposite spins (**Figure 5.34**). Just as we write electron configurations for atoms, we can write the molecular electronic configuration by listing the orbitals with superscripts indicating the number of electrons present. For clarity, we place parentheses around molecular orbitals with the same energy. In this case, each orbital is at a different energy, so parentheses separate each orbital. Thus we would expect a diatomic molecule or ion containing seven electrons (such as $Be_2{}^+$) would have the molecular electron configuration $(\sigma_{1s})^2 (\sigma_{1s}^*)^2 (\sigma_{2s})^2 (\sigma_{2s}^*)^1$. It is common to omit the core electrons from molecular orbital diagrams and configurations and include only the valence electrons.

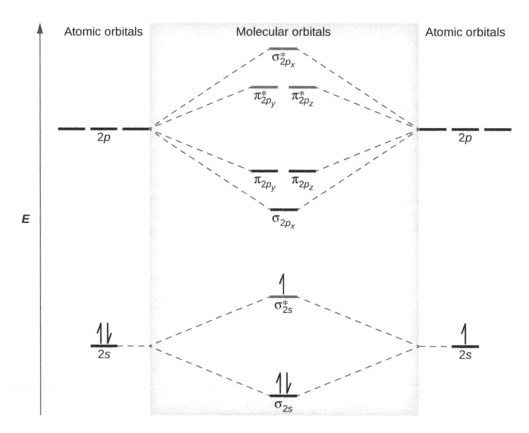

Figure 5.34 This is the molecular orbital diagram for the homonuclear diatomic $Be_2{}^+$, showing the molecular orbitals of the valence shell only. The molecular orbitals are filled in the same manner as atomic orbitals, using the Aufbau principle and Hund's rule.

Bond Order

The filled molecular orbital diagram shows the number of electrons in both bonding and antibonding molecular orbitals. The net contribution of the electrons to the bond strength of a molecule is identified by determining the **bond order** that results from the filling of the molecular orbitals by electrons.

When using Lewis structures to describe the distribution of electrons in molecules, we define bond order as the number of bonding pairs of electrons between two atoms. Thus a single bond has a bond order of 1, a double bond has a bond order of 2, and a triple bond has a bond order of 3. We define bond order differently when we use the molecular orbital description of the distribution of electrons, but the resulting bond order is usually the same. The MO technique is more accurate and can handle cases when the Lewis structure method fails, but both methods describe the same phenomenon.

In the molecular orbital model, an electron contributes to a bonding interaction if it occupies a bonding orbital and it contributes to an antibonding interaction if it occupies an antibonding orbital. The bond order is calculated by subtracting the destabilizing (antibonding) electrons from the stabilizing (bonding) electrons. Since a bond consists of two electrons, we divide by two to get the bond order. We can determine bond order with the following equation:

$$\text{bond order} = \frac{(\text{number of bonding electrons}) - (\text{number of antibonding electrons})}{2}$$

The order of a covalent bond is a guide to its strength; a bond between two given atoms becomes stronger as the bond order increases. If the distribution of electrons in the molecular orbitals between two atoms is such that the resulting bond would have a bond order of zero, a stable bond does not form. We next look at some specific examples of MO diagrams and bond orders.

Bonding in Diatomic Molecules

A dihydrogen molecule (H_2) forms from two hydrogen atoms. When the atomic orbitals of the two atoms combine, the electrons occupy the molecular orbital of lowest energy, the σ_{1s} bonding orbital. A dihydrogen molecule, H_2, readily forms because the energy of a H_2 molecule is lower than that of two H atoms. The σ_{1s} orbital that contains both electrons is lower in energy than either of the two $1s$ atomic orbitals.

A molecular orbital can hold two electrons, so both electrons in the H_2 molecule are in the σ_{1s} bonding orbital; the electron configuration is $(\sigma_{1s})^2$. We represent this configuration by a molecular orbital energy diagram (**Figure 5.35**) in which a single upward arrow indicates one electron in an orbital, and two (upward and downward) arrows indicate two electrons of opposite spin.

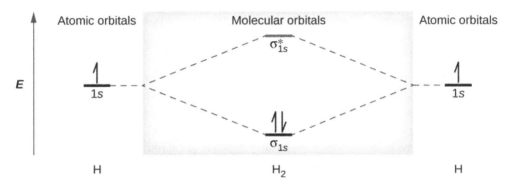

Figure 5.35 The molecular orbital energy diagram predicts that H_2 will be a stable molecule with lower energy than the separated atoms.

A dihydrogen molecule contains two bonding electrons and no antibonding electrons so we have

$$\text{bond order in } H_2 = \frac{(2 - 0)}{2} = 1$$

Because the bond order for the H–H bond is equal to 1, the bond is a single bond.

A helium atom has two electrons, both of which are in its $1s$ orbital. Two helium atoms do not combine to form a dihelium molecule, He_2, with four electrons, because the stabilizing effect of the two electrons in the lower-energy bonding orbital would be offset by the destabilizing effect of the two electrons in the higher-energy antibonding molecular orbital. We would write the hypothetical electron configuration of He_2 as $(\sigma_{1s})^2(\sigma_{1s}^*)^2$ as in **Figure 5.36**.

The net energy change would be zero, so there is no driving force for helium atoms to form the diatomic molecule. In fact, helium exists as discrete atoms rather than as diatomic molecules. The bond order in a hypothetical dihelium molecule would be zero.

$$\text{bond order in } He_2 = \frac{(2 - 2)}{2} = 0$$

A bond order of zero indicates that no bond is formed between two atoms.

Figure 5.36 The molecular orbital energy diagram predicts that He_2 will not be a stable molecule, since it has equal numbers of bonding and antibonding electrons.

The Diatomic Molecules of the Second Period

Eight possible homonuclear diatomic molecules might be formed by the atoms of the second period of the periodic table: Li_2, Be_2, B_2, C_2, N_2, O_2, F_2, and Ne_2. However, we can predict that the Be_2 molecule and the Ne_2 molecule would not be stable. We can see this by a consideration of the molecular electron configurations (**Table 5.2**).

We predict valence molecular orbital electron configurations just as we predict electron configurations of atoms. Valence electrons are assigned to valence molecular orbitals with the lowest possible energies. Consistent with Hund's rule, whenever there are two or more degenerate molecular orbitals, electrons fill each orbital of that type singly before any pairing of electrons takes place.

As we saw in valence bond theory, σ bonds are generally more stable than π bonds formed from degenerate atomic orbitals. Similarly, in molecular orbital theory, σ orbitals are usually more stable than π orbitals. However, this is not always the case. The MOs for the valence orbitals of the second period are shown in **Figure 5.37**. Looking at Ne_2 molecular orbitals, we see that the order is consistent with the generic diagram shown in the previous section. However, for atoms with three or fewer electrons in the p orbitals (Li through N) we observe a different pattern, in which the $σ_p$ orbital is higher in energy than the $π_p$ set. Obtain the molecular orbital diagram for a homonuclear diatomic ion by adding or subtracting electrons from the diagram for the neutral molecule.

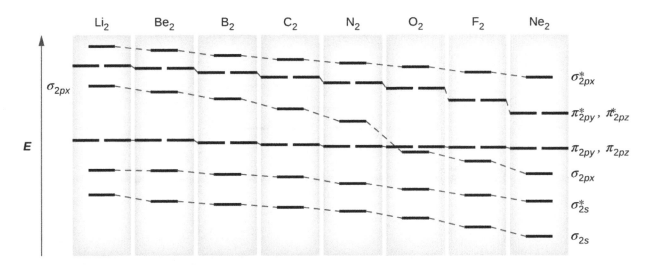

Figure 5.37 This shows the MO diagrams for each homonuclear diatomic molecule in the second period. The orbital energies decrease across the period as the effective nuclear charge increases and atomic radius decreases. Between N_2 and O_2, the order of the orbitals changes.

Link to Learning

You can practice labeling and filling molecular orbitals with this interactive tutorial (http://openstaxcollege.org/l/16labelorbital) from the University of Sydney.

This switch in orbital ordering occurs because of a phenomenon called **s-p mixing**. s-p mixing does not create new orbitals; it merely influences the energies of the existing molecular orbitals. The σ_s wavefunction mathematically combines with the σ_p wavefunction, with the result that the σ_s orbital becomes more stable, and the σ_p orbital becomes less stable (**Figure 5.38**). Similarly, the antibonding orbitals also undergo s-p mixing, with the σ_{s*} becoming more stable and the σ_{p*} becoming less stable.

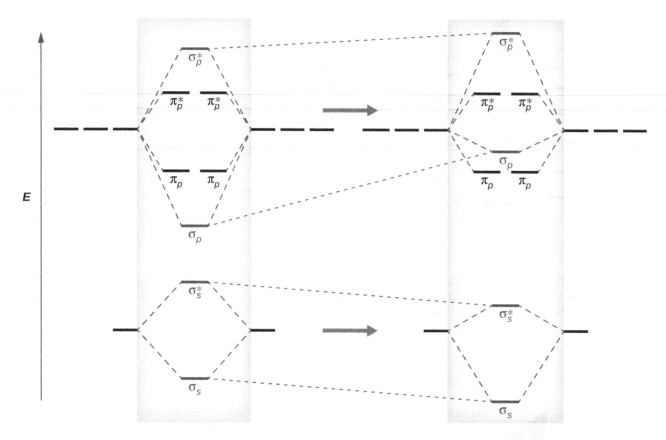

Figure 5.38 Without mixing, the MO pattern occurs as expected, with the σ_p orbital lower in energy than the σ_p orbitals. When s-p mixing occurs, the orbitals shift as shown, with the σ_p orbital higher in energy than the π_p orbitals.

s-p mixing occurs when the s and p orbitals have similar energies. When a single p orbital contains a pair of electrons, the act of pairing the electrons raises the energy of the orbital. Thus the $2p$ orbitals for O, F, and Ne are higher in energy than the $2p$ orbitals for Li, Be, B, C, and N. Because of this, O_2, F_2, and N_2 only have negligible s-p mixing (not sufficient to change the energy ordering), and their MO diagrams follow the normal pattern, as shown in **Figure 5.37**. All of the other period 2 diatomic molecules do have s-p mixing, which leads to the pattern where the σ_p orbital is raised above the π_p set.

Using the MO diagrams shown in **Figure 5.37**, we can add in the electrons and determine the molecular electron configuration and bond order for each of the diatomic molecules. As shown in **Table 5.2**, Be_2 and Ne_2 molecules would have a bond order of 0, and these molecules do not exist.

Electron Configuration and Bond Order for Molecular Orbitals in Homonuclear Diatomic Molecules of Period Two Elements

Molecule	Electron Configuration	Bond Order
Li_2	$(\sigma_{2s})^2$	1
Be_2 (unstable)	$(\sigma_{2s})^2(\sigma_{2s}^*)^2$	0
B_2	$(\sigma_{2s})^2(\sigma_{2s}^*)^2(\pi_{2py},\ \pi_{2pz})^2$	1

Table 5.2

Electron Configuration and Bond Order for Molecular Orbitals in Homonuclear Diatomic Molecules of Period Two Elements

Molecule	Electron Configuration	Bond Order
C_2	$(\sigma_{2s})^2 (\sigma_{2s}^*)^2 (\pi_{2py}, \ \pi_{2pz})^4$	2
N_2	$(\sigma_{2s})^2 (\sigma_{2s}^*)^2 (\pi_{2py}, \ \pi_{2pz})^4 (\sigma_{2px})^2$	3
O_2	$(\sigma_{2s})^2 (\sigma_{2s}^*)^2 (\sigma_{2px})^2 (\pi_{2py}, \ \pi_{2pz})^4 (\pi_{2py}^*, \ \pi_{2pz}^*)^2$	2
F_2	$(\sigma_{2s})^2 (\sigma_{2s}^*)^2 (\sigma_{2px})^2 (\pi_{2py}, \ \pi_{2pz})^4 (\pi_{2py}^*, \ \pi_{2pz}^*)^4$	1
Ne_2 (unstable)	$(\sigma_{2s})^2 (\sigma_{2s}^*)^2 (\sigma_{2px})^2 (\pi_{2py}, \ \pi_{2pz})^4 (\pi_{2py}^*, \ \pi_{2pz}^*)^4 (\sigma_{2px}^*)^2$	0

Table 5.2

The combination of two lithium atoms to form a lithium molecule, Li_2, is analogous to the formation of H_2, but the atomic orbitals involved are the valence $2s$ orbitals. Each of the two lithium atoms has one valence electron. Hence, we have two valence electrons available for the σ_{2s} bonding molecular orbital. Because both valence electrons would be in a bonding orbital, we would predict the Li_2 molecule to be stable. The molecule is, in fact, present in appreciable concentration in lithium vapor at temperatures near the boiling point of the element. All of the other molecules in Table 5.2 with a bond order greater than zero are also known.

The O_2 molecule has enough electrons to half fill the $\left(\pi_{2py}^*, \ \pi_{2pz}^* \right)$ level. We expect the two electrons that occupy these two degenerate orbitals to be unpaired, and this molecular electronic configuration for O_2 is in accord with the fact that the oxygen molecule has two unpaired electrons (Figure 5.40). The presence of two unpaired electrons has proved to be difficult to explain using Lewis structures, but the molecular orbital theory explains it quite well. In fact, the unpaired electrons of the oxygen molecule provide a strong piece of support for the molecular orbital theory.

How Sciences Interconnect

Band Theory

When two identical atomic orbitals on different atoms combine, two molecular orbitals result (see Figure 5.29). The bonding orbital is lower in energy than the original atomic orbitals because the atomic orbitals are in-phase in the molecular orbital. The antibonding orbital is higher in energy than the original atomic orbitals because the atomic orbitals are out-of-phase.

In a solid, similar things happen, but on a much larger scale. Remember that even in a small sample there are a huge number of atoms (typically > 10^{23} atoms), and therefore a huge number of atomic orbitals that may be combined into molecular orbitals. When N valence atomic orbitals, all of the same energy and each containing one (1) electron, are combined, $N/2$ (filled) bonding orbitals and $N/2$ (empty) antibonding orbitals will result. Each bonding orbital will show an energy lowering as the atomic orbitals are *mostly* in-phase, but each of the bonding orbitals will be a little different and have slightly different energies. The antibonding orbitals will show an increase in energy as the atomic orbitals are *mostly* out-of-phase, but each of the antibonding orbitals will also be a little different and have slightly different energies. The allowed energy levels for all the bonding orbitals are so close together that they form a band, called the valence band. Likewise, all the antibonding orbitals are very close together and form a band, called the conduction band. Figure 5.39 shows the bands for three important classes of materials: insulators, semiconductors, and conductors.

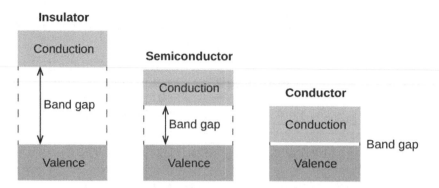

Figure 5.39 Molecular orbitals in solids are so closely spaced that they are described as bands. The valence band is lower in energy and the conduction band is higher in energy. The type of solid is determined by the size of the "band gap" between the valence and conduction bands. Only a very small amount of energy is required to move electrons from the valance band to the conduction band in a conductor, and so they conduct electricity well. In an insulator, the band gap is large, so that very few electrons move, and they are poor conductors of electricity. Semiconductors are in between: they conduct electricity better than insulators, but not as well as conductors.

In order to conduct electricity, electrons must move from the filled valence band to the empty conduction band where they can move throughout the solid. The size of the band gap, or the energy difference between the top of the valence band and the bottom of the conduction band, determines how easy it is to move electrons between the bands. Only a small amount of energy is required in a conductor because the band gap is very small. This small energy difference is "easy" to overcome, so they are good conductors of electricity. In an insulator, the band gap is so "large" that very few electrons move into the conduction band; as a result, insulators are poor conductors of electricity. Semiconductors conduct electricity when "moderate" amounts of energy are provided to move electrons out of the valence band and into the conduction band. Semiconductors, such as silicon, are found in many electronics.

Semiconductors are used in devices such as computers, smartphones, and solar cells. Solar cells produce electricity when light provides the energy to move electrons out of the valence band. The electricity that is generated may then be used to power a light or tool, or it can be stored for later use by charging a battery. As of December 2014, up to 46% of the energy in sunlight could be converted into electricity using solar cells.

Example 5.7

Molecular Orbital Diagrams, Bond Order, and Number of Unpaired Electrons

Draw the molecular orbital diagram for the oxygen molecule, O_2. From this diagram, calculate the bond order for O_2. How does this diagram account for the paramagnetism of O_2?

Solution

We draw a molecular orbital energy diagram similar to that shown in Figure 5.37. Each oxygen atom contributes six electrons, so the diagram appears as shown in Figure 5.40.

Figure 5.40 The molecular orbital energy diagram for O_2 predicts two unpaired electrons.

We calculate the bond order as

$$O_2 = \frac{(8-4)}{2} = 2$$

Oxygen's paramagnetism is explained by the presence of two unpaired electrons in the $(\pi_{2py}, \pi_{2pz})^*$ molecular orbitals.

Check Your Learning

The main component of air is N_2. From the molecular orbital diagram of N_2, predict its bond order and whether it is diamagnetic or paramagnetic.

Answer: N_2 has a bond order of 3 and is diamagnetic.

Example 5.8

Ion Predictions with MO Diagrams

Give the molecular orbital configuration for the valence electrons in $C_2{}^{2-}$. Will this ion be stable?

Solution

Looking at the appropriate MO diagram, we see that the π orbitals are lower in energy than the σ_p orbital. The valence electron configuration for C_2 is $(\sigma_{2s})^2(\sigma_{2s}^*)^2(\pi_{2py}, \pi_{2pz})^4$. Adding two more electrons to generate the $C_2{}^{2-}$ anion will give a valence electron configuration of $(\sigma_{2s})^2(\sigma_{2s}^*)^2(\pi_{2py},\ \pi_{2pz})^4(\sigma_{2px})^2$. Since this has six more bonding electrons than antibonding, the bond order will be 3, and the ion should be stable.

Check Your Learning

How many unpaired electrons would be present on a $Be_2{}^{2-}$ ion? Would it be paramagnetic or diamagnetic?

Answer: two, paramagnetic

Link to Learning

Creating molecular orbital diagrams for molecules with more than two atoms relies on the same basic ideas as the diatomic examples presented here. However, with more atoms, computers are required to calculate how the atomic orbitals combine. See **three-dimensional drawings (http://openstaxcollege.org/l/16orbitaldiag)** of the molecular orbitals for C_6H_6.

Key Terms

antibonding orbital molecular orbital located outside of the region between two nuclei; electrons in an antibonding orbital destabilize the molecule

bond order number of pairs of electrons between two atoms; it can be found by the number of bonds in a Lewis structure or by the difference between the number of bonding and antibonding electrons divided by two

bonding orbital molecular orbital located between two nuclei; electrons in a bonding orbital stabilize a molecule

degenerate orbitals orbitals that have the same energy

diamagnetism phenomenon in which a material is not magnetic itself but is repelled by a magnetic field; it occurs when there are only paired electrons present

homonuclear diatomic molecule molecule consisting of two identical atoms

hybrid orbital orbital created by combining atomic orbitals on a central atom

hybridization model that describes the changes in the atomic orbitals of an atom when it forms a covalent compound

linear combination of atomic orbitals technique for combining atomic orbitals to create molecular orbitals

molecular orbital region of space in which an electron has a high probability of being found in a molecule

molecular orbital diagram visual representation of the relative energy levels of molecular orbitals

molecular orbital theory model that describes the behavior of electrons delocalized throughout a molecule in terms of the combination of atomic wave functions

node plane separating different lobes of orbitals, where the probability of finding an electron is zero

overlap coexistence of orbitals from two different atoms sharing the same region of space, leading to the formation of a covalent bond

paramagnetism phenomenon in which a material is not magnetic itself but is attracted to a magnetic field; it occurs when there are unpaired electrons present

pi bond (π bond) covalent bond formed by side-by-side overlap of atomic orbitals; the electron density is found on opposite sides of the internuclear axis

s-p mixing change that causes σ_p orbitals to be less stable than π_p orbitals due to the mixing of s and p-based molecular orbitals of similar energies.

sigma bond (σ bond) covalent bond formed by overlap of atomic orbitals along the internuclear axis

***sp* hybrid orbital** one of a set of two orbitals with a linear arrangement that results from combining one s and one p orbital

***sp^2* hybrid orbital** one of a set of three orbitals with a trigonal planar arrangement that results from combining one s and two p orbitals

***sp^3* hybrid orbital** one of a set of four orbitals with a tetrahedral arrangement that results from combining one s and three p orbitals

***sp^{3}d* hybrid orbital** one of a set of five orbitals with a trigonal bipyramidal arrangement that results from combining one *s*, three *p*, and one *d* orbital

sp^3d^2 **hybrid orbital** one of a set of six orbitals with an octahedral arrangement that results from combining one *s*, three *p*, and two *d* orbitals

valence bond theory description of bonding that involves atomic orbitals overlapping to form σ or π bonds, within which pairs of electrons are shared

π bonding orbital molecular orbital formed by side-by-side overlap of atomic orbitals, in which the electron density is found on opposite sides of the internuclear axis

π* bonding orbital antibonding molecular orbital formed by out of phase side-by-side overlap of atomic orbitals, in which the electron density is found on both sides of the internuclear axis, and there is a node between the nuclei

σ bonding orbital molecular orbital in which the electron density is found along the axis of the bond

σ* bonding orbital antibonding molecular orbital formed by out-of-phase overlap of atomic orbital along the axis of the bond, generating a node between the nuclei

Key Equations

- $$\text{bond order} = \frac{(\text{number of bonding electron}) - (\text{number of antibonding electrons})}{2}$$

Summary

5.1 Valence Bond Theory

Valence bond theory describes bonding as a consequence of the overlap of two separate atomic orbitals on different atoms that creates a region with one pair of electrons shared between the two atoms. When the orbitals overlap along an axis containing the nuclei, they form a σ bond. When they overlap in a fashion that creates a node along this axis, they form a π bond. Dipole moments can be used to determine partial separations of charges between atoms.

5.2 Hybrid Atomic Orbitals

We can use hybrid orbitals, which are mathematical combinations of some or all of the valence atomic orbitals, to describe the electron density around covalently bonded atoms. These hybrid orbitals either form sigma (σ) bonds directed toward other atoms of the molecule or contain lone pairs of electrons. We can determine the type of hybridization around a central atom from the geometry of the regions of electron density about it. Two such regions imply *sp* hybridization; three, sp^2 hybridization; four, sp^3 hybridization; five, sp^3d hybridization; and six, sp^3d^2 hybridization. Pi (π) bonds are formed from unhybridized atomic orbitals (*p* or *d* orbitals).

5.3 Multiple Bonds

Multiple bonds consist of a σ bond located along the axis between two atoms and one or two π bonds. The σ bonds are usually formed by the overlap of hybridized atomic orbitals, while the π bonds are formed by the side-by-side overlap of unhybridized orbitals. Resonance occurs when there are multiple unhybridized orbitals with the appropriate alignment to overlap, so the placement of π bonds can vary.

5.4 Molecular Orbital Theory

Molecular orbital (MO) theory describes the behavior of electrons in a molecule in terms of combinations of the atomic wave functions. The resulting molecular orbitals may extend over all the atoms in the molecule. Bonding molecular orbitals are formed by in-phase combinations of atomic wave functions, and electrons in these orbitals stabilize a molecule. Antibonding molecular orbitals result from out-of-phase combinations of atomic wave functions and electrons in these orbitals make a molecule less stable. Molecular orbitals located along an internuclear axis are called σ MOs. They can be formed from *s* orbitals or from *p* orbitals oriented in an end-to-end fashion. Molecular orbitals formed from *p* orbitals oriented in a side-by-side fashion have electron density on opposite sides of the internuclear axis and are called π orbitals.

We can describe the electronic structure of diatomic molecules by applying molecular orbital theory to the valence electrons of the atoms. Electrons fill molecular orbitals following the same rules that apply to filling atomic orbitals; Hund's rule and the Aufbau principle tell us that lower-energy orbitals will fill first, electrons will spread out before they pair up, and each orbital can hold a maximum of two electrons with opposite spins. Materials with unpaired electrons are paramagnetic and attracted to a magnetic field, while those with all-paired electrons are diamagnetic and repelled by a magnetic field. Correctly predicting the magnetic properties of molecules is in advantage of molecular orbital theory over Lewis structures and valence bond theory.

Exercises

5.1 Valence Bond Theory

1. Explain how σ and π bonds are similar and how they are different.

2. Use valence bond theory to explain the bonding in F_2, HF, and ClBr. Sketch the overlap of the atomic orbitals involved in the bonds.

3. Use valence bond theory to explain the bonding in O_2. Sketch the overlap of the atomic orbitals involved in the bonds in O_2.

4. How many σ and π bonds are present in the molecule HCN?

5. A friend tells you N_2 has three π bonds due to overlap of the three *p*-orbitals on each N atom. Do you agree?

6. Draw the Lewis structures for CO_2 and CO, and predict the number of σ and π bonds for each molecule.

(a) CO_2

(b) CO

5.2 Hybrid Atomic Orbitals

7. Why is the concept of hybridization required in valence bond theory?

8. Give the shape that describes each hybrid orbital set:

(a) sp^2

(b) sp^3d

(c) sp

(d) sp^3d^2

9. Explain why a carbon atom cannot form five bonds using sp^3d hybrid orbitals.

10. What is the hybridization of the central atom in each of the following?

(a) BeH_2

(b) SF_6

(c) PO_4^{3-}

(d) PCl_5

11. A molecule with the formula AB_3 could have one of four different shapes. Give the shape and the hybridization of the central A atom for each.

12. Methionine, $CH_3SCH_2CH_2CH(NH_2)CO_2H$, is an amino acid found in proteins. Draw a Lewis structure of this compound. What is the hybridization type of each carbon, oxygen, the nitrogen, and the sulfur?

13. Sulfuric acid is manufactured by a series of reactions represented by the following equations:

$$S_8(s) + 8O_2(g) \longrightarrow 8SO_2(g)$$
$$2SO_2(g) + O_2(g) \longrightarrow 2SO_3(g)$$
$$SO_3(g) + H_2O(l) \longrightarrow H_2SO_4(l)$$

Draw a Lewis structure, predict the molecular geometry by VSEPR, and determine the hybridization of sulfur for the following:

(a) circular S_8 molecule

(b) SO_2 molecule

(c) SO_3 molecule

(d) H_2SO_4 molecule (the hydrogen atoms are bonded to oxygen atoms)

14. Two important industrial chemicals, ethene, C_2H_4, and propene, C_3H_6, are produced by the steam (or thermal) cracking process:

$$2C_3H_8(g) \longrightarrow C_2H_4(g) + C_3H_6(g) + CH_4(g) + H_2(g)$$

For each of the four carbon compounds, do the following:

(a) Draw a Lewis structure.

(b) Predict the geometry about the carbon atom.

(c) Determine the hybridization of each type of carbon atom.

15. For many years after they were discovered, it was believed that the noble gases could not form compounds. Now we know that belief to be incorrect. A mixture of xenon and fluorine gases, confined in a quartz bulb and placed on a windowsill, is found to slowly produce a white solid. Analysis of the compound indicates that it contains 77.55% Xe and 22.45% F by mass.

(a) What is the formula of the compound?

(b) Write a Lewis structure for the compound.

(c) Predict the shape of the molecules of the compound.

(d) What hybridization is consistent with the shape you predicted?

16. Consider nitrous acid, HNO_2 (HONO).

(a) Write a Lewis structure.

(b) What are the electron pair and molecular geometries of the internal oxygen and nitrogen atoms in the HNO_2 molecule?

(c) What is the hybridization on the internal oxygen and nitrogen atoms in HNO_2?

17. Strike-anywhere matches contain a layer of $KClO_3$ and a layer of P_4S_3. The heat produced by the friction of striking the match causes these two compounds to react vigorously, which sets fire to the wooden stem of the match. $KClO_3$ contains the ClO_3^- ion. P_4S_3 is an unusual molecule with the skeletal structure.

(a) Write Lewis structures for P_4S_3 and the ClO_3^- ion.

(b) Describe the geometry about the P atoms, the S atom, and the Cl atom in these species.

(c) Assign a hybridization to the P atoms, the S atom, and the Cl atom in these species.

(d) Determine the oxidation states and formal charge of the atoms in P_4S_3 and the ClO_3^- ion.

18. Identify the hybridization of each carbon atom in the following molecule. (The arrangement of atoms is given; you need to determine how many bonds connect each pair of atoms.)

19. Write Lewis structures for NF_3 and PF_5. On the basis of hybrid orbitals, explain the fact that NF_3, PF_3, and PF_5 are stable molecules, but NF_5 does not exist.

20. In addition to NF_3, two other fluoro derivatives of nitrogen are known: N_2F_4 and N_2F_2. What shapes do you predict for these two molecules? What is the hybridization for the nitrogen in each molecule?

5.3 Multiple Bonds

21. The bond energy of a C–C single bond averages 347 kJ mol^{-1}; that of a $C \equiv C$ triple bond averages 839 kJ mol^{-1}. Explain why the triple bond is not three times as strong as a single bond.

22. For the carbonate ion, CO_3^{2-}, draw all of the resonance structures. Identify which orbitals overlap to create each bond.

23. A useful solvent that will dissolve salts as well as organic compounds is the compound acetonitrile, H_3CCN. It is present in paint strippers.

(a) Write the Lewis structure for acetonitrile, and indicate the direction of the dipole moment in the molecule.

(b) Identify the hybrid orbitals used by the carbon atoms in the molecule to form σ bonds.

(c) Describe the atomic orbitals that form the π bonds in the molecule. Note that it is not necessary to hybridize the nitrogen atom.

24. For the molecule allene, $H_2C = C = CH_2$, give the hybridization of each carbon atom. Will the hydrogen atoms be in the same plane or perpendicular planes?

25. Identify the hybridization of the central atom in each of the following molecules and ions that contain multiple bonds:

(a) ClNO (N is the central atom)

(b) CS_2

(c) Cl_2CO (C is the central atom)

(d) Cl_2SO (S is the central atom)

(e) SO_2F_2 (S is the central atom)

(f) XeO_2F_2 (Xe is the central atom)

(g) $ClOF_2^+$ (Cl is the central atom)

26. Describe the molecular geometry and hybridization of the N, P, or S atoms in each of the following compounds.

(a) H_3PO_4, phosphoric acid, used in cola soft drinks

(b) NH_4NO_3, ammonium nitrate, a fertilizer and explosive

(c) S_2Cl_2, disulfur dichloride, used in vulcanizing rubber

(d) $K_4[O_3POPO_3]$, potassium pyrophosphate, an ingredient in some toothpastes

27. For each of the following molecules, indicate the hybridization requested and whether or not the electrons will be delocalized:

(a) ozone (O_3) central O hybridization

(b) carbon dioxide (CO_2) central C hybridization

(c) nitrogen dioxide (NO_2) central N hybridization

(d) phosphate ion $(PO_4{}^{3-})$ central P hybridization

28. For each of the following structures, determine the hybridization requested and whether the electrons will be delocalized:

(a) Hybridization of each carbon

(b) Hybridization of sulfur

(c) All atoms

29. Draw the orbital diagram for carbon in CO_2 showing how many carbon atom electrons are in each orbital.

5.4 Molecular Orbital Theory

30. Sketch the distribution of electron density in the bonding and antibonding molecular orbitals formed from two *s* orbitals and from two *p* orbitals.

31. How are the following similar, and how do they differ?

(a) σ molecular orbitals and π molecular orbitals

(b) ψ for an atomic orbital and ψ for a molecular orbital

(c) bonding orbitals and antibonding orbitals

32. If molecular orbitals are created by combining five atomic orbitals from atom A and five atomic orbitals from atom B combine, how many molecular orbitals will result?

33. Can a molecule with an odd number of electrons ever be diamagnetic? Explain why or why not.

34. Can a molecule with an even number of electrons ever be paramagnetic? Explain why or why not.

35. Why are bonding molecular orbitals lower in energy than the parent atomic orbitals?

36. Calculate the bond order for an ion with this configuration:

$$(\sigma_{2s})^2 (\sigma_{2s}^*)^2 (\sigma_{2px})^2 (\pi_{2py},\ \pi_{2pz})^4 (\pi_{2py}^*,\ \pi_{2pz}^*)^3$$

37. Explain why an electron in the bonding molecular orbital in the H_2 molecule has a lower energy than an electron in the $1s$ atomic orbital of either of the separated hydrogen atoms.

38. Predict the valence electron molecular orbital configurations for the following, and state whether they will be stable or unstable ions.

(a) Na_2^{2+}

(b) Mg_2^{2+}

(c) Al_2^{2+}

(d) Si_2^{2+}

(e) P_2^{2+}

(f) S_2^{2+}

(g) F_2^{2+}

(h) Ar_2^{2+}

39. Determine the bond order of each member of the following groups, and determine which member of each group is predicted by the molecular orbital model to have the strongest bond.

(a) H_2, H_2^+, H_2^-

(b) O_2, O_2^{2+}, O_2^{2-}

(c) Li_2, Be_2^+, Be_2

(d) F_2, F_2^+, F_2^-

(e) N_2, N_2^+, N_2^-

40. For the first ionization energy for an N_2 molecule, what molecular orbital is the electron removed from?

41. Compare the atomic and molecular orbital diagrams to identify the member of each of the following pairs that has the highest first ionization energy (the most tightly bound electron) in the gas phase:

(a) H and H_2

(b) N and N_2

(c) O and O_2

(d) C and C_2

(e) B and B_2

42. Which of the period 2 homonuclear diatomic molecules are predicted to be paramagnetic?

43. A friend tells you that the $2s$ orbital for fluorine starts off at a much lower energy than the $2s$ orbital for lithium, so the resulting σ_{2s} molecular orbital in F_2 is more stable than in Li_2. Do you agree?

44. True or false: Boron contains $2s^2 2p^1$ valence electrons, so only one p orbital is needed to form molecular orbitals.

45. What charge would be needed on F_2 to generate an ion with a bond order of 2?

46. Predict whether the MO diagram for S_2 would show s-p mixing or not.

47. Explain why N_2^{2+} is diamagnetic, while O_2^{4+}, which has the same number of valence electrons, is paramagnetic.

48. Using the MO diagrams, predict the bond order for the stronger bond in each pair:

(a) B_2 or B_2^+

(b) F_2 or F_2^+

(c) O_2 or O_2^{2+}

(d) C_2^+ or C_2^-

Chapter 6

Composition of Substances and Solutions

Figure 6.1 The water in a swimming pool is a complex mixture of substances whose relative amounts must be carefully maintained to ensure the health and comfort of people using the pool. (credit: modification of work by Vic Brincat)

Chapter Outline

6.1 Formula Mass and the Mole Concept

6.2 Determining Empirical and Molecular Formulas

6.3 Molarity

6.4 Other Units for Solution Concentrations

Introduction

Swimming pools have long been a popular means of recreation, exercise, and physical therapy. Since it is impractical to refill large pools with fresh water on a frequent basis, pool water is regularly treated with chemicals to prevent the growth of harmful bacteria and algae. Proper pool maintenance requires regular additions of various chemical compounds in carefully measured amounts. For example, the relative amount of calcium ion, Ca^{2+}, in the water should be maintained within certain limits to prevent eye irritation and avoid damage to the pool bed and plumbing. To maintain proper calcium levels, calcium cations are added to the water in the form of an ionic compound that also contains anions; thus, it is necessary to know both the relative amount of Ca^{2+} in the compound and the volume of water in the pool in order to achieve the proper calcium level. Quantitative aspects of the composition of substances (such as the calcium-containing compound) and mixtures (such as the pool water) are the subject of this chapter.

6.1 Formula Mass and the Mole Concept

By the end of this section, you will be able to:

- Calculate formula masses for covalent and ionic compounds

We can argue that modern chemical science began when scientists started exploring the quantitative as well as the qualitative aspects of chemistry. For example, Dalton's atomic theory was an attempt to explain the results of measurements that allowed him to calculate the relative masses of elements combined in various compounds. Understanding the relationship between the masses of atoms and the chemical formulas of compounds allows us to quantitatively describe the composition of substances.

Formula Mass

In an earlier chapter, we described the development of the atomic mass unit, the concept of average atomic masses, and the use of chemical formulas to represent the elemental makeup of substances. These ideas can be extended to calculate the **formula mass** of a substance by summing the average atomic masses of all the atoms represented in the substance's formula.

Formula Mass for Covalent Substances

For covalent substances, the formula represents the numbers and types of atoms composing a single molecule of the substance; therefore, the formula mass may be correctly referred to as a molecular mass. Consider chloroform ($CHCl_3$), a covalent compound once used as a surgical anesthetic and now primarily used in the production of the "anti-stick" polymer, Teflon. The molecular formula of chloroform indicates that a single molecule contains one carbon atom, one hydrogen atom, and three chlorine atoms. The average molecular mass of a chloroform molecule is therefore equal to the sum of the average atomic masses of these atoms. Figure 6.2 outlines the calculations used to derive the molecular mass of chloroform, which is 119.37 amu.

Element	Quantity		Average atomic mass (amu)		Subtotal (amu)
C	1	×	12.01	=	12.01
H	1	×	1.008	=	1.008
Cl	3	×	35.45	=	106.35
			Molecular mass		119.37

Figure 6.2 The average mass of a chloroform molecule, $CHCl_3$, is 119.37 amu, which is the sum of the average atomic masses of each of its constituent atoms. The model shows the molecular structure of chloroform.

Likewise, the molecular mass of an aspirin molecule, $C_9H_8O_4$, is the sum of the atomic masses of nine carbon atoms, eight hydrogen atoms, and four oxygen atoms, which amounts to 180.15 amu (**Figure 6.3**).

Element	Quantity		Average atomic mass (amu)		Subtotal (amu)
C	9	×	12.01	=	108.09
H	8	×	1.008	=	8.064
O	4	×	16.00	=	64.00
			Molecular mass		180.15

Figure 6.3 The average mass of an aspirin molecule is 180.15 amu. The model shows the molecular structure of aspirin, $C_9H_8O_4$.

Example 6.1

Computing Molecular Mass for a Covalent Compound

Ibuprofen, $C_{13}H_{18}O_2$, is a covalent compound and the active ingredient in several popular nonprescription pain medications, such as Advil and Motrin. What is the molecular mass (amu) for this compound?

Solution

Molecules of this compound are comprised of 13 carbon atoms, 18 hydrogen atoms, and 2 oxygen atoms. Following the approach described above, the average molecular mass for this compound is therefore:

Element	Quantity		Average atomic mass (amu)		Subtotal (amu)
C	13	×	12.01	=	156.13
H	18	×	1.008	=	18.114
O	2	×	16.00	=	32.00
			Molecular mass		206.27

Check Your Learning

Acetaminophen, $C_8H_9NO_2$, is a covalent compound and the active ingredient in several popular nonprescription pain medications, such as Tylenol. What is the molecular mass (amu) for this compound?

Answer: 151.16 amu

Formula Mass for Ionic Compounds

Ionic compounds are composed of discrete cations and anions combined in ratios to yield electrically neutral bulk matter. The formula mass for an ionic compound is calculated in the same way as the formula mass for covalent compounds: by summing the average atomic masses of all the atoms in the compound's formula. Keep in mind, however, that the formula for an ionic compound does not represent the composition of a discrete molecule, so it may not correctly be referred to as the "molecular mass."

As an example, consider sodium chloride, NaCl, the chemical name for common table salt. Sodium chloride is an ionic compound composed of sodium cations, Na^+, and chloride anions, Cl^-, combined in a 1:1 ratio. The formula mass for this compound is computed as 58.44 amu (see Figure 6.4).

Element	Quantity		Average atomic mass (amu)		Subtotal
Na	1	×	22.99	=	22.99
Cl	1	×	35.45	=	35.45
			Formula mass		58.44

Figure 6.4 Table salt, NaCl, contains an array of sodium and chloride ions combined in a 1:1 ratio. Its formula mass is 58.44 amu.

Note that the average masses of neutral sodium and chlorine atoms were used in this computation, rather than the masses for sodium cations and chlorine anions. This approach is perfectly acceptable when computing the formula mass of an ionic compound. Even though a sodium cation has a slightly smaller mass than a sodium atom (since it is missing an electron), this difference will be offset by the fact that a chloride anion is slightly more massive than a chloride atom (due to the extra electron). Moreover, the mass of an electron is negligibly small with respect to the mass of a typical atom. Even when calculating the mass of an isolated ion, the missing or additional electrons can generally be ignored, since their contribution to the overall mass is negligible, reflected only in the nonsignificant digits that will be lost when the computed mass is properly rounded. The few exceptions to this guideline are very light ions derived from elements with precisely known atomic masses.

Example 6.2

Computing Formula Mass for an Ionic Compound

Aluminum sulfate, $Al_2(SO_4)_3$, is an ionic compound that is used in the manufacture of paper and in various water purification processes. What is the formula mass (amu) of this compound?

Solution

The formula for this compound indicates it contains Al^{3+} and SO_4^{2-} ions combined in a 2:3 ratio. For purposes of computing a formula mass, it is helpful to rewrite the formula in the simpler format, $Al_2S_3O_{12}$. Following the approach outlined above, the formula mass for this compound is calculated as follows:

Element	Quantity		Average atomic mass (amu)		Subtotal (amu)
Al	2	×	26.98	=	53.96
S	3	×	32.06	=	96.18
O	12	×	16.00	=	192.00
			Molecular mass		342.14

Check Your Learning

Calcium phosphate, $Ca_3(PO_4)_2$, is an ionic compound and a common anti-caking agent added to food products. What is the formula mass (amu) of calcium phosphate?

Answer: 310.18 amu

6.2 Determining Empirical and Molecular Formulas

By the end of this section, you will be able to:

- Compute the percent composition of a compound
- Determine the empirical formula of a compound
- Determine the molecular formula of a compound

In the previous section, we discussed the relationship between the bulk mass of a substance and the number of atoms or molecules it contains (moles). Given the chemical formula of the substance, we were able to determine the amount of the substance (moles) from its mass, and vice versa. But what if the chemical formula of a substance is unknown? In this section, we will explore how to apply these very same principles in order to derive the chemical formulas of unknown substances from experimental mass measurements.

Percent Composition

The elemental makeup of a compound defines its chemical identity, and chemical formulas are the most succinct way of representing this elemental makeup. When a compound's formula is unknown, measuring the mass of each of its constituent elements is often the first step in the process of determining the formula experimentally. The results of these measurements permit the calculation of the compound's **percent composition**, defined as the percentage by mass of each element in the compound. For example, consider a gaseous compound composed solely of carbon and hydrogen. The percent composition of this compound could be represented as follows:

$$\% \, H = \frac{mass \, H}{mass \, compound} \times 100\%$$

$$\% \, C = \frac{mass \, C}{mass \, compound} \times 100\%$$

If analysis of a 10.0-g sample of this gas showed it to contain 2.5 g H and 7.5 g C, the percent composition would be calculated to be 25% H and 75% C:

$$\% \, H = \frac{2.5 \, g \, H}{10.0 \, g \, compound} \times 100\% = 25\%$$

$$\% \, C = \frac{7.5 \, g \, C}{10.0 \, g \, compound} \times 100\% = 75\%$$

Example 6.3

Calculation of Percent Composition

Analysis of a 12.04-g sample of a liquid compound composed of carbon, hydrogen, and nitrogen showed it to contain 7.34 g C, 1.85 g H, and 2.85 g N. What is the percent composition of this compound?

Solution

To calculate percent composition, we divide the experimentally derived mass of each element by the overall mass of the compound, and then convert to a percentage:

$$\% \, C = \frac{7.34 \, g \, C}{12.04 \, g \, compound} \times 100\% = 61.0\%$$

$$\% \, H = \frac{1.85 \, g \, H}{12.04 \, g \, compound} \times 100\% = 15.4\%$$

$$\% \, N = \frac{2.85 \, g \, N}{12.04 \, g \, compound} \times 100\% = 23.7\%$$

The analysis results indicate that the compound is 61.0% C, 15.4% H, and 23.7% N by mass.

Check Your Learning

A 24.81-g sample of a gaseous compound containing only carbon, oxygen, and chlorine is determined to contain 3.01 g C, 4.00 g O, and 17.81 g Cl. What is this compound's percent composition?

Answer: 12.1% C, 16.1% O, 71.8% Cl

Determining Percent Composition from Formula Mass

Percent composition is also useful for evaluating the relative abundance of a given element in different compounds of known formulas. As one example, consider the common nitrogen-containing fertilizers ammonia (NH_3), ammonium nitrate (NH_4NO_3), and urea (CH_4N_2O). The element nitrogen is the active ingredient for agricultural purposes, so the mass percentage of nitrogen in the compound is a practical and economic concern for consumers choosing among these fertilizers. For these sorts of applications, the percent composition of a compound is easily derived from its formula mass and the atomic masses of its constituent elements. A molecule of NH_3 contains one N atom weighing 14.01 amu and three H atoms weighing a total of (3×1.008 amu) = 3.024 amu. The formula mass of ammonia is therefore (14.01 amu + 3.024 amu) = 17.03 amu, and its percent composition is:

$$\% N = \frac{14.01 \text{ amu N}}{17.03 \text{ amu NH}_3} \times 100\% = 82.27\%$$

$$\% H = \frac{3.024 \text{ amu N}}{17.03 \text{ amu NH}_3} \times 100\% = 17.76\%$$

This same approach may be taken considering a pair of molecules, a dozen molecules, or a mole of molecules, etc. The latter amount is most convenient and would simply involve the use of molar masses instead of atomic and formula masses, as demonstrated Example 6.4. As long as we know the chemical formula of the substance in question, we can easily derive percent composition from the formula mass or molar mass.

Example 6.4

Determining Percent Composition from a Molecular Formula

Aspirin is a compound with the molecular formula $C_9H_8O_4$. What is its percent composition?

Solution

To calculate the percent composition, we need to know the masses of C, H, and O in a known mass of $C_9H_8O_4$. It is convenient to consider 1 mol of $C_9H_8O_4$ and use its molar mass (180.159 g/mole, determined from the chemical formula) to calculate the percentages of each of its elements:

$$\% C = \frac{9 \text{ mol C} \times \text{molar mass C}}{\text{molar mass C}_9\text{H}_{18}\text{O}_4} \times 100 = \frac{9 \times 12.01 \text{ g/mol}}{180.159 \text{ g/mol}} \times 100 = \frac{108.09 \text{ g/mol}}{180.159 \text{ g/mol}} \times 100$$

$$\% C = 60.00\% \text{ C}$$

$$\% H = \frac{8 \text{ mol H} \times \text{molar mass H}}{\text{molar mass C}_9\text{H}_{18}\text{O}_4} \times 100 = \frac{8 \times 1.008 \text{ g/mol}}{180.159 \text{ g/mol}} \times 100 = \frac{8.064 \text{ g/mol}}{180.159 \text{ g/mol}} \times 100$$

$$\% H = 4.476\% \text{ H}$$

$$\% O = \frac{4 \text{ mol O} \times \text{molar mass O}}{\text{molar mass C}_9\text{H}_{18}\text{O}_4} \times 100 = \frac{4 \times 16.00 \text{ g/mol}}{180.159 \text{ g/mol}} \times 100 = \frac{64.00 \text{ g/mol}}{180.159 \text{ g/mol}} \times 100$$

$$\% O = 35.52\%$$

Note that these percentages sum to equal 100.00% when appropriately rounded.

Check Your Learning

To three significant digits, what is the mass percentage of iron in the compound Fe_2O_3?

Answer: 69.9% Fe

Determination of Empirical Formulas

As previously mentioned, the most common approach to determining a compound's chemical formula is to first measure the masses of its constituent elements. However, we must keep in mind that chemical formulas represent the relative *numbers*, not masses, of atoms in the substance. Therefore, any experimentally derived data involving mass must be used to derive the corresponding numbers of atoms in the compound. To accomplish this, we can use molar masses to convert the mass of each element to a number of moles. We then consider the moles of each element relative to each other, converting these numbers into a whole-number ratio that can be used to derive the empirical formula of the substance. Consider a sample of compound determined to contain 1.71 g C and 0.287 g H. The corresponding numbers of atoms (in moles) are:

$$1.17 \text{ g C} \times \frac{1 \text{ mol C}}{12.01 \text{ g C}} = 0.142 \text{ mol C}$$

$$0.287 \text{ g H} \times \frac{1 \text{ mol H}}{1.008 \text{ g H}} = 0.284 \text{ mol H}$$

Thus, we can accurately represent this compound with the formula $C_{0.142}H_{0.248}$. Of course, per accepted convention, formulas contain whole-number subscripts, which can be achieved by dividing each subscript by the smaller subscript:

$$C_{\frac{0.142}{0.142}} \text{ H}_{\frac{0.248}{0.142}} \text{ or } CH_2$$

(Recall that subscripts of "1" are not written but rather assumed if no other number is present.)

The empirical formula for this compound is thus CH_2. This may or not be the compound's *molecular formula* as well; however, we would need additional information to make that determination (as discussed later in this section).

Consider as another example a sample of compound determined to contain 5.31 g Cl and 8.40 g O. Following the same approach yields a tentative empirical formula of:

$$Cl_{0.150}O_{0.525} = Cl_{\frac{0.150}{0.150}} \text{ O}_{\frac{0.525}{0.150}} = ClO_{3.5}$$

In this case, dividing by the smallest subscript still leaves us with a decimal subscript in the empirical formula. To convert this into a whole number, we must multiply each of the subscripts by two, retaining the same atom ratio and yielding Cl_2O_7 as the final empirical formula.

In summary, empirical formulas are derived from experimentally measured element masses by:

1. Deriving the number of moles of each element from its mass

2. Dividing each element's molar amount by the smallest molar amount to yield subscripts for a tentative empirical formula

3. Multiplying all coefficients by an integer, if necessary, to ensure that the smallest whole-number ratio of subscripts is obtained

Figure 6.5 outlines this procedure in flow chart fashion for a substance containing elements A and X.

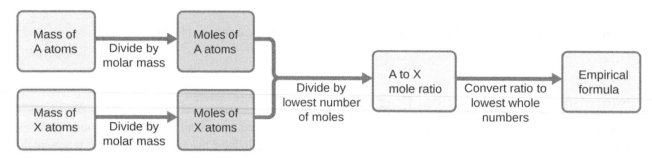

Figure 6.5 The empirical formula of a compound can be derived from the masses of all elements in the sample.

Example 6.5

Determining a Compound's Empirical Formula from the Masses of Its Elements

A sample of the black mineral hematite (Figure 6.6), an oxide of iron found in many iron ores, contains 34.97 g of iron and 15.03 g of oxygen. What is the empirical formula of hematite?

Figure 6.6 Hematite is an iron oxide that is used in jewelry. (credit: Mauro Cateb)

Solution

For this problem, we are given the mass in grams of each element. Begin by finding the moles of each:

$$34.97 \text{ g Fe}\left(\frac{\text{mol Fe}}{55.85 \text{ g}}\right) = 0.6261 \text{ mol Fe}$$

$$15.03 \text{ g O}\left(\frac{\text{mol O}}{16.00 \text{ g}}\right) = 0.9394 \text{ mol O}$$

Next, derive the iron-to-oxygen molar ratio by dividing by the lesser number of moles:

$$\frac{0.6261}{0.6261} = 1.000 \text{ mol Fe}$$

$$\frac{0.9394}{0.6261} = 1.500 \text{ mol O}$$

The ratio is 1.000 mol of iron to 1.500 mol of oxygen ($Fe_1O_{1.5}$). Finally, multiply the ratio by two to get the smallest possible whole number subscripts while still maintaining the correct iron-to-oxygen ratio:

$$2(Fe_1 O_{1.5}) = Fe_2 O_3$$

The empirical formula is Fe_2O_3.

Check Your Learning

What is the empirical formula of a compound if a sample contains 0.130 g of nitrogen and 0.370 g of oxygen?

Answer: N_2O_5

Link to Learning

For additional worked examples illustrating the derivation of empirical formulas, watch the brief video (http://openstaxcollege.org/l/16empforms) clip.

Deriving Empirical Formulas from Percent Composition

Finally, with regard to deriving empirical formulas, consider instances in which a compound's percent composition is available rather than the absolute masses of the compound's constituent elements. In such cases, the percent composition can be used to calculate the masses of elements present in any convenient mass of compound; these masses can then be used to derive the empirical formula in the usual fashion.

Example 6.6

Determining an Empirical Formula from Percent Composition

The bacterial fermentation of grain to produce ethanol forms a gas with a percent composition of 27.29% C and 72.71% O (Figure 6.7). What is the empirical formula for this gas?

Figure 6.7 An oxide of carbon is removed from these fermentation tanks through the large copper pipes at the top. (credit: "Dual Freq"/Wikimedia Commons)

Solution

Since the scale for percentages is 100, it is most convenient to calculate the mass of elements present in a sample weighing 100 g. The calculation is "most convenient" because, per the definition for percent composition, the mass of a given element in grams is numerically equivalent to the element's mass percentage. This numerical equivalence results from the definition of the "percentage" unit, whose name is derived from the Latin phrase *per centum* meaning "by the hundred." Considering this definition, the mass percentages provided may be more conveniently expressed as fractions:

$$27.29\% \, C \; = \; \frac{27.29 \, g \, C}{100 \, g \, compound}$$

$$72.71\% \, O \; = \; \frac{72.71 \, g \, O}{100 \, g \, compound}$$

The molar amounts of carbon and hydrogen in a 100-g sample are calculated by dividing each element's mass by its molar mass:

$$27.29 \, g \, C \left(\frac{mol \, C}{12.01 \, g} \right) \; = \; 2.272 \, mol \, C$$

$$72.71 \, g \, O \left(\frac{mol \, O}{16.00 \, g} \right) \; = \; 4.544 \, mol \, O$$

Coefficients for the tentative empirical formula are derived by dividing each molar amount by the lesser of the two:

$$\frac{2.272 \, mol \, C}{2.272} = 1$$

$$\frac{4.544 \, mol \, O}{2.272} = 2$$

Since the resulting ratio is one carbon to two oxygen atoms, the empirical formula is CO_2.

Check Your Learning

What is the empirical formula of a compound containing 40.0% C, 6.71% H, and 53.28% O?

Answer: CH_2O

Derivation of Molecular Formulas

Recall that empirical formulas are symbols representing the *relative* numbers of a compound's elements. Determining the *absolute* numbers of atoms that compose a single molecule of a covalent compound requires knowledge of both its empirical formula and its molecular mass or molar mass. These quantities may be determined experimentally by various measurement techniques. Molecular mass, for example, is often derived from the mass spectrum of the compound (see discussion of this technique in a previous chapter on atoms and molecules). Molar mass can be measured by a number of experimental methods, many of which will be introduced in later chapters of this text.

Molecular formulas are derived by comparing the compound's molecular or molar mass to its **empirical formula mass**. As the name suggests, an empirical formula mass is the sum of the average atomic masses of all the atoms represented in an empirical formula. If we know the molecular (or molar) mass of the substance, we can divide this by the empirical formula mass in order to identify the number of empirical formula units per molecule, which we designate as *n*:

$$\frac{\text{molecular or molar mass}\left(\text{amu or } \frac{\text{g}}{\text{mol}}\right)}{\text{empirical formula mass}\left(\text{amu or } \frac{\text{g}}{\text{mol}}\right)} = n \text{ formula units/molecule}$$

The molecular formula is then obtained by multiplying each subscript in the empirical formula by *n*, as shown by the generic empirical formula A_xB_y:

$$(A_x B_y)_n = A_{nx} B_{ny}$$

For example, consider a covalent compound whose empirical formula is determined to be CH_2O. The empirical formula mass for this compound is approximately 30 amu (the sum of 12 amu for one C atom, 2 amu for two H atoms, and 16 amu for one O atom). If the compound's molecular mass is determined to be 180 amu, this indicates that molecules of this compound contain six times the number of atoms represented in the empirical formula:

$$\frac{180 \text{ amu/molecule}}{30 \frac{\text{amu}}{\text{formula unit}}} = 6 \text{ formula units/molecule}$$

Molecules of this compound are then represented by molecular formulas whose subscripts are six times greater than those in the empirical formula:

$$(CH_2 O)_6 = C_6 H_{12} O_6$$

Note that this same approach may be used when the molar mass (g/mol) instead of the molecular mass (amu) is used. In this case, we are merely considering one mole of empirical formula units and molecules, as opposed to single units and molecules.

Example 6.7

Determination of the Molecular Formula for Nicotine

Nicotine, an alkaloid in the nightshade family of plants that is mainly responsible for the addictive nature of cigarettes, contains 74.02% C, 8.710% H, and 17.27% N. If 40.57 g of nicotine contains 0.2500 mol nicotine, what is the molecular formula?

Solution

Determining the molecular formula from the provided data will require comparison of the compound's empirical formula mass to its molar mass. As the first step, use the percent composition to derive the compound's empirical formula. Assuming a convenient, a 100-g sample of nicotine yields the following molar amounts of its elements:

$$(74.02 \text{ g C})\left(\frac{1 \text{ mol C}}{12.01 \text{ g C}}\right) = 6.163 \text{ mol C}$$

$$(8.710 \text{ g H})\left(\frac{1 \text{ mol H}}{1.01 \text{ g H}}\right) = 8.624 \text{ mol H}$$

$$(17.27 \text{ g N})\left(\frac{1 \text{ mol N}}{14.01 \text{ g N}}\right) = 1.233 \text{ mol N}$$

Next, we calculate the molar ratios of these elements relative to the least abundant element, N.

$$6.163 \text{ mol C} / 1.233 \text{ mol N} = 5$$
$$8.264 \text{ mol H} / 1.233 \text{ mol N} = 7$$
$$1.233 \text{ mol N} / 1.233 \text{ mol N} = 1$$
$$\frac{1.233}{1.233} = 1.000 \text{ mol N}$$
$$\frac{6.163}{1.233} = 4.998 \text{ mol C}$$
$$\frac{8.624}{1.233} = 6.994 \text{ mol H}$$

The C-to-N and H-to-N molar ratios are adequately close to whole numbers, and so the empirical formula is C_5H_7N. The empirical formula mass for this compound is therefore 81.13 amu/formula unit, or 81.13 g/mol formula unit.

We calculate the molar mass for nicotine from the given mass and molar amount of compound:

$$\frac{40.57 \text{ g nicotine}}{0.2500 \text{ mol nicotine}} = \frac{162.3 \text{ g}}{\text{mol}}$$

Comparing the molar mass and empirical formula mass indicates that each nicotine molecule contains two formula units:

$$\frac{162.3 \text{ g/mol}}{81.13 \frac{\text{g}}{\text{formula unit}}} = 2 \text{ formula units/molecule}$$

Thus, we can derive the molecular formula for nicotine from the empirical formula by multiplying each subscript by two:

$$(C_5H_7N)_2 = C_{10}H_{14}N_2$$

Check Your Learning

What is the molecular formula of a compound with a percent composition of 49.47% C, 5.201% H, 28.84% N, and 16.48% O, and a molecular mass of 194.2 amu?

Answer: $C_8H_{10}N_4O_2$

6.3 Molarity

By the end of this section, you will be able to:

- Describe the fundamental properties of solutions
- Calculate solution concentrations using molarity
- Perform dilution calculations using the dilution equation

In preceding sections, we focused on the composition of substances: samples of matter that contain only one type of element or compound. However, mixtures—samples of matter containing two or more substances physically combined—are more commonly encountered in nature than are pure substances. Similar to a pure substance, the relative composition of a mixture plays an important role in determining its properties. The relative amount of oxygen in a planet's atmosphere determines its ability to sustain aerobic life. The relative amounts of iron, carbon, nickel, and other elements in steel (a mixture known as an "alloy") determine its physical strength and resistance to corrosion. The relative amount of the active ingredient in a medicine determines its effectiveness in achieving the desired pharmacological effect. The relative amount of sugar in a beverage determines its sweetness (see Figure 6.8). In this section, we will describe one of the most common ways in which the relative compositions of mixtures may be quantified.

Figure 6.8 Sugar is one of many components in the complex mixture known as coffee. The amount of sugar in a given amount of coffee is an important determinant of the beverage's sweetness. (credit: Jane Whitney)

Solutions

We have previously defined solutions as homogeneous mixtures, meaning that the composition of the mixture (and therefore its properties) is uniform throughout its entire volume. Solutions occur frequently in nature and have also been implemented in many forms of manmade technology. We will explore a more thorough treatment of solution properties in the chapter on solutions and colloids, but here we will introduce some of the basic properties of solutions.

The relative amount of a given solution component is known as its **concentration**. Often, though not always, a solution contains one component with a concentration that is significantly greater than that of all other components. This component is called the **solvent** and may be viewed as the medium in which the other components are dispersed, or **dissolved**. Solutions in which water is the solvent are, of course, very common on our planet. A solution in which water is the solvent is called an **aqueous solution**.

A **solute** is a component of a solution that is typically present at a much lower concentration than the solvent. Solute concentrations are often described with qualitative terms such as **dilute** (of relatively low concentration) and **concentrated** (of relatively high concentration).

Concentrations may be quantitatively assessed using a wide variety of measurement units, each convenient for particular applications. **Molarity (*M*)** is a useful concentration unit for many applications in chemistry. Molarity is defined as the number of moles of solute in exactly 1 liter (1 L) of the solution:

$$M = \frac{\text{mol solute}}{\text{L solution}}$$

Example 6.8

Calculating Molar Concentrations

A 355-mL soft drink sample contains 0.133 mol of sucrose (table sugar). What is the molar concentration of sucrose in the beverage?

Solution

Since the molar amount of solute and the volume of solution are both given, the molarity can be calculated using the definition of molarity. Per this definition, the solution volume must be converted from mL to L:

$$M = \frac{\text{mol solute}}{\text{L solution}} = \frac{0.133 \text{ mol}}{355 \text{ mL} \times \frac{1 \text{ L}}{1000 \text{ mL}}} = 0.375 \, M$$

Check Your Learning

A teaspoon of table sugar contains about 0.01 mol sucrose. What is the molarity of sucrose if a teaspoon of sugar has been dissolved in a cup of tea with a volume of 200 mL?

Answer: $0.05 \, M$

Example 6.9

Deriving Moles and Volumes from Molar Concentrations

How much sugar (mol) is contained in a modest sip (~10 mL) of the soft drink from Example 6.8?

Solution

In this case, we can rearrange the definition of molarity to isolate the quantity sought, moles of sugar. We then substitute the value for molarity that we derived in Example 6.8, 0.375 M:

$$M = \frac{\text{mol solute}}{\text{L solution}}$$

$$\text{mol solute} = M \times \text{L solution}$$

$$\text{mol solute} = 0.375 \, \frac{\text{mol sugar}}{\text{L}} \times \left(10 \text{ mL} \times \frac{1 \text{ L}}{1000 \text{ mL}}\right) = 0.004 \text{ mol sugar}$$

Check Your Learning

What volume (mL) of the sweetened tea described in Example 6.8 contains the same amount of sugar (mol) as 10 mL of the soft drink in this example?

Answer: 80 mL

Example 6.10

Calculating Molar Concentrations from the Mass of Solute

Distilled white vinegar (Figure 6.9) is a solution of acetic acid, CH_3CO_2H, in water. A 0.500-L vinegar solution contains 25.2 g of acetic acid. What is the concentration of the acetic acid solution in units of molarity?

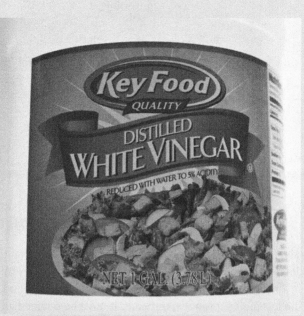

Figure 6.9 Distilled white vinegar is a solution of acetic acid in water.

Solution

As in previous examples, the definition of molarity is the primary equation used to calculate the quantity sought. In this case, the mass of solute is provided instead of its molar amount, so we must use the solute's molar mass to obtain the amount of solute in moles:

$$M = \frac{\text{mol solute}}{\text{L solution}} = \frac{25.2 \text{ g CH}_3\text{CO}_2\text{H} \times \frac{1 \text{ mol CH}_3\text{CO}_2\text{H}}{60.052 \text{ g CH}_3\text{CO}_2\text{H}}}{0.500 \text{ L solution}} = 0.839\ M$$

$$M = \frac{\text{mol solute}}{\text{L solution}} = 0.839\ M$$

$$M = \frac{0.839 \text{ mol solute}}{1.00 \text{ L solution}}$$

Check Your Learning

Calculate the molarity of 6.52 g of $CoCl_2$ (128.9 g/mol) dissolved in an aqueous solution with a total volume of 75.0 mL.

Answer: $0.674\ M$

Example 6.11

Determining the Mass of Solute in a Given Volume of Solution

How many grams of NaCl are contained in 0.250 L of a 5.30-M solution?

Solution

The volume and molarity of the solution are specified, so the amount (mol) of solute is easily computed as demonstrated in Example 6.9:

$$M = \frac{\text{mol solute}}{\text{L solution}}$$

$$\text{mol solute} = M \times \text{L solution}$$

$$\text{mol solute} = 5.30 \frac{\text{mol NaCl}}{\text{L}} \times 0.250 \text{ L} = 1.325 \text{ mol NaCl}$$

Finally, this molar amount is used to derive the mass of NaCl:

$$1.325 \text{ mol NaCl} \times \frac{58.44 \text{ g NaCl}}{\text{mol NaCl}} = 77.4 \text{ g NaCl}$$

Check Your Learning

How many grams of $CaCl_2$ (110.98 g/mol) are contained in 250.0 mL of a 0.200-M solution of calcium chloride?

Answer: 5.55 g $CaCl_2$

When performing calculations stepwise, as in **Example 6.11**, it is important to refrain from rounding any intermediate calculation results, which can lead to rounding errors in the final result. In **Example 6.11**, the molar amount of NaCl computed in the first step, 1.325 mol, would be properly rounded to 1.32 mol if it were to be reported; however, although the last digit (5) is not significant, it must be retained as a guard digit in the intermediate calculation. If we had not retained this guard digit, the final calculation for the mass of NaCl would have been 77.1 g, a difference of 0.3 g.

In addition to retaining a guard digit for intermediate calculations, we can also avoid rounding errors by performing computations in a single step (see **Example 6.12**). This eliminates intermediate steps so that only the final result is rounded.

Example 6.12

Determining the Volume of Solution Containing a Given Mass of Solute

In **Example 6.10**, we found the typical concentration of vinegar to be 0.839 M. What volume of vinegar contains 75.6 g of acetic acid?

Solution

First, use the molar mass to calculate moles of acetic acid from the given mass:

$$\text{g solute} \times \frac{\text{mol solute}}{\text{g solute}} = \text{mol solute}$$

Then, use the molarity of the solution to calculate the volume of solution containing this molar amount of solute:

$$\text{mol solute} \times \frac{\text{L solution}}{\text{mol solute}} = \text{L solution}$$

Combining these two steps into one yields:

$$\text{g solute} \times \frac{\text{mol solute}}{\text{g solute}} \times \frac{\text{L solution}}{\text{mol solute}} = \text{L solution}$$

$$75.6 \text{ g } CH_3CO_2H \left(\frac{\text{mol } CH_3CO_2H}{60.05 \text{ g}} \right) \left(\frac{\text{L solution}}{0.839 \text{ mol } CH_3CO_2H} \right) = 1.50 \text{ L solution}$$

Check Your Learning

What volume of a 1.50-M KBr solution contains 66.0 g KBr?

Answer: 0.370 L

Dilution of Solutions

Dilution is the process whereby the concentration of a solution is lessened by the addition of solvent. For example, we might say that a glass of iced tea becomes increasingly diluted as the ice melts. The water from the melting ice increases the volume of the solvent (water) and the overall volume of the solution (iced tea), thereby reducing the relative concentrations of the solutes that give the beverage its taste (**Figure 6.10**).

Figure 6.10 Both solutions contain the same mass of copper nitrate. The solution on the right is more dilute because the copper nitrate is dissolved in more solvent. (credit: Mark Ott)

Dilution is also a common means of preparing solutions of a desired concentration. By adding solvent to a measured portion of a more concentrated *stock solution*, we can achieve a particular concentration. For example, commercial pesticides are typically sold as solutions in which the active ingredients are far more concentrated than is appropriate for their application. Before they can be used on crops, the pesticides must be diluted. This is also a very common practice for the preparation of a number of common laboratory reagents (**Figure 6.11**).

Figure 6.11 A solution of KMnO4 is prepared by mixing water with 4.74 g of KMnO4 in a flask. (credit: modification of work by Mark Ott)

A simple mathematical relationship can be used to relate the volumes and concentrations of a solution before and after the dilution process. According to the definition of molarity, the molar amount of solute in a solution is equal to the product of the solution's molarity and its volume in liters:

$$n = ML$$

Expressions like these may be written for a solution before and after it is diluted:

$$n_1 = M_1 L_1$$

$$n_2 = M_2 L_2$$

where the subscripts "1" and "2" refer to the solution before and after the dilution, respectively. Since the dilution process *does not change the amount of solute in the solution,* $n_1 = n_2$. Thus, these two equations may be set equal to one another:

$$M_1 L_1 = M_2 L_2$$

This relation is commonly referred to as the dilution equation. Although we derived this equation using molarity as the unit of concentration and liters as the unit of volume, other units of concentration and volume may be used, so long as the units properly cancel per the factor-label method. Reflecting this versatility, the dilution equation is often written in the more general form:

$$C_1 V_1 = C_2 V_2$$

where C and V are concentration and volume, respectively.

Link to Learning

Use the simulation (http://openstaxcollege.org/l/16Phetsolvents) to explore the relations between solute amount, solution volume, and concentration and to confirm the dilution equation.

Example 6.13

Determining the Concentration of a Diluted Solution

If 0.850 L of a 5.00-*M* solution of copper nitrate, $Cu(NO_3)_2$, is diluted to a volume of 1.80 L by the addition of water, what is the molarity of the diluted solution?

Solution

We are given the volume and concentration of a stock solution, V_1 and C_1, and the volume of the resultant diluted solution, V_2. We need to find the concentration of the diluted solution, C_2. We thus rearrange the dilution equation in order to isolate C_2:

$$C_1 V_1 = C_2 V_2$$
$$C_2 = \frac{C_1 V_1}{V_2}$$

Since the stock solution is being diluted by more than two-fold (volume is increased from 0.85 L to 1.80 L), we would expect the diluted solution's concentration to be less than one-half 5 *M*. We will compare this ballpark estimate to the calculated result to check for any gross errors in computation (for example, such as an improper substitution of the given quantities). Substituting the given values for the terms on the right side of this equation yields:

$$C_2 = \frac{0.850\,\text{L} \times 5.00\,\frac{\text{mol}}{\text{L}}}{1.80\,\text{L}} = 2.36\,M$$

This result compares well to our ballpark estimate (it's a bit less than one-half the stock concentration, 5 *M*).

Example 6.14

Volume of a Diluted Solution

What volume of 0.12 M HBr can be prepared from 11 mL (0.011 L) of 0.45 M HBr?

Solution

We are given the volume and concentration of a stock solution, V_1 and C_1, and the concentration of the resultant diluted solution, C_2. We need to find the volume of the diluted solution, V_2. We thus rearrange the dilution equation in order to isolate V_2:

$$C_1 V_1 = C_2 V_2$$
$$V_2 = \frac{C_1 V_1}{C_2}$$

Since the diluted concentration (0.12 M) is slightly more than one-fourth the original concentration (0.45 M), we would expect the volume of the diluted solution to be roughly four times the original volume, or around 44 mL. Substituting the given values and solving for the unknown volume yields:

$$V_2 = \frac{(0.45\ M)(0.011\ L)}{(0.12\ M)}$$

$$V_2 = 0.041\ L$$

The volume of the 0.12-M solution is 0.041 L (41 mL). The result is reasonable and compares well with our rough estimate.

Check Your Learning

A laboratory experiment calls for 0.125 M HNO_3. What volume of 0.125 M HNO_3 can be prepared from 0.250 L of 1.88 M HNO_3?

Answer: 3.76 L

Example 6.15

Volume of a Concentrated Solution Needed for Dilution

What volume of 1.59 M KOH is required to prepare 5.00 L of 0.100 M KOH?

Solution

We are given the concentration of a stock solution, C_1, and the volume and concentration of the resultant diluted solution, V_2 and C_2. We need to find the volume of the stock solution, V_1. We thus rearrange the dilution equation in order to isolate V_1:

$$C_1 V_1 = C_2 V_2$$
$$V_1 = \frac{C_2 V_2}{C_1}$$

Since the concentration of the diluted solution 0.100 M is roughly one-sixteenth that of the stock solution

(1.59 M), we would expect the volume of the stock solution to be about one-sixteenth that of the diluted solution, or around 0.3 liters. Substituting the given values and solving for the unknown volume yields:

$$V_1 = \frac{(0.100\,M)(5.00\,L)}{1.59\,M}$$

$$V_1 = 0.314\,L$$

Thus, we would need 0.314 L of the 1.59-M solution to prepare the desired solution. This result is consistent with our rough estimate.

Check Your Learning

What volume of a 0.575-M solution of glucose, $C_6H_{12}O_6$, can be prepared from 50.00 mL of a 3.00-M glucose solution?

Answer: 0.261 L

6.4 Other Units for Solution Concentrations

By the end of this section, you will be able to:

- Define the concentration units of mass percentage, volume percentage, mass-volume percentage, parts-per-million (ppm), and parts-per-billion (ppb)

- Perform computations relating a solution's concentration and its components' volumes and/or masses using these units

In the previous section, we introduced molarity, a very useful measurement unit for evaluating the concentration of solutions. However, molarity is only one measure of concentration. In this section, we will introduce some other units of concentration that are commonly used in various applications, either for convenience or by convention.

Mass Percentage

Earlier in this chapter, we introduced percent composition as a measure of the relative amount of a given element in a compound. Percentages are also commonly used to express the composition of mixtures, including solutions. The **mass percentage** of a solution component is defined as the ratio of the component's mass to the solution's mass, expressed as a percentage:

$$\text{mass percentage} = \frac{\text{mass of component}}{\text{mass of solution}} \times 100\%$$

We are generally most interested in the mass percentages of solutes, but it is also possible to compute the mass percentage of solvent.

Mass percentage is also referred to by similar names such as *percent mass, percent weight, weight/weight percent*, and other variations on this theme. The most common symbol for mass percentage is simply the percent sign, %, although more detailed symbols are often used including %mass, %weight, and (w/w)%. Use of these more detailed symbols can prevent confusion of mass percentages with other types of percentages, such as volume percentages (to be discussed later in this section).

Mass percentages are popular concentration units for consumer products. The label of a typical liquid bleach bottle (**Figure 6.12**) cites the concentration of its active ingredient, sodium hypochlorite (NaOCl), as being 7.4%. A 100.0-g sample of bleach would therefore contain 7.4 g of NaOCl.

Figure 6.12 Liquid bleach is an aqueous solution of sodium hypochlorite (NaOCl). This brand has a concentration of 7.4% NaOCl by mass.

Example 6.16

Calculation of Percent by Mass

A 5.0-g sample of spinal fluid contains 3.75 mg (0.00375 g) of glucose. What is the percent by mass of glucose in spinal fluid?

Solution

The spinal fluid sample contains roughly 4 mg of glucose in 5000 mg of fluid, so the mass fraction of glucose should be a bit less than one part in 1000, or about 0.1%. Substituting the given masses into the equation defining mass percentage yields:

$$\% \text{ glucose} = \frac{3.75 \text{ mg glucose} \times \frac{1 \text{ g}}{1000 \text{ mg}}}{5.0 \text{ g spinal fluid}} = 0.075\%$$

The computed mass percentage agrees with our rough estimate (it's a bit less than 0.1%).

Note that while any mass unit may be used to compute a mass percentage (mg, g, kg, oz, and so on), the same unit must be used for both the solute and the solution so that the mass units cancel, yielding a dimensionless ratio. In this case, we converted the units of solute in the numerator from mg to g to match the units in the denominator. We could just as easily have converted the denominator from g to mg instead. As long as identical mass units are used for both solute and solution, the computed mass percentage will be correct.

Check Your Learning

A bottle of a tile cleanser contains 135 g of HCl and 775 g of water. What is the percent by mass of HCl in this cleanser?

Answer: 14.8%

Example 6.17

Calculations using Mass Percentage

"Concentrated" hydrochloric acid is an aqueous solution of 37.2% HCl that is commonly used as a laboratory reagent. The density of this solution is 1.19 g/mL. What mass of HCl is contained in 0.500 L of this solution?

Solution

The HCl concentration is near 40%, so a 100-g portion of this solution would contain about 40 g of HCl. Since the solution density isn't greatly different from that of water (1 g/mL), a reasonable estimate of the HCl mass in 500 g (0.5 L) of the solution is about five times greater than that in a 100 g portion, or $5 \times 40 = 200$ g. In order to derive the mass of solute in a solution from its mass percentage, we need to know the corresponding mass of the solution. Using the solution density given, we can convert the solution's volume to mass, and then use the given mass percentage to calculate the solute mass. This mathematical approach is outlined in this flowchart:

For proper unit cancellation, the 0.500-L volume is converted into 500 mL, and the mass percentage is expressed as a ratio, 37.2 g HCl/g solution:

$$500 \text{ mL solution} \left(\frac{1.19 \text{ g solution}}{\text{mL solution}} \right) \left(\frac{37.2 \text{ g HCl}}{100 \text{ g solution}} \right) = 221 \text{ g HCl}$$

This mass of HCl is consistent with our rough estimate of approximately 200 g.

Check Your Learning

What volume of concentrated HCl solution contains 125 g of HCl?

Answer: 282 mL

Volume Percentage

Liquid volumes over a wide range of magnitudes are conveniently measured using common and relatively inexpensive laboratory equipment. The concentration of a solution formed by dissolving a liquid solute in a liquid solvent is therefore often expressed as a **volume percentage**, %vol or (v/v)%:

$$\text{volume percentage} = \frac{\text{volume solute}}{\text{volume solution}} \times 100\%$$

Example 6.18

Calculations using Volume Percentage

Rubbing alcohol (isopropanol) is usually sold as a 70%vol aqueous solution. If the density of isopropyl alcohol is 0.785 g/mL, how many grams of isopropyl alcohol are present in a 355 mL bottle of rubbing alcohol?

Solution

Per the definition of volume percentage, the isopropanol volume is 70% of the total solution volume. Multiplying the isopropanol volume by its density yields the requested mass:

$$(355 \text{ mL solution})\left(\frac{70 \text{ mL isopropyl alcohol}}{100 \text{ mL solution}}\right)\left(\frac{0.785 \text{ g isopropyl alcohol}}{1 \text{ mL isopropyl alcohol}}\right) = 195 \text{ g isopropyl alchol}$$

Check Your Learning

Wine is approximately 12% ethanol (CH_3CH_2OH) by volume. Ethanol has a molar mass of 46.06 g/mol and a density 0.789 g/mL. How many moles of ethanol are present in a 750-mL bottle of wine?

Answer: 1.5 mol ethanol

Mass-Volume Percentage

"Mixed" percentage units, derived from the mass of solute and the volume of solution, are popular for certain biochemical and medical applications. A **mass-volume percent** is a ratio of a solute's mass to the solution's volume expressed as a percentage. The specific units used for solute mass and solution volume may vary, depending on the solution. For example, physiological saline solution, used to prepare intravenous fluids, has a concentration of 0.9% mass/volume (m/v), indicating that the composition is 0.9 g of solute per 100 mL of solution. The concentration of glucose in blood (commonly referred to as "blood sugar") is also typically expressed in terms of a mass-volume ratio. Though not expressed explicitly as a percentage, its concentration is usually given in milligrams of glucose per deciliter (100 mL) of blood (**Figure 6.13**).

(a)

(b)

Figure 6.13 "Mixed" mass-volume units are commonly encountered in medical settings. (a) The NaCl concentration of physiological saline is 0.9% (m/v). (b) This device measures glucose levels in a sample of blood. The normal range for glucose concentration in blood (fasting) is around 70–100 mg/dL. (credit a: modification of work by "The National Guard"/Flickr; credit b: modification of work by Biswarup Ganguly)

Parts per Million and Parts per Billion

Very low solute concentrations are often expressed using appropriately small units such as **parts per million (ppm)** or **parts per billion (ppb)**. Like percentage ("part per hundred") units, ppm and ppb may be defined in terms of masses, volumes, or mixed mass-volume units. There are also ppm and ppb units defined with respect to numbers of atoms and molecules.

The mass-based definitions of ppm and ppb are given here:

$$ppm = \frac{\text{mass solute}}{\text{mass solution}} \times 10^6 \text{ ppm}$$

$$ppb = \frac{\text{mass solute}}{\text{mass solution}} \times 10^9 \text{ ppb}$$

Both ppm and ppb are convenient units for reporting the concentrations of pollutants and other trace contaminants in water. Concentrations of these contaminants are typically very low in treated and natural waters, and their levels cannot exceed relatively low concentration thresholds without causing adverse effects on health and wildlife. For example, the EPA has identified the maximum safe level of fluoride ion in tap water to be 4 ppm. Inline water filters are designed to reduce the concentration of fluoride and several other trace-level contaminants in tap water (**Figure 6.14**).

(a)

(b)

Figure 6.14 (a) In some areas, trace-level concentrations of contaminants can render unfiltered tap water unsafe for drinking and cooking. (b) Inline water filters reduce the concentration of solutes in tap water. (credit a: modification of work by Jenn Durfey; credit b: modification of work by "vastateparkstaff"/Wikimedia commons)

Example 6.19

Calculation of Parts per Million and Parts per Billion Concentrations

According to the EPA, when the concentration of lead in tap water reaches 15 ppb, certain remedial actions must be taken. What is this concentration in ppm? At this concentration, what mass of lead (μg) would be contained in a typical glass of water (300 mL)?

Solution

The definitions of the ppm and ppb units may be used to convert the given concentration from ppb to ppm. Comparing these two unit definitions shows that ppm is 1000 times greater than ppb (1 ppm = 10^3 ppb). Thus:

$$15 \text{ ppb} \times \frac{1 \text{ ppm}}{10^3 \text{ ppb}} = 0.015 \text{ ppm}$$

The definition of the ppb unit may be used to calculate the requested mass if the mass of the solution is provided. However, only the volume of solution (300 mL) is given, so we must use the density to derive the corresponding mass. We can assume the density of tap water to be roughly the same as that of pure water (~1.00 g/mL), since the concentrations of any dissolved substances should not be very large. Rearranging the equation defining the ppb unit and substituting the given quantities yields:

$$\text{ppb} = \frac{\text{mass solute}}{\text{mass solution}} \times 10^9 \text{ ppb}$$

$$\text{mass solute} = \frac{\text{ppb} \times \text{mass solution}}{10^9 \text{ ppb}}$$

$$\text{mass solute} = \frac{15 \text{ ppb} \times 300 \text{ mL} \times \frac{1.00 \text{ g}}{\text{mL}}}{10^9 \text{ ppb}} = 4.5 \times 10^{-6} \text{ g}$$

Finally, convert this mass to the requested unit of micrograms:

$$4.5 \times 10^{-6} \text{ g} \times \frac{1 \text{ μg}}{10^{-6} \text{ g}} = 4.5 \text{ μg}$$

Check Your Learning

A 50.0-g sample of industrial wastewater was determined to contain 0.48 mg of mercury. Express the mercury concentration of the wastewater in ppm and ppb units.

Answer: 9.6 ppm, 9600 ppb

Key Terms

aqueous solution solution for which water is the solvent

Avogadro's number (N_A) experimentally determined value of the number of entities comprising 1 mole of substance, equal to 6.022×10^{23} mol^{-1}

concentrated qualitative term for a solution containing solute at a relatively high concentration

concentration quantitative measure of the relative amounts of solute and solvent present in a solution

dilute qualitative term for a solution containing solute at a relatively low concentration

dilution process of adding solvent to a solution in order to lower the concentration of solutes

dissolved describes the process by which solute components are dispersed in a solvent

empirical formula mass sum of average atomic masses for all atoms represented in an empirical formula

formula mass sum of the average masses for all atoms represented in a chemical formula; for covalent compounds, this is also the molecular mass

mass percentage ratio of solute-to-solution mass expressed as a percentage

mass-volume percent ratio of solute mass to solution volume, expressed as a percentage

molar mass mass in grams of 1 mole of a substance

molarity (M) unit of concentration, defined as the number of moles of solute dissolved in 1 liter of solution

mole amount of substance containing the same number of atoms, molecules, ions, or other entities as the number of atoms in exactly 12 grams of ^{12}C

parts per billion (ppb) ratio of solute-to-solution mass multiplied by 10^9

parts per million (ppm) ratio of solute-to-solution mass multiplied by 10^6

percent composition percentage by mass of the various elements in a compound

solute solution component present in a concentration less than that of the solvent

solvent solution component present in a concentration that is higher relative to other components

volume percentage ratio of solute-to-solution volume expressed as a percentage

Key Equations

- $\% X = \dfrac{\text{mass X}}{\text{mass compound}} \times 100\%$

- $\dfrac{\text{molecular or molar mass}\left(\text{amu or } \frac{\text{g}}{\text{mol}}\right)}{\text{empirical formula mass}\left(\text{amu or } \frac{\text{g}}{\text{mol}}\right)} = n \text{ formula units/molecule}$

- $(A_xB_y)_n = A_{nx}B_{ny}$

- $M = \dfrac{\text{mol solute}}{\text{L solution}}$

- $C_1V_1 = C_2V_2$

- Percent by mass $= \dfrac{\text{mass of solute}}{\text{mass of solution}} \times 100$

- $\text{ppm} = \dfrac{\text{mass solute}}{\text{mass solution}} \times 10^6$ ppm

- $\text{ppb} = \dfrac{\text{mass solute}}{\text{mass solution}} \times 10^9$ ppb

Summary

6.1 Formula Mass and the Mole Concept
The formula mass of a substance is the sum of the average atomic masses of each atom represented in the chemical formula and is expressed in atomic mass units. The formula mass of a covalent compound is also called the molecular mass. Due to the use of the same reference substance in defining the atomic mass unit and the mole, the formula mass (amu) and molar mass (g/mol) for any substance are numerically equivalent (for example, one H_2O molecule weighs approximately18 amu and 1 mole of H_2O molecules weighs approximately 18 g).

6.2 Determining Empirical and Molecular Formulas
The chemical identity of a substance is defined by the types and relative numbers of atoms composing its fundamental entities (molecules in the case of covalent compounds, ions in the case of ionic compounds). A compound's percent composition provides the mass percentage of each element in the compound, and it is often experimentally determined and used to derive the compound's empirical formula. The empirical formula mass of a covalent compound may be compared to the compound's molecular or molar mass to derive a molecular formula.

6.3 Molarity
Solutions are homogeneous mixtures. Many solutions contain one component, called the solvent, in which other components, called solutes, are dissolved. An aqueous solution is one for which the solvent is water. The concentration of a solution is a measure of the relative amount of solute in a given amount of solution. Concentrations may be measured using various units, with one very useful unit being molarity, defined as the number of moles of solute per liter of solution. The solute concentration of a solution may be decreased by adding solvent, a process referred to as dilution. The dilution equation is a simple relation between concentrations and volumes of a solution before and after dilution.

6.4 Other Units for Solution Concentrations
In addition to molarity, a number of other solution concentration units are used in various applications. Percentage concentrations based on the solution components' masses, volumes, or both are useful for expressing relatively high concentrations, whereas lower concentrations are conveniently expressed using ppm or ppb units. These units are popular in environmental, medical, and other fields where mole-based units such as molarity are not as commonly used.

Exercises

6.1 Formula Mass and the Mole Concept
1. What is the total mass (amu) of carbon in each of the following molecules?

(a) CH_4

(b) $CHCl_3$

(c) $C_{12}H_{10}O_6$

(d) $CH_3CH_2CH_2CH_2CH_3$

2. What is the total mass of hydrogen in each of the molecules?

(a) CH_4

(b) $CHCl_3$

(c) $C_{12}H_{10}O_6$

(d) $CH_3CH_2CH_2CH_2CH_3$

3. Calculate the molecular or formula mass of each of the following:

(a) P_4

(b) H_2O

(c) $Ca(NO_3)_2$

(d) CH_3CO_2H (acetic acid)

(e) $C_{12}H_{22}O_{11}$ (sucrose, cane sugar).

4. Determine the molecular mass of the following compounds:

(a)

(b)

(c)

(d)

5. Determine the molecular mass of the following compounds:

(a)

(b)

(c)

(d)

6. Which molecule has a molecular mass of 28.05 amu?

(a)

$$H-C\equiv C-H$$

(b)

(c)

6.2 Determining Empirical and Molecular Formulas

7. What information do we need to determine the molecular formula of a compound from the empirical formula?

8. Calculate the following to four significant figures:

(a) the percent composition of ammonia, NH_3

(b) the percent composition of photographic "hypo," $Na_2S_2O_3$

(c) the percent of calcium ion in $Ca_3(PO_4)_2$

9. Determine the following to four significant figures:

(a) the percent composition of hydrazoic acid, HN_3

(b) the percent composition of TNT, $C_6H_2(CH_3)(NO_2)_3$

(c) the percent of SO_4^{2-} in $Al_2(SO_4)_3$

10. Determine the percent ammonia, NH_3, in $Co(NH_3)_6Cl_3$, to three significant figures.

11. Determine the percent water in $CuSO_4 \cdot 5H_2O$ to three significant figures.

12. Determine the empirical formulas for compounds with the following percent compositions:

(a) 15.8% carbon and 84.2% sulfur

(b) 40.0% carbon, 6.7% hydrogen, and 53.3% oxygen

13. Determine the empirical formulas for compounds with the following percent compositions:

(a) 43.6% phosphorus and 56.4% oxygen

(b) 28.7% K, 1.5% H, 22.8% P, and 47.0% O

14. A compound of carbon and hydrogen contains 92.3% C and has a molar mass of 78.1 g/mol. What is its molecular formula?

15. Dichloroethane, a compound that is often used for dry cleaning, contains carbon, hydrogen, and chlorine. It has a molar mass of 99 g/mol. Analysis of a sample shows that it contains 24.3% carbon and 4.1% hydrogen. What is its molecular formula?

16. Determine the empirical and molecular formula for chrysotile asbestos. Chrysotile has the following percent composition: 28.03% Mg, 21.60% Si, 1.16% H, and 49.21% O. The molar mass for chrysotile is 520.8 g/mol.

17. Polymers are large molecules composed of simple units repeated many times. Thus, they often have relatively simple empirical formulas. Calculate the empirical formulas of the following polymers:

(a) Lucite (Plexiglas); 59.9% C, 8.06% H, 32.0% O

(b) Saran; 24.8% C, 2.0% H, 73.1% Cl

(c) polyethylene; 86% C, 14% H

(d) polystyrene; 92.3% C, 7.7% H

(e) Orlon; 67.9% C, 5.70% H, 26.4% N

18. A major textile dye manufacturer developed a new yellow dye. The dye has a percent composition of 75.95% C, 17.72% N, and 6.33% H by mass with a molar mass of about 240 g/mol. Determine the molecular formula of the dye.

6.3 Molarity

19. Explain what changes and what stays the same when 1.00 L of a solution of NaCl is diluted to 1.80 L.

20. What information do we need to calculate the molarity of a sulfuric acid solution?

21. What does it mean when we say that a 200-mL sample and a 400-mL sample of a solution of salt have the same molarity? In what ways are the two samples identical? In what ways are these two samples different?

22. Determine the molarity for each of the following solutions:

(a) 0.444 mol of $CoCl_2$ in 0.654 L of solution

(b) 98.0 g of phosphoric acid, H_3PO_4, in 1.00 L of solution

(c) 0.2074 g of calcium hydroxide, $Ca(OH)_2$, in 40.00 mL of solution

(d) 10.5 kg of $Na_2SO_4 \cdot 10H_2O$ in 18.60 L of solution

(e) 7.0×10^{-3} mol of I_2 in 100.0 mL of solution

(f) 1.8×10^4 mg of HCl in 0.075 L of solution

23. Determine the molarity of each of the following solutions:

(a) 1.457 mol KCl in 1.500 L of solution

(b) 0.515 g of H_2SO_4 in 1.00 L of solution

(c) 20.54 g of $Al(NO_3)_3$ in 1575 mL of solution

(d) 2.76 kg of $CuSO_4 \cdot 5H_2O$ in 1.45 L of solution

(e) 0.005653 mol of Br_2 in 10.00 mL of solution

(f) 0.000889 g of glycine, $C_2H_5NO_2$, in 1.05 mL of solution

24. Consider this question: What is the mass of the solute in 0.500 L of 0.30 M glucose, $C_6H_{12}O_6$, used for intravenous injection?

(a) Outline the steps necessary to answer the question.

(b) Answer the question.

25. Consider this question: What is the mass of solute in 200.0 L of a 1.556-M solution of KBr?

(a) Outline the steps necessary to answer the question.

(b) Answer the question.

26. Calculate the number of moles and the mass of the solute in each of the following solutions:

(a) 2.00 L of 18.5 M H_2SO_4, concentrated sulfuric acid

(b) 100.0 mL of 3.8×10^{-5} M NaCN, the minimum lethal concentration of sodium cyanide in blood serum

(c) 5.50 L of 13.3 M H_2CO, the formaldehyde used to "fix" tissue samples

(d) 325 mL of 1.8×10^{-6} M $FeSO_4$, the minimum concentration of iron sulfate detectable by taste in drinking water

27. Calculate the number of moles and the mass of the solute in each of the following solutions:

(a) 325 mL of 8.23×10^{-5} M KI, a source of iodine in the diet

(b) 75.0 mL of 2.2×10^{-5} M H_2SO_4, a sample of acid rain

(c) 0.2500 L of 0.1135 M K_2CrO_4, an analytical reagent used in iron assays

(d) 10.5 L of 3.716 M $(NH_4)_2SO_4$, a liquid fertilizer

28. Consider this question: What is the molarity of $KMnO_4$ in a solution of 0.0908 g of $KMnO_4$ in 0.500 L of solution?

(a) Outline the steps necessary to answer the question.

(b) Answer the question.

29. Consider this question: What is the molarity of HCl if 35.23 mL of a solution of HCl contain 0.3366 g of HCl?

(a) Outline the steps necessary to answer the question.

(b) Answer the question.

30. Calculate the molarity of each of the following solutions:

(a) 0.195 g of cholesterol, $C_{27}H_{46}O$, in 0.100 L of serum, the average concentration of cholesterol in human serum

(b) 4.25 g of NH_3 in 0.500 L of solution, the concentration of NH_3 in household ammonia

(c) 1.49 kg of isopropyl alcohol, C_3H_7OH, in 2.50 L of solution, the concentration of isopropyl alcohol in rubbing alcohol

(d) 0.029 g of I_2 in 0.100 L of solution, the solubility of I_2 in water at 20 °C

31. Calculate the molarity of each of the following solutions:

(a) 293 g HCl in 666 mL of solution, a concentrated HCl solution

(b) 2.026 g $FeCl_3$ in 0.1250 L of a solution used as an unknown in general chemistry laboratories

(c) 0.001 mg Cd^{2+} in 0.100 L, the maximum permissible concentration of cadmium in drinking water

(d) 0.0079 g $C_7H_5SNO_3$ in one ounce (29.6 mL), the concentration of saccharin in a diet soft drink.

32. There is about 1.0 g of calcium, as Ca^{2+}, in 1.0 L of milk. What is the molarity of Ca^{2+} in milk?

33. What volume of a 1.00-M $Fe(NO_3)_3$ solution can be diluted to prepare 1.00 L of a solution with a concentration of 0.250 M?

34. If 0.1718 L of a 0.3556-M C_3H_7OH solution is diluted to a concentration of 0.1222 M, what is the volume of the resulting solution?

35. If 4.12 L of a 0.850 M-H_3PO_4 solution is be diluted to a volume of 10.00 L, what is the concentration of the resulting solution?

36. What volume of a 0.33-M $C_{12}H_{22}O_{11}$ solution can be diluted to prepare 25 mL of a solution with a concentration of 0.025 M?

37. What is the concentration of the NaCl solution that results when 0.150 L of a 0.556-M solution is allowed to evaporate until the volume is reduced to 0.105 L?

38. What is the molarity of the diluted solution when each of the following solutions is diluted to the given final volume?

(a) 1.00 L of a 0.250-M solution of $Fe(NO_3)_3$ is diluted to a final volume of 2.00 L

(b) 0.5000 L of a 0.1222-M solution of C_3H_7OH is diluted to a final volume of 1.250 L

(c) 2.35 L of a 0.350-M solution of H_3PO_4 is diluted to a final volume of 4.00 L

(d) 22.50 mL of a 0.025-M solution of $C_{12}H_{22}O_{11}$ is diluted to 100.0 mL

39. What is the final concentration of the solution produced when 225.5 mL of a 0.09988-M solution of Na_2CO_3 is allowed to evaporate until the solution volume is reduced to 45.00 mL?

40. A 2.00-L bottle of a solution of concentrated HCl was purchased for the general chemistry laboratory. The solution contained 868.8 g of HCl. What is the molarity of the solution?

41. An experiment in a general chemistry laboratory calls for a 2.00-M solution of HCl. How many mL of 11.9 M HCl would be required to make 250 mL of 2.00 M HCl?

42. What volume of a 0.20-M K_2SO_4 solution contains 57 g of K_2SO_4?

43. The US Environmental Protection Agency (EPA) places limits on the quantities of toxic substances that may be discharged into the sewer system. Limits have been established for a variety of substances, including hexavalent chromium, which is limited to 0.50 mg/L. If an industry is discharging hexavalent chromium as potassium dichromate ($K_2Cr_2O_7$), what is the maximum permissible molarity of that substance?

6.4 Other Units for Solution Concentrations

44. Consider this question: What mass of a concentrated solution of nitric acid (68.0% HNO_3 by mass) is needed to prepare 400.0 g of a 10.0% solution of HNO_3 by mass?

(a) Outline the steps necessary to answer the question.

(b) Answer the question.

45. What mass of a 4.00% NaOH solution by mass contains 15.0 g of NaOH?

46. What mass of solid NaOH (97.0% NaOH by mass) is required to prepare 1.00 L of a 10.0% solution of NaOH by mass? The density of the 10.0% solution is 1.109 g/mL.

47. What mass of HCl is contained in 45.0 mL of an aqueous HCl solution that has a density of 1.19 g cm^{-3} and contains 37.21% HCl by mass?

48. The hardness of water (hardness count) is usually expressed in parts per million (by mass) of $CaCO_3$, which is equivalent to milligrams of $CaCO_3$ per liter of water. What is the molar concentration of Ca^{2+} ions in a water sample with a hardness count of 175 mg $CaCO_3$/L?

49. The level of mercury in a stream was suspected to be above the minimum considered safe (1 part per billion by weight). An analysis indicated that the concentration was 0.68 parts per billion. Assume a density of 1.0 g/mL and calculate the molarity of mercury in the stream.

50. In Canada and the United Kingdom, devices that measure blood glucose levels provide a reading in millimoles per liter. If a measurement of 5.3 mM is observed, what is the concentration of glucose ($C_6H_{12}O_6$) in mg/dL?

51. A throat spray is 1.40% by mass phenol, C_6H_5OH, in water. If the solution has a density of 0.9956 g/mL, calculate the molarity of the solution.

52. Copper(I) iodide (CuI) is often added to table salt as a dietary source of iodine. How many moles of CuI are contained in 1.00 lb (454 g) of table salt containing 0.0100% CuI by mass?

53. A cough syrup contains 5.0% ethyl alcohol, C_2H_5OH, by mass. If the density of the solution is 0.9928 g/mL, determine the molarity of the alcohol in the cough syrup.

54. D5W is a solution used as an intravenous fluid. It is a 5.0% by mass solution of dextrose ($C_6H_{12}O_6$) in water. If the density of D5W is 1.029 g/mL, calculate the molarity of dextrose in the solution.

55. Find the molarity of a 40.0% by mass aqueous solution of sulfuric acid, H_2SO_4, for which the density is 1.3057 g/mL.

Chapter 7

Stoichiometry of Chemical Reactions

Figure 7.1 Many modern rocket fuels are solid mixtures of substances combined in carefully measured amounts and ignited to yield a thrust-generating chemical reaction. (credit: modification of work by NASA)

Chapter Outline

7.1 Writing and Balancing Chemical Equations

7.2 Classifying Chemical Reactions

7.3 Reaction Stoichiometry

7.4 Reaction Yields

7.5 Quantitative Chemical Analysis

Introduction

Solid-fuel rockets are a central feature in the world's space exploration programs, including the new Space Launch System being developed by the National Aeronautics and Space Administration (NASA) to replace the retired Space Shuttle fleet (Figure 7.1). The engines of these rockets rely on carefully prepared solid mixtures of chemicals combined in precisely measured amounts. Igniting the mixture initiates a vigorous chemical reaction that rapidly generates large amounts of gaseous products. These gases are ejected from the rocket engine through its nozzle, providing the thrust needed to propel heavy payloads into space. Both the nature of this chemical reaction and the relationships between the amounts of the substances being consumed and produced by the reaction are critically important considerations that determine the success of the technology. This chapter will describe how to symbolize chemical reactions using chemical equations, how to classify some common chemical reactions by identifying patterns of reactivity, and how to determine the quantitative relations between the amounts of substances involved in chemical reactions—that is, the reaction *stoichiometry*.

7.1 Writing and Balancing Chemical Equations

By the end of this section, you will be able to:

- Derive chemical equations from narrative descriptions of chemical reactions.
- Write and balance chemical equations in molecular, total ionic, and net ionic formats.

The preceding chapter introduced the use of element symbols to represent individual atoms. When atoms gain or lose electrons to yield ions, or combine with other atoms to form molecules, their symbols are modified or combined to generate chemical formulas that appropriately represent these species. Extending this symbolism to represent both the identities and the relative quantities of substances undergoing a chemical (or physical) change involves writing and balancing a **chemical equation**. Consider as an example the reaction between one methane molecule (CH_4) and two diatomic oxygen molecules (O_2) to produce one carbon dioxide molecule (CO_2) and two water molecules (H_2O). The chemical equation representing this process is provided in the upper half of **Figure 7.2**, with space-filling molecular models shown in the lower half of the figure.

Figure 7.2 The reaction between methane and oxygen to yield carbon dioxide and water (shown at bottom) may be represented by a chemical equation using formulas (top).

This example illustrates the fundamental aspects of any chemical equation:

1. The substances undergoing reaction are called **reactants**, and their formulas are placed on the left side of the equation.

2. The substances generated by the reaction are called **products**, and their formulas are placed on the right sight of the equation.

3. Plus signs (+) separate individual reactant and product formulas, and an arrow ($\longrightarrow$) separates the reactant and product (left and right) sides of the equation.

4. The relative numbers of reactant and product species are represented by **coefficients** (numbers placed immediately to the left of each formula). A coefficient of 1 is typically omitted.

It is common practice to use the smallest possible whole-number coefficients in a chemical equation, as is done in this example. Realize, however, that these coefficients represent the *relative* numbers of reactants and products, and, therefore, they may be correctly interpreted as ratios. Methane and oxygen react to yield carbon dioxide and water in a 1:2:1:2 ratio. This ratio is satisfied if the numbers of these molecules are, respectively, 1-2-1-2, or 2-4-2-4, or 3-6-3-6, and so on (**Figure 7.3**). Likewise, these coefficients may be interpreted with regard to any amount (number) unit, and so this equation may be correctly read in many ways, including:

- *One* methane molecule and *two* oxygen molecules react to yield *one* carbon dioxide molecule and *two* water molecules.

- *One dozen* methane molecules and *two dozen* oxygen molecules react to yield *one dozen* carbon dioxide molecules and *two dozen* water molecules.

- *One mole* of methane molecules and *2 moles* of oxygen molecules react to yield *1 mole* of carbon dioxide molecules and *2 moles* of water molecules.

Mixture before reaction   Mixture after reaction

Figure 7.3 Regardless of the absolute numbers of molecules involved, the ratios between numbers of molecules of each species that react (the reactants) and molecules of each species that form (the products) are the same and are given by the chemical reaction equation.

Balancing Equations

The chemical equation described in section 4.1 is **balanced**, meaning that equal numbers of atoms for each element involved in the reaction are represented on the reactant and product sides. This is a requirement the equation must satisfy to be consistent with the law of conservation of matter. It may be confirmed by simply summing the numbers of atoms on either side of the arrow and comparing these sums to ensure they are equal. Note that the number of atoms for a given element is calculated by multiplying the coefficient of any formula containing that element by the element's subscript in the formula. If an element appears in more than one formula on a given side of the equation, the number of atoms represented in each must be computed and then added together. For example, both product species in the example reaction, CO_2 and H_2O, contain the element oxygen, and so the number of oxygen atoms on the product side of the equation is

$$\left(1\ CO_2\ \text{molecule} \times \frac{2\ O\ \text{atoms}}{CO_2\ \text{molecule}}\right) + \left(2\ H_2O\ \text{molecule} \times \frac{1\ O\ \text{atom}}{H_2O\ \text{molecule}}\right) = 4\ O\ \text{atoms}$$

The equation for the reaction between methane and oxygen to yield carbon dioxide and water is confirmed to be balanced per this approach, as shown here:

$$CH_4 + 2O_2 \longrightarrow CO_2 + 2H_2O$$

Element	Reactants	Products	Balanced?
C	$1 \times 1 = 1$	$1 \times 1 = 1$	1 = 1, yes
H	$4 \times 1 = 4$	$2 \times 2 = 4$	4 = 4, yes
O	$2 \times 2 = 4$	$(1 \times 2) + (2 \times 1) = 4$	4 = 4, yes

A balanced chemical equation often may be derived from a qualitative description of some chemical reaction by a fairly simple approach known as balancing by inspection. Consider as an example the decomposition of water to yield molecular hydrogen and oxygen. This process is represented qualitatively by an *unbalanced* chemical equation:

$$H_2O \longrightarrow H_2 + O_2 \qquad \text{(unbalanced)}$$

Comparing the number of H and O atoms on either side of this equation confirms its imbalance:

Element	Reactants	Products	Balanced?
H	$1 \times 2 = 2$	$1 \times 2 = 2$	2 = 2, yes
O	$1 \times 1 = 1$	$1 \times 2 = 2$	1 ≠ 2, no

The numbers of H atoms on the reactant and product sides of the equation are equal, but the numbers of O atoms are not. To achieve balance, the *coefficients* of the equation may be changed as needed. Keep in mind, of course, that the *formula subscripts* define, in part, the identity of the substance, and so these cannot be changed without altering the qualitative meaning of the equation. For example, changing the reactant formula from H_2O to H_2O_2 would yield balance in the number of atoms, but doing so also changes the reactant's identity (it's now hydrogen peroxide and not water). The O atom balance may be achieved by changing the coefficient for H_2O to 2.

$$2H_2O \longrightarrow H_2 + O_2 \qquad \text{(unbalanced)}$$

Element	Reactants	Products	Balanced?
H	$\mathbf{2} \times 2 = 4$	$1 \times 2 = 2$	4 ≠ 2, no
O	$2 \times 1 = 2$	$1 \times 2 = 2$	2 = 2, yes

The H atom balance was upset by this change, but it is easily reestablished by changing the coefficient for the H_2 product to 2.

$$2H_2O \longrightarrow 2H_2 + O_2 \qquad \text{(balanced)}$$

Element	Reactants	Products	Balanced?
H	$2 \times 2 = 4$	$\mathbf{2} \times 2 = 4$	4 = 4, yes
O	$2 \times 1 = 2$	$1 \times 2 = 2$	2 = 2, yes

These coefficients yield equal numbers of both H and O atoms on the reactant and product sides, and the balanced equation is, therefore:

$$2H_2O \longrightarrow 2H_2 + O_2$$

Example 7.1

Balancing Chemical Equations

Write a balanced equation for the reaction of molecular nitrogen (N_2) and oxygen (O_2) to form dinitrogen pentoxide.

Solution

First, write the unbalanced equation.

$$N_2 + O_2 \longrightarrow N_2O_5 \qquad \text{(unbalanced)}$$

Next, count the number of each type of atom present in the unbalanced equation.

Element	Reactants	Products	Balanced?
N	1 × 2 = 2	1 × 2 = 2	2 = 2, yes
O	1 × 2 = 2	1 × 5 = 5	2 ≠ 5, no

Though nitrogen is balanced, changes in coefficients are needed to balance the number of oxygen atoms. To balance the number of oxygen atoms, a reasonable first attempt would be to change the coefficients for the O_2 and N_2O_5 to integers that will yield 10 O atoms (the least common multiple for the O atom subscripts in these two formulas).

$$N_2 + 5O_2 \longrightarrow 2N_2O_5 \qquad \text{(unbalanced)}$$

Element	Reactants	Products	Balanced?
N	1 × 2 = 2	2 × 2 = 4	2 ≠ 4, no
O	5 × 2 = 10	2 × 5 = 10	10 = 10, yes

The N atom balance has been upset by this change; it is restored by changing the coefficient for the reactant N_2 to 2.

$$2N_2 + 5O_2 \longrightarrow 2N_2O_5$$

Element	Reactants	Products	Balanced?
N	2 × 2 = 4	2 × 2 = 4	4 = 4, yes
O	5 × 2 = 10	2 × 5 = 10	10 = 10, yes

The numbers of N and O atoms on either side of the equation are now equal, and so the equation is balanced.

Check Your Learning

Write a balanced equation for the decomposition of ammonium nitrate to form molecular nitrogen, molecular oxygen, and water. (Hint: Balance oxygen last, since it is present in more than one molecule on the right side of the equation.)

Answer: $2NH_4NO_3 \longrightarrow 2N_2 + O_2 + 4H_2O$

It is sometimes convenient to use fractions instead of integers as intermediate coefficients in the process of balancing a chemical equation. When balance is achieved, all the equation's coefficients may then be multiplied by a whole number to convert the fractional coefficients to integers without upsetting the atom balance. For example, consider the reaction of ethane (C_2H_6) with oxygen to yield H_2O and CO_2, represented by the unbalanced equation:

$$C_2H_6 + O_2 \longrightarrow H_2O + CO_2 \qquad \text{(unbalanced)}$$

Following the usual inspection approach, one might first balance C and H atoms by changing the coefficients for the two product species, as shown:

$$C_2H_6 + O_2 \longrightarrow 3H_2O + 2CO_2 \qquad \text{(unbalanced)}$$

This results in seven O atoms on the product side of the equation, an odd number—no integer coefficient can be used with the O_2 reactant to yield an odd number, so a fractional coefficient, $\frac{7}{2}$, is used instead to yield a provisional balanced equation:

$$C_2H_6 + \frac{7}{2}O_2 \longrightarrow 3H_2O + 2CO_2$$

A conventional balanced equation with integer-only coefficients is derived by multiplying each coefficient by 2:

$$2C_2H_6 + 7O_2 \longrightarrow 6H_2O + 4CO_2$$

Finally with regard to balanced equations, recall that convention dictates use of the *smallest whole-number coefficients*. Although the equation for the reaction between molecular nitrogen and molecular hydrogen to produce ammonia is, indeed, balanced,

$$3N_2 + 9H_2 \longrightarrow 6NH_3$$

the coefficients are not the smallest possible integers representing the relative numbers of reactant and product molecules. Dividing each coefficient by the greatest common factor, 3, gives the preferred equation:

$$N_2 + 3H_2 \longrightarrow 2NH_3$$

Link to Learning

Use this interactive tutorial (http://openstaxcollege.org/l/16BalanceEq) for additional practice balancing equations.

Additional Information in Chemical Equations

The physical states of reactants and products in chemical equations very often are indicated with a parenthetical abbreviation following the formulas. Common abbreviations include *s* for solids, *l* for liquids, *g* for gases, and *aq* for substances dissolved in water (*aqueous solutions*, as introduced in the preceding chapter). These notations are illustrated in the example equation here:

$$2Na(s) + 2H_2O(l) \longrightarrow 2NaOH(aq) + H_2(g)$$

This equation represents the reaction that takes place when sodium metal is placed in water. The solid sodium reacts with liquid water to produce molecular hydrogen gas and the ionic compound sodium hydroxide (a solid in pure form, but readily dissolved in water).

Special conditions necessary for a reaction are sometimes designated by writing a word or symbol above or below the equation's arrow. For example, a reaction carried out by heating may be indicated by the uppercase Greek letter delta (Δ) over the arrow.

$$CaCO_3(s) \xrightarrow{\Delta} CaO(s) + CO_2(g)$$

Other examples of these special conditions will be encountered in more depth in later chapters.

Equations for Ionic Reactions

Given the abundance of water on earth, it stands to reason that a great many chemical reactions take place in aqueous media. When ions are involved in these reactions, the chemical equations may be written with various levels of detail appropriate to their intended use. To illustrate this, consider a reaction between ionic compounds taking place in an aqueous solution. When aqueous solutions of $CaCl_2$ and $AgNO_3$ are mixed, a reaction takes place producing aqueous $Ca(NO_3)_2$ and solid AgCl:

$$CaCl_2(aq) + 2AgNO_3(aq) \longrightarrow Ca(NO_3)_2(aq) + 2AgCl(s)$$

This balanced equation, derived in the usual fashion, is called a **molecular equation** because it doesn't explicitly represent the ionic species that are present in solution. When ionic compounds dissolve in water, they may *dissociate* into their constituent ions, which are subsequently dispersed homogenously throughout the resulting solution (a thorough discussion of this important process is provided in the chapter on solutions). Ionic compounds dissolved in water are, therefore, more realistically represented as dissociated ions, in this case:

$$CaCl_2(aq) \longrightarrow Ca^{2+}(aq) + 2Cl^-(aq)$$
$$2AgNO_3(aq) \longrightarrow 2Ag^+(aq) + 2NO_3{}^-(aq)$$
$$Ca(NO_3)_2(aq) \longrightarrow Ca^{2+}(aq) + 2NO_3{}^-(aq)$$

Unlike these three ionic compounds, AgCl does not dissolve in water to a significant extent, as signified by its physical state notation, *s*.

Explicitly representing all dissolved ions results in a **complete ionic equation**. In this particular case, the formulas for the dissolved ionic compounds are replaced by formulas for their dissociated ions:

$$Ca^{2+}(aq) + 2Cl^-(aq) + 2Ag^+(aq) + 2NO_3{}^-(aq) \longrightarrow Ca^{2+}(aq) + 2NO_3{}^-(aq) + 2AgCl(s)$$

Examining this equation shows that two chemical species are present in identical form on both sides of the arrow, $Ca^{2+}(aq)$ and $NO_3{}^-(aq)$. These **spectator ions**—ions whose presence is required to maintain charge neutrality—are neither chemically nor physically changed by the process, and so they may be eliminated from the equation to yield a more succinct representation called a **net ionic equation**:

$$\cancel{Ca^{2+}(aq)} + 2Cl^-(aq) + 2Ag^+(aq) + \cancel{2NO_3{}^-(aq)} \longrightarrow \cancel{Ca^{2+}(aq)} + \cancel{2NO_3{}^-(aq)} + 2AgCl(s)$$
$$2Cl^-(aq) + 2Ag^+(aq) \longrightarrow 2AgCl(s)$$

Following the convention of using the smallest possible integers as coefficients, this equation is then written:

$$Cl^-(aq) + Ag^+(aq) \longrightarrow AgCl(s)$$

This net ionic equation indicates that solid silver chloride may be produced from dissolved chloride and silver(I) ions, regardless of the source of these ions. These molecular and complete ionic equations provide additional information, namely, the ionic compounds used as sources of Cl^- and Ag^+.

Example 7.2

Molecular and Ionic Equations

When carbon dioxide is dissolved in an aqueous solution of sodium hydroxide, the mixture reacts to yield aqueous sodium carbonate and liquid water. Write balanced molecular, complete ionic, and net ionic equations for this process.

Solution

Begin by identifying formulas for the reactants and products and arranging them properly in chemical equation form:

$$CO_2(aq) + NaOH(aq) \longrightarrow Na_2CO_3(aq) + H_2O(l) \qquad \text{(unbalanced)}$$

Balance is achieved easily in this case by changing the coefficient for NaOH to 2, resulting in the molecular equation for this reaction:

$$CO_2(aq) + 2NaOH(aq) \longrightarrow Na_2CO_3(aq) + H_2O(l)$$

The two dissolved ionic compounds, NaOH and Na_2CO_3, can be represented as dissociated ions to yield the complete ionic equation:

$$CO_2(aq) + 2Na^+(aq) + 2OH^-(aq) \longrightarrow 2Na^+(aq) + CO_3{}^{2-}(aq) + H_2O(l)$$

Finally, identify the spectator ion(s), in this case $Na^+(aq)$, and remove it from each side of the equation to generate the net ionic equation:

$$CO_2(aq) + \cancel{2Na^+(aq)} + 2OH^-(aq) \longrightarrow \cancel{2Na^+(aq)} + CO_3{}^{2-}(aq) + H_2O(l)$$

$$CO_2(aq) + 2OH^-(aq) \longrightarrow CO_3{}^{2-}(aq) + H_2O(l)$$

Check Your Learning

Diatomic chlorine and sodium hydroxide (lye) are commodity chemicals produced in large quantities, along with diatomic hydrogen, via the electrolysis of brine, according to the following unbalanced equation:

$$NaCl(aq) + H_2O(l) \xrightarrow{\text{electricity}} NaOH(aq) + H_2(g) + Cl_2(g)$$

Write balanced molecular, complete ionic, and net ionic equations for this process.

Answer: $2NaCl(aq) + 2H_2O(l) \longrightarrow 2NaOH(aq) + H_2(g) + Cl_2(g)$ (molecular)

$2Na^+(aq) + 2Cl^-(aq) + 2H_2O(l) \longrightarrow 2Na^+(aq) + 2OH^-(aq) + H_2(g) + Cl_2(g)$ (complete ionic)

$2Cl^-(aq) + 2H_2O(l) \longrightarrow 2OH^-(aq) + H_2(g) + Cl_2(g)$ (net ionic)

7.2 Classifying Chemical Reactions

By the end of this section, you will be able to:

- Define three common types of chemical reactions (precipitation, acid-base, and oxidation-reduction)
- Classify chemical reactions as one of these three types given appropriate descriptions or chemical equations
- Identify common acids and bases
- Predict the solubility of common inorganic compounds by using solubility rules
- Compute the oxidation states for elements in compounds

Humans interact with one another in various and complex ways, and we classify these interactions according to common patterns of behavior. When two humans exchange information, we say they are communicating. When they exchange blows with their fists or feet, we say they are fighting. Faced with a wide range of varied interactions between chemical substances, scientists have likewise found it convenient (or even necessary) to classify chemical interactions by identifying common patterns of reactivity. This module will provide an introduction to three of the most prevalent types of chemical reactions: precipitation, acid-base, and oxidation-reduction.

Precipitation Reactions and Solubility Rules

A **precipitation reaction** is one in which dissolved substances react to form one (or more) solid products. Many reactions of this type involve the exchange of ions between ionic compounds in aqueous solution and are sometimes referred to as *double displacement*, *double replacement*, or *metathesis* reactions. These reactions are common in nature and are responsible for the formation of coral reefs in ocean waters and kidney stones in animals. They are used widely in industry for production of a number of commodity and specialty chemicals. Precipitation reactions also play a central role in many chemical analysis techniques, including spot tests used to identify metal ions and *gravimetric methods* for determining the composition of matter (see the last module of this chapter).

The extent to which a substance may be dissolved in water, or any solvent, is quantitatively expressed as its **solubility**, defined as the maximum concentration of a substance that can be achieved under specified conditions. Substances with relatively large solubilities are said to be **soluble**. A substance will **precipitate** when solution conditions are such that its concentration exceeds its solubility. Substances with relatively low solubilities are said to be **insoluble**, and these are the substances that readily precipitate from solution. More information on these important concepts is provided in the text chapter on solutions. For purposes of predicting the identities of solids formed by precipitation reactions, one may simply refer to patterns of solubility that have been observed for many ionic compounds (Table 7.1).

Solubilities of Common Ionic Compounds in Water

Soluble compounds contain • group 1 metal cations (Li^+, Na^+, K^+, Rb^+, and Cs^+) and ammonium ion $(NH_4{}^+)$ • the halide ions (Cl^-, Br^-, and I^-) • the acetate $(C_2H_3O_2{}^-)$, bicarbonate $(HCO_3{}^-)$, nitrate $(NO_3{}^-)$, and chlorate $(ClO_3{}^-)$ ions • the sulfate $(SO_4{}^{2-})$ ion	**Exceptions** to these solubility rules include • halides of Ag^+, $Hg_2{}^{2+}$, and Pb^{2+} • sulfates of Ag^+, Ba^{2+}, Ca^{2+}, $Hg_2{}^{2+}$, Pb^{2+}, and Sr^{2+}
Insoluble compounds contain • carbonate $(CO_3{}^{2-})$, chromate $(CrO_4{}^{2-})$, phosphate $(PO_4{}^{3-})$, and sulfide (S^{2-}) ions • hydroxide ion (OH^-)	**Exceptions** to these insolubility rules include • compounds of these anions with group 1 metal cations and ammonium ion • hydroxides of group 1 metal cations and Ba^{2+}

Table 7.1

A vivid example of precipitation is observed when solutions of potassium iodide and lead nitrate are mixed, resulting in the formation of solid lead iodide:

$$2KI(aq) + Pb(NO_3)_2(aq) \longrightarrow PbI_2(s) + 2KNO_3(aq)$$

This observation is consistent with the solubility guidelines: The only insoluble compound among all those involved is lead iodide, one of the exceptions to the general solubility of iodide salts.

The net ionic equation representing this reaction is:

$$Pb^{2+}(aq) + 2I^-(aq) \longrightarrow PbI_2(s)$$

Lead iodide is a bright yellow solid that was formerly used as an artist's pigment known as iodine yellow (Figure 7.4). The properties of pure PbI_2 crystals make them useful for fabrication of X-ray and gamma ray detectors.

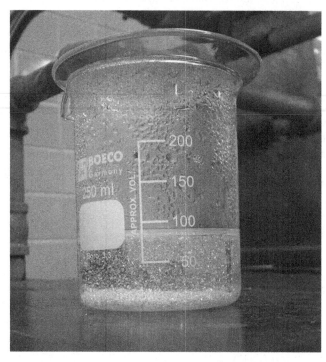

Figure 7.4 A precipitate of PbI_2 forms when solutions containing Pb^{2+} and I^- are mixed. (credit: Der Kreole/Wikimedia Commons)

The solubility guidelines in Table 7.2 may be used to predict whether a precipitation reaction will occur when solutions of soluble ionic compounds are mixed together. One merely needs to identify all the ions present in the solution and then consider if possible cation/anion pairing could result in an insoluble compound. For example, mixing solutions of silver nitrate and sodium fluoride will yield a solution containing Ag^+, $NO_3{}^-$, Na^+, and F^- ions. Aside from the two ionic compounds originally present in the solutions, $AgNO_3$ and NaF, two additional ionic compounds may be derived from this collection of ions: $NaNO_3$ and AgF. The solubility guidelines indicate all nitrate salts are soluble but that AgF is one of the exceptions to the general solubility of fluoride salts. A precipitation reaction, therefore, is predicted to occur, as described by the following equations:

$$NaF(aq) + AgNO_3(aq) \longrightarrow AgF(s) + NaNO_3(aq) \qquad \text{(molecular)}$$

$$Ag^+(aq) + F^-(aq) \longrightarrow AgF(s) \qquad \text{(net ionic)}$$

Example 7.3

Predicting Precipitation Reactions

Predict the result of mixing reasonably concentrated solutions of the following ionic compounds. If precipitation is expected, write a balanced net ionic equation for the reaction.

(a) potassium sulfate and barium nitrate

(b) lithium chloride and silver acetate

(c) lead nitrate and ammonium carbonate

Solution

(a) The two possible products for this combination are KNO_3 and $BaSO_4$. The solubility guidelines indicate $BaSO_4$ is insoluble, and so a precipitation reaction is expected. The net ionic equation for this reaction, derived in the manner detailed in the previous module, is

$$Ba^{2+}(aq) + SO_4^{2-}(aq) \longrightarrow BaSO_4(s)$$

(b) The two possible products for this combination are $LiC_2H_3O_2$ and $AgCl$. The solubility guidelines indicate $AgCl$ is insoluble, and so a precipitation reaction is expected. The net ionic equation for this reaction, derived in the manner detailed in the previous module, is

$$Ag^+(aq) + Cl^-(aq) \longrightarrow AgCl(s)$$

(c) The two possible products for this combination are $PbCO_3$ and NH_4NO_3. The solubility guidelines indicate $PbCO_3$ is insoluble, and so a precipitation reaction is expected. The net ionic equation for this reaction, derived in the manner detailed in the previous module, is

$$Pb^{2+}(aq) + CO_3^{2-}(aq) \longrightarrow PbCO_3(s)$$

Check Your Learning

Which solution could be used to precipitate the barium ion, Ba^{2+}, in a water sample: sodium chloride, sodium hydroxide, or sodium sulfate? What is the formula for the expected precipitate?

Answer: sodium sulfate, $BaSO_4$

Acid-Base Reactions

An **acid-base reaction** is one in which a hydrogen ion, H^+, is transferred from one chemical species to another. Such reactions are of central importance to numerous natural and technological processes, ranging from the chemical transformations that take place within cells and the lakes and oceans, to the industrial-scale production of fertilizers, pharmaceuticals, and other substances essential to society. The subject of acid-base chemistry, therefore, is worthy of thorough discussion, and a full chapter is devoted to this topic later in the text.

For purposes of this brief introduction, we will consider only the more common types of acid-base reactions that take place in aqueous solutions. In this context, an **acid** is a substance that will dissolve in water to yield hydronium ions, H_3O^+. As an example, consider the equation shown here:

$$HCl(aq) + H_2O(aq) \longrightarrow Cl^-(aq) + H_3O^+(aq)$$

The process represented by this equation confirms that hydrogen chloride is an acid. When dissolved in water, H_3O^+ ions are produced by a chemical reaction in which H^+ ions are transferred from HCl molecules to H_2O molecules (Figure 7.5).

Figure 7.5 When hydrogen chloride gas dissolves in water, (a) it reacts as an acid, transferring protons to water molecules to yield (b) hydronium ions (and solvated chloride ions).

The nature of HCl is such that its reaction with water as just described is essentially 100% efficient: Virtually every HCl molecule that dissolves in water will undergo this reaction. Acids that completely react in this fashion are called **strong acids**, and HCl is one among just a handful of common acid compounds that are classified as strong (Table 7.2). A far greater number of compounds behave as **weak acids** and only partially react with water, leaving a large majority of dissolved molecules in their original form and generating a relatively small amount of hydronium ions. Weak acids are commonly encountered in nature, being the substances partly responsible for the tangy taste of citrus fruits, the stinging sensation of insect bites, and the unpleasant smells associated with body odor. A familiar example of a weak acid is acetic acid, the main ingredient in food vinegars:

$$CH_3CO_2H(aq) + H_2O(l) \rightleftharpoons CH_3CO_2{}^-(aq) + H_3O^+(aq)$$

When dissolved in water under typical conditions, only about 1% of acetic acid molecules are present in the ionized form, $CH_3CO_2{}^-$ (**Figure 7.6**). (The use of a double-arrow in the equation above denotes the partial reaction aspect of this process, a concept addressed fully in the chapters on chemical equilibrium.)

(a)   (b)

Figure 7.6   (a) Fruits such as oranges, lemons, and grapefruit contain the weak acid citric acid. (b) Vinegars contain the weak acid acetic acid. (credit a: modification of work by Scott Bauer; credit b: modification of work by Brücke-Osteuropa/Wikimedia Commons)

Common Strong Acids

Compound Formula	Name in Aqueous Solution
HBr	hydrobromic acid
HCl	hydrochloric acid
HI	hydroiodic acid
HNO_3	nitric acid
$HClO_4$	perchloric acid
H_2SO_4	sulfuric acid

Table 7.2

A **base** is a substance that will dissolve in water to yield hydroxide ions, OH^-. The most common bases are ionic compounds composed of alkali or alkaline earth metal cations (groups 1 and 2) combined with the hydroxide ion—for example, NaOH and $Ca(OH)_2$. When these compounds dissolve in water, hydroxide ions are released directly into the solution. For example, KOH and $Ba(OH)_2$ dissolve in water and dissociate completely to produce cations (K^+ and Ba^{2+}, respectively) and hydroxide ions, OH^-. These bases, along with other hydroxides that completely dissociate in water, are considered **strong bases**.

Consider as an example the dissolution of lye (sodium hydroxide) in water:

$$NaOH(s) \longrightarrow Na^+(aq) + OH^-(aq)$$

This equation confirms that sodium hydroxide is a base. When dissolved in water, NaOH dissociates to yield Na^+ and OH^- ions. This is also true for any other ionic compound containing hydroxide ions. Since the dissociation process is essentially complete when ionic compounds dissolve in water under typical conditions, NaOH and other ionic hydroxides are all classified as strong bases.

Unlike ionic hydroxides, some compounds produce hydroxide ions when dissolved by chemically reacting with water molecules. In all cases, these compounds react only partially and so are classified as **weak bases**. These types of compounds are also abundant in nature and important commodities in various technologies. For example, global production of the weak base ammonia is typically well over 100 metric tons annually, being widely used as an agricultural fertilizer, a raw material for chemical synthesis of other compounds, and an active ingredient in household cleaners (Figure 7.7). When dissolved in water, ammonia reacts partially to yield hydroxide ions, as shown here:

$$NH_3(aq) + H_2O(l) \rightleftharpoons NH_4{}^+(aq) + OH^-(aq)$$

This is, by definition, an acid-base reaction, in this case involving the transfer of H^+ ions from water molecules to ammonia molecules. Under typical conditions, only about 1% of the dissolved ammonia is present as $NH_4{}^+$ ions.

(a)   (b)

Figure 7.7 Ammonia is a weak base used in a variety of applications. (a) Pure ammonia is commonly applied as an agricultural fertilizer. (b) Dilute solutions of ammonia are effective household cleansers. (credit a: modification of work by National Resources Conservation Service; credit b: modification of work by pat00139)

The chemical reactions described in which acids and bases dissolved in water produce hydronium and hydroxide ions, respectively, are, by definition, acid-base reactions. In these reactions, water serves as both a solvent *and* a reactant. A **neutralization reaction** is a specific type of acid-base reaction in which the reactants are an acid and a base, the products are often a **salt** and water, and neither reactant is the water itself:

$$\text{acid} + \text{base} \longrightarrow \text{salt} + \text{water}$$

To illustrate a neutralization reaction, consider what happens when a typical antacid such as milk of magnesia (an aqueous suspension of solid $Mg(OH)_2$) is ingested to ease symptoms associated with excess stomach acid (HCl):

$$Mg(OH)_2(s) + 2HCl(aq) \longrightarrow MgCl_2(aq) + 2H_2O(l).$$

Note that in addition to water, this reaction produces a salt, magnesium chloride.

Example 7.4

Writing Equations for Acid-Base Reactions

Write balanced chemical equations for the acid-base reactions described here:

(a) the weak acid hydrogen hypochlorite reacts with water

(b) a solution of barium hydroxide is neutralized with a solution of nitric acid

Solution

(a) The two reactants are provided, HOCl and H_2O. Since the substance is reported to be an acid, its reaction with water will involve the transfer of H^+ from HOCl to H_2O to generate hydronium ions, H_3O^+ and hypochlorite ions, OCl^-.

$$HOCl(aq) + H_2O(l) \rightleftharpoons OCl^-(aq) + H_3O^+(aq)$$

A double-arrow is appropriate in this equation because it indicates the HOCl is a weak acid that has not reacted completely.

(b) The two reactants are provided, $Ba(OH)_2$ and HNO_3. Since this is a neutralization reaction, the two products will be water and a salt composed of the cation of the ionic hydroxide (Ba^{2+}) and the anion generated when the acid transfers its hydrogen ion $(NO_3{}^-)$.

$$Ba(OH)_2(aq) + 2HNO_3(aq) \longrightarrow Ba(NO_3)_2(aq) + 2H_2O(l)$$

Check Your Learning

Write the net ionic equation representing the neutralization of any strong acid with an ionic hydroxide. (Hint: Consider the ions produced when a strong acid is dissolved in water.)

Answer: $H_3O^+(aq) + OH^-(aq) \longrightarrow 2H_2O(l)$

Link to Learning

Explore the microscopic view (http://openstaxcollege.org/l/16AcidsBases) of strong and weak acids and bases.

Oxidation-Reduction Reactions

Earth's atmosphere contains about 20% molecular oxygen, O_2, a chemically reactive gas that plays an essential role in the metabolism of aerobic organisms and in many environmental processes that shape the world. The term **oxidation** was originally used to describe chemical reactions involving O_2, but its meaning has evolved to refer to a broad and important reaction class known as *oxidation-reduction (redox) reactions*. A few examples of such reactions will be used to develop a clear picture of this classification.

Some redox reactions involve the transfer of electrons between reactant species to yield ionic products, such as the reaction between sodium and chlorine to yield sodium chloride:

$$2Na(s) + Cl_2(g) \longrightarrow 2NaCl(s)$$

It is helpful to view the process with regard to each individual reactant, that is, to represent the fate of each reactant in the form of an equation called a **half-reaction**:

$$2Na(s) \longrightarrow 2Na^+(s) + 2e^-$$
$$Cl_2(g) + 2e^- \longrightarrow 2Cl^-(s)$$

These equations show that Na atoms *lose electrons* while Cl atoms (in the Cl_2 molecule) *gain electrons*, the "*s*" subscripts for the resulting ions signifying they are present in the form of a solid ionic compound. For redox reactions of this sort, the loss and gain of electrons define the complementary processes that occur:

$$\textbf{oxidation} \quad = \quad \text{loss of electrons}$$
$$\textbf{reduction} \quad = \quad \text{gain of electrons}$$

In this reaction, then, sodium is *oxidized* and chlorine undergoes **reduction**. Viewed from a more active perspective, sodium functions as a **reducing agent (reductant)**, since it provides electrons to (or reduces) chlorine. Likewise, chlorine functions as an **oxidizing agent (oxidant)**, as it effectively removes electrons from (oxidizes) sodium.

$$\textbf{reducing agent} \quad = \quad \text{species that is oxidized}$$
$$\textbf{oxidizing agent} \quad = \quad \text{species that is reduced}$$

Some redox processes, however, do not involve the transfer of electrons. Consider, for example, a reaction similar to the one yielding NaCl:

$$H_2(g) + Cl_2(g) \longrightarrow 2HCl(g)$$

The product of this reaction is a covalent compound, so transfer of electrons in the explicit sense is not involved. To clarify the similarity of this reaction to the previous one and permit an unambiguous definition of redox reactions, a property called *oxidation number* has been defined. The **oxidation number** (or **oxidation state**) of an element in a compound is the charge its atoms would possess *if the compound was ionic*. The following guidelines are used to assign oxidation numbers to each element in a molecule or ion.

1.   The oxidation number of an atom in an elemental substance is zero.

2.   The oxidation number of a monatomic ion is equal to the ion's charge.

3.   Oxidation numbers for common nonmetals are usually assigned as follows:

     •   Hydrogen: +1 when combined with nonmetals, −1 when combined with metals

     •   Oxygen: −2 in most compounds, sometimes −1 (so-called peroxides, O_2^{2-}), very rarely $-\frac{1}{2}$ (so-called superoxides, O_2^{-}), positive values when combined with F (values vary)

     •   Halogens: −1 for F always, −1 for other halogens except when combined with oxygen or other halogens (positive oxidation numbers in these cases, varying values)

4.   The sum of oxidation numbers for all atoms in a molecule or polyatomic ion equals the charge on the molecule or ion.

Note: The proper convention for reporting charge is to write the number first, followed by the sign (e.g., 2+), while oxidation number is written with the reversed sequence, sign followed by number (e.g., +2). This convention aims to emphasize the distinction between these two related properties.

Example 7.5

Assigning Oxidation Numbers

Follow the guidelines in this section of the text to assign oxidation numbers to all the elements in the following species:

(a) H_2S

(b) SO_3^{2-}

(c) Na_2SO_4

Solution

(a) According to guideline 1, the oxidation number for H is +1.

Using this oxidation number and the compound's formula, guideline 4 may then be used to calculate the oxidation number for sulfur:

$$\text{charge on } H_2S = 0 = (2 \times +1) + (1 \times x)$$
$$x = 0 - (2 \times +1) = -2$$

(b) Guideline 3 suggests the oxidation number for oxygen is −2.

Using this oxidation number and the ion's formula, guideline 4 may then be used to calculate the oxidation number for sulfur:

$$\text{charge on } SO_3^{2-} = -2 = (3 \times -2) + (1 \times x)$$
$$x = -2 - (3 \times -2) = +4$$

(c) For ionic compounds, it's convenient to assign oxidation numbers for the cation and anion separately.

According to guideline 2, the oxidation number for sodium is +1.

Assuming the usual oxidation number for oxygen (−2 per guideline 3), the oxidation number for sulfur is calculated as directed by guideline 4:

$$\text{charge on } SO_4{}^{2-} = -2 = (4 \times -2) + (1 \times x)$$
$$x = -2 - (4 \times -2) = +6$$

Check Your Learning

Assign oxidation states to the elements whose atoms are underlined in each of the following compounds or ions:

(a) K$\underline{N}$O$_3$

(b) $\underline{Al}$H$_3$

(c) $\underline{N}$H$_4{}^+$

(d) H$_2$$\underline{P}O_4{}^-$

Answer: (a) N, +5; (b) Al, +3; (c) N, −3; (d) P, +5

Using the oxidation number concept, an all-inclusive definition of redox reaction has been established. **Oxidation-reduction (redox) reactions** are those in which one or more elements involved undergo a change in oxidation number. (While the vast majority of redox reactions involve changes in oxidation number for two or more elements, a few interesting exceptions to this rule do exist Example 7.6.) Definitions for the complementary processes of this reaction class are correspondingly revised as shown here:

$$\textbf{oxidation} = \text{increase in oxidation number}$$
$$\textbf{reduction} = \text{decrease in oxidation number}$$

Returning to the reactions used to introduce this topic, they may now both be identified as redox processes. In the reaction between sodium and chlorine to yield sodium chloride, sodium is oxidized (its oxidation number increases from 0 in Na to +1 in NaCl) and chlorine is reduced (its oxidation number decreases from 0 in Cl_2 to −1 in NaCl). In the reaction between molecular hydrogen and chlorine, hydrogen is oxidized (its oxidation number increases from 0 in H_2 to +1 in HCl) and chlorine is reduced (its oxidation number decreases from 0 in Cl_2 to −1 in HCl).

Several subclasses of redox reactions are recognized, including **combustion reactions** in which the reductant (also called a *fuel*) and oxidant (often, but not necessarily, molecular oxygen) react vigorously and produce significant amounts of heat, and often light, in the form of a flame. Solid rocket-fuel reactions such as the one depicted in Figure 7.1 are combustion processes. A typical propellant reaction in which solid aluminum is oxidized by ammonium perchlorate is represented by this equation:

$$10Al(s) + 6NH_4ClO_4(s) \longrightarrow 4Al_2O_3(s) + 2AlCl_3(s) + 12H_2O(g) + 3N_2(g)$$

Link to Learning

Watch a brief **video (http://openstaxcollege.org/l/16hybridrocket)** showing the test firing of a small-scale, prototype, hybrid rocket engine planned for use in the new Space Launch System being developed by NASA. The first engines firing at 3 s (green flame) use a liquid fuel/oxidant mixture, and the second, more powerful engines firing at 4 s (yellow flame) use a solid mixture.

Single-displacement (replacement) reactions are redox reactions in which an ion in solution is displaced (or replaced) via the oxidation of a metallic element. One common example of this type of reaction is the acid oxidation of certain metals:

$$Zn(s) + 2HCl(aq) \longrightarrow ZnCl_2(aq) + H_2(g)$$

Metallic elements may also be oxidized by solutions of other metal salts; for example:

$$Cu(s) + 2AgNO_3(aq) \longrightarrow Cu(NO_3)_2(aq) + 2Ag(s)$$

This reaction may be observed by placing copper wire in a solution containing a dissolved silver salt. Silver ions in solution are reduced to elemental silver at the surface of the copper wire, and the resulting Cu^{2+} ions dissolve in the solution to yield a characteristic blue color (**Figure 7.8**).

(a) (b) (c)

Figure 7.8 (a) A copper wire is shown next to a solution containing silver(I) ions. (b) Displacement of dissolved silver ions by copper ions results in (c) accumulation of gray-colored silver metal on the wire and development of a blue color in the solution, due to dissolved copper ions. (credit: modification of work by Mark Ott)

Example 7.6

Describing Redox Reactions

Identify which equations represent redox reactions, providing a name for the reaction if appropriate. For those reactions identified as redox, name the oxidant and reductant.

(a) $ZnCO_3(s) \longrightarrow ZnO(s) + CO_2(g)$

(b) $2Ga(l) + 3Br_2(l) \longrightarrow 2GaBr_3(s)$

(c) $2H_2O_2(aq) \longrightarrow 2H_2O(l) + O_2(g)$

(d) $BaCl_2(aq) + K_2SO_4(aq) \longrightarrow BaSO_4(s) + 2KCl(aq)$

(e) $C_2H_4(g) + 3O_2(g) \longrightarrow 2CO_2(g) + 2H_2O(l)$

Solution

Redox reactions are identified per definition if one or more elements undergo a change in oxidation number.

(a) This is not a redox reaction, since oxidation numbers remain unchanged for all elements.

(b) This is a redox reaction. Gallium is oxidized, its oxidation number increasing from 0 in Ga(l) to +3 in $GaBr_3(s)$. The reducing agent is Ga(l). Bromine is reduced, its oxidation number decreasing from 0 in $Br_2(l)$ to −1 in $GaBr_3(s)$. The oxidizing agent is $Br_2(l)$.

(c) This is a redox reaction. It is a particularly interesting process, as it involves the same element, oxygen, undergoing both oxidation and reduction (a so-called *disproportionation reaction*). Oxygen is oxidized, its oxidation number increasing from −1 in $H_2O_2(aq)$ to 0 in $O_2(g)$. Oxygen is also reduced, its oxidation number decreasing from −1 in $H_2O_2(aq)$ to −2 in $H_2O(l)$. For disproportionation reactions, the same substance functions as an oxidant and a reductant.

(d) This is not a redox reaction, since oxidation numbers remain unchanged for all elements.

(e) This is a redox reaction (combustion). Carbon is oxidized, its oxidation number increasing from −2 in $C_2H_4(g)$ to +4 in $CO_2(g)$. The reducing agent (fuel) is $C_2H_4(g)$. Oxygen is reduced, its oxidation number decreasing from 0 in $O_2(g)$ to −2 in $H_2O(l)$. The oxidizing agent is $O_2(g)$.

Check Your Learning

This equation describes the production of tin(II) chloride:

$$Sn(s) + 2HCl(g) \longrightarrow SnCl_2(s) + H_2(g)$$

Is this a redox reaction? If so, provide a more specific name for the reaction if appropriate, and identify the oxidant and reductant.

Answer: Yes, a single-replacement reaction. $Sn(s)$ is the reductant, $HCl(g)$ is the oxidant.

Balancing Redox Reactions via the Half-Reaction Method

Redox reactions that take place in aqueous media often involve water, hydronium ions, and hydroxide ions as reactants or products. Although these species are not oxidized or reduced, they do participate in chemical change in other ways (e.g., by providing the elements required to form oxyanions). Equations representing these reactions are sometimes very difficult to balance by inspection, so systematic approaches have been developed to assist in the process. One very useful approach is to use the method of half-reactions, which involves the following steps:

1. Write the two half-reactions representing the redox process.

2. Balance all elements except oxygen and hydrogen.

3. Balance oxygen atoms by adding H_2O molecules.

4. Balance hydrogen atoms by adding H^+ ions.

5. Balance charge[1] by adding electrons.

6. If necessary, multiply each half-reaction's coefficients by the smallest possible integers to yield equal numbers of electrons in each.

7. Add the balanced half-reactions together and simplify by removing species that appear on both sides of the equation.

8. For reactions occurring in basic media (excess hydroxide ions), carry out these additional steps:

   a.   Add OH^- ions to both sides of the equation in numbers equal to the number of H^+ ions.

   b.   On the side of the equation containing both H^+ and OH^- ions, combine these ions to yield water molecules.

   c.   Simplify the equation by removing any redundant water molecules.

9. Finally, check to see that both the number of atoms and the total charges[2] are balanced.

Example 7.7

Balancing Redox Reactions in Acidic Solution

Write a balanced equation for the reaction between dichromate ion and iron(II) to yield iron(III) and chromium(III) in acidic solution.

$$Cr_2O_7{}^{2-} + Fe^{2+} \longrightarrow Cr^{3+} + Fe^{3+}$$

---

1.   The requirement of "charge balance" is just a specific type of "mass balance" in which the species in question are electrons. An equation must represent equal numbers of electrons on the reactant and product sides, and so both atoms and charges must be balanced.

2.   The requirement of "charge balance" is just a specific type of "mass balance" in which the species in question are electrons. An equation must represent equal numbers of electrons on the reactant and product sides, and so both atoms and charges must be balanced.

Solution

Step 1.   *Write the two half-reactions.*
Each half-reaction will contain one reactant and one product with one element in common.

$$Fe^{2+} \longrightarrow Fe^{3+}$$

$$Cr_2O_7{}^{2-} \longrightarrow Cr^{3+}$$

Step 2.   *Balance all elements except oxygen and hydrogen.* The iron half-reaction is already balanced, but the chromium half-reaction shows two Cr atoms on the left and one Cr atom on the right. Changing the coefficient on the right side of the equation to 2 achieves balance with regard to Cr atoms.

$$Fe^{2+} \longrightarrow Fe^{3+}$$

$$Cr_2O_7{}^{2-} \longrightarrow 2Cr^{3+}$$

Step 3.   *Balance oxygen atoms by adding* H_2O *molecules.* The iron half-reaction does not contain O atoms. The chromium half-reaction shows seven O atoms on the left and none on the right, so seven water molecules are added to the right side.

$$Fe^{2+} \longrightarrow Fe^{3+}$$

$$Cr_2O_7{}^{2-} \longrightarrow 2Cr^{3+} + 7H_2O$$

Step 4.   *Balance hydrogen atoms by adding* H^+ *ions.* The iron half-reaction does not contain H atoms. The chromium half-reaction shows 14 H atoms on the right and none on the left, so 14 hydrogen ions are added to the left side.

$$Fe^{2+} \longrightarrow Fe^{3+}$$

$$Cr_2O_7{}^{2-} + 14H^+ + \longrightarrow 2Cr^{3+} + 7H_2O$$

Step 5.   *Balance charge by adding electrons.* The iron half-reaction shows a total charge of 2+ on the left side (1 Fe^{2+} ion) and 3+ on the right side (1 Fe^{3+} ion). Adding one electron to the right side bring that side's total charge to $(3+) + (1-) = 2+$, and charge balance is achieved.
The chromium half-reaction shows a total charge of $(1 \times 2-) + (14 \times 1+) = 12+$ on the left side (1 $Cr_2O_7{}^{2-}$ ion and 14 H^+ ions). The total charge on the right side is $(2 \times 3+) = 6 + (2\ Cr^{3+}$ ions). Adding six electrons to the left side will bring that side's total charge to $(12+ + 6-) = 6+$, and charge balance is achieved.

$$Fe^{2+} \longrightarrow Fe^{3+} + e^-$$

$$Cr_2O_7{}^{2-} + 14H^+ + 6e^- \longrightarrow 2Cr^{3+} + 7H_2O$$

Step 6.   *Multiply the two half-reactions so the number of electrons in one reaction equals the number of electrons in the other reaction.* To be consistent with mass conservation, and the idea that redox reactions involve the transfer (not creation or destruction) of electrons, the iron half-reaction's coefficient must be multiplied by 6.

$$6Fe^{2+} \longrightarrow 6Fe^{3+} + 6e^-$$

$$Cr_2O_7{}^{2-} + 6e^- + 14H^+ \longrightarrow 2Cr^{3+} + 7H_2O$$

Step 7.   *Add the balanced half-reactions and cancel species that appear on both sides of the equation.*

$$6Fe^{2+} + Cr_2O_7{}^{2-} + 6e^- + 14H^+ \longrightarrow 6Fe^{3+} + 6e^- + 2Cr^{3+} + 7H_2O$$

Only the six electrons are redundant species. Removing them from each side of the equation yields the simplified, balanced equation here:

$$6Fe^{2+} + Cr_2O_7{}^{2-} + 14H^+ \longrightarrow 6Fe^{3+} + 2Cr^{3+} + 7H_2O$$

A final check of atom and charge balance confirms the equation is balanced.

	Reactants	Products
Fe	6	6
Cr	2	2
O	7	7
H	14	14
charge	24+	24+

Check Your Learning

In acidic solution, hydrogen peroxide reacts with Fe^{2+} to produce Fe^{3+} and H_2O. Write a balanced equation for this reaction.

Answer: $H_2O_2(aq) + 2H^+(aq) + 2Fe^{2+} \longrightarrow 2H_2O(l) + 2Fe^{3+}$

7.3 Reaction Stoichiometry

By the end of this section, you will be able to:

- Explain the concept of stoichiometry as it pertains to chemical reactions
- Use balanced chemical equations to derive stoichiometric factors relating amounts of reactants and products
- Perform stoichiometric calculations involving mass, moles, and solution molarity

A balanced chemical equation provides a great deal of information in a very succinct format. Chemical formulas provide the identities of the reactants and products involved in the chemical change, allowing classification of the reaction. Coefficients provide the relative numbers of these chemical species, allowing a quantitative assessment of the relationships between the amounts of substances consumed and produced by the reaction. These quantitative relationships are known as the reaction's **stoichiometry**, a term derived from the Greek words *stoicheion* (meaning "element") and *metron* (meaning "measure"). In this module, the use of balanced chemical equations for various stoichiometric applications is explored.

The general approach to using stoichiometric relationships is similar in concept to the way people go about many common activities. Food preparation, for example, offers an appropriate comparison. A recipe for making eight pancakes calls for 1 cup pancake mix, $\frac{3}{4}$ cup milk, and one egg. The "equation" representing the preparation of pancakes per this recipe is

$$1 \text{ cup mix} + \frac{3}{4}\text{cup milk} + 1 \text{ egg} \longrightarrow 8 \text{ pancakes}$$

If two dozen pancakes are needed for a big family breakfast, the ingredient amounts must be increased proportionally according to the amounts given in the recipe. For example, the number of eggs required to make 24 pancakes is

$$24 \text{ pancakes} \times \frac{1 \text{ egg}}{8 \text{ pancakes}} = 3 \text{ eggs}$$

Balanced chemical equations are used in much the same fashion to determine the amount of one reactant required to react with a given amount of another reactant, or to yield a given amount of product, and so forth. The coefficients in the balanced equation are used to derive **stoichiometric factors** that permit computation of the desired quantity. To illustrate this idea, consider the production of ammonia by reaction of hydrogen and nitrogen:

$$N_2(g) + 3H_2(g) \longrightarrow 2NH_3(g)$$

This equation shows ammonia molecules are produced from hydrogen molecules in a 2:3 ratio, and stoichiometric factors may be derived using any amount (number) unit:

$$\frac{2 \text{ NH}_3 \text{ molecules}}{3 \text{ H}_2 \text{ molecules}} \quad \text{or} \quad \frac{2 \text{ doz NH}_3 \text{ molecules}}{3 \text{ doz H}_2 \text{ molecules}} \quad \text{or} \quad \frac{2 \text{ mol NH}_3 \text{ molecules}}{3 \text{ mol H}_2 \text{ molecules}}$$

These stoichiometric factors can be used to compute the number of ammonia molecules produced from a given number of hydrogen molecules, or the number of hydrogen molecules required to produce a given number of ammonia molecules. Similar factors may be derived for any pair of substances in any chemical equation.

Example 7.8

Moles of Reactant Required in a Reaction

How many moles of I_2 are required to react with 0.429 mol of Al according to the following equation (see Figure 7.9)?

$$2Al + 3I_2 \longrightarrow 2AlI_3$$

Figure 7.9 Aluminum and iodine react to produce aluminum iodide. The heat of the reaction vaporizes some of the solid iodine as a purple vapor. (credit: modification of work by Mark Ott)

Solution

Referring to the balanced chemical equation, the stoichiometric factor relating the two substances of interest is $\frac{3 \text{ mol } I_2}{2 \text{ mol Al}}$. The molar amount of iodine is derived by multiplying the provided molar amount of aluminum by this factor:

$$\text{mol } I_2 = 0.429 \text{ mol Al} \times \frac{3 \text{ mol } I_2}{2 \text{ mol Al}}$$
$$= 0.644 \text{ mol } I_2$$

Check Your Learning

How many moles of $Ca(OH)_2$ are required to react with 1.36 mol of H_3PO_4 to produce $Ca_3(PO_4)_2$ according to the equation $3Ca(OH)_2 + 2H_3PO_4 \longrightarrow Ca_3(PO_4)_2 + 6H_2O$?

Answer: 2.04 mol

Example 7.9

Number of Product Molecules Generated by a Reaction

How many carbon dioxide molecules are produced when 0.75 mol of propane is combusted according to this equation?

$$C_3H_8 + 5O_2 \longrightarrow 3CO_2 + 4H_2O$$

Solution

The approach here is the same as for Example 7.8, though the absolute number of molecules is requested, not the number of moles of molecules. This will simply require use of the moles-to-numbers conversion factor, Avogadro's number.

The balanced equation shows that carbon dioxide is produced from propane in a 3:1 ratio:

$$\frac{3 \text{ mol } CO_2}{1 \text{ mol } C_3H_8}$$

Using this stoichiometric factor, the provided molar amount of propane, and Avogadro's number,

$$0.75 \text{ mol } C_3H_8 \times \frac{3 \text{ mol } CO_2}{1 \text{ mol } C_3H_8} \times \frac{6.022 \times 10^{23} \text{ } CO_2 \text{ molecules}}{\text{mol } CO_2} = 1.4 \times 10^{24} \text{ } CO_2 \text{ molecules}$$

Check Your Learning

How many NH_3 molecules are produced by the reaction of 4.0 mol of $Ca(OH)_2$ according to the following equation:

$$(NH_4)_2SO_4 + Ca(OH)_2 \longrightarrow 2NH_3 + CaSO_4 + 2H_2O$$

Answer: 4.8×10^{24} NH_3 molecules

These examples illustrate the ease with which the amounts of substances involved in a chemical reaction of known stoichiometry may be related. Directly measuring numbers of atoms and molecules is, however, not an easy task, and the practical application of stoichiometry requires that we use the more readily measured property of mass.

Example 7.10

Relating Masses of Reactants and Products

What mass of sodium hydroxide, NaOH, would be required to produce 16 g of the antacid milk of magnesia [magnesium hydroxide, $Mg(OH)_2$] by the following reaction?

$$MgCl_2(aq) + 2NaOH(aq) \longrightarrow Mg(OH)_2(s) + 2NaCl(aq)$$

Solution

The approach used previously in Example 7.8 and Example 7.9 is likewise used here; that is, we must derive an appropriate stoichiometric factor from the balanced chemical equation and use it to relate the amounts of the two substances of interest. In this case, however, masses (not molar amounts) are provided and requested, so additional steps of the sort learned in the previous chapter are required. The calculations required are outlined in this flowchart:

$$16 \; \cancel{\text{g Mg(OH)}_2} \times \frac{1 \; \cancel{\text{mol Mg(OH)}_2}}{58.3 \; \cancel{\text{g Mg(OH)}_2}} \times \frac{2 \; \cancel{\text{mol NaOH}}}{1 \; \cancel{\text{mol Mg(OH)}_2}} \times \frac{40.0 \text{ g NaOH}}{\cancel{\text{mol NaOH}}} = 22 \text{ g NaOH}$$

Check Your Learning

What mass of gallium oxide, Ga_2O_3, can be prepared from 29.0 g of gallium metal? The equation for the reaction is $4Ga + 3O_2 \longrightarrow 2Ga_2O_3$.

Answer: 39.0 g

Example 7.11

Relating Masses of Reactants

What mass of oxygen gas, O_2, from the air is consumed in the combustion of 702 g of octane, C_8H_{18}, one of the principal components of gasoline?

$$2C_8H_{18} + 25O_2 \longrightarrow 16CO_2 + 18H_2O$$

Solution

The approach required here is the same as for the Example 7.10, differing only in that the provided and requested masses are both for reactant species.

$$702 \; \cancel{\text{g C}_8\text{H}_{18}} \times \frac{1 \; \cancel{\text{mol C}_8\text{H}_{18}}}{114.23 \; \cancel{\text{g C}_8\text{H}_{18}}} \times \frac{25 \; \cancel{\text{mol O}_2}}{2 \; \cancel{\text{mol C}_8\text{H}_{18}}} \times \frac{32.00 \text{ g O}_2}{\cancel{\text{mol O}_2}} = 2.46 \times 10^3 \text{ g O}_2$$

Check Your Learning

What mass of CO is required to react with 25.13 g of Fe_2O_3 according to the equation

$$Fe_2O_3 + 3CO \longrightarrow 2Fe + 3CO_2?$$

Answer: 13.22 g

These examples illustrate just a few instances of reaction stoichiometry calculations. Numerous variations on the beginning and ending computational steps are possible depending upon what particular quantities are provided and sought (volumes, solution concentrations, and so forth). Regardless of the details, all these calculations share a common essential component: the use of stoichiometric factors derived from balanced chemical equations. **Figure 7.10** provides a general outline of the various computational steps associated with many reaction stoichiometry calculations.

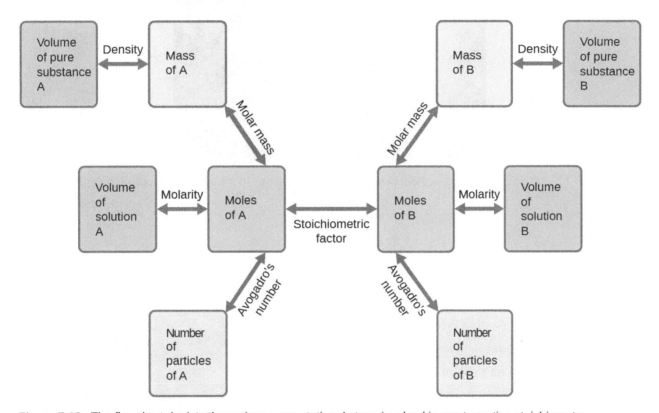

Figure 7.10 The flowchart depicts the various computational steps involved in most reaction stoichiometry calculations.

Chemistry in Everyday Life

Airbags

Airbags (**Figure 7.11**) are a safety feature provided in most automobiles since the 1990s. The effective operation of an airbag requires that it be rapidly inflated with an appropriate amount (volume) of gas when the vehicle is involved in a collision. This requirement is satisfied in many automotive airbag systems through use of explosive chemical reactions, one common choice being the decomposition of sodium azide, NaN_3. When sensors in the vehicle detect a collision, an electrical current is passed through a carefully measured amount of NaN_3 to initiate its decomposition:

$$2NaN_3(s) \longrightarrow 3N_2(g) + 2Na(s)$$

This reaction is very rapid, generating gaseous nitrogen that can deploy and fully inflate a typical airbag in a fraction of a second (~0.03–0.1 s). Among many engineering considerations, the amount of sodium azide used must be appropriate for generating enough nitrogen gas to fully inflate the air bag and ensure its proper function. For example, a small mass (~100 g) of NaN_3 will generate approximately 50 L of N_2.

Figure 7.11   Airbags deploy upon impact to minimize serious injuries to passengers. (credit: Jon Seidman)

7.4 Reaction Yields

By the end of this section, you will be able to:

- Explain the concepts of theoretical yield and limiting reactants/reagents.
- Derive the theoretical yield for a reaction under specified conditions.
- Calculate the percent yield for a reaction.

The relative amounts of reactants and products represented in a balanced chemical equation are often referred to as *stoichiometric amounts*. All the exercises of the preceding module involved stoichiometric amounts of reactants. For example, when calculating the amount of product generated from a given amount of reactant, it was assumed that any other reactants required were available in stoichiometric amounts (or greater). In this module, more realistic situations are considered, in which reactants are not present in stoichiometric amounts.

Limiting Reactant

Consider another food analogy, making grilled cheese sandwiches (Figure 7.12):

$$1 \text{ slice of cheese } + \text{ 2 slices of bread } \longrightarrow 1 \text{ sandwich}$$

Stoichiometric amounts of sandwich ingredients for this recipe are bread and cheese slices in a 2:1 ratio. Provided with 28 slices of bread and 11 slices of cheese, one may prepare 11 sandwiches per the provided recipe, using all the provided cheese and having six slices of bread left over. In this scenario, the number of sandwiches prepared has been *limited* by the number of cheese slices, and the bread slices have been provided in *excess*.

1 sandwich = 2 slices of bread + 1 slice of cheese

Provided with: 28 slices of bread   + 11 slices of cheese

We can make: 11 sandwiches   + 6 slices bread left over

Figure 7.12 Sandwich making can illustrate the concepts of limiting and excess reactants.

Consider this concept now with regard to a chemical process, the reaction of hydrogen with chlorine to yield hydrogen chloride:

$$H_2(s) + Cl_2(g) \longrightarrow 2HCl(g)$$

The balanced equation shows the hydrogen and chlorine react in a 1:1 stoichiometric ratio. If these reactants are provided in any other amounts, one of the reactants will nearly always be entirely consumed, thus limiting the amount of product that may be generated. This substance is the **limiting reactant**, and the other substance is the **excess reactant**. Identifying the limiting and excess reactants for a given situation requires computing the molar amounts of each reactant provided and comparing them to the stoichiometric amounts represented in the balanced chemical equation. For example, imagine combining 3 moles of H_2 and 2 moles of Cl_2. This represents a 3:2 (or 1.5:1) ratio of hydrogen to chlorine present for reaction, which is greater than the stoichiometric ratio of 1:1. Hydrogen, therefore, is present in excess, and chlorine is the limiting reactant. Reaction of all the provided chlorine (2 mol) will consume 2 mol of the 3 mol of hydrogen provided, leaving 1 mol of hydrogen unreacted.

An alternative approach to identifying the limiting reactant involves comparing the amount of product expected for the complete reaction of each reactant. Each reactant amount is used to separately calculate the amount of product that would be formed per the reaction's stoichiometry. The reactant yielding the lesser amount of product is the limiting reactant. For the example in the previous paragraph, complete reaction of the hydrogen would yield

$$\text{mol HCl produced} = 3 \text{ mol } H_2 \times \frac{2 \text{ mol HCl}}{1 \text{ mol } H_2} = 6 \text{ mol HCl}$$

Complete reaction of the provided chlorine would produce

$$\text{mol HCl produced} = 2 \text{ mol } Cl_2 \times \frac{2 \text{ mol HCl}}{1 \text{ mol } Cl_2} = 4 \text{ mol HCl}$$

The chlorine will be completely consumed once 4 moles of HCl have been produced. Since enough hydrogen was provided to yield 6 moles of HCl, there will be unreacted hydrogen remaining once this reaction is complete. Chlorine, therefore, is the limiting reactant and hydrogen is the excess reactant (**Figure 7.13**).

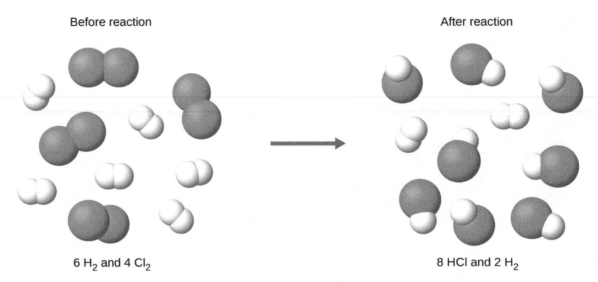

Before reaction   After reaction

6 H$_2$ and 4 Cl$_2$ 8 HCl and 2 H$_2$

Figure 7.13 When H$_2$ and Cl$_2$ are combined in nonstoichiometric amounts, one of these reactants will limit the amount of HCl that can be produced. This illustration shows a reaction in which hydrogen is present in excess and chlorine is the limiting reactant.

Link to Learning

View this interactive **simulation (http://openstaxcollege.org/l/16reactantprod)** illustrating the concepts of limiting and excess reactants.

Example 7.12

Identifying the Limiting Reactant

Silicon nitride is a very hard, high-temperature-resistant ceramic used as a component of turbine blades in jet engines. It is prepared according to the following equation:

$$3Si(s) + 2N_2(g) \longrightarrow Si_3N_4(s)$$

Which is the limiting reactant when 2.00 g of Si and 1.50 g of N$_2$ react?

Solution

Compute the provided molar amounts of reactants, and then compare these amounts to the balanced equation to identify the limiting reactant.

$$\text{mol Si} = 2.00 \text{ g Si} \times \frac{1 \text{ mol Si}}{28.09 \text{ g Si}} = 0.0712 \text{ mol Si}$$

$$\text{mol N}_2 = 1.50 \text{ g N}_2 \times \frac{1 \text{ mol N}_2}{28.02 \text{ g N}_2} = 0.0535 \text{ mol N}_2$$

The provided Si:N$_2$ molar ratio is:

$$\frac{0.0712 \text{ mol Si}}{0.0535 \text{ mol N}_2} = \frac{1.33 \text{ mol Si}}{1 \text{ mol N}_2}$$

The stoichiometric Si:N_2 ratio is:

$$\frac{3 \text{ mol Si}}{2 \text{ mol N}_2} = \frac{1.5 \text{ mol Si}}{1 \text{ mol N}_2}$$

Comparing these ratios shows that Si is provided in a less-than-stoichiometric amount, and so is the limiting reactant.

Alternatively, compute the amount of product expected for complete reaction of each of the provided reactants. The 0.0712 moles of silicon would yield

$$\text{mol Si}_3\text{N}_4 \text{ produced} = 0.0712 \text{ mol Si} \times \frac{1 \text{ mol Si}_3\text{N}_4}{3 \text{ mol Si}} = 0.0237 \text{ mol Si}_3\text{N}_4$$

while the 0.0535 moles of nitrogen would produce

$$\text{mol Si}_3\text{N}_4 \text{ produced} = 0.0535 \text{ mol N}_2 \times \frac{1 \text{ mol Si}_3\text{N}_4}{2 \text{ mol N}_2} = 0.0268 \text{ mol Si}_3\text{N}_4$$

Since silicon yields the lesser amount of product, it is the limiting reactant.

Check Your Learning

Which is the limiting reactant when 5.00 g of H_2 and 10.0 g of O_2 react and form water?

Answer: O_2

Percent Yield

The amount of product that *may be* produced by a reaction under specified conditions, as calculated per the stoichiometry of an appropriate balanced chemical equation, is called the **theoretical yield** of the reaction. In practice, the amount of product obtained is called the **actual yield**, and it is often less than the theoretical yield for a number of reasons. Some reactions are inherently inefficient, being accompanied by *side reactions* that generate other products. Others are, by nature, incomplete (consider the partial reactions of weak acids and bases discussed earlier in this chapter). Some products are difficult to collect without some loss, and so less than perfect recovery will reduce the actual yield. The extent to which a reaction's theoretical yield is achieved is commonly expressed as its **percent yield**:

$$\text{percent yield} = \frac{\text{actual yield}}{\text{theoretical yield}} \times 100\%$$

Actual and theoretical yields may be expressed as masses or molar amounts (or any other appropriate property; e.g., volume, if the product is a gas). As long as both yields are expressed using the same units, these units will cancel when percent yield is calculated.

Example 7.13

Calculation of Percent Yield

Upon reaction of 1.274 g of copper sulfate with excess zinc metal, 0.392 g copper metal was obtained according to the equation:

$$CuSO_4(aq) + Zn(s) \longrightarrow Cu(s) + ZnSO_4(aq)$$

What is the percent yield?

Solution

The provided information identifies copper sulfate as the limiting reactant, and so the theoretical yield is found by the approach illustrated in the previous module, as shown here:

$$1.274 \; \cancel{\text{g CuSO}_4} \times \frac{1 \; \cancel{\text{mol CuSO}_4}}{159.62 \; \cancel{\text{g CuSO}_4}} \times \frac{1 \; \cancel{\text{mol Cu}}}{1 \; \cancel{\text{mol CuSO}_4}} \times \frac{63.55 \; \text{g Cu}}{1 \; \cancel{\text{mol Cu}}} = 0.5072 \; \text{g Cu}$$

Using this theoretical yield and the provided value for actual yield, the percent yield is calculated to be

$$\text{percent yield} = \left(\frac{\text{actual yield}}{\text{theoretical yield}} \right) \times 100$$

$$\text{percent yield} = \left(\frac{0.392 \; \text{g Cu}}{0.5072 \; \text{g Cu}} \right) \times 100$$

$$= 77.3\%$$

Check Your Learning

What is the percent yield of a reaction that produces 12.5 g of the gas Freon CF_2Cl_2 from 32.9 g of CCl_4 and excess HF?

$$CCl_4 + 2HF \longrightarrow CF_2Cl_2 + 2HCl$$

Answer: 48.3%

How Sciences Interconnect

Green Chemistry and Atom Economy

The purposeful design of chemical products and processes that minimize the use of environmentally hazardous substances and the generation of waste is known as *green chemistry*. Green chemistry is a philosophical approach that is being applied to many areas of science and technology, and its practice is summarized by guidelines known as the "Twelve Principles of Green Chemistry" (see details at this website (http://openstaxcollege.org/l/16greenchem)). One of the 12 principles is aimed specifically at maximizing the efficiency of processes for synthesizing chemical products. The *atom economy* of a process is a measure of this efficiency, defined as the percentage by mass of the final product of a synthesis relative to the masses of *all* the reactants used:

$$\text{atom economy} = \frac{\text{mass of product}}{\text{mass of reactants}} \times 100\%$$

Though the definition of atom economy at first glance appears very similar to that for percent yield, be aware that this property represents a difference in the *theoretical* efficiencies of *different* chemical processes. The percent yield of a given chemical process, on the other hand, evaluates the efficiency of a process by comparing the yield of product actually obtained to the maximum yield predicted by stoichiometry.

The synthesis of the common nonprescription pain medication, ibuprofen, nicely illustrates the success of a green chemistry approach (Figure 7.14). First marketed in the early 1960s, ibuprofen was produced using a six-step synthesis that required 514 g of reactants to generate each mole (206 g) of ibuprofen, an atom economy of 40%. In the 1990s, an alternative process was developed by the BHC Company (now BASF Corporation) that requires only three steps and has an atom economy of ~80%, nearly twice that of the original process. The BHC process generates significantly less chemical waste; uses less-hazardous and recyclable materials; and provides significant cost-savings to the manufacturer (and, subsequently, the consumer). In recognition of the positive environmental impact of the BHC process, the company received the Environmental Protection Agency's Greener Synthetic Pathways Award in 1997.

(a)   (b)

Figure 7.14   (a) Ibuprofen is a popular nonprescription pain medication commonly sold as 200 mg tablets. (b) The BHC process for synthesizing ibuprofen requires only three steps and exhibits an impressive atom economy. (credit a: modification of work by Derrick Coetzee)

7.5 Quantitative Chemical Analysis

By the end of this section, you will be able to:

- Describe the fundamental aspects of titrations and gravimetric analysis.
- Perform stoichiometric calculations using typical titration and gravimetric data.

In the 18th century, the strength (actually the concentration) of vinegar samples was determined by noting the amount of potassium carbonate, K_2CO_3, which had to be added, a little at a time, before bubbling ceased. The greater the weight of potassium carbonate added to reach the point where the bubbling ended, the more concentrated the vinegar.

We now know that the effervescence that occurred during this process was due to reaction with acetic acid, CH_3CO_2H, the compound primarily responsible for the odor and taste of vinegar. Acetic acid reacts with potassium carbonate according to the following equation:

$$2CH_3CO_2H(aq) + K_2CO_3(s) \longrightarrow KCH_3CO_3(aq) + CO_2(g) + H_2O(l)$$

The bubbling was due to the production of CO_2.

The test of vinegar with potassium carbonate is one type of **quantitative analysis**—the determination of the amount or concentration of a substance in a sample. In the analysis of vinegar, the concentration of the solute (acetic acid) was determined from the amount of reactant that combined with the solute present in a known volume of the solution. In other types of chemical analyses, the amount of a substance present in a sample is determined by measuring the amount of product that results.

Titration

The described approach to measuring vinegar strength was an early version of the analytical technique known as **titration analysis**. A typical titration analysis involves the use of a **buret** (Figure 7.15) to make incremental additions of a solution containing a known concentration of some substance (the **titrant**) to a sample solution containing the substance whose concentration is to be measured (the **analyte**). The titrant and analyte undergo a chemical reaction of known stoichiometry, and so measuring the volume of titrant solution required for complete reaction with the analyte (the **equivalence point** of the titration) allows calculation of the analyte concentration. The equivalence point of a titration may be detected visually if a distinct change in the appearance of the sample solution accompanies the completion of the reaction. The halt of bubble formation in the classic vinegar analysis is one such example, though, more commonly, special dyes called **indicators** are added to the sample solutions to impart a change in color at or very near the equivalence point of the titration. Equivalence points may also be detected by measuring some solution property that changes in a predictable way during the course of the titration. Regardless of the approach taken to detect a titration's equivalence point, the volume of titrant actually measured is called the **end point**. Properly designed titration methods typically ensure that the difference between the equivalence and end points is negligible. Though any type of chemical reaction may serve as the basis for a titration analysis, the three described in this chapter (precipitation, acid-base, and redox) are most common. Additional details regarding titration analysis are provided in the chapter on acid-base equilibria.

(a)   (b)

Figure 7.15   (a) A student fills a buret in preparation for a titration analysis. (b) A typical buret permits volume measurements to the nearest 0.1 mL. (credit a: modification of work by Mark Blaser and Matt Evans; credit b: modification of work by Mark Blaser and Matt Evans)

Example 7.14

Titration Analysis

The end point in a titration of a 50.00-mL sample of aqueous HCl was reached by addition of 35.23 mL of 0.250 M NaOH titrant. The titration reaction is:

$$HCl(aq) + NaOH(aq) \longrightarrow NaCl(aq) + H_2O(l)$$

What is the molarity of the HCl?

Solution

As for all reaction stoichiometry calculations, the key issue is the relation between the molar amounts of the chemical species of interest as depicted in the balanced chemical equation. The approach outlined in previous modules of this chapter is followed, with additional considerations required, since the amounts of reactants provided and requested are expressed as solution concentrations.

For this exercise, the calculation will follow the following outlined steps:

The molar amount of HCl is calculated to be:

$$35.23 \text{ mL NaOH} \times \frac{1 \text{ L}}{1000 \text{ mL}} \times \frac{0.250 \text{ mol NaOH}}{1 \text{ L}} \times \frac{1 \text{ mol HCl}}{1 \text{ mol NaOH}} = 8.81 \times 10^{-3} \text{ mol HCl}$$

Using the provided volume of HCl solution and the definition of molarity, the HCl concentration is:

$$M = \frac{\text{mol HCl}}{\text{L solution}}$$

$$M = \frac{8.81 \times 10^{-3} \text{ mol HCl}}{50.00 \text{ mL} \times \frac{1 \text{ L}}{1000 \text{ mL}}}$$

$$M = 0.176 \, M$$

Note: For these types of titration calculations, it is convenient to recognize that solution molarity is also equal to the number of *milli*moles of solute per *milli*liter of solution:

$$M = \frac{\text{mol solute}}{\text{L solution}} \times \frac{\frac{10^3 \text{ mmol}}{\text{mol}}}{\frac{10^3 \text{ mL}}{\text{L}}} = \frac{\text{mmol solute}}{\text{mL solution}}$$

Using this version of the molarity unit will shorten the calculation by eliminating two conversion factors:

$$\frac{35.23 \text{ mL NaOH} \times \frac{0.250 \text{ mmol NaOH}}{\text{mL NaOH}} \times \frac{1 \text{ mmol HCl}}{1 \text{ mmol NaOH}}}{50.00 \text{ mL solution}} = 0.176 \, M \text{ HCl}$$

Check Your Learning

A 20.00-mL sample of aqueous oxalic acid, $H_2C_2O_4$, was titrated with a 0.09113-M solution of potassium permanganate, $KMnO_4$.

$$2MnO_4{}^-(aq) + 5H_2C_2O_4(aq) + 6H^+(aq) \longrightarrow 10CO_2(g) + 2Mn^{2+}(aq) + 8H_2O(l)$$

A volume of 23.24 mL was required to reach the end point. What is the oxalic acid molarity?

Answer: 0.2648 M

Gravimetric Analysis

A **gravimetric analysis** is one in which a sample is subjected to some treatment that causes a change in the physical state of the analyte that permits its separation from the other components of the sample. Mass measurements of the sample, the isolated analyte, or some other component of the analysis system, used along with the known stoichiometry of the compounds involved, permit calculation of the analyte concentration. Gravimetric methods were the first techniques used for quantitative chemical analysis, and they remain important tools in the modern chemistry laboratory.

The required change of state in a gravimetric analysis may be achieved by various physical and chemical processes. For example, the moisture (water) content of a sample is routinely determined by measuring the mass of a sample before and after it is subjected to a controlled heating process that evaporates the water. Also common are gravimetric techniques in which the analyte is subjected to a precipitation reaction of the sort described earlier in this chapter. The precipitate is typically isolated from the reaction mixture by filtration, carefully dried, and then weighed (**Figure 7.16**). The mass of the precipitate may then be used, along with relevant stoichiometric relationships, to calculate analyte concentration.

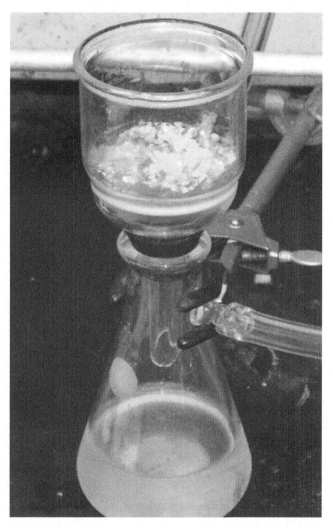

Figure 7.16 Precipitate may be removed from a reaction mixture by filtration.

Example 7.15

Gravimetric Analysis

A 0.4550-g solid mixture containing $MgSO_4$ is dissolved in water and treated with an excess of $Ba(NO_3)_2$, resulting in the precipitation of 0.6168 g of $BaSO_4$.

$$MgSO_4(aq) + Ba(NO_3)_2(aq) \longrightarrow BaSO_4(s) + Mg(NO_3)_2(aq)$$

What is the concentration (percent) of $MgSO_4$ in the mixture?

Solution

The plan for this calculation is similar to others used in stoichiometric calculations, the central step being the connection between the moles of $BaSO_4$ and $MgSO_4$ through their stoichiometric factor. Once the mass of $MgSO_4$ is computed, it may be used along with the mass of the sample mixture to calculate the requested percentage concentration.

The mass of $MgSO_4$ that would yield the provided precipitate mass is

$$0.6168 \text{ g BaSO}_4 \times \frac{1 \text{ mol BaSO}_4}{233.43 \text{ g BaSO}_4} \times \frac{1 \text{ mol MgSO}_4}{1 \text{ mol BaSO}_4} \times \frac{120.37 \text{ g MgSO}_4}{1 \text{ mol MgSO}_4} = 0.3181 \text{ g MgSO}_4$$

The concentration of $MgSO_4$ in the sample mixture is then calculated to be

$$\text{percent MgSO}_4 = \frac{\text{mass MgSO}_4}{\text{mass sample}} \times 100\%$$

$$\frac{0.3181 \text{ g}}{0.4550 \text{ g}} \times 100\% = 69.91\%$$

Check Your Learning

What is the percent of chloride ion in a sample if 1.1324 g of the sample produces 1.0881 g of AgCl when treated with excess Ag^+?

$$Ag^+(aq) + Cl^-(aq) \longrightarrow AgCl(s)$$

Answer: 23.76%

The elemental composition of hydrocarbons and related compounds may be determined via a gravimetric method known as **combustion analysis**. In a combustion analysis, a weighed sample of the compound is heated to a high temperature under a stream of oxygen gas, resulting in its complete combustion to yield gaseous products of known identities. The complete combustion of hydrocarbons, for example, will yield carbon dioxide and water as the only products. The gaseous combustion products are swept through separate, preweighed collection devices containing compounds that selectively absorb each product (**Figure 7.17**). The mass increase of each device corresponds to the mass of the absorbed product and may be used in an appropriate stoichiometric calculation to derive the mass of the relevant element.

Figure 7.17 This schematic diagram illustrates the basic components of a combustion analysis device for determining the carbon and hydrogen content of a sample.

Example 7.16

Combustion Analysis

Polyethylene is a hydrocarbon polymer used to produce food-storage bags and many other flexible plastic items. A combustion analysis of a 0.00126-g sample of polyethylene yields 0.00394 g of CO_2 and 0.00161 g of H_2O. What is the empirical formula of polyethylene?

Solution

The primary assumption in this exercise is that all the carbon in the sample combusted is converted to carbon dioxide, and all the hydrogen in the sample is converted to water:

$$C_x H_y(s) + \text{ excess } O_2(g) \longrightarrow xCO_2(g) + \frac{y}{2}H_2O(g)$$

Note that a balanced equation is not necessary for the task at hand. To derive the empirical formula of the compound, only the subscripts x and y are needed.

First, calculate the molar amounts of carbon and hydrogen in the sample, using the provided masses of the carbon dioxide and water, respectively. With these molar amounts, the empirical formula for the compound may be written as described in the previous chapter of this text. An outline of this approach is given in the following flow chart:

$$\text{mol C} = 0.00394 \text{ g CO}_2 \times \frac{1 \text{ mol CO}_2}{44.01 \text{ g/mol}} \times \frac{1 \text{ mol C}}{1 \text{ mol CO}_2} = 8.95 \times 10^{-5} \text{ mol C}$$

$$\text{mol H} = 0.00161 \text{ g H}_2\text{O} \times \frac{1 \text{ mol H}_2\text{O}}{18.02 \text{ g/mol}} \times \frac{2 \text{ mol H}}{1 \text{ mol H}_2\text{O}} = 1.79 \times 10^{-4} \text{ mol H}$$

The empirical formula for the compound is then derived by identifying the smallest whole-number multiples for these molar amounts. The H-to-C molar ratio is

$$\frac{\text{mol H}}{\text{mol C}} = \frac{1.79 \times 10^{-4} \text{ mol H}}{8.95 \times 10^{-5} \text{ mol C}} = \frac{2 \text{ mol H}}{1 \text{ mol C}}$$

and the empirical formula for polyethylene is CH_2.

Check Your Learning

A 0.00215-g sample of polystyrene, a polymer composed of carbon and hydrogen, produced 0.00726 g of CO_2 and 0.00148 g of H_2O in a combustion analysis. What is the empirical formula for polystyrene?

Answer: CH

Key Terms

acid substance that produces H_3O^+ when dissolved in water

acid-base reaction reaction involving the transfer of a hydrogen ion between reactant species

actual yield amount of product formed in a reaction

analyte chemical species of interest

balanced equation chemical equation with equal numbers of atoms for each element in the reactant and product

base substance that produces OH^- when dissolved in water

buret device used for the precise delivery of variable liquid volumes, such as in a titration analysis

chemical equation symbolic representation of a chemical reaction

coefficient number placed in front of symbols or formulas in a chemical equation to indicate their relative amount

combustion analysis gravimetric technique used to determine the elemental composition of a compound via the collection and weighing of its gaseous combustion products

combustion reaction vigorous redox reaction producing significant amounts of energy in the form of heat and, sometimes, light

complete ionic equation chemical equation in which all dissolved ionic reactants and products, including spectator ions, are explicitly represented by formulas for their dissociated ions

end point measured volume of titrant solution that yields the change in sample solution appearance or other property expected for stoichiometric equivalence (see *equivalence point*)

equivalence point volume of titrant solution required to react completely with the analyte in a titration analysis; provides a stoichiometric amount of titrant for the sample's analyte according to the titration reaction

excess reactant reactant present in an amount greater than required by the reaction stoichiometry

gravimetric analysis quantitative chemical analysis method involving the separation of an analyte from a sample by a physical or chemical process and subsequent mass measurements of the analyte, reaction product, and/or sample

half-reaction an equation that shows whether each reactant loses or gains electrons in a reaction.

indicator substance added to the sample in a titration analysis to permit visual detection of the end point

insoluble of relatively low solubility; dissolving only to a slight extent

limiting reactant reactant present in an amount lower than required by the reaction stoichiometry, thus limiting the amount of product generated

molecular equation chemical equation in which all reactants and products are represented as neutral substances

net ionic equation chemical equation in which only those dissolved ionic reactants and products that undergo a chemical or physical change are represented (excludes spectator ions)

neutralization reaction reaction between an acid and a base to produce salt and water

oxidation process in which an element's oxidation number is increased by loss of electrons

oxidation number (also, oxidation state) the charge each atom of an element would have in a compound if the compound were ionic

oxidation-reduction reaction (also, redox reaction) reaction involving a change in oxidation number for one or more reactant elements

oxidizing agent (also, oxidant) substance that brings about the oxidation of another substance, and in the process becomes reduced

percent yield measure of the efficiency of a reaction, expressed as a percentage of the theoretical yield

precipitate insoluble product that forms from reaction of soluble reactants

precipitation reaction reaction that produces one or more insoluble products; when reactants are ionic compounds, sometimes called double-displacement or metathesis

product substance formed by a chemical or physical change; shown on the right side of the arrow in a chemical equation

quantitative analysis the determination of the amount or concentration of a substance in a sample

reactant substance undergoing a chemical or physical change; shown on the left side of the arrow in a chemical equation

reducing agent (also, reductant) substance that brings about the reduction of another substance, and in the process becomes oxidized

reduction process in which an element's oxidation number is decreased by gain of electrons

salt ionic compound that can be formed by the reaction of an acid with a base that contains a cation and an anion other than hydroxide or oxide

single-displacement reaction (also, replacement) redox reaction involving the oxidation of an elemental substance by an ionic species

solubility the extent to which a substance may be dissolved in water, or any solvent

soluble of relatively high solubility; dissolving to a relatively large extent

spectator ion ion that does not undergo a chemical or physical change during a reaction, but its presence is required to maintain charge neutrality

stoichiometric factor ratio of coefficients in a balanced chemical equation, used in computations relating amounts of reactants and products

stoichiometry relationships between the amounts of reactants and products of a chemical reaction

strong acid acid that reacts completely when dissolved in water to yield hydronium ions

strong base base that reacts completely when dissolved in water to yield hydroxide ions

theoretical yield amount of product that may be produced from a given amount of reactant(s) according to the reaction stoichiometry

titrant solution containing a known concentration of substance that will react with the analyte in a titration analysis

titration analysis quantitative chemical analysis method that involves measuring the volume of a reactant solution required to completely react with the analyte in a sample

weak acid acid that reacts only to a slight extent when dissolved in water to yield hydronium ions

weak base base that reacts only to a slight extent when dissolved in water to yield hydroxide ions

Key Equations

- $\text{percent yield} = \left(\dfrac{\text{actual yield}}{\text{theoretical yield}} \right) \times 100$

Summary

7.1 Writing and Balancing Chemical Equations
Chemical equations are symbolic representations of chemical and physical changes. Formulas for the substances undergoing the change (reactants) and substances generated by the change (products) are separated by an arrow and preceded by integer coefficients indicating their relative numbers. Balanced equations are those whose coefficients result in equal numbers of atoms for each element in the reactants and products. Chemical reactions in aqueous solution that involve ionic reactants or products may be represented more realistically by complete ionic equations and, more succinctly, by net ionic equations.

7.2 Classifying Chemical Reactions
Chemical reactions are classified according to similar patterns of behavior. A large number of important reactions are included in three categories: precipitation, acid-base, and oxidation-reduction (redox). Precipitation reactions involve the formation of one or more insoluble products. Acid-base reactions involve the transfer of hydrogen ions between reactants. Redox reactions involve a change in oxidation number for one or more reactant elements. Writing balanced equations for some redox reactions that occur in aqueous solutions is simplified by using a systematic approach called the half-reaction method.

7.3 Reaction Stoichiometry
A balanced chemical equation may be used to describe a reaction's stoichiometry (the relationships between amounts of reactants and products). Coefficients from the equation are used to derive stoichiometric factors that subsequently may be used for computations relating reactant and product masses, molar amounts, and other quantitative properties.

7.4 Reaction Yields
When reactions are carried out using less-than-stoichiometric quantities of reactants, the amount of product generated will be determined by the limiting reactant. The amount of product generated by a chemical reaction is its actual yield. This yield is often less than the amount of product predicted by the stoichiometry of the balanced chemical equation representing the reaction (its theoretical yield). The extent to which a reaction generates the theoretical amount of product is expressed as its percent yield.

7.5 Quantitative Chemical Analysis
The stoichiometry of chemical reactions may serve as the basis for quantitative chemical analysis methods. Titrations involve measuring the volume of a titrant solution required to completely react with a sample solution. This volume is then used to calculate the concentration of analyte in the sample using the stoichiometry of the titration reaction. Gravimetric analysis involves separating the analyte from the sample by a physical or chemical process, determining its mass, and then calculating its concentration in the sample based on the stoichiometry of the relevant process. Combustion analysis is a gravimetric method used to determine the elemental composition of a compound by collecting and weighing the gaseous products of its combustion.

Exercises

7.1 Writing and Balancing Chemical Equations

1. What does it mean to say an equation is balanced? Why is it important for an equation to be balanced?

2. Consider molecular, complete ionic, and net ionic equations.

(a) What is the difference between these types of equations?

(b) In what circumstance would the complete and net ionic equations for a reaction be identical?

3. Balance the following equations:

(a) $PCl_5(s) + H_2O(l) \longrightarrow POCl_3(l) + HCl(aq)$

(b) $Cu(s) + HNO_3(aq) \longrightarrow Cu(NO_3)_2(aq) + H_2O(l) + NO(g)$

(c) $H_2(g) + I_2(s) \longrightarrow HI(s)$

(d) $Fe(s) + O_2(g) \longrightarrow Fe_2O_3(s)$

(e) $Na(s) + H_2O(l) \longrightarrow NaOH(aq) + H_2(g)$

(f) $(NH_4)_2Cr_2O_7(s) \longrightarrow Cr_2O_3(s) + N_2(g) + H_2O(g)$

(g) $P_4(s) + Cl_2(g) \longrightarrow PCl_3(l)$

(h) $PtCl_4(s) \longrightarrow Pt(s) + Cl_2(g)$

4. Balance the following equations:

(a) $Ag(s) + H_2S(g) + O_2(g) \longrightarrow Ag_2S(s) + H_2O(l)$

(b) $P_4(s) + O_2(g) \longrightarrow P_4O_{10}(s)$

(c) $Pb(s) + H_2O(l) + O_2(g) \longrightarrow Pb(OH)_2(s)$

(d) $Fe(s) + H_2O(l) \longrightarrow Fe_3O_4(s) + H_2(g)$

(e) $Sc_2O_3(s) + SO_3(l) \longrightarrow Sc_2(SO_4)_3(s)$

(f) $Ca_3(PO_4)_2(aq) + H_3PO_4(aq) \longrightarrow Ca(H_2PO_4)_2(aq)$

(g) $Al(s) + H_2SO_4(aq) \longrightarrow Al_2(SO_4)_3(s) + H_2(g)$

(h) $TiCl_4(s) + H_2O(g) \longrightarrow TiO_2(s) + HCl(g)$

5. Write a balanced molecular equation describing each of the following chemical reactions.

(a) Solid calcium carbonate is heated and decomposes to solid calcium oxide and carbon dioxide gas.

(b) Gaseous butane, C_4H_{10}, reacts with diatomic oxygen gas to yield gaseous carbon dioxide and water vapor.

(c) Aqueous solutions of magnesium chloride and sodium hydroxide react to produce solid magnesium hydroxide and aqueous sodium chloride.

(d) Water vapor reacts with sodium metal to produce solid sodium hydroxide and hydrogen gas.

6. Write a balanced equation describing each of the following chemical reactions.

(a) Solid potassium chlorate, $KClO_3$, decomposes to form solid potassium chloride and diatomic oxygen gas.

(b) Solid aluminum metal reacts with solid diatomic iodine to form solid Al_2I_6.

(c) When solid sodium chloride is added to aqueous sulfuric acid, hydrogen chloride gas and aqueous sodium sulfate are produced.

(d) Aqueous solutions of phosphoric acid and potassium hydroxide react to produce aqueous potassium dihydrogen phosphate and liquid water.

7. Colorful fireworks often involve the decomposition of barium nitrate and potassium chlorate and the reaction of the metals magnesium, aluminum, and iron with oxygen.

(a) Write the formulas of barium nitrate and potassium chlorate.

(b) The decomposition of solid potassium chlorate leads to the formation of solid potassium chloride and diatomic oxygen gas. Write an equation for the reaction.

(c) The decomposition of solid barium nitrate leads to the formation of solid barium oxide, diatomic nitrogen gas, and diatomic oxygen gas. Write an equation for the reaction.

(d) Write separate equations for the reactions of the solid metals magnesium, aluminum, and iron with diatomic oxygen gas to yield the corresponding metal oxides. (Assume the iron oxide contains Fe^{3+} ions.)

8. Fill in the blank with a single chemical formula for a covalent compound that will balance the equation:

$$
\begin{array}{c}
\overset{\displaystyle H}{|}\ \overset{\displaystyle H}{|}\ \overset{\displaystyle O}{\|}\\
H-C-C-C-O-H\\
\underset{\displaystyle H}{|}\ \underset{\displaystyle H}{|}
\end{array}
\ +\ NaOH\ \longrightarrow\
\begin{array}{c}
\overset{\displaystyle H}{|}\ \overset{\displaystyle H}{|}\ \overset{\displaystyle O}{\|}\\
H-C-C-C-O^{-}\\
\underset{\displaystyle H}{|}\ \underset{\displaystyle H}{|}
\end{array}
\ +\ Na^{+}\ +\ \underline{\quad}
$$

9. Aqueous hydrogen fluoride (hydrofluoric acid) is used to etch glass and to analyze minerals for their silicon content. Hydrogen fluoride will also react with sand (silicon dioxide).

(a) Write an equation for the reaction of solid silicon dioxide with hydrofluoric acid to yield gaseous silicon tetrafluoride and liquid water.

(b) The mineral fluorite (calcium fluoride) occurs extensively in Illinois. Solid calcium fluoride can also be prepared by the reaction of aqueous solutions of calcium chloride and sodium fluoride, yielding aqueous sodium chloride as the other product. Write complete and net ionic equations for this reaction.

10. A novel process for obtaining magnesium from sea water involves several reactions. Write a balanced chemical equation for each step of the process.

(a) The first step is the decomposition of solid calcium carbonate from seashells to form solid calcium oxide and gaseous carbon dioxide.

(b) The second step is the formation of solid calcium hydroxide as the only product from the reaction of the solid calcium oxide with liquid water.

(c) Solid calcium hydroxide is then added to the seawater, reacting with dissolved magnesium chloride to yield solid magnesium hydroxide and aqueous calcium chloride.

(d) The solid magnesium hydroxide is added to a hydrochloric acid solution, producing dissolved magnesium chloride and liquid water.

(e) Finally, the magnesium chloride is melted and electrolyzed to yield liquid magnesium metal and diatomic chlorine gas.

11. From the balanced molecular equations, write the complete ionic and net ionic equations for the following:

(a) $K_2C_2O_4(aq) + Ba(OH)_2(aq) \longrightarrow 2KOH(aq) + BaC_2O_4(s)$

(b) $Pb(NO_3)_2(aq) + H_2SO_4(aq) \longrightarrow PbSO_4(s) + 2HNO_3(aq)$

(c) $CaCO_3(s) + H_2SO_4(aq) \longrightarrow CaSO_4(s) + CO_2(g) + H_2O(l)$

7.2 Classifying Chemical Reactions

12. Use the following equations to answer the next four questions:

i. $H_2O(s) \longrightarrow H_2O(l)$

ii. $Na^+(aq) + Cl^-(aq) + Ag^+(aq) + NO_3^-(aq) \longrightarrow AgCl(s) + Na^+(aq) + NO_3^-(aq)$

iii. $CH_3OH(g) + O_2(g) \longrightarrow CO_2(g) + H_2O(g)$

iv. $2H_2O(l) \longrightarrow 2H_2(g) + O_2(g)$

v. $H^+(aq) + OH^-(aq) \longrightarrow H_2O(l)$

(a) Which equation describes a physical change?

(b) Which equation identifies the reactants and products of a combustion reaction?

(c) Which equation is not balanced?

(d) Which is a net ionic equation?

13. Indicate what type, or types, of reaction each of the following represents:

(a) $Ca(s) + Br_2(l) \longrightarrow CaBr_2(s)$

(b) $Ca(OH)_2(aq) + 2HBr(aq) \longrightarrow CaBr_2(aq) + 2H_2O(l)$

(c) $C_6H_{12}(l) + 9O_2(g) \longrightarrow 6CO_2(g) + 6H_2O(g)$

14. Indicate what type, or types, of reaction each of the following represents:

(a) $H_2O(g) + C(s) \longrightarrow CO(g) + H_2(g)$

(b) $2KClO_3(s) \longrightarrow 2KCl(s) + 3O_2(g)$

(c) $Al(OH)_3(aq) + 3HCl(aq) \longrightarrow AlCl_3(aq) + 3H_2O(l)$

(d) $Pb(NO_3)_2(aq) + H_2SO_4(aq) \longrightarrow PbSO_4(s) + 2HNO_3(aq)$

15. Silver can be separated from gold because silver dissolves in nitric acid while gold does not. Is the dissolution of silver in nitric acid an acid-base reaction or an oxidation-reduction reaction? Explain your answer.

16. Determine the oxidation states of the elements in the following compounds:

(a) NaI

(b) $GdCl_3$

(c) $LiNO_3$

(d) H_2Se

(e) Mg_2Si

(f) RbO_2, rubidium superoxide

(g) HF

17. Determine the oxidation states of the elements in the compounds listed. None of the oxygen-containing compounds are peroxides or superoxides.

(a) H_3PO_4

(b) $Al(OH)_3$

(c) SeO_2

(d) KNO_2

(e) In_2S_3

(f) P_4O_6

18. Determine the oxidation states of the elements in the compounds listed. None of the oxygen-containing compounds are peroxides or superoxides.

(a) H_2SO_4

(b) $Ca(OH)_2$

(c) BrOH

(d) $ClNO_2$

(e) $TiCl_4$

(f) NaH

19. Classify the following as acid-base reactions or oxidation-reduction reactions:

(a) $Na_2S(aq) + 2HCl(aq) \longrightarrow 2NaCl(aq) + H_2S(g)$

(b) $2Na(s) + 2HCl(aq) \longrightarrow 2NaCl(aq) + H_2(g)$

(c) $Mg(s) + Cl_2(g) \longrightarrow MgCl_2(s)$

(d) $MgO(s) + 2HCl(aq) \longrightarrow MgCl_2(aq) + H_2O(l)$

(e) $K_3P(s) + 2O_2(g) \longrightarrow K_3PO_4(s)$

(f) $3KOH(aq) + H_3PO_4(aq) \longrightarrow K_3PO_4(aq) + 3H_2O(l)$

20. Identify the atoms that are oxidized and reduced, the change in oxidation state for each, and the oxidizing and reducing agents in each of the following equations:

(a) $Mg(s) + NiCl_2(aq) \longrightarrow MgCl_2(aq) + Ni(s)$

(b) $PCl_3(l) + Cl_2(g) \longrightarrow PCl_5(s)$

(c) $C_2H_4(g) + 3O_2(g) \longrightarrow 2CO_2(g) + 2H_2O(g)$

(d) $Zn(s) + H_2SO_4(aq) \longrightarrow ZnSO_4(aq) + H_2(g)$

(e) $2K_2S_2O_3(s) + I_2(s) \longrightarrow K_2S_4O_6(s) + 2KI(s)$

(f) $3Cu(s) + 8HNO_3(aq) \longrightarrow 3Cu(NO_3)_2(aq) + 2NO(g) + 4H_2O(l)$

21. Complete and balance the following acid-base equations:

(a) HCl gas reacts with solid $Ca(OH)_2(s)$.

(b) A solution of $Sr(OH)_2$ is added to a solution of HNO_3.

22. Complete and balance the following acid-base equations:

(a) A solution of $HClO_4$ is added to a solution of LiOH.

(b) Aqueous H_2SO_4 reacts with NaOH.

(c) $Ba(OH)_2$ reacts with HF gas.

23. Complete and balance the following oxidation-reduction reactions, which give the highest possible oxidation state for the oxidized atoms.

(a) $Al(s) + F_2(g) \longrightarrow$

(b) $Al(s) + CuBr_2(aq) \longrightarrow$ (single displacement)

(c) $P_4(s) + O_2(g) \longrightarrow$

(d) $Ca(s) + H_2O(l) \longrightarrow$ (products are a strong base and a diatomic gas)

24. Complete and balance the following oxidation-reduction reactions, which give the highest possible oxidation state for the oxidized atoms.

(a) $K(s) + H_2O(l) \longrightarrow$

(b) $Ba(s) + HBr(aq) \longrightarrow$

(c) $Sn(s) + I_2(s) \longrightarrow$

25. Complete and balance the equations for the following acid-base neutralization reactions. If water is used as a solvent, write the reactants and products as aqueous ions. In some cases, there may be more than one correct answer, depending on the amounts of reactants used.

(a) $Mg(OH)_2(s) + HClO_4(aq) \longrightarrow$

(b) $SO_3(g) + H_2O(l) \longrightarrow$ (assume an excess of water and that the product dissolves)

(c) $SrO(s) + H_2SO_4(l) \longrightarrow$

26. When heated to 700–800 °C, diamonds, which are pure carbon, are oxidized by atmospheric oxygen. (They burn!) Write the balanced equation for this reaction.

27. The military has experimented with lasers that produce very intense light when fluorine combines explosively with hydrogen. What is the balanced equation for this reaction?

28. Write the molecular, total ionic, and net ionic equations for the following reactions:

(a) $Ca(OH)_2(aq) + HC_2H_3O_2(aq) \longrightarrow$

(b) $H_3PO_4(aq) + CaCl_2(aq) \longrightarrow$

29. Great Lakes Chemical Company produces bromine, Br_2, from bromide salts such as NaBr, in Arkansas brine by treating the brine with chlorine gas. Write a balanced equation for the reaction of NaBr with Cl_2.

30. In a common experiment in the general chemistry laboratory, magnesium metal is heated in air to produce MgO. MgO is a white solid, but in these experiments it often looks gray, due to small amounts of Mg_3N_2, a compound formed as some of the magnesium reacts with nitrogen. Write a balanced equation for each reaction.

31. Lithium hydroxide may be used to absorb carbon dioxide in enclosed environments, such as manned spacecraft and submarines. Write an equation for the reaction that involves 2 mol of LiOH per 1 mol of CO_2. (Hint: Water is one of the products.)

32. Calcium propionate is sometimes added to bread to retard spoilage. This compound can be prepared by the reaction of calcium carbonate, $CaCO_3$, with propionic acid, $C_2H_5CO_2H$, which has properties similar to those of acetic acid. Write the balanced equation for the formation of calcium propionate.

33. Complete and balance the equations of the following reactions, each of which could be used to remove hydrogen sulfide from natural gas:

(a) $Ca(OH)_2(s) + H_2S(g) \longrightarrow$

(b) $Na_2CO_3(aq) + H_2S(g) \longrightarrow$

34. Copper(II) sulfide is oxidized by molecular oxygen to produce gaseous sulfur trioxide and solid copper(II) oxide. The gaseous product then reacts with liquid water to produce liquid hydrogen sulfate as the only product. Write the two equations which represent these reactions.

35. Write balanced chemical equations for the reactions used to prepare each of the following compounds from the given starting material(s). In some cases, additional reactants may be required.

(a) solid ammonium nitrate from gaseous molecular nitrogen via a two-step process (first reduce the nitrogen to ammonia, then neutralize the ammonia with an appropriate acid)

(b) gaseous hydrogen bromide from liquid molecular bromine via a one-step redox reaction

(c) gaseous H_2S from solid Zn and S via a two-step process (first a redox reaction between the starting materials, then reaction of the product with a strong acid)

36. Calcium cyclamate $Ca(C_6H_{11}NHSO_3)_2$ is an artificial sweetener used in many countries around the world but is banned in the United States. It can be purified industrially by converting it to the barium salt through reaction of the acid $C_6H_{11}NHSO_3H$ with barium carbonate, treatment with sulfuric acid (barium sulfate is very insoluble), and then neutralization with calcium hydroxide. Write the balanced equations for these reactions.

37. Complete and balance each of the following half-reactions (steps 2–5 in half-reaction method):

(a) $Sn^{4+}(aq) \longrightarrow Sn^{2+}(aq)$

(b) $[Ag(NH_3)_2]^+(aq) \longrightarrow Ag(s) + NH_3(aq)$

(c) $Hg_2Cl_2(s) \longrightarrow Hg(l) + Cl^-(aq)$

(d) $H_2O(l) \longrightarrow O_2(g)$ (in acidic solution)

(e) $IO_3^-(aq) \longrightarrow I_2(s)$

(f) $SO_3^{2-}(aq) \longrightarrow SO_4^{2-}(aq)$ (in acidic solution)

(g) $MnO_4^-(aq) \longrightarrow Mn^{2+}(aq)$ (in acidic solution)

(h) $Cl^-(aq) \longrightarrow ClO_3^-(aq)$ (in basic solution)

38. Complete and balance each of the following half-reactions (steps 2–5 in half-reaction method):

(a) $Cr^{2+}(aq) \longrightarrow Cr^{3+}(aq)$

(b) $Hg(l) + Br^-(aq) \longrightarrow HgBr_4^{2-}(aq)$

(c) $ZnS(s) \longrightarrow Zn(s) + S^{2-}(aq)$

(d) $H_2(g) \longrightarrow H_2O(l)$ (in basic solution)

(e) $H_2(g) \longrightarrow H_3O^+(aq)$ (in acidic solution)

(f) $NO_3^-(aq) \longrightarrow HNO_2(aq)$ (in acidic solution)

(g) $MnO_2(s) \longrightarrow MnO_4^-(aq)$ (in basic solution)

(h) $Cl^-(aq) \longrightarrow ClO_3^-(aq)$ (in acidic solution)

39. Balance each of the following equations according to the half-reaction method:

(a) $Sn^{2+}(aq) + Cu^{2+}(aq) \longrightarrow Sn^{4+}(aq) + Cu^{+}(aq)$

(b) $H_2S(g) + Hg_2^{2+}(aq) \longrightarrow Hg(l) + S(s)$ (in acid)

(c) $CN^{-}(aq) + ClO_2(aq) \longrightarrow CNO^{-}(aq) + Cl^{-}(aq)$ (in acid)

(d) $Fe^{2+}(aq) + Ce^{4+}(aq) \longrightarrow Fe^{3+}(aq) + Ce^{3+}(aq)$

(e) $HBrO(aq) \longrightarrow Br^{-}(aq) + O_2(g)$ (in acid)

40. Balance each of the following equations according to the half-reaction method:

(a) $Zn(s) + NO_3^{-}(aq) \longrightarrow Zn^{2+}(aq) + N_2(g)$ (in acid)

(b) $Zn(s) + NO_3^{-}(aq) \longrightarrow Zn^{2+}(aq) + NH_3(aq)$ (in base)

(c) $CuS(s) + NO_3^{-}(aq) \longrightarrow Cu^{2+}(aq) + S(s) + NO(g)$ (in acid)

(d) $NH_3(aq) + O_2(g) \longrightarrow NO_2(g)$ (gas phase)

(e) $Cl_2(g) + OH^{-}(aq) \longrightarrow Cl^{-}(aq) + ClO_3^{-}(aq)$ (in base)

(f) $H_2O_2(aq) + MnO_4^{-}(aq) \longrightarrow Mn^{2+}(aq) + O_2(g)$ (in acid)

(g) $NO_2(g) \longrightarrow NO_3^{-}(aq) + NO_2^{-}(aq)$ (in base)

(h) $Fe^{3+}(aq) + I^{-}(aq) \longrightarrow Fe^{2+}(aq) + I_2(aq)$

41. Balance each of the following equations according to the half-reaction method:

(a) $MnO_4^{-}(aq) + NO_2^{-}(aq) \longrightarrow MnO_2(s) + NO_3^{-}(aq)$ (in base)

(b) $MnO_4^{2-}(aq) \longrightarrow MnO_4^{-}(aq) + MnO_2(s)$ (in base)

(c) $Br_2(l) + SO_2(g) \longrightarrow Br^{-}(aq) + SO_4^{2-}(aq)$ (in acid)

7.3 Reaction Stoichiometry

42. Write the balanced equation, then outline the steps necessary to determine the information requested in each of the following:

(a) The number of moles and the mass of chlorine, Cl_2, required to react with 10.0 g of sodium metal, Na, to produce sodium chloride, NaCl.

(b) The number of moles and the mass of oxygen formed by the decomposition of 1.252 g of mercury(II) oxide.

(c) The number of moles and the mass of sodium nitrate, $NaNO_3$, required to produce 128 g of oxygen. ($NaNO_2$ is the other product.)

(d) The number of moles and the mass of carbon dioxide formed by the combustion of 20.0 kg of carbon in an excess of oxygen.

(e) The number of moles and the mass of copper(II) carbonate needed to produce 1.500 kg of copper(II) oxide. (CO_2 is the other product.)

(f)

The number of moles and the mass of $\begin{array}{c} H \quad H \\ | \quad\; | \\ Br-C-C-Br \\ | \quad\; | \\ H \quad H \end{array}$ formed by the reaction of 12.85 g of $\begin{array}{c} H \qquad\quad H \\ \backslash \qquad\quad / \\ C=C \\ / \qquad\quad \backslash \\ H \qquad\quad H \end{array}$

with an excess of Br_2.

43. Determine the number of moles and the mass requested for each reaction in **Exercise 7.42**.

44. Write the balanced equation, then outline the steps necessary to determine the information requested in each of the following:

(a) The number of moles and the mass of Mg required to react with 5.00 g of HCl and produce $MgCl_2$ and H_2.

(b) The number of moles and the mass of oxygen formed by the decomposition of 1.252 g of silver(I) oxide.

(c) The number of moles and the mass of magnesium carbonate, $MgCO_3$, required to produce 283 g of carbon dioxide. (MgO is the other product.)

(d) The number of moles and the mass of water formed by the combustion of 20.0 kg of acetylene, C_2H_2, in an excess of oxygen.

(e) The number of moles and the mass of barium peroxide, BaO_2, needed to produce 2.500 kg of barium oxide, BaO (O_2 is the other product.)

(f)

The number of moles and the mass of $\overset{\textstyle H \quad\quad H}{\underset{\textstyle H \quad\quad H}{C=C}}$ required to react with H_2O to produce 9.55 g of $H-\overset{H}{\underset{H}{C}}-\overset{H}{\underset{H}{C}}-O-H$.

45. Determine the number of moles and the mass requested for each reaction in **Exercise 7.44**.

46. H_2 is produced by the reaction of 118.5 mL of a 0.8775-M solution of H_3PO_4 according to the following equation: $2Cr + 2H_3PO_4 \longrightarrow 3H_2 + 2CrPO_4$.

(a) Outline the steps necessary to determine the number of moles and mass of H_2.

(b) Perform the calculations outlined.

47. Gallium chloride is formed by the reaction of 2.6 L of a 1.44 M solution of HCl according to the following equation: $2Ga + 6HCl \longrightarrow 2GaCl_3 + 3H_2$.

(a) Outline the steps necessary to determine the number of moles and mass of gallium chloride.

(b) Perform the calculations outlined.

48. I_2 is produced by the reaction of 0.4235 mol of $CuCl_2$ according to the following equation: $2CuCl_2 + 4KI \longrightarrow 2CuI + 4KCl + I_2$.

(a) How many molecules of I_2 are produced?

(b) What mass of I_2 is produced?

49. Silver is often extracted from ores such as $K[Ag(CN)_2]$ and then recovered by the reaction $2K[Ag(CN)_2](aq) + Zn(s) \longrightarrow 2Ag(s) + Zn(CN)_2(aq) + 2KCN(aq)$

(a) How many molecules of $Zn(CN)_2$ are produced by the reaction of 35.27 g of $K[Ag(CN)_2]$?

(b) What mass of $Zn(CN)_2$ is produced?

50. What mass of silver oxide, Ag_2O, is required to produce 25.0 g of silver sulfadiazine, $AgC_{10}H_9N_4SO_2$, from the reaction of silver oxide and sulfadiazine?
$2C_{10}H_{10}N_4SO_2 + Ag_2O \longrightarrow 2AgC_{10}H_9N_4SO_2 + H_2O$

51. Carborundum is silicon carbide, SiC, a very hard material used as an abrasive on sandpaper and in other applications. It is prepared by the reaction of pure sand, SiO_2, with carbon at high temperature. Carbon monoxide, CO, is the other product of this reaction. Write the balanced equation for the reaction, and calculate how much SiO_2 is required to produce 3.00 kg of SiC.

52. Automotive air bags inflate when a sample of sodium azide, NaN_3, is very rapidly decomposed.

$$2NaN_3(s) \longrightarrow 2Na(s) + 3N_2(g)$$

What mass of sodium azide is required to produce 2.6 ft^3 (73.6 L) of nitrogen gas with a density of 1.25 g/L?

53. Urea, $CO(NH_2)_2$, is manufactured on a large scale for use in producing urea-formaldehyde plastics and as a fertilizer. What is the maximum mass of urea that can be manufactured from the CO_2 produced by combustion of 1.00×10^3 kg of carbon followed by the reaction?

$$CO_2(g) + 2NH_3(g) \longrightarrow CO(NH_2)_2(s) + H_2O(l)$$

54. In an accident, a solution containing 2.5 kg of nitric acid was spilled. Two kilograms of Na_2CO_3 was quickly spread on the area and CO_2 was released by the reaction. Was sufficient Na_2CO_3 used to neutralize all of the acid?

55. A compact car gets 37.5 miles per gallon on the highway. If gasoline contains 84.2% carbon by mass and has a density of 0.8205 g/mL, determine the mass of carbon dioxide produced during a 500-mile trip (3.785 liters per gallon).

56. What volume of 0.750 M hydrochloric acid solution can be prepared from the HCl produced by the reaction of 25.0 g of NaCl with excess sulfuric acid?

$$NaCl(s) + H_2SO_4(l) \longrightarrow HCl(g) + NaHSO_4(s)$$

57. What volume of a 0.2089 M KI solution contains enough KI to react exactly with the $Cu(NO_3)_2$ in 43.88 mL of a 0.3842 M solution of $Cu(NO_3)_2$?

$$2Cu(NO_3)_2 + 4KI \longrightarrow 2CuI + I_2 + 4KNO_3$$

58. A mordant is a substance that combines with a dye to produce a stable fixed color in a dyed fabric. Calcium acetate is used as a mordant. It is prepared by the reaction of acetic acid with calcium hydroxide.

$$2CH_3CO_2H + Ca(OH)_2 \longrightarrow Ca(CH_3CO_2)_2 + 2H_2O$$

What mass of $Ca(OH)_2$ is required to react with the acetic acid in 25.0 mL of a solution having a density of 1.065 g/mL and containing 58.0% acetic acid by mass?

59. The toxic pigment called white lead, $Pb_3(OH)_2(CO_3)_2$, has been replaced in white paints by rutile, TiO_2. How much rutile (g) can be prepared from 379 g of an ore that contains 88.3% ilmenite ($FeTiO_3$) by mass?

$$2FeTiO_3 + 4HCl + Cl_2 \longrightarrow 2FeCl_3 + 2TiO_2 + 2H_2O$$

7.4 Reaction Yields

60. The following quantities are placed in a container: 1.5×10^{24} atoms of hydrogen, 1.0 mol of sulfur, and 88.0 g of diatomic oxygen.

(a) What is the total mass in grams for the collection of all three elements?

(b) What is the total number of moles of atoms for the three elements?

(c) If the mixture of the three elements formed a compound with molecules that contain two hydrogen atoms, one sulfur atom, and four oxygen atoms, which substance is consumed first?

(d) How many atoms of each remaining element would remain unreacted in the change described in (c)?

61. What is the limiting reactant in a reaction that produces sodium chloride from 8 g of sodium and 8 g of diatomic chlorine?

62. Which of the postulates of Dalton's atomic theory explains why we can calculate a theoretical yield for a chemical reaction?

63. A student isolated 25 g of a compound following a procedure that would theoretically yield 81 g. What was his percent yield?

64. A sample of 0.53 g of carbon dioxide was obtained by heating 1.31 g of calcium carbonate. What is the percent yield for this reaction?

$$CaCO_3(s) \longrightarrow CaO(s) + CO_2(s)$$

65. Freon-12, CCl_2F_2, is prepared from CCl_4 by reaction with HF. The other product of this reaction is HCl. Outline the steps needed to determine the percent yield of a reaction that produces 12.5 g of CCl_2F_2 from 32.9 g of CCl_4. Freon-12 has been banned and is no longer used as a refrigerant because it catalyzes the decomposition of ozone and has a very long lifetime in the atmosphere. Determine the percent yield.

66. Citric acid, $C_6H_8O_7$, a component of jams, jellies, and fruity soft drinks, is prepared industrially via fermentation of sucrose by the mold *Aspergillus niger*. The equation representing this reaction is

$$C_{12}H_{22}O_{11} + H_2O + 3O_2 \longrightarrow 2C_6H_8O_7 + 4H_2O$$

What mass of citric acid is produced from exactly 1 metric ton (1.000×10^3 kg) of sucrose if the yield is 92.30%?

67. Toluene, $C_6H_5CH_3$, is oxidized by air under carefully controlled conditions to benzoic acid, $C_6H_5CO_2H$, which is used to prepare the food preservative sodium benzoate, $C_6H_5CO_2Na$. What is the percent yield of a reaction that converts 1.000 kg of toluene to 1.21 kg of benzoic acid?

$$2C_6H_5CH_3 + 3O_2 \longrightarrow 2C_6H_5CO_2H + 2H_2O$$

68. In a laboratory experiment, the reaction of 3.0 mol of H_2 with 2.0 mol of I_2 produced 1.0 mol of HI. Determine the theoretical yield in grams and the percent yield for this reaction.

69. Outline the steps needed to solve the following problem, then do the calculations. Ether, $(C_2H_5)_2O$, which was originally used as an anesthetic but has been replaced by safer and more effective medications, is prepared by the reaction of ethanol with sulfuric acid.

$$2C_2H_5OH + H_2SO_4 \longrightarrow (C_2H_5)_2O + H_2SO_4{\cdot}H_2O$$

What is the percent yield of ether if 1.17 L (d = 0.7134 g/mL) is isolated from the reaction of 1.500 L of C_2H_5OH (d = 0.7894 g/mL)?

70. Outline the steps needed to determine the limiting reactant when 30.0 g of propane, C_3H_8, is burned with 75.0 g of oxygen.

Determine the limiting reactant.

71. Outline the steps needed to determine the limiting reactant when 0.50 mol of Cr and 0.75 mol of H_3PO_4 react according to the following chemical equation.

$$2Cr + 2H_3PO_4 \longrightarrow 2CrPO_4 + 3H_2$$

Determine the limiting reactant.

72. What is the limiting reactant when 1.50 g of lithium and 1.50 g of nitrogen combine to form lithium nitride, a component of advanced batteries, according to the following unbalanced equation?

$$Li + N_2 \longrightarrow Li_3N$$

73. Uranium can be isolated from its ores by dissolving it as $UO_2(NO_3)_2$, then separating it as solid $UO_2(C_2O_4){\cdot}3H_2O$. Addition of 0.4031 g of sodium oxalate, $Na_2C_2O_4$, to a solution containing 1.481 g of uranyl nitrate, $UO_2(NO_3)_2$, yields 1.073 g of solid $UO_2(C_2O_4){\cdot}3H_2O$.

$$Na_2C_2O_4 + UO_2(NO_3)_2 + 3H_2O \longrightarrow UO_2(C_2O_4){\cdot}3H_2O + 2NaNO_3$$

Determine the limiting reactant and the percent yield of this reaction.

74. How many molecules of $C_2H_4Cl_2$ can be prepared from 15 C_2H_4 molecules and 8 Cl_2 molecules?

75. How many molecules of the sweetener saccharin can be prepared from 30 C atoms, 25 H atoms, 12 O atoms, 8 S atoms, and 14 N atoms?

76. The phosphorus pentoxide used to produce phosphoric acid for cola soft drinks is prepared by burning phosphorus in oxygen.

(a) What is the limiting reactant when 0.200 mol of P_4 and 0.200 mol of O_2 react according to

$$P_4 + 5O_2 \longrightarrow P_4O_{10}$$

(b) Calculate the percent yield if 10.0 g of P_4O_{10} is isolated from the reaction.

77. Would you agree to buy 1 trillion (1,000,000,000,000) gold atoms for \$5? Explain why or why not. Find the current price of gold at http://money.cnn.com/data/commodities/ (1 troy ounce = 31.1 g)

7.5 Quantitative Chemical Analysis

78. What volume of 0.0105-M HBr solution is required to titrate 125 mL of a 0.0100-M $Ca(OH)_2$ solution?

$$Ca(OH)_2(aq) + 2HBr(aq) \longrightarrow CaBr_2(aq) + 2H_2O(l)$$

79. Titration of a 20.0-mL sample of acid rain required 1.7 mL of 0.0811 M NaOH to reach the end point. If we assume that the acidity of the rain is due to the presence of sulfuric acid, what was the concentration of sulfuric acid in this sample of rain?

80. What is the concentration of NaCl in a solution if titration of 15.00 mL of the solution with 0.2503 M $AgNO_3$ requires 20.22 mL of the $AgNO_3$ solution to reach the end point?

$$AgNO_3(aq) + NaCl(aq) \longrightarrow AgCl(s) + NaNO_3(aq)$$

81. In a common medical laboratory determination of the concentration of free chloride ion in blood serum, a serum sample is titrated with a $Hg(NO_3)_2$ solution.

$$2Cl^-(aq) + Hg(NO_3)_2(aq) \longrightarrow 2NO_3^-(aq) + HgCl_2(s)$$

What is the Cl^- concentration in a 0.25-mL sample of normal serum that requires 1.46 mL of 8.25×10^{-4} M $Hg(NO_3)_2(aq)$ to reach the end point?

82. Potatoes can be peeled commercially by soaking them in a 3-M to 6-M solution of sodium hydroxide, then removing the loosened skins by spraying them with water. Does a sodium hydroxide solution have a suitable concentration if titration of 12.00 mL of the solution requires 30.6 mL of 1.65 M HCl to reach the end point?

83. A sample of gallium bromide, $GaBr_2$, weighing 0.165 g was dissolved in water and treated with silver nitrate, $AgNO_3$, resulting in the precipitation of 0.299 g AgBr. Use these data to compute the %Ga (by mass) $GaBr_2$.

84. The principal component of mothballs is naphthalene, a compound with a molecular mass of about 130 amu, containing only carbon and hydrogen. A 3.000-mg sample of naphthalene burns to give 10.3 mg of CO_2. Determine its empirical and molecular formulas.

85. A 0.025-g sample of a compound composed of boron and hydrogen, with a molecular mass of ~28 amu, burns spontaneously when exposed to air, producing 0.063 g of B_2O_3. What are the empirical and molecular formulas of the compound?

86. Sodium bicarbonate (baking soda), $NaHCO_3$, can be purified by dissolving it in hot water (60 °C), filtering to remove insoluble impurities, cooling to 0 °C to precipitate solid $NaHCO_3$, and then filtering to remove the solid, leaving soluble impurities in solution. Any $NaHCO_3$ that remains in solution is not recovered. The solubility of $NaHCO_3$ in hot water of 60 °C is 164 g/L. Its solubility in cold water of 0 °C is 69 g/L. What is the percent yield of $NaHCO_3$ when it is purified by this method?

87. What volume of 0.600 M HCl is required to react completely with 2.50 g of sodium hydrogen carbonate?

$$NaHCO_3(aq) + HCl(aq) \longrightarrow NaCl(aq) + CO_2(g) + H_2O(l)$$

88. What volume of 0.08892 M HNO_3 is required to react completely with 0.2352 g of potassium hydrogen phosphate?

$$2HNO_3(aq) + K_2HPO_4(aq) \longrightarrow H_2PO_4(aq) + 2KNO_3(aq)$$

89. What volume of a 0.3300-M solution of sodium hydroxide would be required to titrate 15.00 mL of 0.1500 M oxalic acid?

$$C_2O_4H_2(aq) + 2NaOH(aq) \longrightarrow Na_2C_2O_4(aq) + 2H_2O(l)$$

90. What volume of a 0.00945-M solution of potassium hydroxide would be required to titrate 50.00 mL of a sample of acid rain with a H_2SO_4 concentration of 1.23×10^{-4} M.

$$H_2SO_4(aq) + 2KOH(aq) \longrightarrow K_2SO_4(aq) + 2H_2O(l)$$

91. A sample of solid calcium hydroxide, $Ca(OH)_2$, is allowed to stand in water until a saturated solution is formed. A titration of 75.00 mL of this solution with 5.00×10^{-2} M HCl requires 36.6 mL of the acid to reach the end point.

$$Ca(OH)_2(aq) + 2HCl(aq) \longrightarrow CaCl_2(aq) + 2H_2O(l)$$

What is the molarity?

92. What mass of $Ca(OH)_2$ will react with 25.0 g of propionic acid to form the preservative calcium propionate according to the equation?

93. How many milliliters of a 0.1500-M solution of KOH will be required to titrate 40.00 mL of a 0.0656-M solution of H_3PO_4?

$$H_3PO_4(aq) + 2KOH(aq) \longrightarrow K_2HPO_4(aq) + 2H_2O(l)$$

94. Potassium acid phthalate, $KHC_6H_4O_4$, or KHP, is used in many laboratories, including general chemistry laboratories, to standardize solutions of base. KHP is one of only a few stable solid acids that can be dried by warming and weighed. A 0.3420-g sample of $KHC_6H_4O_4$ reacts with 35.73 mL of a NaOH solution in a titration. What is the molar concentration of the NaOH?

$$KHC_6H_4O_4(aq) + NaOH(aq) \longrightarrow KNaC_6H_4O_4(aq) + H_2O(aq)$$

95. The reaction of WCl_6 with Al at ~400 °C gives black crystals of a compound containing only tungsten and chlorine. A sample of this compound, when reduced with hydrogen, gives 0.2232 g of tungsten metal and hydrogen chloride, which is absorbed in water. Titration of the hydrochloric acid thus produced requires 46.2 mL of 0.1051 M NaOH to reach the end point. What is the empirical formula of the black tungsten chloride?

Chapter 8

Gases

Figure 8.1 The hot air inside these balloons is less dense than the surrounding cool air. This results in a buoyant force that causes the balloons to rise when their guy lines are untied. (credit: modification of work by Anthony Quintano)

Chapter Outline

8.1 Gas Pressure

8.2 Relating Pressure, Volume, Amount, and Temperature: The Ideal Gas Law

8.3 Stoichiometry of Gaseous Substances, Mixtures, and Reactions

8.4 Effusion and Diffusion of Gases

8.5 The Kinetic-Molecular Theory

8.6 Non-Ideal Gas Behavior

Introduction

We are surrounded by an ocean of gas—the atmosphere—and many of the properties of gases are familiar to us from our daily activities. Heated gases expand, which can make a hot air balloon rise (**Figure 8.1**) or cause a blowout in a bicycle tire left in the sun on a hot day.

Gases have played an important part in the development of chemistry. In the seventeenth and eighteenth centuries, many scientists investigated gas behavior, providing the first mathematical descriptions of the behavior of matter.

In this chapter, we will examine the relationships between gas temperature, pressure, amount, and volume. We will study a simple theoretical model and use it to analyze the experimental behavior of gases. The results of these analyses will show us the limitations of the theory and how to improve on it.

8.1 Gas Pressure

By the end of this section, you will be able to:

* Define the property of pressure
* Define and convert among the units of pressure measurements
* Describe the operation of common tools for measuring gas pressure
* Calculate pressure from manometer data

The earth's atmosphere exerts a pressure, as does any other gas. Although we do not normally notice atmospheric pressure, we are sensitive to pressure changes—for example, when your ears "pop" during take-off and landing while flying, or when you dive underwater. Gas pressure is caused by the force exerted by gas molecules colliding with the surfaces of objects (Figure 8.2). Although the force of each collision is very small, any surface of appreciable area experiences a large number of collisions in a short time, which can result in a high pressure. In fact, normal air pressure is strong enough to crush a metal container when not balanced by equal pressure from inside the container.

Figure 8.2   The atmosphere above us exerts a large pressure on objects at the surface of the earth, roughly equal to the weight of a bowling ball pressing on an area the size of a human thumbnail.

Link to Learning

A dramatic illustration (http://openstaxcollege.org/l/16atmospressur1) of atmospheric pressure is provided in this brief video, which shows a railway tanker car imploding when its internal pressure is decreased.

A smaller scale demonstration (http://openstaxcollege.org/l/16atmospressur2) of this phenomenon is briefly explained.

Atmospheric pressure is caused by the weight of the column of air molecules in the atmosphere above an object, such as the tanker car. At sea level, this pressure is roughly the same as that exerted by a full-grown African elephant standing on a doormat, or a typical bowling ball resting on your thumbnail. These may seem like huge amounts, and they are, but life on earth has evolved under such atmospheric pressure. If you actually perch a bowling ball on your thumbnail, the pressure experienced is *twice* the usual pressure, and the sensation is unpleasant.

In general, **pressure** is defined as the force exerted on a given area: $P = \frac{F}{A}$. Note that pressure is directly proportional to force and inversely proportional to area. Thus, pressure can be increased either by increasing the amount of force or by decreasing the area over which it is applied; pressure can be decreased by decreasing the force or increasing the area.

Let's apply this concept to determine which would be more likely to fall through thin ice in **Figure 8.3**—the elephant or the figure skater? A large African elephant can weigh 7 tons, supported on four feet, each with a diameter of about 1.5 ft (footprint area of 250 in^2), so the pressure exerted by each foot is about 14 lb/in^2:

$$\text{pressure per elephant foot} = 14{,}000 \frac{\text{lb}}{\text{elephant}} \times \frac{1 \text{ elephant}}{4 \text{ feet}} \times \frac{1 \text{ foot}}{250 \text{ in}^2} = 14 \text{ lb/in}^2$$

The figure skater weighs about 120 lbs, supported on two skate blades, each with an area of about 2 in^2, so the pressure exerted by each blade is about 30 lb/in^2:

$$\text{pressure per skate blade} = 120 \frac{\text{lb}}{\text{skater}} \times \frac{1 \text{ skater}}{2 \text{ blades}} \times \frac{1 \text{ blade}}{2 \text{ in}^2} = 30 \text{ lb/in}^2$$

Even though the elephant is more than one hundred-times heavier than the skater, it exerts less than one-half of the pressure and would therefore be less likely to fall though thin ice. On the other hand, if the skater removes her skates and stands with bare feet (or regular footwear) on the ice, the larger area over which her weight is applied greatly reduces the pressure exerted:

$$\text{pressure per human foot} = 120 \frac{\text{lb}}{\text{skater}} \times \frac{1 \text{ skater}}{2 \text{ feet}} \times \frac{1 \text{ foot}}{30 \text{ in}^2} = 2 \text{ lb/in}^2$$

(a)   (b)

Figure 8.3 Although (a) an elephant's weight is large, creating a very large force on the ground, (b) the figure skater exerts a much higher pressure on the ice due to the small surface area of her skates. (credit a: modification of work by Guido da Rozze; credit b: modification of work by Ryosuke Yagi)

The SI unit of pressure is the **pascal (Pa)**, with 1 Pa = 1 N/m^2, where N is the newton, a unit of force defined as 1 kg m/s^2. One pascal is a small pressure; in many cases, it is more convenient to use units of kilopascal (1 kPa = 1000 Pa) or **bar** (1 bar = 100,000 Pa). In the United States, pressure is often measured in pounds of force on an area of one square inch—**pounds per square inch (psi)**—for example, in car tires. Pressure can also be measured using the unit **atmosphere (atm)**, which originally represented the average sea level air pressure at the approximate latitude of Paris (45°). **Table 8.1** provides some information on these and a few other common units for pressure measurements

Pressure Units

Unit Name and Abbreviation	Definition or Relation to Other Unit
pascal (Pa)	1 Pa = 1 N/m^2 recommended IUPAC unit

Table 8.1

Pressure Units

Unit Name and Abbreviation	Definition or Relation to Other Unit
kilopascal (kPa)	1 kPa = 1000 Pa
pounds per square inch (psi)	air pressure at sea level is ~14.7 psi
atmosphere (atm)	1 atm = 101,325 Pa air pressure at sea level is ~1 atm
bar (bar, or b)	1 bar = 100,000 Pa (exactly) commonly used in meteorology
millibar (mbar, or mb)	1000 mbar = 1 bar
inches of mercury (in. Hg)	1 in. Hg = 3386 Pa used by aviation industry, also some weather reports
torr	$1 \text{ torr} = \frac{1}{760} \text{ atm}$ named after Evangelista Torricelli, inventor of the barometer
millimeters of mercury (mm Hg)	1 mm Hg ~1 torr

Table 8.1

Example 8.1

Conversion of Pressure Units

The United States National Weather Service reports pressure in both inches of Hg and millibars. Convert a pressure of 29.2 in. Hg into:

(a) torr

(b) atm

(c) kPa

(d) mbar

Solution

This is a unit conversion problem. The relationships between the various pressure units are given in Table 8.1.

(a) $29.2 \text{ in Hg} \times \frac{25.4 \text{ mm}}{1 \text{ in}} \times \frac{1 \text{ torr}}{1 \text{ mm Hg}} = 742 \text{ torr}$

(b) $742 \text{ torr} \times \frac{1 \text{ atm}}{760 \text{ torr}} = 0.976 \text{ atm}$

(c) $742 \text{ torr} \times \frac{101.325 \text{ kPa}}{760 \text{ torr}} = 98.9 \text{ kPa}$

(d) $98.9 \text{ kPa} \times \frac{1000 \text{ Pa}}{1 \text{ kPa}} \times \frac{1 \text{ bar}}{100,000 \text{ Pa}} \times \frac{1000 \text{ mbar}}{1 \text{ bar}} = 989 \text{ mbar}$

Check Your Learning

A typical barometric pressure in Kansas City is 740 torr. What is this pressure in atmospheres, in millimeters of mercury, in kilopascals, and in bar?

Answer: 0.974 atm; 740 mm Hg; 98.7 kPa; 0.987 bar

We can measure atmospheric pressure, the force exerted by the atmosphere on the earth's surface, with a **barometer** (Figure 8.4). A barometer is a glass tube that is closed at one end, filled with a nonvolatile liquid such as mercury, and then inverted and immersed in a container of that liquid. The atmosphere exerts pressure on the liquid outside the tube, the column of liquid exerts pressure inside the tube, and the pressure at the liquid surface is the same inside and outside the tube. The height of the liquid in the tube is therefore proportional to the pressure exerted by the atmosphere.

Figure 8.4 In a barometer, the height, h, of the column of liquid is used as a measurement of the air pressure. Using very dense liquid mercury (left) permits the construction of reasonably sized barometers, whereas using water (right) would require a barometer more than 30 feet tall.

If the liquid is water, normal atmospheric pressure will support a column of water over 10 meters high, which is rather inconvenient for making (and reading) a barometer. Because mercury (Hg) is about 13.6-times denser than water, a mercury barometer only needs to be $\frac{1}{13.6}$ as tall as a water barometer—a more suitable size. Standard atmospheric pressure of 1 atm at sea level (101,325 Pa) corresponds to a column of mercury that is about 760 mm (29.92 in.) high. The **torr** was originally intended to be a unit equal to one millimeter of mercury, but it no longer corresponds exactly. The pressure exerted by a fluid due to gravity is known as **hydrostatic pressure**, p:

$$p = h\rho g$$

where h is the height of the fluid, ρ is the density of the fluid, and g is acceleration due to gravity.

Example 8.2

Calculation of Barometric Pressure

Show the calculation supporting the claim that atmospheric pressure near sea level corresponds to the pressure exerted by a column of mercury that is about 760 mm high. The density of mercury = 13.6 g/cm^3.

Solution

The hydrostatic pressure is given by $p = h\rho g$, with h = 760 mm, ρ = 13.6 g/cm^3, and g = 9.81 m/s^2. Plugging these values into the equation and doing the necessary unit conversions will give us the value we seek.

(Note: We are expecting to find a pressure of ~101,325 Pa:)

$$101{,}325\ N/m^2 = 101{,}325\ \frac{kg\cdot m/s^2}{m^2} = 101{,}325\ \frac{kg}{m\cdot s^2}$$

$$p = \left(760\ mm \times \frac{1\ m}{1000\ mm}\right) \times \left(\frac{13.6\ g}{1\ cm^3} \times \frac{1\ kg}{1000\ g} \times \frac{(100\ cm)^3}{(1\ m)^3}\right) \times \left(\frac{9.81\ m}{1\ s^2}\right)$$

$$= (0.760\ m)(13{,}600\ kg/m^3)(9.81\ m/s^2) = 1.01 \times 10^5\ kg/ms^2 = 1.01 \times 10^5\ N/m^2$$

$$= 1.01 \times 10^5\ Pa$$

Check Your Learning

Calculate the height of a column of water at 25 °C that corresponds to normal atmospheric pressure. The density of water at this temperature is 1.0 g/cm^3.

Answer: 10.3 m

A **manometer** is a device similar to a barometer that can be used to measure the pressure of a gas trapped in a container. A closed-end manometer is a U-shaped tube with one closed arm, one arm that connects to the gas to be measured, and a nonvolatile liquid (usually mercury) in between. As with a barometer, the distance between the liquid levels in the two arms of the tube (*h* in the diagram) is proportional to the pressure of the gas in the container. An open-end manometer (**Figure 8.5**) is the same as a closed-end manometer, but one of its arms is open to the atmosphere. In this case, the distance between the liquid levels corresponds to the difference in pressure between the gas in the container and the atmosphere.

Figure 8.5 A manometer can be used to measure the pressure of a gas. The (difference in) height between the liquid levels (*h*) is a measure of the pressure. Mercury is usually used because of its large density.

Example 8.3

Calculation of Pressure Using a Closed-End Manometer

The pressure of a sample of gas is measured with a closed-end manometer, as shown to the right. The liquid in the manometer is mercury. Determine the pressure of the gas in:

(a) torr

(b) Pa

(c) bar

Solution

The pressure of the gas is equal to a column of mercury of height 26.4 cm. (The pressure at the bottom horizontal line is equal on both sides of the tube. The pressure on the left is due to the gas and the pressure on the right is due to 26.4 cm Hg, or mercury.) We could use the equation $p = h\rho g$ as in **Example 8.2**, but it is simpler to just convert between units using **Table 8.1**.

(a) $26.4 \cancel{\text{cm Hg}} \times \dfrac{10 \cancel{\text{mm Hg}}}{1 \cancel{\text{cm Hg}}} \times \dfrac{1 \text{ torr}}{1 \cancel{\text{mm Hg}}} = 264 \text{ torr}$

(b) $264 \cancel{\text{torr}} \times \dfrac{1 \cancel{\text{atm}}}{760 \cancel{\text{torr}}} \times \dfrac{101{,}325 \text{ Pa}}{1 \cancel{\text{atm}}} = 35{,}200 \text{ Pa}$

(c) $35{,}200 \cancel{\text{Pa}} \times \dfrac{1 \text{ bar}}{100{,}000 \cancel{\text{Pa}}} = 0.352 \text{ bar}$

Check Your Learning

The pressure of a sample of gas is measured with a closed-end manometer. The liquid in the manometer is mercury. Determine the pressure of the gas in:

(a) torr

(b) Pa

(c) bar

Answer: (a) ~150 torr; (b) ~20,000 Pa; (c) ~0.20 bar

Example 8.4

Calculation of Pressure Using an Open-End Manometer

The pressure of a sample of gas is measured at sea level with an open-end Hg (mercury) manometer, as shown to the right. Determine the pressure of the gas in:

(a) mm Hg

(b) atm

(c) kPa

Solution

The pressure of the gas equals the hydrostatic pressure due to a column of mercury of height 13.7 cm plus the pressure of the atmosphere at sea level. (The pressure at the bottom horizontal line is equal on both sides of the tube. The pressure on the left is due to the gas and the pressure on the right is due to 13.7 cm of Hg plus atmospheric pressure.)

(a) In mm Hg, this is: 137 mm Hg + 760 mm Hg = 897 mm Hg

(b) $897 \text{ mm Hg} \times \dfrac{1 \text{ atm}}{760 \text{ mm Hg}} = 1.18 \text{ atm}$

(c) $1.18 \text{ atm} \times \dfrac{101.325 \text{ kPa}}{1 \text{ atm}} = 1.20 \times 10^2 \text{ kPa}$

Check Your Learning

The pressure of a sample of gas is measured at sea level with an open-end Hg manometer, as shown to the right. Determine the pressure of the gas in:

(a) mm Hg

(b) atm

(c) kPa

Answer: (a) 642 mm Hg; (b) 0.845 atm; (c) 85.6 kPa

Chemistry in Everyday Life

Measuring Blood Pressure

Blood pressure is measured using a device called a sphygmomanometer (Greek *sphygmos* = "pulse"). It consists of an inflatable cuff to restrict blood flow, a manometer to measure the pressure, and a method of determining when blood flow begins and when it becomes impeded (Figure 8.6). Since its invention in 1881, it has been an essential medical device. There are many types of sphygmomanometers: manual ones that require a stethoscope and are used by medical professionals; mercury ones, used when the most accuracy is required; less accurate mechanical ones; and digital ones that can be used with little training but that have limitations. When using a sphygmomanometer, the cuff is placed around the upper arm and inflated until blood flow is completely blocked, then slowly released. As the heart beats, blood forced through the arteries causes a rise in pressure. This rise in pressure at which blood flow begins is the *systolic pressure*—the peak pressure in the cardiac cycle. When the cuff's pressure equals the arterial systolic pressure, blood flows past the cuff, creating audible sounds that can be heard using a stethoscope. This is followed by a decrease in pressure as the heart's ventricles prepare for another beat. As cuff pressure continues to decrease, eventually sound is no longer heard; this is the *diastolic pressure*—the lowest pressure (resting phase) in the cardiac cycle. Blood pressure units from a sphygmomanometer are in terms of millimeters of mercury (mm Hg).

(a)   (b)

Figure 8.6 (a) A medical technician prepares to measure a patient's blood pressure with a sphygmomanometer. (b) A typical sphygmomanometer uses a valved rubber bulb to inflate the cuff and a diaphragm gauge to measure pressure. (credit a: modification of work by Master Sgt. Jeffrey Allen)

How Sciences Interconnect

Meteorology, Climatology, and Atmospheric Science

Throughout the ages, people have observed clouds, winds, and precipitation, trying to discern patterns and make predictions: when it is best to plant and harvest; whether it is safe to set out on a sea voyage; and much more. We now face complex weather and atmosphere-related challenges that will have a major impact on our civilization and the ecosystem. Several different scientific disciplines use chemical principles to help us better understand weather, the atmosphere, and climate. These are meteorology, climatology, and atmospheric science. Meteorology is the study of the atmosphere, atmospheric phenomena, and atmospheric effects on earth's weather. Meteorologists seek to understand and predict the weather in the short term, which can save lives and benefit the economy. Weather forecasts (Figure 8.7) are the result of thousands of measurements of air pressure, temperature, and the like, which are compiled, modeled, and analyzed in weather centers worldwide.

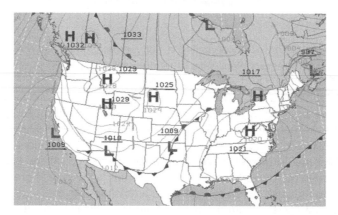

Figure 8.7 Meteorologists use weather maps to describe and predict weather. Regions of high (H) and low (L) pressure have large effects on weather conditions. The gray lines represent locations of constant pressure known as isobars. (credit: modification of work by National Oceanic and Atmospheric Administration)

In terms of weather, low-pressure systems occur when the earth's surface atmospheric pressure is lower than the surrounding environment: Moist air rises and condenses, producing clouds. Movement of moisture and air within various weather fronts instigates most weather events.

The atmosphere is the gaseous layer that surrounds a planet. Earth's atmosphere, which is roughly 100–125 km thick, consists of roughly 78.1% nitrogen and 21.0% oxygen, and can be subdivided further into the regions shown in **Figure 8.8**: the exosphere (furthest from earth, > 700 km above sea level), the thermosphere (80–700 km), the mesosphere (50–80 km), the stratosphere (second lowest level of our atmosphere, 12–50 km above sea level), and the troposphere (up to 12 km above sea level, roughly 80% of the earth's atmosphere by mass and the layer where most weather events originate). As you go higher in the troposphere, air density and temperature both decrease.

Figure 8.8 Earth's atmosphere has five layers: the troposphere, the stratosphere, the mesosphere, the thermosphere, and the exosphere.

Climatology is the study of the climate, averaged weather conditions over long time periods, using atmospheric data. However, climatologists study patterns and effects that occur over decades, centuries, and millennia, rather than shorter time frames of hours, days, and weeks like meteorologists. Atmospheric science is an even broader field, combining meteorology, climatology, and other scientific disciplines that study the atmosphere.

8.2 Relating Pressure, Volume, Amount, and Temperature: The Ideal Gas Law

By the end of this section, you will be able to:

- Identify the mathematical relationships between the various properties of gases
- Use the ideal gas law, and related gas laws, to compute the values of various gas properties under specified conditions

During the seventeenth and especially eighteenth centuries, driven both by a desire to understand nature and a quest to make balloons in which they could fly (**Figure 8.9**), a number of scientists established the relationships between the macroscopic physical properties of gases, that is, pressure, volume, temperature, and amount of gas. Although their measurements were not precise by today's standards, they were able to determine the mathematical relationships between pairs of these variables (e.g., pressure and temperature, pressure and volume) that hold for an *ideal* gas—a hypothetical construct that real gases approximate under certain conditions. Eventually, these individual laws were combined into a single equation—the *ideal gas law*—that relates gas quantities for gases and is quite accurate for low pressures and moderate temperatures. We will consider the key developments in individual relationships (for pedagogical reasons not quite in historical order), then put them together in the ideal gas law.

(a)

(b)

(c)

Figure 8.9   In 1783, the first (a) hydrogen-filled balloon flight, (b) manned hot air balloon flight, and (c) manned hydrogen-filled balloon flight occurred. When the hydrogen-filled balloon depicted in (a) landed, the frightened villagers of Gonesse reportedly destroyed it with pitchforks and knives. The launch of the latter was reportedly viewed by 400,000 people in Paris.

Pressure and Temperature: Amontons's Law

Imagine filling a rigid container attached to a pressure gauge with gas and then sealing the container so that no gas may escape. If the container is cooled, the gas inside likewise gets colder and its pressure is observed to decrease. Since the container is rigid and tightly sealed, both the volume and number of moles of gas remain constant. If we heat the sphere, the gas inside gets hotter (**Figure 8.10**) and the pressure increases.

Figure 8.10 The effect of temperature on gas pressure: When the hot plate is off, the pressure of the gas in the sphere is relatively low. As the gas is heated, the pressure of the gas in the sphere increases.

This relationship between temperature and pressure is observed for any sample of gas confined to a constant volume. An example of experimental pressure-temperature data is shown for a sample of air under these conditions in **Figure 8.11**. We find that temperature and pressure are linearly related, and if the temperature is on the kelvin scale, then P and T are directly proportional (again, when *volume and moles of gas are held constant*); if the temperature on the kelvin scale increases by a certain factor, the gas pressure increases by the same factor.

Temperature (°C)	Temperature (K)	Pressure (kPa)
−150	173	36.0
−100	223	46.4
−50	273	56.7
0	323	67.1
50	373	77.5
100	423	88.0

Figure 8.11 For a constant volume and amount of air, the pressure and temperature are directly proportional, provided the temperature is in kelvin. (Measurements cannot be made at lower temperatures because of the condensation of the gas.) When this line is extrapolated to lower pressures, it reaches a pressure of 0 at −273 °C, which is 0 on the kelvin scale and the lowest possible temperature, called absolute zero.

Guillaume Amontons was the first to empirically establish the relationship between the pressure and the temperature of a gas (~1700), and Joseph Louis Gay-Lussac determined the relationship more precisely (~1800). Because of this, the *P-T* relationship for gases is known as either **Amontons's law** or **Gay-Lussac's law**. Under either name, it states that *the pressure of a given amount of gas is directly proportional to its temperature on the kelvin scale when the volume is held constant*. Mathematically, this can be written:

$$P \propto T \text{ or } P = \text{constant} \times T \text{ or } P = k \times T$$

where $\propto$ means "is proportional to," and k is a proportionality constant that depends on the identity, amount, and volume of the gas.

For a confined, constant volume of gas, the ratio $\frac{P}{T}$ is therefore constant (i.e., $\frac{P}{T} = k$). If the gas is initially in "Condition 1" (with $P = P_1$ and $T = T_1$), and then changes to "Condition 2" (with $P = P_2$ and $T = T_2$), we have that $\frac{P_1}{T_1} = k$ and $\frac{P_2}{T_2} = k$, which reduces to $\frac{P_1}{T_1} = \frac{P_2}{T_2}$. This equation is useful for pressure-temperature calculations for a confined gas at constant volume. Note that temperatures must be on the kelvin scale for any gas law calculations (0 on the kelvin scale and the lowest possible temperature is called **absolute zero**). (Also note that there are at least three ways we can describe how the pressure of a gas changes as its temperature changes: We can use a table of values, a graph, or a mathematical equation.)

Example 8.5

Predicting Change in Pressure with Temperature

A can of hair spray is used until it is empty except for the propellant, isobutane gas.

(a) On the can is the warning "Store only at temperatures below 120 °F (48.8 °C). Do not incinerate." Why?

(b) The gas in the can is initially at 24 °C and 360 kPa, and the can has a volume of 350 mL. If the can is left in a car that reaches 50 °C on a hot day, what is the new pressure in the can?

Solution

(a) The can contains an amount of isobutane gas at a constant volume, so if the temperature is increased by heating, the pressure will increase proportionately. High temperature could lead to high pressure, causing the can to burst. (Also, isobutane is combustible, so incineration could cause the can to explode.)

(b) We are looking for a pressure change due to a temperature change at constant volume, so we will use Amontons's/Gay-Lussac's law. Taking P_1 and T_1 as the initial values, T_2 as the temperature where the pressure is unknown and P_2 as the unknown pressure, and converting °C to K, we have:

$$\frac{P_1}{T_1} = \frac{P_2}{T_2} \text{ which means that } \frac{360\,\text{kPa}}{297\,\text{K}} = \frac{P_2}{323\,\text{K}}$$

Rearranging and solving gives: $P_2 = \dfrac{360\,\text{kPa} \times 323\,\cancel{\text{K}}}{297\,\cancel{\text{K}}} = 390\,\text{kPa}$

Check Your Learning

A sample of nitrogen, N_2, occupies 45.0 mL at 27 °C and 600 torr. What pressure will it have if cooled to −73 °C while the volume remains constant?

Answer: 400 torr

Volume and Temperature: Charles's Law

If we fill a balloon with air and seal it, the balloon contains a specific amount of air at atmospheric pressure, let's say 1 atm. If we put the balloon in a refrigerator, the gas inside gets cold and the balloon shrinks (although both the amount of gas and its pressure remain constant). If we make the balloon very cold, it will shrink a great deal, and it expands again when it warms up.

Link to Learning

This video (http://openstaxcollege.org/l/16CharlesLaw) shows how cooling and heating a gas causes its volume to decrease or increase, respectively.

These examples of the effect of temperature on the volume of a given amount of a confined gas at constant pressure are true in general: The volume increases as the temperature increases, and decreases as the temperature decreases. Volume-temperature data for a 1-mole sample of methane gas at 1 atm are listed and graphed in Figure 8.12.

Temperature (°C)	Temperature (K)	Volume (L)
−3	270	22
−23	250	21
−53	220	18
−162	111	9

Figure 8.12 The volume and temperature are linearly related for 1 mole of methane gas at a constant pressure of 1 atm. If the temperature is in kelvin, volume and temperature are directly proportional. The line stops at 111 K because methane liquefies at this temperature; when extrapolated, it intersects the graph's origin, representing a temperature of absolute zero.

The relationship between the volume and temperature of a given amount of gas at constant pressure is known as Charles's law in recognition of the French scientist and balloon flight pioneer Jacques Alexandre César Charles. **Charles's law** states that *the volume of a given amount of gas is directly proportional to its temperature on the kelvin scale when the pressure is held constant.*

Mathematically, this can be written as:

$$V \propto T \text{ or } V = \text{constant} \cdot T \text{ or } V = k \cdot T \text{ or } V_1/T_1 = V_2/T_2$$

with k being a proportionality constant that depends on the amount and pressure of the gas.

For a confined, constant pressure gas sample, $\frac{V}{T}$ is constant (i.e., the ratio = k), and as seen with the P-T relationship, this leads to another form of Charles's law: $\frac{V_1}{T_1} = \frac{V_2}{T_2}$.

Example 8.6

Predicting Change in Volume with Temperature

A sample of carbon dioxide, CO_2, occupies 0.300 L at 10 °C and 750 torr. What volume will the gas have at 30 °C and 750 torr?

Solution

Because we are looking for the volume change caused by a temperature change at constant pressure, this is a job for Charles's law. Taking V_1 and T_1 as the initial values, T_2 as the temperature at which the volume is unknown and V_2 as the unknown volume, and converting °C into K we have:

$$\frac{V_1}{T_1} = \frac{V_2}{T_2} \text{ which means that } \frac{0.300\,\text{L}}{283\,\text{K}} = \frac{V_2}{303\,\text{K}}$$

Rearranging and solving gives: $V_2 = \dfrac{0.300\,\text{L} \times 303\,\cancel{\text{K}}}{283\,\cancel{\text{K}}} = 0.321\,\text{L}$

This answer supports our expectation from Charles's law, namely, that raising the gas temperature (from 283 K to 303 K) at a constant pressure will yield an increase in its volume (from 0.300 L to 0.321 L).

Check Your Learning

A sample of oxygen, O_2, occupies 32.2 mL at 30 °C and 452 torr. What volume will it occupy at –70 °C and the same pressure?

Answer: 21.6 mL

Example 8.7

Measuring Temperature with a Volume Change

Temperature is sometimes measured with a gas thermometer by observing the change in the volume of the gas as the temperature changes at constant pressure. The hydrogen in a particular hydrogen gas thermometer has a volume of 150.0 cm^3 when immersed in a mixture of ice and water (0.00 °C). When immersed in boiling liquid ammonia, the volume of the hydrogen, at the same pressure, is 131.7 cm^3. Find the temperature of boiling ammonia on the kelvin and Celsius scales.

Solution

A volume change caused by a temperature change at constant pressure means we should use Charles's law. Taking V_1 and T_1 as the initial values, T_2 as the temperature at which the volume is unknown and V_2 as the unknown volume, and converting °C into K we have:

$$\frac{V_1}{T_1} = \frac{V_2}{T_2} \text{ which means that } \frac{150.0\,\text{cm}^3}{273.15\,\text{K}} = \frac{131.7\,\text{cm}^3}{T_2}$$

Rearrangement gives $T_2 = \dfrac{131.7\,\cancel{\text{cm}^3} \times 273.15\,\text{K}}{150.0\,\cancel{\text{cm}^3}} = 239.8\,\text{K}$

Subtracting 273.15 from 239.8 K, we find that the temperature of the boiling ammonia on the Celsius scale is –33.4 °C.

Check Your Learning

What is the volume of a sample of ethane at 467 K and 1.1 atm if it occupies 405 mL at 298 K and 1.1 atm?

Answer: 635 mL

Volume and Pressure: Boyle's Law

If we partially fill an airtight syringe with air, the syringe contains a specific amount of air at constant temperature, say 25 °C. If we slowly push in the plunger while keeping temperature constant, the gas in the syringe is compressed into a smaller volume and its pressure increases; if we pull out the plunger, the volume increases and the pressure decreases.

This example of the effect of volume on the pressure of a given amount of a confined gas is true in general. Decreasing the volume of a contained gas will increase its pressure, and increasing its volume will decrease its pressure. In fact, if the volume increases by a certain factor, the pressure decreases by the same factor, and vice versa. Volume-pressure data for an air sample at room temperature are graphed in Figure 8.13.

Figure 8.13 When a gas occupies a smaller volume, it exerts a higher pressure; when it occupies a larger volume, it exerts a lower pressure (assuming the amount of gas and the temperature do not change). Since P and V are inversely proportional, a graph of $\frac{1}{P}$ vs. V is linear.

Unlike the *P-T* and *V-T* relationships, pressure and volume are not directly proportional to each other. Instead, *P* and *V* exhibit inverse proportionality: Increasing the pressure results in a decrease of the volume of the gas. Mathematically this can be written:

$$P \propto 1/V \text{ or } P = k \cdot 1/V \text{ or } P \cdot V = k \text{ or } P_1 V_1 = P_2 V_2$$

with *k* being a constant. Graphically, this relationship is shown by the straight line that results when plotting the inverse of the pressure $\left(\frac{1}{P}\right)$ versus the volume (*V*), or the inverse of volume $\left(\frac{1}{V}\right)$ versus the pressure (*P*). Graphs with curved lines are difficult to read accurately at low or high values of the variables, and they are more difficult to use in fitting theoretical equations and parameters to experimental data. For those reasons, scientists often try to find a way to "linearize" their data. If we plot *P* versus *V*, we obtain a hyperbola (see Figure 8.14).

Figure 8.14   The relationship between pressure and volume is inversely proportional. (a) The graph of P vs. V is a hyperbola, whereas (b) the graph of $\left(\frac{1}{P}\right)$ vs. V is linear.

The relationship between the volume and pressure of a given amount of gas at constant temperature was first published by the English natural philosopher Robert Boyle over 300 years ago. It is summarized in the statement now known as **Boyle's law**: *The volume of a given amount of gas held at constant temperature is inversely proportional to the pressure under which it is measured.*

Example 8.8

Volume of a Gas Sample

The sample of gas in **Figure 8.13** has a volume of 15.0 mL at a pressure of 13.0 psi. Determine the pressure of the gas at a volume of 7.5 mL, using:

(a) the $P\text{-}V$ graph in **Figure 8.13**

(b) the $\frac{1}{P}$ vs. V graph in **Figure 8.13**

(c) the Boyle's law equation

Comment on the likely accuracy of each method.

Solution

(a) Estimating from the $P\text{-}V$ graph gives a value for P somewhere around 27 psi.

(b) Estimating from the $\frac{1}{P}$ versus V graph give a value of about 26 psi.

(c) From Boyle's law, we know that the product of pressure and volume (PV) for a given sample of gas at a constant temperature is always equal to the same value. Therefore we have $P_1V_1 = k$ and $P_2V_2 = k$ which means that $P_1V_1 = P_2V_2$.

Using P_1 and V_1 as the known values 13.0 psi and 15.0 mL, P_2 as the pressure at which the volume is unknown, and V_2 as the unknown volume, we have:

$$P_1V_1 = P_2V_2 \text{ or } 13.0 \text{ psi} \times 15.0 \text{ mL} = P_2 \times 7.5 \text{ mL}$$

Solving:

$$P_2 = \frac{13.0 \text{ psi} \times 15.0 \text{ mL}}{7.5 \text{ mL}} = 26 \text{ psi}$$

It was more difficult to estimate well from the $P\text{-}V$ graph, so (a) is likely more inaccurate than (b) or (c). The calculation will be as accurate as the equation and measurements allow.

Check Your Learning

The sample of gas in **Figure 8.13** has a volume of 30.0 mL at a pressure of 6.5 psi. Determine the volume of the gas at a pressure of 11.0 psi, using:

(a) the *P-V* graph in Figure 8.13

(b) the $\frac{1}{P}$ vs. *V* graph in Figure 8.13

(c) the Boyle's law equation

Comment on the likely accuracy of each method.

Answer: (a) about 17–18 mL; (b) ~18 mL; (c) 17.7 mL; it was more difficult to estimate well from the *P-V* graph, so (a) is likely more inaccurate than (b); the calculation will be as accurate as the equation and measurements allow

Chemistry in Everyday Life

Breathing and Boyle's Law

What do you do about 20 times per minute for your whole life, without break, and often without even being aware of it? The answer, of course, is respiration, or breathing. How does it work? It turns out that the gas laws apply here. Your lungs take in gas that your body needs (oxygen) and get rid of waste gas (carbon dioxide). Lungs are made of spongy, stretchy tissue that expands and contracts while you breathe. When you inhale, your diaphragm and intercostal muscles (the muscles between your ribs) contract, expanding your chest cavity and making your lung volume larger. The increase in volume leads to a decrease in pressure (Boyle's law). This causes air to flow into the lungs (from high pressure to low pressure). When you exhale, the process reverses: Your diaphragm and rib muscles relax, your chest cavity contracts, and your lung volume decreases, causing the pressure to increase (Boyle's law again), and air flows out of the lungs (from high pressure to low pressure). You then breathe in and out again, and again, repeating this Boyle's law cycle for the rest of your life (Figure 8.15).

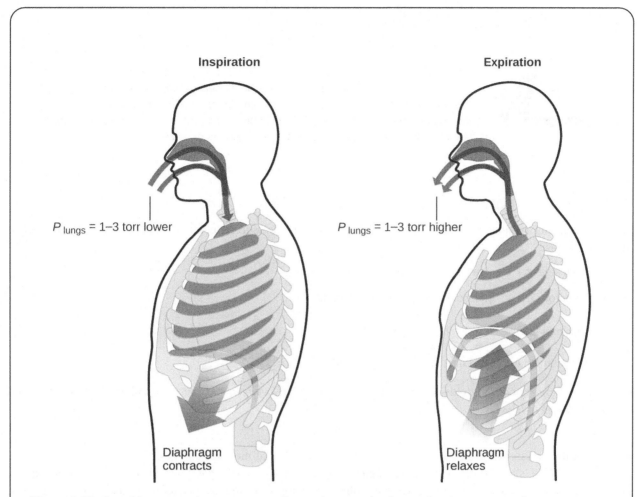

Figure 8.15 Breathing occurs because expanding and contracting lung volume creates small pressure differences between your lungs and your surroundings, causing air to be drawn into and forced out of your lungs.

Moles of Gas and Volume: Avogadro's Law

The Italian scientist Amedeo Avogadro advanced a hypothesis in 1811 to account for the behavior of gases, stating that equal volumes of all gases, measured under the same conditions of temperature and pressure, contain the same number of molecules. Over time, this relationship was supported by many experimental observations as expressed by **Avogadro's law**: *For a confined gas, the volume (V) and number of moles (n) are directly proportional if the pressure and temperature both remain constant.*

In equation form, this is written as:

$$V \propto n \ \text{ or } \ V = k \times n \ \text{ or } \ \frac{V_1}{n_1} = \frac{V_2}{n_2}$$

Mathematical relationships can also be determined for the other variable pairs, such as P versus n, and n versus T.

The Ideal Gas Law

To this point, four separate laws have been discussed that relate pressure, volume, temperature, and the number of moles of the gas:

- Boyle's law: PV = constant at constant T and n

- Amontons's law: $\frac{P}{T}$ = constant at constant V and n

- Charles's law: $\frac{V}{T}$ = constant at constant P and n

- Avogadro's law: $\frac{V}{n}$ = constant at constant P and T

Combining these four laws yields the **ideal gas law**, a relation between the pressure, volume, temperature, and number of moles of a gas:

$$PV = nRT$$

where P is the pressure of a gas, V is its volume, n is the number of moles of the gas, T is its temperature on the kelvin scale, and R is a constant called the **ideal gas constant** or the universal gas constant. The units used to express pressure, volume, and temperature will determine the proper form of the gas constant as required by dimensional analysis, the most commonly encountered values being 0.08206 L atm mol^{-1} K^{-1} and 8.314 kPa L mol^{-1} K^{-1}.

Gases whose properties of P, V, and T are accurately described by the ideal gas law (or the other gas laws) are said to exhibit *ideal behavior* or to approximate the traits of an **ideal gas**. An ideal gas is a hypothetical construct that may be used along with *kinetic molecular theory* to effectively explain the gas laws as will be described in a later module of this chapter. Although all the calculations presented in this module assume ideal behavior, this assumption is only reasonable for gases under conditions of relatively low pressure and high temperature. In the final module of this chapter, a modified gas law will be introduced that accounts for the *non-ideal* behavior observed for many gases at relatively high pressures and low temperatures.

The ideal gas equation contains five terms, the gas constant R and the variable properties P, V, n, and T. Specifying any four of these terms will permit use of the ideal gas law to calculate the fifth term as demonstrated in the following example exercises.

Example 8.9

Using the Ideal Gas Law

Methane, CH_4, is being considered for use as an alternative automotive fuel to replace gasoline. One gallon of gasoline could be replaced by 655 g of CH_4. What is the volume of this much methane at 25 °C and 745 torr?

Solution

We must rearrange $PV = nRT$ to solve for V: $V = \frac{nRT}{P}$

If we choose to use $R = 0.08206$ L atm mol^{-1} K^{-1}, then the amount must be in moles, temperature must be in kelvin, and pressure must be in atm.

Converting into the "right" units:

$$n = 6\,55 \; \text{g CH}_4 \times \frac{1 \text{ mol}}{16.043 \text{ g CH}_4} = 40.8 \text{ mol}$$

$$T = 25 \,^{\circ}\text{C} + 273 = 298 \text{ K}$$

$$P = 745 \text{ torr} \times \frac{1 \text{ atm}}{760 \text{ torr}} = 0.980 \text{ atm}$$

$$V = \frac{nRT}{P} = \frac{(40.8 \text{ mol})(0.08206 \text{ L atm mol}^{-1} \text{ K}^{-1})(298 \text{ K})}{0.980 \text{ atm}} = 1.02 \times 10^3 \text{ L}$$

It would require 1020 L (269 gal) of gaseous methane at about 1 atm of pressure to replace 1 gal of gasoline. It requires a large container to hold enough methane at 1 atm to replace several gallons of gasoline.

Check Your Learning

Calculate the pressure in bar of 2520 moles of hydrogen gas stored at 27 °C in the 180-L storage tank of a modern hydrogen-powered car.

Answer: 350 bar

If the number of moles of an ideal gas are kept constant under two different sets of conditions, a useful mathematical relationship called the combined gas law is obtained: $\frac{P_1 V_1}{T_1} = \frac{P_2 V_2}{T_2}$ using units of atm, L, and K. Both sets of conditions are equal to the product of $n \times R$ (where n = the number of moles of the gas and R is the ideal gas law constant).

Example 8.10

Using the Combined Gas Law

When filled with air, a typical scuba tank with a volume of 13.2 L has a pressure of 153 atm (Figure 8.16). If the water temperature is 27 °C, how many liters of air will such a tank provide to a diver's lungs at a depth of approximately 70 feet in the ocean where the pressure is 3.13 atm?

Figure 8.16 Scuba divers use compressed air to breathe while underwater. (credit: modification of work by Mark Goodchild)

Letting *1* represent the air in the scuba tank and *2* represent the air in the lungs, and noting that body temperature (the temperature the air will be in the lungs) is 37 °C, we have:

$$\frac{P_1 V_1}{T_1} = \frac{P_2 V_2}{T_2} \longrightarrow \frac{(153 \text{ atm})(13.2 \text{ L})}{(300 \text{ K})} = \frac{(3.13 \text{ atm})(V_2)}{(310 \text{ K})}$$

Solving for V_2:

$$V_2 = \frac{(153 \text{ atm})(13.2 \text{ L})(310 \text{ K})}{(300 \text{ K})(3.13 \text{ atm})} = 667 \text{ L}$$

(Note: Be advised that this particular example is one in which the assumption of ideal gas behavior is not very reasonable, since it involves gases at relatively high pressures and low temperatures. Despite this limitation, the calculated volume can be viewed as a good "ballpark" estimate.)

Check Your Learning

A sample of ammonia is found to occupy 0.250 L under laboratory conditions of 27 °C and 0.850 atm. Find the volume of this sample at 0 °C and 1.00 atm.

Answer: 0.193 L

Chemistry in Everyday Life

The Interdependence between Ocean Depth and Pressure in Scuba Diving

Whether scuba diving at the Great Barrier Reef in Australia (shown in Figure 8.17) or in the Caribbean, divers must understand how pressure affects a number of issues related to their comfort and safety.

Figure 8.17   Scuba divers, whether at the Great Barrier Reef or in the Caribbean, must be aware of buoyancy, pressure equalization, and the amount of time they spend underwater, to avoid the risks associated with pressurized gases in the body. (credit: Kyle Taylor)

Pressure increases with ocean depth, and the pressure changes most rapidly as divers reach the surface. The pressure a diver experiences is the sum of all pressures above the diver (from the water and the air). Most pressure measurements are given in units of atmospheres, expressed as "atmospheres absolute" or ATA in the diving community: Every 33 feet of salt water represents 1 ATA of pressure in addition to 1 ATA of pressure from the atmosphere at sea level. As a diver descends, the increase in pressure causes the body's air pockets in the ears and lungs to compress; on the ascent, the decrease in pressure causes these air pockets to expand, potentially rupturing eardrums or bursting the lungs. Divers must therefore undergo equalization by adding air to body airspaces on the descent by breathing normally and adding air to the mask by breathing out of the nose or adding air to the ears and sinuses by equalization techniques; the corollary is also true on ascent, divers must release air from the body to maintain equalization. Buoyancy, or the ability to control whether a diver sinks or floats, is controlled by the buoyancy compensator (BCD). If a diver is ascending, the air in his BCD expands because of lower pressure according to Boyle's law (decreasing the pressure of gases increases the volume). The expanding air increases the buoyancy of the diver, and she or he begins to ascend. The diver must vent air from the BCD or risk an uncontrolled ascent that could rupture the lungs. In descending, the increased pressure causes the air in the BCD to compress and the diver sinks much more quickly; the diver must add air to the BCD or risk an uncontrolled descent, facing much higher pressures near the ocean floor. The pressure also impacts how long a diver can stay underwater before ascending. The deeper a diver dives, the more compressed the air that is breathed because of increased pressure: If a diver dives 33 feet, the pressure is 2 ATA and the air would be compressed to one-half of its original volume. The diver uses up available air twice as fast as at the surface.

Standard Conditions of Temperature and Pressure

We have seen that the volume of a given quantity of gas and the number of molecules (moles) in a given volume of gas vary with changes in pressure and temperature. Chemists sometimes make comparisons against a **standard temperature and pressure (STP)** for reporting properties of gases: 273.15 K and 1 atm (101.325 kPa). At STP, an ideal gas has a volume of about 22.4 L—this is referred to as the **standard molar volume** (Figure 8.18).

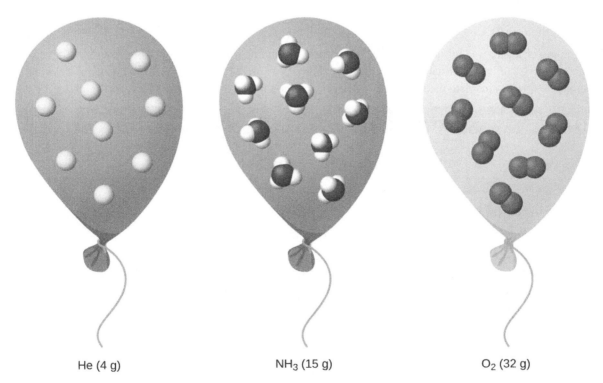

He (4 g) NH_3 (15 g) O_2 (32 g)

Figure 8.18 Since the number of moles in a given volume of gas varies with pressure and temperature changes, chemists use standard temperature and pressure (273.15 K and 1 atm or 101.325 kPa) to report properties of gases.

8.3 Stoichiometry of Gaseous Substances, Mixtures, and Reactions

By the end of this section, you will be able to:

- Use the ideal gas law to compute gas densities and molar masses
- Perform stoichiometric calculations involving gaseous substances
- State Dalton's law of partial pressures and use it in calculations involving gaseous mixtures

The study of the chemical behavior of gases was part of the basis of perhaps the most fundamental chemical revolution in history. French nobleman Antoine Lavoisier, widely regarded as the "father of modern chemistry," changed chemistry from a qualitative to a quantitative science through his work with gases. He discovered the law of conservation of matter, discovered the role of oxygen in combustion reactions, determined the composition of air, explained respiration in terms of chemical reactions, and more. He was a casualty of the French Revolution, guillotined in 1794. Of his death, mathematician and astronomer Joseph-Louis Lagrange said, "It took the mob only a moment to remove his head; a century will not suffice to reproduce it."[1]

As described in an earlier chapter of this text, we can turn to chemical stoichiometry for answers to many of the questions that ask "How much?" We can answer the question with masses of substances or volumes of solutions. However, we can also answer this question another way: with volumes of gases. We can use the ideal gas equation to relate the pressure, volume, temperature, and number of moles of a gas. Here we will combine the ideal gas equation with other equations to find gas density and molar mass. We will deal with mixtures of different gases, and calculate amounts of substances in reactions involving gases. This section will not introduce any new material or ideas, but will provide examples of applications and ways to integrate concepts we have already discussed.

Density of a Gas

Recall that the density of a gas is its mass to volume ratio, $\rho = \frac{m}{V}$. Therefore, if we can determine the mass of some volume of a gas, we will get its density. The density of an unknown gas can used to determine its molar mass and thereby assist in its identification. The ideal gas law, $PV = nRT$, provides us with a means of deriving such a mathematical formula to relate the density of a gas to its volume in the proof shown in **Example 8.11**.

Example 8.11

Derivation of a Density Formula from the Ideal Gas Law

Use $PV = nRT$ to derive a formula for the density of gas in g/L

Solution

    Step 1. $PV = nRT$

    Step 2. *Rearrange to get (mol/L):* $\frac{n}{V} = \frac{P}{RT}$

    Step 3. *Multiply each side of the equation by the molar mass,* $\mathcal{M}$. When moles are multiplied by $\mathcal{M}$ in g/mol, g are obtained:

$$(\mathcal{M})\left(\frac{n}{V}\right) = \left(\frac{P}{RT}\right)(\mathcal{M})$$

    Step 4. $g/L = \rho = \frac{P\mathcal{M}}{RT}$

---

1. "Quotations by Joseph-Louis Lagrange," last modified February 2006, accessed February 10, 2015, http://www-history.mcs.st-andrews.ac.uk/Quotations/Lagrange.html

Check Your Learning

A gas was found to have a density of 0.0847 g/L at 17.0 °C and a pressure of 760 torr. What is its molar mass? What is the gas?

Answer: $\rho = \dfrac{P\mathcal{M}}{RT}$

$$0.0847 \text{ g/L} = 760 \text{ torr} \times \frac{1 \text{ atm}}{760 \text{ torr}} \times \frac{\mathcal{M}}{0.0821 \text{ L atm/mol K}} \times 290 \text{ K}$$

$\mathcal{M} = 2.02$ g/mol; therefore, the gas must be hydrogen (H_2, 2.02 g/mol)

We must specify both the temperature and the pressure of a gas when calculating its density because the number of moles of a gas (and thus the mass of the gas) in a liter changes with temperature or pressure. Gas densities are often reported at STP.

Example 8.12

Empirical/Molecular Formula Problems Using the Ideal Gas Law and Density of a Gas

Cyclopropane, a gas once used with oxygen as a general anesthetic, is composed of 85.7% carbon and 14.3% hydrogen by mass. Find the empirical formula. If 1.56 g of cyclopropane occupies a volume of 1.00 L at 0.984 atm and 50 °C, what is the molecular formula for cyclopropane?

Solution

Strategy: First solve the empirical formula problem using methods discussed earlier. Assume 100 g and convert the percentage of each element into grams. Determine the number of moles of carbon and hydrogen in the 100-g sample of cyclopropane. Divide by the smallest number of moles to relate the number of moles of carbon to the number of moles of hydrogen. In the last step, realize that the smallest whole number ratio is the empirical formula:

$$85.7 \text{ g C} \times \frac{1 \text{ mol C}}{12.01 \text{ g C}} = 7.136 \text{ mol C} \qquad \frac{7.136}{7.136} = 1.00 \text{ mol C}$$

$$14.3 \text{ g H} \times \frac{1 \text{ mol H}}{1.01 \text{ g H}} = 14.158 \text{ mol H} \qquad \frac{14.158}{7.136} = 1.98 \text{ mol H}$$

Empirical formula is CH_2 [empirical mass (EM) of 14.03 g/empirical unit].

Next, use the density equation related to the ideal gas law to determine the molar mass:

$$d = \frac{P\mathcal{M}}{RT} \qquad \frac{1.56 \text{ g}}{1.00 \text{ L}} = 0.984 \text{ atm} \times \frac{\mathcal{M}}{0.0821 \text{ L atm/mol K}} \times 323 \text{ K}$$

$\mathcal{M} = 42.0$ g/mol, $\dfrac{\mathcal{M}}{\text{E}\mathcal{M}} = \dfrac{42.0}{14.03} = 2.99$, so $(3)(CH_2) = C_3H_6$ (molecular formula)

Check Your Learning

Acetylene, a fuel used welding torches, is comprised of 92.3% C and 7.7% H by mass. Find the empirical formula. If 1.10 g of acetylene occupies of volume of 1.00 L at 1.15 atm and 59.5 °C, what is the molecular formula for acetylene?

Answer: Empirical formula, CH; Molecular formula, C_2H_2

Molar Mass of a Gas

Another useful application of the ideal gas law involves the determination of molar mass. By definition, the molar mass of a substance is the ratio of its mass in grams, m, to its amount in moles, n:

$$\mathcal{M} = \frac{\text{grams of substance}}{\text{moles of substance}} = \frac{m}{n}$$

The ideal gas equation can be rearranged to isolate n:

$$n = \frac{PV}{RT}$$

and then combined with the molar mass equation to yield:

$$\mathcal{M} = \frac{mRT}{PV}$$

This equation can be used to derive the molar mass of a gas from measurements of its pressure, volume, temperature, and mass.

Example 8.13

Determining the Molar Mass of a Volatile Liquid

The approximate molar mass of a volatile liquid can be determined by:

1. Heating a sample of the liquid in a flask with a tiny hole at the top, which converts the liquid into gas that may escape through the hole

2. Removing the flask from heat at the instant when the last bit of liquid becomes gas, at which time the flask will be filled with only gaseous sample at ambient pressure

3. Sealing the flask and permitting the gaseous sample to condense to liquid, and then weighing the flask to determine the sample's mass (see **Figure 8.19**)

Figure 8.19   When the volatile liquid in the flask is heated past its boiling point, it becomes gas and drives air out of the flask. At $t_{l \longrightarrow g}$,   the flask is filled with volatile liquid gas at the same pressure as the atmosphere. If the flask is then cooled to room temperature, the gas condenses and the mass of the gas that filled the flask, and is now liquid, can be measured. (credit: modification of work by Mark Ott)

Using this procedure, a sample of chloroform gas weighing 0.494 g is collected in a flask with a volume of 129 cm^3 at 99.6 °C when the atmospheric pressure is 742.1 mm Hg. What is the approximate molar mass of chloroform?

Solution

Since $\mathcal{M} = \frac{m}{n}$ and $n = \frac{PV}{RT}$, substituting and rearranging gives $\mathcal{M} = \frac{mRT}{PV}$,

then

$$\mathcal{M} = \frac{mRT}{PV} = \frac{(0.494 \text{ g}) \times 0.08206 \text{ L·atm/mol K} \times 372.8 \text{ K}}{0.976 \text{ atm} \times 0.129 \text{ L}} = 120 \text{ g/mol.}$$

Check Your Learning

A sample of phosphorus that weighs 3.243×10^{-2} g exerts a pressure of 31.89 kPa in a 56.0-mL bulb at 550 °C. What are the molar mass and molecular formula of phosphorus vapor?

Answer: 124 g/mol P$_4$

The Pressure of a Mixture of Gases: Dalton's Law

Unless they chemically react with each other, the individual gases in a mixture of gases do not affect each other's pressure. Each individual gas in a mixture exerts the same pressure that it would exert if it were present alone in the container (**Figure 8.20**). The pressure exerted by each individual gas in a mixture is called its **partial pressure**. This observation is summarized by **Dalton's law of partial pressures**: *The total pressure of a mixture of ideal gases is equal to the sum of the partial pressures of the component gases*:

$$P_{Total} = P_A + P_B + P_C + ... = \Sigma_i P_i$$

In the equation P_{Total} is the total pressure of a mixture of gases, P_A is the partial pressure of gas A; P_B is the partial pressure of gas B; P_C is the partial pressure of gas C; and so on.

Figure 8.20 If equal-volume cylinders containing gas A at a pressure of 300 kPa, gas B at a pressure of 600 kPa, and gas C at a pressure of 450 kPa are all combined in the same-size cylinder, the total pressure of the mixture is 1350 kPa.

The partial pressure of gas A is related to the total pressure of the gas mixture via its **mole fraction (X)**, a unit of concentration defined as the number of moles of a component of a solution divided by the total number of moles of all components:

$$P_A = X_A \times P_{Total} \qquad \text{where} \qquad X_A = \frac{n_A}{n_{Total}}$$

where P_A, X_A, and n_A are the partial pressure, mole fraction, and number of moles of gas A, respectively, and n_{Total} is the number of moles of all components in the mixture.

Example 8.14

The Pressure of a Mixture of Gases

A 10.0-L vessel contains 2.50×10^{-3} mol of H_2, 1.00×10^{-3} mol of He, and 3.00×10^{-4} mol of Ne at 35 °C.

(a) What are the partial pressures of each of the gases?

(b) What is the total pressure in atmospheres?

Solution

The gases behave independently, so the partial pressure of each gas can be determined from the ideal gas equation, using $P = \frac{nRT}{V}$:

$$P_{H_2} = \frac{(2.50 \times 10^{-3} \ \text{mol})(0.08206 \ \text{L atm mol}^{-1} \text{K}^{-1})(308 \ \text{K})}{10.0 \ \text{L}} = 6.32 \times 10^{-3} \ \text{atm}$$

$$P_{He} = \frac{(1.00 \times 10^{-3} \ \text{mol})(0.08206 \ \text{L atm mol}^{-1} \text{K}^{-1})(308 \ \text{K})}{10.0 \ \text{L}} = 2.53 \times 10^{-3} \ \text{atm}$$

$$P_{Ne} = \frac{(3.00 \times 10^{-4} \ \text{mol})(0.08206 \ \text{L atm mol}^{-1} \text{K}^{-1})(308 \ \text{K})}{10.0 \ \text{L}} = 7.58 \times 10^{-4} \ \text{atm}$$

The total pressure is given by the sum of the partial pressures:

$$P_T = P_{H_2} + P_{He} + P_{Ne} = (0.00632 + 0.00253 + 0.00076) \ \text{atm} = 9.61 \times 10^{-3} \ \text{atm}$$

Check Your Learning

A 5.73-L flask at 25 °C contains 0.0388 mol of N_2, 0.147 mol of CO, and 0.0803 mol of H_2. What is the total pressure in the flask in atmospheres?

Answer: 1.137 atm

Here is another example of this concept, but dealing with mole fraction calculations.

Example 8.15

The Pressure of a Mixture of Gases

A gas mixture used for anesthesia contains 2.83 mol oxygen, O_2, and 8.41 mol nitrous oxide, N_2O. The total pressure of the mixture is 192 kPa.

(a) What are the mole fractions of O_2 and N_2O?

(b) What are the partial pressures of O_2 and N_2O?

Solution

The mole fraction is given by $X_A = \frac{n_A}{n_{Total}}$ and the partial pressure is $P_A = X_A \times P_{Total}$.

For O_2,

$$X_{O_2} = \frac{n_{O_2}}{n_{Total}} = \frac{2.83 \ \text{mol}}{(2.83 + 8.41) \ \text{mol}} = 0.252$$

and $P_{O_2} = X_{O_2} \times P_{Total} = 0.252 \times 192 \ \text{kPa} = 48.4 \ \text{kPa}$

For N_2O,

$$X_{N_2} = \frac{n_{N_2}}{n_{Total}} = \frac{8.41 \ \text{mol}}{(2.83 + 8.41) \ \text{mol}} = 0.748$$

and

$$P_{N_2} = X_{N_2} \times P_{Total} = 0.748 \times 192 \ \text{kPa} = 143.6 \ \text{kPa}$$

Check Your Learning

What is the pressure of a mixture of 0.200 g of H_2, 1.00 g of N_2, and 0.820 g of Ar in a container with a volume of 2.00 L at 20 °C?

Answer: 1.87 atm

Collection of Gases over Water

A simple way to collect gases that do not react with water is to capture them in a bottle that has been filled with water and inverted into a dish filled with water. The pressure of the gas inside the bottle can be made equal to the air pressure outside by raising or lowering the bottle. When the water level is the same both inside and outside the bottle (**Figure 8.21**), the pressure of the gas is equal to the atmospheric pressure, which can be measured with a barometer.

Figure 8.21 When a reaction produces a gas that is collected above water, the trapped gas is a mixture of the gas produced by the reaction and water vapor. If the collection flask is appropriately positioned to equalize the water levels both within and outside the flask, the pressure of the trapped gas mixture will equal the atmospheric pressure outside the flask (see the earlier discussion of manometers).

However, there is another factor we must consider when we measure the pressure of the gas by this method. Water evaporates and there is always gaseous water (water vapor) above a sample of liquid water. As a gas is collected over water, it becomes saturated with water vapor and the total pressure of the mixture equals the partial pressure of the gas plus the partial pressure of the water vapor. The pressure of the pure gas is therefore equal to the total pressure minus the pressure of the water vapor—this is referred to as the "dry" gas pressure, that is, the pressure of the gas only, without water vapor. The **vapor pressure of water**, which is the pressure exerted by water vapor in equilibrium with liquid water in a closed container, depends on the temperature (**Figure 8.22**); more detailed information on the temperature dependence of water vapor can be found in **Table 8.2**, and vapor pressure will be discussed in more detail in the chapter on liquids.

Figure 8.22 This graph shows the vapor pressure of water at sea level as a function of temperature.

Vapor Pressure of Ice and Water in Various Temperatures at Sea Level

Temperature (°C)	Pressure (torr)	Temperature (°C)	Pressure (torr)	Temperature (°C)	Pressure (torr)
−10	1.95	18	15.5	30	31.8
−5	3.0	19	16.5	35	42.2
−2	3.9	20	17.5	40	55.3
0	4.6	21	18.7	50	92.5
2	5.3	22	19.8	60	149.4
4	6.1	23	21.1	70	233.7
6	7.0	24	22.4	80	355.1
8	8.0	25	23.8	90	525.8
10	9.2	26	25.2	95	633.9
12	10.5	27	26.7	99	733.2
14	12.0	28	28.3	100.0	760.0
16	13.6	29	30.0	101.0	787.6

Table 8.2

Example 8.16

Pressure of a Gas Collected Over Water

If 0.200 L of argon is collected over water at a temperature of 26 °C and a pressure of 750 torr in a system like that shown in **Figure 8.21**, what is the partial pressure of argon?

Solution

According to Dalton's law, the total pressure in the bottle (750 torr) is the sum of the partial pressure of argon and the partial pressure of gaseous water:

$$P_T = P_{Ar} + P_{H_2O}$$

Rearranging this equation to solve for the pressure of argon gives:

$$P_{Ar} = P_T - P_{H_2O}$$

The pressure of water vapor above a sample of liquid water at 26 °C is 25.2 torr (Appendix E), so:

$$P_{Ar} = 750 \text{ torr} - 25.2 \text{ torr} = 725 \text{ torr}$$

Check Your Learning

A sample of oxygen collected over water at a temperature of 29.0 °C and a pressure of 764 torr has a volume of 0.560 L. What volume would the dry oxygen have under the same conditions of temperature and pressure?

Answer: 0.583 L

Chemical Stoichiometry and Gases

Chemical stoichiometry describes the quantitative relationships between reactants and products in chemical reactions.

We have previously measured quantities of reactants and products using masses for solids and volumes in conjunction with the molarity for solutions; now we can also use gas volumes to indicate quantities. If we know the volume, pressure, and temperature of a gas, we can use the ideal gas equation to calculate how many moles of the gas are present. If we know how many moles of a gas are involved, we can calculate the volume of a gas at any temperature and pressure.

Avogadro's Law Revisited

Sometimes we can take advantage of a simplifying feature of the stoichiometry of gases that solids and solutions do not exhibit: All gases that show ideal behavior contain the same number of molecules in the same volume (at the same temperature and pressure). Thus, the ratios of volumes of gases involved in a chemical reaction are given by the coefficients in the equation for the reaction, provided that the gas volumes are measured at the same temperature and pressure.

We can extend Avogadro's law (that the volume of a gas is directly proportional to the number of moles of the gas) to chemical reactions with gases: Gases combine, or react, in definite and simple proportions by volume, provided that all gas volumes are measured at the same temperature and pressure. For example, since nitrogen and hydrogen gases react to produce ammonia gas according to $N_2(g) + 3H_2(g) \longrightarrow 2NH_3(g)$, a given volume of nitrogen gas reacts with three times that volume of hydrogen gas to produce two times that volume of ammonia gas, if pressure and temperature remain constant.

The explanation for this is illustrated in Figure 8.23. According to Avogadro's law, equal volumes of gaseous N_2, H_2, and NH_3, at the same temperature and pressure, contain the same number of molecules. Because one molecule of N_2 reacts with three molecules of H_2 to produce two molecules of NH_3, the volume of H_2 required is three times the volume of N_2, and the volume of NH_3 produced is two times the volume of N_2.

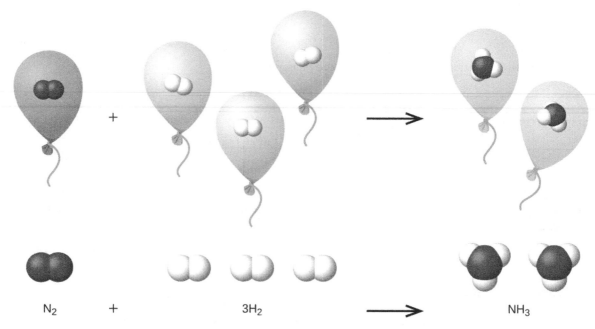

Figure 8.23   One volume of N_2 combines with three volumes of H_2 to form two volumes of NH_3.

Example 8.17

Reaction of Gases

Propane, $C_3H_8(g)$, is used in gas grills to provide the heat for cooking. What volume of $O_2(g)$ measured at 25 °C and 760 torr is required to react with 2.7 L of propane measured under the same conditions of temperature and pressure? Assume that the propane undergoes complete combustion.

Solution

The ratio of the volumes of C_3H_8 and O_2 will be equal to the ratio of their coefficients in the balanced equation for the reaction:

$$C_3H_8(g) + 5O_2(g) \longrightarrow 3CO_2(g) + 4H_2O(l)$$
$$\text{1 volume + 5 volumes} \qquad \text{3 volumes + 4 volumes}$$

From the equation, we see that one volume of C_3H_8 will react with five volumes of O_2:

$$2.7 \ \text{L } C_3H_8 \times \frac{5 \text{ L } O_2}{1 \ \text{L } C_3H_8} = 13.5 \text{ L } O_2$$

A volume of 13.5 L of O_2 will be required to react with 2.7 L of C_3H_8.

Check Your Learning

An acetylene tank for an oxyacetylene welding torch provides 9340 L of acetylene gas, C_2H_2, at 0 °C and 1 atm. How many tanks of oxygen, each providing 7.00×10^3 L of O_2 at 0 °C and 1 atm, will be required to burn the acetylene?

$$2C_2H_2 + 5O_2 \longrightarrow 4CO_2 + 2H_2O$$

Answer: 3.34 tanks (2.34×10^4 L)

Example 8.18

Volumes of Reacting Gases

Ammonia is an important fertilizer and industrial chemical. Suppose that a volume of 683 billion cubic feet of gaseous ammonia, measured at 25 °C and 1 atm, was manufactured. What volume of $H_2(g)$, measured under the same conditions, was required to prepare this amount of ammonia by reaction with N_2?

$$N_2(g) + 3H_2(g) \longrightarrow 2NH_3(g)$$

Solution

Because equal volumes of H_2 and NH_3 contain equal numbers of molecules and each three molecules of H_2 that react produce two molecules of NH_3, the ratio of the volumes of H_2 and NH_3 will be equal to 3:2. Two volumes of NH_3, in this case in units of billion ft^3, will be formed from three volumes of H_2:

$$683 \text{ billion ft}^3 \text{ NH}_3 \times \frac{3 \text{ billion ft}^3 \text{ H}_2}{2 \text{ billion ft}^3 \text{ NH}_3} = 1.02 \times 10^3 \text{ billion ft}^3 \text{ H}_2$$

The manufacture of 683 billion ft^3 of NH_3 required 1020 billion ft^3 of H_2. (At 25 °C and 1 atm, this is the volume of a cube with an edge length of approximately 1.9 miles.)

Check Your Learning

What volume of $O_2(g)$ measured at 25 °C and 760 torr is required to react with 17.0 L of ethylene, $C_2H_4(g)$, measured under the same conditions of temperature and pressure? The products are CO_2 and water vapor.

Answer: 51.0 L

Example 8.19

Volume of Gaseous Product

What volume of hydrogen at 27 °C and 723 torr may be prepared by the reaction of 8.88 g of gallium with an excess of hydrochloric acid?

$$2Ga(s) + 6HCl(aq) \longrightarrow 2GaCl_3(aq) + 3H_2(g)$$

Solution

To convert from the mass of gallium to the volume of $H_2(g)$, we need to do something like this:

The first two conversions are:

$$8.88 \text{ g Ga} \times \frac{1 \text{ mol Ga}}{69.723 \text{ g Ga}} \times \frac{3 \text{ mol H}_2}{2 \text{ mol Ga}} = 0.191 \text{ mol H}_2$$

Finally, we can use the ideal gas law:

$$V_{H_2} = \left(\frac{nRT}{P}\right)_{H_2} = \frac{0.191 \text{ mol} \times 0.08206 \text{ L atm mol}^{-1} \text{ K}^{-1} \times 300 \text{ K}}{0.951 \text{ atm}} = 4.94 \text{ L}$$

Check Your Learning

Sulfur dioxide is an intermediate in the preparation of sulfuric acid. What volume of SO_2 at 343 °C and 1.21 atm is produced by burning l.00 kg of sulfur in oxygen?

Answer: 1.30×10^3 L

How Sciences Interconnect

Greenhouse Gases and Climate Change

The thin skin of our atmosphere keeps the earth from being an ice planet and makes it habitable. In fact, this is due to less than 0.5% of the air molecules. Of the energy from the sun that reaches the earth, almost $\frac{1}{3}$ is reflected back into space, with the rest absorbed by the atmosphere and the surface of the earth. Some of the energy that the earth absorbs is re-emitted as infrared (IR) radiation, a portion of which passes back out through the atmosphere into space. However, most of this IR radiation is absorbed by certain substances in the atmosphere, known as greenhouse gases, which re-emit this energy in all directions, trapping some of the heat. This maintains favorable living conditions—without atmosphere, the average global average temperature of 14 °C (57 °F) would be about –19 °C (–2 °F). The major greenhouse gases (GHGs) are water vapor, carbon dioxide, methane, and ozone. Since the Industrial Revolution, human activity has been increasing the concentrations of GHGs, which have changed the energy balance and are significantly altering the earth's climate (Figure 8.24).

Figure 8.24 Greenhouse gases trap enough of the sun's energy to make the planet habitable—this is known as the greenhouse effect. Human activities are increasing greenhouse gas levels, warming the planet and causing more extreme weather events.

There is strong evidence from multiple sources that higher atmospheric levels of CO_2 are caused by human activity, with fossil fuel burning accounting for about $\frac{3}{4}$ of the recent increase in CO_2. Reliable data from ice cores reveals that CO_2 concentration in the atmosphere is at the highest level in the past 800,000 years; other evidence indicates that it may be at its highest level in 20 million years. In recent years, the CO_2 concentration has increased from historical levels of below 300 ppm to almost 400 ppm today (Figure 8.25).

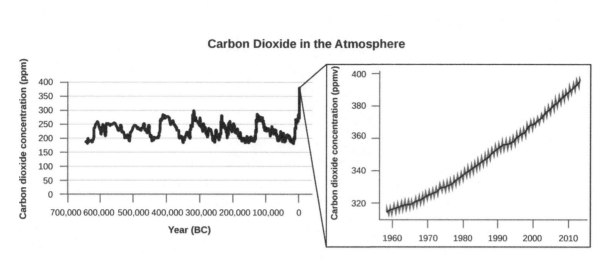

Figure 8.25 CO$_2$ levels over the past 700,000 years were typically from 200–300 ppm, with a steep, unprecedented increase over the past 50 years.

Link to Learning

Click here (http://openstaxcollege.org/l/16GlobalWarming) to see a 2-minute video explaining greenhouse gases and global warming.

Portrait of a Chemist

Susan Solomon

Atmospheric and climate scientist Susan Solomon (Figure 8.26) is the author of one of *The New York Times* books of the year (*The Coldest March*, 2001), one of Time magazine's 100 most influential people in the world (2008), and a working group leader of the Intergovernmental Panel on Climate Change (IPCC), which was the recipient of the 2007 Nobel Peace Prize. She helped determine and explain the cause of the formation of the ozone hole over Antarctica, and has authored many important papers on climate change. She has been awarded the top scientific honors in the US and France (the National Medal of Science and the Grande Medaille, respectively), and is a member of the National Academy of Sciences, the Royal Society, the French Academy of Sciences, and the European Academy of Sciences. Formerly a professor at the University of Colorado, she is now at MIT, and continues to work at NOAA.

For more information, watch this video (http://openstaxcollege.org/l/16SusanSolomon) about Susan Solomon.

Figure 8.26   Susan Solomon's research focuses on climate change and has been instrumental in determining the cause of the ozone hole over Antarctica. (credit: National Oceanic and Atmospheric Administration)

8.4 Effusion and Diffusion of Gases

By the end of this section, you will be able to:

- Define and explain effusion and diffusion
- State Graham's law and use it to compute relevant gas properties

If you have ever been in a room when a piping hot pizza was delivered, you have been made aware of the fact that gaseous molecules can quickly spread throughout a room, as evidenced by the pleasant aroma that soon reaches your nose. Although gaseous molecules travel at tremendous speeds (hundreds of meters per second), they collide with other gaseous molecules and travel in many different directions before reaching the desired target. At room temperature, a gaseous molecule will experience billions of collisions per second. The **mean free path** is the average distance a molecule travels between collisions. The mean free path increases with decreasing pressure; in general, the mean free path for a gaseous molecule will be hundreds of times the diameter of the molecule

In general, we know that when a sample of gas is introduced to one part of a closed container, its molecules very quickly disperse throughout the container; this process by which molecules disperse in space in response to differences in concentration is called **diffusion** (shown in Figure 8.27). The gaseous atoms or molecules are, of course, unaware of any concentration gradient, they simply move randomly—regions of higher concentration have more particles than regions of lower concentrations, and so a net movement of species from high to low concentration areas takes place. In a closed environment, diffusion will ultimately result in equal concentrations of gas throughout, as depicted in Figure 8.27. The gaseous atoms and molecules continue to move, but since their concentrations are the same in both bulbs, the rates of transfer between the bulbs are equal (no *net* transfer of molecules occurs).

Figure 8.27 (a) Two gases, H_2 and O_2, are initially separated. (b) When the stopcock is opened, they mix together. The lighter gas, H_2, passes through the opening faster than O_2, so just after the stopcock is opened, more H_2 molecules move to the O_2 side than O_2 molecules move to the H_2 side. (c) After a short time, both the slower-moving O_2 molecules and the faster-moving H_2 molecules have distributed themselves evenly on both sides of the vessel.

We are often interested in the **rate of diffusion**, the amount of gas passing through some area per unit time:

$$\text{rate of diffusion} = \frac{\text{amount of gas passing through an area}}{\text{unit of time}}$$

The diffusion rate depends on several factors: the concentration gradient (the increase or decrease in concentration from one point to another); the amount of surface area available for diffusion; and the distance the gas particles must travel. Note also that the time required for diffusion to occur is inversely proportional to the rate of diffusion, as shown in the rate of diffusion equation.

A process involving movement of gaseous species similar to diffusion is **effusion**, the escape of gas molecules through a tiny hole such as a pinhole in a balloon into a vacuum (**Figure 8.28**). Although diffusion and effusion rates both depend on the molar mass of the gas involved, their rates are not equal; however, the ratios of their rates are the same.

Diffusion   Effusion

Figure 8.28 Diffusion occurs when gas molecules disperse throughout a container. Effusion occurs when a gas passes through an opening that is smaller than the mean free path of the particles, that is, the average distance traveled between collisions. Effectively, this means that only one particle passes through at a time.

If a mixture of gases is placed in a container with porous walls, the gases effuse through the small openings in the walls. The lighter gases pass through the small openings more rapidly (at a higher rate) than the heavier ones (**Figure 8.29**). In 1832, Thomas Graham studied the rates of effusion of different gases and formulated **Graham's law of effusion**: *The rate of effusion of a gas is inversely proportional to the square root of the mass of its particles*:

$$\text{rate of effusion} \propto \frac{1}{\sqrt{\mathcal{M}}}$$

This means that if two gases A and B are at the same temperature and pressure, the ratio of their effusion rates is inversely proportional to the ratio of the square roots of the masses of their particles:

$$\frac{\text{rate of effusion of A}}{\text{rate of effusion of B}} = \frac{\sqrt{\mathcal{M}_B}}{\sqrt{\mathcal{M}_A}}$$

Figure 8.29 A balloon filled with air (the blue one) remains full overnight. A balloon filled with helium (the green one) partially deflates because the smaller, light helium atoms effuse through small holes in the rubber much more readily than the heavier molecules of nitrogen and oxygen found in air. (credit: modification of work by Mark Ott)

Example 8.20

Applying Graham's Law to Rates of Effusion

Calculate the ratio of the rate of effusion of hydrogen to the rate of effusion of oxygen.

Solution

From Graham's law, we have:

$$\frac{\text{rate of effusion of hydrogen}}{\text{rate of effusion of oxygen}} = \frac{\sqrt{1.43\ \cancel{g\,L^{-1}}}}{\sqrt{0.0899\ \cancel{g\,L^{-1}}}} = \frac{1.20}{0.300} = \frac{4}{1}$$

Using molar masses:

$$\frac{\text{rate of effusion of hydrogen}}{\text{rate of effusion of oxygen}} = \frac{\sqrt{32\ \cancel{g\,mol^{-1}}}}{\sqrt{2\ \cancel{g\,mol^{-1}}}} = \frac{\sqrt{16}}{\sqrt{1}} = \frac{4}{1}$$

Hydrogen effuses four times as rapidly as oxygen.

Check Your Learning

At a particular pressure and temperature, nitrogen gas effuses at the rate of 79 mL/s. Using the same apparatus at the same temperature and pressure, at what rate will sulfur dioxide effuse?

Answer: 52 mL/s

Here's another example, making the point about how determining times differs from determining rates.

Example 8.21

Effusion Time Calculations

It takes 243 s for 4.46×10^{-5} mol Xe to effuse through a tiny hole. Under the same conditions, how long will it take 4.46×10^{-5} mol Ne to effuse?

Solution

It is important to resist the temptation to use the times directly, and to remember how rate relates to time as well as how it relates to mass. Recall the definition of rate of effusion:

$$\text{rate of effusion} = \frac{\text{amount of gas transferred}}{\text{time}}$$

and combine it with Graham's law:

$$\frac{\text{rate of effusion of gas Xe}}{\text{rate of effusion of gas Ne}} = \frac{\sqrt{\mathcal{M}_{Ne}}}{\sqrt{\mathcal{M}_{Xe}}}$$

To get:

$$\frac{\frac{\text{amount of Xe transferred}}{\text{time for Xe}}}{\frac{\text{amount of Ne transferred}}{\text{time for Ne}}} = \frac{\sqrt{\mathcal{M}_{Ne}}}{\sqrt{\mathcal{M}_{Xe}}}$$

Noting that *amount of A = amount of B*, and solving for *time for Ne*:

$$\frac{\frac{\cancel{\text{amount of Xe}}}{\text{time for Xe}}}{\frac{\cancel{\text{amount of Ne}}}{\text{time for Ne}}} = \frac{\text{time for Ne}}{\text{time for Xe}} = \frac{\sqrt{\mathcal{M}_{Ne}}}{\sqrt{\mathcal{M}_{Xe}}} = \frac{\sqrt{\mathcal{M}_{Ne}}}{\sqrt{\mathcal{M}_{Xe}}}$$

and substitute values:

$$\frac{\text{time for Ne}}{243 \text{ s}} = \sqrt{\frac{20.2 \cancel{\text{ g mol}}}{131.3 \cancel{\text{ g mol}}}} = 0.392$$

Finally, solve for the desired quantity:

$$\text{time for Ne} = 0.392 \times 243 \text{ s} = 95.3 \text{ s}$$

Note that this answer is reasonable: Since Ne is lighter than Xe, the effusion rate for Ne will be larger than that for Xe, which means the time of effusion for Ne will be smaller than that for Xe.

Check Your Learning

A party balloon filled with helium deflates to $\frac{2}{3}$ of its original volume in 8.0 hours. How long will it take an identical balloon filled with the same number of moles of air ($\mathcal{M}$ = 28.2 g/mol) to deflate to $\frac{1}{2}$ of its original volume?

Answer: 32 h

Finally, here is one more example showing how to calculate molar mass from effusion rate data.

Example 8.22

Determining Molar Mass Using Graham's Law

An unknown gas effuses 1.66 times more rapidly than CO_2. What is the molar mass of the unknown gas? Can you make a reasonable guess as to its identity?

Solution

From Graham's law, we have:

$$\frac{\text{rate of effusion of Unknown}}{\text{rate of effusion of } CO_2} = \frac{\sqrt{\mathcal{M}_{CO_2}}}{\sqrt{\mathcal{M}_{Unknown}}}$$

Plug in known data:

$$\frac{1.66}{1} = \frac{\sqrt{44.0 \text{ g/mol}}}{\sqrt{\mathcal{M}_{Unknown}}}$$

Solve:

$$\mathcal{M}_{Unknown} = \frac{44.0 \text{ g/mol}}{(1.66)^2} = 16.0 \text{ g/mol}$$

The gas could well be CH_4, the only gas with this molar mass.

Check Your Learning

Hydrogen gas effuses through a porous container 8.97-times faster than an unknown gas. Estimate the molar mass of the unknown gas.

Answer: 163 g/mol

How Sciences Interconnect

Use of Diffusion for Nuclear Energy Applications: Uranium Enrichment

Gaseous diffusion has been used to produce enriched uranium for use in nuclear power plants and weapons. Naturally occurring uranium contains only 0.72% of ^{235}U, the kind of uranium that is "fissile," that is, capable of sustaining a nuclear fission chain reaction. Nuclear reactors require fuel that is 2–5% ^{235}U, and nuclear bombs need even higher concentrations. One way to enrich uranium to the desired levels is to take advantage of Graham's law. In a gaseous diffusion enrichment plant, uranium hexafluoride (UF_6, the only uranium compound that is volatile enough to work) is slowly pumped through large cylindrical vessels called diffusers, which contain porous barriers with microscopic openings. The process is one of diffusion because the other side of the barrier is not evacuated. The $^{235}UF_6$ molecules have a higher average speed and diffuse through the barrier a little faster than the heavier $^{238}UF_6$ molecules. The gas that has passed through the barrier is slightly enriched in $^{235}UF_6$ and the residual gas is slightly depleted. The small difference in molecular weights between $^{235}UF_6$ and $^{238}UF_6$ only about 0.4% enrichment, is achieved in one diffuser (Figure 8.30). But by connecting many diffusers in a sequence of stages (called a cascade), the desired level of enrichment can be attained.

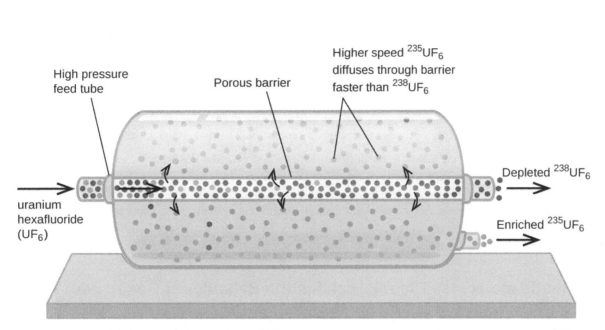

Figure 8.30 In a diffuser, gaseous UF_6 is pumped through a porous barrier, which partially separates $^{235}UF_6$ from $^{238}UF_6$ The UF_6 must pass through many large diffuser units to achieve sufficient enrichment in ^{235}U.

The large scale separation of gaseous $^{235}UF_6$ from $^{238}UF_6$ was first done during the World War II, at the atomic energy installation in Oak Ridge, Tennessee, as part of the Manhattan Project (the development of the first atomic bomb). Although the theory is simple, this required surmounting many daunting technical challenges to make it work in practice. The barrier must have tiny, uniform holes (about 10^{-6} cm in diameter) and be porous enough to produce high flow rates. All materials (the barrier, tubing, surface coatings, lubricants, and gaskets) need to be able to contain, but not react with, the highly reactive and corrosive UF_6.

Because gaseous diffusion plants require very large amounts of energy (to compress the gas to the high pressures required and drive it through the diffuser cascade, to remove the heat produced during compression, and so on), it is now being replaced by gas centrifuge technology, which requires far less energy. A current hot political issue is how to deny this technology to Iran, to prevent it from producing enough enriched uranium for them to use to make nuclear weapons.

8.5 The Kinetic-Molecular Theory

- State the postulates of the kinetic-molecular theory
- Use this theory's postulates to explain the gas laws

The gas laws that we have seen to this point, as well as the ideal gas equation, are empirical, that is, they have been derived from experimental observations. The mathematical forms of these laws closely describe the macroscopic behavior of most gases at pressures less than about 1 or 2 atm. Although the gas laws describe relationships that have been verified by many experiments, they do not tell us why gases follow these relationships.

The **kinetic molecular theory** (KMT) is a simple microscopic model that effectively explains the gas laws described in previous modules of this chapter. This theory is based on the following five postulates described here. (Note: The term "molecule" will be used to refer to the individual chemical species that compose the gas, although some gases are composed of atomic species, for example, the noble gases.)

1. Gases are composed of molecules that are in continuous motion, travelling in straight lines and changing

direction only when they collide with other molecules or with the walls of a container.

2. The molecules composing the gas are negligibly small compared to the distances between them.

3. The pressure exerted by a gas in a container results from collisions between the gas molecules and the container walls.

4. Gas molecules exert no attractive or repulsive forces on each other or the container walls; therefore, their collisions are *elastic* (do not involve a loss of energy).

5. The average kinetic energy of the gas molecules is proportional to the kelvin temperature of the gas.

The test of the KMT and its postulates is its ability to explain and describe the behavior of a gas. The various gas laws can be derived from the assumptions of the KMT, which have led chemists to believe that the assumptions of the theory accurately represent the properties of gas molecules. We will first look at the individual gas laws (Boyle's, Charles's, Amontons's, Avogadro's, and Dalton's laws) conceptually to see how the KMT explains them. Then, we will more carefully consider the relationships between molecular masses, speeds, and kinetic energies with temperature, and explain Graham's law.

The Kinetic-Molecular Theory Explains the Behavior of Gases, Part I

Recalling that gas pressure is exerted by rapidly moving gas molecules and depends directly on the number of molecules hitting a unit area of the wall per unit of time, we see that the KMT conceptually explains the behavior of a gas as follows:

- *Amontons's law.* If the temperature is increased, the average speed and kinetic energy of the gas molecules increase. If the volume is held constant, the increased speed of the gas molecules results in more frequent and more forceful collisions with the walls of the container, therefore increasing the pressure (**Figure 8.31**).

- *Charles's law.* If the temperature of a gas is increased, a constant pressure may be maintained only if the volume occupied by the gas increases. This will result in greater average distances traveled by the molecules to reach the container walls, as well as increased wall surface area. These conditions will decrease the both the frequency of molecule-wall collisions and the number of collisions per unit area, the combined effects of which balance the effect of increased collision forces due to the greater kinetic energy at the higher temperature.

- *Boyle's law.* If the gas volume is decreased, the container wall area decreases and the molecule-wall collision frequency increases, both of which increase the pressure exerted by the gas (**Figure 8.31**).

- *Avogadro's law.* At constant pressure and temperature, the frequency and force of molecule-wall collisions are constant. Under such conditions, increasing the number of gaseous molecules will require a proportional increase in the container volume in order to yield a decrease in the number of collisions per unit area to compensate for the increased frequency of collisions (**Figure 8.31**).

- *Dalton's Law.* Because of the large distances between them, the molecules of one gas in a mixture bombard the container walls with the same frequency whether other gases are present or not, and the total pressure of a gas mixture equals the sum of the (partial) pressures of the individual gases.

Figure 8.31 (a) When gas temperature increases, gas pressure increases due to increased force and frequency of molecular collisions. (b) When volume decreases, gas pressure increases due to increased frequency of molecular collisions. (c) When the amount of gas increases at a constant pressure, volume increases to yield a constant number of collisions per unit wall area per unit time.

Molecular Velocities and Kinetic Energy

The previous discussion showed that the KMT qualitatively explains the behaviors described by the various gas laws. The postulates of this theory may be applied in a more quantitative fashion to derive these individual laws. To do this, we must first look at velocities and kinetic energies of gas molecules, and the temperature of a gas sample.

In a gas sample, individual molecules have widely varying speeds; however, because of the *vast* number of molecules and collisions involved, the molecular speed distribution and average speed are constant. This molecular speed distribution is known as a Maxwell-Boltzmann distribution, and it depicts the relative numbers of molecules in a bulk sample of gas that possesses a given speed (Figure 8.32).

Figure 8.32 The molecular speed distribution for oxygen gas at 300 K is shown here. Very few molecules move at either very low or very high speeds. The number of molecules with intermediate speeds increases rapidly up to a maximum, which is the most probable speed, then drops off rapidly. Note that the most probable speed, v_p, is a little less than 400 m/s, while the root mean square speed, u_{rms}, is closer to 500 m/s.

The kinetic energy (KE) of a particle of mass (m) and speed (u) is given by:

$$KE = \frac{1}{2}mu^2$$

Expressing mass in kilograms and speed in meters per second will yield energy values in units of joules (J = kg m^2 s^{-2}). To deal with a large number of gas molecules, we use averages for both speed and kinetic energy. In the KMT, the **root mean square velocity** of a particle, **u_{rms}**, is defined as the square root of the average of the squares of the velocities with n = the number of particles:

$$u_{rms} = \sqrt{\overline{u^2}} = \sqrt{\frac{u_1^2 + u_2^2 + u_3^2 + u_4^2 + \cdots}{n}}$$

The average kinetic energy, KE$_{avg}$, is then equal to:

$$KE_{avg} = \frac{1}{2}mu_{rms}^2$$

The KE$_{avg}$ of a collection of gas molecules is also directly proportional to the temperature of the gas and may be described by the equation:

$$KE_{avg} = \frac{3}{2}RT$$

where R is the gas constant and T is the kelvin temperature. When used in this equation, the appropriate form of the gas constant is 8.314 J/mol·K (8.314 kg m^{2}s^{-2}mol^{-1}K^{-1}). These two separate equations for KE$_{avg}$ may be combined and rearranged to yield a relation between molecular speed and temperature:

$$\frac{1}{2}mu_{rms}^2 = \frac{3}{2}RT$$

$$u_{rms} = \sqrt{\frac{3RT}{m}}$$

Example 8.23

Calculation of u_{rms}

Calculate the root-mean-square velocity for a nitrogen molecule at 30 °C.

Solution

Convert the temperature into Kelvin:

$$30\,°C + 273 = 303\ K$$

Determine the mass of a nitrogen molecule in kilograms:

$$\frac{28.0\ g}{1\ mol} \times \frac{1\ kg}{1000\ g} = 0.028\ kg/mol$$

Replace the variables and constants in the root-mean-square velocity equation, replacing Joules with the equivalent kg m^{2}s^{-2}:

$$u_{rms} = \sqrt{\frac{3RT}{m}}$$

$$u_{rms} = \sqrt{\frac{3(8.314\ J/mol\ K)(303\ K)}{(0.028\ kg/mol)}} = \sqrt{2.70 \times 10^5\ m^2\,s^{-2}} = 519\ m/s$$

Check Your Learning

Calculate the root-mean-square velocity for an oxygen molecule at –23 °C.

Answer: 441 m/s

If the temperature of a gas increases, its KE_{avg} increases, more molecules have higher speeds and fewer molecules have lower speeds, and the distribution shifts toward higher speeds overall, that is, to the right. If temperature decreases, KE_{avg} decreases, more molecules have lower speeds and fewer molecules have higher speeds, and the distribution shifts toward lower speeds overall, that is, to the left. This behavior is illustrated for nitrogen gas in Figure 8.33.

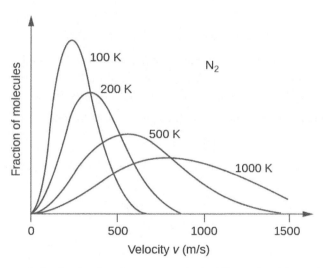

Figure 8.33 The molecular speed distribution for nitrogen gas (N_2) shifts to the right and flattens as the temperature increases; it shifts to the left and heightens as the temperature decreases.

At a given temperature, all gases have the same KE_{avg} for their molecules. Gases composed of lighter molecules have more high-speed particles and a higher u_{rms}, with a speed distribution that peaks at relatively higher velocities. Gases consisting of heavier molecules have more low-speed particles, a lower u_{rms}, and a speed distribution that peaks at relatively lower velocities. This trend is demonstrated by the data for a series of noble gases shown in Figure 8.34.

Figure 8.34 Molecular velocity is directly related to molecular mass. At a given temperature, lighter molecules move faster on average than heavier molecules.

Link to Learning

The **gas simulator (http://openstaxcollege.org/l/16MolecVelocity)** may be used to examine the effect of temperature on molecular velocities. Examine the simulator's "energy histograms" (molecular speed distributions) and "species information" (which gives average speed values) for molecules of different masses at various temperatures.

The Kinetic-Molecular Theory Explains the Behavior of Gases, Part II

According to Graham's law, the molecules of a gas are in rapid motion and the molecules themselves are small. The average distance between the molecules of a gas is large compared to the size of the molecules. As a consequence, gas molecules can move past each other easily and diffuse at relatively fast rates.

The rate of effusion of a gas depends directly on the (average) speed of its molecules:

$$\text{effusion rate} \propto u_{\text{rms}}$$

Using this relation, and the equation relating molecular speed to mass, Graham's law may be easily derived as shown here:

$$u_{\text{rms}} = \sqrt{\frac{3RT}{m}}$$

$$m = \frac{3RT}{u_{\text{rms}}^2} = \frac{3RT}{\bar{u}^2}$$

$$\frac{\text{effusion rate A}}{\text{effusion rate B}} = \frac{u_{\text{rms A}}}{u_{\text{rms B}}} = \frac{\sqrt{\frac{3RT}{m_A}}}{\sqrt{\frac{3RT}{m_B}}} = \sqrt{\frac{m_B}{m_A}}$$

The ratio of the rates of effusion is thus derived to be inversely proportional to the ratio of the square roots of their masses. This is the same relation observed experimentally and expressed as Graham's law.

8.6 Non-Ideal Gas Behavior

By the end of this section, you will be able to:

- Describe the physical factors that lead to deviations from ideal gas behavior

- Explain how these factors are represented in the van der Waals equation

- Define compressibility (Z) and describe how its variation with pressure reflects non-ideal behavior

- Quantify non-ideal behavior by comparing computations of gas properties using the ideal gas law and the van der Waals equation

Thus far, the ideal gas law, $PV = nRT$, has been applied to a variety of different types of problems, ranging from reaction stoichiometry and empirical and molecular formula problems to determining the density and molar mass of a gas. As mentioned in the previous modules of this chapter, however, the behavior of a gas is often non-ideal, meaning that the observed relationships between its pressure, volume, and temperature are not accurately described by the gas laws. In this section, the reasons for these deviations from ideal gas behavior are considered.

One way in which the accuracy of $PV = nRT$ can be judged is by comparing the actual volume of 1 mole of gas (its molar volume, V_m) to the molar volume of an ideal gas at the same temperature and pressure. This ratio is called the **compressibility factor (Z)** with:

$$Z = \frac{\text{molar volume of gas at same } T \text{ and } P}{\text{molar volume of ideal gas at same } T \text{ and } P} = \left(\frac{PV_m}{RT}\right)_{\text{measured}}$$

Ideal gas behavior is therefore indicated when this ratio is equal to 1, and any deviation from 1 is an indication of non-ideal behavior. **Figure 8.35** shows plots of Z over a large pressure range for several common gases.

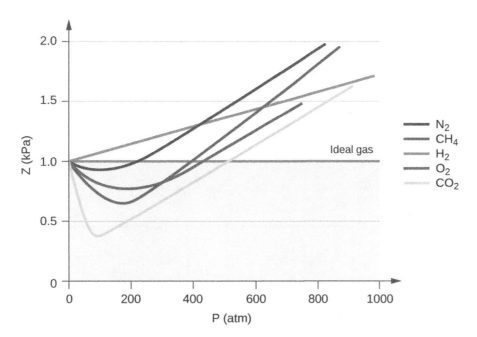

Figure 8.35 A graph of the compressibility factor (Z) vs. pressure shows that gases can exhibit significant deviations from the behavior predicted by the ideal gas law.

As is apparent from **Figure 8.35**, the ideal gas law does not describe gas behavior well at relatively high pressures. To determine why this is, consider the differences between real gas properties and what is expected of a hypothetical ideal gas.

Particles of a hypothetical ideal gas have no significant volume and do not attract or repel each other. In general, real gases approximate this behavior at relatively low pressures and high temperatures. However, at high pressures, the molecules of a gas are crowded closer together, and the amount of empty space between the molecules is reduced. At these higher pressures, the volume of the gas molecules themselves becomes appreciable relative to the total volume occupied by the gas (Figure 8.36). The gas therefore becomes less compressible at these high pressures, and although its volume continues to decrease with increasing pressure, this decrease is not *proportional* as predicted by Boyle's law.

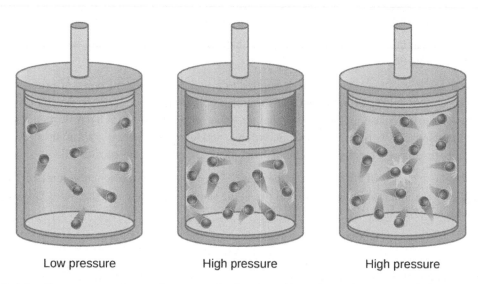

| Low pressure | High pressure | High pressure |

Figure 8.36   Raising the pressure of a gas increases the fraction of its volume that is occupied by the gas molecules and makes the gas less compressible.

At relatively low pressures, gas molecules have practically no attraction for one another because they are (on average) so far apart, and they behave almost like particles of an ideal gas. At higher pressures, however, the force of attraction is also no longer insignificant. This force pulls the molecules a little closer together, slightly decreasing the pressure (if the volume is constant) or decreasing the volume (at constant pressure) (Figure 8.37). This change is more pronounced at low temperatures because the molecules have lower KE relative to the attractive forces, and so they are less effective in overcoming these attractions after colliding with one another.

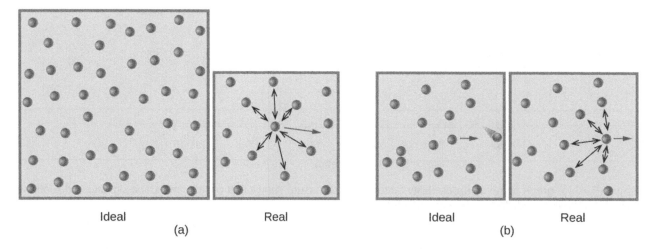

Figure 8.37   (a) Attractions between gas molecules serve to decrease the gas volume at constant pressure compared to an ideal gas whose molecules experience no attractive forces. (b) These attractive forces will decrease the force of collisions between the molecules and container walls, therefore reducing the pressure exerted compared to an ideal gas.

There are several different equations that better approximate gas behavior than does the ideal gas law. The first, and simplest, of these was developed by the Dutch scientist Johannes van der Waals in 1879. The **van der Waals equation** improves upon the ideal gas law by adding two terms: one to account for the volume of the gas molecules and another for the attractive forces between them.

$$PV = nRT \longrightarrow \left(P + \frac{an^2}{V^2} \right) (V - nb) = nRT$$

Correction for molecular attraction

Correction for volume of molecules

The constant a corresponds to the strength of the attraction between molecules of a particular gas, and the constant b corresponds to the size of the molecules of a particular gas. The "correction" to the pressure term in the ideal gas law is $\frac{n^2 a}{V^2}$, and the "correction" to the volume is nb. Note that when V is relatively large and n is relatively small, both of these correction terms become negligible, and the van der Waals equation reduces to the ideal gas law, $PV = nRT$. Such a condition corresponds to a gas in which a relatively low number of molecules is occupying a relatively large volume, that is, a gas at a relatively low pressure. Experimental values for the van der Waals constants of some common gases are given in Table 8.3.

Values of van der Waals Constants for Some Common Gases

Gas	a (L^2 atm/mol^2)	b (L/mol)
N_2	1.39	0.0391
O_2	1.36	0.0318
CO_2	3.59	0.0427
H_2O	5.46	0.0305
He	0.0342	0.0237
CCl_4	20.4	0.1383

Table 8.3

At low pressures, the correction for intermolecular attraction, a, is more important than the one for molecular volume, b. At high pressures and small volumes, the correction for the volume of the molecules becomes important because the molecules themselves are incompressible and constitute an appreciable fraction of the total volume. At some intermediate pressure, the two corrections have opposing influences and the gas appears to follow the relationship given by $PV = nRT$ over a small range of pressures. This behavior is reflected by the "dips" in several of the compressibility curves shown in Figure 8.35. The attractive force between molecules initially makes the gas more compressible than an ideal gas, as pressure is raised (Z decreases with increasing P). At very high pressures, the gas becomes less compressible (Z increases with P), as the gas molecules begin to occupy an increasingly significant fraction of the total gas volume.

Strictly speaking, the ideal gas equation functions well when intermolecular attractions between gas molecules are negligible and the gas molecules themselves do not occupy an appreciable part of the whole volume. These criteria are satisfied under conditions of *low pressure and high temperature*. Under such conditions, the gas is said to behave ideally, and deviations from the gas laws are small enough that they may be disregarded—this is, however, very often not the case.

Example 8.24

Comparison of Ideal Gas Law and van der Waals Equation

A 4.25-L flask contains 3.46 mol CO_2 at 229 °C. Calculate the pressure of this sample of CO_2:

(a) from the ideal gas law

(b) from the van der Waals equation

(c) Explain the reason(s) for the difference.

Solution

(a) From the ideal gas law:

$$P = \frac{nRT}{V} = \frac{3.46 \text{ mol} \times 0.08206 \text{ L atm mol}^{-1} \text{ K}^{-1} \times 502 \text{ K}}{4.25 \text{ L}} = 33.5 \text{ atm}$$

(b) From the van der Waals equation:

$$\left(P + \frac{n^2 a}{V^2}\right) \times (V - nb) = nRT \longrightarrow P = \frac{nRT}{(V - nb)} - \frac{n^2 a}{V^2}$$

$$P = \frac{3.46 \text{ mol} \times 0.08206 \text{ L atm mol}^{-1} \text{ K}^{-1} \times 502 \text{ K}}{\left(4.25 \text{ L} - 3.46 \text{ mol} \times 0.0427 \text{ L mol}^{-1}\right)} - \frac{(3.46 \text{ mol})^2 \times 3.59 \text{ L}^2 \text{ atm mol}^2}{(4.25 \text{ L})^2}$$

This finally yields $P = 32.4$ atm.

(c) This is not very different from the value from the ideal gas law because the pressure is not very high and the temperature is not very low. The value is somewhat different because CO_2 molecules do have some volume and attractions between molecules, and the ideal gas law assumes they do not have volume or attractions.

Check your Learning

A 560-mL flask contains 21.3 g N_2 at 145 °C. Calculate the pressure of N_2:

(a) from the ideal gas law

(b) from the van der Waals equation

(c) Explain the reason(s) for the difference.

Answer: (a) 46.562 atm; (b) 46.594 atm; (c) The van der Waals equation takes into account the volume of the gas molecules themselves as well as intermolecular attractions.

Key Terms

absolute zero temperature at which the volume of a gas would be zero according to Charles's law.

Amontons's law (also, Gay-Lussac's law) pressure of a given number of moles of gas is directly proportional to its kelvin temperature when the volume is held constant

atmosphere (atm) unit of pressure; 1 atm = 101,325 Pa

Avogadro's law volume of a gas at constant temperature and pressure is proportional to the number of gas molecules

bar (bar or b) unit of pressure; 1 bar = 100,000 Pa

barometer device used to measure atmospheric pressure

Boyle's law volume of a given number of moles of gas held at constant temperature is inversely proportional to the pressure under which it is measured

Charles's law volume of a given number of moles of gas is directly proportional to its kelvin temperature when the pressure is held constant

compressibility factor (Z) ratio of the experimentally measured molar volume for a gas to its molar volume as computed from the ideal gas equation

Dalton's law of partial pressures total pressure of a mixture of ideal gases is equal to the sum of the partial pressures of the component gases.

diffusion movement of an atom or molecule from a region of relatively high concentration to one of relatively low concentration (discussed in this chapter with regard to gaseous species, but applicable to species in any phase)

effusion transfer of gaseous atoms or molecules from a container to a vacuum through very small openings

Graham's law of effusion rates of diffusion and effusion of gases are inversely proportional to the square roots of their molecular masses

hydrostatic pressure pressure exerted by a fluid due to gravity

ideal gas hypothetical gas whose physical properties are perfectly described by the gas laws

ideal gas constant (R) constant derived from the ideal gas equation $R = 0.08226$ L atm mol^{-1} K^{-1} or 8.314 L kPa mol^{-1} K^{-1}

ideal gas law relation between the pressure, volume, amount, and temperature of a gas under conditions derived by combination of the simple gas laws

kinetic molecular theory theory based on simple principles and assumptions that effectively explains ideal gas behavior

manometer device used to measure the pressure of a gas trapped in a container

mean free path average distance a molecule travels between collisions

mole fraction (X) concentration unit defined as the ratio of the molar amount of a mixture component to the total number of moles of all mixture components

partial pressure pressure exerted by an individual gas in a mixture

pascal (Pa) SI unit of pressure; $1\ Pa = 1\ N/m^2$

pounds per square inch (psi) unit of pressure common in the US

pressure force exerted per unit area

rate of diffusion amount of gas diffusing through a given area over a given time

root mean square velocity (u_{rms}) measure of average velocity for a group of particles calculated as the square root of the average squared velocity

standard conditions of temperature and pressure (STP) 273.15 K (0 °C) and 1 atm (101.325 kPa)

standard molar volume volume of 1 mole of gas at STP, approximately 22.4 L for gases behaving ideally

torr unit of pressure; $1\ torr = \dfrac{1}{760}\ atm$

van der Waals equation modified version of the ideal gas equation containing additional terms to account for non-ideal gas behavior

vapor pressure of water pressure exerted by water vapor in equilibrium with liquid water in a closed container at a specific temperature

Key Equations

- $P = \dfrac{F}{A}$

- $p = h\rho g$

- $PV = nRT$

- $P_{Total} = P_A + P_B + P_C + \ldots = \Sigma_i P_i$

- $P_A = X_A\, P_{Total}$

- $X_A = \dfrac{n_A}{n_{Total}}$

- $\text{rate of diffusion} = \dfrac{\text{amount of gas passing through an area}}{\text{unit of time}}$

- $\dfrac{\text{rate of effusion of gas A}}{\text{rate of effusion of gas B}} = \dfrac{\sqrt{m_B}}{\sqrt{m_A}} = \dfrac{\sqrt{\mathscr{M}_B}}{\sqrt{\mathscr{M}_A}}$

- $u_{rms} = \sqrt{\overline{u^2}} = \sqrt{\dfrac{u_1^2 + u_2^2 + u_3^2 + u_4^2 + \ldots}{n}}$

- $KE_{avg} = \dfrac{3}{2}RT$

- $u_{rms} = \sqrt{\dfrac{3RT}{m}}$

- $Z = \dfrac{\text{molar volume of gas at same } T \text{ and } P}{\text{molar volume of ideal gas at same } T \text{ and } P} = \left(\dfrac{P \times V_m}{R \times T}\right)_{measured}$

- $\left(P + \dfrac{n^2 a}{V^2}\right) \times (V - nb) = nRT$

Summary

8.1 Gas Pressure

Gases exert pressure, which is force per unit area. The pressure of a gas may be expressed in the SI unit of pascal or kilopascal, as well as in many other units including torr, atmosphere, and bar. Atmospheric pressure is measured using a barometer; other gas pressures can be measured using one of several types of manometers.

8.2 Relating Pressure, Volume, Amount, and Temperature: The Ideal Gas Law

The behavior of gases can be described by several laws based on experimental observations of their properties. The pressure of a given amount of gas is directly proportional to its absolute temperature, provided that the volume does not change (Amontons's law). The volume of a given gas sample is directly proportional to its absolute temperature at constant pressure (Charles's law). The volume of a given amount of gas is inversely proportional to its pressure when temperature is held constant (Boyle's law). Under the same conditions of temperature and pressure, equal volumes of all gases contain the same number of molecules (Avogadro's law).

The equations describing these laws are special cases of the ideal gas law, $PV = nRT$, where P is the pressure of the gas, V is its volume, n is the number of moles of the gas, T is its kelvin temperature, and R is the ideal (universal) gas constant.

8.3 Stoichiometry of Gaseous Substances, Mixtures, and Reactions

The ideal gas law can be used to derive a number of convenient equations relating directly measured quantities to properties of interest for gaseous substances and mixtures. Appropriate rearrangement of the ideal gas equation may be made to permit the calculation of gas densities and molar masses. Dalton's law of partial pressures may be used to relate measured gas pressures for gaseous mixtures to their compositions. Avogadro's law may be used in stoichiometric computations for chemical reactions involving gaseous reactants or products.

8.4 Effusion and Diffusion of Gases

Gaseous atoms and molecules move freely and randomly through space. Diffusion is the process whereby gaseous atoms and molecules are transferred from regions of relatively high concentration to regions of relatively low concentration. Effusion is a similar process in which gaseous species pass from a container to a vacuum through very small orifices. The rates of effusion of gases are inversely proportional to the square roots of their densities or to the square roots of their atoms/molecules' masses (Graham's law).

8.5 The Kinetic-Molecular Theory

The kinetic molecular theory is a simple but very effective model that effectively explains ideal gas behavior. The theory assumes that gases consist of widely separated molecules of negligible volume that are in constant motion, colliding elastically with one another and the walls of their container with average velocities determined by their absolute temperatures. The individual molecules of a gas exhibit a range of velocities, the distribution of these velocities being dependent on the temperature of the gas and the mass of its molecules.

8.6 Non-Ideal Gas Behavior

Gas molecules possess a finite volume and experience forces of attraction for one another. Consequently, gas behavior is not necessarily described well by the ideal gas law. Under conditions of low pressure and high temperature, these factors are negligible, the ideal gas equation is an accurate description of gas behavior, and the gas is said to exhibit ideal behavior. However, at lower temperatures and higher pressures, corrections for molecular volume and molecular attractions are required to account for finite molecular size and attractive forces. The van der Waals equation is a modified version of the ideal gas law that can be used to account for the non-ideal behavior of gases under these conditions.

Exercises

8.1 Gas Pressure

1.   Why are sharp knives more effective than dull knives (Hint: think about the definition of pressure)?

2.   Why do some small bridges have weight limits that depend on how many wheels or axles the crossing vehicle has?

3.   Why should you roll or belly-crawl rather than walk across a thinly-frozen pond?

4.   A typical barometric pressure in Redding, California, is about 750 mm Hg. Calculate this pressure in atm and kPa.

5.   A typical barometric pressure in Denver, Colorado, is 615 mm Hg. What is this pressure in atmospheres and kilopascals?

6.   A typical barometric pressure in Kansas City is 740 torr. What is this pressure in atmospheres, in millimeters of mercury, and in kilopascals?

7.   Canadian tire pressure gauges are marked in units of kilopascals. What reading on such a gauge corresponds to 32 psi?

8.   During the Viking landings on Mars, the atmospheric pressure was determined to be on the average about 6.50 millibars (1 bar = 0.987 atm). What is that pressure in torr and kPa?

9.   The pressure of the atmosphere on the surface of the planet Venus is about 88.8 atm. Compare that pressure in psi to the normal pressure on earth at sea level in psi.

10.   A medical laboratory catalog describes the pressure in a cylinder of a gas as 14.82 MPa. What is the pressure of this gas in atmospheres and torr?

11.   Consider this scenario and answer the following questions: On a mid-August day in the northeastern United States, the following information appeared in the local newspaper: atmospheric pressure at sea level 29.97 in. Hg, 1013.9 mbar.

(a) What was the pressure in kPa?

(b) The pressure near the seacoast in the northeastern United States is usually reported near 30.0 in. Hg. During a hurricane, the pressure may fall to near 28.0 in. Hg. Calculate the drop in pressure in torr.

12.   Why is it necessary to use a nonvolatile liquid in a barometer or manometer?

13.   The pressure of a sample of gas is measured at sea level with a closed-end manometer. The liquid in the manometer is mercury. Determine the pressure of the gas in:

(a) torr

(b) Pa

(c) bar

14. The pressure of a sample of gas is measured with an open-end manometer, partially shown to the right. The liquid in the manometer is mercury. Assuming atmospheric pressure is 29.92 in. Hg, determine the pressure of the gas in:

(a) torr

(b) Pa

(c) bar

15. The pressure of a sample of gas is measured at sea level with an open-end mercury manometer. Assuming atmospheric pressure is 760.0 mm Hg, determine the pressure of the gas in:

(a) mm Hg

(b) atm

(c) kPa

16. The pressure of a sample of gas is measured at sea level with an open-end mercury manometer. Assuming atmospheric pressure is 760 mm Hg, determine the pressure of the gas in:

(a) mm Hg

(b) atm

(c) kPa

17. How would the use of a volatile liquid affect the measurement of a gas using open-ended manometers vs. closed-end manometers?

8.2 Relating Pressure, Volume, Amount, and Temperature: The Ideal Gas Law

18. Sometimes leaving a bicycle in the sun on a hot day will cause a blowout. Why?

19. Explain how the volume of the bubbles exhausted by a scuba diver (**Figure 8.16**) change as they rise to the surface, assuming that they remain intact.

20. One way to state Boyle's law is "All other things being equal, the pressure of a gas is inversely proportional to its volume." (a) What is the meaning of the term "inversely proportional?" (b) What are the "other things" that must be equal?

21. An alternate way to state Avogadro's law is "All other things being equal, the number of molecules in a gas is directly proportional to the volume of the gas." (a) What is the meaning of the term "directly proportional?" (b) What are the "other things" that must be equal?

22. How would the graph in **Figure 8.12** change if the number of moles of gas in the sample used to determine the curve were doubled?

23. How would the graph in **Figure 8.13** change if the number of moles of gas in the sample used to determine the curve were doubled?

24. In addition to the data found in **Figure 8.13**, what other information do we need to find the mass of the sample of air used to determine the graph?

25. Determine the volume of 1 mol of CH_4 gas at 150 K and 1 atm, using **Figure 8.12**.

26. Determine the pressure of the gas in the syringe shown in **Figure 8.13** when its volume is 12.5 mL, using:

(a) the appropriate graph

(b) Boyle's law

27. A spray can is used until it is empty except for the propellant gas, which has a pressure of 1344 torr at 23 °C. If the can is thrown into a fire (T = 475 °C), what will be the pressure in the hot can?

28. What is the temperature of an 11.2-L sample of carbon monoxide, CO, at 744 torr if it occupies 13.3 L at 55 °C and 744 torr?

29. A 2.50-L volume of hydrogen measured at –196 °C is warmed to 100 °C. Calculate the volume of the gas at the higher temperature, assuming no change in pressure.

30. A balloon inflated with three breaths of air has a volume of 1.7 L. At the same temperature and pressure, what is the volume of the balloon if five more same-sized breaths are added to the balloon?

31. A weather balloon contains 8.80 moles of helium at a pressure of 0.992 atm and a temperature of 25 °C at ground level. What is the volume of the balloon under these conditions?

32. The volume of an automobile air bag was 66.8 L when inflated at 25 °C with 77.8 g of nitrogen gas. What was the pressure in the bag in kPa?

33. How many moles of gaseous boron trifluoride, BF_3, are contained in a 4.3410-L bulb at 788.0 K if the pressure is 1.220 atm? How many grams of BF_3?

34. Iodine, I_2, is a solid at room temperature but sublimes (converts from a solid into a gas) when warmed. What is the temperature in a 73.3-mL bulb that contains 0.292 g of I_2 vapor at a pressure of 0.462 atm?

35. How many grams of gas are present in each of the following cases?

(a) 0.100 L of CO_2 at 307 torr and 26 °C

(b) 8.75 L of C_2H_4, at 378.3 kPa and 483 K

(c) 221 mL of Ar at 0.23 torr and −54 °C

36. A high altitude balloon is filled with 1.41×10^4 L of hydrogen at a temperature of 21 °C and a pressure of 745 torr. What is the volume of the balloon at a height of 20 km, where the temperature is −48 °C and the pressure is 63.1 torr?

37. A cylinder of medical oxygen has a volume of 35.4 L, and contains O_2 at a pressure of 151 atm and a temperature of 25 °C. What volume of O_2 does this correspond to at normal body conditions, that is, 1 atm and 37 °C?

38. A large scuba tank (Figure 8.16) with a volume of 18 L is rated for a pressure of 220 bar. The tank is filled at 20 °C and contains enough air to supply 1860 L of air to a diver at a pressure of 2.37 atm (a depth of 45 feet). Was the tank filled to capacity at 20 °C?

39. A 20.0-L cylinder containing 11.34 kg of butane, C_4H_{10}, was opened to the atmosphere. Calculate the mass of the gas remaining in the cylinder if it were opened and the gas escaped until the pressure in the cylinder was equal to the atmospheric pressure, 0.983 atm, and a temperature of 27 °C.

40. While resting, the average 70-kg human male consumes 14 L of pure O_2 per hour at 25 °C and 100 kPa. How many moles of O_2 are consumed by a 70 kg man while resting for 1.0 h?

41. For a given amount of gas showing ideal behavior, draw labeled graphs of:

(a) the variation of P with V

(b) the variation of V with T

(c) the variation of P with T

(d) the variation of $\frac{1}{P}$ with V

42. A liter of methane gas, CH_4, at STP contains more atoms of hydrogen than does a liter of pure hydrogen gas, H_2, at STP. Using Avogadro's law as a starting point, explain why.

43. The effect of chlorofluorocarbons (such as CCl_2F_2) on the depletion of the ozone layer is well known. The use of substitutes, such as $CH_3CH_2F(g)$, for the chlorofluorocarbons, has largely corrected the problem. Calculate the volume occupied by 10.0 g of each of these compounds at STP:

(a) $CCl_2F_2(g)$

(b) $CH_3CH_2F(g)$

44. As 1 g of the radioactive element radium decays over 1 year, it produces 1.16×10^{18} alpha particles (helium nuclei). Each alpha particle becomes an atom of helium gas. What is the pressure in pascal of the helium gas produced if it occupies a volume of 125 mL at a temperature of 25 °C?

45. A balloon that is 100.21 L at 21 °C and 0.981 atm is released and just barely clears the top of Mount Crumpet in British Columbia. If the final volume of the balloon is 144.53 L at a temperature of 5.24 °C, what is the pressure experienced by the balloon as it clears Mount Crumpet?

46. If the temperature of a fixed amount of a gas is doubled at constant volume, what happens to the pressure?

47. If the volume of a fixed amount of a gas is tripled at constant temperature, what happens to the pressure?

8.3 Stoichiometry of Gaseous Substances, Mixtures, and Reactions

48. What is the density of laughing gas, dinitrogen monoxide, N_2O, at a temperature of 325 K and a pressure of 113.0 kPa?

49. Calculate the density of Freon 12, CF_2Cl_2, at 30.0 °C and 0.954 atm.

50. Which is denser at the same temperature and pressure, dry air or air saturated with water vapor? Explain.

51. A cylinder of $O_2(g)$ used in breathing by emphysema patients has a volume of 3.00 L at a pressure of 10.0 atm. If the temperature of the cylinder is 28.0 °C, what mass of oxygen is in the cylinder?

52. What is the molar mass of a gas if 0.0494 g of the gas occupies a volume of 0.100 L at a temperature 26 °C and a pressure of 307 torr?

53. What is the molar mass of a gas if 0.281 g of the gas occupies a volume of 125 mL at a temperature 126 °C and a pressure of 777 torr?

54. How could you show experimentally that the molecular formula of propene is C_3H_6, not CH_2?

55. The density of a certain gaseous fluoride of phosphorus is 3.93 g/L at STP. Calculate the molar mass of this fluoride and determine its molecular formula.

56. Consider this question: What is the molecular formula of a compound that contains 39% C, 45% N, and 16% H if 0.157 g of the compound occupies l25 mL with a pressure of 99.5 kPa at 22 °C?

(a) Outline the steps necessary to answer the question.

(b) Answer the question.

57. A 36.0–L cylinder of a gas used for calibration of blood gas analyzers in medical laboratories contains 350 g CO_2, 805 g O_2, and 4,880 g N_2. At 25 degrees C, what is the pressure in the cylinder in atmospheres?

58. A cylinder of a gas mixture used for calibration of blood gas analyzers in medical laboratories contains 5.0% CO_2, 12.0% O_2, and the remainder N_2 at a total pressure of 146 atm. What is the partial pressure of each component of this gas? (The percentages given indicate the percent of the total pressure that is due to each component.)

59. A sample of gas isolated from unrefined petroleum contains 90.0% CH_4, 8.9% C_2H_6, and 1.1% C_3H_8 at a total pressure of 307.2 kPa. What is the partial pressure of each component of this gas? (The percentages given indicate the percent of the total pressure that is due to each component.)

60. A mixture of 0.200 g of H_2, 1.00 g of N_2, and 0.820 g of Ar is stored in a closed container at STP. Find the volume of the container, assuming that the gases exhibit ideal behavior.

61. Most mixtures of hydrogen gas with oxygen gas are explosive. However, a mixture that contains less than 3.0 % O_2 is not. If enough O_2 is added to a cylinder of H_2 at 33.2 atm to bring the total pressure to 34.5 atm, is the mixture explosive?

62. A commercial mercury vapor analyzer can detect, in air, concentrations of gaseous Hg atoms (which are poisonous) as low as 2×10^{-6} mg/L of air. At this concentration, what is the partial pressure of gaseous mercury if the atmospheric pressure is 733 torr at 26 °C?

63. A sample of carbon monoxide was collected over water at a total pressure of 756 torr and a temperature of 18 °C. What is the pressure of the carbon monoxide? (See Table 8.2 for the vapor pressure of water.)

64. In an experiment in a general chemistry laboratory, a student collected a sample of a gas over water. The volume of the gas was 265 mL at a pressure of 753 torr and a temperature of 27 °C. The mass of the gas was 0.472 g. What was the molar mass of the gas?

65. Joseph Priestley first prepared pure oxygen by heating mercuric oxide, HgO:
$$2HgO(s) \longrightarrow 2Hg(l) + O_2(g)$$

(a) Outline the steps necessary to answer the following question: What volume of O_2 at 23 °C and 0.975 atm is produced by the decomposition of 5.36 g of HgO?

(b) Answer the question.

66. Cavendish prepared hydrogen in 1766 by the novel method of passing steam through a red-hot gun barrel:
$$4H_2O(g) + 3Fe(s) \longrightarrow Fe_3O_4(s) + 4H_2(g)$$

(a) Outline the steps necessary to answer the following question: What volume of H_2 at a pressure of 745 torr and a temperature of 20 °C can be prepared from the reaction of 15.O g of H_2O?

(b) Answer the question.

67. The chlorofluorocarbon CCl_2F_2 can be recycled into a different compound by reaction with hydrogen to produce $CH_2F_2(g)$, a compound useful in chemical manufacturing:

$$CCl_2F_2(g) + 4H_2(g) \longrightarrow CH_2F_2(g) + 2HCl(g)$$

(a) Outline the steps necessary to answer the following question: What volume of hydrogen at 225 atm and 35.5 °C would be required to react with 1 ton (1.000×10^3 kg) of CCl_2F_2?

(b) Answer the question.

68. Automobile air bags are inflated with nitrogen gas, which is formed by the decomposition of solid sodium azide (NaN_3). The other product is sodium metal. Calculate the volume of nitrogen gas at 27 °C and 756 torr formed by the decomposition of 125 g of sodium azide.

69. Lime, CaO, is produced by heating calcium carbonate, $CaCO_3$; carbon dioxide is the other product.

(a) Outline the steps necessary to answer the following question: What volume of carbon dioxide at 875° and 0.966 atm is produced by the decomposition of 1 ton (1.000×10^3 kg) of calcium carbonate?

(b) Answer the question.

70. Before small batteries were available, carbide lamps were used for bicycle lights. Acetylene gas, C_2H_2, and solid calcium hydroxide were formed by the reaction of calcium carbide, CaC_2, with water. The ignition of the acetylene gas provided the light. Currently, the same lamps are used by some cavers, and calcium carbide is used to produce acetylene for carbide cannons.

(a) Outline the steps necessary to answer the following question: What volume of C_2H_2 at 1.005 atm and 12.2 °C is formed by the reaction of 15.48 g of CaC_2 with water?

(b) Answer the question.

71. Calculate the volume of oxygen required to burn 12.00 L of ethane gas, C_2H_6, to produce carbon dioxide and water, if the volumes of C_2H_6 and O_2 are measured under the same conditions of temperature and pressure.

72. What volume of O_2 at STP is required to oxidize 8.0 L of NO at STP to NO_2? What volume of NO_2 is produced at STP?

73. Consider the following questions:

(a) What is the total volume of the $CO_2(g)$ and $H_2O(g)$ at 600 °C and 0.888 atm produced by the combustion of 1.00 L of $C_2H_6(g)$ measured at STP?

(b) What is the partial pressure of H_2O in the product gases?

74. Methanol, CH_3OH, is produced industrially by the following reaction:

$$CO(g) + 2H_2(g) \xrightarrow{\text{copper catalyst 300 °C, 300 atm}} CH_3OH(g)$$

Assuming that the gases behave as ideal gases, find the ratio of the total volume of the reactants to the final volume.

75. What volume of oxygen at 423.0 K and a pressure of 127.4 kPa is produced by the decomposition of 129.7 g of BaO_2 to BaO and O_2?

76. A 2.50-L sample of a colorless gas at STP decomposed to give 2.50 L of N_2 and 1.25 L of O_2 at STP. What is the colorless gas?

77. Ethanol, C_2H_5OH, is produced industrially from ethylene, C_2H_4, by the following sequence of reactions:

$$3C_2H_4 + 2H_2SO_4 \longrightarrow C_2H_5HSO_4 + (C_2H_5)_2SO_4$$
$$C_2H_5HSO_4 + (C_2H_5)_2SO_4 + 3H_2O \longrightarrow 3C_2H_5OH + 2H_2SO_4$$

What volume of ethylene at STP is required to produce 1.000 metric ton (1000 kg) of ethanol if the overall yield of ethanol is 90.1%?

78. One molecule of hemoglobin will combine with four molecules of oxygen. If 1.0 g of hemoglobin combines with 1.53 mL of oxygen at body temperature (37 °C) and a pressure of 743 torr, what is the molar mass of hemoglobin?

79. A sample of a compound of xenon and fluorine was confined in a bulb with a pressure of 18 torr. Hydrogen was added to the bulb until the pressure was 72 torr. Passage of an electric spark through the mixture produced Xe and HF. After the HF was removed by reaction with solid KOH, the final pressure of xenon and unreacted hydrogen in the bulb was 36 torr. What is the empirical formula of the xenon fluoride in the original sample? (Note: Xenon fluorides contain only one xenon atom per molecule.)

80. One method of analyzing amino acids is the van Slyke method. The characteristic amino groups ($-NH_2$) in protein material are allowed to react with nitrous acid, HNO_2, to form N_2 gas. From the volume of the gas, the amount of amino acid can be determined. A 0.0604-g sample of a biological sample containing glycine, $CH_2(NH_2)COOH$, was analyzed by the van Slyke method and yielded 3.70 mL of N_2 collected over water at a pressure of 735 torr and 29 °C. What was the percentage of glycine in the sample?

$$CH_2(NH_2)CO_2H + HNO_2 \longrightarrow CH_2(OH)CO_2H + H_2O + N_2$$

8.4 Effusion and Diffusion of Gases

81. A balloon filled with helium gas is found to take 6 hours to deflate to 50% of its original volume. How long will it take for an identical balloon filled with the same volume of hydrogen gas (instead of helium) to decrease its volume by 50%?

82. Explain why the numbers of molecules are not identical in the left- and right-hand bulbs shown in the center illustration of **Figure 8.27**.

83. Starting with the definition of rate of effusion and Graham's finding relating rate and molar mass, show how to derive the Graham's law equation, relating the relative rates of effusion for two gases to their molecular masses.

84. Heavy water, D_2O (molar mass = 20.03 g mol^{-1}), can be separated from ordinary water, H_2O (molar mass = 18.01), as a result of the difference in the relative rates of diffusion of the molecules in the gas phase. Calculate the relative rates of diffusion of H_2O and D_2O.

85. Which of the following gases diffuse more slowly than oxygen? F_2, Ne, N_2O, C_2H_2, NO, Cl_2, H_2S

86. During the discussion of gaseous diffusion for enriching uranium, it was claimed that $^{235}UF_6$ diffuses 0.4% faster than $^{238}UF_6$. Show the calculation that supports this value. The molar mass of $^{235}UF_6$ = 235.043930 + 6 × 18.998403 = 349.034348 g/mol, and the molar mass of $^{238}UF_6$ = 238.050788 + 6 × 18.998403 = 352.041206 g/mol.

87. Calculate the relative rate of diffusion of $^1H_2$ (molar mass 2.0 g/mol) compared to that of $^2H_2$ (molar mass 4.0 g/mol) and the relative rate of diffusion of O_2 (molar mass 32 g/mol) compared to that of O_3 (molar mass 48 g/mol).

88. A gas of unknown identity diffuses at a rate of 83.3 mL/s in a diffusion apparatus in which carbon dioxide diffuses at the rate of 102 mL/s. Calculate the molecular mass of the unknown gas.

89. When two cotton plugs, one moistened with ammonia and the other with hydrochloric acid, are simultaneously inserted into opposite ends of a glass tube that is 87.0 cm long, a white ring of NH_4Cl forms where gaseous NH_3 and gaseous HCl first come into contact. (Hint: Calculate the rates of diffusion for both NH_3 and HCl, and find out how much faster NH_3 diffuses than HCl.)

$$NH_3(g) + HCl(g) \longrightarrow NH_4Cl(s)$$

At approximately what distance from the ammonia moistened plug does this occur?

8.5 The Kinetic-Molecular Theory

90. Using the postulates of the kinetic molecular theory, explain why a gas uniformly fills a container of any shape.

91. Can the speed of a given molecule in a gas double at constant temperature? Explain your answer.

92. Describe what happens to the average kinetic energy of ideal gas molecules when the conditions are changed as follows:

(a) The pressure of the gas is increased by reducing the volume at constant temperature.

(b) The pressure of the gas is increased by increasing the temperature at constant volume.

(c) The average velocity of the molecules is increased by a factor of 2.

93. The distribution of molecular velocities in a sample of helium is shown in Figure 8.34. If the sample is cooled, will the distribution of velocities look more like that of H_2 or of H_2O? Explain your answer.

94. What is the ratio of the average kinetic energy of a SO_2 molecule to that of an O_2 molecule in a mixture of two gases? What is the ratio of the root mean square speeds, u_{rms}, of the two gases?

95. A 1-L sample of CO initially at STP is heated to 546 °C, and its volume is increased to 2 L.

(a) What effect do these changes have on the number of collisions of the molecules of the gas per unit area of the container wall?

(b) What is the effect on the average kinetic energy of the molecules?

(c) What is the effect on the root mean square speed of the molecules?

96. The root mean square speed of H_2 molecules at 25 °C is about 1.6 km/s. What is the root mean square speed of a N_2 molecule at 25 °C?

97. Answer the following questions:

(a) Is the pressure of the gas in the hot air balloon shown at the opening of this chapter greater than, less than, or equal to that of the atmosphere outside the balloon?

(b) Is the density of the gas in the hot air balloon shown at the opening of this chapter greater than, less than, or equal to that of the atmosphere outside the balloon?

(c) At a pressure of 1 atm and a temperature of 20 °C, dry air has a density of 1.2256 g/L. What is the (average) molar mass of dry air?

(d) The average temperature of the gas in a hot air balloon is 1.30×10^2 °F. Calculate its density, assuming the molar mass equals that of dry air.

(e) The lifting capacity of a hot air balloon is equal to the difference in the mass of the cool air displaced by the balloon and the mass of the gas in the balloon. What is the difference in the mass of 1.00 L of the cool air in part (c) and the hot air in part (d)?

(f) An average balloon has a diameter of 60 feet and a volume of 1.1×10^5 ft^3. What is the lifting power of such a balloon? If the weight of the balloon and its rigging is 500 pounds, what is its capacity for carrying passengers and cargo?

(g) A balloon carries 40.0 gallons of liquid propane (density 0.5005 g/L). What volume of CO_2 and H_2O gas is produced by the combustion of this propane?

(h) A balloon flight can last about 90 minutes. If all of the fuel is burned during this time, what is the approximate rate of heat loss (in kJ/min) from the hot air in the bag during the flight?

98. Show that the ratio of the rate of diffusion of Gas 1 to the rate of diffusion of Gas 2, $\dfrac{R_1}{R_2}$, is the same at 0 °C and 100 °C.

8.6 Non-Ideal Gas Behavior

99.   Graphs showing the behavior of several different gases follow. Which of these gases exhibit behavior significantly different from that expected for ideal gases?

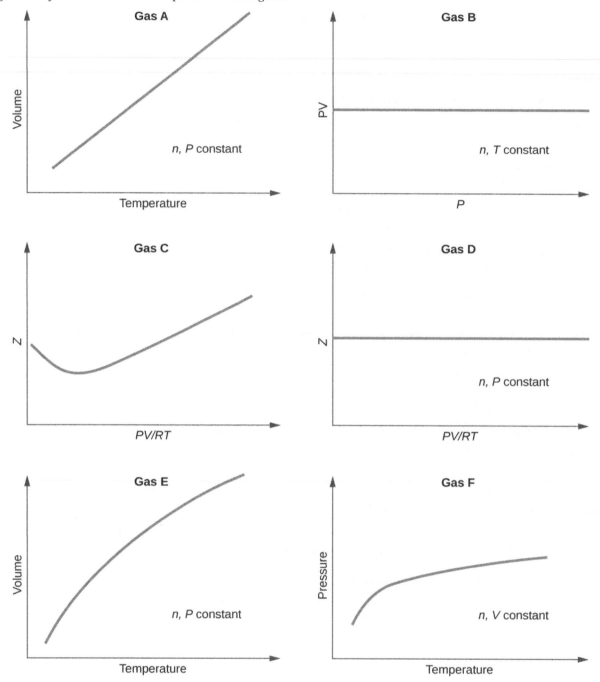

100. Explain why the plot of PV for CO_2 differs from that of an ideal gas.

101. Under which of the following sets of conditions does a real gas behave most like an ideal gas, and for which conditions is a real gas expected to deviate from ideal behavior? Explain.

(a) high pressure, small volume

(b) high temperature, low pressure

(c) low temperature, high pressure

102. Describe the factors responsible for the deviation of the behavior of real gases from that of an ideal gas.

103. For which of the following gases should the correction for the molecular volume be largest:

CO, CO_2, H_2, He, NH_3, SF_6?

104. A 0.245-L flask contains 0.467 mol CO_2 at 159 °C. Calculate the pressure:

(a) using the ideal gas law

(b) using the van der Waals equation

(c) Explain the reason for the difference.

(d) Identify which correction (that for P or V) is dominant and why.

105. Answer the following questions:

(a) If XX behaved as an ideal gas, what would its graph of Z vs. P look like?

(b) For most of this chapter, we performed calculations treating gases as ideal. Was this justified?

(c) What is the effect of the volume of gas molecules on Z? Under what conditions is this effect small? When is it large? Explain using an appropriate diagram.

(d) What is the effect of intermolecular attractions on the value of Z? Under what conditions is this effect small? When is it large? Explain using an appropriate diagram.

(e) In general, under what temperature conditions would you expect Z to have the largest deviations from the Z for an ideal gas?

Chapter 9

Thermochemistry

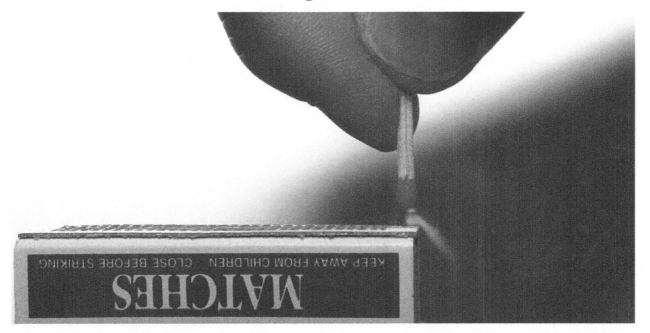

Figure 9.1 Sliding a match head along a rough surface initiates a combustion reaction that produces energy in the form of heat and light. (credit: modification of work by Laszlo Ilyes)

Chapter Outline

9.1 Energy Basics

9.2 Calorimetry

9.3 Enthalpy

9.4 Strengths of Ionic and Covalent Bonds

Introduction

Chemical reactions, such as those that occur when you light a match, involve changes in energy as well as matter. Societies at all levels of development could not function without the energy released by chemical reactions. In 2012, about 85% of US energy consumption came from the combustion of petroleum products, coal, wood, and garbage. We use this energy to produce electricity (38%); to transport food, raw materials, manufactured goods, and people (27%); for industrial production (21%); and to heat and power our homes and businesses (10%).[1] While these combustion reactions help us meet our essential energy needs, they are also recognized by the majority of the scientific community as a major contributor to global climate change.

Useful forms of energy are also available from a variety of chemical reactions other than combustion. For example, the energy produced by the batteries in a cell phone, car, or flashlight results from chemical reactions. This chapter introduces many of the basic ideas necessary to explore the relationships between chemical changes and energy, with a focus on thermal energy.

The chemical bond is simply another form of energy, and its strength is indicated in exactly the same units as any other

1. US Energy Information Administration, *Primary Energy Consumption by Source and Sector, 2012*, http://www.eia.gov/totalenergy/data/monthly/pdf/flow/css_2012_energy.pdf. Data derived from US Energy Information Administration, *Monthly Energy Review* (January 2014).

process involving energy. That is, in joules (or kilojoules) – or, when taken on a molar basis, in J/mol or kJ/mol. All of the principles involving energy we have examined up to now apply to bond energies exactly as they do to all other forms of energy: that is, energy may change form or be absorbed or released, but it cannot be created or destroyed. The energy of a chemical bond is indicated by the bond enthalpy, taken by convention to be the energy required to break a chemical bond. The same energy is released when a chemical bond is formed. Given that a chemical reaction involves breaking some bonds and making others, the enthalpy change for a chemical reaction can be estimated by analyzing the bonds broken and formed during the reaction. While this procedure gives an estimate of the overall enthalpy, it should be noted that a far more precise method involves using enthalpies of formation; the fact that there can be significant differences between, for example, an O–H bond in water and that in acetic acid accounts for the discrepancy in calculating ΔH using bond enthalpies versus the use of enthalpies of formation.

9.1 Energy Basics

By the end of this section, you will be able to:

- Define energy, distinguish types of energy, and describe the nature of energy changes that accompany chemical and physical changes

- Distinguish the related properties of heat, thermal energy, and temperature

- Define and distinguish specific heat and heat capacity, and describe the physical implications of both

- Perform calculations involving heat, specific heat, and temperature change

Chemical changes and their accompanying changes in energy are important parts of our everyday world (**Figure 9.2**). The macronutrients in food (proteins, fats, and carbohydrates) undergo metabolic reactions that provide the energy to keep our bodies functioning. We burn a variety of fuels (gasoline, natural gas, coal) to produce energy for transportation, heating, and the generation of electricity. Industrial chemical reactions use enormous amounts of energy to produce raw materials (such as iron and aluminum). Energy is then used to manufacture those raw materials into useful products, such as cars, skyscrapers, and bridges.

(a) (b) (c)

Figure 9.2 The energy involved in chemical changes is important to our daily lives: (a) A cheeseburger for lunch provides the energy you need to get through the rest of the day; (b) the combustion of gasoline provides the energy that moves your car (and you) between home, work, and school; and (c) coke, a processed form of coal, provides the energy needed to convert iron ore into iron, which is essential for making many of the products we use daily. (credit a: modification of work by "Pink Sherbet Photography"/Flickr; credit b: modification of work by Jeffery Turner)

Over 90% of the energy we use comes originally from the sun. Every day, the sun provides the earth with almost 10,000 times the amount of energy necessary to meet all of the world's energy needs for that day. Our challenge is to find ways to convert and store incoming solar energy so that it can be used in reactions or chemical processes that are both convenient and nonpolluting. Plants and many bacteria capture solar energy through photosynthesis. We release the energy stored in plants when we burn wood or plant products such as ethanol. We also use this energy to fuel our bodies by eating food that comes directly from plants or from animals that got their energy by eating plants. Burning coal and petroleum also releases stored solar energy: These fuels are fossilized plant and animal matter.

This chapter will introduce the basic ideas of an important area of science concerned with the amount of heat absorbed or released during chemical and physical changes—an area called **thermochemistry**. The concepts introduced in this chapter are widely used in almost all scientific and technical fields. Food scientists use them to determine the energy content of foods. Biologists study the energetics of living organisms, such as the metabolic combustion of sugar into carbon dioxide and water. The oil, gas, and transportation industries, renewable energy providers, and many others endeavor to find better methods to produce energy for our commercial and personal needs. Engineers strive to improve energy efficiency, find better ways to heat and cool our homes, refrigerate our food and drinks, and meet the energy and cooling needs of computers and electronics, among other applications. Understanding thermochemical principles is essential for chemists, physicists, biologists, geologists, every type of engineer, and just about anyone who studies or does any kind of science.

Energy

Energy can be defined as the capacity to supply heat or do work. One type of **work (*w*)** is the process of causing matter to move against an opposing force. For example, we do work when we inflate a bicycle tire—we move matter (the air in the pump) against the opposing force of the air already in the tire.

Like matter, energy comes in different types. One scheme classifies energy into two types: **potential energy**, the energy an object has because of its relative position, composition, or condition, and **kinetic energy**, the energy that an object possesses because of its motion. Water at the top of a waterfall or dam has potential energy because of its position; when it flows downward through generators, it has kinetic energy that can be used to do work and produce electricity in a hydroelectric plant (**Figure 9.3**). A battery has potential energy because the chemicals within it can produce electricity that can do work.

(a)   (b)

Figure 9.3   (a) Water that is higher in elevation, for example, at the top of Victoria Falls, has a higher potential energy than water at a lower elevation. As the water falls, some of its potential energy is converted into kinetic energy. (b) If the water flows through generators at the bottom of a dam, such as the Hoover Dam shown here, its kinetic energy is converted into electrical energy. (credit a: modification of work by Steve Jurvetson; credit b: modification of work by "curimedia"/Wikimedia commons)

Energy can be converted from one form into another, but all of the energy present before a change occurs always exists in some form after the change is completed. This observation is expressed in the law of conservation of energy: during a chemical or physical change, energy can be neither created nor destroyed, although it can be changed in form. (This is also one version of the first law of thermodynamics, as you will learn later.)

When one substance is converted into another, there is always an associated conversion of one form of energy into another. Heat is usually released or absorbed, but sometimes the conversion involves light, electrical energy, or some other form of energy. For example, chemical energy (a type of potential energy) is stored in the molecules that compose gasoline. When gasoline is combusted within the cylinders of a car's engine, the rapidly expanding gaseous products of this chemical reaction generate mechanical energy (a type of kinetic energy) when they move the cylinders' pistons.

According to the law of conservation of matter (seen in an earlier chapter), there is no detectable change in the total amount of matter during a chemical change. When chemical reactions occur, the energy changes are relatively modest and the mass changes are too small to measure, so the laws of conservation of matter and energy hold well. However, in nuclear reactions, the energy changes are much larger (by factors of a million or so), the mass changes are measurable, and matter-energy conversions are significant. This will be examined in more detail in a later chapter on nuclear chemistry. To encompass both chemical and nuclear changes, we combine these laws into one statement: The total quantity of matter and energy in the universe is fixed.

Thermal Energy, Temperature, and Heat

Thermal energy is kinetic energy associated with the random motion of atoms and molecules. **Temperature** is a quantitative measure of "hot" or "cold." When the atoms and molecules in an object are moving or vibrating quickly, they have a higher average kinetic energy (KE), and we say that the object is "hot." When the atoms and molecules are moving slowly, they have lower KE, and we say that the object is "cold" (**Figure 9.4**). Assuming that no chemical reaction or phase change (such as melting or vaporizing) occurs, increasing the amount of thermal energy in a sample of matter will cause its temperature to increase. And, assuming that no chemical reaction or phase change (such as condensation or freezing) occurs, decreasing the amount of thermal energy in a sample of matter will cause its temperature to decrease.

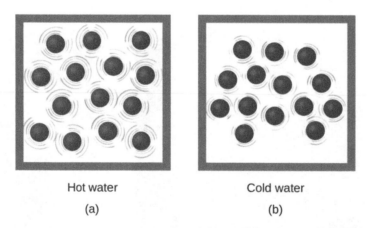

Hot water
(a)

Cold water
(b)

Figure 9.4   (a) The molecules in a sample of hot water move more rapidly than (b) those in a sample of cold water.

Link to Learning

Click on this **interactive simulation (http://openstaxcollege.org/l/ 16PHETtempFX)** to view the effects of temperature on molecular motion.

Most substances expand as their temperature increases and contract as their temperature decreases. This property can be used to measure temperature changes, as shown in **Figure 9.5**. The operation of many thermometers depends on the expansion and contraction of substances in response to temperature changes.

Figure 9.5   (a) In an alcohol or mercury thermometer, the liquid (dyed red for visibility) expands when heated and contracts when cooled, much more so than the glass tube that contains the liquid. (b) In a bimetallic thermometer, two different metals (such as brass and steel) form a two-layered strip. When heated or cooled, one of the metals (brass) expands or contracts more than the other metal (steel), causing the strip to coil or uncoil. Both types of thermometers have a calibrated scale that indicates the temperature. (credit a: modification of work by "dwstucke"/Flickr)

Link to Learning

The following demonstration (http://openstaxcollege.org/l/16Bimetallic) allows one to view the effects of heating and cooling a coiled bimetallic strip.

Heat (q) is the transfer of thermal energy between two bodies at different temperatures. Heat flow (a redundant term, but one commonly used) increases the thermal energy of one body and decreases the thermal energy of the other. Suppose we initially have a high temperature (and high thermal energy) substance (H) and a low temperature (and low thermal energy) substance (L). The atoms and molecules in H have a higher average KE than those in L. If we place substance H in contact with substance L, the thermal energy will flow spontaneously from substance H to substance L. The temperature of substance H will decrease, as will the average KE of its molecules; the temperature of substance L will increase, along with the average KE of its molecules. Heat flow will continue until the two substances are at the same temperature (**Figure 9.6**).

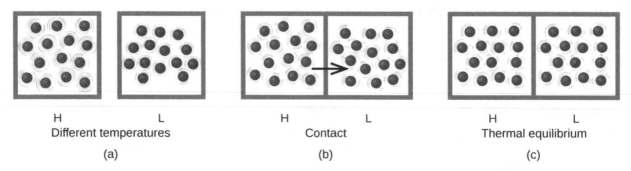

H   L   H   L   H   L
Different temperatures   Contact   Thermal equilibrium
(a)   (b)   (c)

Figure 9.6   (a) Substances H and L are initially at different temperatures, and their atoms have different average kinetic energies. (b) When they are put into contact with each other, collisions between the molecules result in the transfer of kinetic (thermal) energy from the hotter to the cooler matter. (c) The two objects reach "thermal equilibrium" when both substances are at the same temperature, and their molecules have the same average kinetic energy.

Link to Learning

Click on the PhET simulation (http://openstaxcollege.org/l/16PHETenergy) to explore energy forms and changes. Visit the Energy Systems tab to create combinations of energy sources, transformation methods, and outputs. Click on Energy Symbols to visualize the transfer of energy.

Matter undergoing chemical reactions and physical changes can release or absorb heat. A change that releases heat is called an **exothermic process**. For example, the combustion reaction that occurs when using an oxyacetylene torch is an exothermic process—this process also releases energy in the form of light as evidenced by the torch's flame (**Figure 9.7**). A reaction or change that absorbs heat is an **endothermic process**. A cold pack used to treat muscle strains provides an example of an endothermic process. When the substances in the cold pack (water and a salt like ammonium nitrate) are brought together, the resulting process absorbs heat, leading to the sensation of cold.

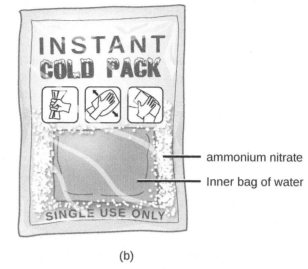

(a)   (b)

Figure 9.7   (a) An oxyacetylene torch produces heat by the combustion of acetylene in oxygen. The energy released by this exothermic reaction heats and then melts the metal being cut. The sparks are tiny bits of the molten metal flying away. (b) A cold pack uses an endothermic process to create the sensation of cold. (credit a: modification of work by "Skatebiker"/Wikimedia commons)

Historically, energy was measured in units of **calories (cal)**. A calorie is the amount of energy required to raise one gram of water by 1 degree C (1 kelvin). However, this quantity depends on the atmospheric pressure and the starting temperature of the water. The ease of measurement of energy changes in calories has meant that the calorie is still frequently used. The Calorie (with a capital C), or large calorie, commonly used in quantifying food energy content, is a kilocalorie. The SI unit of heat, work, and energy is the joule. A **joule (J)** is defined as the amount of energy used when a force of 1 newton moves an object 1 meter. It is named in honor of the English physicist James Prescott Joule. One joule is equivalent to 1 kg m^2/s^2, which is also called 1 newton–meter. A kilojoule (kJ) is 1000 joules. To standardize its definition, 1 calorie has been set to equal 4.184 joules.

We now introduce two concepts useful in describing heat flow and temperature change. The **heat capacity (C)** of a body of matter is the quantity of heat (q) it absorbs or releases when it experiences a temperature change (ΔT) of 1 degree Celsius (or equivalently, 1 kelvin):

$$C = \frac{q}{\Delta T}$$

Heat capacity is determined by both the type and amount of substance that absorbs or releases heat. It is therefore an extensive property—its value is proportional to the amount of the substance.

For example, consider the heat capacities of two cast iron frying pans. The heat capacity of the large pan is five times greater than that of the small pan because, although both are made of the same material, the mass of the large pan is five times greater than the mass of the small pan. More mass means more atoms are present in the larger pan, so it takes more energy to make all of those atoms vibrate faster. The heat capacity of the small cast iron frying pan is found by observing that it takes 18,150 J of energy to raise the temperature of the pan by 50.0 °C:

$$C_{\text{small pan}} = \frac{18{,}140 \text{ J}}{50.0 \text{ °C}} = 363 \text{ J/°C}$$

The larger cast iron frying pan, while made of the same substance, requires 90,700 J of energy to raise its temperature by 50.0 °C. The larger pan has a (proportionally) larger heat capacity because the larger amount of material requires a (proportionally) larger amount of energy to yield the same temperature change:

$$C_{\text{large pan}} = \frac{90{,}700 \text{ J}}{50.0 \text{ °C}} = 1814 \text{ J/°C}$$

The **specific heat capacity** (*c*) of a substance, commonly called its "specific heat," is the quantity of heat required to raise the temperature of 1 gram of a substance by 1 degree Celsius (or 1 kelvin):

$$c = \frac{q}{m\Delta T}$$

Specific heat capacity depends only on the kind of substance absorbing or releasing heat. It is an intensive property—the type, but not the amount, of the substance is all that matters. For example, the small cast iron frying pan has a mass of 808 g. The specific heat of iron (the material used to make the pan) is therefore:

$$c_{iron} = \frac{18{,}140 \text{ J}}{(808 \text{ g})(50.0 \text{ °C})} = 0.449 \text{ J/g °C}$$

The large frying pan has a mass of 4040 g. Using the data for this pan, we can also calculate the specific heat of iron:

$$c_{iron} = \frac{90{,}700 \text{ J}}{(4040 \text{ g})(50.0 \text{ °C})} = 0.449 \text{ J/g °C}$$

Although the large pan is more massive than the small pan, since both are made of the same material, they both yield the same value for specific heat (for the material of construction, iron). Note that specific heat is measured in units of energy per temperature per mass and is an intensive property, being derived from a ratio of two extensive properties (heat and mass). The molar heat capacity, also an intensive property, is the heat capacity per mole of a particular substance and has units of J/mol °C (**Figure 9.8**).

Figure 9.8   Due to its larger mass, a large frying pan has a larger heat capacity than a small frying pan. Because they are made of the same material, both frying pans have the same specific heat. (credit: Mark Blaser)

Liquid water has a relatively high specific heat (about 4.2 J/g °C); most metals have much lower specific heats (usually less than 1 J/g °C). The specific heat of a substance varies somewhat with temperature. However, this variation is usually small enough that we will treat specific heat as constant over the range of temperatures that will be considered in this chapter. Specific heats of some common substances are listed in **Table 9.1**.

Specific Heats of Common Substances at 25 °C and 1 bar

Substance	Symbol (*state*)	Specific Heat (J/g °C)
helium	He(*g*)	5.193
water	$H_2O(l)$	4.184
ethanol	$C_2H_6O(l)$	2.376
ice	$H_2O(s)$	2.093 (at −10 °C)
water vapor	$H_2O(g)$	1.864
nitrogen	$N_2(g)$	1.040

Table 9.1

Specific Heats of Common Substances at 25 °C and 1 bar

Substance	Symbol (*state*)	Specific Heat (J/g °C)
air		1.007
oxygen	$O_2(g)$	0.918
aluminum	$Al(s)$	0.897
carbon dioxide	$CO_2(g)$	0.853
argon	$Ar(g)$	0.522
iron	$Fe(s)$	0.449
copper	$Cu(s)$	0.385
lead	$Pb(s)$	0.130
gold	$Au(s)$	0.129
silicon	$Si(s)$	0.712

Table 9.1

If we know the mass of a substance and its specific heat, we can determine the amount of heat, q, entering or leaving the substance by measuring the temperature change before and after the heat is gained or lost:

$$q = (\text{specific heat}) \times (\text{mass of substance}) \times (\text{temperature change})$$
$$q = c \times m \times \Delta T = c \times m \times (T_{final} - T_{initial})$$

In this equation, c is the specific heat of the substance, m is its mass, and ΔT (which is read "delta T") is the temperature change, $T_{final} - T_{initial}$. If a substance gains thermal energy, its temperature increases, its final temperature is higher than its initial temperature, $T_{final} - T_{initial}$ has a positive value, and the value of q is positive. If a substance loses thermal energy, its temperature decreases, the final temperature is lower than the initial temperature, $T_{final} - T_{initial}$ has a negative value, and the value of q is negative.

Example 9.1

Measuring Heat

A flask containing 8.0×10^2 g of water is heated, and the temperature of the water increases from 21 °C to 85 °C. How much heat did the water absorb?

Solution

To answer this question, consider these factors:

- the specific heat of the substance being heated (in this case, water)

- the amount of substance being heated (in this case, 800 g)

- the magnitude of the temperature change (in this case, from 21 °C to 85 °C).

The specific heat of water is 4.184 J/g °C, so to heat 1 g of water by 1 °C requires 4.184 J. We note that since 4.184 J is required to heat 1 g of water by 1 °C, we will need *800 times as much* to heat 800 g of water by 1 °C. Finally, we observe that since 4.184 J are required to heat 1 g of water by 1 °C, we will need *64 times as much* to heat it by 64 °C (that is, from 21 °C to 85 °C).

This can be summarized using the equation:

$$q = c \times m \times \Delta T = c \times m \times (T_{final} - T_{initial})$$
$$= (4.184 \text{ J/g °C}) \times (800 \text{ g}) \times (85 - 21) \text{ °C}$$
$$= (4.184 \text{ J/g °C}) \times (800 \text{ g}) \times (64) \text{ °C}$$
$$= 210,000 \text{ J } (= 210 \text{ kJ})$$

Because the temperature increased, the water absorbed heat and q is positive.

Check Your Learning

How much heat, in joules, must be added to a 5.00×10^2-g iron skillet to increase its temperature from 25 °C to 250 °C? The specific heat of iron is 0.451 J/g °C.

Answer: 5.05×10^4 J

Note that the relationship between heat, specific heat, mass, and temperature change can be used to determine any of these quantities (not just heat) if the other three are known or can be deduced.

Example 9.2

Determining Other Quantities

A piece of unknown metal weighs 348 g. When the metal piece absorbs 6.64 kJ of heat, its temperature increases from 22.4 °C to 43.6 °C. Determine the specific heat of this metal (which might provide a clue to its identity).

Solution

Since mass, heat, and temperature change are known for this metal, we can determine its specific heat using the relationship:

$$q = c \times m \times \Delta T = c \times m \times (T_{final} - T_{initial})$$

Substituting the known values:

$$6640 \text{ J} = c \times (348 \text{ g}) \times (43.6 - 22.4) \text{ °C}$$

Solving:

$$c = \frac{6640 \text{ J}}{(348 \text{ g}) \times (21.2 \text{ °C})} = 0.900 \text{ J/g °C}$$

Comparing this value with the values in Table 9.1, this value matches the specific heat of aluminum, which suggests that the unknown metal may be aluminum.

Check Your Learning

A piece of unknown metal weighs 217 g. When the metal piece absorbs 1.43 kJ of heat, its temperature increases from 24.5 °C to 39.1 °C. Determine the specific heat of this metal, and predict its identity.

Answer: $c = 0.45$ J/g °C; the metal is likely to be iron

Chemistry in Everyday Life

Solar Thermal Energy Power Plants

The sunlight that reaches the earth contains thousands of times more energy than we presently capture. Solar thermal systems provide one possible solution to the problem of converting energy from the sun into energy we can use. Large-scale solar thermal plants have different design specifics, but all concentrate sunlight to heat some substance; the heat "stored" in that substance is then converted into electricity.

The Solana Generating Station in Arizona's Sonora Desert produces 280 megawatts of electrical power. It uses parabolic mirrors that focus sunlight on pipes filled with a heat transfer fluid (HTF) (Figure 9.9). The HTF then does two things: It turns water into steam, which spins turbines, which in turn produces electricity, and it melts and heats a mixture of salts, which functions as a thermal energy storage system. After the sun goes down, the molten salt mixture can then release enough of its stored heat to produce steam to run the turbines for 6 hours. Molten salts are used because they possess a number of beneficial properties, including high heat capacities and thermal conductivities.

Figure 9.9   This solar thermal plant uses parabolic trough mirrors to concentrate sunlight. (credit a: modification of work by Bureau of Land Management)

The 377-megawatt Ivanpah Solar Generating System, located in the Mojave Desert in California, is the largest solar thermal power plant in the world (Figure 9.10). Its 170,000 mirrors focus huge amounts of sunlight on three water-filled towers, producing steam at over 538 °C that drives electricity-producing turbines. It produces enough energy to power 140,000 homes. Water is used as the working fluid because of its large heat capacity and heat of vaporization.

(a)   (b)

Figure 9.10   (a) The Ivanpah solar thermal plant uses 170,000 mirrors to concentrate sunlight on water-filled towers. (b) It covers 4000 acres of public land near the Mojave Desert and the California-Nevada border. (credit a: modification of work by Craig Dietrich; credit b: modification of work by "USFWS Pacific Southwest Region"/Flickr)

9.2 Calorimetry

By the end of this section, you will be able to:

- Explain the technique of calorimetry
- Calculate and interpret heat and related properties using typical calorimetry data

One technique we can use to measure the amount of heat involved in a chemical or physical process is known as **calorimetry**. Calorimetry is used to measure amounts of heat transferred to or from a substance. To do so, the heat is exchanged with a calibrated object (calorimeter). The change in temperature of the measuring part of the calorimeter is converted into the amount of heat (since the previous calibration was used to establish its heat capacity). The measurement of heat transfer using this approach requires the definition of a **system** (the substance or substances undergoing the chemical or physical change) and its **surroundings** (the other components of the measurement apparatus that serve to either provide heat to the system or absorb heat from the system). Knowledge of the heat capacity of the surroundings, and careful measurements of the masses of the system and surroundings and their temperatures before and after the process allows one to calculate the heat transferred as described in this section.

A **calorimeter** is a device used to measure the amount of heat involved in a chemical or physical process. For example, when an exothermic reaction occurs in solution in a calorimeter, the heat produced by the reaction is absorbed by the solution, which increases its temperature. When an endothermic reaction occurs, the heat required is absorbed from the thermal energy of the solution, which decreases its temperature (Figure 9.11). The temperature change, along with the specific heat and mass of the solution, can then be used to calculate the amount of heat involved in either case.

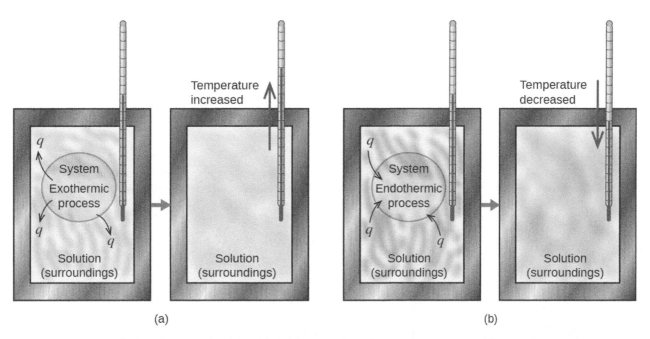

Figure 9.11 In a calorimetric determination, either (a) an exothermic process occurs and heat, q, is negative, indicating that thermal energy is transferred from the system to its surroundings, or (b) an endothermic process occurs and heat, q, is positive, indicating that thermal energy is transferred from the surroundings to the system.

Scientists use well-insulated calorimeters that all but prevent the transfer of heat between the calorimeter and its environment. This enables the accurate determination of the heat involved in chemical processes, the energy content of foods, and so on. General chemistry students often use simple calorimeters constructed from polystyrene cups (**Figure 9.12**). These easy-to-use "coffee cup" calorimeters allow more heat exchange with their surroundings, and therefore produce less accurate energy values.

Figure 9.12 A simple calorimeter can be constructed from two polystyrene cups. A thermometer and stirrer extend through the cover into the reaction mixture.

Commercial solution calorimeters are also available. Relatively inexpensive calorimeters often consist of two thin-walled cups that are nested in a way that minimizes thermal contact during use, along with an insulated cover, handheld stirrer, and simple thermometer. More expensive calorimeters used for industry and research typically have a well-insulated, fully enclosed reaction vessel, motorized stirring mechanism, and a more accurate temperature sensor (**Figure 9.13**).

Figure 9.13 Commercial solution calorimeters range from (a) simple, inexpensive models for student use to (b) expensive, more accurate models for industry and research.

Before we practice calorimetry problems involving chemical reactions, consider a simpler example that illustrates the core idea behind calorimetry. Suppose we initially have a high-temperature substance, such as a hot piece of metal (M), and a low-temperature substance, such as cool water (W). If we place the metal in the water, heat will flow from M to W. The temperature of M will decrease, and the temperature of W will increase, until the two substances have the same temperature—that is, when they reach thermal equilibrium (**Figure 9.14**). If this occurs in a calorimeter, ideally all of this heat transfer occurs between the two substances, with no heat gained or lost by either the calorimeter or the calorimeter's surroundings. Under these ideal circumstances, the net heat change is zero:

$$q_{\text{substance M}} + q_{\text{substance W}} = 0$$

This relationship can be rearranged to show that the heat gained by substance M is equal to the heat lost by substance W:

$$q_{\text{substance M}} = -q_{\text{substance W}}$$

The magnitude of the heat (change) is therefore the same for both substances, and the negative sign merely shows that $q_{\text{substance M}}$ and $q_{\text{substance W}}$ are opposite in direction of heat flow (gain or loss) but does not indicate the arithmetic sign of either q value (that is determined by whether the matter in question gains or loses heat, per definition). In the specific situation described, $q_{\text{substance M}}$ is a negative value and $q_{\text{substance W}}$ is positive, since heat is transferred from M to W.

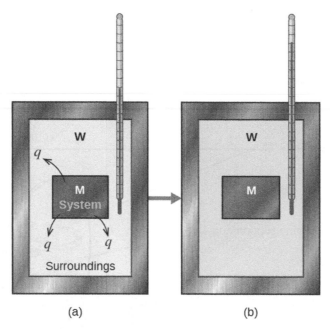

Figure 9.14 In a simple calorimetry process, (a) heat, q, is transferred from the hot metal, M, to the cool water, W, until (b) both are at the same temperature.

Example 9.3

Heat Transfer between Substances at Different Temperatures

A 360-g piece of rebar (a steel rod used for reinforcing concrete) is dropped into 425 mL of water at 24.0 °C. The final temperature of the water was measured as 42.7 °C. Calculate the initial temperature of the piece of rebar. Assume the specific heat of steel is approximately the same as that for iron (Table 9.1), and that all heat transfer occurs between the rebar and the water (there is no heat exchange with the surroundings).

Solution

The temperature of the water increases from 24.0 °C to 42.7 °C, so the water absorbs heat. That heat came from the piece of rebar, which initially was at a higher temperature. Assuming that all heat transfer was between the rebar and the water, with no heat "lost" to the surroundings, then *heat given off by rebar = −heat taken in by water*, or:

$$q_{\text{rebar}} = -q_{\text{water}}$$

Since we know how heat is related to other measurable quantities, we have:

$$(c \times m \times \Delta T)_{\text{rebar}} = -(c \times m \times \Delta T)_{\text{water}}$$

Letting f = final and i = initial, in expanded form, this becomes:

$$c_{\text{rebar}} \times m_{\text{rebar}} \times (T_{\text{f,rebar}} - T_{\text{i,rebar}}) = -c_{\text{water}} \times m_{\text{water}} \times (T_{\text{f,water}} - T_{\text{i,water}})$$

The density of water is 1.0 g/mL, so 425 mL of water = 425 g. Noting that the final temperature of both the rebar and water is 42.7 °C, substituting known values yields:

$$(0.449 \text{ J/g °C})(360 \text{ g})(42.7 \text{ °C} - T_{\text{i,rebar}}) = (4.184 \text{ J/g °C})(425 \text{ g})(42.7 \text{ °C} - 24.0 \text{ °C})$$

$$T_{i,rebar} = \frac{(4.184 \text{ J/g °C})(425 \text{ g})(42.7 \text{ °C} - 24.0 \text{ °C})}{(0.449 \text{ J/g °C})(360 \text{ g})} + 42.7 \text{ °C}$$

Solving this gives $T_{\text{i,rebar}}$= 248 °C, so the initial temperature of the rebar was 248 °C.

Check Your Learning

A 248-g piece of copper is dropped into 390 mL of water at 22.6 °C. The final temperature of the water was measured as 39.9 °C. Calculate the initial temperature of the piece of copper. Assume that all heat transfer occurs between the copper and the water.

Answer: The initial temperature of the copper was 335.6 °C.

Check Your Learning

A 248-g piece of copper initially at 314 °C is dropped into 390 mL of water initially at 22.6 °C. Assuming that all heat transfer occurs between the copper and the water, calculate the final temperature.

Answer: The final temperature (reached by both copper and water) is 38.7 °C.

This method can also be used to determine other quantities, such as the specific heat of an unknown metal.

Example 9.4

Identifying a Metal by Measuring Specific Heat

A 59.7 g piece of metal that had been submerged in boiling water was quickly transferred into 60.0 mL of water initially at 22.0 °C. The final temperature is 28.5 °C. Use these data to determine the specific heat of the metal. Use this result to identify the metal.

Solution

Assuming perfect heat transfer, *heat given off by metal = −heat taken in by water*, or:

$$q_{metal} = -q_{water}$$

In expanded form, this is:

$$c_{metal} \times m_{metal} \times (T_{f,metal} - T_{i, metal}) = -c_{water} \times m_{water} \times (T_{f,water} - T_{i,water})$$

Noting that since the metal was submerged in boiling water, its initial temperature was 100.0 °C; and that for water, 60.0 mL = 60.0 g; we have:

$$(c_{metal})(59.7 \text{ g})(28.5 \text{ °C} - 100.0 \text{ °C}) = -(4.18 \text{ J/g °C})(60.0 \text{ g})(28.5 \text{ °C} - 22.0 \text{ °C})$$

Solving this:

$$c_{metal} = \frac{-(4.184 \text{ J/g °C})(60.0 \text{ g})(6.5 \text{ °C})}{(59.7 \text{ g})(-71.5 \text{ °C})} = 0.38 \text{ J/g °C}$$

Comparing this with values in Table 9.1, our experimental specific heat is closest to the value for copper (0.39 J/g °C), so we identify the metal as copper.

Check Your Learning

A 92.9-g piece of a silver/gray metal is heated to 178.0 °C, and then quickly transferred into 75.0 mL of water initially at 24.0 °C. After 5 minutes, both the metal and the water have reached the same temperature: 29.7 °C. Determine the specific heat and the identity of the metal. (Note: You should find that the specific heat is close to that of two different metals. Explain how you can confidently determine the identity of the metal).

Answer: c_{metal}= 0.13 J/g °C This specific heat is close to that of either gold or lead. It would be difficult to determine which metal this was based solely on the numerical values. However, the observation that the metal is silver/gray in addition to the value for the specific heat indicates that the metal is lead.

When we use calorimetry to determine the heat involved in a chemical reaction, the same principles we have been discussing apply. The amount of heat absorbed by the calorimeter is often small enough that we can neglect it (though not for highly accurate measurements, as discussed later), and the calorimeter minimizes energy exchange with the surroundings. Because energy is neither created nor destroyed during a chemical reaction, there is no overall energy change during the reaction. The heat produced or consumed in the reaction (the "system"), $q_{reaction}$, plus the heat absorbed or lost by the solution (the "surroundings"), $q_{solution}$, must add up to zero:

$$q_{reaction} + q_{solution} = 0$$

This means that the amount of heat produced or consumed in the reaction equals the amount of heat absorbed or lost by the solution:

$$q_{reaction} = -q_{solution}$$

This concept lies at the heart of all calorimetry problems and calculations.

Example 9.5

Heat Produced by an Exothermic Reaction

When 50.0 mL of 1.00 M HCl(aq) and 50.0 mL of 1.00 M NaOH(aq), both at 22.0 °C, are added to a coffee cup calorimeter, the temperature of the mixture reaches a maximum of 28.9 °C. What is the approximate amount of heat produced by this reaction?

$$HCl(aq) + NaOH(aq) \longrightarrow NaCl(aq) + H_2O(l)$$

Solution

To visualize what is going on, imagine that you could combine the two solutions so quickly that no reaction took place while they mixed; then after mixing, the reaction took place. At the instant of mixing, you have 100.0 mL of a mixture of HCl and NaOH at 22.0 °C. The HCl and NaOH then react until the solution temperature reaches 28.9 °C.

The heat given off by the reaction is equal to that taken in by the solution. Therefore:

$$q_{reaction} = -q_{solution}$$

(It is important to remember that this relationship only holds if the calorimeter does not absorb any heat from the reaction, and there is no heat exchange between the calorimeter and its surroundings.)

Next, we know that the heat absorbed by the solution depends on its specific heat, mass, and temperature change:

$$q_{solution} = (c \times m \times \Delta T)_{solution}$$

To proceed with this calculation, we need to make a few more reasonable assumptions or approximations. Since the solution is aqueous, we can proceed as if it were water in terms of its specific heat and mass values. The density of water is approximately 1.0 g/mL, so 100.0 mL has a mass of about 1.0×10^2 g (two significant figures). The specific heat of water is approximately 4.18 J/g °C, so we use that for the specific heat of the solution. Substituting these values gives:

$$q_{solution} = (4.184 \text{ J/g °C})(1.0 \times 10^2 \text{ g})(28.9 \text{ °C} - 22.0 \text{ °C}) = 2.89 \times 10^3 \text{ J}$$

Finally, since we are trying to find the heat of the reaction, we have:

$$q_{reaction} = -q_{solution} = -2.89 \times 10^3 \text{ J}$$

The negative sign indicates that the reaction is exothermic. It produces 2.89 kJ of heat.

Check Your Learning

When 100 mL of 0.200 M NaCl(aq) and 100 mL of 0.200 M AgNO$_3$(aq), both at 21.9 °C, are mixed in a coffee cup calorimeter, the temperature increases to 23.5 °C as solid AgCl forms. How much heat is produced by this precipitation reaction? What assumptions did you make to determine your value?

Answer: 1.34×10^3 J; assume no heat is absorbed by the calorimeter, no heat is exchanged between the calorimeter and its surroundings, and that the specific heat and mass of the solution are the same as those for water

Chemistry in Everyday Life

Thermochemistry of Hand Warmers

When working or playing outdoors on a cold day, you might use a hand warmer to warm your hands (Figure 9.15). A common reusable hand warmer contains a supersaturated solution of $NaC_2H_3O_2$ (sodium acetate) and a metal disc. Bending the disk creates nucleation sites around which the metastable $NaC_2H_3O_2$ quickly crystallizes (a later chapter on solutions will investigate saturation and supersaturation in more detail).

The process $NaC_2H_3O_2(aq) \longrightarrow NaC_2H_3O_2(s)$ is exothermic, and the heat produced by this process is absorbed by your hands, thereby warming them (at least for a while). If the hand warmer is reheated, the $NaC_2H_3O_2$ redissolves and can be reused.

Figure 9.15 Chemical hand warmers produce heat that warms your hand on a cold day. In this one, you can see the metal disc that initiates the exothermic precipitation reaction. (credit: modification of work by Science Buddies TV/YouTube)

Another common hand warmer produces heat when it is ripped open, exposing iron and water in the hand warmer to oxygen in the air. One simplified version of this exothermic reaction is $2Fe(s) + \frac{3}{2}O_2(g) \longrightarrow Fe_2O_3(s)$. Salt in the hand warmer catalyzes the reaction, so it produces heat more rapidly; cellulose, vermiculite, and activated carbon help distribute the heat evenly. Other types of hand warmers use lighter fluid (a platinum catalyst helps lighter fluid oxidize exothermically), charcoal (charcoal oxidizes in a special case), or electrical units that produce heat by passing an electrical current from a battery through resistive wires.

Link to Learning

This link (http://openstaxcollege.org/l/16Handwarmer) shows the precipitation reaction that occurs when the disk in a chemical hand warmer is flexed.

Example 9.6

Heat Flow in an Instant Ice Pack

When solid ammonium nitrate dissolves in water, the solution becomes cold. This is the basis for an "instant ice pack" (Figure 9.16). When 3.21 g of solid NH_4NO_3 dissolves in 50.0 g of water at 24.9 °C in a calorimeter, the temperature decreases to 20.3 °C.

Calculate the value of q for this reaction and explain the meaning of its arithmetic sign. State any assumptions that you made.

ammonium nitrate

Inner bag of water

Figure 9.16 An instant cold pack consists of a bag containing solid ammonium nitrate and a second bag of water. When the bag of water is broken, the pack becomes cold because the dissolution of ammonium nitrate is an endothermic process that removes thermal energy from the water. The cold pack then removes thermal energy from your body.

Solution

We assume that the calorimeter prevents heat transfer between the solution and its external environment (including the calorimeter itself), in which case:

$$q_{rxn} = -q_{soln}$$

with "rxn" and "soln" used as shorthand for "reaction" and "solution," respectively.

Assuming also that the specific heat of the solution is the same as that for water, we have:

$$q_{rxn} = -q_{soln} = -(c \times m \times \Delta T)_{soln}$$
$$= -[(4.184 \text{ J/g} \,°\text{C}) \times (53.2 \text{ g}) \times (20.3 \,°\text{C} - 24.9 \,°\text{C})]$$
$$= -[(4.184 \text{ J/g} \,°\text{C}) \times (53.2 \text{ g}) \times (-4.6 \,°\text{C})]$$
$$+1.0 \times 10^3 \text{ J} = +1.0 \text{ kJ}$$

The positive sign for q indicates that the dissolution is an endothermic process.

Check Your Learning

When a 3.00-g sample of KCl was added to 3.00×10^2 g of water in a coffee cup calorimeter, the temperature decreased by 1.05 °C. How much heat is involved in the dissolution of the KCl? What assumptions did you make?

Answer: 1.33 kJ; assume that the calorimeter prevents heat transfer between the solution and its external environment (including the calorimeter itself) and that the specific heat of the solution is the same as that for water

If the amount of heat absorbed by a calorimeter is too large to neglect or if we require more accurate results, then we must take into account the heat absorbed both by the solution and by the calorimeter.

The calorimeters described are designed to operate at constant (atmospheric) pressure and are convenient to measure heat flow accompanying processes that occur in solution. A different type of calorimeter that operates at constant volume, colloquially known as a **bomb calorimeter**, is used to measure the energy produced by reactions that yield large amounts of heat and gaseous products, such as combustion reactions. (The term "bomb" comes from the observation that these reactions can be vigorous enough to resemble explosions that would damage other calorimeters.) This type of calorimeter consists of a robust steel container (the "bomb") that contains the reactants and is itself submerged in water (**Figure 9.17**). The sample is placed in the bomb, which is then filled with oxygen at high pressure. A small electrical spark is used to ignite the sample. The energy produced by the reaction is trapped in the steel bomb and the surrounding water. The temperature increase is measured and, along with the known heat capacity of the calorimeter, is used to calculate the energy produced by the reaction. Bomb calorimeters require calibration to determine the heat capacity of the calorimeter and ensure accurate results. The calibration is accomplished using a reaction with a known q, such as a measured quantity of benzoic acid ignited by a spark from a nickel fuse wire that is weighed before and after the reaction. The temperature change produced by the known reaction is used to determine the heat capacity of the calorimeter. The calibration is generally performed each time before the calorimeter is used to gather research data.

Figure 9.17 (a) A bomb calorimeter is used to measure heat produced by reactions involving gaseous reactants or products, such as combustion. (b) The reactants are contained in the gas-tight "bomb," which is submerged in water and surrounded by insulating materials. (credit a: modification of work by "Harbor1"/Wikimedia commons)

Link to Learning

Click on this link (http://openstaxcollege.org/l/16BombCal) to view how a bomb calorimeter is prepared for action.

This site (http://openstaxcollege.org/l/16Calorcalcs) shows calorimetric calculations using sample data.

Example 9.7

Bomb Calorimetry

When 3.12 g of glucose, $C_6H_{12}O_6$, is burned in a bomb calorimeter, the temperature of the calorimeter increases from 23.8 °C to 35.6 °C. The calorimeter contains 775 g of water, and the bomb itself has a heat capacity of 893 J/°C. How much heat was produced by the combustion of the glucose sample?

Solution

The combustion produces heat that is primarily absorbed by the water and the bomb. (The amounts of heat absorbed by the reaction products and the unreacted excess oxygen are relatively small and dealing with them is beyond the scope of this text. We will neglect them in our calculations.)

The heat produced by the reaction is absorbed by the water and the bomb:

$$q_{rxn} = -(q_{water} + q_{bomb})$$
$$= -[(4.184 \text{ J/g °C}) \times (775 \text{ g}) \times (35.6 \text{ °C} - 23.8 \text{ °C}) + 893 \text{ J/°C} \times (35.6 \text{ °C} - 23.8 \text{ °C})]$$
$$= -(38,300 \text{ J} + 10,500 \text{ J})$$
$$= -48,800 \text{ J} = -48.8 \text{ kJ}$$

This reaction released 48.7 kJ of heat when 3.12 g of glucose was burned.

Check Your Learning

When 0.963 g of benzene, C_6H_6, is burned in a bomb calorimeter, the temperature of the calorimeter increases by 8.39 °C. The bomb has a heat capacity of 784 J/°C and is submerged in 925 mL of water. How much heat was produced by the combustion of the glucose sample?

Answer: 39.0 kJ

Since the first one was constructed in 1899, 35 calorimeters have been built to measure the heat produced by a living person.[2] These whole-body calorimeters of various designs are large enough to hold an individual human being. More recently, whole-room calorimeters allow for relatively normal activities to be performed, and these calorimeters generate data that more closely reflect the real world. These calorimeters are used to measure the metabolism of individuals under different environmental conditions, different dietary regimes, and with different health conditions, such as diabetes. In humans, metabolism is typically measured in Calories per day. A **nutritional calorie (Calorie)** is the energy unit used to quantify the amount of energy derived from the metabolism of foods; one Calorie is equal to 1000 calories (1 kcal), the amount of energy needed to heat 1 kg of water by 1 °C.

Chemistry in Everyday Life

Measuring Nutritional Calories

In your day-to-day life, you may be more familiar with energy being given in Calories, or nutritional calories, which are used to quantify the amount of energy in foods. One calorie (cal) = exactly 4.184 joules, and one Calorie (note the capitalization) = 1000 cal, or 1 kcal. (This is approximately the amount of energy needed to heat 1 kg of water by 1 °C.)

The macronutrients in food are proteins, carbohydrates, and fats or oils. Proteins provide about 4 Calories per gram, carbohydrates also provide about 4 Calories per gram, and fats and oils provide about 9 Calories/g. Nutritional labels on food packages show the caloric content of one serving of the food, as well as the breakdown into Calories from each of the three macronutrients (Figure 9.18).

2.   Francis D. Reardon et al. "The Snellen human calorimeter revisited, re-engineered and upgraded: Design and performance characteristics." *Medical and Biological Engineering and Computing* 8 (2006)721–28, http://link.springer.com/article/10.1007/s11517-006-0086-5.

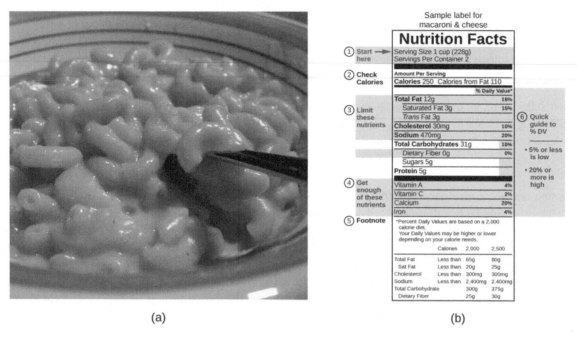

(a)   (b)

Figure 9.18 (a) Macaroni and cheese contain energy in the form of the macronutrients in the food. (b) The food's nutritional information is shown on the package label. In the US, the energy content is given in Calories (per serving); the rest of the world usually uses kilojoules. (credit a: modification of work by "Rex Roof"/Flickr)

For the example shown in (b), the total energy per 228-g portion is calculated by:

$$(5 \text{ g protein} \times 4 \text{ Calories/g}) + (31 \text{ g carb} \times 4 \text{ Calories/g}) + (12 \text{ g fat} \times 9 \text{ Calories/g}) = 252 \text{ Calories}$$

So, you can use food labels to count your Calories. But where do the values come from? And how accurate are they? The caloric content of foods can be determined by using bomb calorimetry; that is, by burning the food and measuring the energy it contains. A sample of food is weighed, mixed in a blender, freeze-dried, ground into powder, and formed into a pellet. The pellet is burned inside a bomb calorimeter, and the measured temperature change is converted into energy per gram of food.

Today, the caloric content on food labels is derived using a method called the Atwater system that uses the average caloric content of the different chemical constituents of food, protein, carbohydrate, and fats. The average amounts are those given in the equation and are derived from the various results given by bomb calorimetry of whole foods. The carbohydrate amount is discounted a certain amount for the fiber content, which is indigestible carbohydrate. To determine the energy content of a food, the quantities of carbohydrate, protein, and fat are each multiplied by the average Calories per gram for each and the products summed to obtain the total energy.

Link to Learning

Click on this link (http://openstaxcollege.org/l/16USDA) to access the US Department of Agriculture (USDA) National Nutrient Database, containing nutritional information on over 8000 foods.

9.3 Enthalpy

By the end of this section, you will be able to:

- State the first law of thermodynamics

- Define enthalpy and explain its classification as a state function

- Write and balance thermochemical equations

- Calculate enthalpy changes for various chemical reactions

- Explain Hess's law and use it to compute reaction enthalpies

Thermochemistry is a branch of **chemical thermodynamics**, the science that deals with the relationships between heat, work, and other forms of energy in the context of chemical and physical processes. As we concentrate on thermochemistry in this chapter, we need to consider some widely used concepts of thermodynamics.

Substances act as reservoirs of energy, meaning that energy can be added to them or removed from them. Energy is stored in a substance when the kinetic energy of its atoms or molecules is raised. The greater kinetic energy may be in the form of increased translations (travel or straight-line motions), vibrations, or rotations of the atoms or molecules. When thermal energy is lost, the intensities of these motions decrease and the kinetic energy falls. The total of all possible kinds of energy present in a substance is called the **internal energy (U)**, sometimes symbolized as E.

As a system undergoes a change, its internal energy can change, and energy can be transferred from the system to the surroundings, or from the surroundings to the system. Energy is transferred into a system when it absorbs heat (q) from the surroundings or when the surroundings do work (w) on the system. For example, energy is transferred into room-temperature metal wire if it is immersed in hot water (the wire absorbs heat from the water), or if you rapidly bend the wire back and forth (the wire becomes warmer because of the work done on it). Both processes increase the internal energy of the wire, which is reflected in an increase in the wire's temperature. Conversely, energy is transferred out of a system when heat is lost from the system, or when the system does work on the surroundings.

The relationship between internal energy, heat, and work can be represented by the equation:

$$\Delta U = q + w$$

as shown in Figure 9.19. This is one version of the **first law of thermodynamics**, and it shows that the internal energy of a system changes through heat flow into or out of the system (positive q is heat flow in; negative q is heat flow out) or work done on or by the system. The work, w, is positive if it is done on the system and negative if it is done by the system.

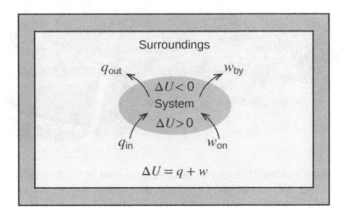

Figure 9.19 The internal energy, U, of a system can be changed by heat flow and work. If heat flows into the system, q_{in}, or work is done on the system, w_{on}, its internal energy increases, $\Delta U > 0$. If heat flows out of the system, q_{out}, or work is done by the system, w_{by}, its internal energy decreases, $\Delta U < 0$.

A type of work called **expansion work** (or pressure-volume work) occurs when a system pushes back the surroundings against a restraining pressure, or when the surroundings compress the system. An example of this occurs during the operation of an internal combustion engine. The reaction of gasoline and oxygen is exothermic. Some of this energy is given off as heat, and some does work pushing the piston in the cylinder. The substances involved in the reaction are the system, and the engine and the rest of the universe are the surroundings. The system loses energy by both heating and doing work on the surroundings, and its internal energy decreases. (The engine is able to keep the car moving because this process is repeated many times per second while the engine is running.) We will consider how to determine the amount of work involved in a chemical or physical change in the chapter on thermodynamics.

Link to Learning

This view of an internal combustion engine (http://openstaxcollege.org/l/16combustion) illustrates the conversion of energy produced by the exothermic combustion reaction of a fuel such as gasoline into energy of motion.

As discussed, the relationship between internal energy, heat, and work can be represented as $\Delta U = q + w$. Internal energy is a type of quantity known as a **state function** (or state variable), whereas heat and work are not state functions. The value of a state function depends only on the state that a system is in, and not on how that state is reached. If a quantity is not a state function, then its value *does* depend on how the state is reached. An example of a state function is altitude or elevation. If you stand on the summit of Mt. Kilimanjaro, you are at an altitude of 5895 m, and it does not matter whether you hiked there or parachuted there. The distance you traveled to the top of Kilimanjaro, however, is not a state function. You could climb to the summit by a direct route or by a more roundabout, circuitous path (Figure 9.20). The distances traveled would differ (distance is not a state function) but the elevation reached would be the same (altitude is a state function).

Figure 9.20 Paths X and Y represent two different routes to the summit of Mt. Kilimanjaro. Both have the same change in elevation (altitude or elevation on a mountain is a state function; it does not depend on path), but they have very different distances traveled (distance walked is not a state function; it depends on the path). (credit: modification of work by Paul Shaffner)

Chemists ordinarily use a property known as **enthalpy (H)** to describe the thermodynamics of chemical and physical processes. Enthalpy is defined as the sum of a system's internal energy (U) and the mathematical product of its pressure (P) and volume (V):

$$H = U + PV$$

Since it is derived from three state functions (U, P, and V), enthalpy is also a state function. Enthalpy values for specific substances cannot be measured directly; only enthalpy *changes* for chemical or physical processes can be determined. For processes that take place at constant pressure (a common condition for many chemical and physical changes), the **enthalpy change (ΔH)** is:

$$\Delta H = \Delta U + P\Delta V$$

The mathematical product $P\Delta V$ represents work (w), namely, expansion or pressure-volume work as noted. By their definitions, the arithmetic signs of ΔV and w will always be opposite:

$$P\Delta V = -w$$

Substituting this equation and the definition of internal energy into the enthalpy-change equation yields:

$$\begin{aligned} \Delta H &= \Delta U + P\Delta V \\ &= q_p + w - w \\ &= q_p \end{aligned}$$

where q_p is the heat of reaction under conditions of constant pressure.

And so, if a chemical or physical process is carried out at constant pressure with the only work done caused by expansion or contraction, then the heat flow (q_p) and enthalpy change (ΔH) for the process are equal.

The heat given off when you operate a Bunsen burner is equal to the enthalpy change of the methane combustion reaction that takes place, since it occurs at the essentially constant pressure of the atmosphere. On the other hand, the heat produced by a reaction measured in a bomb calorimeter (**Figure 9.17**) is not equal to ΔH because the closed, constant-volume metal container prevents expansion work from occurring. Chemists usually perform experiments under normal atmospheric conditions, at constant external pressure with $q = \Delta H$, which makes enthalpy the most convenient choice for determining heat.

The following conventions apply when we use ΔH:

1. Chemists use a thermochemical equation to represent the changes in both matter and energy. In a thermochemical equation, the enthalpy change of a reaction is shown as a ΔH value following the equation for the reaction. This ΔH value indicates the amount of heat associated with the reaction involving the number of moles of reactants and products *as shown in the chemical equation*. For example, consider this equation:

$$H_2(g) + \frac{1}{2}O_2(g) \longrightarrow H_2O(l) \qquad \Delta H = -286 \text{ kJ}$$

   This equation indicates that when 1 mole of hydrogen gas and $\frac{1}{2}$ mole of oxygen gas at some temperature and pressure change to 1 mole of liquid water at the same temperature and pressure, 286 kJ of heat are released to the surroundings. If the coefficients of the chemical equation are multiplied by some factor, the enthalpy change must be multiplied by that same factor (ΔH is an extensive property):

   (two-fold increase in amounts)
   $$2H_2(g) + O_2(g) \longrightarrow 2H_2O(l) \qquad \Delta H = 2 \times (-286 \text{ kJ}) = -572 \text{ kJ}$$
   (two-fold decrease in amounts)
   $$\frac{1}{2}H_2(g) + \frac{1}{4}O_2(g) \longrightarrow \frac{1}{2}H_2O(l) \qquad \Delta H = \frac{1}{2} \times (-286 \text{ kJ}) = -143 \text{ kJ}$$

2. The enthalpy change of a reaction depends on the physical state of the reactants and products of the reaction (whether we have gases, liquids, solids, or aqueous solutions), so these must be shown. For example, when 1 mole of hydrogen gas and $\frac{1}{2}$ mole of oxygen gas change to 1 mole of liquid water at the same temperature and pressure, 286 kJ of heat are released. If gaseous water forms, only 242 kJ of heat are released.

$$H_2(g) + \frac{1}{2}O_2(g) \longrightarrow H_2O(g) \qquad \Delta H = -242 \text{ kJ}$$

3. A negative value of an enthalpy change, ΔH, indicates an exothermic reaction; a positive value of ΔH indicates an endothermic reaction. If the direction of a chemical equation is reversed, the arithmetic sign of its ΔH is changed (a process that is endothermic in one direction is exothermic in the opposite direction).

Example 9.8

Measurement of an Enthalpy Change

When 0.0500 mol of HCl(aq) reacts with 0.0500 mol of NaOH(aq) to form 0.0500 mol of NaCl(aq), 2.9 kJ of heat are produced. What is ΔH, the enthalpy change, per mole of acid reacting, for the acid-base reaction run under the conditions described in Example 9.5?

$$HCl(aq) + NaOH(aq) \longrightarrow NaCl(aq) + H_2O(l)$$

Solution

For the reaction of 0.0500 mol acid (HCl), $q = -2.9$ kJ. This ratio $\dfrac{-2.9 \text{ kJ}}{0.0500 \text{ mol HCl}}$ can be used as a conversion factor to find the heat produced when 1 mole of HCl reacts:

$$\Delta H = 1 \text{ mol HCl} \times \frac{-2.9 \text{ kJ}}{0.0500 \text{ mol HCl}} = -58 \text{ kJ}$$

The enthalpy change when 1 mole of HCl reacts is −58 kJ. Since that is the number of moles in the chemical equation, we write the thermochemical equation as:

$$HCl(aq) + NaOH(aq) \longrightarrow NaCl(aq) + H_2O(l) \qquad \Delta H = -58 \text{ kJ}$$

Check Your Learning

When 1.34 g Zn(s) reacts with 60.0 mL of 0.750 M HCl(aq), 3.14 kJ of heat are produced. Determine the enthalpy change per mole of zinc reacting for the reaction:

$$Zn(s) + 2HCl(aq) \longrightarrow ZnCl_2(aq) + H_2(g)$$

Answer: $\Delta H = -153$ kJ

Be sure to take both stoichiometry and limiting reactants into account when determining the ΔH for a chemical reaction.

Example 9.9

Another Example of the Measurement of an Enthalpy Change

A gummy bear contains 2.67 g sucrose, $C_{12}H_{22}O_{11}$. When it reacts with 7.19 g potassium chlorate, $KClO_3$, 43.7 kJ of heat are produced. Determine the enthalpy change for the reaction

$$C_{12}H_{22}O_{11}(aq) + 8KClO_3(aq) \longrightarrow 12CO_2(g) + 11H_2O(l) + 8KCl(aq).$$

Solution

We have $\qquad 2.67 \text{ g} \times \dfrac{1 \text{ mol}}{342.3 \text{ g}} = 0.00780 \text{ mol } C_{12}H_{22}O_{11} \qquad$ available, and

$7.19 \text{ g} \times \dfrac{1 \text{ mol}}{122.5 \text{ g}} = 0.0587 \text{ mol } KClO_3 \qquad\qquad$ available. Since

$0.0587 \text{ mol } KClO_3 \times \dfrac{1 \text{ mol } C_{12}H_{22}O_{11}}{8 \text{ mol } KClO_3} = 0.00734 \text{ mol } C_{12}H_{22}O_{11}$ is needed, $C_{12}H_{22}O_{11}$ is the excess reactant and $KClO_3$ is the limiting reactant.

The reaction uses 8 mol $KClO_3$, and the conversion factor is $\dfrac{-43.7\,\text{kJ}}{0.0587\,\text{mol }KClO_3}$, so we have

$\Delta H = 8\,\text{mol} \times \dfrac{-43.7\,\text{kJ}}{0.0587\,\text{mol }KClO_3} = -5960\,\text{kJ}$. The enthalpy change for this reaction is -5960 kJ, and the thermochemical equation is:

$$C_{12}H_{22}O_{11} + 8KClO_3 \longrightarrow 12CO_2 + 11H_2O + 8KCl \qquad \Delta H = -5960\,\text{kJ}$$

Check Your Learning

When 1.42 g of iron reacts with 1.80 g of chlorine, 3.22 g of $FeCl_2(s)$ and 8.60 kJ of heat is produced. What is the enthalpy change for the reaction when 1 mole of $FeCl_2(s)$ is produced?

Answer: $\Delta H = -338$ kJ

Enthalpy changes are typically tabulated for reactions in which both the reactants and products are at the same conditions. A **standard state** is a commonly accepted set of conditions used as a reference point for the determination of properties under other different conditions. For chemists, the IUPAC standard state refers to materials under a pressure of 1 bar and solutions at 1 M, and does not specify a temperature. Many thermochemical tables list values with a standard state of 1 atm. Because the ΔH of a reaction changes very little with such small changes in pressure (1 bar = 0.987 atm), ΔH values (except for the most precisely measured values) are essentially the same under both sets of standard conditions. We will include a superscripted "o" in the enthalpy change symbol to designate standard state. Since the usual (but not technically standard) temperature is 298.15 K, we will use a subscripted "298" to designate this temperature. Thus, the symbol (ΔH°_{298}) is used to indicate an enthalpy change for a process occurring under these conditions. (The symbol ΔH is used to indicate an enthalpy change for a reaction occurring under nonstandard conditions.)

The enthalpy changes for many types of chemical and physical processes are available in the reference literature, including those for combustion reactions, phase transitions, and formation reactions. As we discuss these quantities, it is important to pay attention to the *extensive* nature of enthalpy and enthalpy changes. Since the enthalpy change for a given reaction is proportional to the amounts of substances involved, it may be reported on that basis (i.e., as the ΔH for specific amounts of reactants). However, we often find it more useful to divide one extensive property (ΔH) by another (amount of substance), and report a per-amount *intensive* value of ΔH, often "normalized" to a per-mole basis. (Note that this is similar to determining the intensive property specific heat from the extensive property heat capacity, as seen previously.)

Enthalpy of Combustion

Standard enthalpy of combustion (ΔH°_C) is the enthalpy change when 1 mole of a substance burns (combines vigorously with oxygen) under standard state conditions; it is sometimes called "heat of combustion." For example, the enthalpy of combustion of ethanol, -1366.8 kJ/mol, is the amount of heat produced when one mole of ethanol undergoes complete combustion at 25 °C and 1 atmosphere pressure, yielding products also at 25 °C and 1 atm.

$$C_2H_5OH(l) + 3O_2(g) \longrightarrow 2CO_2 + 3H_2O(l) \qquad \Delta H^{\circ}_{298} = -1366.8\,\text{kJ}$$

Enthalpies of combustion for many substances have been measured; a few of these are listed in Table 9.2. Many readily available substances with large enthalpies of combustion are used as fuels, including hydrogen, carbon (as coal or charcoal), and **hydrocarbons** (compounds containing only hydrogen and carbon), such as methane, propane, and the major components of gasoline.

Standard Molar Enthalpies of Combustion

Substance	Combustion Reaction	Enthalpy of Combustion, ΔH_c° $(\frac{kJ}{mol} \text{ at } 25\,^\circ C)$
carbon	$C(s) + O_2(g) \longrightarrow CO_2(g)$	−393.5
hydrogen	$H_2(g) + \frac{1}{2}O_2(g) \longrightarrow H_2O(l)$	−285.8
magnesium	$Mg(s) + \frac{1}{2}O_2(g) \longrightarrow MgO(s)$	−601.6
sulfur	$S(s) + O_2(g) \longrightarrow SO_2(g)$	−296.8
carbon monoxide	$CO(g) + \frac{1}{2}O_2(g) \longrightarrow CO_2(g)$	−283.0
methane	$CH_4(g) + 2O_2(g) \longrightarrow CO_2(g) + 2H_2O(l)$	−890.8
acetylene	$C_2H_2(g) + \frac{5}{2}O_2(g) \longrightarrow 2CO_2(g) + H_2O(l)$	−1301.1
ethanol	$C_2H_5OH(l) + 3O_2(g) \longrightarrow 2CO_2(g) + 3H_2O(l)$	−1366.8
methanol	$CH_3OH(l) + \frac{3}{2}O_2(g) \longrightarrow CO_2(g) + 2H_2O(l)$	−726.1
isooctane	$C_8H_{18}(l) + \frac{25}{2}O_2(g) \longrightarrow 8CO_2(g) + 9H_2O(l)$	−5461

Table 9.2

Example 9.10

Using Enthalpy of Combustion

As Figure 9.21 suggests, the combustion of gasoline is a highly exothermic process. Let us determine the approximate amount of heat produced by burning 1.00 L of gasoline, assuming the enthalpy of combustion of gasoline is the same as that of isooctane, a common component of gasoline. The density of isooctane is 0.692 g/mL.

Figure 9.21   The combustion of gasoline is very exothermic. (credit: modification of work by "AlexEagle"/Flickr)

Solution

Starting with a known amount (1.00 L of isooctane), we can perform conversions between units until we arrive at the desired amount of heat or energy. The enthalpy of combustion of isooctane provides one of the necessary conversions. Table 9.2 gives this value as −5460 kJ per 1 mole of isooctane (C_8H_{18}).

Using these data,

$$1.00 \; \text{L} \, C_8H_{18} \times \frac{1000 \; \text{mL} \, C_8H_{18}}{1 \; \text{L} \, C_8H_{18}} \times \frac{0.692 \; \text{g} \, C_8H_{18}}{1 \; \text{mL} \, C_8H_{18}} \times \frac{1 \; \text{mol} \, C_8H_{18}}{114 \; \text{g} \, C_8H_{18}} \times \frac{-5460 \; \text{kJ}}{1 \; \text{mol} \, C_8H_{18}} = -3.31 \times 10^4 \, \text{kJ}$$

The combustion of 1.00 L of isooctane produces 33,100 kJ of heat. (This amount of energy is enough to melt 99.2 kg, or about 218 lbs, of ice.)

Note: If you do this calculation one step at a time, you would find:

$$1.00 \, \text{L} \, C_8H_{18} \longrightarrow 1.00 \times 10^3 \; \text{mL} \, C_8H_{18}$$

$$1.00 \times 10^3 \; \text{mL} \, C_8H_{18} \longrightarrow 692 \, \text{g} \, C_8H_{18}$$

$$692 \, \text{g} \, C_8H_{18} \longrightarrow 6.07 \, \text{mol} \, C_8H_{18}$$

$$692 \, \text{g} \, C_8H_{18} \longrightarrow -3.31 \times 10^4 \, \text{kJ}$$

Check Your Learning

How much heat is produced by the combustion of 125 g of acetylene?

Answer: $6.25 \times 10^3 \, \text{kJ}$

Chemistry in Everyday Life

Emerging Algae-Based Energy Technologies (Biofuels)

As reserves of fossil fuels diminish and become more costly to extract, the search is ongoing for replacement fuel sources for the future. Among the most promising biofuels are those derived from algae (Figure 9.22). The species of algae used are nontoxic, biodegradable, and among the world's fastest growing organisms. About 50% of algal weight is oil, which can be readily converted into fuel such as biodiesel. Algae can yield 26,000 gallons of biofuel per hectare—much more energy per acre than other crops. Some strains of algae can flourish in brackish water that is not usable for growing other crops. Algae can produce biodiesel, biogasoline, ethanol, butanol, methane, and even jet fuel.

(a)   (b)   (c)

Figure 9.22   (a) Tiny algal organisms can be (b) grown in large quantities and eventually (c) turned into a useful fuel such as biodiesel. (credit a: modification of work by Micah Sittig; credit b: modification of work by Robert Kerton; credit c: modification of work by John F. Williams)

According to the US Department of Energy, only 39,000 square kilometers (about 0.4% of the land mass of the US or less than $\frac{1}{7}$ of the area used to grow corn) can produce enough algal fuel to replace all the petroleum-based fuel used in the US. The cost of algal fuels is becoming more competitive—for instance, the US Air Force is producing jet fuel from algae at a total cost of under $5 per gallon.[3] The process used to produce algal fuel is as follows: grow the algae (which use sunlight as their energy source and CO_2 as a raw material); harvest the algae; extract the fuel compounds (or precursor compounds); process as necessary (e.g., perform a transesterification reaction to make biodiesel); purify; and distribute (Figure 9.23).

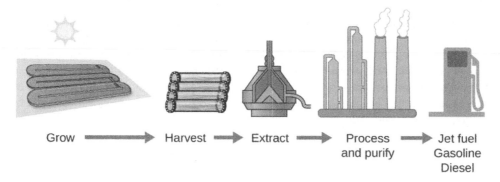

Grow ⟶ Harvest ⟶ Extract ⟶ Process and purify ⟶ Jet fuel Gasoline Diesel

Figure 9.23   Algae convert sunlight and carbon dioxide into oil that is harvested, extracted, purified, and transformed into a variety of renewable fuels.

3. For more on algal fuel, see http://www.theguardian.com/environment/2010/feb/13/algae-solve-pentagon-fuel-problem.

Standard Enthalpy of Formation

A **standard enthalpy of formation** is an enthalpy change for a reaction in which exactly 1 mole of a pure substance is formed from free elements in their most stable states under standard state conditions. These values are especially useful for computing or predicting enthalpy changes for chemical reactions that are impractical or dangerous to carry out, or for processes for which it is difficult to make measurements. If we have values for the appropriate standard enthalpies of formation, we can determine the enthalpy change for any reaction, which we will practice in the next section on Hess's law.

The standard enthalpy of formation of $CO_2(g)$ is −393.5 kJ/mol. This is the enthalpy change for the exothermic reaction:

$$C(s) + O_2(g) \longrightarrow CO_2(g) \qquad \Delta H_f^\circ = \Delta H_{298}^\circ = -393.5 \text{ kJ}$$

starting with the reactants at a pressure of 1 atm and 25 °C (with the carbon present as graphite, the most stable form of carbon under these conditions) and ending with one mole of CO_2, also at 1 atm and 25 °C. For nitrogen dioxide, $NO_2(g)$, ΔH_f° is 33.2 kJ/mol. This is the enthalpy change for the reaction:

$$\tfrac{1}{2}N_2(g) + O_2(g) \longrightarrow NO_2(g) \qquad \Delta H_f^\circ = \Delta H_{298}^\circ = +33.2 \text{ kJ}$$

A reaction equation with $\tfrac{1}{2}$ mole of N_2 and 1 mole of O_2 is correct in this case because the standard enthalpy of formation always refers to 1 mole of product, $NO_2(g)$.

You will find a table of standard enthalpies of formation of many common substances in **Appendix G**. These values indicate that formation reactions range from highly exothermic (such as −2984 kJ/mol for the formation of P_4O_{10}) to strongly endothermic (such as +226.7 kJ/mol for the formation of acetylene, C_2H_2). By definition, the standard enthalpy of formation of an element in its most stable form is equal to zero under standard conditions, which is 1 atm for gases and 1 M for solutions.

Example 9.11

Evaluating an Enthalpy of Formation

Ozone, $O_3(g)$, forms from oxygen, $O_2(g)$, by an endothermic process. Ultraviolet radiation is the source of the energy that drives this reaction in the upper atmosphere. Assuming that both the reactants and products of the reaction are in their standard states, determine the standard enthalpy of formation, ΔH_f° of ozone from the following information:

$$3O_2(g) \longrightarrow 2O_3(g) \qquad \Delta H_{298}^\circ = +286 \text{ kJ}$$

Solution

ΔH_f° is the enthalpy change for the formation of one mole of a substance in its standard state from the elements in their standard states. Thus, ΔH_f° for $O_3(g)$ is the enthalpy change for the reaction:

$$\tfrac{3}{2}O_2(g) \longrightarrow O_3(g)$$

For the formation of 2 mol of $O_3(g)$, $\Delta H^\circ_{298} = +286$ kJ. This ratio, $\left(\dfrac{286\text{ kJ}}{2\text{ mol }O_3}\right)$, can be used as a conversion factor to find the heat produced when 1 mole of $O_3(g)$ is formed, which is the enthalpy of formation for $O_3(g)$:

$$\Delta H^\circ \text{ for 1 mole of } O_3(g) = 1\ \cancel{\text{mol }O_3} \times \frac{286\text{ kJ}}{2\ \cancel{\text{mol }O_3}} = 143\text{ kJ}$$

Therefore, ΔH°_f $[O_3(g)] = +143$ kJ/mol.

Check Your Learning

Hydrogen gas, H_2, reacts explosively with gaseous chlorine, Cl_2, to form hydrogen chloride, $HCl(g)$. What is the enthalpy change for the reaction of 1 mole of $H_2(g)$ with 1 mole of $Cl_2(g)$ if both the reactants and products are at standard state conditions? The standard enthalpy of formation of $HCl(g)$ is −92.3 kJ/mol.

Answer: For the reaction $H_2(g) + Cl_2(g) \longrightarrow 2HCl(g)$ $\Delta H^\circ_{298} = -184.6$ kJ

Example 9.12

Writing Reaction Equations for ΔH°_f

Write the heat of formation reaction equations for:

(a) $C_2H_5OH(l)$

(b) $Ca_3(PO_4)_2(s)$

Solution

Remembering that ΔH°_f reaction equations are for forming 1 mole of the compound from its constituent elements under standard conditions, we have:

(a) $2C(s,\ \text{graphite}) + 3H_2(g) + \frac{1}{2}O_2(g) \longrightarrow C_2H_5OH(l)$

(b) $3Ca(s) + \frac{1}{2}P_4(s) + 4O_2(g) \longrightarrow Ca_3(PO_4)_2(s)$

Note: The standard state of carbon is graphite, and phosphorus exists as P_4.

Check Your Learning

Write the heat of formation reaction equations for:

(a) $C_2H_5OC_2H_5(l)$

(b) $Na_2CO_3(s)$

Answer: (a) $4C(s,\ \text{graphite}) + 5H_2(g) + \frac{1}{2}O_2(g) \longrightarrow C_2H_5OC_2H_5(l)$; (b) $2Na(s) + C(s,\ \text{graphite}) + \frac{3}{2}O_2(g) \longrightarrow Na_2CO_3(s)$

Hess's Law

There are two ways to determine the amount of heat involved in a chemical change: measure it experimentally, or calculate it from other experimentally determined enthalpy changes. Some reactions are difficult, if not impossible, to investigate and make accurate measurements for experimentally. And even when a reaction is not hard to perform or measure, it is convenient to be able to determine the heat involved in a reaction without having to perform an experiment.

This type of calculation usually involves the use of **Hess's law**, which states: *If a process can be written as the sum* *of several stepwise processes, the enthalpy change of the total process equals the sum of the enthalpy changes of the various steps.* Hess's law is valid because enthalpy is a state function: Enthalpy changes depend only on where a chemical process starts and ends, but not on the path it takes from start to finish. For example, we can think of the reaction of carbon with oxygen to form carbon dioxide as occurring either directly or by a two-step process. The direct process is written:

$$C(s) + O_2(g) \longrightarrow CO_2(g) \qquad \Delta H^\circ_{298} = -394 \text{ kJ}$$

In the two-step process, first carbon monoxide is formed:

$$C(s) + \tfrac{1}{2}O_2(g) \longrightarrow CO(g) \qquad \Delta H^\circ_{298} = -111 \text{ kJ}$$

Then, carbon monoxide reacts further to form carbon dioxide:

$$CO(g) + \tfrac{1}{2}O_2(g) \longrightarrow CO_2(g) \qquad \Delta H^\circ_{298} = -283 \text{ kJ}$$

The equation describing the overall reaction is the sum of these two chemical changes:

$$\text{Step 1: } C(s) + \tfrac{1}{2}O_2(g) \longrightarrow CO(g)$$

$$\text{Step 2: } CO(g) + \tfrac{1}{2}O_2(g) \longrightarrow CO_2(g)$$

$$\overline{\text{Sum: } C(s) + \tfrac{1}{2}O_2(g) + CO(g) + \tfrac{1}{2}O_2(g) \longrightarrow CO(g) + CO_2(g)}$$

Because the CO produced in Step 1 is consumed in Step 2, the net change is:

$$C(s) + O_2(g) \longrightarrow CO_2(g)$$

According to Hess's law, the enthalpy change of the reaction will equal the sum of the enthalpy changes of the steps. We can apply the data from the experimental enthalpies of combustion in **Table 9.2** to find the enthalpy change of the entire reaction from its two steps:

$$C(s) + \tfrac{1}{2}O_2(g) \longrightarrow CO(g) \qquad \Delta H^\circ_{298} = -111 \text{ kJ}$$

$$\underline{CO(g) + \tfrac{1}{2}O_2(g) \longrightarrow CO_2(g) \quad \Delta H^\circ_{298} = -283 \text{ kJ}}$$

$$C(s) + O_2(g) \longrightarrow CO_2(g) \qquad \Delta H^\circ_{298} = -394 \text{ kJ}$$

The result is shown in **Figure 9.24**. We see that ΔH of the overall reaction is the same whether it occurs in one step or two. This finding (overall ΔH for the reaction = sum of ΔH values for reaction "steps" in the overall reaction) is true in general for chemical and physical processes.

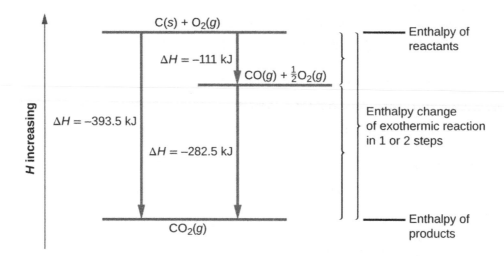

Figure 9.24 The formation of $CO_2(g)$ from its elements can be thought of as occurring in two steps, which sum to the overall reaction, as described by Hess's law. The horizontal blue lines represent enthalpies. For an exothermic process, the products are at lower enthalpy than are the reactants.

Before we further practice using Hess's law, let us recall two important features of ΔH.

1. ΔH is directly proportional to the quantities of reactants or products. For example, the enthalpy change for the reaction forming 1 mole of $NO_2(g)$ is +33.2 kJ:

$$\tfrac{1}{2}N_2(g) + O_2(g) \longrightarrow NO_2(g) \qquad \Delta H = +33.2 \text{ kJ}$$

When 2 moles of NO_2 (twice as much) are formed, the ΔH will be twice as large:

$$N_2(g) + 2O_2(g) \longrightarrow 2NO_2(g) \qquad \Delta H = +66.4 \text{ kJ}$$

In general, if we multiply or divide an equation by a number, then the enthalpy change should also be multiplied or divided by the same number.

2. ΔH for a reaction in one direction is equal in magnitude and opposite in sign to ΔH for the reaction in the reverse direction. For example, given that:

$$H_2(g) + Cl_2(g) \longrightarrow 2HCl(g) \qquad \Delta H = -184.6 \text{ kJ}$$

Then, for the "reverse" reaction, the enthalpy change is also "reversed":

$$2HCl(g) \longrightarrow H_2(g) + Cl_2(g) \qquad \Delta H = +184.6 \text{ kJ}$$

Example 9.13

Stepwise Calculation of ΔH_f° Using Hess's Law

Determine the enthalpy of formation, ΔH_f°, of $FeCl_3(s)$ from the enthalpy changes of the following two-step process that occurs under standard state conditions:

$$Fe(s) + Cl_2(g) \longrightarrow FeCl_2(s) \qquad \Delta H^\circ = -341.8 \text{ kJ}$$
$$FeCl_2(s) + \tfrac{1}{2}Cl_2(g) \longrightarrow FeCl_3(s) \qquad \Delta H^\circ = -57.7 \text{ kJ}$$

Solution

We are trying to find the standard enthalpy of formation of $FeCl_3(s)$, which is equal to ΔH° for the reaction:

$$Fe(s) + \tfrac{3}{2}Cl_2(g) \longrightarrow FeCl_3(s) \qquad \Delta H_f^\circ = ?$$

Looking at the reactions, we see that the reaction for which we want to find $\Delta H°$ is the sum of the two reactions with known ΔH values, so we must sum their ΔHs:

$$Fe(s) + Cl_2(g) \longrightarrow FeCl_2(s) \qquad \Delta H° = -341.8 \text{ kJ}$$

$$\underline{FeCl_2(s) + \tfrac{1}{2}Cl_2(g) \longrightarrow FeCl_3(s) \qquad \Delta H° = -57.7 \text{ kJ}}$$

$$Fe(s) + \tfrac{1}{2}Cl_2(g) \longrightarrow FeCl_3(s) \qquad \Delta H° = -399.5 \text{ kJ}$$

The enthalpy of formation, $\Delta H_f°$, of $FeCl_3(s)$ is -399.5 kJ/mol.

Check Your Learning

Calculate ΔH for the process:

$$N_2(g) + 2O_2(g) \longrightarrow 2NO_2(g)$$

from the following information:

$$N_2(g) + O_2(g) \longrightarrow 2NO(g) \qquad \Delta H = 180.5 \text{ kJ}$$

$$NO(g) + \tfrac{1}{2}O_2(g) \longrightarrow NO_2(g) \qquad \Delta H = -57.06 \text{ kJ}$$

Answer: 66.4 kJ

Here is a less straightforward example that illustrates the thought process involved in solving many Hess's law problems. It shows how we can find many standard enthalpies of formation (and other values of ΔH) if they are difficult to determine experimentally.

Example 9.14

A More Challenging Problem Using Hess's Law

Chlorine monofluoride can react with fluorine to form chlorine trifluoride:

(i) $ClF(g) + F_2(g) \longrightarrow ClF_3(g) \qquad \Delta H° = ?$

Use the reactions here to determine the $\Delta H°$ for reaction *(i)*:

(ii) $2OF_2(g) \longrightarrow O_2(g) + 2F_2(g) \qquad \Delta H°_{(ii)} = -49.4 \text{ kJ}$

(iii) $2ClF(g) + O_2(g) \longrightarrow Cl_2O(g) + OF_2(g) \qquad \Delta H°_{(iii)} = +205.6 \text{ kJ}$

(iv) $ClF_3(g) + O_2(g) \longrightarrow \tfrac{1}{2}Cl_2O(g) + \tfrac{3}{2}OF_2(g) \qquad \Delta H°_{(iv)} = +266.7 \text{ kJ}$

Solution

Our goal is to manipulate and combine reactions *(ii)*, *(iii)*, and *(iv)* such that they add up to reaction *(i)*. Going from left to right in *(i)*, we first see that $ClF(g)$ is needed as a reactant. This can be obtained by multiplying reaction *(iii)* by $\tfrac{1}{2}$, which means that the $\Delta H°$ change is also multiplied by $\tfrac{1}{2}$:

$$ClF(g) + \tfrac{1}{2}O_2(g) \longrightarrow \tfrac{1}{2}Cl_2O(g) + \tfrac{1}{2}OF_2(g) \qquad \Delta H° = \tfrac{1}{2}(205.6) = +102.8 \text{ kJ}$$

Next, we see that F_2 is also needed as a reactant. To get this, reverse and halve reaction *(ii)*, which means that the $\Delta H°$ changes sign and is halved:

$$\tfrac{1}{2}O_2(g) + F_2(g) \longrightarrow OF_2(g) \qquad \Delta H° = +24.7 \text{ kJ}$$

To get ClF_3 as a product, reverse *(iv)*, changing the sign of $\Delta H°$:

$$\tfrac{1}{2}Cl_2O(g) + \tfrac{3}{2}OF_2(g) \longrightarrow ClF_3(g) + O_2(g) \qquad \Delta H° = -266.7 \text{ kJ}$$

Now check to make sure that these reactions add up to the reaction we want:

$$ClF(g) + \frac{1}{2}O_2(g) \longrightarrow \frac{1}{2}Cl_2O(g) + \frac{1}{2}OF_2(g) \qquad \Delta H° = +102.8 \text{ kJ}$$

$$\frac{1}{2}O_2(g) + F_2(g) \longrightarrow OF_2(g) \qquad\qquad\qquad\qquad \Delta H° = +24.7 \text{ kJ}$$

$$\frac{1}{2}Cl_2O(g) + \frac{3}{2}OF_2(g) \longrightarrow ClF_3(g) + O_2(g) \qquad \Delta H° = -266.7 \text{ kJ}$$

$$ClF(g) + F_2 \longrightarrow ClF_3(g) \qquad\qquad\qquad\qquad \Delta H° = -139.2 \text{ kJ}$$

Reactants $\frac{1}{2}O_2$ and $\frac{1}{2}O_2$ cancel out product O_2; product $\frac{1}{2}Cl_2O$ cancels reactant $\frac{1}{2}Cl_2O$; and reactant $\frac{3}{2}OF_2$ is cancelled by products $\frac{1}{2}OF_2$ and OF_2. This leaves only reactants $ClF(g)$ and $F_2(g)$ and product $ClF_3(g)$, which are what we want. Since summing these three modified reactions yields the reaction of interest, summing the three modified $\Delta H°$ values will give the desired $\Delta H°$:

$$\Delta H° = (+102.8 \text{ kJ}) + (24.7 \text{ kJ}) + (-266.7 \text{ kJ}) = -139.2 \text{ kJ}$$

Check Your Learning

Aluminum chloride can be formed from its elements:

(i) $2Al(s) + 3Cl_2(g) \longrightarrow 2AlCl_3(s) \qquad \Delta H° = ?$

Use the reactions here to determine the $\Delta H°$ for reaction *(i)*:

(ii) $HCl(g) \longrightarrow HCl(aq) \qquad \Delta H°_{(ii)} = -74.8 \text{ kJ}$

(iii) $H_2(g) + Cl_2(g) \longrightarrow 2HCl(g) \qquad \Delta H°_{(iii)} = -185 \text{ kJ}$

(iv) $AlCl_3(aq) \longrightarrow AlCl_3(s) \qquad \Delta H°_{(iv)} = +323 \text{ kJ/mol}$

(v) $2Al(s) + 6HCl(aq) \longrightarrow 2AlCl_3(aq) + 3H_2(g) \qquad \Delta H°_{(v)} = -1049 \text{ kJ}$

Answer: -1407 kJ

We also can use Hess's law to determine the enthalpy change of any reaction if the corresponding enthalpies of formation of the reactants and products are available. The stepwise reactions we consider are: (i) decompositions of the reactants into their component elements (for which the enthalpy changes are proportional to the negative of the enthalpies of formation of the reactants), followed by (ii) re-combinations of the elements to give the products (with the enthalpy changes proportional to the enthalpies of formation of the products). The standard enthalpy change of the overall reaction is therefore equal to: (ii) the sum of the standard enthalpies of formation of all the products plus (i) the sum of the negatives of the standard enthalpies of formation of the reactants. This is usually rearranged slightly to be written as follows, with $\sum$ representing "the sum of" and n standing for the stoichiometric coefficients:

$$\Delta H°_{reaction} = \sum n \times \Delta H°_f \text{ (products)} - \sum n \times \Delta H°_f \text{ (reactants)}$$

The following example shows in detail why this equation is valid, and how to use it to calculate the enthalpy change for a reaction of interest.

Example 9.15

Using Hess's Law

What is the standard enthalpy change for the reaction:

$$3NO_2(g) + H_2O(l) \longrightarrow 2HNO_3(aq) + NO(g) \qquad \Delta H° = ?$$

Solution: Using the Equation

Use the special form of Hess's law given previously:

$$\Delta H^\circ_{\text{reaction}} = \sum n \times \Delta H^\circ_{\text{f}} \text{ (products)} - \sum n \times \Delta H^\circ_{\text{f}} \text{ (reactants)}$$

$$= \left[2 \text{ mol HNO}_3 \times \frac{-207.4 \text{ kJ}}{\text{mol HNO}_3(aq)} + 1 \text{ mol NO}(g) \times \frac{+90.2 \text{ kJ}}{\text{mol NO}(g)} \right]$$

$$- \left[3 \text{ mol NO}_2(g) \times \frac{+33.2 \text{ kJ}}{\text{mol NO}_2(g)} + 1 \text{ mol H}_2\text{O}(l) \times \frac{-285.8 \text{ kJ}}{\text{mol H}_2\text{O}(l)} \right]$$

$$= 2(-207.4 \text{ kJ}) + 1(+90.2 \text{ kJ}) - 3(+33.2 \text{ kJ}) - 1(-285.8 \text{ kJ})$$

$$= -138.4 \text{ kJ}$$

Solution: Supporting Why the General Equation Is Valid

Alternatively, we can write this reaction as the sum of the decompositions of $3NO_2(g)$ and $1H_2O(l)$ into their constituent elements, and the formation of $2HNO_3(aq)$ and $1NO(g)$ from their constituent elements. Writing out these reactions, and noting their relationships to the $\Delta H^\circ_{\text{f}}$ values for these compounds (from Appendix G), we have:

$$3NO_2(g) \longrightarrow 3/2N_2(g) + 3O_2(g) \qquad \Delta H^\circ_1 = -99.6 \text{ kJ}$$

$$H_2O(l) \longrightarrow H_2(g) + \tfrac{1}{2}O_2(g) \qquad \Delta H^\circ_2 = +285.8 \text{ kJ} \, [-1 \times \Delta H^\circ_{\text{f}} \, (H_2O)]$$

$$H_2(g) + N_2(g) + 3O_2(g) \longrightarrow 2HNO_3(aq) \qquad \Delta H^\circ_3 = -414.8 \text{ kJ} \, [2 \times \Delta H^\circ_{\text{f}} \, (HNO_3)]$$

$$\tfrac{1}{2}N_2(g) + \tfrac{1}{2}O_2(g) \longrightarrow NO(g) \qquad \Delta H^\circ_4 = +90.2 \text{ kJ} \, [1 \times (NO)]$$

Summing these reaction equations gives the reaction we are interested in:

$$3NO_2(g) + H_2O(l) \longrightarrow 2HNO_3(aq) + NO(g)$$

Summing their enthalpy changes gives the value we want to determine:

$$\Delta H^\circ_{\text{rxn}} = \Delta H^\circ_1 + \Delta H^\circ_2 + \Delta H^\circ_3 + \Delta H^\circ_4 = (-99.6 \text{ kJ}) + (+285.8 \text{ kJ}) + (-414.8 \text{ kJ}) + (+90.2 \text{ kJ})$$

$$= -138.4 \text{ kJ}$$

So the standard enthalpy change for this reaction is $\Delta H^\circ = -138.4$ kJ.

Note that this result was obtained by (1) multiplying the $\Delta H^\circ_{\text{f}}$ of each product by its stoichiometric coefficient and summing those values, (2) multiplying the $\Delta H^\circ_{\text{f}}$ of each reactant by its stoichiometric coefficient and summing those values, and then (3) subtracting the result found in (2) from the result found in (1). This is also the procedure in using the general equation, as shown.

Check Your Learning

Calculate the heat of combustion of 1 mole of ethanol, $C_2H_5OH(l)$, when $H_2O(l)$ and $CO_2(g)$ are formed. Use the following enthalpies of formation: $C_2H_5OH(l)$, −278 kJ/mol; $H_2O(l)$, −286 kJ/mol; and $CO_2(g)$, −394 kJ/mol.

Answer: −1368 kJ/mol

9.4 Strengths of Ionic and Covalent Bonds

By the end of this section, you will be able to:

- Describe the energetics of covalent and ionic bond formation and breakage
- Use the Born-Haber cycle to compute lattice energies for ionic compounds
- Use average covalent bond energies to estimate enthalpies of reaction

A bond's strength describes how strongly each atom is joined to another atom, and therefore how much energy is required to break the bond between the two atoms.

It is essential to remember that energy must be added to break chemical bonds (an endothermic process), whereas forming chemical bonds releases energy (an exothermic process). In the case of H_2, the covalent bond is very strong; a large amount of energy, 436 kJ, must be added to break the bonds in one mole of hydrogen molecules and cause the atoms to separate:

$$H_2(g) \longrightarrow 2H(g) \qquad \text{bond energy} = 436\,\text{kJ}$$

Conversely, the same amount of energy is released when one mole of H_2 molecules forms from two moles of H atoms:

$$2H(g) \longrightarrow H_2(g) \qquad \text{bond energy} = -436\,\text{kJ}$$

Bond Strength: Covalent Bonds

Stable molecules exist because covalent bonds hold the atoms together. We measure the strength of a covalent bond by the energy required to break it, that is, the energy necessary to separate the bonded atoms. Separating any pair of bonded atoms requires energy (see Figure 4.4). The stronger a bond, the greater the energy required to break it.

The energy required to break a specific covalent bond in one mole of gaseous molecules is called the bond energy or the bond dissociation energy. The bond energy for a diatomic molecule, D_{X-Y}, is defined as the standard enthalpy change for the endothermic reaction:

$$XY(g) \longrightarrow X(g) + Y(g) \qquad D_{X-Y} = \Delta H°$$

For example, the bond energy of the pure covalent H–H bond, D_{H-H}, is 436 kJ per mole of H–H bonds broken:

$$H_2(g) \longrightarrow 2H(g) \qquad D_{H-H} = \Delta H° = 436\,\text{kJ}$$

Molecules with three or more atoms have two or more bonds. The sum of all bond energies in such a molecule is equal to the standard enthalpy change for the endothermic reaction that breaks all the bonds in the molecule. For example, the sum of the four C–H bond energies in CH_4, 1660 kJ, is equal to the standard enthalpy change of the reaction:

The average C–H bond energy, D_{C-H}, is 1660/4 = 415 kJ/mol because there are four moles of C–H bonds broken per mole of the reaction. Although the four C–H bonds are equivalent in the original molecule, they do not each require the same energy to break; once the first bond is broken (which requires 439 kJ/mol), the remaining bonds are easier to break. The 415 kJ/mol value is the average, not the exact value required to break any one bond.

The strength of a bond between two atoms increases as the number of electron pairs in the bond increases. Generally, as the bond strength increases, the bond length decreases. Thus, we find that triple bonds are stronger and shorter than double bonds between the same two atoms; likewise, double bonds are stronger and shorter than single bonds between the same two atoms. Average bond energies for some common bonds appear in Table 9.3, and a comparison of bond lengths and bond strengths for some common bonds appears in Table 9.4. When one atom bonds to various atoms in a group, the bond strength typically decreases as we move down the group. For example, C–F is 439 kJ/mol, C–Cl is 330 kJ/mol, and C–Br is 275 kJ/mol.

Bond Energies (kJ/mol)

Bond	Bond Energy	Bond	Bond Energy	Bond	Bond Energy
H–H	436	C–S	260	F–Cl	255
H–C	415	C–Cl	330	F–Br	235
H–N	390	C–Br	275	Si–Si	230

Table 9.3

Bond Energies (kJ/mol)

Bond	Bond Energy	Bond	Bond Energy	Bond	Bond Energy
H–O	464	C–I	240	Si–P	215
H–F	569	N–N	160	Si–S	225
H–Si	395	N = N	418	Si–Cl	359
H–P	320	N ≡ N	946	Si–Br	290
H–S	340	N–O	200	Si–I	215
H–Cl	432	N–F	270	P–P	215
H–Br	370	N–P	210	P–S	230
H–I	295	N–Cl	200	P–Cl	330
C–C	345	N–Br	245	P–Br	270
C = C	611	O–O	140	P–I	215
C ≡ C	837	O = O	498	S–S	215
C–N	290	O–F	160	S–Cl	250
C = N	615	O–Si	370	S–Br	215
C ≡ N	891	O–P	350	Cl–Cl	243
C–O	350	O–Cl	205	Cl–Br	220
C = O	741	O–I	200	Cl–I	210
C ≡ O	1080	F–F	160	Br–Br	190
C–F	439	F–Si	540	Br–I	180
C–Si	360	F–P	489	I–I	150
C–P	265	F–S	285		

Table 9.3

Average Bond Lengths and Bond Energies for Some Common Bonds

Bond	Bond Length (Å)	Bond Energy (kJ/mol)
C–C	1.54	345
C = C	1.34	611
C ≡ C	1.20	837
C–N	1.43	290
C = N	1.38	615
C ≡ N	1.16	891

Table 9.4

Average Bond Lengths and Bond Energies for Some Common Bonds

Bond	Bond Length (Å)	Bond Energy (kJ/mol)
C–O	1.43	350
C = O	1.23	741
C ≡ O	1.13	1080

Table 9.4

The bond energy is the difference between the energy minimum (which occurs at the bond distance) and the energy of the two separated atoms. This is the quantity of energy released when the bond is formed. Conversely, the same amount of energy is required to break the bond. For the H_2 molecule shown in **Figure 5.2**, at the bond distance of 74 pm the system is 7.24×10^{-19} J lower in energy than the two separated hydrogen atoms. This may seem like a small number. However, as we will learn in more detail later, bond energies are often discussed on a per-mole basis. For example, it requires 7.24×10^{-19} J to break one H–H bond, but it takes 4.36×10^5 J to break 1 mole of H–H bonds. A comparison of some bond lengths and energies is shown in **m61763 (http://cnx.org/content/m61763/ 1.4/#CNX_Chem_08_01Morse)** and **Table 9.3**. We can find many of these bonds in a variety of molecules, and this table provides average values. For example, breaking the first C–H bond in CH_4 requires 439.3 kJ/mol, while breaking the first C–H bond in $H–CH_2C_6H_5$ (a common paint thinner) requires 375.5 kJ/mol.

As seen in **Table 9.3** and **Table 9.4**, an average carbon-carbon single bond is 347 kJ/mol, while in a carbon-carbon double bond, the π bond increases the bond strength by 267 kJ/mol. Adding an additional π bond causes a further increase of 225 kJ/mol. We can see a similar pattern when we compare other σ and π bonds. Thus, each individual π bond is generally weaker than a corresponding σ bond between the same two atoms. In a σ bond, there is a greater degree of orbital overlap than in a π bond.

We can use bond energies to calculate approximate enthalpy changes for reactions where enthalpies of formation are not available. Calculations of this type will also tell us whether a reaction is exothermic or endothermic. An exothermic reaction (ΔH negative, heat produced) results when the bonds in the products are stronger than the bonds in the reactants. An endothermic reaction (ΔH positive, heat absorbed) results when the bonds in the products are weaker than those in the reactants.

The enthalpy change, ΔH, for a chemical reaction is approximately equal to the sum of the energy required to break all bonds in the reactants (energy "in", positive sign) plus the energy released when all bonds are formed in the products (energy "out," negative sign). This can be expressed mathematically in the following way:

$$\Delta H = \Sigma D_{\text{bonds broken}} - \Sigma D_{\text{bonds formed}}$$

In this expression, the symbol Σ means "the sum of" and D represents the bond energy in kilojoules per mole, which is always a positive number. The bond energy is obtained from a table (like **Table 9.4**) and will depend on whether the particular bond is a single, double, or triple bond. Thus, in calculating enthalpies in this manner, it is important that we consider the bonding in all reactants and products. Because D values are typically averages for one type of bond in many different molecules, this calculation provides a rough estimate, not an exact value, for the enthalpy of reaction.

Consider the following reaction:

$$H_2(g) + Cl_2(g) \longrightarrow 2HCl(g)$$

or

$$H–H(g) + Cl–Cl(g) \longrightarrow 2H–Cl(g)$$

To form two moles of HCl, one mole of H–H bonds and one mole of Cl–Cl bonds must be broken. The energy required to break these bonds is the sum of the bond energy of the H–H bond (436 kJ/mol) and the Cl–Cl bond (243 kJ/mol). During the reaction, two moles of H–Cl bonds are formed (bond energy = 432 kJ/mol), releasing 2×432

kJ; or 864 kJ. Because the bonds in the products are stronger than those in the reactants, the reaction releases more energy than it consumes:

$$\Delta H = \Sigma D_{\text{bonds broken}} - \Sigma D_{\text{bonds formed}}$$
$$\Delta H = [D_{\text{H-H}} + D_{\text{Cl-Cl}}] - 2D_{\text{H-Cl}}$$
$$= [436 + 243] - 2(432) = -185 \text{ kJ}$$

This excess energy is released as heat, so the reaction is exothermic. Appendix G gives a value for the standard molar enthalpy of formation of HCl(g), ΔH_f°, of −92.307 kJ/mol. Twice that value is −184.6 kJ, which agrees well with the answer obtained earlier for the formation of two moles of HCl.

Example 9.16

Using Bond Energies to Calculate Approximate Enthalpy Changes

Methanol, CH_3OH, may be an excellent alternative fuel. The high-temperature reaction of steam and carbon produces a mixture of the gases carbon monoxide, CO, and hydrogen, H_2, from which methanol can be produced. Using the bond energies in Table 9.4, calculate the approximate enthalpy change, ΔH, for the reaction here:

$$CO(g) + 2H_2(g) \longrightarrow CH_3OH(g)$$

Solution

First, we need to write the Lewis structures of the reactants and the products:

From this, we see that ΔH for this reaction involves the energy required to break a C–O triple bond and two H–H single bonds, as well as the energy produced by the formation of three C–H single bonds, a C–O single bond, and an O–H single bond. We can express this as follows:

$$\Delta H = \Sigma D_{\text{bonds broken}} - \Sigma D_{\text{bonds formed}}$$
$$\Delta H = [D_{C \equiv O} + 2(D_{H-H})] - [3(D_{C-H}) + D_{C-O} + D_{O-H}]$$

Using the bond energy values in Table 9.4, we obtain:

$$\Delta H = [1080 + 2(436)] - [3(415) + 350 + 464]$$
$$= -107 \text{ kJ}$$

We can compare this value to the value calculated based on ΔH_f° data from Appendix G:

$$\Delta H = [\Delta H_f^\circ \ CH_3OH(g)] - [\Delta H_f^\circ \ CO(g) + 2 \times \Delta H_f^\circ \ H_2]$$
$$= [-201.0] - [-110.52 + 2 \times 0]$$
$$= -90.5 \text{ kJ}$$

Note that there is a fairly significant gap between the values calculated using the two different methods. This occurs because D values are the *average* of different bond strengths; therefore, they often give only rough agreement with other data.

Check Your Learning

Ethyl alcohol, CH_3CH_2OH, was one of the first organic chemicals deliberately synthesized by humans. It has many uses in industry, and it is the alcohol contained in alcoholic beverages. It can be obtained by the fermentation of sugar or synthesized by the hydration of ethylene in the following reaction:

Using the bond energies in Table 9.4, calculate an approximate enthalpy change, ΔH, for this reaction.

Answer: -35 kJ

Ionic Bond Strength and Lattice Energy

An ionic compound is stable because of the electrostatic attraction between its positive and negative ions. The lattice energy of a compound is a measure of the strength of this attraction. The **lattice energy ($\Delta H_{lattice}$)** of an ionic compound is defined as the energy required to separate one mole of the solid into its component gaseous ions. For the ionic solid MX, the lattice energy is the enthalpy change of the process:

$$MX(s) \longrightarrow M^{n+}(g) + X^{n-}(g) \qquad \Delta H_{lattice}$$

Note that we are using the convention where the ionic solid is separated into ions, so our lattice energies will be *endothermic* (positive values). Some texts use the equivalent but opposite convention, defining lattice energy as the energy released when separate ions combine to form a lattice and giving negative (exothermic) values. Thus, if you are looking up lattice energies in another reference, be certain to check which definition is being used. In both cases, a larger magnitude for lattice energy indicates a more stable ionic compound. For sodium chloride, $\Delta H_{lattice} = 769$ kJ. Thus, it requires 769 kJ to separate one mole of solid NaCl into gaseous Na^+ and Cl^- ions. When one mole each of gaseous Na^+ and Cl^- ions form solid NaCl, 769 kJ of heat is released.

The lattice energy $\Delta H_{lattice}$ of an ionic crystal can be expressed by the following equation (derived from Coulomb's law, governing the forces between electric charges):

$$\Delta H_{lattice} = \frac{C(Z^+)(Z^-)}{R_0}$$

in which C is a constant that depends on the type of crystal structure; Z^+ and Z^- are the charges on the ions; and R_0 is the interionic distance (the sum of the radii of the positive and negative ions). Thus, the lattice energy of an ionic crystal increases rapidly as the charges of the ions increase and the sizes of the ions decrease. When all other parameters are kept constant, doubling the charge of both the cation and anion quadruples the lattice energy. For example, the lattice energy of LiF (Z^+ and $Z^- = 1$) is 1023 kJ/mol, whereas that of MgO (Z^+ and $Z^- = 2$) is 3900 kJ/mol (R_0 is nearly the same—about 200 pm for both compounds).

Different interatomic distances produce different lattice energies. For example, we can compare the lattice energy of MgF_2 (2957 kJ/mol) to that of MgI_2 (2327 kJ/mol) to observe the effect on lattice energy of the smaller ionic size of F^- as compared to I^-.

Example 9.17

Lattice Energy Comparisons

The precious gem ruby is aluminum oxide, Al_2O_3, containing traces of Cr^{3+}. The compound Al_2Se_3 is used in the fabrication of some semiconductor devices. Which has the larger lattice energy, Al_2O_3 or Al_2Se_3?

Solution

In these two ionic compounds, the charges Z^+ and Z^- are the same, so the difference in lattice energy will depend upon R_0. The O^{2-} ion is smaller than the Se^{2-} ion. Thus, Al_2O_3 would have a shorter interionic distance than Al_2Se_3, and Al_2O_3 would have the larger lattice energy.

Check Your Learning

Zinc oxide, ZnO, is a very effective sunscreen. How would the lattice energy of ZnO compare to that of NaCl?

Answer: ZnO would have the larger lattice energy because the Z values of both the cation and the anion in ZnO are greater, and the interionic distance of ZnO is smaller than that of NaCl.

The Born-Haber Cycle

It is not possible to measure lattice energies directly. However, the lattice energy can be calculated using the equation given in the previous section or by using a thermochemical cycle. The **Born-Haber cycle** is an application of Hess's law that breaks down the formation of an ionic solid into a series of individual steps:

- ΔH_f°, the standard enthalpy of formation of the compound

- *IE*, the ionization energy of the metal

- *EA*, the electron affinity of the nonmetal

- ΔH_s°, the enthalpy of sublimation of the metal

- *D*, the bond dissociation energy of the nonmetal

- $\Delta H_{lattice}$, the lattice energy of the compound

Figure 9.25 diagrams the Born-Haber cycle for the formation of solid cesium fluoride.

Figure 9.25 The Born-Haber cycle shows the relative energies of each step involved in the formation of an ionic solid from the necessary elements in their reference states.

We begin with the elements in their most common states, Cs(*s*) and F$_2$(*g*). The ΔH_s° represents the conversion of solid cesium into a gas, and then the ionization energy converts the gaseous cesium atoms into cations. In the next step, we account for the energy required to break the F–F bond to produce fluorine atoms. Converting one mole of fluorine atoms into fluoride ions is an exothermic process, so this step gives off energy (the electron affinity) and is shown as decreasing along the *y*-axis. We now have one mole of Cs cations and one mole of F anions. These ions combine to produce solid cesium fluoride. The enthalpy change in this step is the negative of the lattice energy, so it is also an exothermic quantity. The total energy involved in this conversion is equal to the experimentally determined enthalpy of formation, ΔH_f°, of the compound from its elements. In this case, the overall change is exothermic.

Hess's law can also be used to show the relationship between the enthalpies of the individual steps and the enthalpy of formation. Table 9.5 shows this for cesium chloride, $CsCl_2$.

Enthalpy of sublimation of Cs(s)	$Cs(s) \longrightarrow Cs(g) \qquad \Delta H = \Delta H_s^\circ = 76.5 kJ$
One-half of the bond energy of Cl_2	$\frac{1}{2} Cl_2(g) \longrightarrow Cl(g) \qquad \Delta H = \frac{1}{2} D = 122 kJ$
Ionization energy of Na(g)	$Na(g) \longrightarrow Na^+(g) + e^- \qquad \Delta H = IE = 496 kJ$
Negative of the electron affinity of Cl	$Cl(g) + e^- \longrightarrow Cl^-(g) \qquad \Delta H = -EA = -368 kJ$
Negative of the lattice energy of NaCl(s)	$Na^+(g) + Cl^-(g) \longrightarrow NaCl(s) \qquad \Delta H = -\Delta H_{lattice} = ?$
Enthalpy of formation of NaCl(s), add steps 1–5	$\Delta H = \Delta H_f^\circ = \Delta H_s^\circ + \frac{1}{2}D + IE + (-EA) + (-\Delta H_{lattice})$ $Na(s) + \frac{1}{2} Cl_2(g) \longrightarrow NaCl(s) = -411 kJ$

Table 9.5

Thus, the lattice energy can be calculated from other values. For cesium chloride, using this data, the lattice energy is:

$$\Delta H_{lattice} = (411 + 109 + 122 + 496 + 368) \, kJ = 770 \, kJ$$

The Born-Haber cycle may also be used to calculate any one of the other quantities in the equation for lattice energy, provided that the remainder is known. For example, if the relevant enthalpy of sublimation ΔH_s°, ionization energy (IE), bond dissociation enthalpy (D), lattice energy $\Delta H_{lattice}$, and standard enthalpy of formation ΔH_f° are known, the Born-Haber cycle can be used to determine the electron affinity of an atom.

Lattice energies calculated for ionic compounds are typically much higher than bond dissociation energies measured for covalent bonds. Whereas lattice energies typically fall in the range of 600–4000 kJ/mol (some even higher), covalent bond dissociation energies are typically between 150–400 kJ/mol for single bonds. Keep in mind, however, that these are not directly comparable values. For ionic compounds, lattice energies are associated with many interactions, as cations and anions pack together in an extended lattice. For covalent bonds, the bond dissociation energy is associated with the interaction of just two atoms.

Key Terms

bomb calorimeter device designed to measure the energy change for processes occurring under conditions of constant volume; commonly used for reactions involving solid and gaseous reactants or products

bond energy (also, bond dissociation energy) energy required to break a covalent bond in a gaseous substance

Born-Haber cycle thermochemical cycle relating the various energetic steps involved in the formation of an ionic solid from the relevant elements

calorie (cal) unit of heat or other energy; the amount of energy required to raise 1 gram of water by 1 degree Celsius; 1 cal is defined as 4.184 J

calorimeter device used to measure the amount of heat absorbed or released in a chemical or physical process

calorimetry process of measuring the amount of heat involved in a chemical or physical process

chemical thermodynamics area of science that deals with the relationships between heat, work, and all forms of energy associated with chemical and physical processes

endothermic process chemical reaction or physical change that absorbs heat

energy capacity to supply heat or do work

enthalpy (H) sum of a system's internal energy and the mathematical product of its pressure and volume

enthalpy change (ΔH) heat released or absorbed by a system under constant pressure during a chemical or physical process

exothermic process chemical reaction or physical change that releases heat

expansion work (pressure-volume work) work done as a system expands or contracts against external pressure

first law of thermodynamics internal energy of a system changes due to heat flow in or out of the system or work done on or by the system

heat (q) transfer of thermal energy between two bodies

heat capacity (C) extensive property of a body of matter that represents the quantity of heat required to increase its temperature by 1 degree Celsius (or 1 kelvin)

Hess's law if a process can be represented as the sum of several steps, the enthalpy change of the process equals the sum of the enthalpy changes of the steps

hydrocarbon compound composed only of hydrogen and carbon; the major component of fossil fuels

internal energy (U) total of all possible kinds of energy present in a substance or substances

joule (J) SI unit of energy; 1 joule is the kinetic energy of an object with a mass of 2 kilograms moving with a velocity of 1 meter per second, 1 J = 1 kg m^2/s and 4.184 J = 1 cal

kinetic energy energy of a moving body, in joules, equal to $\frac{1}{2}mv^2$ (where m = mass and v = velocity)

lattice energy ($\Delta H_{lattice}$) energy required to separate one mole of an ionic solid into its component gaseous ions

nutritional calorie (Calorie) unit used for quantifying energy provided by digestion of foods, defined as 1000 cal or 1 kcal

potential energy energy of a particle or system of particles derived from relative position, composition, or condition

specific heat capacity (c) intensive property of a substance that represents the quantity of heat required to raise the temperature of 1 gram of the substance by 1 degree Celsius (or 1 kelvin)

standard enthalpy of combustion (ΔH_c°) heat released when one mole of a compound undergoes complete combustion under standard conditions

standard enthalpy of formation (ΔH_f°) enthalpy change of a chemical reaction in which 1 mole of a pure substance is formed from its elements in their most stable states under standard state conditions

standard state set of physical conditions as accepted as common reference conditions for reporting thermodynamic properties; 1 bar of pressure, and solutions at 1 molar concentrations, usually at a temperature of 298.15 K

state function property depending only on the state of a system, and not the path taken to reach that state

surroundings all matter other than the system being studied

system portion of matter undergoing a chemical or physical change being studied

temperature intensive property of matter that is a quantitative measure of "hotness" and "coldness"

thermal energy kinetic energy associated with the random motion of atoms and molecules

thermochemistry study of measuring the amount of heat absorbed or released during a chemical reaction or a physical change

work (w) energy transfer due to changes in external, macroscopic variables such as pressure and volume; or causing matter to move against an opposing force

Key Equations

- $q = c \times m \times \Delta T = c \times m \times (T_{\text{final}} - T_{\text{initial}})$

- $\Delta U = q + w$

- $\Delta H^\circ_{\text{reaction}} = \sum n \times \Delta H_f^\circ \text{ (products)} - \sum n \times \Delta H_f^\circ \text{ (reactants)}$

- Bond energy for a diatomic molecule: $XY(g) \longrightarrow X(g) + Y(g)$ $D_{X-Y} = \Delta H^\circ$

- Enthalpy change: $\Delta H = \Sigma D_{\text{bonds broken}} - \Sigma D_{\text{bonds formed}}$

- Lattice energy for a solid MX: $MX(s) \longrightarrow M^{n+}(g) + X^{n-}(g)$ $\Delta H_{\text{lattice}}$

- Lattice energy for an ionic crystal: $\Delta H_{\text{lattice}} = \dfrac{C(Z^+)(Z^-)}{R_0}$

Summary

9.1 Energy Basics

Energy is the capacity to do work (applying a force to move matter). Kinetic energy (KE) is the energy of motion; potential energy is energy due to relative position, composition, or condition. When energy is converted from one form into another, energy is neither created nor destroyed (law of conservation of energy or first law of thermodynamics).

Matter has thermal energy due to the KE of its molecules and temperature that corresponds to the average KE of its molecules. Heat is energy that is transferred between objects at different temperatures; it flows from a high to a low temperature. Chemical and physical processes can absorb heat (endothermic) or release heat (exothermic). The SI unit of energy, heat, and work is the joule (J).

Specific heat and heat capacity are measures of the energy needed to change the temperature of a substance or object. The amount of heat absorbed or released by a substance depends directly on the type of substance, its mass, and the temperature change it undergoes.

9.2 Calorimetry

Calorimetry is used to measure the amount of thermal energy transferred in a chemical or physical process. This requires careful measurement of the temperature change that occurs during the process and the masses of the system and surroundings. These measured quantities are then used to compute the amount of heat produced or consumed in the process using known mathematical relations.

Calorimeters are designed to minimize energy exchange between the system being studied and its surroundings. They range from simple coffee cup calorimeters used by introductory chemistry students to sophisticated bomb calorimeters used to determine the energy content of food.

9.3 Enthalpy

If a chemical change is carried out at constant pressure and the only work done is caused by expansion or contraction, q for the change is called the enthalpy change with the symbol ΔH, or ΔH°_{298} for reactions occurring under standard state conditions. The value of ΔH for a reaction in one direction is equal in magnitude, but opposite in sign, to ΔH for the reaction in the opposite direction, and ΔH is directly proportional to the quantity of reactants and products. Examples of enthalpy changes include enthalpy of combustion, enthalpy of fusion, enthalpy of vaporization, and standard enthalpy of formation. The standard enthalpy of formation, ΔH°_f , is the enthalpy change accompanying the formation of 1 mole of a substance from the elements in their most stable states at 1 bar (standard state). Many of the processes are carried out at 298.15 K. If the enthalpies of formation are available for the reactants and products of a reaction, the enthalpy change can be calculated using Hess's law: If a process can be written as the sum of several stepwise processes, the enthalpy change of the total process equals the sum of the enthalpy changes of the various steps.

9.4 Strengths of Ionic and Covalent Bonds

The strength of a covalent bond is measured by its bond dissociation energy, that is, the amount of energy required to break that particular bond in a mole of molecules. Multiple bonds are stronger than single bonds between the same atoms. The enthalpy of a reaction can be estimated based on the energy input required to break bonds and the energy released when new bonds are formed. For ionic bonds, the lattice energy is the energy required to separate one mole of a compound into its gas phase ions. Lattice energy increases for ions with higher charges and shorter distances between ions. Lattice energies are often calculated using the Born-Haber cycle, a thermochemical cycle including all of the energetic steps involved in converting elements into an ionic compound.

Exercises

9.1 Energy Basics

1. A burning match and a bonfire may have the same temperature, yet you would not sit around a burning match on a fall evening to stay warm. Why not?

2. Prepare a table identifying several energy transitions that take place during the typical operation of an automobile.

3. Explain the difference between heat capacity and specific heat of a substance.

4. Calculate the heat capacity, in joules and in calories per degree, of the following:

(a) 28.4 g of water

(b) 1.00 oz of lead

5. Calculate the heat capacity, in joules and in calories per degree, of the following:

(a) 45.8 g of nitrogen gas

(b) 1.00 pound of aluminum metal

6. How much heat, in joules and in calories, must be added to a 75.0–g iron block with a specific heat of 0.449 J/g °C to increase its temperature from 25 °C to its melting temperature of 1535 °C?

7. How much heat, in joules and in calories, is required to heat a 28.4-g (1-oz) ice cube from −23.0 °C to −1.0 °C?

8. How much would the temperature of 275 g of water increase if 36.5 kJ of heat were added?

9. If 14.5 kJ of heat were added to 485 g of liquid water, how much would its temperature increase?

10. A piece of unknown substance weighs 44.7 g and requires 2110 J to increase its temperature from 23.2 °C to 89.6 °C.

(a) What is the specific heat of the substance?

(b) If it is one of the substances found in Table 9.1, what is its likely identity?

11. A piece of unknown solid substance weighs 437.2 g, and requires 8460 J to increase its temperature from 19.3 °C to 68.9 °C.

(a) What is the specific heat of the substance?

(b) If it is one of the substances found in Table 9.1, what is its likely identity?

12. An aluminum kettle weighs 1.05 kg.

(a) What is the heat capacity of the kettle?

(b) How much heat is required to increase the temperature of this kettle from 23.0 °C to 99.0 °C?

(c) How much heat is required to heat this kettle from 23.0 °C to 99.0 °C if it contains 1.25 L of water (density of 0.997 g/mL and a specific heat of 4.184 J/g °C)?

13. Most people find waterbeds uncomfortable unless the water temperature is maintained at about 85 °F. Unless it is heated, a waterbed that contains 892 L of water cools from 85 °F to 72 °F in 24 hours. Estimate the amount of electrical energy required over 24 hours, in kWh, to keep the bed from cooling. Note that 1 kilowatt-hour (kWh) = 3.6×10^6 J, and assume that the density of water is 1.0 g/mL (independent of temperature). What other assumptions did you make? How did they affect your calculated result (i.e., were they likely to yield "positive" or "negative" errors)?

9.2 Calorimetry

14. A 500-mL bottle of water at room temperature and a 2-L bottle of water at the same temperature were placed in a refrigerator. After 30 minutes, the 500-mL bottle of water had cooled to the temperature of the refrigerator. An hour later, the 2-L of water had cooled to the same temperature. When asked which sample of water lost the most heat, one student replied that both bottles lost the same amount of heat because they started at the same temperature and finished at the same temperature. A second student thought that the 2-L bottle of water lost more heat because there was more water. A third student believed that the 500-mL bottle of water lost more heat because it cooled more quickly. A fourth student thought that it was not possible to tell because we do not know the initial temperature and the final temperature of the water. Indicate which of these answers is correct and describe the error in each of the other answers.

15. Would the amount of heat measured for the reaction in Example 9.5 be greater, lesser, or remain the same if we used a calorimeter that was a poorer insulator than a coffee cup calorimeter? Explain your answer.

16. Would the amount of heat absorbed by the dissolution in Example 9.6 appear greater, lesser, or remain the same if the experimenter used a calorimeter that was a poorer insulator than a coffee cup calorimeter? Explain your answer.

17. Would the amount of heat absorbed by the dissolution in Example 9.6 appear greater, lesser, or remain the same if the heat capacity of the calorimeter were taken into account? Explain your answer.

18. How many milliliters of water at 23 °C with a density of 1.00 g/mL must be mixed with 180 mL (about 6 oz) of coffee at 95 °C so that the resulting combination will have a temperature of 60 °C? Assume that coffee and water have the same density and the same specific heat.

19. How much will the temperature of a cup (180 g) of coffee at 95 °C be reduced when a 45 g silver spoon (specific heat 0.24 J/g °C) at 25 °C is placed in the coffee and the two are allowed to reach the same temperature? Assume that the coffee has the same density and specific heat as water.

20. A 45-g aluminum spoon (specific heat 0.88 J/g °C) at 24 °C is placed in 180 mL (180 g) of coffee at 85 °C and the temperature of the two become equal.

(a) What is the final temperature when the two become equal? Assume that coffee has the same specific heat as water.

(b) The first time a student solved this problem she got an answer of 88 °C. Explain why this is clearly an incorrect answer.

21. The temperature of the cooling water as it leaves the hot engine of an automobile is 240 °F. After it passes through the radiator it has a temperature of 175 °F. Calculate the amount of heat transferred from the engine to the surroundings by one gallon of water with a specific heat of 4.184 J/g °C.

22. A 70.0-g piece of metal at 80.0 °C is placed in 100 g of water at 22.0 °C contained in a calorimeter like that shown in **Figure 9.12**. The metal and water come to the same temperature at 24.6 °C. How much heat did the metal give up to the water? What is the specific heat of the metal?

23. If a reaction produces 1.506 kJ of heat, which is trapped in 30.0 g of water initially at 26.5 °C in a calorimeter like that in **Figure 9.12**, what is the resulting temperature of the water?

24. A 0.500-g sample of KCl is added to 50.0 g of water in a calorimeter (**Figure 9.12**). If the temperature decreases by 1.05 °C, what is the approximate amount of heat involved in the dissolution of the KCl, assuming the heat capacity of the resulting solution is 4.18 J/g °C? Is the reaction exothermic or endothermic?

25. Dissolving 3.0 g of $CaCl_2(s)$ in 150.0 g of water in a calorimeter (**Figure 9.12**) at 22.4 °C causes the temperature to rise to 25.8 °C. What is the approximate amount of heat involved in the dissolution, assuming the heat capacity of the resulting solution is 4.18 J/g °C? Is the reaction exothermic or endothermic?

26. When 50.0 g of 0.200 M NaCl(aq) at 24.1 °C is added to 100.0 g of 0.100 M $AgNO_3$(aq) at 24.1 °C in a calorimeter, the temperature increases to 25.2 °C as AgCl(s) forms. Assuming the specific heat of the solution and products is 4.20 J/g °C, calculate the approximate amount of heat in joules produced.

27. The addition of 3.15 g of $Ba(OH)_2 \cdot 8H_2O$ to a solution of 1.52 g of NH_4SCN in 100 g of water in a calorimeter caused the temperature to fall by 3.1 °C. Assuming the specific heat of the solution and products is 4.20 J/g °C, calculate the approximate amount of heat absorbed by the reaction, which can be represented by the following equation:

$$Ba(OH)_2 \cdot 8H_2O(s) + 2NH_4SCN(aq) \longrightarrow Ba(SCN)_2(aq) + 2NH_3(aq) + 10H_2O(l)$$

28. The reaction of 50 mL of acid and 50 mL of base described in **Example 9.5** increased the temperature of the solution by 6.9 degrees. How much would the temperature have increased if 100 mL of acid and 100 mL of base had been used in the same calorimeter starting at the same temperature of 22.0 °C? Explain your answer.

29. If the 3.21 g of NH_4NO_3 in **Example 9.6** were dissolved in 100.0 g of water under the same conditions, how much would the temperature change? Explain your answer.

30. When 1.0 g of fructose, $C_6H_{12}O_6(s)$, a sugar commonly found in fruits, is burned in oxygen in a bomb calorimeter, the temperature of the calorimeter increases by 1.58 °C. If the heat capacity of the calorimeter and its contents is 9.90 kJ/°C, what is q for this combustion?

31. When a 0.740-g sample of trinitrotoluene (TNT), $C_7H_5N_2O_6$, is burned in a bomb calorimeter, the temperature increases from 23.4 °C to 26.9 °C. The heat capacity of the calorimeter is 534 J/°C, and it contains 675 mL of water. How much heat was produced by the combustion of the TNT sample?

32. One method of generating electricity is by burning coal to heat water, which produces steam that drives an electric generator. To determine the rate at which coal is to be fed into the burner in this type of plant, the heat of combustion per ton of coal must be determined using a bomb calorimeter. When 1.00 g of coal is burned in a bomb calorimeter (**Figure 9.17**), the temperature increases by 1.48 °C. If the heat capacity of the calorimeter is 21.6 kJ/°C, determine the heat produced by combustion of a ton of coal (2.000×10^3 pounds).

33. The amount of fat recommended for someone with a daily diet of 2000 Calories is 65 g. What percent of the calories in this diet would be supplied by this amount of fat if the average number of Calories for fat is 9.1 Calories/g?

34. A teaspoon of the carbohydrate sucrose (common sugar) contains 16 Calories (16 kcal). What is the mass of one teaspoon of sucrose if the average number of Calories for carbohydrates is 4.1 Calories/g?

35. What is the maximum mass of carbohydrate in a 6-oz serving of diet soda that contains less than 1 Calorie per can if the average number of Calories for carbohydrates is 4.1 Calories/g?

36. A pint of premium ice cream can contain 1100 Calories. What mass of fat, in grams and pounds, must be produced in the body to store an extra 1.1×10^3 Calories if the average number of Calories for fat is 9.1 Calories/g?

37. A serving of a breakfast cereal contains 3 g of protein, 18 g of carbohydrates, and 6 g of fat. What is the Calorie content of a serving of this cereal if the average number of Calories for fat is 9.1 Calories/g, for carbohydrates is 4.1 Calories/g, and for protein is 4.1 Calories/g?

38. Which is the least expensive source of energy in kilojoules per dollar: a box of breakfast cereal that weighs 32 ounces and costs $4.23, or a liter of isooctane (density, 0.6919 g/mL) that costs $0.45? Compare the nutritional value of the cereal with the heat produced by combustion of the isooctane under standard conditions. A 1.0-ounce serving of the cereal provides 130 Calories.

9.3 Enthalpy

39. Explain how the heat measured in **Example 9.5** differs from the enthalpy change for the exothermic reaction described by the following equation:

$$HCl(aq) + NaOH(aq) \longrightarrow NaCl(aq) + H_2O(l)$$

40. Using the data in the check your learning section of **Example 9.5**, calculate ΔH in kJ/mol of $AgNO_3(aq)$ for the reaction: $NaCl(aq) + AgNO_3(aq) \longrightarrow AgCl(s) + NaNO_3(aq)$

41. Calculate the enthalpy of solution (ΔH for the dissolution) per mole of NH_4NO_3 under the conditions described in **Example 9.6**.

42. Calculate ΔH for the reaction described by the equation. (*Hint*: use the value for the approximate amount of heat absorbed by the reaction that you calculated in a previous exercise.)

$$Ba(OH)_2 \cdot 8H_2O(s) + 2NH_4SCN(aq) \longrightarrow Ba(SCN)_2(aq) + 2NH_3(aq) + 10H_2O(l)$$

43. Calculate the enthalpy of solution (ΔH for the dissolution) per mole of $CaCl_2$.

44. Although the gas used in an oxyacetylene torch (**Figure 9.7**) is essentially pure acetylene, the heat produced by combustion of one mole of acetylene in such a torch is likely not equal to the enthalpy of combustion of acetylene listed in **Table 9.2**. Considering the conditions for which the tabulated data are reported, suggest an explanation.

45. How much heat is produced by burning 4.00 moles of acetylene under standard state conditions?

46. How much heat is produced by combustion of 125 g of methanol under standard state conditions?

47. How many moles of isooctane must be burned to produce 100 kJ of heat under standard state conditions?

48. What mass of carbon monoxide must be burned to produce 175 kJ of heat under standard state conditions?

49. When 2.50 g of methane burns in oxygen, 125 kJ of heat is produced. What is the enthalpy of combustion per mole of methane under these conditions?

50. How much heat is produced when 100 mL of 0.250 M HCl (density, 1.00 g/mL) and 200 mL of 0.150 M NaOH (density, 1.00 g/mL) are mixed?

$$HCl(aq) + NaOH(aq) \longrightarrow NaCl(aq) + H_2O(l) \qquad \Delta H^\circ_{298} = -58 \text{ kJ}$$

If both solutions are at the same temperature and the heat capacity of the products is 4.19 J/g °C, how much will the temperature increase? What assumption did you make in your calculation?

51. A sample of 0.562 g of carbon is burned in oxygen in a bomb calorimeter, producing carbon dioxide. Assume both the reactants and products are under standard state conditions, and that the heat released is directly proportional to the enthalpy of combustion of graphite. The temperature of the calorimeter increases from 26.74 °C to 27.93 °C. What is the heat capacity of the calorimeter and its contents?

52. Before the introduction of chlorofluorocarbons, sulfur dioxide (enthalpy of vaporization, 6.00 kcal/mol) was used in household refrigerators. What mass of SO_2 must be evaporated to remove as much heat as evaporation of 1.00 kg of CCl_2F_2 (enthalpy of vaporization is 17.4 kJ/mol)?

The vaporization reactions for SO_2 and CCl_2F_2 are $SO_2(l) \longrightarrow SO_2(g)$ and $CCl_2F(l) \longrightarrow CCl_2F_2(g)$, respectively.

53. Homes may be heated by pumping hot water through radiators. What mass of water will provide the same amount of heat when cooled from 95.0 to 35.0 °C, as the heat provided when 100 g of steam is cooled from 110 °C to 100 °C.

54. Which of the enthalpies of combustion in Table 9.2 the table are also standard enthalpies of formation?

55. Does the standard enthalpy of formation of $H_2O(g)$ differ from ΔH° for the reaction
$$2H_2(g) + O_2(g) \longrightarrow 2H_2O(g)?$$

56. Joseph Priestly prepared oxygen in 1774 by heating red mercury(II) oxide with sunlight focused through a lens. How much heat is required to decompose exactly 1 mole of red $HgO(s)$ to $Hg(l)$ and $O_2(g)$ under standard conditions?

57. How many kilojoules of heat will be released when exactly 1 mole of manganese, Mn, is burned to form $Mn_3O_4(s)$ at standard state conditions?

58. How many kilojoules of heat will be released when exactly 1 mole of iron, Fe, is burned to form $Fe_2O_3(s)$ at standard state conditions?

59. The following sequence of reactions occurs in the commercial production of aqueous nitric acid:

$$4NH_3(g) + 5O_2(g) \longrightarrow 4NO(g) + 6H_2O(l) \qquad \Delta H = -907 \text{ kJ}$$
$$2NO(g) + O_2(g) \longrightarrow 2NO_2(g) \qquad \Delta H = -113 \text{ kJ}$$
$$3NO_2 + H_2O(l) \longrightarrow 2HNO_3(aq) + NO(g) \qquad \Delta H = -139 \text{ kJ}$$

Determine the total energy change for the production of one mole of aqueous nitric acid by this process.

60. Both graphite and diamond burn.
$$C(s, \text{ diamond}) + O_2(g) \longrightarrow CO_2(g)$$

For the conversion of graphite to diamond:
$$C(s, \text{ graphite}) \longrightarrow C(s, \text{ diamond}) \qquad \Delta H^\circ_{298} = 1.90 \text{ kJ}$$

Which produces more heat, the combustion of graphite or the combustion of diamond?

61. From the molar heats of formation in Appendix G, determine how much heat is required to evaporate one mole of water: $H_2O(l) \longrightarrow H_2O(g)$

62. Which produces more heat?
$$Os(s) \longrightarrow 2O_2(g) \longrightarrow OsO_4(s)$$

or

$$Os(s) \longrightarrow 2O_2(g) \longrightarrow OsO_4(g)$$

for the phase change $OsO_4(s) \longrightarrow OsO_4(g) \qquad \Delta H = 56.4 \text{ kJ}$

63. Calculate ΔH°_{298} for the process

$$Sb(s) + \tfrac{5}{2}Cl_2(g) \longrightarrow SbCl_5(g)$$

from the following information:

$$Sb(s) + \tfrac{3}{2}Cl_2(g) \longrightarrow SbCl_3(g) \qquad \Delta H^\circ_{298} = -314\,kJ$$

$$SbCl_3(s) + Cl_2(g) \longrightarrow SbCl_5(g) \qquad \Delta H^\circ_{298} = -80\,kJ$$

64. Calculate ΔH°_{298} for the process $Zn(s) + S(s) + 2O_2(g) \longrightarrow ZnSO_4(s)$

from the following information:

$$Zn(s) + S(s) \longrightarrow ZnS(s) \qquad \Delta H^\circ_{298} = -206.0\,kJ$$

$$ZnS(s) + 2O_2(g) \longrightarrow ZnSO_4(s) \qquad \Delta H^\circ_{298} = -776.8\,kJ$$

65. Calculate ΔH for the process $Hg_2Cl_2(s) \longrightarrow 2Hg(l) + Cl_2(g)$

from the following information:

$$Hg(l) + Cl_2(g) \longrightarrow HgCl_2(s) \qquad \Delta H = -224\,kJ$$
$$Hg(l) + HgCl_2(s) \longrightarrow Hg_2Cl_2(s) \qquad \Delta H = -41.2\,kJ$$

66. Calculate ΔH°_{298} for the process $Co_3O_4(s) \longrightarrow 3Co(s) + 2O_2(g)$

from the following information:

$$Co(s) + \tfrac{1}{2}O_2(g) \longrightarrow CoO(s) \qquad \Delta H^\circ_{298} = -237.9kJ$$

$$3CoO(s) + \tfrac{1}{2}O_2(g) \longrightarrow Co_3O_4(s) \qquad \Delta H^\circ_{298} = -177.5kJ$$

67. Calculate the standard molar enthalpy of formation of NO(g) from the following data:

$$N_2(g) + 2O_2 \longrightarrow 2NO_2(g) \qquad \Delta H^\circ_{298} = 66.4\,kJ$$

$$2NO(g) + O_2 \longrightarrow 2NO_2(g) \qquad \Delta H^\circ_{298} = -114.1\,kJ$$

68. Using the data in **Appendix G**, calculate the standard enthalpy change for each of the following reactions:

(a) $N_2(g) + O_2(g) \longrightarrow 2NO(g)$

(b) $Si(s) + 2Cl_2(g) \longrightarrow SiCl_4(g)$

(c) $Fe_2O_3(s) + 3H_2(g) \longrightarrow 2Fe(s) + 3H_2O(l)$

(d) $2LiOH(s) + CO_2(g) \longrightarrow Li_2CO_3(s) + H_2O(g)$

69. Using the data in **Appendix G**, calculate the standard enthalpy change for each of the following reactions:

(a) $Si(s) + 2F_2(g) \longrightarrow SiF_4(g)$

(b) $2C(s) + 2H_2(g) + O_2(g) \longrightarrow CH_3CO_2H(l)$

(c) $CH_4(g) + N_2(g) \longrightarrow HCN(g) + NH_3(g);$

(d) $CS_2(g) + 3Cl_2(g) \longrightarrow CCl_4(g) + S_2Cl_2(g)$

70. The following reactions can be used to prepare samples of metals. Determine the enthalpy change under standard state conditions for each.

(a) $2Ag_2O(s) \longrightarrow 4Ag(s) + O_2(g)$

(b) $SnO(s) + CO(g) \longrightarrow Sn(s) + CO_2(g)$

(c) $Cr_2O_3(s) + 3H_2(g) \longrightarrow 2Cr(s) + 3H_2O(l)$

(d) $2Al(s) + Fe_2O_3(s) \longrightarrow Al_2O_3(s) + 2Fe(s)$

71. The decomposition of hydrogen peroxide, H_2O_2, has been used to provide thrust in the control jets of various space vehicles. Using the data in **Appendix G**, determine how much heat is produced by the decomposition of exactly 1 mole of H_2O_2 under standard conditions.

$$2H_2O_2(l) \longrightarrow 2H_2O(g) + O_2(g)$$

72. Calculate the enthalpy of combustion of propane, $C_3H_8(g)$, for the formation of $H_2O(g)$ and $CO_2(g)$. The enthalpy of formation of propane is −104 kJ/mol.

73. Calculate the enthalpy of combustion of butane, $C_4H_{10}(g)$ for the formation of $H_2O(g)$ and $CO_2(g)$. The enthalpy of formation of butane is −126 kJ/mol.

74. Both propane and butane are used as gaseous fuels. Which compound produces more heat per gram when burned?

75. The white pigment TiO_2 is prepared by the reaction of titanium tetrachloride, $TiCl_4$, with water vapor in the gas phase: $TiCl_4(g) + 2H_2O(g) \longrightarrow TiO_2(s) + 4HCl(g)$.

How much heat is evolved in the production of exactly 1 mole of $TiO_2(s)$ under standard state conditions?

76. Water gas, a mixture of H_2 and CO, is an important industrial fuel produced by the reaction of steam with red hot coke, essentially pure carbon: $C(s) + H_2O(g) \longrightarrow CO(g) + H_2(g)$.

(a) Assuming that coke has the same enthalpy of formation as graphite, calculate ΔH°_{298} for this reaction.

(b) Methanol, a liquid fuel that could possibly replace gasoline, can be prepared from water gas and additional hydrogen at high temperature and pressure in the presence of a suitable catalyst: $2H_2(g) + CO(g) \longrightarrow CH_3OH(g)$.

Under the conditions of the reaction, methanol forms as a gas. Calculate ΔH°_{298} for this reaction and for the condensation of gaseous methanol to liquid methanol.

(c) Calculate the heat of combustion of 1 mole of liquid methanol to $H_2O(g)$ and $CO_2(g)$.

77. In the early days of automobiles, illumination at night was provided by burning acetylene, C_2H_2. Though no longer used as auto headlamps, acetylene is still used as a source of light by some cave explorers. The acetylene is (was) prepared in the lamp by the reaction of water with calcium carbide, CaC_2:

$$CaC_2(s) + 2H_2O(l) \longrightarrow Ca(OH)_2(s) + C_2H_2(g).$$

Calculate the standard enthalpy of the reaction. The ΔH°_f of CaC_2 is −15.14 kcal/mol.

78. From the data in **Table 9.2**, determine which of the following fuels produces the greatest amount of heat per gram when burned under standard conditions: $CO(g)$, $CH_4(g)$, or $C_2H_2(g)$.

79. The enthalpy of combustion of hard coal averages −35 kJ/g, that of gasoline, 1.28×10^5 kJ/gal. How many kilograms of hard coal provide the same amount of heat as is available from 1.0 gallon of gasoline? Assume that the density of gasoline is 0.692 g/mL (the same as the density of isooctane).

80. Ethanol, C_2H_5OH, is used as a fuel for motor vehicles, particularly in Brazil.

(a) Write the balanced equation for the combustion of ethanol to $CO_2(g)$ and $H_2O(g)$, and, using the data in **Appendix G**, calculate the enthalpy of combustion of 1 mole of ethanol.

(b) The density of ethanol is 0.7893 g/mL. Calculate the enthalpy of combustion of exactly 1 L of ethanol.

(c) Assuming that an automobile's mileage is directly proportional to the heat of combustion of the fuel, calculate how much farther an automobile could be expected to travel on 1 L of gasoline than on 1 L of ethanol. Assume that gasoline has the heat of combustion and the density of n–octane, C_8H_{18} (ΔH°_f = −208.4 kJ/mol; density = 0.7025 g/mL).

81. Among the substances that react with oxygen and that have been considered as potential rocket fuels are diborane [B_2H_6, produces $B_2O_3(s)$ and $H_2O(g)$], methane [CH_4, produces $CO_2(g)$ and $H_2O(g)$], and hydrazine [N_2H_4, produces $N_2(g)$ and $H_2O(g)$]. On the basis of the heat released by 1.00 g of each substance in its reaction with oxygen, which of these compounds offers the best possibility as a rocket fuel? The ΔH°_f of $B_2H_6(g)$, $CH_4(g)$, and $N_2H_4(l)$ may be found in **Appendix G**.

82. How much heat is produced when 1.25 g of chromium metal reacts with oxygen gas under standard conditions?

83. Ethylene, C_2H_2, a byproduct from the fractional distillation of petroleum, is fourth among the 50 chemical compounds produced commercially in the largest quantities. About 80% of synthetic ethanol is manufactured from ethylene by its reaction with water in the presence of a suitable catalyst. $C_2H_4(g) + H_2O(g) \longrightarrow C_2H_5OH(l)$

Using the data in the table in **Appendix G**, calculate $\Delta H°$ for the reaction.

84. The oxidation of the sugar glucose, $C_6H_{12}O_6$, is described by the following equation:

$$C_6H_{12}O_6(s) + 6O_2(g) \longrightarrow 6CO_2(g) + 6H_2O(l) \qquad \Delta H = -2816 \text{ kJ}$$

The metabolism of glucose gives the same products, although the glucose reacts with oxygen in a series of steps in the body.

(a) How much heat in kilojoules can be produced by the metabolism of 1.0 g of glucose?

(b) How many Calories can be produced by the metabolism of 1.0 g of glucose?

85. Propane, C_3H_8, is a hydrocarbon that is commonly used as a fuel.

(a) Write a balanced equation for the complete combustion of propane gas.

(b) Calculate the volume of air at 25 °C and 1.00 atmosphere that is needed to completely combust 25.0 grams of propane. Assume that air is 21.0 percent O_2 by volume. (Hint: we will see how to do this calculation in a later chapter on gases—for now use the information that 1.00 L of air at 25 °C and 1.00 atm contains 0.275 g of O_2 per liter.)

(c) The heat of combustion of propane is −2,219.2 kJ/mol. Calculate the heat of formation, $\Delta H_f°$ of propane given that $\Delta H_f°$ of $H_2O(l) = -285.8$ kJ/mol and $\Delta H_f°$ of $CO_2(g) = -393.5$ kJ/mol.

(d) Assuming that all of the heat released in burning 25.0 grams of propane is transferred to 4.00 kilograms of water, calculate the increase in temperature of the water.

86. During a recent winter month in Sheboygan, Wisconsin, it was necessary to obtain 3500 kWh of heat provided by a natural gas furnace with 89% efficiency to keep a small house warm (the efficiency of a gas furnace is the percent of the heat produced by combustion that is transferred into the house).

(a) Assume that natural gas is pure methane and determine the volume of natural gas in cubic feet that was required to heat the house. The average temperature of the natural gas was 56 °F; at this temperature and a pressure of 1 atm, natural gas has a density of 0.681 g/L.

(b) How many gallons of LPG (liquefied petroleum gas) would be required to replace the natural gas used? Assume the LPG is liquid propane [C_3H_8: density, 0.5318 g/mL; enthalpy of combustion, 2219 kJ/mol for the formation of $CO_2(g)$ and $H_2O(l)$] and the furnace used to burn the LPG has the same efficiency as the gas furnace.

(c) What mass of carbon dioxide is produced by combustion of the methane used to heat the house?

(d) What mass of water is produced by combustion of the methane used to heat the house?

(e) What volume of air is required to provide the oxygen for the combustion of the methane used to heat the house? Air contains 23% oxygen by mass. The average density of air during the month was 1.22 g/L.

(f) How many kilowatt–hours (1 kWh = 3.6 × 10^6 J) of electricity would be required to provide the heat necessary to heat the house? Note electricity is 100% efficient in producing heat inside a house.

(g) Although electricity is 100% efficient in producing heat inside a house, production and distribution of electricity is not 100% efficient. The efficiency of production and distribution of electricity produced in a coal-fired power plant is about 40%. A certain type of coal provides 2.26 kWh per pound upon combustion. What mass of this coal in kilograms will be required to produce the electrical energy necessary to heat the house if the efficiency of generation and distribution is 40%?

9.4 Strengths of Ionic and Covalent Bonds

87. Which bond in each of the following pairs of bonds is the strongest?

(a) C–C or $C = C$

(b) C–N or $C \equiv N$

(c) $C \equiv O$ or $C = O$

(d) H–F or H–Cl

(e) C–H or O–H

(f) C–N or C–O

88. Using the bond energies in **Table 9.3**, determine the approximate enthalpy change for each of the following reactions:

(a) $H_2(g) + Br_2(g) \longrightarrow 2HBr(g)$

(b) $CH_4(g) + I_2(g) \longrightarrow CH_3 I(g) + HI(g)$

(c) $C_2 H_4(g) + 3O_2(g) \longrightarrow 2CO_2(g) + 2H_2 O(g)$

89. Using the bond energies in **Table 9.3**, determine the approximate enthalpy change for each of the following reactions:

(a) $Cl_2(g) + 3F_2(g) \longrightarrow 2ClF_3(g)$

(b) $H_2 C = CH_2(g) + H_2(g) \longrightarrow H_3 CCH_3(g)$

(c) $2C_2 H_6(g) + 7O_2(g) \longrightarrow 4CO_2(g) + 6H_2 O(g)$

90. Draw a curve that describes the energy of a system with H and Cl atoms at varying distances. Then, find the minimum energy of this curve two ways (**Figure 5.2**).

(a) Use the bond energy found in **Table 9.3** and **Table 9.4** to calculate the energy for one single HCl bond (Hint: How many bonds are in a mole?)

(b) Use the enthalpy of reaction and the bond energies for H_2 and Cl_2 to solve for the energy of one mole of HCl bonds.

$$H_2(g) + Cl_2(g) \rightleftharpoons 2HCl(g) \qquad \Delta H^\circ_{rxn} = -184.7 \text{ kJ/mol}$$

91. Explain why bonds occur at specific average bond distances instead of the atoms approaching each other infinitely close (**Figure 5.2**).

92. When a molecule can form two different structures, the structure with the stronger bonds is usually the more stable form. Use bond energies to predict the correct structure of the hydroxylamine molecule:

$$H-\overset{\cdot\cdot}{\underset{\underset{H}{|}}{N}}-\overset{\cdot\cdot}{O}-H \quad \text{or} \quad H-\overset{\overset{H}{|}}{\underset{\underset{H}{|}}{N}}-\overset{\cdot\cdot}{\underset{\cdot\cdot}{O}}:$$

93. How does the bond energy of HCl(g) differ from the standard enthalpy of formation of HCl(g)?

94. Using the standard enthalpy of formation data in **Appendix G**, show how the standard enthalpy of formation of HCl(g) can be used to determine the bond energy.

95. Using the standard enthalpy of formation data in **Appendix G**, calculate the bond energy of the carbon-sulfur double bond in CS_2.

96. Using the standard enthalpy of formation data in **Appendix G**, determine which bond is stronger: the S–F bond in $SF_4(g)$ or in $SF_6(g)$?

97. Using the standard enthalpy of formation data in **Appendix G**, determine which bond is stronger: the P–Cl bond in $PCl_3(g)$ or in $PCl_5(g)$?

98. Complete the following Lewis structure by adding bonds (not atoms), and then indicate the longest bond:

$$\begin{array}{ccccccccc} & H & H & & & H & H & \\ H & C & C & C & C & C & C & H \\ & H & H & & & H & H & \end{array}$$

99. Use the bond energy to calculate an approximate value of ΔH for the following reaction. Which is the more stable form of FNO_2?

100. Use principles of atomic structure to answer each of the following:[4]

(a) The radius of the Ca atom is 197 pm; the radius of the Ca^{2+} ion is 99 pm. Account for the difference.

(b) The lattice energy of $CaO(s)$ is –3460 kJ/mol; the lattice energy of K_2O is –2240 kJ/mol. Account for the difference.

(c) Given these ionization values, explain the difference between Ca and K with regard to their first and second ionization energies.

Element	First Ionization Energy (kJ/mol)	Second Ionization Energy (kJ/mol)
K	419	3050
Ca	590	1140

(d) The first ionization energy of Mg is 738 kJ/mol and that of Al is 578 kJ/mol. Account for this difference.

101. The lattice energy of LiF is 1023 kJ/mol, and the Li–F distance is 200.8 pm. NaF crystallizes in the same structure as LiF but with a Na–F distance of 231 pm. Which of the following values most closely approximates the lattice energy of NaF: 510, 890, 1023, 1175, or 4090 kJ/mol? Explain your choice.

102. For which of the following substances is the least energy required to convert one mole of the solid into separate ions?

(a) MgO

(b) SrO

(c) KF

(d) CsF

(e) MgF_2

---

4. This question is taken from the Chemistry Advanced Placement Examination and is used with the permission of the Educational Testing Service.

103. The reaction of a metal, M, with a halogen, X_2, proceeds by an exothermic reaction as indicated by this equation: $M(s) + X_2(g) \longrightarrow MX_2(s)$. For each of the following, indicate which option will make the reaction more exothermic. Explain your answers.

(a) a large radius vs. a small radius for M^{+2}

(b) a high ionization energy vs. a low ionization energy for M

(c) an increasing bond energy for the halogen

(d) a decreasing electron affinity for the halogen

(e) an increasing size of the anion formed by the halogen

104. The lattice energy of LiF is 1023 kJ/mol, and the Li–F distance is 201 pm. MgO crystallizes in the same structure as LiF but with a Mg–O distance of 205 pm. Which of the following values most closely approximates the lattice energy of MgO: 256 kJ/mol, 512 kJ/mol, 1023 kJ/mol, 2046 kJ/mol, or 4008 kJ/mol? Explain your choice.

105. Which compound in each of the following pairs has the larger lattice energy? Note: Mg^{2+} and Li^+ have similar radii; O^{2-} and F^- have similar radii. Explain your choices.

(a) MgO or MgSe

(b) LiF or MgO

(c) Li_2O or LiCl

(d) Li_2Se or MgO

106. Which compound in each of the following pairs has the larger lattice energy? Note: Ba^{2+} and

K^+ have similar radii; S^{2-} and Cl^- have similar radii. Explain your choices.

(a) K_2O or Na_2O

(b) K_2S or BaS

(c) KCl or BaS

(d) BaS or $BaCl_2$

107. Which of the following compounds requires the most energy to convert one mole of the solid into separate ions?

(a) MgO

(b) SrO

(c) KF

(d) CsF

(e) MgF_2

108. Which of the following compounds requires the most energy to convert one mole of the solid into separate ions?

(a) K_2S

(b) K_2O

(c) CaS

(d) Cs_2S

(e) CaO

109. The lattice energy of KF is 794 kJ/mol, and the interionic distance is 269 pm. The Na–F

distance in NaF, which has the same structure as KF, is 231 pm. Which of the following values is the closest approximation of the lattice energy of NaF: 682 kJ/mol, 794 kJ/mol, 924 kJ/mol, 1588 kJ/mol, or 3175 kJ/mol? Explain your answer.

Chapter 10

Liquids and Solids

Figure 10.1 Solid carbon dioxide ("dry ice", left) sublimes vigorously when placed in a liquid (right), cooling the liquid and generating a fog of condensed water vapor above the cylinder. (credit: modification of work by Paul Flowers)

Chapter Outline

10.1 Intermolecular Forces

10.2 Properties of Liquids

10.3 Phase Transitions

10.4 Phase Diagrams

10.5 The Solid State of Matter

10.6 Lattice Structures in Crystalline Solids

Introduction

The great distances between atoms and molecules in a gaseous phase, and the corresponding absence of any significant interactions between them, allows for simple descriptions of many physical properties that are the same for all gases, regardless of their chemical identities. As described in the final module of the chapter on gases, this situation changes at high pressures and low temperatures—conditions that permit the atoms and molecules to interact to a much greater extent. In the liquid and solid states, these interactions are of considerable strength and play an important role in determining a number of physical properties that *do* depend on the chemical identity of the substance. In this chapter, the nature of these interactions and their effects on various physical properties of liquid and solid phases will be examined.

10.1 Intermolecular Forces

By the end of this section, you will be able to:

- Describe the types of intermolecular forces possible between atoms or molecules in condensed phases (dispersion forces, dipole-dipole attractions, and hydrogen bonding)

- Identify the types of intermolecular forces experienced by specific molecules based on their structures

- Explain the relation between the intermolecular forces present within a substance and the temperatures associated with changes in its physical state

As was the case for gaseous substances, the kinetic molecular theory may be used to explain the behavior of solids and liquids. In the following description, the term *particle* will be used to refer to an atom, molecule, or ion. Note that we will use the popular phrase "intermolecular attraction" to refer to attractive forces between the particles of a substance, regardless of whether these particles are molecules, atoms, or ions.

Consider these two aspects of the molecular-level environments in solid, liquid, and gaseous matter:

- Particles in a solid are tightly packed together and often arranged in a regular pattern; in a liquid, they are close together with no regular arrangement; in a gas, they are far apart with no regular arrangement.

- Particles in a solid vibrate about fixed positions and do not generally move in relation to one another; in a liquid, they move past each other but remain in essentially constant contact; in a gas, they move independently of one another except when they collide.

The differences in the properties of a solid, liquid, or gas reflect the strengths of the attractive forces between the atoms, molecules, or ions that make up each phase. The phase in which a substance exists depends on the relative extents of its **intermolecular forces** (IMFs) and the kinetic energies (KE) of its molecules. IMFs are the various forces of attraction that may exist between the atoms and molecules of a substance due to electrostatic phenomena, as will be detailed in this module. These forces serve to hold particles close together, whereas the particles' KE provides the energy required to overcome the attractive forces and thus increase the distance between particles. **Figure 10.2** illustrates how changes in physical state may be induced by changing the temperature, hence, the average KE, of a given substance.

Figure 10.2 Transitions between solid, liquid, and gaseous states of a substance occur when conditions of temperature or pressure favor the associated changes in intermolecular forces. (Note: The space between particles in the gas phase is much greater than shown.)

As an example of the processes depicted in this figure, consider a sample of water. When gaseous water is cooled sufficiently, the attractions between H_2O molecules will be capable of holding them together when they come into contact with each other; the gas condenses, forming liquid H_2O. For example, liquid water forms on the outside of a cold glass as the water vapor in the air is cooled by the cold glass, as seen in Figure 10.3.

(a)   (b)

Figure 10.3   Condensation forms when water vapor in the air is cooled enough to form liquid water, such as (a) on the outside of a cold beverage glass or (b) in the form of fog. (credit a: modification of work by Jenny Downing; credit b: modification of work by Cory Zanker)

We can also liquefy many gases by compressing them, if the temperature is not too high. The increased pressure brings the molecules of a gas closer together, such that the attractions between the molecules become strong relative to their KE. Consequently, they form liquids. Butane, C_4H_{10}, is the fuel used in disposable lighters and is a gas at standard temperature and pressure. Inside the lighter's fuel compartment, the butane is compressed to a pressure that results in its condensation to the liquid state, as shown in Figure 10.4.

Figure 10.4   Gaseous butane is compressed within the storage compartment of a disposable lighter, resulting in its condensation to the liquid state. (credit: modification of work by "Sam-Cat"/Flickr)

Finally, if the temperature of a liquid becomes sufficiently low, or the pressure on the liquid becomes sufficiently high, the molecules of the liquid no longer have enough KE to overcome the IMF between them, and a solid forms. A more thorough discussion of these and other changes of state, or phase transitions, is provided in a later module of this chapter.

Link to Learning

Access this interactive simulation (http://openstaxcollege.org/l/16phetvisual) on states of matter, phase transitions, and intermolecular forces. This simulation is useful for visualizing concepts introduced throughout this chapter.

Forces between Molecules

Under appropriate conditions, the attractions between all gas molecules will cause them to form liquids or solids. This is due to intermolecular forces, not *intra*molecular forces. *Intra*molecular forces are those *within* the molecule that keep the molecule together, for example, the bonds between the atoms. *Inter*molecular forces are the attractions *between* molecules, which determine many of the physical properties of a substance. Figure 10.5 illustrates these different molecular forces. The strengths of these attractive forces vary widely, though usually the IMFs between small molecules are weak compared to the intramolecular forces that bond atoms together within a molecule. For example, to overcome the IMFs in one mole of liquid HCl and convert it into gaseous HCl requires only about 17 kilojoules. However, to break the covalent bonds between the hydrogen and chlorine atoms in one mole of HCl requires about 25 times more energy—430 kilojoules.

Figure 10.5 *Intra*molecular forces keep a molecule intact. *Inter*molecular forces hold multiple molecules together and determine many of a substance's properties.

All of the attractive forces between neutral atoms and molecules are known as **van der Waals forces**, although they are usually referred to more informally as intermolecular attraction. We will consider the various types of IMFs in the next three sections of this module.

Dispersion Forces

One of the three van der Waals forces is present in all condensed phases, regardless of the nature of the atoms or molecules composing the substance. This attractive force is called the London dispersion force in honor of German-born American physicist Fritz London who, in 1928, first explained it. This force is often referred to as simply the **dispersion force**. Because the electrons of an atom or molecule are in constant motion (or, alternatively, the electron's location is subject to quantum-mechanical variability), at any moment in time, an atom or molecule can develop a temporary, **instantaneous dipole** if its electrons are distributed asymmetrically. The presence of this dipole can, in turn, distort the electrons of a neighboring atom or molecule, producing an **induced dipole**. These two rapidly fluctuating, temporary dipoles thus result in a relatively weak electrostatic attraction between the species—a so-called dispersion force like that illustrated in Figure 10.6.

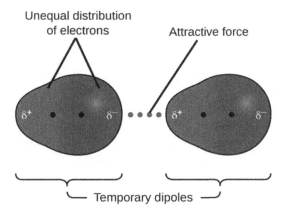

Figure 10.6 Dispersion forces result from the formation of temporary dipoles, as illustrated here for two nonpolar diatomic molecules.

Dispersion forces that develop between atoms in different molecules can attract the two molecules to each other. The forces are relatively weak, however, and become significant only when the molecules are very close. Larger and heavier atoms and molecules exhibit stronger dispersion forces than do smaller and lighter atoms and molecules. F_2 and Cl_2 are gases at room temperature (reflecting weaker attractive forces); Br_2 is a liquid, and I_2 is a solid (reflecting stronger attractive forces). Trends in observed melting and boiling points for the halogens clearly demonstrate this effect, as seen in Table 10.1.

Melting and Boiling Points of the Halogens

Halogen	Molar Mass	Atomic Radius	Melting Point	Boiling Point
fluorine, F_2	38 g/mol	72 pm	53 K	85 K
chlorine, Cl_2	71 g/mol	99 pm	172 K	238 K
bromine, Br_2	160 g/mol	114 pm	266 K	332 K
iodine, I_2	254 g/mol	133 pm	387 K	457 K
astatine, At_2	420 g/mol	150 pm	575 K	610 K

Table 10.1

The increase in melting and boiling points with increasing atomic/molecular size may be rationalized by considering how the strength of dispersion forces is affected by the electronic structure of the atoms or molecules in the substance. In a larger atom, the valence electrons are, on average, farther from the nuclei than in a smaller atom. Thus, they are less tightly held and can more easily form the temporary dipoles that produce the attraction. The measure of how easy or difficult it is for another electrostatic charge (for example, a nearby ion or polar molecule) to distort a molecule's charge distribution (its electron cloud) is known as **polarizability**. A molecule that has a charge cloud that is easily distorted is said to be very polarizable and will have large dispersion forces; one with a charge cloud that is difficult to distort is not very polarizable and will have small dispersion forces.

Example 10.1

London Forces and Their Effects

Order the following compounds of a group 14 element and hydrogen from lowest to highest boiling point: CH_4, SiH_4, GeH_4, and SnH_4. Explain your reasoning.

Solution

Applying the skills acquired in the chapter on chemical bonding and molecular geometry, all of these compounds are predicted to be nonpolar, so they may experience only dispersion forces: the smaller the molecule, the less polarizable and the weaker the dispersion forces; the larger the molecule, the larger the dispersion forces. The molar masses of CH_4, SiH_4, GeH_4, and SnH_4 are approximately 16 g/mol, 32 g/mol, 77 g/mol, and 123 g/mol, respectively. Therefore, CH_4 is expected to have the lowest boiling point and SnH_4 the highest boiling point. The ordering from lowest to highest boiling point is expected to be $CH_4 < SiH_4 < GeH_4 < SnH_4$.

A graph of the actual boiling points of these compounds versus the period of the group 14 element shows this prediction to be correct:

Check Your Learning

Order the following hydrocarbons from lowest to highest boiling point: C_2H_6, C_3H_8, and C_4H_{10}.

Answer: $C_2H_6 < C_3H_8 < C_4H_{10}$. All of these compounds are nonpolar and only have London dispersion forces: the larger the molecule, the larger the dispersion forces and the higher the boiling point. The ordering from lowest to highest boiling point is therefore $C_2H_6 < C_3H_8 < C_4H_{10}$.

The shapes of molecules also affect the magnitudes of the dispersion forces between them. For example, boiling points for the isomers *n*-pentane, isopentane, and neopentane (shown in **Figure 10.7**) are 36 °C, 27 °C, and 9.5 °C, respectively. Even though these compounds are composed of molecules with the same chemical formula, C_5H_{12}, the difference in boiling points suggests that dispersion forces in the liquid phase are different, being greatest for *n*-pentane and least for neopentane. The elongated shape of *n*-pentane provides a greater surface area available for contact between molecules, resulting in correspondingly stronger dispersion forces. The more compact shape of isopentane offers a smaller surface area available for intermolecular contact and, therefore, weaker dispersion forces. Neopentane molecules are the most compact of the three, offering the least available surface area for intermolecular contact and, hence, the weakest dispersion forces. This behavior is analogous to the connections that may be formed between strips of VELCRO brand fasteners: the greater the area of the strip's contact, the stronger the connection.

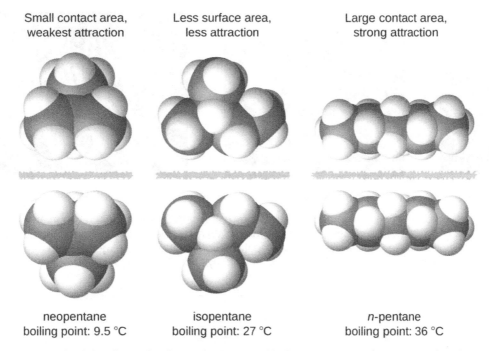

Small contact area, weakest attraction   Less surface area, less attraction   Large contact area, strong attraction

neopentane
boiling point: 9.5 °C

isopentane
boiling point: 27 °C

n-pentane
boiling point: 36 °C

Figure 10.7 The strength of the dispersion forces increases with the contact area between molecules, as demonstrated by the boiling points of these pentane isomers.

Chemistry in Everyday Life

Geckos and Intermolecular Forces

Geckos have an amazing ability to adhere to most surfaces. They can quickly run up smooth walls and across ceilings that have no toe-holds, and they do this without having suction cups or a sticky substance on their toes. And while a gecko can lift its feet easily as it walks along a surface, if you attempt to pick it up, it sticks to the surface. How are geckos (as well as spiders and some other insects) able to do this? Although this phenomenon has been investigated for hundreds of years, scientists only recently uncovered the details of the process that allows geckos' feet to behave this way.

Geckos' toes are covered with hundreds of thousands of tiny hairs known as *setae*, with each seta, in turn, branching into hundreds of tiny, flat, triangular tips called *spatulae*. The huge numbers of spatulae on its setae provide a gecko, shown in **Figure 10.8**, with a large total surface area for sticking to a surface. In 2000, Kellar Autumn, who leads a multi-institutional gecko research team, found that geckos adhered equally well to both polar silicon dioxide and nonpolar gallium arsenide. This proved that geckos stick to surfaces because of dispersion forces—weak intermolecular attractions arising from temporary, synchronized charge distributions between adjacent molecules. Although dispersion forces are very weak, the total attraction over millions of spatulae is large enough to support many times the gecko's weight.

In 2014, two scientists developed a model to explain how geckos can rapidly transition from "sticky" to "nonsticky." Alex Greaney and Congcong Hu at Oregon State University described how geckos can achieve this by changing the angle between their spatulae and the surface. Geckos' feet, which are normally nonsticky, become sticky when a small shear force is applied. By curling and uncurling their toes, geckos can alternate between sticking and unsticking from a surface, and thus easily move across it. Further investigations may eventually lead to the development of better adhesives and other applications.

Setae   Spatulae

Figure 10.8 Geckos' toes contain large numbers of tiny hairs (setae), which branch into many triangular tips (spatulae). Geckos adhere to surfaces because of van der Waals attractions between the surface and a gecko's millions of spatulae. By changing how the spatulae contact the surface, geckos can turn their stickiness "on" and "off." (credit photo: modification of work by "JC*+A!"/Flickr)

Link to Learning

Watch this video (http://openstaxcollege.org/l/16kellaraut) to learn more about Kellar Autumn's research that determined that van der Waals forces are responsible for a gecko's ability to cling and climb.

Dipole-Dipole Attractions

Recall from the chapter on chemical bonding and molecular geometry that *polar* molecules have a partial positive charge on one side and a partial negative charge on the other side of the molecule—a separation of charge called a *dipole*. Consider a polar molecule such as hydrogen chloride, HCl. In the HCl molecule, the more electronegative Cl atom bears the partial negative charge, whereas the less electronegative H atom bears the partial positive charge. An attractive force between HCl molecules results from the attraction between the positive end of one HCl molecule and the negative end of another. This attractive force is called a **dipole-dipole attraction**—the electrostatic force between the partially positive end of one polar molecule and the partially negative end of another, as illustrated in Figure 10.9.

Figure 10.9 This image shows two arrangements of polar molecules, such as HCl, that allow an attraction between the partial negative end of one molecule and the partial positive end of another.

The effect of a dipole-dipole attraction is apparent when we compare the properties of HCl molecules to nonpolar F_2 molecules. Both HCl and F_2 consist of the same number of atoms and have approximately the same molecular mass. At a temperature of 150 K, molecules of both substances would have the same average KE. However, the dipole-dipole attractions between HCl molecules are sufficient to cause them to "stick together" to form a liquid, whereas the relatively weaker dispersion forces between nonpolar F_2 molecules are not, and so this substance is gaseous at this temperature. The higher normal boiling point of HCl (188 K) compared to F_2 (85 K) is a reflection of the greater strength of dipole-dipole attractions between HCl molecules, compared to the attractions between nonpolar F_2 molecules. We will often use values such as boiling or freezing points, or enthalpies of vaporization or fusion, as indicators of the relative strengths of IMFs of attraction present within different substances.

Example 10.2

Dipole-Dipole Forces and Their Effects

Predict which will have the higher boiling point: N_2 or CO. Explain your reasoning.

Solution

CO and N_2 are both diatomic molecules with masses of about 28 amu, so they experience similar London dispersion forces. Because CO is a polar molecule, it experiences dipole-dipole attractions. Because N_2 is nonpolar, its molecules cannot exhibit dipole-dipole attractions. The dipole-dipole attractions between CO molecules are comparably stronger than the dispersion forces between nonpolar N_2 molecules, so CO is expected to have the higher boiling point.

Check Your Learning

Predict which will have the higher boiling point: ICl or Br_2. Explain your reasoning.

Answer: ICl. ICl and Br_2 have similar masses (~160 amu) and therefore experience similar London dispersion forces. ICl is polar and thus also exhibits dipole-dipole attractions; Br_2 is nonpolar and does not. The relatively stronger dipole-dipole attractions require more energy to overcome, so ICl will have the higher boiling point.

Hydrogen Bonding

Nitrosyl fluoride (ONF, molecular mass 49 amu) is a gas at room temperature. Water (H_2O, molecular mass 18 amu) is a liquid, even though it has a lower molecular mass. We clearly cannot attribute this difference between the two compounds to dispersion forces. Both molecules have about the same shape and ONF is the heavier and larger molecule. It is, therefore, expected to experience more significant dispersion forces. Additionally, we cannot attribute this difference in boiling points to differences in the dipole moments of the molecules. Both molecules are polar and exhibit comparable dipole moments. The large difference between the boiling points is due to a particularly strong dipole-dipole attraction that may occur when a molecule contains a hydrogen atom bonded to a fluorine, oxygen, or nitrogen atom (the three most electronegative elements). The very large difference in electronegativity between the H atom (2.1) and the atom to which it is bonded (4.0 for an F atom, 3.5 for an O atom, or 3.0 for a N atom), combined with the very small size of a H atom and the relatively small sizes of F, O, or N atoms, leads to *highly concentrated partial charges* with these atoms. Molecules with F-H, O-H, or N-H moieties are very strongly attracted to similar moieties in nearby molecules, a particularly strong type of dipole-dipole attraction called **hydrogen bonding**. Examples of hydrogen bonds include HF$\cdots$HF, $H_2O\cdots$HOH, and $H_3N\cdots$HNH$_2$, in which the hydrogen bonds are denoted by dots. **Figure 10.10** illustrates hydrogen bonding between water molecules.

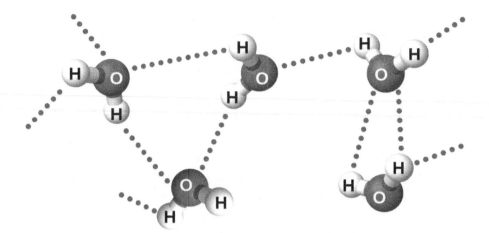

Figure 10.10   Water molecules participate in multiple hydrogen-bonding interactions with nearby water molecules.

Despite use of the word "bond," keep in mind that hydrogen bonds are *intermolecular* attractive forces, not *intramolecular* attractive forces (covalent bonds). Hydrogen bonds are much weaker than covalent bonds, only about 5 to 10% as strong, but are generally much stronger than other dipole-dipole attractions and dispersion forces.

Hydrogen bonds have a pronounced effect on the properties of condensed phases (liquids and solids). For example, consider the trends in boiling points for the binary hydrides of group 15 (NH_3, PH_3, AsH_3, and SbH_3), group 16 hydrides (H_2O, H_2S, H_2Se, and H_2Te), and group 17 hydrides (HF, HCl, HBr, and HI). The boiling points of the heaviest three hydrides for each group are plotted in Figure 10.11. As we progress down any of these groups, the polarities of the molecules decrease slightly, whereas the sizes of the molecules increase substantially. The effect of increasingly stronger dispersion forces dominates that of increasingly weaker dipole-dipole attractions, and the boiling points are observed to increase steadily.

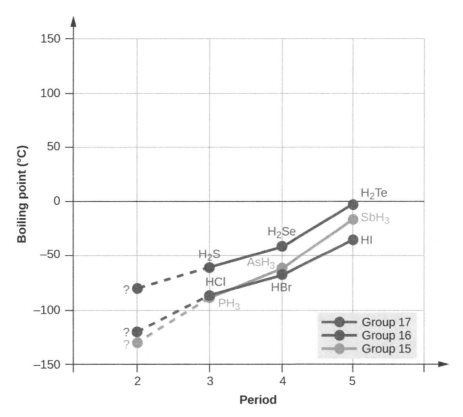

Figure 10.11 For the group 15, 16, and 17 hydrides, the boiling points for each class of compounds increase with increasing molecular mass for elements in periods 3, 4, and 5.

If we use this trend to predict the boiling points for the lightest hydride for each group, we would expect NH_3 to boil at about −120 °C, H_2O to boil at about −80 °C, and HF to boil at about −110 °C. However, when we measure the boiling points for these compounds, we find that they are dramatically higher than the trends would predict, as shown in **Figure 10.12**. The stark contrast between our naïve predictions and reality provides compelling evidence for the strength of hydrogen bonding.

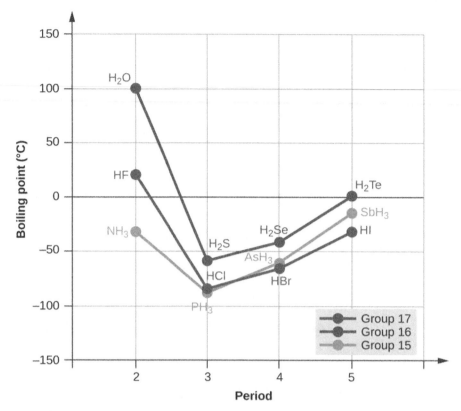

Figure 10.12 In comparison to periods 3–5, the binary hydrides of period 2 elements in groups 17, 16 and 15 (F, O and N, respectively) exhibit anomalously high boiling points due to hydrogen bonding.

Example 10.3

Effect of Hydrogen Bonding on Boiling Points

Consider the compounds dimethylether (CH_3OCH_3), ethanol (CH_3CH_2OH), and propane ($CH_3CH_2CH_3$). Their boiling points, not necessarily in order, are −42.1 °C, −24.8 °C, and 78.4 °C. Match each compound with its boiling point. Explain your reasoning.

Solution

The VSEPR-predicted shapes of CH_3OCH_3, CH_3CH_2OH, and $CH_3CH_2CH_3$ are similar, as are their molar masses (46 g/mol, 46 g/mol, and 44 g/mol, respectively), so they will exhibit similar dispersion forces. Since $CH_3CH_2CH_3$ is nonpolar, it may exhibit *only* dispersion forces. Because CH_3OCH_3 is polar, it will also experience dipole-dipole attractions. Finally, CH_3CH_2OH has an −OH group, and so it will experience the uniquely strong dipole-dipole attraction known as hydrogen bonding. So the ordering in terms of strength of IMFs, and thus boiling points, is $CH_3CH_2CH_3 < CH_3OCH_3 < CH_3CH_2OH$. The boiling point of propane is −42.1 °C, the boiling point of dimethylether is −24.8 °C, and the boiling point of ethanol is 78.5 °C.

Check Your Learning

Ethane (CH_3CH_3) has a melting point of −183 °C and a boiling point of −89 °C. Predict the melting and boiling points for methylamine (CH_3NH_2). Explain your reasoning.

Answer: The melting point and boiling point for methylamine are predicted to be significantly greater than those of ethane. CH_3CH_3 and CH_3NH_2 are similar in size and mass, but methylamine possesses an −NH group and therefore may exhibit hydrogen bonding. This greatly increases its IMFs, and therefore its melting and boiling points. It is difficult to predict values, but the known values are a melting point of −93 °C and a boiling point of −6 °C.

How Sciences Interconnect

Hydrogen Bonding and DNA

Deoxyribonucleic acid (DNA) is found in every living organism and contains the genetic information that determines the organism's characteristics, provides the blueprint for making the proteins necessary for life, and serves as a template to pass this information on to the organism's offspring. A DNA molecule consists of two (anti-)parallel chains of repeating nucleotides, which form its well-known double helical structure, as shown in Figure 10.13.

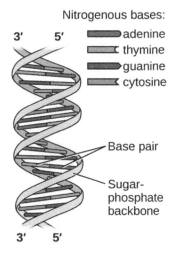

Figure 10.13 Two separate DNA molecules form a double-stranded helix in which the molecules are held together via hydrogen bonding. (credit: modification of work by Jerome Walker, Dennis Myts)

Each nucleotide contains a (deoxyribose) sugar bound to a phosphate group on one side, and one of four nitrogenous bases on the other. Two of the bases, cytosine (C) and thymine (T), are single-ringed structures known as pyrimidines. The other two, adenine (A) and guanine (G), are double-ringed structures called purines. These bases form complementary base pairs consisting of one purine and one pyrimidine, with adenine pairing with thymine, and cytosine with guanine. Each base pair is held together by hydrogen bonding. A and T share two hydrogen bonds, C and G share three, and both pairings have a similar shape and structure Figure 10.14.

Figure 10.14 The geometries of the base molecules result in maximum hydrogen bonding between adenine and thymine (AT) and between guanine and cytosine (GC), so-called "complementary base pairs."

The cumulative effect of millions of hydrogen bonds effectively holds the two strands of DNA together. Importantly, the two strands of DNA can relatively easily "unzip" down the middle since hydrogen bonds are relatively weak compared to the covalent bonds that hold the atoms of the individual DNA molecules together. This allows both strands to function as a template for replication.

10.2 Properties of Liquids

By the end of this section, you will be able to:

- Distinguish between adhesive and cohesive forces
- Define viscosity, surface tension, and capillary rise
- Describe the roles of intermolecular attractive forces in each of these properties/phenomena

When you pour a glass of water, or fill a car with gasoline, you observe that water and gasoline flow freely. But when you pour syrup on pancakes or add oil to a car engine, you note that syrup and motor oil do not flow as readily. The **viscosity** of a liquid is a measure of its resistance to flow. Water, gasoline, and other liquids that flow freely have a low viscosity. Honey, syrup, motor oil, and other liquids that do not flow freely, like those shown in Figure 10.15, have higher viscosities. We can measure viscosity by measuring the rate at which a metal ball falls through a liquid (the ball falls more slowly through a more viscous liquid) or by measuring the rate at which a liquid flows through a narrow tube (more viscous liquids flow more slowly).

(a)   (b)

Figure 10.15   (a) Honey and (b) motor oil are examples of liquids with high viscosities; they flow slowly. (credit a: modification of work by Scott Bauer; credit b: modification of work by David Nagy)

The IMFs between the molecules of a liquid, the size and shape of the molecules, and the temperature determine how easily a liquid flows. As Table 10.2 shows, the more structurally complex are the molecules in a liquid and the stronger the IMFs between them, the more difficult it is for them to move past each other and the greater is the viscosity of the liquid. As the temperature increases, the molecules move more rapidly and their kinetic energies are better able to overcome the forces that hold them together; thus, the viscosity of the liquid decreases.

Viscosities of Common Substances at 25 °C

Substance	Formula	Viscosity (mPa·s)
water	H_2O	0.890
mercury	Hg	1.526
ethanol	C_2H_5OH	1.074
octane	C_8H_{18}	0.508
ethylene glycol	$CH_2(OH)CH_2(OH)$	16.1
honey	variable	~2,000–10,000
motor oil	variable	~50–500

Table 10.2

The various IMFs between identical molecules of a substance are examples of **cohesive forces**. The molecules within a liquid are surrounded by other molecules and are attracted equally in all directions by the cohesive forces within the liquid. However, the molecules on the surface of a liquid are attracted only by about one-half as many molecules. Because of the unbalanced molecular attractions on the surface molecules, liquids contract to form a shape that minimizes the number of molecules on the surface—that is, the shape with the minimum surface area. A small drop of liquid tends to assume a spherical shape, as shown in Figure 10.16, because in a sphere, the ratio of surface area to volume is at a minimum. Larger drops are more greatly affected by gravity, air resistance, surface interactions, and so on, and as a result, are less spherical.

Figure 10.16 Attractive forces result in a spherical water drop that minimizes surface area; cohesive forces hold the sphere together; adhesive forces keep the drop attached to the web. (credit photo: modification of work by "OliBac"/Flickr)

Surface tension is defined as the energy required to increase the surface area of a liquid, or the force required to increase the length of a liquid surface by a given amount. This property results from the cohesive forces between molecules at the surface of a liquid, and it causes the surface of a liquid to behave like a stretched rubber membrane. Surface tensions of several liquids are presented in Table 10.3. Among common liquids, water exhibits a distinctly high surface tension due to strong hydrogen bonding between its molecules. As a result of this high surface tension, the surface of water represents a relatively "tough skin" that can withstand considerable force without breaking. A steel needle carefully placed on water will float. Some insects, like the one shown in Figure 10.17, even though they are denser than water, move on its surface because they are supported by the surface tension.

Surface Tensions of Common Substances at 25 °C

Substance	Formula	Surface Tension (mN/m)
water	H_2O	71.99
mercury	Hg	458.48
ethanol	C_2H_5OH	21.97
octane	C_8H_{18}	21.14
ethylene glycol	$CH_2(OH)CH_2(OH)$	47.99

Table 10.3

Figure 10.17 Surface tension (right) prevents this insect, a "water strider," from sinking into the water.

The IMFs of attraction between two *different* molecules are called **adhesive forces**. Consider what happens when water comes into contact with some surface. If the adhesive forces between water molecules and the molecules of the surface are weak compared to the cohesive forces between the water molecules, the water does not "wet" the surface. For example, water does not wet waxed surfaces or many plastics such as polyethylene. Water forms drops on these surfaces because the cohesive forces within the drops are greater than the adhesive forces between the water and the plastic. Water spreads out on glass because the adhesive force between water and glass is greater than the cohesive forces within the water. When water is confined in a glass tube, its meniscus (surface) has a concave shape because the water wets the glass and creeps up the side of the tube. On the other hand, the cohesive forces between mercury atoms are much greater than the adhesive forces between mercury and glass. Mercury therefore does not wet glass, and it forms a convex meniscus when confined in a tube because the cohesive forces within the mercury tend to draw it into a drop (**Figure 10.18**).

Figure 10.18   Differences in the relative strengths of cohesive and adhesive forces result in different meniscus shapes for mercury (left) and water (right) in glass tubes. (credit: Mark Ott)

If you place one end of a paper towel in spilled wine, as shown in **Figure 10.19**, the liquid wicks up the paper towel. A similar process occurs in a cloth towel when you use it to dry off after a shower. These are examples of **capillary action**—when a liquid flows within a porous material due to the attraction of the liquid molecules to the surface of the material and to other liquid molecules. The adhesive forces between the liquid and the porous material, combined with the cohesive forces within the liquid, may be strong enough to move the liquid upward against gravity.

Figure 10.19 Wine wicks up a paper towel (left) because of the strong attractions of water (and ethanol) molecules to the −OH groups on the towel's cellulose fibers and the strong attractions of water molecules to other water (and ethanol) molecules (right). (credit photo: modification of work by Mark Blaser)

Towels soak up liquids like water because the fibers of a towel are made of molecules that are attracted to water molecules. Most cloth towels are made of cotton, and paper towels are generally made from paper pulp. Both consist of long molecules of cellulose that contain many −OH groups. Water molecules are attracted to these −OH groups and form hydrogen bonds with them, which draws the H_2O molecules up the cellulose molecules. The water molecules are also attracted to each other, so large amounts of water are drawn up the cellulose fibers.

Capillary action can also occur when one end of a small diameter tube is immersed in a liquid, as illustrated in Figure 10.20. If the liquid molecules are strongly attracted to the tube molecules, the liquid creeps up the inside of the tube until the weight of the liquid and the adhesive forces are in balance. The smaller the diameter of the tube is, the higher the liquid climbs. It is partly by capillary action occurring in plant cells called xylem that water and dissolved nutrients are brought from the soil up through the roots and into a plant. Capillary action is the basis for thin layer chromatography, a laboratory technique commonly used to separate small quantities of mixtures. You depend on a constant supply of tears to keep your eyes lubricated and on capillary action to pump tear fluid away.

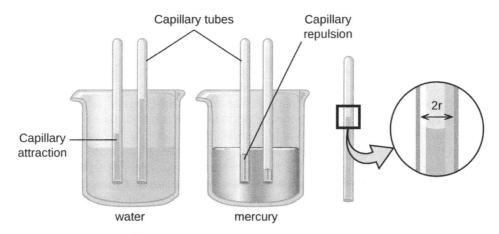

Figure 10.20 Depending upon the relative strengths of adhesive and cohesive forces, a liquid may rise (such as water) or fall (such as mercury) in a glass capillary tube. The extent of the rise (or fall) is directly proportional to the surface tension of the liquid and inversely proportional to the density of the liquid and the radius of the tube.

The height to which a liquid will rise in a capillary tube is determined by several factors as shown in the following equation:

$$h = \frac{2T \cos \theta}{r\rho g}$$

In this equation, h is the height of the liquid inside the capillary tube relative to the surface of the liquid outside the tube, T is the surface tension of the liquid, θ is the contact angle between the liquid and the tube, r is the radius of the tube, ρ is the density of the liquid, and g is the acceleration due to gravity, 9.8 m/s². When the tube is made of a material to which the liquid molecules are strongly attracted, they will spread out completely on the surface, which corresponds to a contact angle of 0°. This is the situation for water rising in a glass tube.

Example 10.4

Capillary Rise

At 25 °C, how high will water rise in a glass capillary tube with an inner diameter of 0.25 mm?

For water, T = 71.99 mN/m and ρ = 1.0 g/cm³.

Solution

The liquid will rise to a height h given by: $h = \frac{2T \cos \theta}{r\rho g}$

The Newton is defined as a kg m/s², and so the provided surface tension is equivalent to 0.07199 kg/s². The provided density must be converted into units that will cancel appropriately: ρ = 1000 kg/m³. The diameter of the tube in meters is 0.00025 m, so the radius is 0.000125 m. For a glass tube immersed in water, the contact angle is θ = 0°, so cos θ = 1. Finally, acceleration due to gravity on the earth is g = 9.8 m/s². Substituting these values into the equation, and cancelling units, we have:

$$h = \frac{2(0.07199 \text{ kg/s}^2)}{(0.000125 \text{ m})(1000 \text{ kg/m}^3)(9.8 \text{ m/s}^2)} = 0.12 \text{ m} = 12 \text{ cm}$$

Check Your Learning

Water rises in a glass capillary tube to a height of 8.4 cm. What is the diameter of the capillary tube?

Answer: diameter = 0.36 mm

Biomedical Applications of Capillary Action

Many medical tests require drawing a small amount of blood, for example to determine the amount of glucose in someone with diabetes or the hematocrit level in an athlete. This procedure can be easily done because of capillary action, the ability of a liquid to flow up a small tube against gravity, as shown in Figure 10.21. When your finger is pricked, a drop of blood forms and holds together due to surface tension—the unbalanced intermolecular attractions at the surface of the drop. Then, when the open end of a narrow-diameter glass tube touches the drop of blood, the adhesive forces between the molecules in the blood and those at the glass surface draw the blood up the tube. How far the blood goes up the tube depends on the diameter of the tube (and the type of fluid). A small tube has a relatively large surface area for a given volume of blood, which results in larger (relative) attractive forces, allowing the blood to be drawn farther up the tube. The liquid itself is held together by its own cohesive forces. When the weight of the liquid in the tube generates a downward force equal to the upward force associated with capillary action, the liquid stops rising.

Figure 10.21   Blood is collected for medical analysis by capillary action, which draws blood into a small diameter glass tube. (credit: modification of work by Centers for Disease Control and Prevention)

10.3 Phase Transitions

By the end of this section, you will be able to:

- Define phase transitions and phase transition temperatures
- Explain the relation between phase transition temperatures and intermolecular attractive forces
- Describe the processes represented by typical heating and cooling curves, and compute heat flows and enthalpy changes accompanying these processes

We witness and utilize changes of physical state, or phase transitions, in a great number of ways. As one example of global significance, consider the evaporation, condensation, freezing, and melting of water. These changes of state are essential aspects of our earth's water cycle as well as many other natural phenomena and technological processes of central importance to our lives. In this module, the essential aspects of phase transitions are explored.

Vaporization and Condensation

When a liquid vaporizes in a closed container, gas molecules cannot escape. As these gas phase molecules move randomly about, they will occasionally collide with the surface of the condensed phase, and in some cases, these collisions will result in the molecules re-entering the condensed phase. The change from the gas phase to the liquid is called **condensation**. When the rate of condensation becomes equal to the rate of **vaporization**, neither the amount of the liquid nor the amount of the vapor in the container changes. The vapor in the container is then said to be *in equilibrium* with the liquid. Keep in mind that this is not a static situation, as molecules are continually exchanged between the condensed and gaseous phases. Such is an example of a **dynamic equilibrium**, the status of a system in

Chapter 10 | Liquids and Solids
539

which reciprocal processes (for example, vaporization and condensation) occur at equal rates. The pressure exerted by the vapor in equilibrium with a liquid in a closed container at a given temperature is called the liquid's **vapor pressure** (or equilibrium vapor pressure). The area of the surface of the liquid in contact with a vapor and the size of the vessel have no effect on the vapor pressure, although they do affect the time required for the equilibrium to be reached. We can measure the vapor pressure of a liquid by placing a sample in a closed container, like that illustrated in Figure 10.22, and using a manometer to measure the increase in pressure that is due to the vapor in equilibrium with the condensed phase.

Figure 10.22 In a closed container, dynamic equilibrium is reached when (a) the rate of molecules escaping from the liquid to become the gas (b) increases and eventually (c) equals the rate of gas molecules entering the liquid. When this equilibrium is reached, the vapor pressure of the gas is constant, although the vaporization and condensation processes continue.

The chemical identities of the molecules in a liquid determine the types (and strengths) of intermolecular attractions possible; consequently, different substances will exhibit different equilibrium vapor pressures. Relatively strong intermolecular attractive forces will serve to impede vaporization as well as favoring "recapture" of gas-phase molecules when they collide with the liquid surface, resulting in a relatively low vapor pressure. Weak intermolecular attractions present less of a barrier to vaporization, and a reduced likelihood of gas recapture, yielding relatively high vapor pressures. The following example illustrates this dependence of vapor pressure on intermolecular attractive forces.

Example 10.5

Explaining Vapor Pressure in Terms of IMFs

Given the shown structural formulas for these four compounds, explain their relative vapor pressures in terms of types and extents of IMFs:

ethanol   ethylene glycol   diethyl ether   water

Solution

Diethyl ether has a very small dipole and most of its intermolecular attractions are London forces. Although this molecule is the largest of the four under consideration, its IMFs are the weakest and, as a result, its molecules most readily escape from the liquid. It also has the highest vapor pressure. Due to its smaller size, ethanol exhibits weaker dispersion forces than diethyl ether. However, ethanol is capable of hydrogen bonding and, therefore, exhibits stronger overall IMFs, which means that fewer molecules escape from the liquid at any given temperature, and so ethanol has a lower vapor pressure than diethyl ether. Water is much smaller than either of the previous substances and exhibits weaker dispersion forces, but its extensive hydrogen bonding provides stronger intermolecular attractions, fewer molecules escaping the liquid, and a lower vapor pressure than for either diethyl ether or ethanol. Ethylene glycol has two −OH groups, so, like water, it exhibits extensive hydrogen bonding. It is much larger than water and thus experiences larger London forces. Its overall IMFs are the largest of these four substances, which means its vaporization rate will be the slowest and, consequently, its vapor pressure the lowest.

Check Your Learning

At 20 °C, the vapor pressures of several alcohols are given in this table. Explain these vapor pressures in terms of types and extents of IMFs for these alcohols:

Compound	methanol CH_3OH	ethanol C_2H_5OH	propanol C_3H_7OH	butanol C_4H_9OH
Vapor Pressure at 20 °C	11.9 kPa	5.95 kPa	2.67 kPa	0.56 kPa

Answer: All these compounds exhibit hydrogen bonding; these strong IMFs are difficult for the molecules to overcome, so the vapor pressures are relatively low. As the size of molecule increases from methanol to butanol, dispersion forces increase, which means that the vapor pressures decrease as observed: $P_{methanol} > P_{ethanol} > P_{propanol} > P_{butanol}$.

As temperature increases, the vapor pressure of a liquid also increases due to the increased average KE of its molecules. Recall that at any given temperature, the molecules of a substance experience a range of kinetic energies, with a certain fraction of molecules having a sufficient energy to overcome IMF and escape the liquid (vaporize). At a higher temperature, a greater fraction of molecules have enough energy to escape from the liquid, as shown in Figure 10.23. The escape of more molecules per unit of time and the greater average speed of the molecules that escape both contribute to the higher vapor pressure.

Figure 10.23 Temperature affects the distribution of kinetic energies for the molecules in a liquid. At the higher temperature, more molecules have the necessary kinetic energy, KE, to escape from the liquid into the gas phase.

Boiling Points

When the vapor pressure increases enough to equal the external atmospheric pressure, the liquid reaches its boiling point. The **boiling point** of a liquid is the temperature at which its equilibrium vapor pressure is equal to the pressure exerted on the liquid by its gaseous surroundings. For liquids in open containers, this pressure is that due to the earth's atmosphere. The **normal boiling point** of a liquid is defined as its boiling point when surrounding pressure is equal to 1 atm (101.3 kPa). Figure 10.24 shows the variation in vapor pressure with temperature for several different substances. Considering the definition of boiling point, these curves may be seen as depicting the dependence of a liquid's boiling point on surrounding pressure.

Figure 10.24 The boiling points of liquids are the temperatures at which their equilibrium vapor pressures equal the pressure of the surrounding atmosphere. Normal boiling points are those corresponding to a pressure of 1 atm (101.3 kPa.)

Example 10.6

A Boiling Point at Reduced Pressure

A typical atmospheric pressure in Leadville, Colorado (elevation 10,200 feet) is 68 kPa. Use the graph in Figure 10.24 to determine the boiling point of water at this elevation.

Solution

The graph of the vapor pressure of water versus temperature in Figure 10.24 indicates that the vapor pressure of water is 68 kPa at about 90 °C. Thus, at about 90 °C, the vapor pressure of water will equal the atmospheric pressure in Leadville, and water will boil.

Check Your Learning

The boiling point of ethyl ether was measured to be 10 °C at a base camp on the slopes of Mount Everest. Use Figure 10.24 to determine the approximate atmospheric pressure at the camp.

Answer: Approximately 40 kPa (0.4 atm)

The quantitative relation between a substance's vapor pressure and its temperature is described by the **Clausius-Clapeyron equation**:

$$P = Ae^{-\Delta H_{vap}/RT}$$

where ΔH_{vap} is the enthalpy of vaporization for the liquid, R is the gas constant, and $\ln A$ is a constant whose value depends on the chemical identity of the substance. This equation is often rearranged into logarithmic form to yield the linear equation:

$$\ln P = -\frac{\Delta H_{vap}}{RT} + \ln A$$

This linear equation may be expressed in a two-point format that is convenient for use in various computations, as demonstrated in the example exercises that follow. If at temperature T_1, the vapor pressure is P_1, and at temperature T_2, the vapor pressure is T_2, the corresponding linear equations are:

$$\ln P_1 = -\frac{\Delta H_{vap}}{RT_1} + \ln A \qquad\qquad \text{and} \qquad\qquad \ln P_2 = -\frac{\Delta H_{vap}}{RT_2} + \ln A$$

Since the constant, $\ln A$, is the same, these two equations may be rearranged to isolate $\ln A$ and then set them equal to one another:

$$\ln P_1 + \frac{\Delta H_{vap}}{RT_1} = \ln P_2 + \frac{\Delta H_{vap}}{RT_2}$$

which can be combined into:

$$\ln\left(\frac{P_2}{P_1}\right) = \frac{\Delta H_{vap}}{R}\left(\frac{1}{T_1} - \frac{1}{T_2}\right)$$

Example 10.7

Estimating Enthalpy of Vaporization

Isooctane (2,2,4-trimethylpentane) has an octane rating of 100. It is used as one of the standards for the octane-rating system for gasoline. At 34.0 °C, the vapor pressure of isooctane is 10.0 kPa, and at 98.8 °C, its vapor pressure is 100.0 kPa. Use this information to estimate the enthalpy of vaporization for isooctane.

Solution

The enthalpy of vaporization, ΔH_{vap}, can be determined by using the Clausius-Clapeyron equation:

$$\ln\left(\frac{P_2}{P_1}\right) = \frac{\Delta H_{vap}}{R}\left(\frac{1}{T_1} - \frac{1}{T_2}\right)$$

Since we have two vapor pressure-temperature values (T_1 = 34.0 °C = 307.2 K, P_1 = 10.0 kPa and T_2 = 98.8 °C = 372.0 K, P_2 = 100 kPa), we can substitute them into this equation and solve for ΔH_{vap}. Rearranging the Clausius-Clapeyron equation and solving for ΔH_{vap} yields:

$$\Delta H_{vap} = \frac{R \cdot \ln\left(\frac{P_2}{P_1}\right)}{\left(\frac{1}{T_1} - \frac{1}{T_2}\right)} = \frac{(8.3145 \text{ J/mol·K}) \cdot \ln\left(\frac{100 \text{ kPa}}{10.0 \text{ kPa}}\right)}{\left(\frac{1}{307.2 \text{ K}} - \frac{1}{372.0 \text{ K}}\right)} = 33{,}800 \text{ J/mol} = 33.8 \text{ kJ/mol}$$

Note that the pressure can be in any units, so long as they agree for both P values, but the temperature must be in kelvin for the Clausius-Clapeyron equation to be valid.

Check Your Learning

At 20.0 °C, the vapor pressure of ethanol is 5.95 kPa, and at 63.5 °C, its vapor pressure is 53.3 kPa. Use this information to estimate the enthalpy of vaporization for ethanol.

Answer: 47,782 J/mol = 47.8 kJ/mol

Example 10.8

Estimating Temperature (or Vapor Pressure)

For benzene (C_6H_6), the normal boiling point is 80.1 °C and the enthalpy of vaporization is 30.8 kJ/mol. What is the boiling point of benzene in Denver, where atmospheric pressure = 83.4 kPa?

Solution

If the temperature and vapor pressure are known at one point, along with the enthalpy of vaporization, ΔH_{vap}, then the temperature that corresponds to a different vapor pressure (or the vapor pressure that corresponds to a different temperature) can be determined by using the Clausius-Clapeyron equation:

$$\ln\left(\frac{P_2}{P_1}\right) = \frac{\Delta H_{vap}}{R}\left(\frac{1}{T_1} - \frac{1}{T_2}\right)$$

Since the normal boiling point is the temperature at which the vapor pressure equals atmospheric pressure at sea level, we know one vapor pressure-temperature value ($T_1 = 80.1\ °C = 353.3\ K$, $P_1 = 101.3\ kPa$, $\Delta H_{vap} = 30.8\ kJ/mol$) and want to find the temperature (T_2) that corresponds to vapor pressure $P_2 = 83.4\ kPa$. We can substitute these values into the Clausius-Clapeyron equation and then solve for T_2. Rearranging the Clausius-Clapeyron equation and solving for T_2 yields:

$$T_2 = \left(\frac{-R\cdot\ln\left(\frac{P_2}{P_1}\right)}{\Delta H_{vap}} + \frac{1}{T_1}\right)^{-1} = \left(\frac{-(8.3145\ J/mol\cdot K)\cdot\ln\left(\frac{83.4\ kPa}{101.3\ kPa}\right)}{30,800\ J/mol} + \frac{1}{353.3\ K}\right)^{-1} = 346.9\ K\ \text{or}\ 73.8°\,C$$

Check Your Learning

For acetone $(CH_3)_2CO$, the normal boiling point is 56.5 °C and the enthalpy of vaporization is 31.3 kJ/mol. What is the vapor pressure of acetone at 25.0 °C?

Answer: 30.1 kPa

Enthalpy of Vaporization

Vaporization is an endothermic process. The cooling effect can be evident when you leave a swimming pool or a shower. When the water on your skin evaporates, it removes heat from your skin and causes you to feel cold. The energy change associated with the vaporization process is the enthalpy of vaporization, ΔH_{vap}. For example, the vaporization of water at standard temperature is represented by:

$$H_2O(l) \longrightarrow H_2O(g) \qquad \Delta H_{vap} = 44.01\ kJ/mol$$

As described in the chapter on thermochemistry, the reverse of an endothermic process is exothermic. And so, the condensation of a gas releases heat:

$$H_2O(g) \longrightarrow H_2O(l) \qquad \Delta H_{con} = -\Delta H_{vap} = -44.01\ kJ/mol$$

Example 10.9

Using Enthalpy of Vaporization

One way our body is cooled is by evaporation of the water in sweat (Figure 10.25). In very hot climates, we can lose as much as 1.5 L of sweat per day. Although sweat is not pure water, we can get an approximate value of the amount of heat removed by evaporation by assuming that it is. How much heat is required to evaporate 1.5 L of water (1.5 kg) at $T = 37\ °C$ (normal body temperature); $\Delta H_{vap} = 43.46\ kJ/mol$ at 37 °C.

Figure 10.25   Evaporation of sweat helps cool the body. (credit: "Kullez"/Flickr)

Solution

We start with the known volume of sweat (approximated as just water) and use the given information to convert to the amount of heat needed:

$$1.5 \, \cancel{L} \times \frac{1000 \, \cancel{g}}{1 \, \cancel{L}} \times \frac{1 \, \cancel{mol}}{18 \, \cancel{g}} \times \frac{43.46 \, kJ}{1 \, \cancel{mol}} = 3.6 \times 10^3 \, kJ$$

Thus, 3600 kJ of heat are removed by the evaporation of 1.5 L of water.

Check Your Learning

How much heat is required to evaporate 100.0 g of liquid ammonia, NH_3, at its boiling point if its enthalpy of vaporization is 4.8 kJ/mol?

Answer: 28 kJ

Melting and Freezing

When we heat a crystalline solid, we increase the average energy of its atoms, molecules, or ions and the solid gets hotter. At some point, the added energy becomes large enough to partially overcome the forces holding the molecules or ions of the solid in their fixed positions, and the solid begins the process of transitioning to the liquid state, or **melting**. At this point, the temperature of the solid stops rising, despite the continual input of heat, and it remains constant until all of the solid is melted. Only after all of the solid has melted will continued heating increase the temperature of the liquid (Figure 10.26).

(a)   (b)   (c)   (d)

Figure 10.26   (a) This beaker of ice has a temperature of −12.0 °C. (b) After 10 minutes the ice has absorbed enough heat from the air to warm to 0 °C. A small amount has melted. (c) Thirty minutes later, the ice has absorbed more heat, but its temperature is still 0 °C. The ice melts without changing its temperature. (d) Only after all the ice has melted does the heat absorbed cause the temperature to increase to 22.2 °C. (credit: modification of work by Mark Ott)

If we stop heating during melting and place the mixture of solid and liquid in a perfectly insulated container so no heat can enter or escape, the solid and liquid phases remain in equilibrium. This is almost the situation with a mixture of ice and water in a very good thermos bottle; almost no heat gets in or out, and the mixture of solid ice and liquid water remains for hours. In a mixture of solid and liquid at equilibrium, the reciprocal processes of melting and **freezing** occur at equal rates, and the quantities of solid and liquid therefore remain constant. The temperature at which the solid and liquid phases of a given substance are in equilibrium is called the **melting point** of the solid or the **freezing point** of the liquid. Use of one term or the other is normally dictated by the direction of the phase transition being considered, for example, solid to liquid (melting) or liquid to solid (freezing).

The enthalpy of fusion and the melting point of a crystalline solid depend on the strength of the attractive forces between the units present in the crystal. Molecules with weak attractive forces form crystals with low melting points. Crystals consisting of particles with stronger attractive forces melt at higher temperatures.

The amount of heat required to change one mole of a substance from the solid state to the liquid state is the enthalpy of fusion, ΔH_{fus} of the substance. The enthalpy of fusion of ice is 6.0 kJ/mol at 0 °C. Fusion (melting) is an endothermic process:

$$H_2O(s) \longrightarrow H_2O(l) \qquad\qquad \Delta H_{fus} = 6.01 \text{ kJ/mol}$$

The reciprocal process, freezing, is an exothermic process whose enthalpy change is −6.0 kJ/mol at 0 °C:

$$H_2O(l) \longrightarrow H_2O(s) \qquad\qquad \Delta H_{frz} = -\Delta H_{fus} = -6.01 \text{ kJ/mol}$$

Sublimation and Deposition

Some solids can transition directly into the gaseous state, bypassing the liquid state, via a process known as **sublimation**. At room temperature and standard pressure, a piece of dry ice (solid CO_2) sublimes, appearing to gradually disappear without ever forming any liquid. Snow and ice sublime at temperatures below the melting point of water, a slow process that may be accelerated by winds and the reduced atmospheric pressures at high altitudes. When solid iodine is warmed, the solid sublimes and a vivid purple vapor forms (Figure 10.27). The reverse of sublimation is called **deposition**, a process in which gaseous substances condense directly into the solid state, bypassing the liquid state. The formation of frost is an example of deposition.

Figure 10.27 Sublimation of solid iodine in the bottom of the tube produces a purple gas that subsequently deposits as solid iodine on the colder part of the tube above. (credit: modification of work by Mark Ott)

Like vaporization, the process of sublimation requires an input of energy to overcome intermolecular attractions. The enthalpy of sublimation, ΔH_{sub}, is the energy required to convert one mole of a substance from the solid to the gaseous state. For example, the sublimation of carbon dioxide is represented by:

$$CO_2(s) \longrightarrow CO_2(g) \qquad\qquad \Delta H_{sub} = 26.1 \text{ kJ/mol}$$

Likewise, the enthalpy change for the reverse process of deposition is equal in magnitude but opposite in sign to that for sublimation:

$$CO_2(g) \longrightarrow CO_2(s) \qquad\qquad \Delta H_{dep} = -\Delta H_{sub} = -26.1 \text{ kJ/mol}$$

Consider the extent to which intermolecular attractions must be overcome to achieve a given phase transition. Converting a solid into a liquid requires that these attractions be only partially overcome; transition to the gaseous state requires that they be completely overcome. As a result, the enthalpy of fusion for a substance is less than its enthalpy of vaporization. This same logic can be used to derive an approximate relation between the enthalpies of all phase changes for a given substance. Though not an entirely accurate description, sublimation may be conveniently modeled as a sequential two-step process of melting followed by vaporization in order to apply Hess's Law. Viewed in this manner, the enthalpy of sublimation for a substance may be estimated as the sum of its enthalpies of fusion and vaporization, as illustrated in **Figure 10.28**. For example:

$$\text{solid} \longrightarrow \text{liquid} \qquad \Delta H_{\text{fus}}$$
$$\text{liquid} \longrightarrow \text{gas} \qquad \Delta H_{\text{vap}}$$

$$\overline{\text{solid} \longrightarrow \text{gas} \qquad \Delta H_{\text{sub}} = \Delta H_{\text{fus}} + \Delta H_{\text{vap}}}$$

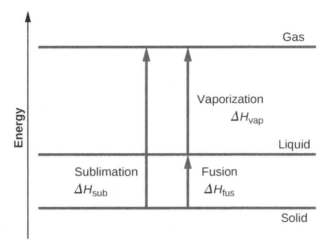

Figure 10.28 For a given substance, the sum of its enthalpy of fusion and enthalpy of vaporization is approximately equal to its enthalpy of sublimation.

Heating and Cooling Curves

In the chapter on thermochemistry, the relation between the amount of heat absorbed or related by a substance, q, and its accompanying temperature change, ΔT, was introduced:

$$q = mc\Delta T$$

where m is the mass of the substance and c is its specific heat. The relation applies to matter being heated or cooled, but not undergoing a change in state. When a substance being heated or cooled reaches a temperature corresponding to one of its phase transitions, further gain or loss of heat is a result of diminishing or enhancing intermolecular attractions, instead of increasing or decreasing molecular kinetic energies. While a substance is undergoing a change in state, its temperature remains constant. **Figure 10.29** shows a typical heating curve.

Consider the example of heating a pot of water to boiling. A stove burner will supply heat at a roughly constant rate; initially, this heat serves to increase the water's temperature. When the water reaches its boiling point, the temperature remains constant despite the continued input of heat from the stove burner. This same temperature is maintained by the water as long as it is boiling. If the burner setting is increased to provide heat at a greater rate, the water temperature does not rise, but instead the boiling becomes more vigorous (rapid). This behavior is observed for other phase transitions as well: For example, temperature remains constant while the change of state is in progress.

Figure 10.29   A typical heating curve for a substance depicts changes in temperature that result as the substance absorbs increasing amounts of heat. Plateaus in the curve (regions of constant temperature) are exhibited when the substance undergoes phase transitions.

Example 10.10

Total Heat Needed to Change Temperature and Phase for a Substance

How much heat is required to convert 135 g of ice at −15 °C into water vapor at 120 °C?

Solution

The transition described involves the following steps:

1. Heat ice from −15 °C to 0 °C

2. Melt ice

3. Heat water from 0 °C to 100 °C

4. Boil water

5. Heat steam from 100 °C to 120 °C

The heat needed to change the temperature of a given substance (with no change in phase) is: $q = m \times c \times \Delta T$ (see previous chapter on thermochemistry). The heat needed to induce a given change in phase is given by $q = n \times \Delta H$.

Using these equations with the appropriate values for specific heat of ice, water, and steam, and enthalpies of fusion and vaporization, we have:

$$q_{total} = (m \cdot c \cdot \Delta T)_{ice} + n \cdot \Delta H_{fus} + (m \cdot c \cdot \Delta T)_{water} + n \cdot \Delta H_{vap} + (m \cdot c \cdot \Delta T)_{steam}$$

$$= (135 \text{ g} \cdot 2.09 \text{ J/g} \cdot °C \cdot 15°C) + \left(135 \cdot \frac{1 \text{ mol}}{18.02 \text{ g}} \cdot 6.01 \text{ kJ/mol}\right)$$

$$+(135 \text{ g} \cdot 4.18 \text{ J/g} \cdot °C \cdot 100°C) + \left(135 \text{ g} \cdot \frac{1 \text{ mol}}{18.02 \text{ g}} \cdot 40.67 \text{ kJ/mol}\right)$$

$$+(135 \text{ g} \cdot 1.84 \text{ J/g} \cdot °C \cdot 20°C)$$
$$= 4230 \text{ J} + 45.0 \text{ kJ} + 56{,}500 \text{ J} + 305 \text{ kJ} + 4970 \text{ J}$$

Converting the quantities in J to kJ permits them to be summed, yielding the total heat required:

$$= 4.23 \text{ kJ} + 45.0 \text{ kJ} + 56.5 \text{ kJ} + 305 \text{ kJ} + 4.97 \text{ kJ} = 416 \text{ kJ}$$

Check Your Learning

What is the total amount of heat released when 94.0 g water at 80.0 °C cools to form ice at −30.0 °C?

Answer: 40.5 kJ

10.4 Phase Diagrams

By the end of this section, you will be able to:

- Explain the construction and use of a typical phase diagram
- Use phase diagrams to identify stable phases at given temperatures and pressures, and to describe phase transitions resulting from changes in these properties
- Describe the supercritical fluid phase of matter

In the previous module, the variation of a liquid's equilibrium vapor pressure with temperature was described. Considering the definition of boiling point, plots of vapor pressure versus temperature represent how the boiling point of the liquid varies with pressure. Also described was the use of heating and cooling curves to determine a substance's melting (or freezing) point. Making such measurements over a wide range of pressures yields data that may be presented graphically as a phase diagram. A **phase diagram** combines plots of pressure versus temperature for the liquid-gas, solid-liquid, and solid-gas phase-transition equilibria of a substance. These diagrams indicate the physical states that exist under specific conditions of pressure and temperature, and also provide the pressure dependence of the phase-transition temperatures (melting points, sublimation points, boiling points). A typical phase diagram for a pure substance is shown in Figure 10.30.

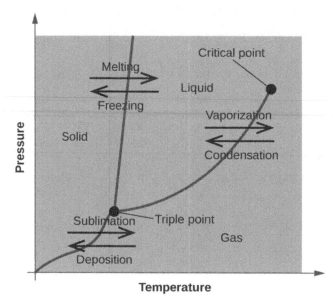

Figure 10.30 The physical state of a substance and its phase-transition temperatures are represented graphically in a phase diagram.

To illustrate the utility of these plots, consider the phase diagram for water shown in **Figure 10.31**.

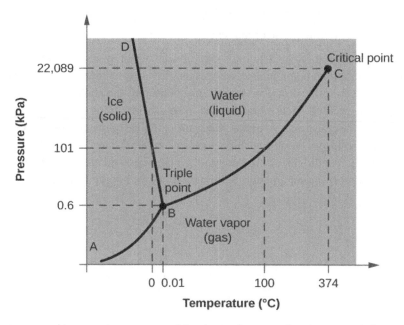

Figure 10.31 The pressure and temperature axes on this phase diagram of water are not drawn to constant scale in order to illustrate several important properties.

We can use the phase diagram to identify the physical state of a sample of water under specified conditions of pressure and temperature. For example, a pressure of 50 kPa and a temperature of −10 °C correspond to the region of the diagram labeled "ice." Under these conditions, water exists only as a solid (ice). A pressure of 50 kPa and a temperature of 50 °C correspond to the "water" region—here, water exists only as a liquid. At 25 kPa and 200 °C, water exists only in the gaseous state. Note that on the H_2O phase diagram, the pressure and temperature axes are not drawn to a constant scale in order to permit the illustration of several important features as described here.

The curve BC in Figure 10.31 is the plot of vapor pressure versus temperature as described in the previous module of this chapter. This "liquid-vapor" curve separates the liquid and gaseous regions of the phase diagram and provides the boiling point for water at any pressure. For example, at 1 atm, the boiling point is 100 °C. Notice that the liquid-vapor curve terminates at a temperature of 374 °C and a pressure of 218 atm, indicating that water cannot exist as a liquid above this temperature, regardless of the pressure. The physical properties of water under these conditions are intermediate between those of its liquid and gaseous phases. This unique state of matter is called a supercritical fluid, a topic that will be described in the next section of this module.

The solid-vapor curve, labeled AB in Figure 10.31, indicates the temperatures and pressures at which ice and water vapor are in equilibrium. These temperature-pressure data pairs correspond to the sublimation, or deposition, points for water. If we could zoom in on the solid-gas line in Figure 10.31, we would see that ice has a vapor pressure of about 0.20 kPa at −10 °C. Thus, if we place a frozen sample in a vacuum with a pressure less than 0.20 kPa, ice will sublime. This is the basis for the "freeze-drying" process often used to preserve foods, such as the ice cream shown in Figure 10.32.

Figure 10.32   Freeze-dried foods, like this ice cream, are dehydrated by sublimation at pressures below the triple point for water. (credit: "Iwao"/Flickr)

The solid-liquid curve labeled BD shows the temperatures and pressures at which ice and liquid water are in equilibrium, representing the melting/freezing points for water. Note that this curve exhibits a slight negative slope (greatly exaggerated for clarity), indicating that the melting point for water decreases slightly as pressure increases. Water is an unusual substance in this regard, as most substances exhibit an increase in melting point with increasing pressure. This behavior is partly responsible for the movement of glaciers, like the one shown in Figure 10.33. The bottom of a glacier experiences an immense pressure due to its weight that can melt some of the ice, forming a layer of liquid water on which the glacier may more easily slide.

Figure 10.33   The immense pressures beneath glaciers result in partial melting to produce a layer of water that provides lubrication to assist glacial movement. This satellite photograph shows the advancing edge of the Perito Moreno glacier in Argentina. (credit: NASA)

The point of intersection of all three curves is labeled B in **Figure 10.31**. At the pressure and temperature represented by this point, all three phases of water coexist in equilibrium. This temperature-pressure data pair is called the **triple point**. At pressures lower than the triple point, water cannot exist as a liquid, regardless of the temperature.

Example 10.11

Determining the State of Water

Using the phase diagram for water given in **Figure 10.31**, determine the state of water at the following temperatures and pressures:

(a) −10 °C and 50 kPa

(b) 25 °C and 90 kPa

(c) 50 °C and 40 kPa

(d) 80 °C and 5 kPa

(e) −10 °C and 0.3 kPa

(f) 50 °C and 0.3 kPa

Solution

Using the phase diagram for water, we can determine that the state of water at each temperature and pressure given are as follows: (a) solid; (b) liquid; (c) liquid; (d) gas; (e) solid; (f) gas.

Check Your Learning

What phase changes can water undergo as the temperature changes if the pressure is held at 0.3 kPa? If the pressure is held at 50 kPa?

Answer: At 0.3 kPa: s ⟶ g at −58 °C. At 50 kPa: s ⟶ l at 0 °C, l ⟶ g at 78 °C

Consider the phase diagram for carbon dioxide shown in **Figure 10.34** as another example. The solid-liquid curve exhibits a positive slope, indicating that the melting point for CO_2 increases with pressure as it does for most substances (water being a notable exception as described previously). Notice that the triple point is well above 1 atm, indicating that carbon dioxide cannot exist as a liquid under ambient pressure conditions. Instead, cooling gaseous carbon dioxide at 1 atm results in its deposition into the solid state. Likewise, solid carbon dioxide does not melt at 1 atm pressure but instead sublimes to yield gaseous CO_2. Finally, notice that the critical point for carbon dioxide is observed at a relatively modest temperature and pressure in comparison to water.

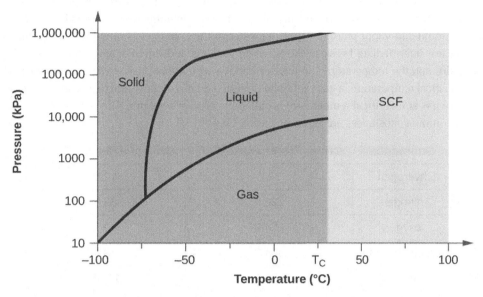

Figure 10.34 The pressure and temperature axes on this phase diagram of carbon dioxide are not drawn to constant scale in order to illustrate several important properties.

Example 10.12

Determining the State of Carbon Dioxide

Using the phase diagram for carbon dioxide shown in Figure 10.34, determine the state of CO_2 at the following temperatures and pressures:

(a) −30 °C and 2000 kPa

(b) −60 °C and 1000 kPa

(c) −60 °C and 100 kPa

(d) 20 °C and 1500 kPa

(e) 0 °C and 100 kPa

(f) 20 °C and 100 kPa

Solution

Using the phase diagram for carbon dioxide provided, we can determine that the state of CO_2 at each temperature and pressure given are as follows: (a) liquid; (b) solid; (c) gas; (d) liquid; (e) gas; (f) gas.

Check Your Learning

Determine the phase changes carbon dioxide undergoes when its temperature is varied, thus holding its pressure constant at 1500 kPa? At 500 kPa? At what approximate temperatures do these phase changes occur?

Answer: at 1500 kPa: s ⟶ l at −45 °C, l ⟶ g at −10 °C; at 500 kPa: s ⟶ g at −58 °C

Supercritical Fluids

If we place a sample of water in a sealed container at 25 °C, remove the air, and let the vaporization-condensation equilibrium establish itself, we are left with a mixture of liquid water and water vapor at a pressure of 0.03 atm.

A distinct boundary between the more dense liquid and the less dense gas is clearly observed. As we increase the temperature, the pressure of the water vapor increases, as described by the liquid-gas curve in the phase diagram for water (Figure 10.31), and a two-phase equilibrium of liquid and gaseous phases remains. At a temperature of 374 °C, the vapor pressure has risen to 218 atm, and any further increase in temperature results in the disappearance of the boundary between liquid and vapor phases. All of the water in the container is now present in a single phase whose physical properties are intermediate between those of the gaseous and liquid states. This phase of matter is called a **supercritical fluid**, and the temperature and pressure above which this phase exists is the **critical point** (Figure 10.35). Above its critical temperature, a gas cannot be liquefied no matter how much pressure is applied. The pressure required to liquefy a gas at its critical temperature is called the critical pressure. The critical temperatures and critical pressures of some common substances are given in Table 10.4.

Substance	Critical Temperature (K)	Critical Pressure (atm)
hydrogen	33.2	12.8
nitrogen	126.0	33.5
oxygen	154.3	49.7
carbon dioxide	304.2	73.0
ammonia	405.5	111.5
sulfur dioxide	430.3	77.7
water	647.1	217.7

Table 10.4

Figure 10.35 (a) A sealed container of liquid carbon dioxide slightly below its critical point is heated, resulting in (b) the formation of the supercritical fluid phase. Cooling the supercritical fluid lowers its temperature and pressure below the critical point, resulting in the reestablishment of separate liquid and gaseous phases (c and d). Colored floats illustrate differences in density between the liquid, gaseous, and supercritical fluid states. (credit: modification of work by "mrmrobin"/YouTube)

Link to Learning

Observe the liquid-to-supercritical fluid transition (http://openstaxcollege.org/l/16supercrit) for carbon dioxide.

Like a gas, a supercritical fluid will expand and fill a container, but its density is much greater than typical gas densities, typically being close to those for liquids. Similar to liquids, these fluids are capable of dissolving nonvolatile solutes. They exhibit essentially no surface tension and very low viscosities, however, so they can more effectively penetrate very small openings in a solid mixture and remove soluble components. These properties make supercritical fluids extremely useful solvents for a wide range of applications. For example, supercritical carbon dioxide has become a very popular solvent in the food industry, being used to decaffeinate coffee, remove fats from potato chips, and extract flavor and fragrance compounds from citrus oils. It is nontoxic, relatively inexpensive, and not considered to be a pollutant. After use, the CO_2 can be easily recovered by reducing the pressure and collecting the resulting gas.

Example 10.13

The Critical Temperature of Carbon Dioxide

If we shake a carbon dioxide fire extinguisher on a cool day (18 °C), we can hear liquid CO_2 sloshing around inside the cylinder. However, the same cylinder appears to contain no liquid on a hot summer day (35 °C). Explain these observations.

Solution

On the cool day, the temperature of the CO_2 is below the critical temperature of CO_2, 304 K or 31 °C (Table 10.4), so liquid CO_2 is present in the cylinder. On the hot day, the temperature of the CO_2 is greater than its critical temperature of 31 °C. Above this temperature no amount of pressure can liquefy CO_2 so no liquid CO_2 exists in the fire extinguisher.

Check Your Learning

Ammonia can be liquefied by compression at room temperature; oxygen cannot be liquefied under these conditions. Why do the two gases exhibit different behavior?

Answer: The critical temperature of ammonia is 405.5 K, which is higher than room temperature. The critical temperature of oxygen is below room temperature; thus oxygen cannot be liquefied at room temperature.

Chemistry in Everyday Life

Decaffeinating Coffee Using Supercritical CO_2

Coffee is the world's second most widely traded commodity, following only petroleum. Across the globe, people love coffee's aroma and taste. Many of us also depend on one component of coffee—caffeine—to help us get going in the morning or stay alert in the afternoon. But late in the day, coffee's stimulant effect can keep you from sleeping, so you may choose to drink decaffeinated coffee in the evening.

Since the early 1900s, many methods have been used to decaffeinate coffee. All have advantages and disadvantages, and all depend on the physical and chemical properties of caffeine. Because caffeine is a somewhat polar molecule, it dissolves well in water, a polar liquid. However, since many of the other 400-plus compounds that contribute to coffee's taste and aroma also dissolve in H_2O, hot water decaffeination processes can also remove some of these compounds, adversely affecting the smell and taste of the decaffeinated coffee. Dichloromethane (CH_2Cl_2) and ethyl acetate ($CH_3CO_2C_2H_5$) have similar polarity to caffeine, and are therefore very effective solvents for caffeine extraction, but both also remove some flavor and aroma components, and their use requires long extraction and cleanup times. Because both of these solvents are toxic, health concerns have been raised regarding the effect of residual solvent remaining in the decaffeinated coffee.

Supercritical fluid extraction using carbon dioxide is now being widely used as a more effective and environmentally friendly decaffeination method (Figure 10.36). At temperatures above 304.2 K and pressures above 7376 kPa, CO_2 is a supercritical fluid, with properties of both gas and liquid. Like a gas, it penetrates deep into the coffee beans; like a liquid, it effectively dissolves certain substances. Supercritical carbon dioxide extraction of steamed coffee beans removes 97–99% of the caffeine, leaving coffee's flavor and aroma compounds intact. Because CO_2 is a gas under standard conditions, its removal from the extracted coffee beans is easily accomplished, as is the recovery of the caffeine from the extract. The caffeine recovered from coffee beans via this process is a valuable product that can be used subsequently as an additive to other foods or drugs.

Figure 10.36   (a) Caffeine molecules have both polar and nonpolar regions, making it soluble in solvents of varying polarities. (b) The schematic shows a typical decaffeination process involving supercritical carbon dioxide.

10.5 The Solid State of Matter

By the end of this section, you will be able to:

- Define and describe the bonding and properties of ionic, molecular, metallic, and covalent network crystalline solids

- Describe the main types of crystalline solids: ionic solids, metallic solids, covalent network solids, and molecular solids

- Explain the ways in which crystal defects can occur in a solid

When most liquids are cooled, they eventually freeze and form **crystalline solids**, solids in which the atoms, ions, or molecules are arranged in a definite repeating pattern. It is also possible for a liquid to freeze before its molecules become arranged in an orderly pattern. The resulting materials are called **amorphous solids** or noncrystalline solids (or, sometimes, glasses). The particles of such solids lack an ordered internal structure and are randomly arranged (**Figure 10.37**).

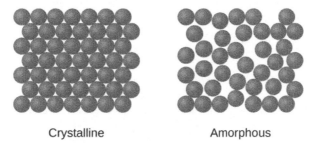

Crystalline   Amorphous

Figure 10.37 The entities of a solid phase may be arranged in a regular, repeating pattern (crystalline solids) or randomly (amorphous).

Metals and ionic compounds typically form ordered, crystalline solids. Substances that consist of large molecules, or a mixture of molecules whose movements are more restricted, often form amorphous solids. For examples, candle waxes are amorphous solids composed of large hydrocarbon molecules. Some substances, such as boron oxide (shown in **Figure 10.38**), can form either crystalline or amorphous solids, depending on the conditions under which it is produced. Also, amorphous solids may undergo a transition to the crystalline state under appropriate conditions.

(a)   (b)

Figure 10.38 (a) Diboron trioxide, B_2O_3, is normally found as a white, amorphous solid (a glass), which has a high degree of disorder in its structure. (b) By careful, extended heating, it can be converted into a crystalline form of B_2O_3, which has a very ordered arrangement.

Crystalline solids are generally classified according the nature of the forces that hold its particles together. These forces are primarily responsible for the physical properties exhibited by the bulk solids. The following sections provide descriptions of the major types of crystalline solids: ionic, metallic, covalent network, and molecular.

Ionic Solids

Ionic solids, such as sodium chloride and nickel oxide, are composed of positive and negative ions that are held together by electrostatic attractions, which can be quite strong (**Figure 10.39**). Many ionic crystals also have high melting points. This is due to the very strong attractions between the ions—in ionic compounds, the attractions between full charges are (much) larger than those between the partial charges in polar molecular compounds. This will be looked at in more detail in a later discussion of lattice energies. Although they are hard, they also tend to be brittle, and they shatter rather than bend. Ionic solids do not conduct electricity; however, they do conduct when molten or dissolved because their ions are free to move. Many simple compounds formed by the reaction of a metallic element with a nonmetallic element are ionic.

Figure 10.39   Sodium chloride is an ionic solid.

Metallic Solids

Metallic solids such as crystals of copper, aluminum, and iron are formed by metal atoms **Figure 10.40**. The structure of metallic crystals is often described as a uniform distribution of atomic nuclei within a "sea" of delocalized electrons. The atoms within such a metallic solid are held together by a unique force known as *metallic bonding* that gives rise to many useful and varied bulk properties. All exhibit high thermal and electrical conductivity, metallic luster, and malleability. Many are very hard and quite strong. Because of their malleability (the ability to deform under pressure or hammering), they do not shatter and, therefore, make useful construction materials. The melting points of the metals vary widely. Mercury is a liquid at room temperature, and the alkali metals melt below 200 °C. Several post-transition metals also have low melting points, whereas the transition metals melt at temperatures above 1000 °C. These differences reflect differences in strengths of metallic bonding among the metals.

Figure 10.40   Copper is a metallic solid.

Covalent Network Solid

Covalent network solids include crystals of diamond, silicon, some other nonmetals, and some covalent compounds such as silicon dioxide (sand) and silicon carbide (carborundum, the abrasive on sandpaper). Many minerals have networks of covalent bonds. The atoms in these solids are held together by a network of covalent bonds, as shown in **Figure 10.41**. To break or to melt a covalent network solid, covalent bonds must be broken. Because covalent bonds are relatively strong, covalent network solids are typically characterized by hardness, strength, and high melting points. For example, diamond is one of the hardest substances known and melts above 3500 °C.

Figure 10.41 A covalent crystal contains a three-dimensional network of covalent bonds, as illustrated by the structures of diamond, silicon dioxide, silicon carbide, and graphite. Graphite is an exceptional example, composed of planar sheets of covalent crystals that are held together in layers by noncovalent forces. Unlike typical covalent solids, graphite is very soft and electrically conductive.

Molecular Solid

Molecular solids, such as ice, sucrose (table sugar), and iodine, as shown in **Figure 10.42**, are composed of neutral molecules. The strengths of the attractive forces between the units present in different crystals vary widely, as indicated by the melting points of the crystals. Small symmetrical molecules (nonpolar molecules), such as H_2, N_2, O_2, and F_2, have weak attractive forces and form molecular solids with very low melting points (below −200 °C). Substances consisting of larger, nonpolar molecules have larger attractive forces and melt at higher temperatures. Molecular solids composed of molecules with permanent dipole moments (polar molecules) melt at still higher temperatures. Examples include ice (melting point, 0 °C) and table sugar (melting point, 185 °C).

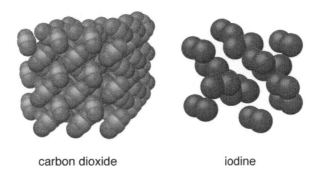

Figure 10.42 Carbon dioxide (CO_2) consists of small, nonpolar molecules and forms a molecular solid with a melting point of −78 °C. Iodine (I_2) consists of larger, nonpolar molecules and forms a molecular solid that melts at 114 °C.

Properties of Solids

A crystalline solid, like those listed in **Table 10.5**, has a precise melting temperature because each atom or molecule of the same type is held in place with the same forces or energy. Thus, the attractions between the units that make up the crystal all have the same strength and all require the same amount of energy to be broken. The gradual softening of an amorphous material differs dramatically from the distinct melting of a crystalline solid. This results from the structural nonequivalence of the molecules in the amorphous solid. Some forces are weaker than others, and when an amorphous material is heated, the weakest intermolecular attractions break first. As the temperature is increased further, the stronger attractions are broken. Thus amorphous materials soften over a range of temperatures.

Types of Crystalline Solids and Their Properties

Type of Solid	Type of Particles	Type of Attractions	Properties	Examples
ionic	ions	ionic bonds	hard, brittle, conducts electricity as a liquid but not as a solid, high to very high melting points	NaCl, Al_2O_3
metallic	atoms of electropositive elements	metallic bonds	shiny, malleable, ductile, conducts heat and electricity well, variable hardness and melting temperature	Cu, Fe, Ti, Pb, U
covalent network	atoms of electronegative elements	covalent bonds	very hard, not conductive, very high melting points	C (diamond), SiO_2, SiC
molecular	molecules (or atoms)	IMFs	variable hardness, variable brittleness, not conductive, low melting points	H_2O, CO_2, I_2, $C_{12}H_{22}O_{11}$

Table 10.5

How Sciences Interconnect

Graphene: Material of the Future

Carbon is an essential element in our world. The unique properties of carbon atoms allow the existence of carbon-based life forms such as ourselves. Carbon forms a huge variety of substances that we use on a daily basis, including those shown in Figure 10.43. You may be familiar with diamond and graphite, the two most common *allotropes* of carbon. (Allotropes are different structural forms of the same element.) Diamond is one of the hardest-known substances, whereas graphite is soft enough to be used as pencil lead. These very different properties stem from the different arrangements of the carbon atoms in the different allotropes.

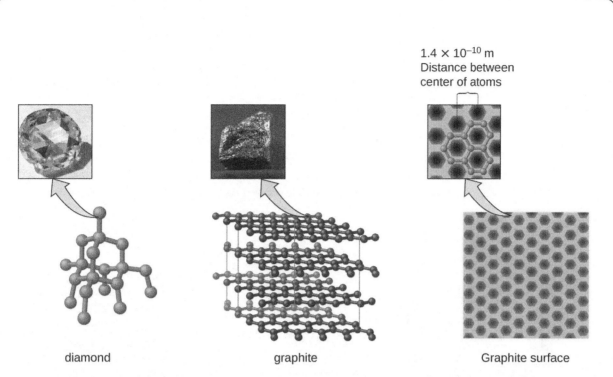

1.4 × 10⁻¹⁰ m
Distance between
center of atoms

diamond   graphite   Graphite surface

Figure 10.43 Diamond is extremely hard because of the strong bonding between carbon atoms in all directions. Graphite (in pencil lead) rubs off onto paper due to the weak attractions between the carbon layers. An image of a graphite surface shows the distance between the centers of adjacent carbon atoms. (credit left photo: modification of work by Steve Jurvetson; credit middle photo: modification of work by United States Geological Survey)

You may be less familiar with a recently discovered form of carbon: graphene. Graphene was first isolated in 2004 by using tape to peel off thinner and thinner layers from graphite. It is essentially a single sheet (one atom thick) of graphite. Graphene, illustrated in Figure 10.44, is not only strong and lightweight, but it is also an excellent conductor of electricity and heat. These properties may prove very useful in a wide range of applications, such as vastly improved computer chips and circuits, better batteries and solar cells, and stronger and lighter structural materials. The 2010 Nobel Prize in Physics was awarded to Andre Geim and Konstantin Novoselov for their pioneering work with graphene.

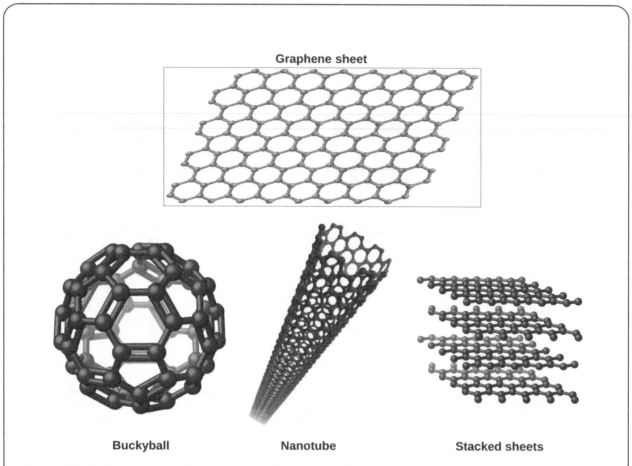

Figure 10.44 Graphene sheets can be formed into buckyballs, nanotubes, and stacked layers.

Crystal Defects

In a crystalline solid, the atoms, ions, or molecules are arranged in a definite repeating pattern, but occasional defects may occur in the pattern. Several types of defects are known, as illustrated in **Figure 10.45**. **Vacancies** are defects that occur when positions that should contain atoms or ions are vacant. Less commonly, some atoms or ions in a crystal may occupy positions, called **interstitial sites**, located between the regular positions for atoms. Other distortions are found in impure crystals, as, for example, when the cations, anions, or molecules of the impurity are too large to fit into the regular positions without distorting the structure. Trace amounts of impurities are sometimes added to a crystal (a process known as *doping*) in order to create defects in the structure that yield desirable changes in its properties. For example, silicon crystals are doped with varying amounts of different elements to yield suitable electrical properties for their use in the manufacture of semiconductors and computer chips.

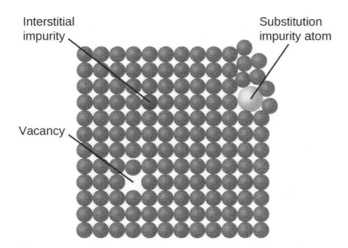

Figure 10.45 Types of crystal defects include vacancies, interstitial atoms, and substitutions impurities.

10.6 Lattice Structures in Crystalline Solids

By the end of this section, you will be able to:

- Describe the arrangement of atoms and ions in crystalline structures
- Compute ionic radii using unit cell dimensions
- Explain the use of X-ray diffraction measurements in determining crystalline structures

Over 90% of naturally occurring and man-made solids are crystalline. Most solids form with a regular arrangement of their particles because the overall attractive interactions between particles are maximized, and the total intermolecular energy is minimized, when the particles pack in the most efficient manner. The regular arrangement at an atomic level is often reflected at a macroscopic level. In this module, we will explore some of the details about the structures of metallic and ionic crystalline solids, and learn how these structures are determined experimentally.

The Structures of Metals

We will begin our discussion of crystalline solids by considering elemental metals, which are relatively simple because each contains only one type of atom. A pure metal is a crystalline solid with metal atoms packed closely together in a repeating pattern. Some of the properties of metals in general, such as their malleability and ductility, are largely due to having identical atoms arranged in a regular pattern. The different properties of one metal compared to another partially depend on the sizes of their atoms and the specifics of their spatial arrangements. We will explore the similarities and differences of four of the most common metal crystal geometries in the sections that follow.

Unit Cells of Metals

The structure of a crystalline solid, whether a metal or not, is best described by considering its simplest repeating unit, which is referred to as its **unit cell**. The unit cell consists of lattice points that represent the locations of atoms or ions. The entire structure then consists of this unit cell repeating in three dimensions, as illustrated in **Figure 10.46**.

Figure 10.46 A unit cell shows the locations of lattice points repeating in all directions.

Let us begin our investigation of crystal lattice structure and unit cells with the most straightforward structure and the most basic unit cell. To visualize this, imagine taking a large number of identical spheres, such as tennis balls, and arranging them uniformly in a container. The simplest way to do this would be to make layers in which the spheres in one layer are directly above those in the layer below, as illustrated in **Figure 10.47**. This arrangement is called **simple cubic structure**, and the unit cell is called the **simple cubic unit cell** or primitive cubic unit cell.

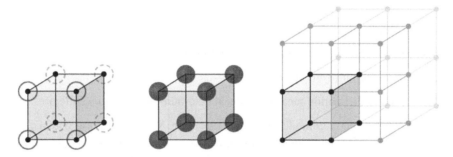

Figure 10.47 When metal atoms are arranged with spheres in one layer directly above or below spheres in another layer, the lattice structure is called simple cubic. Note that the spheres are in contact.

In a simple cubic structure, the spheres are not packed as closely as they could be, and they only "fill" about 52% of the volume of the container. This is a relatively inefficient arrangement, and only one metal (polonium, Po) crystallizes in a simple cubic structure. As shown in **Figure 10.48**, a solid with this type of arrangement consists of planes (or layers) in which each atom contacts only the four nearest neighbors in its layer; one atom directly above it in the layer above; and one atom directly below it in the layer below. The number of other particles that each particle in a crystalline solid contacts is known as its **coordination number**. For a polonium atom in a simple cubic array, the coordination number is, therefore, six.

Figure 10.48 An atom in a simple cubic lattice structure contacts six other atoms, so it has a coordination number of six.

In a simple cubic lattice, the unit cell that repeats in all directions is a cube defined by the centers of eight atoms, as shown in **Figure 10.49**. Atoms at adjacent corners of this unit cell contact each other, so the edge length of this cell is equal to two atomic radii, or one atomic diameter. A cubic unit cell contains only the parts of these atoms that are within it. Since an atom at a corner of a simple cubic unit cell is contained by a total of eight unit cells, only one-eighth of that atom is within a specific unit cell. And since each simple cubic unit cell has one atom at each of its eight "corners," there is $8 \times \frac{1}{8} = 1$ atom within one simple cubic unit cell.

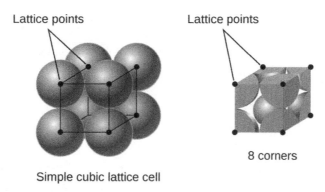

Figure 10.49 A simple cubic lattice unit cell contains one-eighth of an atom at each of its eight corners, so it contains one atom total.

Example 10.14

Calculation of Atomic Radius and Density for Metals, Part 1

The edge length of the unit cell of alpha polonium is 336 pm.

(a) Determine the radius of a polonium atom.

(b) Determine the density of alpha polonium.

Solution

Alpha polonium crystallizes in a simple cubic unit cell:

(a) Two adjacent Po atoms contact each other, so the edge length of this cell is equal to two Po atomic radii: $l = 2r$. Therefore, the radius of Po is $r = \frac{1}{2} = \frac{336\text{ pm}}{2} = 168$ pm.

(b) Density is given by $density = \frac{mass}{volume}$. The density of polonium can be found by determining the density of its unit cell (the mass contained within a unit cell divided by the volume of the unit cell). Since a Po unit cell contains one-eighth of a Po atom at each of its eight corners, a unit cell contains one Po atom.

The mass of a Po unit cell can be found by:

$$1\text{ Po unit cell} \times \frac{1\text{ Po atom}}{1\text{ Po unit cell}} \times \frac{1\text{ mol Po}}{6.022 \times 10^{23}\text{ Po atoms}} \times \frac{208.998\text{ g}}{1\text{ mol Po}} = 3.47 \times 10^{-22}\text{ g}$$

The volume of a Po unit cell can be found by:

$$V = l^3 = \left(336 \times 10^{-10}\text{ cm}\right)^3 = 3.79 \times 10^{-23}\text{ cm}^3$$

(Note that the edge length was converted from pm to cm to get the usual volume units for density.)

Therefore, the density of $Po = \dfrac{3.471 \times 10^{-22}\text{ g}}{3.79 \times 10^{-23}\text{ cm}^3} = 9.16$ g/cm^3

Check Your Learning

The edge length of the unit cell for nickel is 0.3524 nm. The density of Ni is 8.90 g/cm^3. Does nickel crystallize in a simple cubic structure? Explain.

Answer: No. If Ni was simple cubic, its density would be given by:

$$1\text{ Ni atom} \times \frac{1\text{ mol Ni}}{6.022 \times 10^{23}\text{ Ni atoms}} \times \frac{58.693\text{ g}}{1\text{ mol Ni}} = 9.746 \times 10^{-23}\text{ g}$$

$$V = l^3 = \left(3.524 \times 10^{-8}\text{ cm}\right)^3 = 4.376 \times 10^{-23}\text{ cm}^3$$

Then the density of Ni would be $= \dfrac{9.746 \times 10^{-23}\text{ g}}{4.376 \times 10^{-23}\text{ cm}^3} = 2.23$ g/cm^3

Since the actual density of Ni is not close to this, Ni does not form a simple cubic structure.

Most metal crystals are one of the four major types of unit cells. For now, we will focus on the three cubic unit cells: simple cubic (which we have already seen), **body-centered cubic unit cell**, and **face-centered cubic unit cell**—all of which are illustrated in Figure 10.50. (Note that there are actually seven different lattice systems, some of which have more than one type of lattice, for a total of 14 different types of unit cells. We leave the more complicated geometries for later in this module.)

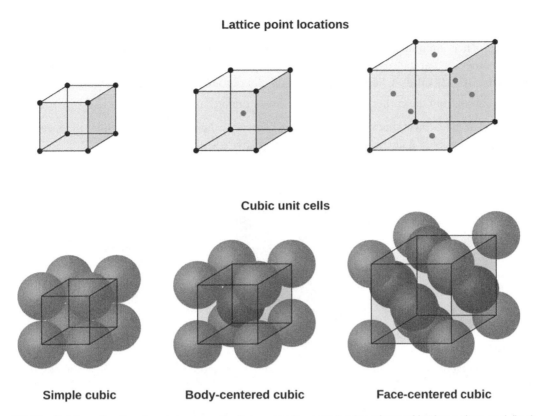

Figure 10.50 Cubic unit cells of metals show (in the upper figures) the locations of lattice points and (in the lower figures) metal atoms located in the unit cell.

Some metals crystallize in an arrangement that has a cubic unit cell with atoms at all of the corners and an atom in the center, as shown in **Figure 10.51**. This is called a **body-centered cubic (BCC) solid**. Atoms in the corners of a BCC unit cell do not contact each other but contact the atom in the center. A BCC unit cell contains two atoms: one-eighth of an atom at each of the eight corners $(8 \times \frac{1}{8} = 1$ atom from the corners) plus one atom from the center. Any atom in this structure touches four atoms in the layer above it and four atoms in the layer below it. Thus, an atom in a BCC structure has a coordination number of eight.

Body-centered cubic structure

Figure 10.51 In a body-centered cubic structure, atoms in a specific layer do not touch each other. Each atom touches four atoms in the layer above it and four atoms in the layer below it.

Atoms in BCC arrangements are much more efficiently packed than in a simple cubic structure, occupying about 68% of the total volume. Isomorphous metals with a BCC structure include K, Ba, Cr, Mo, W, and Fe at room temperature.

(Elements or compounds that crystallize with the same structure are said to be **isomorphous**.)

Many other metals, such as aluminum, copper, and lead, crystallize in an arrangement that has a cubic unit cell with atoms at all of the corners and at the centers of each face, as illustrated in Figure 10.52. This arrangement is called a **face-centered cubic (FCC) solid**. A FCC unit cell contains four atoms: one-eighth of an atom at each of the eight corners $(8 \times \frac{1}{8} = 1$ atom from the corners) and one-half of an atom on each of the six faces $(6 \times \frac{1}{2} = 3$ atoms from the faces). The atoms at the corners touch the atoms in the centers of the adjacent faces along the face diagonals of the cube. Because the atoms are on identical lattice points, they have identical environments.

Face-centered cubic structure

Figure 10.52 A face-centered cubic solid has atoms at the corners and, as the name implies, at the centers of the faces of its unit cells.

Atoms in an FCC arrangement are packed as closely together as possible, with atoms occupying 74% of the volume. This structure is also called **cubic closest packing (CCP)**. In CCP, there are three repeating layers of hexagonally arranged atoms. Each atom contacts six atoms in its own layer, three in the layer above, and three in the layer below. In this arrangement, each atom touches 12 near neighbors, and therefore has a coordination number of 12. The fact that FCC and CCP arrangements are equivalent may not be immediately obvious, but why they are actually the same structure is illustrated in Figure 10.53.

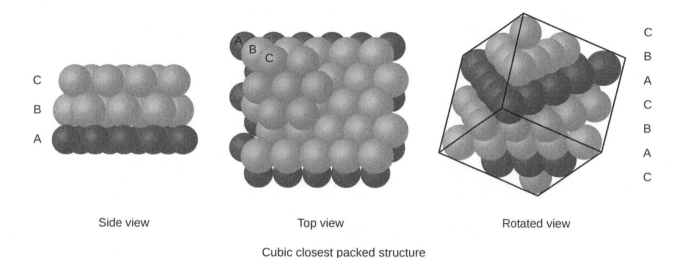

Side view   Top view   Rotated view

Cubic closest packed structure

Figure 10.53 A CCP arrangement consists of three repeating layers (ABCABC…) of hexagonally arranged atoms. Atoms in a CCP structure have a coordination number of 12 because they contact six atoms in their layer, plus three atoms in the layer above and three atoms in the layer below. By rotating our perspective, we can see that a CCP structure has a unit cell with a face containing an atom from layer A at one corner, atoms from layer B across a diagonal (at two corners and in the middle of the face), and an atom from layer C at the remaining corner. This is the same as a face-centered cubic arrangement.

Because closer packing maximizes the overall attractions between atoms and minimizes the total intermolecular energy, the atoms in most metals pack in this manner. We find two types of closest packing in simple metallic crystalline structures: CCP, which we have already encountered, and **hexagonal closest packing (HCP)** shown in **Figure 10.54**. Both consist of repeating layers of hexagonally arranged atoms. In both types, a second layer (B) is placed on the first layer (A) so that each atom in the second layer is in contact with three atoms in the first layer. The third layer is positioned in one of two ways. In HCP, atoms in the third layer are directly above atoms in the first layer (i.e., the third layer is also type A), and the stacking consists of alternating type A and type B close-packed layers (i.e., ABABAB⋯). In CCP, atoms in the third layer are not above atoms in either of the first two layers (i.e., the third layer is type C), and the stacking consists of alternating type A, type B, and type C close-packed layers (i.e., ABCABCABC⋯). About two–thirds of all metals crystallize in closest-packed arrays with coordination numbers of 12. Metals that crystallize in an HCP structure include Cd, Co, Li, Mg, Na, and Zn, and metals that crystallize in a CCP structure include Ag, Al, Ca, Cu, Ni, Pb, and Pt.

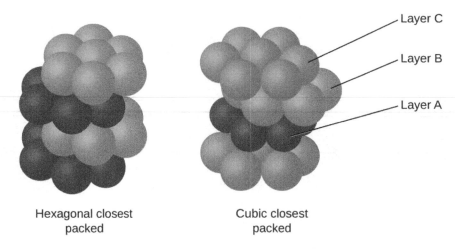

Hexagonal closest
packed

Cubic closest
packed

Figure 10.54 In both types of closest packing, atoms are packed as compactly as possible. Hexagonal closest packing consists of two alternating layers (ABABAB…). Cubic closest packing consists of three alternating layers (ABCABCABC…).

Example 10.15

Calculation of Atomic Radius and Density for Metals, Part 2

Calcium crystallizes in a face-centered cubic structure. The edge length of its unit cell is 558.8 pm.

(a) What is the atomic radius of Ca in this structure?

(b) Calculate the density of Ca.

Solution

(a) In an FCC structure, Ca atoms contact each other across the diagonal of the face, so the length of the diagonal is equal to four Ca atomic radii (d = 4r). Two adjacent edges and the diagonal of the face form a right triangle, with the length of each side equal to 558.8 pm and the length of the hypotenuse equal to four Ca atomic radii:

$$a^2 + a^2 = d^2 \longrightarrow (558.8 \text{ pm})^2 + (558.5 \text{ pm})^2 = (4r)^2$$

Solving this gives $r = \sqrt{\dfrac{(558.8 \text{ pm})^2 + (558.5 \text{ pm})^2}{16}} = 197.6$ pmg for a Ca radius.

(b) Density is given by $\text{density} = \dfrac{\text{mass}}{\text{volume}}$. The density of calcium can be found by determining the density of its unit cell: for example, the mass contained within a unit cell divided by the volume of the unit cell.

A face-centered Ca unit cell has one-eighth of an atom at each of the eight corners $(8 \times \frac{1}{8} = 1$ atom$)$ and one-half of an atom on each of the six faces $6 \times \frac{1}{2} = 3$ atoms$)$, for a total of four atoms in the unit cell.

The mass of the unit cell can be found by:

$$1 \text{ Ca unit cell} \times \frac{4 \text{ Ca atoms}}{1 \text{ Ca unit cell}} \times \frac{1 \text{ mol Ca}}{6.022 \times 10^{23} \text{ Ca atoms}} \times \frac{40.078 \text{ g}}{1 \text{ mol Ca}} = 2.662 \times 10^{-22} \text{ g}$$

The volume of a Ca unit cell can be found by:

$$V = a^3 = \left(558.8 \times 10^{-10} \text{ cm}\right)^3 = 1.745 \times 10^{-22} \text{ cm}^3$$

(Note that the edge length was converted from pm to cm to get the usual volume units for density.)

Then, the density of $\text{Po} = \frac{2.662 \times 10^{-22} \text{ g}}{1.745 \times 10^{-22} \text{ cm}^3} = 1.53 \text{ g/cm}^3$

Check Your Learning

Silver crystallizes in an FCC structure. The edge length of its unit cell is 409 pm.

(a) What is the atomic radius of Ag in this structure?

(b) Calculate the density of Ag.

Answer: (a) 144 pm; (b) 10.5 g/cm^3

In general, a unit cell is defined by the lengths of three axes (a, b, and c) and the angles (α, β, and γ) between them, as illustrated in **Figure 10.55**. The axes are defined as being the lengths between points in the space lattice. Consequently, unit cell axes join points with identical environments.

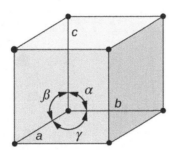

Figure 10.55 A unit cell is defined by the lengths of its three axes (a, b, and c) and the angles (α, β, and γ) between the axes.

There are seven different lattice systems, some of which have more than one type of lattice, for a total of fourteen different unit cells, which have the shapes shown in **Figure 10.56**.

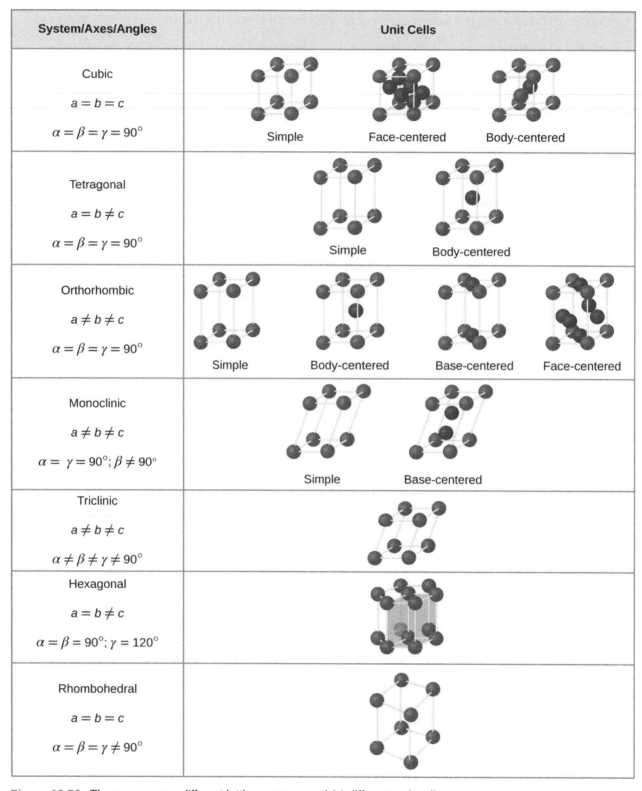

System/Axes/Angles	Unit Cells

Figure 10.56 There are seven different lattice systems and 14 different unit cells.

The Structures of Ionic Crystals

Ionic crystals consist of two or more different kinds of ions that usually have different sizes. The packing of these ions into a crystal structure is more complex than the packing of metal atoms that are the same size.

Most monatomic ions behave as charged spheres, and their attraction for ions of opposite charge is the same in every direction. Consequently, stable structures for ionic compounds result (1) when ions of one charge are surrounded by as many ions as possible of the opposite charge and (2) when the cations and anions are in contact with each other. Structures are determined by two principal factors: the relative sizes of the ions and the ratio of the numbers of positive and negative ions in the compound.

In simple ionic structures, we usually find the anions, which are normally larger than the cations, arranged in a closest-packed array. (As seen previously, additional electrons attracted to the same nucleus make anions larger and fewer electrons attracted to the same nucleus make cations smaller when compared to the atoms from which they are formed.) The smaller cations commonly occupy one of two types of **holes** (or interstices) remaining between the anions. The smaller of the holes is found between three anions in one plane and one anion in an adjacent plane. The four anions surrounding this hole are arranged at the corners of a tetrahedron, so the hole is called a **tetrahedral hole**. The larger type of hole is found at the center of six anions (three in one layer and three in an adjacent layer) located at the corners of an octahedron; this is called an **octahedral hole**. Figure 10.57 illustrates both of these types of holes.

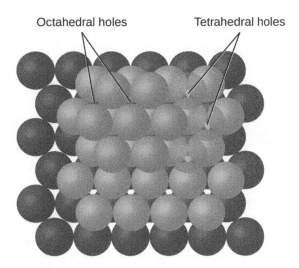

Figure 10.57 Cations may occupy two types of holes between anions: octahedral holes or tetrahedral holes.

Depending on the relative sizes of the cations and anions, the cations of an ionic compound may occupy tetrahedral or octahedral holes, as illustrated in Figure 10.58. Relatively small cations occupy tetrahedral holes, and larger cations occupy octahedral holes. If the cations are too large to fit into the octahedral holes, the anions may adopt a more open structure, such as a simple cubic array. The larger cations can then occupy the larger cubic holes made possible by the more open spacing.

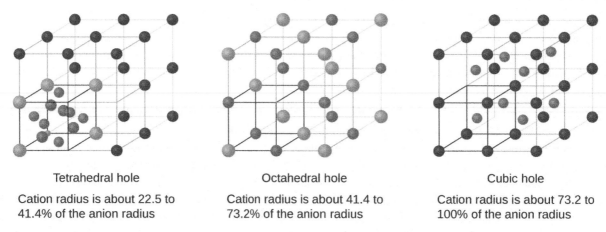

Tetrahedral hole	Octahedral hole	Cubic hole
Cation radius is about 22.5 to 41.4% of the anion radius	Cation radius is about 41.4 to 73.2% of the anion radius	Cation radius is about 73.2 to 100% of the anion radius

Figure 10.58 A cation's size and the shape of the hole occupied by the compound are directly related.

There are two tetrahedral holes for each anion in either an HCP or CCP array of anions. A compound that crystallizes in a closest-packed array of anions with cations in the tetrahedral holes can have a maximum cation:anion ratio of 2:1; all of the tetrahedral holes are filled at this ratio. Examples include Li_2O, Na_2O, Li_2S, and Na_2S. Compounds with a ratio of less than 2:1 may also crystallize in a closest-packed array of anions with cations in the tetrahedral holes, if the ionic sizes fit. In these compounds, however, some of the tetrahedral holes remain vacant.

Example 10.16

Occupancy of Tetrahedral Holes

Zinc sulfide is an important industrial source of zinc and is also used as a white pigment in paint. Zinc sulfide crystallizes with zinc ions occupying one-half of the tetrahedral holes in a closest-packed array of sulfide ions. What is the formula of zinc sulfide?

Solution

Because there are two tetrahedral holes per anion (sulfide ion) and one-half of these holes are occupied by zinc ions, there must be $\frac{1}{2} \times 2$, or 1, zinc ion per sulfide ion. Thus, the formula is ZnS.

Check Your Learning

Lithium selenide can be described as a closest-packed array of selenide ions with lithium ions in all of the tetrahedral holes. What it the formula of lithium selenide?

Answer: Li_2Se

The ratio of octahedral holes to anions in either an HCP or CCP structure is 1:1. Thus, compounds with cations in octahedral holes in a closest-packed array of anions can have a maximum cation:anion ratio of 1:1. In NiO, MnS, NaCl, and KH, for example, all of the octahedral holes are filled. Ratios of less than 1:1 are observed when some of the octahedral holes remain empty.

Example 10.17

Stoichiometry of Ionic Compounds

Sapphire is aluminum oxide. Aluminum oxide crystallizes with aluminum ions in two-thirds of the octahedral holes in a closest-packed array of oxide ions. What is the formula of aluminum oxide?

Solution

Because there is one octahedral hole per anion (oxide ion) and only two-thirds of these holes are occupied, the ratio of aluminum to oxygen must be $\frac{2}{3}$:1, which would give $Al_{2/3}O$. The simplest whole number ratio is 2:3, so the formula is Al_2O_3.

Check Your Learning

The white pigment titanium oxide crystallizes with titanium ions in one-half of the octahedral holes in a closest-packed array of oxide ions. What is the formula of titanium oxide?

Answer: TiO_2

In a simple cubic array of anions, there is one cubic hole that can be occupied by a cation for each anion in the array. In CsCl, and in other compounds with the same structure, all of the cubic holes are occupied. Half of the cubic holes are occupied in SrH_2, UO_2, $SrCl_2$, and CaF_2.

Different types of ionic compounds often crystallize in the same structure when the relative sizes of their ions and their stoichiometries (the two principal features that determine structure) are similar.

Unit Cells of Ionic Compounds

Many ionic compounds crystallize with cubic unit cells, and we will use these compounds to describe the general features of ionic structures.

When an ionic compound is composed of cations and anions of similar size in a 1:1 ratio, it typically forms a simple cubic structure. Cesium chloride, CsCl, (illustrated in **Figure 10.59**) is an example of this, with Cs^+ and Cl^- having radii of 174 pm and 181 pm, respectively. We can think of this as chloride ions forming a simple cubic unit cell, with a cesium ion in the center; or as cesium ions forming a unit cell with a chloride ion in the center; or as simple cubic unit cells formed by Cs^+ ions overlapping unit cells formed by Cl^- ions. Cesium ions and chloride ions touch along the body diagonals of the unit cells. One cesium ion and one chloride ion are present per unit cell, giving the 1:1 stoichiometry required by the formula for cesium chloride. Note that there is no lattice point in the center of the cell, and CsCl is not a BCC structure because a cesium ion is not identical to a chloride ion.

Simple cubic structure

Figure 10.59 Ionic compounds with similar-sized cations and anions, such as CsCl, usually form a simple cubic structure. They can be described by unit cells with either cations at the corners or anions at the corners.

We have said that the location of lattice points is arbitrary. This is illustrated by an alternate description of the CsCl structure in which the lattice points are located in the centers of the cesium ions. In this description, the cesium ions are located on the lattice points at the corners of the cell, and the chloride ion is located at the center of the cell. The two unit cells are different, but they describe identical structures.

When an ionic compound is composed of a 1:1 ratio of cations and anions that differ significantly in size, it typically crystallizes with an FCC unit cell, like that shown in **Figure 10.60**. Sodium chloride, NaCl, is an example of this, with Na^+ and Cl^- having radii of 102 pm and 181 pm, respectively. We can think of this as chloride ions forming an

FCC cell, with sodium ions located in the octahedral holes in the middle of the cell edges and in the center of the cell. The sodium and chloride ions touch each other along the cell edges. The unit cell contains four sodium ions and four chloride ions, giving the 1:1 stoichiometry required by the formula, NaCl.

Face-centered simple cubic structure

Figure 10.60 Ionic compounds with anions that are much larger than cations, such as NaCl, usually form an FCC structure. They can be described by FCC unit cells with cations in the octahedral holes.

The cubic form of zinc sulfide, zinc blende, also crystallizes in an FCC unit cell, as illustrated in **Figure 10.61**. This structure contains sulfide ions on the lattice points of an FCC lattice. (The arrangement of sulfide ions is identical to the arrangement of chloride ions in sodium chloride.) The radius of a zinc ion is only about 40% of the radius of a sulfide ion, so these small Zn^{2+} ions are located in alternating tetrahedral holes, that is, in one half of the tetrahedral holes. There are four zinc ions and four sulfide ions in the unit cell, giving the empirical formula ZnS.

ZnS face-centered unit cell

Figure 10.61 ZnS, zinc sulfide (or zinc blende) forms an FCC unit cell with sulfide ions at the lattice points and much smaller zinc ions occupying half of the tetrahedral holes in the structure.

A calcium fluoride unit cell, like that shown in **Figure 10.62**, is also an FCC unit cell, but in this case, the cations are located on the lattice points; equivalent calcium ions are located on the lattice points of an FCC lattice. All of the tetrahedral sites in the FCC array of calcium ions are occupied by fluoride ions. There are four calcium ions and eight fluoride ions in a unit cell, giving a calcium:fluorine ratio of 1:2, as required by the chemical formula, CaF_2. Close examination of **Figure 10.62** will reveal a simple cubic array of fluoride ions with calcium ions in one half of the cubic holes. The structure cannot be described in terms of a **space lattice** of points on the fluoride ions because the fluoride ions do not all have identical environments. The orientation of the four calcium ions about the fluoride ions differs.

CaF$_2$ face-centered unit cell

Figure 10.62 Calcium fluoride, CaF$_2$, forms an FCC unit cell with calcium ions (green) at the lattice points and fluoride ions (red) occupying all of the tetrahedral sites between them.

Calculation of Ionic Radii

If we know the edge length of a unit cell of an ionic compound and the position of the ions in the cell, we can calculate ionic radii for the ions in the compound if we make assumptions about individual ionic shapes and contacts.

Example 10.18

Calculation of Ionic Radii

The edge length of the unit cell of LiCl (NaCl-like structure, FCC) is 0.514 nm or 5.14 Å. Assuming that the lithium ion is small enough so that the chloride ions are in contact, as in **Figure 10.60**, calculate the ionic radius for the chloride ion.

Note: The length unit angstrom, Å, is often used to represent atomic-scale dimensions and is equivalent to 10^{-10} m.

Solution

On the face of a LiCl unit cell, chloride ions contact each other across the diagonal of the face:

Drawing a right triangle on the face of the unit cell, we see that the length of the diagonal is equal to four chloride radii (one radius from each corner chloride and one diameter—which equals two radii—from the chloride ion in the center of the face), so $d = 4r$. From the Pythagorean theorem, we have:

$$a^2 + a^2 = d^2$$

which yields:

$$(0.514 \text{ nm})^2 + (0.514 \text{ nm})^2 = (4r)^2 = 16r^2$$

Solving this gives:

$$r = \sqrt{\frac{(0.514 \text{ nm})^2 + (0.514 \text{ nm})^2}{16}} = 0.182 \text{ nm} (1.82 \text{ Å}) \text{ for a Cl}^- \text{ radius.}$$

Check Your Learning

The edge length of the unit cell of KCl (NaCl-like structure, FCC) is 6.28 Å. Assuming anion-cation contact along the cell edge, calculate the radius of the potassium ion. The radius of the chloride ion is 1.82 Å.

Answer: The radius of the potassium ion is 1.33 Å.

It is important to realize that values for ionic radii calculated from the edge lengths of unit cells depend on numerous assumptions, such as a perfect spherical shape for ions, which are approximations at best. Hence, such calculated values are themselves approximate and comparisons cannot be pushed too far. Nevertheless, this method has proved useful for calculating ionic radii from experimental measurements such as X-ray crystallographic determinations.

X-Ray Crystallography

The size of the unit cell and the arrangement of atoms in a crystal may be determined from measurements of the *diffraction* of X-rays by the crystal, termed **X-ray crystallography**. **Diffraction** is the change in the direction of travel experienced by an electromagnetic wave when it encounters a physical barrier whose dimensions are comparable to those of the wavelength of the light. X-rays are electromagnetic radiation with wavelengths about as long as the distance between neighboring atoms in crystals (on the order of a few Å).

When a beam of monochromatic X-rays strikes a crystal, its rays are scattered in all directions by the atoms within the crystal. When scattered waves traveling in the same direction encounter one another, they undergo *interference*, a process by which the waves combine to yield either an increase or a decrease in amplitude (intensity) depending upon the extent to which the combining waves' maxima are separated (see **Figure 10.63**).

Figure 10.63   Light waves occupying the same space experience interference, combining to yield waves of greater (a) or lesser (b) intensity, depending upon the separation of their maxima and minima.

When X-rays of a certain wavelength, λ, are scattered by atoms in adjacent crystal planes separated by a distance, d, they may undergo constructive interference when the difference between the distances traveled by the two waves prior to their combination is an integer factor, n, of the wavelength. This condition is satisfied when the angle of the diffracted beam, θ, is related to the wavelength and interatomic distance by the equation:

$$n\lambda = 2d \sin \theta$$

This relation is known as the **Bragg equation** in honor of W. H. Bragg, the English physicist who first explained this phenomenon. **Figure 10.64** illustrates two examples of diffracted waves from the same two crystal planes. The figure on the left depicts waves diffracted at the Bragg angle, resulting in constructive interference, while that on the right shows diffraction and a different angle that does not satisfy the Bragg condition, resulting in destructive interference.

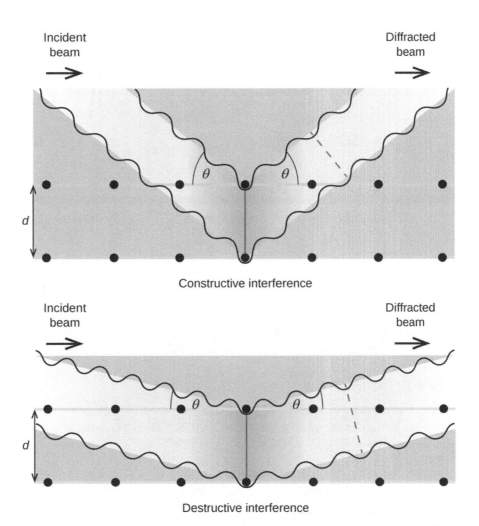

Constructive interference

Destructive interference

Figure 10.64 The diffraction of X-rays scattered by the atoms within a crystal permits the determination of the distance between the atoms. The top image depicts constructive interference between two scattered waves and a resultant diffracted wave of high intensity. The bottom image depicts destructive interference and a low intensity diffracted wave.

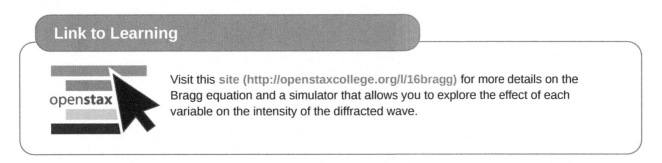

Link to Learning

Visit this **site (http://openstaxcollege.org/l/16bragg)** for more details on the Bragg equation and a simulator that allows you to explore the effect of each variable on the intensity of the diffracted wave.

An X-ray diffractometer, such as the one illustrated in **Figure 10.65**, may be used to measure the angles at which X-rays are diffracted when interacting with a crystal as described earlier. From such measurements, the Bragg equation may be used to compute distances between atoms as demonstrated in the following example exercise.

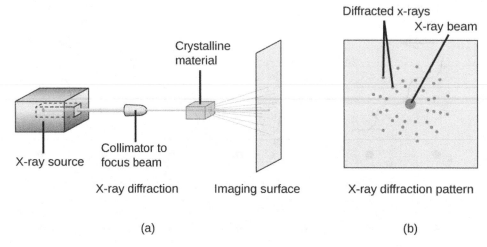

Figure 10.65 (a) In a diffractometer, a beam of X-rays strikes a crystalline material, producing (b) an X-ray diffraction pattern that can be analyzed to determine the crystal structure.

Example 10.19

Using the Bragg Equation

In a diffractometer, X-rays with a wavelength of 0.1315 nm were used to produce a diffraction pattern for copper. The first order diffraction ($n = 1$) occurred at an angle $\theta = 25.25°$. Determine the spacing between the diffracting planes in copper.

Solution

The distance between the planes is found by solving the Bragg equation, $n\lambda = 2d \sin \theta$, for d.

This gives: $d = \dfrac{n\lambda}{2 \sin \theta} = \dfrac{1(0.1315 \text{ nm})}{2 \sin (25.25°)} = 0.154 \text{ nm}$

Check Your Learning

A crystal with spacing between planes equal to 0.394 nm diffracts X-rays with a wavelength of 0.147 nm. What is the angle for the first order diffraction?

Answer: 21.9°.

Portrait of a Chemist

X-ray Crystallographer Rosalind Franklin

The discovery of the structure of DNA in 1953 by Francis Crick and James Watson is one of the great achievements in the history of science. They were awarded the 1962 Nobel Prize in Physiology or Medicine, along with Maurice Wilkins, who provided experimental proof of DNA's structure. British chemist Rosalind Franklin made invaluable contributions to this monumental achievement through her work in measuring X-ray diffraction images of DNA. Early in her career, Franklin's research on the structure of coals proved helpful to the British war effort. After shifting her focus to biological systems in the early 1950s, Franklin and doctoral student Raymond Gosling discovered that DNA consists of two forms: a long, thin fiber formed when wet (type "B") and a short, wide fiber formed when dried (type "A"). Her X-ray diffraction images of DNA (Figure 10.66) provided the crucial information that allowed Watson and Crick to confirm that DNA forms a double helix, and to determine details of its size and structure. Franklin also conducted pioneering research on viruses and the RNA that contains their genetic information, uncovering new information that radically changed the body of knowledge in the field. After developing ovarian cancer, Franklin continued to work until her death in 1958 at age 37. Among many posthumous recognitions of her work, the Chicago Medical School of Finch University of Health Sciences changed its name to the Rosalind Franklin University of Medicine and Science in 2004, and adopted an image of her famous X-ray diffraction image of DNA as its official university logo.

Figure 10.66 This illustration shows an X-ray diffraction image similar to the one Franklin found in her research. (credit: National Institutes of Health)

Key Terms

adhesive force force of attraction between molecules of different chemical identities

amorphous solid (also, noncrystalline solid) solid in which the particles lack an ordered internal structure

body-centered cubic (BCC) solid crystalline structure that has a cubic unit cell with lattice points at the corners and in the center of the cell

body-centered cubic unit cell simplest repeating unit of a body-centered cubic crystal; it is a cube containing lattice points at each corner and in the center of the cube

boiling point temperature at which the vapor pressure of a liquid equals the pressure of the gas above it

Bragg equation equation that relates the angles at which X-rays are diffracted by the atoms within a crystal

capillary action flow of liquid within a porous material due to the attraction of the liquid molecules to the surface of the material and to other liquid molecules

Clausius-Clapeyron equation mathematical relationship between the temperature, vapor pressure, and enthalpy of vaporization for a substance

cohesive force force of attraction between identical molecules

condensation change from a gaseous to a liquid state

coordination number number of atoms closest to any given atom in a crystal or to the central metal atom in a complex

covalent network solid solid whose particles are held together by covalent bonds

critical point temperature and pressure above which a gas cannot be condensed into a liquid

crystalline solid solid in which the particles are arranged in a definite repeating pattern

cubic closest packing (CCP) crystalline structure in which planes of closely packed atoms or ions are stacked as a series of three alternating layers of different relative orientations (ABC)

deposition change from a gaseous state directly to a solid state

diffraction redirection of electromagnetic radiation that occurs when it encounters a physical barrier of appropriate dimensions

dipole-dipole attraction intermolecular attraction between two permanent dipoles

dispersion force (also, London dispersion force) attraction between two rapidly fluctuating, temporary dipoles; significant only when particles are very close together

dynamic equilibrium state of a system in which reciprocal processes are occurring at equal rates

face-centered cubic (FCC) solid crystalline structure consisting of a cubic unit cell with lattice points on the corners and in the center of each face

face-centered cubic unit cell simplest repeating unit of a face-centered cubic crystal; it is a cube containing lattice points at each corner and in the center of each face

freezing change from a liquid state to a solid state

freezing point temperature at which the solid and liquid phases of a substance are in equilibrium; see also *melting point*

hexagonal closest packing (HCP) crystalline structure in which close packed layers of atoms or ions are stacked as a series of two alternating layers of different relative orientations (AB)

hole (also, interstice) space between atoms within a crystal

hydrogen bonding occurs when exceptionally strong dipoles attract; bonding that exists when hydrogen is bonded to one of the three most electronegative elements: F, O, or N

induced dipole temporary dipole formed when the electrons of an atom or molecule are distorted by the instantaneous dipole of a neighboring atom or molecule

instantaneous dipole temporary dipole that occurs for a brief moment in time when the electrons of an atom or molecule are distributed asymmetrically

intermolecular force noncovalent attractive force between atoms, molecules, and/or ions

interstitial sites spaces between the regular particle positions in any array of atoms or ions

ionic solid solid composed of positive and negative ions held together by strong electrostatic attractions

isomorphous possessing the same crystalline structure

melting change from a solid state to a liquid state

melting point temperature at which the solid and liquid phases of a substance are in equilibrium; see also *freezing point*

metallic solid solid composed of metal atoms

molecular solid solid composed of neutral molecules held together by intermolecular forces of attraction

normal boiling point temperature at which a liquid's vapor pressure equals 1 atm (760 torr)

octahedral hole open space in a crystal at the center of six particles located at the corners of an octahedron

phase diagram pressure-temperature graph summarizing conditions under which the phases of a substance can exist

polarizability measure of the ability of a charge to distort a molecule's charge distribution (electron cloud)

simple cubic structure crystalline structure with a cubic unit cell with lattice points only at the corners

simple cubic unit cell (also, primitive cubic unit cell) unit cell in the simple cubic structure

space lattice all points within a crystal that have identical environments

sublimation change from solid state directly to gaseous state

supercritical fluid substance at a temperature and pressure higher than its critical point; exhibits properties intermediate between those of gaseous and liquid states

surface tension energy required to increase the area, or length, of a liquid surface by a given amount

tetrahedral hole tetrahedral space formed by four atoms or ions in a crystal

triple point temperature and pressure at which the vapor, liquid, and solid phases of a substance are in equilibrium

unit cell smallest portion of a space lattice that is repeated in three dimensions to form the entire lattice

vacancy defect that occurs when a position that should contain an atom or ion is vacant

van der Waals force attractive or repulsive force between molecules, including dipole-dipole, dipole-induced dipole, and London dispersion forces; does not include forces due to covalent or ionic bonding, or the attraction between ions and molecules

vapor pressure (also, equilibrium vapor pressure) pressure exerted by a vapor in equilibrium with a solid or a liquid at a given temperature

vaporization change from liquid state to gaseous state

viscosity measure of a liquid's resistance to flow

X-ray crystallography experimental technique for determining distances between atoms in a crystal by measuring the angles at which X-rays are diffracted when passing through the crystal

Key Equations

- $h = \dfrac{2T \cos \theta}{r \rho g}$

- $P = A e^{-\Delta H_{vap}/RT}$

- $\ln P = -\dfrac{\Delta H_{vap}}{RT} + \ln A$

- $\ln\left(\dfrac{P_2}{P_1}\right) = \dfrac{\Delta H_{vap}}{R}\left(\dfrac{1}{T_1} - \dfrac{1}{T_2}\right)$

- $n\lambda = 2d \sin \theta$

Summary

10.1 Intermolecular Forces

The physical properties of condensed matter (liquids and solids) can be explained in terms of the kinetic molecular theory. In a liquid, intermolecular attractive forces hold the molecules in contact, although they still have sufficient KE to move past each other.

Intermolecular attractive forces, collectively referred to as van der Waals forces, are responsible for the behavior of liquids and solids and are electrostatic in nature. Dipole-dipole attractions result from the electrostatic attraction of the partial negative end of one dipolar molecule for the partial positive end of another. The temporary dipole that results from the motion of the electrons in an atom can induce a dipole in an adjacent atom and give rise to the London dispersion force. London forces increase with increasing molecular size. Hydrogen bonds are a special type of dipole-dipole attraction that results when hydrogen is bonded to one of the three most electronegative elements: F, O, or N.

10.2 Properties of Liquids

The intermolecular forces between molecules in the liquid state vary depending upon their chemical identities and result in corresponding variations in various physical properties. Cohesive forces between like molecules are responsible for a liquid's viscosity (resistance to flow) and surface tension (elasticity of a liquid surface). Adhesive forces between the molecules of a liquid and different molecules composing a surface in contact with the liquid are responsible for phenomena such as surface wetting and capillary rise.

10.3 Phase Transitions

Phase transitions are processes that convert matter from one physical state into another. There are six phase transitions between the three phases of matter. Melting, vaporization, and sublimation are all endothermic processes, requiring an input of heat to overcome intermolecular attractions. The reciprocal transitions of freezing, condensation, and deposition are all exothermic processes, involving heat as intermolecular attractive forces are established or strengthened. The temperatures at which phase transitions occur are determined by the relative strengths of intermolecular attractions and are, therefore, dependent on the chemical identity of the substance.

10.4 Phase Diagrams

The temperature and pressure conditions at which a substance exists in solid, liquid, and gaseous states are summarized in a phase diagram for that substance. Phase diagrams are combined plots of three pressure-temperature equilibrium curves: solid-liquid, liquid-gas, and solid-gas. These curves represent the relationships between phase-transition temperatures and pressures. The point of intersection of all three curves represents the substance's triple point—the temperature and pressure at which all three phases are in equilibrium. At pressures below the triple point, a substance cannot exist in the liquid state, regardless of its temperature. The terminus of the liquid-gas curve represents the substance's critical point, the pressure and temperature above which a liquid phase cannot exist.

10.5 The Solid State of Matter

Some substances form crystalline solids consisting of particles in a very organized structure; others form amorphous (noncrystalline) solids with an internal structure that is not ordered. The main types of crystalline solids are ionic solids, metallic solids, covalent network solids, and molecular solids. The properties of the different kinds of crystalline solids are due to the types of particles of which they consist, the arrangements of the particles, and the strengths of the attractions between them. Because their particles experience identical attractions, crystalline solids have distinct melting temperatures; the particles in amorphous solids experience a range of interactions, so they soften gradually and melt over a range of temperatures. Some crystalline solids have defects in the definite repeating pattern of their particles. These defects (which include vacancies, atoms or ions not in the regular positions, and impurities) change physical properties such as electrical conductivity, which is exploited in the silicon crystals used to manufacture computer chips.

10.6 Lattice Structures in Crystalline Solids

The structures of crystalline metals and simple ionic compounds can be described in terms of packing of spheres. Metal atoms can pack in hexagonal closest-packed structures, cubic closest-packed structures, body-centered structures, and simple cubic structures. The anions in simple ionic structures commonly adopt one of these structures, and the cations occupy the spaces remaining between the anions. Small cations usually occupy tetrahedral holes in a closest-packed array of anions. Larger cations usually occupy octahedral holes. Still larger cations can occupy cubic holes in a simple cubic array of anions. The structure of a solid can be described by indicating the size and shape of a unit cell and the contents of the cell. The type of structure and dimensions of the unit cell can be determined by X-ray diffraction measurements.

Exercises

10.1 Intermolecular Forces

1. In terms of their bulk properties, how do liquids and solids differ? How are they similar?

2. In terms of the kinetic molecular theory, in what ways are liquids similar to solids? In what ways are liquids different from solids?

3. In terms of the kinetic molecular theory, in what ways are liquids similar to gases? In what ways are liquids different from gases?

4. Explain why liquids assume the shape of any container into which they are poured, whereas solids are rigid and retain their shape.

5. What is the evidence that all neutral atoms and molecules exert attractive forces on each other?

6. Open the **PhET States of Matter Simulation (http://openstaxcollege.org/l/16phetvisual)** to answer the following questions:

(a) Select the Solid, Liquid, Gas tab. Explore by selecting different substances, heating and cooling the systems, and changing the state. What similarities do you notice between the four substances for each phase (solid, liquid, gas)? What differences do you notice?

(b) For each substance, select each of the states and record the given temperatures. How do the given temperatures for each state correlate with the strengths of their intermolecular attractions? Explain.

(c) Select the Interaction Potential tab, and use the default neon atoms. Move the Ne atom on the right and observe how the potential energy changes. Select the Total Force button, and move the Ne atom as before. When is the total force on each atom attractive and large enough to matter? Then select the Component Forces button, and move the Ne atom. When do the attractive (van der Waals) and repulsive (electron overlap) forces balance? How does this relate to the potential energy versus the distance between atoms graph? Explain.

7. Define the following and give an example of each:

(a) dispersion force

(b) dipole-dipole attraction

(c) hydrogen bond

8. The types of intermolecular forces in a substance are identical whether it is a solid, a liquid, or a gas. Why then does a substance change phase from a gas to a liquid or to a solid?

9. Why do the boiling points of the noble gases increase in the order He < Ne < Ar < Kr < Xe?

10. Neon and HF have approximately the same molecular masses.

(a) Explain why the boiling points of Neon and HF differ.

(b) Compare the change in the boiling points of Ne, Ar, Kr, and Xe with the change of the boiling points of HF, HCl, HBr, and HI, and explain the difference between the changes with increasing atomic or molecular mass.

11. Arrange each of the following sets of compounds in order of increasing boiling point temperature:

(a) HCl, H_2O, SiH_4

(b) F_2, Cl_2, Br_2

(c) CH_4, C_2H_6, C_3H_8

(d) O_2, NO, N_2

12. The molecular mass of butanol, C_4H_9OH, is 74.14; that of ethylene glycol, $CH_2(OH)CH_2OH$, is 62.08, yet their boiling points are 117.2 °C and 174 °C, respectively. Explain the reason for the difference.

13. On the basis of intermolecular attractions, explain the differences in the boiling points of n–butane (−1 °C) and chloroethane (12 °C), which have similar molar masses.

14. On the basis of dipole moments and/or hydrogen bonding, explain in a qualitative way the differences in the boiling points of acetone (56.2 °C) and 1-propanol (97.4 °C), which have similar molar masses.

15. The melting point of $H_2O(s)$ is 0 °C. Would you expect the melting point of $H_2S(s)$ to be −85 °C, 0 °C, or 185 °C? Explain your answer.

16. Silane (SiH_4), phosphine (PH_3), and hydrogen sulfide (H_2S) melt at −185 °C, −133 °C, and −85 °C, respectively. What does this suggest about the polar character and intermolecular attractions of the three compounds?

17. Explain why a hydrogen bond between two water molecules is weaker than a hydrogen bond between two hydrogen fluoride molecules.

18. Under certain conditions, molecules of acetic acid, CH_3COOH, form "dimers," pairs of acetic acid molecules held together by strong intermolecular attractions:

Draw a dimer of acetic acid, showing how two CH_3COOH molecules are held together, and stating the type of IMF that is responsible.

19. Proteins are chains of amino acids that can form in a variety of arrangements, one of which is a helix. What kind of IMF is responsible for holding the protein strand in this shape? On the protein image, show the locations of the IMFs that hold the protein together:

20. The density of liquid NH_3 is 0.64 g/mL; the density of gaseous NH_3 at STP is 0.0007 g/mL. Explain the difference between the densities of these two phases.

21. Identify the intermolecular forces present in the following solids:

(a) CH_3CH_2OH

(b) $CH_3CH_2CH_3$

(c) CH_3CH_2Cl

10.2 Properties of Liquids

22. The test tubes shown here contain equal amounts of the specified motor oils. Identical metal spheres were dropped at the same time into each of the tubes, and a brief moment later, the spheres had fallen to the heights indicated in the illustration.

Rank the motor oils in order of increasing viscosity, and explain your reasoning:

23. Although steel is denser than water, a steel needle or paper clip placed carefully lengthwise on the surface of still water can be made to float. Explain at a molecular level how this is possible:

Figure 10.67   (credit: Cory Zanker)

24. The surface tension and viscosity values for diethyl ether, acetone, ethanol, and ethylene glycol are shown here.

Compound	Molecule	Surface Tension (mN/m)	Viscosity (mPa s)
diethyl ether $C_2H_5OC_2H_5$		17	0.22
acetone CH_3COCH_3		23	0.31
ethanol C_2H_5OH		22	1.07
ethylene glycol $CH_2(OH)CH_2(OH)$		48	16.1

(a) Explain their differences in viscosity in terms of the size and shape of their molecules and their IMFs.

(b) Explain their differences in surface tension in terms of the size and shape of their molecules and their IMFs:

25. You may have heard someone use the figure of speech "slower than molasses in winter" to describe a process that occurs slowly. Explain why this is an apt idiom, using concepts of molecular size and shape, molecular interactions, and the effect of changing temperature.

26. It is often recommended that you let your car engine run idle to warm up before driving, especially on cold winter days. While the benefit of prolonged idling is dubious, it is certainly true that a warm engine is more fuel efficient than a cold one. Explain the reason for this.

27. The surface tension and viscosity of water at several different temperatures are given in this table.

Water	Surface Tension (mN/m)	Viscosity (mPa s)
0 °C	75.6	1.79
20 °C	72.8	1.00
60 °C	66.2	0.47
100 °C	58.9	0.28

(a) As temperature increases, what happens to the surface tension of water? Explain why this occurs, in terms of molecular interactions and the effect of changing temperature.

(b) As temperature increases, what happens to the viscosity of water? Explain why this occurs, in terms of molecular interactions and the effect of changing temperature.

28. At 25 °C, how high will water rise in a glass capillary tube with an inner diameter of 0.63 mm? Refer to Example 10.4 for the required information.

29. Water rises in a glass capillary tube to a height of 17 cm. What is the diameter of the capillary tube?

10.3 Phase Transitions

30. Heat is added to boiling water. Explain why the temperature of the boiling water does not change. What does change?

31. Heat is added to ice at 0 °C. Explain why the temperature of the ice does not change. What does change?

32. What feature characterizes the dynamic equilibrium between a liquid and its vapor in a closed container?

33. Identify two common observations indicating some liquids have sufficient vapor pressures to noticeably evaporate?

34. Identify two common observations indicating some solids, such as dry ice and mothballs, have vapor pressures sufficient to sublime?

35. What is the relationship between the intermolecular forces in a liquid and its vapor pressure?

36. What is the relationship between the intermolecular forces in a solid and its melting temperature?

37. Why does spilled gasoline evaporate more rapidly on a hot day than on a cold day?

38. Carbon tetrachloride, CCl_4, was once used as a dry cleaning solvent, but is no longer used because it is carcinogenic. At 57.8 °C, the vapor pressure of CCl_4 is 54.0 kPa, and its enthalpy of vaporization is 33.05 kJ/mol. Use this information to estimate the normal boiling point for CCl_4.

39. When is the boiling point of a liquid equal to its normal boiling point?

40. How does the boiling of a liquid differ from its evaporation?

41. Use the information in Figure 10.24 to estimate the boiling point of water in Denver when the atmospheric pressure is 83.3 kPa.

42. A syringe at a temperature of 20 °C is filled with liquid ether in such a way that there is no space for any vapor. If the temperature is kept constant and the plunger is withdrawn to create a volume that can be occupied by vapor, what would be the approximate pressure of the vapor produced?

43. Explain the following observations:

(a) It takes longer to cook an egg in Ft. Davis, Texas (altitude, 5000 feet above sea level) than it does in Boston (at sea level).

(b) Perspiring is a mechanism for cooling the body.

44. The enthalpy of vaporization of water is larger than its enthalpy of fusion. Explain why.

45. Explain why the molar enthalpies of vaporization of the following substances increase in the order $CH_4 < C_2H_6 < C_3H_8$, even though the type of IMF (dispersion) is the same.

46. Explain why the enthalpies of vaporization of the following substances increase in the order $CH_4 < NH_3 < H_2O$, even though all three substances have approximately the same molar mass.

47. The enthalpy of vaporization of $CO_2(l)$ is 9.8 kJ/mol. Would you expect the enthalpy of vaporization of $CS_2(l)$ to be 28 kJ/mol, 9.8 kJ/mol, or −8.4 kJ/mol? Discuss the plausibility of each of these answers.

48. The hydrogen fluoride molecule, HF, is more polar than a water molecule, H_2O (for example, has a greater dipole moment), yet the molar enthalpy of vaporization for liquid hydrogen fluoride is lesser than that for water. Explain.

49. Ethyl chloride (boiling point, 13 °C) is used as a local anesthetic. When the liquid is sprayed on the skin, it cools the skin enough to freeze and numb it. Explain the cooling effect of liquid ethyl chloride.

50. Which contains the compounds listed correctly in order of increasing boiling points?

(a) $N_2 < CS_2 < H_2O < KCl$

(b) $H_2O < N_2 < CS_2 < KCl$

(c) $N_2 < KCl < CS_2 < H_2O$

(d) $CS_2 < N_2 < KCl < H_2O$

(e) $KCl < H_2O < CS_2 < N_2$

51. How much heat is required to convert 422 g of liquid H_2O at 23.5 °C into steam at 150 °C?

52. Evaporation of sweat requires energy and thus take excess heat away from the body. Some of the water that you drink may eventually be converted into sweat and evaporate. If you drink a 20-ounce bottle of water that had been in the refrigerator at 3.8 °C, how much heat is needed to convert all of that water into sweat and then to vapor?? (Note: Your body temperature is 36.6 °C. For the purpose of solving this problem, assume that the thermal properties of sweat are the same as for water.)

53. Titanium tetrachloride, $TiCl_4$, has a melting point of −23.2 °C and has a ΔH_{fusion} = 9.37 kJ/mol.

(a) How much energy is required to melt 263.1 g $TiCl_4$?

(b) For $TiCl_4$, which will likely have the larger magnitude: ΔH_{fusion} or $\Delta H_{vaporization}$? Explain your reasoning.

10.4 Phase Diagrams

54. From the phase diagram for water (**Figure 10.31**), determine the state of water at:

(a) 35 °C and 85 kPa

(b) −15 °C and 40 kPa

(c) −15 °C and 0.1 kPa

(d) 75 °C and 3 kPa

(e) 40 °C and 0.1 kPa

(f) 60 °C and 50 kPa

55. What phase changes will take place when water is subjected to varying pressure at a constant temperature of 0.005 °C? At 40 °C? At −40 °C?

56. Pressure cookers allow food to cook faster because the higher pressure inside the pressure cooker increases the boiling temperature of water. A particular pressure cooker has a safety valve that is set to vent steam if the pressure exceeds 3.4 atm. What is the approximate maximum temperature that can be reached inside this pressure cooker? Explain your reasoning.

57. From the phase diagram for carbon dioxide in Figure 10.34, determine the state of CO_2 at:

(a) 20 °C and 1000 kPa

(b) 10 °C and 2000 kPa

(c) 10 °C and 100 kPa

(d) −40 °C and 500 kPa

(e) −80 °C and 1500 kPa

(f) −80 °C and 10 kPa

58. Determine the phase changes that carbon dioxide undergoes as the pressure changes if the temperature is held at −50 °C? If the temperature is held at −40 °C? At 20 °C? (See the phase diagram in Figure 10.34.)

59. Consider a cylinder containing a mixture of liquid carbon dioxide in equilibrium with gaseous carbon dioxide at an initial pressure of 65 atm and a temperature of 20 °C. Sketch a plot depicting the change in the cylinder pressure with time as gaseous carbon dioxide is released at constant temperature.

60. Dry ice, $CO_2(s)$, does not melt at atmospheric pressure. It sublimes at a temperature of −78 °C. What is the lowest pressure at which $CO_2(s)$ will melt to give $CO_2(l)$? At approximately what temperature will this occur? (See Figure 10.34 for the phase diagram.)

61. If a severe storm results in the loss of electricity, it may be necessary to use a clothesline to dry laundry. In many parts of the country in the dead of winter, the clothes will quickly freeze when they are hung on the line. If it does not snow, will they dry anyway? Explain your answer.

62. Is it possible to liquefy nitrogen at room temperature (about 25 °C)? Is it possible to liquefy sulfur dioxide at room temperature? Explain your answers.

63. Elemental carbon has one gas phase, one liquid phase, and two different solid phases, as shown in the phase diagram:

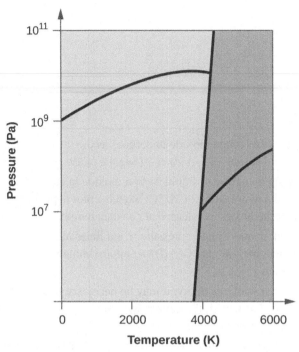

(a) On the phase diagram, label the gas and liquid regions.

(b) Graphite is the most stable phase of carbon at normal conditions. On the phase diagram, label the graphite phase.

(c) If graphite at normal conditions is heated to 2500 K while the pressure is increased to 10^{10} Pa, it is converted into diamond. Label the diamond phase.

(d) Circle each triple point on the phase diagram.

(e) In what phase does carbon exist at 5000 K and 10^8 Pa?

(f) If the temperature of a sample of carbon increases from 3000 K to 5000 K at a constant pressure of 10^6 Pa, which phase transition occurs, if any?

10.5 The Solid State of Matter

64. What types of liquids typically form amorphous solids?

65. At very low temperatures oxygen, O_2, freezes and forms a crystalline solid. Which best describes these crystals?

(a) ionic

(b) covalent network

(c) metallic

(d) amorphous

(e) molecular crystals

66. As it cools, olive oil slowly solidifies and forms a solid over a range of temperatures. Which best describes the solid?

(a) ionic

(b) covalent network

(c) metallic

(d) amorphous

(e) molecular crystals

67. Explain why ice, which is a crystalline solid, has a melting temperature of 0 °C, whereas butter, which is an amorphous solid, softens over a range of temperatures.

68. Identify the type of crystalline solid (metallic, network covalent, ionic, or molecular) formed by each of the following substances:

(a) SiO_2

(b) KCl

(c) Cu

(d) CO_2

(e) C (diamond)

(f) $BaSO_4$

(g) NH_3

(h) NH_4F

(i) C_2H_5OH

69. Identify the type of crystalline solid (metallic, network covalent, ionic, or molecular) formed by each of the following substances:

(a) $CaCl_2$

(b) SiC

(c) N_2

(d) Fe

(e) C (graphite)

(f) $CH_3CH_2CH_2CH_3$

(g) HCl

(h) NH_4NO_3

(i) K_3PO_4

70. Classify each substance in the table as either a metallic, ionic, molecular, or covalent network solid:

Substance	Appearance	Melting Point	Electrical Conductivity	Solubility in Water
X	lustrous, malleable	1500 °C	high	insoluble
Y	soft, yellow	113 °C	none	insoluble
Z	hard, white	800 °C	only if melted/dissolved	soluble

71. Classify each substance in the table as either a metallic, ionic, molecular, or covalent network solid:

Substance	Appearance	Melting Point	Electrical Conductivity	Solubility in Water
X	brittle, white	800 °C	only if melted/dissolved	soluble
Y	shiny, malleable	1100 °C	high	insoluble
Z	hard, colorless	3550 °C	none	insoluble

72. Identify the following substances as ionic, metallic, covalent network, or molecular solids:

Substance A is malleable, ductile, conducts electricity well, and has a melting point of 1135 °C. Substance B is brittle, does not conduct electricity as a solid but does when molten, and has a melting point of 2072 °C. Substance C is very hard, does not conduct electricity, and has a melting point of 3440 °C. Substance D is soft, does not conduct electricity, and has a melting point of 185 °C.

73. Substance A is shiny, conducts electricity well, and melts at 975 °C. Substance A is likely a(n):

(a) ionic solid

(b) metallic solid

(c) molecular solid

(d) covalent network solid

74. Substance B is hard, does not conduct electricity, and melts at 1200 °C. Substance B is likely a(n):

(a) ionic solid

(b) metallic solid

(c) molecular solid

(d) covalent network solid

10.6 Lattice Structures in Crystalline Solids

75. Describe the crystal structure of iron, which crystallizes with two equivalent metal atoms in a cubic unit cell.

76. Describe the crystal structure of Pt, which crystallizes with four equivalent metal atoms in a cubic unit cell.

77. What is the coordination number of a chromium atom in the body-centered cubic structure of chromium?

78. What is the coordination number of an aluminum atom in the face-centered cubic structure of aluminum?

79. Cobalt metal crystallizes in a hexagonal closest packed structure. What is the coordination number of a cobalt atom?

80. Nickel metal crystallizes in a cubic closest packed structure. What is the coordination number of a nickel atom?

81. Tungsten crystallizes in a body-centered cubic unit cell with an edge length of 3.165 Å.

(a) What is the atomic radius of tungsten in this structure?

(b) Calculate the density of tungsten.

82. Platinum (atomic radius = 1.38 Å) crystallizes in a cubic closely packed structure. Calculate the edge length of the face-centered cubic unit cell and the density of platinum.

83. Barium crystallizes in a body-centered cubic unit cell with an edge length of 5.025 Å

(a) What is the atomic radius of barium in this structure?

(b) Calculate the density of barium.

84. Aluminum (atomic radius = 1.43 Å) crystallizes in a cubic closely packed structure. Calculate the edge length of the face-centered cubic unit cell and the density of aluminum.

85. The density of aluminum is 2.7 g/cm^3; that of silicon is 2.3 g/cm^3. Explain why Si has the lower density even though it has heavier atoms.

86. The free space in a metal may be found by subtracting the volume of the atoms in a unit cell from the volume of the cell. Calculate the percentage of free space in each of the three cubic lattices if all atoms in each are of equal size and touch their nearest neighbors. Which of these structures represents the most efficient packing? That is, which packs with the least amount of unused space?

87. Cadmium sulfide, sometimes used as a yellow pigment by artists, crystallizes with cadmium, occupying one-half of the tetrahedral holes in a closest packed array of sulfide ions. What is the formula of cadmium sulfide? Explain your answer.

88. A compound of cadmium, tin, and phosphorus is used in the fabrication of some semiconductors. It crystallizes with cadmium occupying one-fourth of the tetrahedral holes and tin occupying one-fourth of the tetrahedral holes in a closest packed array of phosphide ions. What is the formula of the compound? Explain your answer.

89. What is the formula of the magnetic oxide of cobalt, used in recording tapes, that crystallizes with cobalt atoms occupying one-eighth of the tetrahedral holes and one-half of the octahedral holes in a closely packed array of oxide ions?

90. A compound containing zinc, aluminum, and sulfur crystallizes with a closest-packed array of sulfide ions. Zinc ions are found in one-eighth of the tetrahedral holes and aluminum ions in one-half of the octahedral holes. What is the empirical formula of the compound?

91. A compound of thallium and iodine crystallizes in a simple cubic array of iodide ions with thallium ions in all of the cubic holes. What is the formula of this iodide? Explain your answer.

92. Which of the following elements reacts with sulfur to form a solid in which the sulfur atoms form a closest-packed array with all of the octahedral holes occupied: Li, Na, Be, Ca, or Al?

93. What is the percent by mass of titanium in rutile, a mineral that contains titanium and oxygen, if structure can be described as a closest packed array of oxide ions with titanium ions in one-half of the octahedral holes? What is the oxidation number of titanium?

94. Explain why the chemically similar alkali metal chlorides NaCl and CsCl have different structures, whereas the chemically different NaCl and MnS have the same structure.

95. As minerals were formed from the molten magma, different ions occupied the same cites in the crystals. Lithium often occurs along with magnesium in minerals despite the difference in the charge on their ions. Suggest an explanation.

96. Rubidium iodide crystallizes with a cubic unit cell that contains iodide ions at the corners and a rubidium ion in the center. What is the formula of the compound?

97. One of the various manganese oxides crystallizes with a cubic unit cell that contains manganese ions at the corners and in the center. Oxide ions are located at the center of each edge of the unit cell. What is the formula of the compound?

98. NaH crystallizes with the same crystal structure as NaCl. The edge length of the cubic unit cell of NaH is 4.880 Å.

(a) Calculate the ionic radius of H$^-$. (The ionic radius of Li$^+$ is 0.0.95 Å.)

(b) Calculate the density of NaH.

99. Thallium(I) iodide crystallizes with the same structure as CsCl. The edge length of the unit cell of TlI is 4.20 Å. Calculate the ionic radius of Tl$^+$. (The ionic radius of I$^-$ is 2.16 Å.)

100. A cubic unit cell contains manganese ions at the corners and fluoride ions at the center of each edge.

(a) What is the empirical formula of this compound? Explain your answer.

(b) What is the coordination number of the Mn^{3+} ion?

(c) Calculate the edge length of the unit cell if the radius of a Mn^{3+} ion is 0.65 A.

(d) Calculate the density of the compound.

101. What is the spacing between crystal planes that diffract X-rays with a wavelength of 1.541 nm at an angle θ of 15.55° (first order reflection)?

102. A diffractometer using X-rays with a wavelength of 0.2287 nm produced first-order diffraction peak for a crystal angle $\theta = 16.21°$. Determine the spacing between the diffracting planes in this crystal.

103. A metal with spacing between planes equal to 0.4164 nm diffracts X-rays with a wavelength of 0.2879 nm. What is the diffraction angle for the first order diffraction peak?

104. Gold crystallizes in a face-centered cubic unit cell. The second-order reflection (n = 2) of X-rays for the planes that make up the tops and bottoms of the unit cells is at $\theta = 22.20°$. The wavelength of the X-rays is 1.54 Å. What is the density of metallic gold?

105. When an electron in an excited molybdenum atom falls from the L to the K shell, an X-ray is emitted. These X-rays are diffracted at an angle of 7.75° by planes with a separation of 2.64 Å. What is the difference in energy between the K shell and the L shell in molybdenum assuming a first-order diffraction?

Chapter 11

Solutions and Colloids

Figure 11.1 Coral reefs, such as this one at the Palmyra Atoll National Wildlife Refuge, are vital to the ecosystem of earth's oceans but are threatened by climate change and dissolved pollution. Marine life depends on the specific chemical composition of the complex mixture we know as seawater. (credit: modification of work by "USFWS – Pacific Region"/Wikimedia Commons)

Chapter Outline

11.1 The Dissolution Process

11.2 Electrolytes

11.3 Solubility

11.4 Colligative Properties

11.5 Colloids

Introduction

Coral reefs are home to about 25% of all marine species. They are being threatened by climate change, oceanic acidification, and water pollution, all of which change the composition of the solution we know as seawater. Dissolved oxygen in seawater is critical for sea creatures, but as the oceans warm, oxygen becomes less soluble. As the concentration of carbon dioxide in the atmosphere increases, the concentration of carbon dioxide in the oceans increases, contributing to oceanic acidification. Coral reefs are particularly sensitive to the acidification of the ocean, since the exoskeletons of the coral polyps are soluble in acidic solutions. Humans contribute to the changing of seawater composition by allowing agricultural runoff and other forms of pollution to affect our oceans.

Solutions are crucial to the processes that sustain life and to many other processes involving chemical reactions. In this chapter, we will consider the nature of solutions, and examine factors that determine whether a solution will form and what properties it may have. In addition, we will discuss colloids—systems that resemble solutions but consist of dispersions of particles somewhat larger than ordinary molecules or ions.

11.1 The Dissolution Process

By the end of this section, you will be able to:

- Describe the basic properties of solutions and how they form
- Predict whether a given mixture will yield a solution based on molecular properties of its components
- Explain why some solutions either produce or absorb heat when they form

An earlier chapter of this text introduced *solutions*, defined as homogeneous mixtures of two or more substances. Often, one component of a solution is present at a significantly greater concentration, in which case it is called the *solvent*. The other components of the solution present in relatively lesser concentrations are called *solutes*. Sugar is a covalent solid composed of sucrose molecules, $C_{12}H_{22}O_{11}$. When this compound dissolves in water, its molecules become uniformly distributed among the molecules of water:

$$C_{12}H_{22}O_{11}(s) \longrightarrow C_{12}H_{22}O_{11}(aq)$$

The subscript "*aq*" in the equation signifies that the sucrose molecules are solutes and are therefore *individually dispersed* throughout the *aqueous solution* (water is the solvent). Although sucrose molecules are heavier than water molecules, they remain dispersed throughout the solution; gravity does not cause them to "settle out" over time.

Potassium dichromate, $K_2Cr_2O_7$, is an ionic compound composed of colorless potassium ions, K^+, and orange dichromate ions, $Cr_2O_7{}^{2-}$. When a small amount of solid potassium dichromate is added to water, the compound dissolves and dissociates to yield potassium ions and dichromate ions uniformly distributed throughout the mixture (**Figure 11.2**), as indicated in this equation:

$$K_2Cr_2O_7(s) \longrightarrow 2K^+(aq) + Cr_2O_7{}^{2-}(aq)$$

As with the mixture of sugar and water, this mixture is also an aqueous solution. Its solutes, potassium and dichromate ions, remain individually dispersed among the solvent (water) molecules.

Figure 11.2 When potassium dichromate ($K_2Cr_2O_7$) is mixed with water, it forms a homogeneous orange solution. (credit: modification of work by Mark Ott)

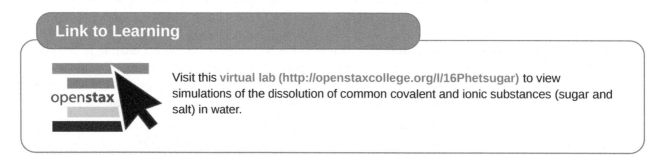

Link to Learning

Visit this **virtual lab (http://openstaxcollege.org/l/16Phetsugar)** to view simulations of the dissolution of common covalent and ionic substances (sugar and salt) in water.

Water is used so often as a solvent that the word solution has come to imply an aqueous solution to many people. However, almost any gas, liquid, or solid can act as a solvent. Many **alloys** are solid solutions of one metal dissolved in another; for example, US five-cent coins contain nickel dissolved in copper. Air is a gaseous solution, a homogeneous mixture of nitrogen, oxygen, and several other gases. Oxygen (a gas), alcohol (a liquid), and sugar (a solid) all dissolve in water (a liquid) to form liquid solutions. Table 11.1 gives examples of several different solutions and the phases of the solutes and solvents.

Different Types of Solutions

Solution	Solute	Solvent
air	$O_2(g)$	$N_2(g)$
soft drinks[1]	$CO_2(g)$	$H_2O(l)$
hydrogen in palladium	$H_2(g)$	$Pd(s)$
rubbing alcohol	$H_2O(l)$	$C_3H_8O(l)$ (2-propanol)
saltwater	$NaCl(s)$	$H_2O(l)$
brass	$Zn(s)$	$Cu(s)$

Table 11.1

Solutions exhibit these defining traits:

- They are homogeneous; that is, after a solution is mixed, it has the same composition at all points throughout (its composition is uniform).

- The physical state of a solution—solid, liquid, or gas—is typically the same as that of the solvent, as demonstrated by the examples in Table 11.1.

- The components of a solution are dispersed on a molecular scale; that is, they consist of a mixture of separated molecules, atoms, and/or ions.

- The dissolved solute in a solution will not settle out or separate from the solvent.

- The composition of a solution, or the concentrations of its components, can be varied continuously, within limits.

The Formation of Solutions

The formation of a solution is an example of a **spontaneous process**, a process that occurs under specified conditions without the requirement of energy from some external source. Sometimes we stir a mixture to speed up the dissolution process, but this is not necessary; a homogeneous solution would form if we waited long enough. The topic of spontaneity is critically important to the study of chemical thermodynamics and is treated more thoroughly in a later chapter of this text. For purposes of this chapter's discussion, it will suffice to consider two criteria that *favor*, but do not guarantee, the spontaneous formation of a solution:

1. a decrease in the internal energy of the system (an exothermic change, as discussed in the previous chapter on thermochemistry)

2. an increase in the disorder in the system (which indicates an increase in the *entropy* of the system, as you will learn about in the later chapter on thermodynamics)

In the process of dissolution, an internal energy change often, but not always, occurs as heat is absorbed or evolved. An increase in disorder always results when a solution forms.

When the strengths of the intermolecular forces of attraction between solute and solvent species in a solution are no different than those present in the separated components, the solution is formed with no accompanying energy change. Such a solution is called an **ideal solution**. A mixture of ideal gases (or gases such as helium and argon, which closely approach ideal behavior) is an example of an ideal solution, since the entities comprising these gases experience no significant intermolecular attractions.

---

1. If bubbles of gas are observed within the liquid, the mixture is not homogeneous and, thus, not a solution.

When containers of helium and argon are connected, the gases spontaneously mix due to diffusion and form a solution (**Figure 11.3**). The formation of this solution clearly involves an increase in disorder, since the helium and argon atoms occupy a volume twice as large as that which each occupied before mixing.

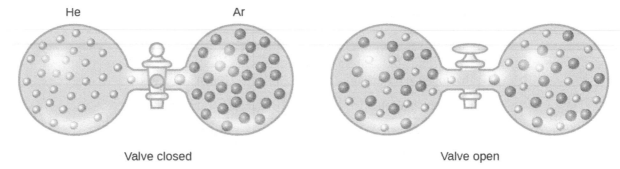

Figure 11.3 Samples of helium and argon spontaneously mix to give a solution in which the disorder of the atoms of the two gases is increased.

Ideal solutions may also form when structurally similar liquids are mixed. For example, mixtures of the alcohols methanol (CH_3OH) and ethanol (C_2H_5OH) form ideal solutions, as do mixtures of the hydrocarbons pentane, C_5H_{12}, and hexane, C_6H_{14}. Placing methanol and ethanol, or pentane and hexane, in the bulbs shown in **Figure 11.3** will result in the same diffusion and subsequent mixing of these liquids as is observed for the He and Ar gases (although at a much slower rate), yielding solutions with no significant change in energy. Unlike a mixture of gases, however, the components of these liquid-liquid solutions do, indeed, experience intermolecular attractive forces. But since the molecules of the two substances being mixed are structurally very similar, the intermolecular attractive forces between like and unlike molecules are essentially the same, and the dissolution process, therefore, does not entail any appreciable increase or decrease in energy. These examples illustrate how diffusion alone can provide the driving force required to cause the spontaneous formation of a solution. In some cases, however, the relative magnitudes of intermolecular forces of attraction between solute and solvent species may prevent dissolution.

Three types of intermolecular attractive forces are relevant to the dissolution process: solute-solute, solvent-solvent, and solute-solvent. As illustrated in **Figure 11.4**, the formation of a solution may be viewed as a stepwise process in which energy is consumed to overcome solute-solute and solvent-solvent attractions (endothermic processes) and released when solute-solvent attractions are established (an exothermic process referred to as **solvation**). The relative magnitudes of the energy changes associated with these stepwise processes determine whether the dissolution process overall will release or absorb energy. In some cases, solutions do not form because the energy required to separate solute and solvent species is so much greater than the energy released by solvation.

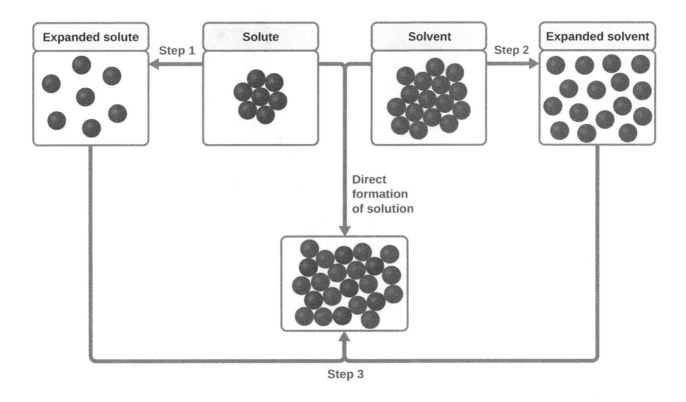

Figure 11.4 This schematic representation of dissolution shows a stepwise process involving the endothermic separation of solute and solvent species (Steps 1 and 2) and exothermic solvation (Step 3).

For example, cooking oils and water will not mix to any appreciable extent to yield solutions (**Figure 11.5**). Hydrogen bonding is the dominant intermolecular attractive force present in liquid water; the nonpolar hydrocarbon molecules of cooking oils are not capable of hydrogen bonding, instead being held together by dispersion forces. Forming an oil-water solution would require overcoming the very strong hydrogen bonding in water, as well as the significantly strong dispersion forces between the relatively large oil molecules. And, since the polar water molecules and nonpolar oil molecules would not experience very strong intermolecular attraction, very little energy would be released by solvation.

Figure 11.5   A mixture of nonpolar cooking oil and polar water does not yield a solution. (credit: Gautam Dogra)

On the other hand, a mixture of ethanol and water will mix in any proportions to yield a solution. In this case, both substances are capable of hydrogen bonding, and so the solvation process is sufficiently exothermic to compensate for the endothermic separations of solute and solvent molecules.

As noted at the beginning of this module, spontaneous solution formation is favored, but not guaranteed, by exothermic dissolution processes. While many soluble compounds do, indeed, dissolve with the release of heat, some dissolve endothermically. Ammonium nitrate (NH_4NO_3) is one such example and is used to make instant cold packs for treating injuries like the one pictured in Figure 11.6. A thin-walled plastic bag of water is sealed inside a larger bag with solid NH_4NO_3. When the smaller bag is broken, a solution of NH_4NO_3 forms, absorbing heat from the surroundings (the injured area to which the pack is applied) and providing a cold compress that decreases swelling. Endothermic dissolutions such as this one require a greater energy input to separate the solute species than is recovered when the solutes are solvated, but they are spontaneous nonetheless due to the increase in disorder that accompanies formation of the solution.

Figure 11.6 An instant cold pack gets cold when certain salts, such as ammonium nitrate, dissolve in water—an endothermic process.

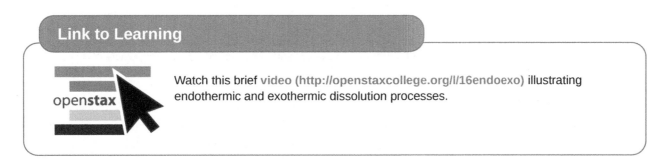

Link to Learning

Watch this brief **video (http://openstaxcollege.org/l/16endoexo)** illustrating endothermic and exothermic dissolution processes.

11.2 Electrolytes

By the end of this module, you will be able to:

- Define and give examples of electrolytes
- Distinguish between the physical and chemical changes that accompany dissolution of ionic and covalent electrolytes
- Relate electrolyte strength to solute-solvent attractive forces

When some substances are dissolved in water, they undergo either a physical or a chemical change that yields ions in solution. These substances constitute an important class of compounds called **electrolytes**. Substances that do not yield ions when dissolved are called **nonelectrolytes**. If the physical or chemical process that generates the ions is essentially 100% efficient (all of the dissolved compound yields ions), then the substance is known as a **strong electrolyte**. If only a relatively small fraction of the dissolved substance undergoes the ion-producing process, it is called a **weak electrolyte**.

Substances may be identified as strong, weak, or nonelectrolytes by measuring the electrical conductance of an aqueous solution containing the substance. To conduct electricity, a substance must contain freely mobile, charged species. Most familiar is the conduction of electricity through metallic wires, in which case the mobile, charged entities are electrons. Solutions may also conduct electricity if they contain dissolved ions, with conductivity increasing as ion concentration increases. Applying a voltage to electrodes immersed in a solution permits assessment of the relative concentration of dissolved ions, either quantitatively, by measuring the electrical current flow, or qualitatively, by observing the brightness of a light bulb included in the circuit (**Figure 11.7**).

Figure 11.7   Solutions of nonelectrolytes such as ethanol do not contain dissolved ions and cannot conduct electricity. Solutions of electrolytes contain ions that permit the passage of electricity. The conductivity of an electrolyte solution is related to the strength of the electrolyte.

Ionic Electrolytes

Water and other polar molecules are attracted to ions, as shown in **Figure 11.8**. The electrostatic attraction between an ion and a molecule with a dipole is called an **ion-dipole attraction**. These attractions play an important role in the dissolution of ionic compounds in water.

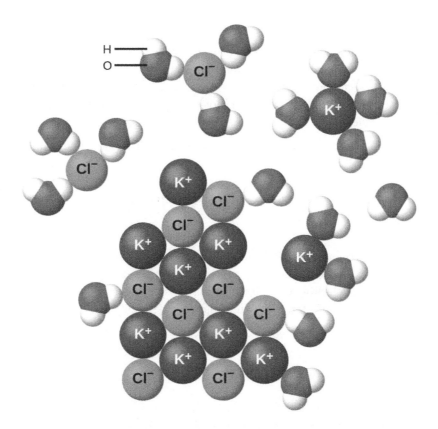

Figure 11.8 As potassium chloride (KCl) dissolves in water, the ions are hydrated. The polar water molecules are attracted by the charges on the K⁺ and Cl⁻ ions. Water molecules in front of and behind the ions are not shown.

When ionic compounds dissolve in water, the ions in the solid separate and disperse uniformly throughout the solution because water molecules surround and solvate the ions, reducing the strong electrostatic forces between them. This process represents a physical change known as **dissociation**. Under most conditions, ionic compounds will dissociate nearly completely when dissolved, and so they are classified as strong electrolytes.

Let us consider what happens at the microscopic level when we add solid KCl to water. Ion-dipole forces attract the positive (hydrogen) end of the polar water molecules to the negative chloride ions at the surface of the solid, and they attract the negative (oxygen) ends to the positive potassium ions. The water molecules penetrate between individual K⁺ and Cl⁻ ions and surround them, reducing the strong interionic forces that bind the ions together and letting them move off into solution as solvated ions, as **Figure 11.8** shows. The reduction of the electrostatic attraction permits the independent motion of each hydrated ion in a dilute solution, resulting in an increase in the disorder of the system as the ions change from their fixed and ordered positions in the crystal to mobile and much more disordered states in solution. This increased disorder is responsible for the dissolution of many ionic compounds, including KCl, which dissolve with absorption of heat.

In other cases, the electrostatic attractions between the ions in a crystal are so large, or the ion-dipole attractive forces between the ions and water molecules are so weak, that the increase in disorder cannot compensate for the energy required to separate the ions, and the crystal is insoluble. Such is the case for compounds such as calcium carbonate (limestone), calcium phosphate (the inorganic component of bone), and iron oxide (rust).

Covalent Electrolytes

Pure water is an extremely poor conductor of electricity because it is only very slightly ionized—only about two out of every 1 billion molecules ionize at 25 °C. Water ionizes when one molecule of water gives up a proton to another molecule of water, yielding hydronium and hydroxide ions.

$$H_2O(l) + H_2O(l) \rightleftharpoons H_3O^+(aq) + OH^-(aq)$$

In some cases, we find that solutions prepared from covalent compounds conduct electricity because the solute molecules react chemically with the solvent to produce ions. For example, pure hydrogen chloride is a gas consisting of covalent HCl molecules. This gas contains no ions. However, when we dissolve hydrogen chloride in water, we find that the solution is a very good conductor. The water molecules play an essential part in forming ions: Solutions of hydrogen chloride in many other solvents, such as benzene, do not conduct electricity and do not contain ions.

Hydrogen chloride is an *acid*, and so its molecules react with water, transferring H^+ ions to form hydronium ions (H_3O^+) and chloride ions (Cl^-):

This reaction is essentially 100% complete for HCl (i.e., it is a *strong acid* and, consequently, a strong electrolyte). Likewise, weak acids and bases that only react partially generate relatively low concentrations of ions when dissolved in water and are classified as weak electrolytes. The reader may wish to review the discussion of strong and weak acids provided in the earlier chapter of this text on reaction classes and stoichiometry.

11.3 Solubility

By the end of this module, you will be able to:

- Describe the effects of temperature and pressure on solubility
- State Henry's law and use it in calculations involving the solubility of a gas in a liquid
- Explain the degrees of solubility possible for liquid-liquid solutions

Imagine adding a small amount of salt to a glass of water, stirring until all the salt has dissolved, and then adding a bit more. You can repeat this process until the salt concentration of the solution reaches its natural limit, a limit determined primarily by the relative strengths of the solute-solute, solute-solvent, and solvent-solvent attractive forces discussed in the previous two modules of this chapter. You can be certain that you have reached this limit because, no matter how long you stir the solution, undissolved salt remains. The concentration of salt in the solution at this point is known as its solubility.

The **solubility** of a solute in a particular solvent is the maximum concentration that may be achieved under given conditions when the dissolution process is *at equilibrium*. Referring to the example of salt in water:

$$NaCl(s) \rightleftharpoons Na^+(aq) + Cl^-(aq)$$

When a solute's concentration is equal to its solubility, the solution is said to be **saturated** with that solute. If the solute's concentration is less than its solubility, the solution is said to be **unsaturated**. A solution that contains a relatively low concentration of solute is called dilute, and one with a relatively high concentration is called concentrated.

If we add more salt to a saturated solution of salt, we see it fall to the bottom and no more seems to dissolve. In fact, the added salt does dissolve, as represented by the forward direction of the dissolution equation. Accompanying this process, dissolved salt will precipitate, as depicted by the reverse direction of the equation. The system is said to be at equilibrium when these two reciprocal processes are occurring at equal rates, and so the amount of undissolved and dissolved salt remains constant. Support for the simultaneous occurrence of the dissolution and precipitation processes is provided by noting that the number and sizes of the undissolved salt crystals will change over time, though their combined mass will remain the same.

Solutions may be prepared in which a solute concentration *exceeds* its solubility. Such solutions are said to be **supersaturated**, and they are interesting examples of *nonequilibrium* states. For example, the carbonated beverage in an open container that has not yet "gone flat" is supersaturated with carbon dioxide gas; given time, the CO_2 concentration will decrease until it reaches its equilibrium value.

Solutions of Gases in Liquids

In an earlier module of this chapter, the effect of intermolecular attractive forces on solution formation was discussed. The chemical structures of the solute and solvent dictate the types of forces possible and, consequently, are important factors in determining solubility. For example, under similar conditions, the water solubility of oxygen is approximately three times greater than that of helium, but 100 times less than the solubility of chloromethane, $CHCl_3$. Considering the role of the solvent's chemical structure, note that the solubility of oxygen in the liquid hydrocarbon hexane, C_6H_{14}, is approximately 20 times greater than it is in water.

Other factors also affect the solubility of a given substance in a given solvent. Temperature is one such factor, with gas solubility typically decreasing as temperature increases (**Figure 11.9**). This is one of the major impacts resulting from the thermal pollution of natural bodies of water.

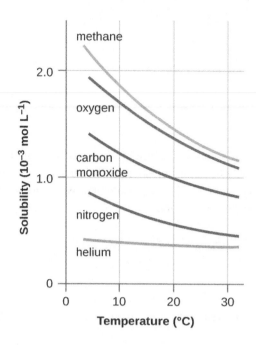

Figure 11.9   The solubilities of these gases in water decrease as the temperature increases. All solubilities were measured with a constant pressure of 101.3 kPa (1 atm) of gas above the solutions.

When the temperature of a river, lake, or stream is raised abnormally high, usually due to the discharge of hot water from some industrial process, the solubility of oxygen in the water is decreased. Decreased levels of dissolved oxygen may have serious consequences for the health of the water's ecosystems and, in severe cases, can result in large-scale fish kills (Figure 11.10).

(a)   (b)

Figure 11.10   (a) The small bubbles of air in this glass of chilled water formed when the water warmed to room temperature and the solubility of its dissolved air decreased. (b) The decreased solubility of oxygen in natural waters subjected to thermal pollution can result in large-scale fish kills. (credit a: modification of work by Liz West; credit b: modification of work by U.S. Fish and Wildlife Service)

The solubility of a gaseous solute is also affected by the partial pressure of solute in the gas to which the solution is exposed. Gas solubility increases as the pressure of the gas increases. Carbonated beverages provide a nice illustration of this relationship. The carbonation process involves exposing the beverage to a relatively high pressure of carbon dioxide gas and then sealing the beverage container, thus saturating the beverage with CO_2 at this pressure. When the beverage container is opened, a familiar hiss is heard as the carbon dioxide gas pressure is released, and some of the dissolved carbon dioxide is typically seen leaving solution in the form of small bubbles (**Figure 11.11**). At this point, the beverage is *supersaturated* with carbon dioxide and, with time, the dissolved carbon dioxide concentration will decrease to its equilibrium value and the beverage will become "flat."

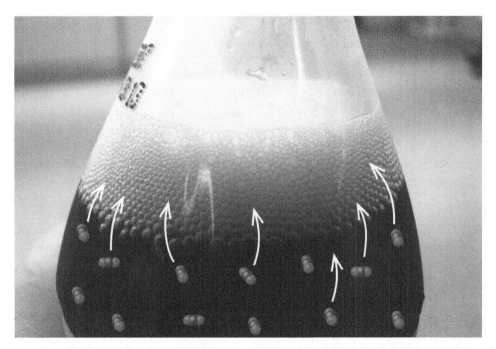

Figure 11.11 Opening the bottle of carbonated beverage reduces the pressure of the *gaseous* carbon dioxide above the beverage. The solubility of CO_2 is thus lowered, and some *dissolved* carbon dioxide may be seen leaving the solution as small gas bubbles. (credit: modification of work by Derrick Coetzee)

For many gaseous solutes, the relation between solubility, C_g, and partial pressure, P_g, is a proportional one:

$$C_g = kP_g$$

where k is a proportionality constant that depends on the identities of the gaseous solute and solvent, and on the solution temperature. This is a mathematical statement of **Henry's law**: *The quantity of an ideal gas that dissolves in a definite volume of liquid is directly proportional to the pressure of the gas.*

Example 11.1

Application of Henry's Law

At 20 °C, the concentration of dissolved oxygen in water exposed to gaseous oxygen at a partial pressure of 101.3 kPa (760 torr) is 1.38×10^{-3} mol L^{-1}. Use Henry's law to determine the solubility of oxygen when its partial pressure is 20.7 kPa (155 torr), the approximate pressure of oxygen in earth's atmosphere.

Solution

According to Henry's law, for an ideal solution the solubility, C_g, of a gas (1.38×10^{-3} mol L^{-1}, in this case) is directly proportional to the pressure, P_g, of the undissolved gas above the solution (101.3 kPa, or 760 torr, in this case). Because we know both C_g and P_g, we can rearrange this expression to solve for k.

$$C_g = kP_g$$

$$k = \frac{C_g}{P_g}$$

$$= \frac{1.38 \times 10^{-3} \text{ mol L}^{-1}}{101.3 \text{ kPa}}$$

$$= 1.36 \times 10^{-5} \text{ mol L}^{-1} \text{ kPa}^{-1}$$

$$\left(1.82 \times 10^{-6} \text{ mol L}^{-1} \text{ torr}^{-1}\right)$$

Now we can use k to find the solubility at the lower pressure.

$$C_g = kP_g$$

$$1.36 \times 10^{-5} \text{ mol L}^{-1} \text{ kPa}^{-1} \times 20.7 \text{ kPa}$$

$$\left(\text{or } 1.82 \times 10^{-6} \text{ mol L}^{-1} \text{ torr}^{-1} \times 155 \text{ torr}\right)$$

$$= 2.82 \times 10^{-4} \text{ mol L}^{-1}$$

Note that various units may be used to express the quantities involved in these sorts of computations. Any combination of units that yield to the constraints of dimensional analysis are acceptable.

Check Your Learning

Exposing a 100.0 mL sample of water at 0 °C to an atmosphere containing a gaseous solute at 20.26 kPa (152 torr) resulted in the dissolution of 1.45×10^{-3} g of the solute. Use Henry's law to determine the solubility of this gaseous solute when its pressure is 101.3 kPa (760 torr).

Answer: 7.25×10^{-3} in 100.0 mL or 0.0725 g/L

Chemistry in Everyday Life

Decompression Sickness or "The Bends"

Decompression sickness (DCS), or "the bends," is an effect of the increased pressure of the air inhaled by scuba divers when swimming underwater at considerable depths. In addition to the pressure exerted by the atmosphere, divers are subjected to additional pressure due to the water above them, experiencing an increase of approximately 1 atm for each 10 m of depth. Therefore, the air inhaled by a diver while submerged contains gases at the corresponding higher ambient pressure, and the concentrations of the gases dissolved in the diver's blood are proportionally higher per Henry's law.

As the diver ascends to the surface of the water, the ambient pressure decreases and the dissolved gases becomes less soluble. If the ascent is too rapid, the gases escaping from the diver's blood may form bubbles that can cause a variety of symptoms ranging from rashes and joint pain to paralysis and death. To avoid DCS, divers must ascend from depths at relatively slow speeds (10 or 20 m/min) or otherwise make several decompression stops, pausing for several minutes at given depths during the ascent. When these preventive measures are unsuccessful, divers with DCS are often provided hyperbaric oxygen therapy in pressurized vessels called decompression (or recompression) chambers (Figure 11.12).

(a)

(b)

Figure 11.12   (a) US Navy divers undergo training in a recompression chamber. (b) Divers receive hyperbaric oxygen therapy.

Deviations from Henry's law are observed when a chemical reaction takes place between the gaseous solute and the solvent. Thus, for example, the solubility of ammonia in water does not increase as rapidly with increasing pressure as predicted by the law because ammonia, being a base, reacts to some extent with water to form ammonium ions and hydroxide ions.

Gases can form supersaturated solutions. If a solution of a gas in a liquid is prepared either at low temperature or under pressure (or both), then as the solution warms or as the gas pressure is reduced, the solution may become supersaturated. In 1986, more than 1700 people in Cameroon were killed when a cloud of gas, almost certainly carbon dioxide, bubbled from Lake Nyos (**Figure 11.13**), a deep lake in a volcanic crater. The water at the bottom of Lake Nyos is saturated with carbon dioxide by volcanic activity beneath the lake. It is believed that the lake underwent a turnover due to gradual heating from below the lake, and the warmer, less-dense water saturated with carbon dioxide reached the surface. Consequently, tremendous quantities of dissolved CO_2 were released, and the colorless gas, which is denser than air, flowed down the valley below the lake and suffocated humans and animals living in the valley.

(a)   (b)

Figure 11.13   (a) It is believed that the 1986 disaster that killed more than 1700 people near Lake Nyos in Cameroon resulted when a large volume of carbon dioxide gas was released from the lake. (b) A CO_2 vent has since been installed to help outgas the lake in a slow, controlled fashion and prevent a similar catastrophe from happening in the future. (credit a: modification of work by Jack Lockwood; credit b: modification of work by Bill Evans)

Solutions of Liquids in Liquids

We know that some liquids mix with each other in all proportions; in other words, they have infinite mutual solubility and are said to be **miscible**. Ethanol, sulfuric acid, and ethylene glycol (popular for use as antifreeze, pictured in Figure 11.14) are examples of liquids that are completely miscible with water. Two-cycle motor oil is miscible with gasoline.

Figure 11.14   Water and antifreeze are miscible; mixtures of the two are homogeneous in all proportions. (credit: "dno1967"/Wikimedia commons)

Liquids that mix with water in all proportions are usually polar substances or substances that form hydrogen bonds. For such liquids, the dipole-dipole attractions (or hydrogen bonding) of the solute molecules with the solvent molecules are at least as strong as those between molecules in the pure solute or in the pure solvent. Hence, the two kinds of molecules mix easily. Likewise, nonpolar liquids are miscible with each other because there is no appreciable difference in the strengths of solute-solute, solvent-solvent, and solute-solvent intermolecular attractions. The solubility of polar molecules in polar solvents and of nonpolar molecules in nonpolar solvents is, again, an illustration of the chemical axiom "like dissolves like."

Two liquids that do not mix to an appreciable extent are called **immiscible**. Layers are formed when we pour immiscible liquids into the same container. Gasoline, oil (**Figure 11.15**), benzene, carbon tetrachloride, some paints, and many other nonpolar liquids are immiscible with water. The attraction between the molecules of such nonpolar liquids and polar water molecules is ineffectively weak. The only strong attractions in such a mixture are between the water molecules, so they effectively squeeze out the molecules of the nonpolar liquid. The distinction between immiscibility and miscibility is really one of degrees, so that miscible liquids are of infinite mutual solubility, while liquids said to be immiscible are of very low (though not zero) mutual solubility.

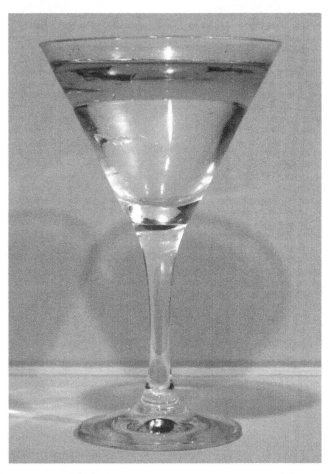

Figure 11.15 Water and oil are immiscible. Mixtures of these two substances will form two separate layers with the less dense oil floating on top of the water. (credit: "Yortw"/Flickr)

Two liquids, such as bromine and water, that are of *moderate* mutual solubility are said to be **partially miscible**. Two partially miscible liquids usually form two layers when mixed. In the case of the bromine and water mixture, the upper layer is water, saturated with bromine, and the lower layer is bromine saturated with water. Since bromine is nonpolar, and, thus, not very soluble in water, the water layer is only slightly discolored by the bright orange bromine dissolved in it. Since the solubility of water in bromine is very low, there is no noticeable effect on the dark color of the bromine layer (Figure 11.16).

Figure 11.16   Bromine (the deep orange liquid on the left) and water (the clear liquid in the middle) are partially miscible. The top layer in the mixture on the right is a saturated solution of bromine in water; the bottom layer is a saturated solution of water in bromine. (credit: Paul Flowers)

Solutions of Solids in Liquids

The dependence of solubility on temperature for a number of inorganic solids in water is shown by the solubility curves in Figure 11.17. Reviewing these data indicate a general trend of increasing solubility with temperature, although there are exceptions, as illustrated by the ionic compound cerium sulfate.

Figure 11.17 This graph shows how the solubility of several solids changes with temperature.

The temperature dependence of solubility can be exploited to prepare supersaturated solutions of certain compounds. A solution may be saturated with the compound at an elevated temperature (where the solute is more soluble) and subsequently cooled to a lower temperature without precipitating the solute. The resultant solution contains solute at a concentration greater than its equilibrium solubility at the lower temperature (i.e., it is supersaturated) and is relatively stable. Precipitation of the excess solute can be initiated by adding a seed crystal (see the video in the Link to Learning earlier in this module) or by mechanically agitating the solution. Some hand warmers, such as the one pictured in **Figure 11.18**, take advantage of this behavior.

Figure 11.18 This hand warmer produces heat when the sodium acetate in a supersaturated solution precipitates. Precipitation of the solute is initiated by a mechanical shockwave generated when the flexible metal disk within the solution is "clicked." (credit: modification of work by "Velela"/Wikimedia Commons)

Link to Learning

This **video (http://openstaxcollege.org/l/16handwarmer)** shows the crystallization process occurring in a hand warmer.

11.4 Colligative Properties

By the end of this section, you will be able to:

- Express concentrations of solution components using mole fraction and molality
- Describe the effect of solute concentration on various solution properties (vapor pressure, boiling point, freezing point, and osmotic pressure)
- Perform calculations using the mathematical equations that describe these various colligative effects
- Describe the process of distillation and its practical applications
- Explain the process of osmosis and describe how it is applied industrially and in nature

The properties of a solution are different from those of either the pure solute(s) or solvent. Many solution properties are dependent upon the chemical identity of the solute. Compared to pure water, a solution of hydrogen chloride is more acidic, a solution of ammonia is more basic, a solution of sodium chloride is more dense, and a solution of sucrose is more viscous. There are a few solution properties, however, that depend *only* upon the total concentration of solute species, regardless of their identities. These **colligative properties** include vapor pressure lowering, boiling point elevation, freezing point depression, and osmotic pressure. This small set of properties is of central importance to many natural phenomena and technological applications, as will be described in this module.

Mole Fraction and Molality

Several units commonly used to express the concentrations of solution components were introduced in an earlier chapter of this text, each providing certain benefits for use in different applications. For example, molarity (M) is a convenient unit for use in stoichiometric calculations, since it is defined in terms of the molar amounts of solute species:

$$M = \frac{\text{mol solute}}{\text{L solution}}$$

Because solution volumes vary with temperature, molar concentrations will likewise vary. When expressed as molarity, the concentration of a solution with identical numbers of solute and solvent species will be different at different temperatures, due to the contraction/expansion of the solution. More appropriate for calculations involving many colligative properties are mole-based concentration units whose values are not dependent on temperature. Two such units are *mole fraction* (introduced in the previous chapter on gases) and *molality*.

The mole fraction, X, of a component is the ratio of its molar amount to the total number of moles of all solution components:

$$X_A = \frac{\text{mol A}}{\text{total mol of all components}}$$

Molality is a concentration unit defined as the ratio of the numbers of moles of solute to the mass of the solvent in kilograms:

$$m = \frac{\text{mol solute}}{\text{kg solvent}}$$

Since these units are computed using only masses and molar amounts, they do not vary with temperature and, thus, are better suited for applications requiring temperature-independent concentrations, including several colligative properties, as will be described in this chapter module.

Example 11.2

Calculating Mole Fraction and Molality

The antifreeze in most automobile radiators is a mixture of equal volumes of ethylene glycol and water, with minor amounts of other additives that prevent corrosion. What are the (a) mole fraction and (b) molality of ethylene glycol, $C_2H_4(OH)_2$, in a solution prepared from 2.22×10^3 g of ethylene glycol and 2.00×10^3 g of water (approximately 2 L of glycol and 2 L of water)?

Solution

(a) The mole fraction of ethylene glycol may be computed by first deriving molar amounts of both solution components and then substituting these amounts into the unit definition.

$$\text{mol } C_2H_4(OH)_2 = 2220 \text{ g} \times \frac{1 \text{ mol } C_2H_4(OH)_2}{62.07 \text{ g } C_2H_4(OH)_2} = 35.8 \text{ mol } C_2H_4(OH)_2$$

$$\text{mol } H_2O = 2000 \text{ g} \times \frac{1 \text{ mol } H_2O}{18.02 \text{ g } H_2O} = 111 \text{ mol } H_2O$$

$$X_{\text{ethylene glycol}} = \frac{35.8 \text{ mol } C_2H_4(OH)_2}{(35.8 + 111) \text{ mol total}} = 0.245$$

Notice that mole fraction is a dimensionless property, being the ratio of properties with identical units (moles).

(b) To find molality, we need to know the moles of the solute and the mass of the solvent (in kg).

First, use the given mass of ethylene glycol and its molar mass to find the moles of solute:

$$2220 \text{ g } C_2H_4(OH)_2 \left(\frac{\text{mol } C_2H_2(OH)_2}{62.07 \text{ g}} \right) = 35.8 \text{ mol } C_2H_4(OH)_2$$

Then, convert the mass of the water from grams to kilograms:

$$2000 \text{ g } H_2O \left(\frac{1 \text{ kg}}{1000 \text{ g}} \right) = 2 \text{ kg } H_2O$$

Finally, calculate molarity per its definition:

$$\text{molality} = \frac{\text{mol solute}}{\text{kg solvent}}$$

$$\text{molality} = \frac{35.8 \text{ mol } C_2H_4(OH)_2}{2 \text{ kg } H_2O}$$

$$\text{molality} = 17.9 \, m$$

Check Your Learning

What are the mole fraction and molality of a solution that contains 0.850 g of ammonia, NH_3, dissolved in 125 g of water?

Answer: 7.14×10^{-3}; $0.399 \, m$

Example 11.3

Converting Mole Fraction and Molal Concentrations

Calculate the mole fraction of solute and solvent in a 3.0 m solution of sodium chloride.

Solution

Converting from one concentration unit to another is accomplished by first comparing the two unit definitions. In this case, both units have the same numerator (moles of solute) but different denominators. The provided molal concentration may be written as:

$$\frac{3.0 \text{ mol NaCl}}{1.0 \text{ kg H}_2\text{O}}$$

The numerator for this solution's mole fraction is, therefore, 3.0 mol NaCl. The denominator may be computed by deriving the molar amount of water corresponding to 1.0 kg

$$1.0 \text{ kg H}_2\text{O}\left(\frac{1000 \text{ g}}{1 \text{ kg}}\right)\left(\frac{\text{mol H}_2\text{O}}{18.02 \text{ g}}\right) = 55 \text{ mol H}_2\text{O}$$

and then substituting these molar amounts into the definition for mole fraction.

$$X_{\text{H}_2\text{O}} = \frac{\text{mol H}_2\text{O}}{\text{mol NaCl} + \text{mol H}_2\text{O}}$$

$$X_{\text{H}_2\text{O}} = \frac{55 \text{ mol H}_2\text{O}}{3.0 \text{ mol NaCl} + 55 \text{ mol H}_2\text{O}}$$

$$X_{\text{H}_2\text{O}} = 0.95$$

$$X_{\text{NaCl}} = \frac{\text{mol NaCl}}{\text{mol NaCl} + \text{mol H}_2\text{O}}$$

$$X_{\text{NaCl}} = \frac{3.0 \text{ mol NaCl}}{3.0 \text{ mol NaCl} + 55 \text{ mol H}_2\text{O}}$$

$$X_{\text{NaCl}} = 0.052$$

Check Your Learning

The mole fraction of iodine, I_2, dissolved in dichloromethane, CH_2Cl_2, is 0.115. What is the molal concentration, m, of iodine in this solution?

Answer: 1.50 m

Vapor Pressure Lowering

As described in the chapter on liquids and solids, the equilibrium vapor pressure of a liquid is the pressure exerted by its gaseous phase when vaporization and condensation are occurring at equal rates:

$$\text{liquid} \rightleftharpoons \text{gas}$$

Dissolving a nonvolatile substance in a volatile liquid results in a lowering of the liquid's vapor pressure. This phenomenon can be rationalized by considering the effect of added solute molecules on the liquid's vaporization and condensation processes. To vaporize, solvent molecules must be present at the surface of the solution. The presence of solute decreases the surface area available to solvent molecules and thereby reduces the rate of solvent vaporization. Since the rate of condensation is unaffected by the presence of solute, the net result is that the vaporization-condensation equilibrium is achieved with fewer solvent molecules in the vapor phase (i.e., at a lower vapor pressure) (Figure 11.19). While this kinetic interpretation is useful, it does not account for several important aspects of the colligative nature of vapor pressure lowering. A more rigorous explanation involves the property of *entropy*, a topic of discussion in a later text chapter on thermodynamics. For purposes of understanding the lowering of a liquid's vapor pressure, it is adequate to note that the greater entropy of a solution in comparison to its separate solvent and solute serves to effectively stabilize the solvent molecules and hinder their vaporization. A lower vapor pressure results, and a correspondingly higher boiling point as described in the next section of this module.

(a) Pure water   (b) Aqueous solution

Figure 11.19 The presence of nonvolatile solutes lowers the vapor pressure of a solution by impeding the evaporation of solvent molecules.

The relationship between the vapor pressures of solution components and the concentrations of those components is described by **Raoult's law**: *The partial pressure exerted by any component of an ideal solution is equal to the vapor pressure of the pure component multiplied by its mole fraction in the solution.*

$$P_A = X_A P_A^\circ$$

where P_A is the partial pressure exerted by component A in the solution, P_A° is the vapor pressure of pure A, and X_A is the mole fraction of A in the solution. (Mole fraction is a concentration unit introduced in the chapter on gases.)

Recalling that the total pressure of a gaseous mixture is equal to the sum of partial pressures for all its components (Dalton's law of partial pressures), the total vapor pressure exerted by a solution containing i components is

$$P_{\text{solution}} = \sum_i P_i = \sum_i X_i P_i^\circ$$

A nonvolatile substance is one whose vapor pressure is negligible ($P^\circ \approx 0$), and so the vapor pressure above a solution containing only nonvolatile solutes is due only to the solvent:

$$P_{\text{solution}} = X_{\text{solvent}} P_{\text{solvent}}^\circ$$

Example 11.4

Calculation of a Vapor Pressure

Compute the vapor pressure of an ideal solution containing 92.1 g of glycerin, $C_3H_5(OH)_3$, and 184.4 g of ethanol, C_2H_5OH, at 40 °C. The vapor pressure of pure ethanol is 0.178 atm at 40 °C. Glycerin is essentially nonvolatile at this temperature.

Solution

Since the solvent is the only volatile component of this solution, its vapor pressure may be computed per Raoult's law as:

$$P_{solution} = X_{solvent} P°_{solvent}$$

First, calculate the molar amounts of each solution component using the provided mass data.

$$92.1 \text{ g } C_3H_5(OH)_3 \times \frac{1 \text{ mol } C_3H_5(OH)_3}{92.094 \text{ g } C_3H_5(OH)_3} = 1.00 \text{ mol } C_3H_5(OH)_3$$

$$184.4 \text{ g } C_2H_5OH \times \frac{1 \text{ mol } C_2H_5OH}{46.069 \text{ g } C_2H_5OH} = 4.000 \text{ mol } C_2H_5OH$$

Next, calculate the mole fraction of the solvent (ethanol) and use Raoult's law to compute the solution's vapor pressure.

$$X_{C_2H_5OH} = \frac{4.000 \text{ mol}}{(1.00 \text{ mol} + 4.000 \text{ mol})} = 0.800$$

$$P_{solv} = X_{solv} P°_{solv} = 0.800 \times 0.178 \text{ atm} = 0.142 \text{ atm}$$

Check Your Learning

A solution contains 5.00 g of urea, $CO(NH_2)_2$ (a nonvolatile solute) and 0.100 kg of water. If the vapor pressure of pure water at 25 °C is 23.7 torr, what is the vapor pressure of the solution?

Answer: 23.4 torr

Elevation of the Boiling Point of a Solvent

As described in the chapter on liquids and solids, the *boiling point* of a liquid is the temperature at which its vapor pressure is equal to ambient atmospheric pressure. Since the vapor pressure of a solution is lowered due to the presence of nonvolatile solutes, it stands to reason that the solution's boiling point will subsequently be increased. Compared to pure solvent, a solution, therefore, will require a higher temperature to achieve any given vapor pressure, including one equivalent to that of the surrounding atmosphere. The increase in boiling point observed when nonvolatile solute is dissolved in a solvent, ΔT_b, is called **boiling point elevation** and is directly proportional to the molal concentration of solute species:

$$\Delta T_b = K_b m$$

where K_b is the **boiling point elevation constant**, or the *ebullioscopic constant* and m is the molal concentration (molality) of all solute species.

Boiling point elevation constants are characteristic properties that depend on the identity of the solvent. Values of K_b for several solvents are listed in Table 11.2.

Boiling Point Elevation and Freezing Point Depression Constants for Several Solvents

Solvent	Boiling Point (°C at 1 atm)	K_b (Cm^{-1})	Freezing Point (°C at 1 atm)	K_f (Cm^{-1})
water	100.0	0.512	0.0	1.86
hydrogen acetate	118.1	3.07	16.6	3.9
benzene	80.1	2.53	5.5	5.12
chloroform	61.26	3.63	−63.5	4.68
nitrobenzene	210.9	5.24	5.67	8.1

Table 11.2

The extent to which the vapor pressure of a solvent is lowered and the boiling point is elevated depends on the total number of solute particles present in a given amount of solvent, not on the mass or size or chemical identities of the particles. A 1 *m* aqueous solution of sucrose (342 g/mol) and a 1 *m* aqueous solution of ethylene glycol (62 g/mol) will exhibit the same boiling point because each solution has one mole of solute particles (molecules) per kilogram of solvent.

Example 11.5

Calculating the Boiling Point of a Solution

What is the boiling point of a 0.33 *m* solution of a nonvolatile solute in benzene?

Solution

Use the equation relating boiling point elevation to solute molality to solve this problem in two steps.

Step 1. *Calculate the change in boiling point.*
$$\Delta T_b = K_b m = 2.53 \,°\text{C} \, m^{-1} \times 0.33 \, m = 0.83 \,°\text{C}$$

Step 2. *Add the boiling point elevation to the pure solvent's boiling point.*
$$\text{Boiling temperature} = 80.1 \,°\text{C} + 0.83 \,°\text{C} = 80.9 \,°\text{C}$$

Check Your Learning

What is the boiling point of the antifreeze described in Example 11.2?

Answer: 109.2 °C

Example 11.6

The Boiling Point of an Iodine Solution

Find the boiling point of a solution of 92.1 g of iodine, I_2, in 800.0 g of chloroform, $CHCl_3$, assuming that the iodine is nonvolatile and that the solution is ideal.

Solution

We can solve this problem using four steps.

Step 1. *Convert from grams to moles of* I_2 *using the molar mass of* I_2 *in the unit conversion factor.*
Result: 0.363 mol
Step 2. *Determine the molality of the solution from the number of moles of solute and the mass of solvent, in kilograms.*
Result: 0.454 *m*
Step 3. *Use the direct proportionality between the change in boiling point and molal concentration to determine how much the boiling point changes.*
Result: 1.65 °C
Step 4. *Determine the new boiling point from the boiling point of the pure solvent and the change.*
Result: 62.91 °C
Check each result as a self-assessment.

Check Your Learning

What is the boiling point of a solution of 1.0 g of glycerin, $C_3H_5(OH)_3$, in 47.8 g of water? Assume an ideal solution.

Answer: 100.12 °C

Distillation of Solutions

Distillation is a technique for separating the components of mixtures that is widely applied in both in the laboratory and in industrial settings. It is used to refine petroleum, to isolate fermentation products, and to purify water. This separation technique involves the controlled heating of a sample mixture to selectively vaporize, condense, and collect one or more components of interest. A typical apparatus for laboratory-scale distillations is shown in **Figure 11.20**.

Boiling point temperature

Still head

Still pot

Sample mixture

Heating bath (oil/sand)

Stirrer speed control

Stirrer/heat plate

Heat source

Still receiver

Receiving flask

(a)   (b)

Figure 11.20 A typical laboratory distillation unit is shown in (a) a photograph and (b) a schematic diagram of the components. (credit a: modification of work by "Rifleman82"/Wikimedia commons; credit b: modification of work by "Slashme"/Wikimedia Commons)

Oil refineries use large-scale *fractional distillation* to separate the components of crude oil. The crude oil is heated to high temperatures at the base of a tall *fractionating column*, vaporizing many of the components that rise within the column. As vaporized components reach adequately cool zones during their ascent, they condense and are collected. The collected liquids are simpler mixtures of hydrocarbons and other petroleum compounds that are of appropriate composition for various applications (e.g., diesel fuel, kerosene, gasoline), as depicted in Figure 11.21.

Figure 11.21 Crude oil is a complex mixture that is separated by large-scale fractional distillation to isolate various simpler mixtures.

Depression of the Freezing Point of a Solvent

Solutions freeze at lower temperatures than pure liquids. This phenomenon is exploited in "de-icing" schemes that use salt (**Figure 11.22**), calcium chloride, or urea to melt ice on roads and sidewalks, and in the use of ethylene glycol as an "antifreeze" in automobile radiators. Seawater freezes at a lower temperature than fresh water, and so the Arctic and Antarctic oceans remain unfrozen even at temperatures below 0 °C (as do the body fluids of fish and other cold-blooded sea animals that live in these oceans).

Figure 11.22 Rock salt (NaCl), calcium chloride (CaCl$_2$), or a mixture of the two are used to melt ice. (credit: modification of work by Eddie Welker)

The decrease in freezing point of a dilute solution compared to that of the pure solvent, ΔT_f, is called the **freezing point depression** and is directly proportional to the molal concentration of the solute

$$\Delta T_f = K_f m$$

where m is the molal concentration of the solute in the solvent and K_f is called the **freezing point depression constant** (or *cryoscopic constant*). Just as for boiling point elevation constants, these are characteristic properties whose values depend on the chemical identity of the solvent. Values of K_f for several solvents are listed in Table 11.2.

Example 11.7

Calculation of the Freezing Point of a Solution

What is the freezing point of the 0.33 m solution of a nonvolatile nonelectrolyte solute in benzene described in Example 11.3?

Solution

Use the equation relating freezing point depression to solute molality to solve this problem in two steps.

Step 1. *Calculate the change in freezing point.*
$$\Delta T_f = K_f m = 5.12\,°C\,m^{-1} \times 0.33\,m = 1.7\,°C$$

Step 2. *Subtract the freezing point change observed from the pure solvent's freezing point.*
$$\text{Freezing Temperature} = 5.5\,°C - 1.7\,°C = 3.8\,°C$$

Check Your Learning

What is the freezing point of a 1.85 m solution of a nonvolatile nonelectrolyte solute in nitrobenzene?

Answer: −9.3 °C

Chemistry in Everyday Life

Colligative Properties and De-Icing

Sodium chloride and its group 2 analogs calcium and magnesium chloride are often used to de-ice roadways and sidewalks, due to the fact that a solution of any one of these salts will have a freezing point lower than 0 °C, the freezing point of pure water. The group 2 metal salts are frequently mixed with the cheaper and more readily available sodium chloride ("rock salt") for use on roads, since they tend to be somewhat less corrosive than the NaCl, and they provide a larger depression of the freezing point, since they dissociate to yield three particles per formula unit, rather than two particles like the sodium chloride.

Because these ionic compounds tend to hasten the corrosion of metal, they would not be a wise choice to use in antifreeze for the radiator in your car or to de-ice a plane prior to takeoff. For these applications, covalent compounds, such as ethylene or propylene glycol, are often used. The glycols used in radiator fluid not only lower the freezing point of the liquid, but they elevate the boiling point, making the fluid useful in both winter and summer. Heated glycols are often sprayed onto the surface of airplanes prior to takeoff in inclement weather in the winter to remove ice that has already formed and prevent the formation of more ice, which would be particularly dangerous if formed on the control surfaces of the aircraft (Figure 11.23).

(a)

(b)

Figure 11.23   Freezing point depression is exploited to remove ice from (a) roadways and (b) the control surfaces of aircraft.

Phase Diagram for an Aqueous Solution of a Nonelectrolyte

The colligative effects on vapor pressure, boiling point, and freezing point described in the previous section are conveniently summarized by comparing the phase diagrams for a pure liquid and a solution derived from that liquid. Phase diagrams for water and an aqueous solution are shown in Figure 11.24.

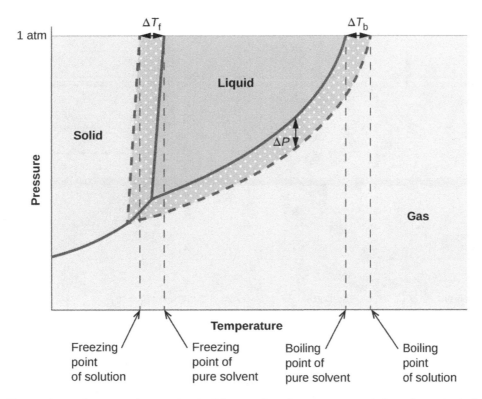

Figure 11.24 These phase diagrams show water (solid curves) and an aqueous solution of nonelectrolyte (dashed curves).

The liquid-vapor curve for the solution is located *beneath* the corresponding curve for the solvent, depicting the vapor pressure *lowering*, ΔP, that results from the dissolution of nonvolatile solute. Consequently, at any given pressure, the solution's boiling point is observed at a higher temperature than that for the pure solvent, reflecting the boiling point elevation, ΔT_b, associated with the presence of nonvolatile solute. The solid-liquid curve for the solution is displaced left of that for the pure solvent, representing the freezing point depression, ΔT_f, that accompanies solution formation. Finally, notice that the solid-gas curves for the solvent and its solution are identical. This is the case for many solutions comprising liquid solvents and nonvolatile solutes. Just as for vaporization, when a solution of this sort is frozen, it is actually just the *solvent* molecules that undergo the liquid-to-solid transition, forming pure solid solvent that excludes solute species. The solid and gaseous phases, therefore, are composed solvent only, and so transitions between these phases are not subject to colligative effects.

Osmosis and Osmotic Pressure of Solutions

A number of natural and synthetic materials exhibit *selective permeation*, meaning that only molecules or ions of a certain size, shape, polarity, charge, and so forth, are capable of passing through (permeating) the material. Biological cell membranes provide elegant examples of selective permeation in nature, while dialysis tubing used to remove metabolic wastes from blood is a more simplistic technological example. Regardless of how they may be fabricated, these materials are generally referred to as **semipermeable membranes**.

Consider the apparatus illustrated in **Figure 11.25**, in which samples of pure solvent and a solution are separated by a membrane that only solvent molecules may permeate. Solvent molecules will diffuse across the membrane in both directions. Since the concentration of *solvent* is greater in the pure solvent than the solution, these molecules will diffuse from the solvent side of the membrane to the solution side at a faster rate than they will in the reverse direction. The result is a net transfer of solvent molecules from the pure solvent to the solution. Diffusion-driven transfer of solvent molecules through a semipermeable membrane is a process known as **osmosis**.

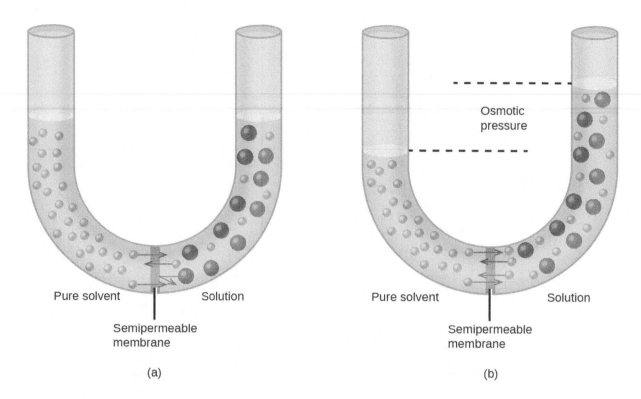

Figure 11.25 Osmosis results in the transfer of solvent molecules from a sample of low (or zero) solute concentration to a sample of higher solute concentration.

When osmosis is carried out in an apparatus like that shown in **Figure 11.25**, the volume of the solution increases as it becomes diluted by accumulation of solvent. This causes the level of the solution to rise, increasing its hydrostatic pressure (due to the weight of the column of solution in the tube) and resulting in a faster transfer of solvent molecules back to the pure solvent side. When the pressure reaches a value that yields a reverse solvent transfer rate equal to the osmosis rate, bulk transfer of solvent ceases. This pressure is called the **osmotic pressure (Π)** of the solution. The osmotic pressure of a dilute solution is related to its solute molarity, M, and absolute temperature, T, according to the equation

$$\Pi = MRT$$

where R is the universal gas constant.

Example 11.8

Calculation of Osmotic Pressure

What is the osmotic pressure (atm) of a 0.30 M solution of glucose in water that is used for intravenous infusion at body temperature, 37 °C?

Solution

We can find the osmotic pressure, Π, using the formula $\Pi = MRT$, where T is on the Kelvin scale (310 K) and the value of R is expressed in appropriate units (0.08206 L atm/mol K).

$$
\begin{aligned}
\Pi &= MRT \\
&= 0.03 \text{ mol/L} \times 0.08206 \text{ L atm/mol K} \times 310 \text{ K} \\
&= 7.6 \text{ atm}
\end{aligned}
$$

Check Your Learning

What is the osmotic pressure (atm) a solution with a volume of 0.750 L that contains 5.0 g of methanol, CH_3OH, in water at 37 °C?

Answer: 5.3 atm

If a solution is placed in an apparatus like the one shown in **Figure 11.26**, applying pressure greater than the osmotic pressure of the solution reverses the osmosis and pushes solvent molecules from the solution into the pure solvent. This technique of reverse osmosis is used for large-scale desalination of seawater and on smaller scales to produce high-purity tap water for drinking.

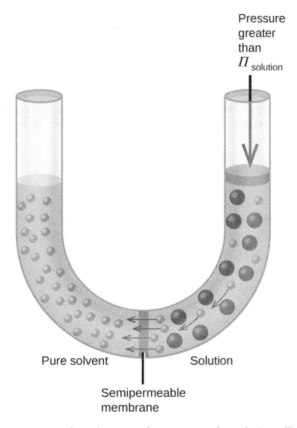

Figure 11.26 Applying a pressure greater than the osmotic pressure of a solution will reverse osmosis. Solvent molecules from the solution are pushed into the pure solvent.

Chemistry in Everyday Life

Reverse Osmosis Water Purification

In the process of osmosis, diffusion serves to move water through a semipermeable membrane from a less concentrated solution to a more concentrated solution. Osmotic pressure is the amount of pressure that must be applied to the more concentrated solution to cause osmosis to stop. If greater pressure is applied, the water will go from the more concentrated solution to a less concentrated (more pure) solution. This is called reverse osmosis. Reverse osmosis (RO) is used to purify water in many applications, from desalination plants in coastal cities, to water-purifying machines in grocery stores (**Figure 11.27**), and smaller reverse-osmosis household units. With a hand-operated pump, small RO units can be used in third-world countries, disaster areas, and in lifeboats. Our military forces have a variety of generator-operated RO units that can be transported in vehicles to remote locations.

(a)   (b)

Figure 11.27   Reverse osmosis systems for purifying drinking water are shown here on (a) small and (b) large scales. (credit a: modification of work by Jerry Kirkhart; credit b: modification of work by Willard J. Lathrop)

Examples of osmosis are evident in many biological systems because cells are surrounded by semipermeable membranes. Carrots and celery that have become limp because they have lost water can be made crisp again by placing them in water. Water moves into the carrot or celery cells by osmosis. A cucumber placed in a concentrated salt solution loses water by osmosis and absorbs some salt to become a pickle. Osmosis can also affect animal cells. Solute concentrations are particularly important when solutions are injected into the body. Solutes in body cell fluids and blood serum give these solutions an osmotic pressure of approximately 7.7 atm. Solutions injected into the body must have the same osmotic pressure as blood serum; that is, they should be **isotonic** with blood serum. If a less concentrated solution, a **hypotonic** solution, is injected in sufficient quantity to dilute the blood serum, water from the diluted serum passes into the blood cells by osmosis, causing the cells to expand and rupture. This process is called **hemolysis**. When a more concentrated solution, a **hypertonic** solution, is injected, the cells lose water to the more concentrated solution, shrivel, and possibly die in a process called **crenation**. These effects are illustrated in Figure 11.28.

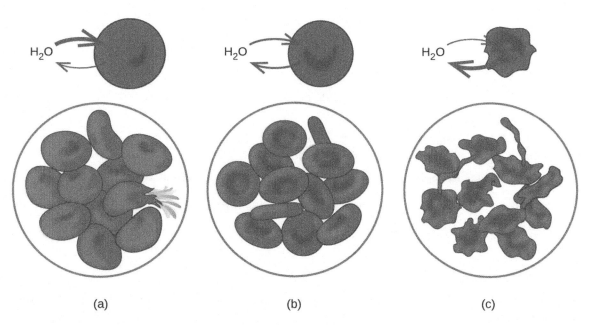

Figure 11.28 Red blood cell membranes are water permeable and will (a) swell and possibly rupture in a hypotonic solution; (b) maintain normal volume and shape in an isotonic solution; and (c) shrivel and possibly die in a hypertonic solution. (credit a/b/c: modifications of work by "LadyofHats"/Wikimedia commons)

Determination of Molar Masses

Osmotic pressure and changes in freezing point, boiling point, and vapor pressure are directly proportional to the concentration of solute present. Consequently, we can use a measurement of one of these properties to determine the molar mass of the solute from the measurements.

Example 11.9

Determination of a Molar Mass from a Freezing Point Depression

A solution of 4.00 g of a nonelectrolyte dissolved in 55.0 g of benzene is found to freeze at 2.32 °C. What is the molar mass of this compound?

Solution

We can solve this problem using the following steps.

Freezing point of solution $\xrightarrow{\ 1\ }$ ΔT_f $\xrightarrow{\ 2\ }$ Molal concentration of compound $\xrightarrow{\ 3\ }$ Moles of compound in sample $\xrightarrow{\ 4\ }$ Molar mass of compound

Step 1. *Determine the change in freezing point from the observed freezing point and the freezing*

point of pure benzene (Table 11.2).

$$\Delta T_f = 5.5\ °C - 2.32\ °C = 3.2\ °C$$

Step 2.   *Determine the molal concentration from K_f, the freezing point depression constant for benzene (Table 11.2), and ΔT_f.*

$$\Delta T_f = K_f m$$

$$m = \frac{\Delta T_f}{K_f} = \frac{3.2\ °C}{5.12\ °C\ m^{-1}} = 0.63\ m$$

Step 3.   *Determine the number of moles of compound in the solution from the molal concentration and the mass of solvent used to make the solution.*

$$\text{Moles of solute} = \frac{0.62\ \text{mol solute}}{1.00\ \text{kg solvent}} \times 0.0550\ \text{kg solvent} = 0.035\ \text{mol}$$

Step 4.   *Determine the molar mass from the mass of the solute and the number of moles in that mass.*

$$\text{Molar mass} = \frac{4.00\ \text{g}}{0.034\ \text{mol}} = 1.2 \times 10^2\ \text{g/mol}$$

Check Your Learning

A solution of 35.7 g of a nonelectrolyte in 220.0 g of chloroform has a boiling point of 64.5 °C. What is the molar mass of this compound?

Answer: 1.8×10^2 g/mol

Example 11.10

Determination of a Molar Mass from Osmotic Pressure

A 0.500 L sample of an aqueous solution containing 10.0 g of hemoglobin has an osmotic pressure of 5.9 torr at 22 °C. What is the molar mass of hemoglobin?

Solution

Here is one set of steps that can be used to solve the problem:

Step 1.   *Convert the osmotic pressure to atmospheres, then determine the molar concentration from the osmotic pressure.*

$$\Pi = \frac{5.9\ \text{torr} \times 1\ \text{atm}}{760\ \text{torr}} = 7.8 \times 10^{-3}\ \text{atm}$$

$$\Pi = MRT$$

$$M = \frac{\Pi}{RT} = \frac{7.8 \times 10^{-3}\ \text{atm}}{(0.08206\ \text{L atm/mol K})(295\ \text{K})} = 3.2 \times 10^{-4}\ M$$

Step 2.   *Determine the number of moles of hemoglobin in the solution from the concentration and the volume of the solution.*

$$\text{moles of hemoglobin} = \frac{3.2 \times 10^{-4}\ \text{mol}}{1\ \text{L solution}} \times 0.500\ \text{L solution} = 1.6 \times 10^{-4}\ \text{mol}$$

Step 3.   *Determine the molar mass from the mass of hemoglobin and the number of moles in that mass.*

$$\text{molar mass} = \frac{10.0\ \text{g}}{1.6 \times 10^{-4}\ \text{mol}} = 6.2 \times 10^4\ \text{g/mol}$$

Colligative Properties of Electrolytes

As noted previously in this module, the colligative properties of a solution depend only on the number, not on the kind, of solute species dissolved. For example, 1 mole of any nonelectrolyte dissolved in 1 kilogram of solvent produces the same lowering of the freezing point as does 1 mole of any other nonelectrolyte. However, 1 mole of sodium chloride (an electrolyte) forms *2 moles* of ions when dissolved in solution. Each individual ion produces the same effect on the freezing point as a single molecule does.

Example 11.11

The Freezing Point of a Solution of an Electrolyte

The concentration of ions in seawater is approximately the same as that in a solution containing 4.2 g of NaCl dissolved in 125 g of water. Assume that each of the ions in the NaCl solution has the same effect on the freezing point of water as a nonelectrolyte molecule, and determine the freezing temperature the solution (which is approximately equal to the freezing temperature of seawater).

Solution

We can solve this problem using the following series of steps.

Step 1. *Convert from grams to moles of NaCl using the molar mass of NaCl in the unit conversion factor.*
Result: 0.072 mol NaCl
Step 2. *Determine the number of moles of ions present in the solution using the number of moles of ions in 1 mole of NaCl as the conversion factor (2 mol ions/1 mol NaCl).*
Result: 0.14 mol ions
Step 3. *Determine the molality of the ions in the solution from the number of moles of ions and the mass of solvent, in kilograms.*
Result: 1.1 *m*
Step 4. *Use the direct proportionality between the change in freezing point and molal concentration to determine how much the freezing point changes.*
Result: 2.0 °C
Step 5. *Determine the new freezing point from the freezing point of the pure solvent and the change.*
Result: −2.0 °C

Check each result as a self-assessment.

Check Your Learning

Assume that each of the ions in calcium chloride, $CaCl_2$, has the same effect on the freezing point of water as a nonelectrolyte molecule. Calculate the freezing point of a solution of 0.724 g of $CaCl_2$ in 175 g of water.

Answer: $-0.208 \, °C$

Assuming complete dissociation, a 1.0 m aqueous solution of NaCl contains 2.0 mole of ions (1.0 mol Na^+ and 1.0 mol Cl^-) per each kilogram of water, and its freezing point depression is expected to be

$$\Delta T_f = 2.0 \text{ mol ions/kg water} \times 1.86 \, °C \text{ kg water/mol ion} = 3.7 \, °C.$$

When this solution is actually prepared and its freezing point depression measured, however, a value of 3.4 °C is obtained. Similar discrepancies are observed for other ionic compounds, and the differences between the measured and expected colligative property values typically become more significant as solute concentrations increase. These observations suggest that the ions of sodium chloride (and other strong electrolytes) are not completely dissociated in solution.

To account for this and avoid the errors accompanying the assumption of total dissociation, an experimentally measured parameter named in honor of Nobel Prize-winning German chemist Jacobus Henricus van't Hoff is used. The **van't Hoff factor (i)** is defined as the ratio of solute particles in solution to the number of formula units dissolved:

$$i = \frac{\text{moles of particles in solution}}{\text{moles of formula units dissolved}}$$

Values for measured van't Hoff factors for several solutes, along with predicted values assuming complete dissociation, are shown in Table 11.3.

Expected and Observed van't Hoff Factors for Several 0.050 m Aqueous Electrolyte Solutions

Electrolyte	Particles in Solution	i (Predicted)	i (Measured)
HCl	H^+, Cl^-	2	1.9
NaCl	Na^+, Cl^-	2	1.9
$MgSO_4$	Mg^{2+}, SO_4^{2-}	2	1.3
$MgCl_2$	Mg^{2+}, $2Cl^-$	3	2.7
$FeCl_3$	Fe^{3+}, $3Cl^-$	4	3.4
glucose[2]	$C_{12}H_{22}O_{11}$	1	1.0

Table 11.3

In 1923, the chemists Peter Debye and Erich Hückel proposed a theory to explain the apparent incomplete ionization of strong electrolytes. They suggested that although interionic attraction in an aqueous solution is very greatly reduced by solvation of the ions and the insulating action of the polar solvent, it is not completely nullified. The residual attractions prevent the ions from behaving as totally independent particles (Figure 11.29). In some cases, a positive and negative ion may actually touch, giving a solvated unit called an ion pair. Thus, the **activity**, or the effective concentration, of any particular kind of ion is less than that indicated by the actual concentration. Ions become more and more widely separated the more dilute the solution, and the residual interionic attractions become less and less. Thus, in extremely dilute solutions, the effective concentrations of the ions (their activities) are essentially equal to the actual concentrations. Note that the van't Hoff factors for the electrolytes in Table 11.3 are for 0.05 m solutions,

---

2. A nonelectrolyte shown for comparison.

at which concentration the value of *i* for NaCl is 1.9, as opposed to an ideal value of 2.

Figure 11.29 Ions become more and more widely separated the more dilute the solution, and the residual interionic attractions become less.

11.5 Colloids

By the end of this section, you will be able to:

- Describe the composition and properties of colloidal dispersions
- List and explain several technological applications of colloids

As a child, you may have made suspensions such as mixtures of mud and water, flour and water, or a suspension of solid pigments in water, known as tempera paint. These suspensions are heterogeneous mixtures composed of relatively large particles that are visible (or that can be seen with a magnifying glass). They are cloudy, and the suspended particles settle out after mixing. On the other hand, when we make a solution, we prepare a homogeneous mixture in which no settling occurs and in which the dissolved species are molecules or ions. Solutions exhibit completely different behavior from suspensions. A solution may be colored, but it is transparent, the molecules or ions are invisible, and they do not settle out on standing. A group of mixtures called **colloids** (or **colloidal dispersions**) exhibit properties intermediate between those of suspensions and solutions (**Figure 11.30**). The particles in a colloid are larger than most simple molecules; however, colloidal particles are small enough that they do not settle out upon standing.

(a)   (b)   (c)

Figure 11.30 (a) A solution is a homogeneous mixture that appears clear, such as the saltwater in this aquarium. (b) In a colloid, such as milk, the particles are much larger but remain dispersed and do not settle. (c) A suspension, such as mud, is a heterogeneous mixture of suspended particles that appears cloudy and in which the particles can settle. (credit a photo: modification of work by Adam Wimsatt; credit b photo: modification of work by Melissa Wiese; credit c photo: modification of work by Peter Burgess)

The particles in a colloid are large enough to scatter light, a phenomenon called the **Tyndall effect**. This can make colloidal mixtures appear cloudy or opaque, such as the searchlight beams shown in **Figure 11.31**. Clouds are colloidal mixtures. They are composed of water droplets that are much larger than molecules, but that are small enough that they do not settle out.

Figure 11.31 The paths of searchlight beams are made visible when light is scattered by colloidal-size particles in the air (fog, smoke, etc.). (credit: "Bahman"/Wikimedia Commons)

The term "colloid"—from the Greek words *kolla*, meaning "glue," and *eidos*, meaning "like"—was first used in 1861 by Thomas Graham to classify mixtures such as starch in water and gelatin. Many colloidal particles are aggregates of hundreds or thousands of molecules, but others (such as proteins and polymer molecules) consist of a single extremely large molecule. The protein and synthetic polymer molecules that form colloids may have molecular masses ranging from a few thousand to many million atomic mass units.

Analogous to the identification of solution components as "solute" and "solvent," the components of a colloid are likewise classified according to their relative amounts. The particulate component typically present in a relatively minor amount is called the **dispersed phase** and the substance or solution throughout which the particulate is dispersed is called the **dispersion medium**. Colloids may involve virtually any combination of physical states (gas in liquid, liquid in solid, solid in gas, etc.), as illustrated by the examples of colloidal systems given in Table 11.4.

Examples of Colloidal Systems

Dispersed Phase	Dispersion Medium	Common Examples	Name
solid	gas	smoke, dust	—
solid	liquid	starch in water, some inks, paints, milk of magnesia	sol
solid	solid	some colored gems, some alloys	—
liquid	gas	clouds, fogs, mists, sprays	aerosol
liquid	liquid	milk, mayonnaise, butter	emulsion
liquid	solid	jellies, gels, pearl, opal (H_2O in SiO_2)	gel
gas	liquid	foams, whipped cream, beaten egg whites	foam

Table 11.4

Examples of Colloidal Systems

Dispersed Phase	Dispersion Medium	Common Examples	Name
gas	solid	pumice, floating soaps	—

Table 11.4

Preparation of Colloidal Systems

We can prepare a colloidal system by producing particles of colloidal dimensions and distributing these particles throughout a dispersion medium. Particles of colloidal size are formed by two methods:

1. Dispersion methods: that is, by breaking down larger particles. For example, paint pigments are produced by dispersing large particles by grinding in special mills.

2. Condensation methods: that is, growth from smaller units, such as molecules or ions. For example, clouds form when water molecules condense and form very small droplets.

A few solid substances, when brought into contact with water, disperse spontaneously and form colloidal systems. Gelatin, glue, starch, and dehydrated milk powder behave in this manner. The particles are already of colloidal size; the water simply disperses them. Powdered milk particles of colloidal size are produced by dehydrating milk spray. Some atomizers produce colloidal dispersions of a liquid in air.

We can prepare an **emulsion** by shaking together or blending two immiscible liquids. This breaks one liquid into droplets of colloidal size, which then disperse throughout the other liquid. Oil spills in the ocean may be difficult to clean up, partly because wave action can cause the oil and water to form an emulsion. In many emulsions, however, the dispersed phase tends to coalesce, form large drops, and separate. Therefore, emulsions are usually stabilized by an **emulsifying agent**, a substance that inhibits the coalescence of the dispersed liquid. For example, a little soap will stabilize an emulsion of kerosene in water. Milk is an emulsion of butterfat in water, with the protein casein as the emulsifying agent. Mayonnaise is an emulsion of oil in vinegar, with egg yolk components as the emulsifying agents.

Condensation methods form colloidal particles by aggregation of molecules or ions. If the particles grow beyond the colloidal size range, drops or precipitates form, and no colloidal system results. Clouds form when water molecules aggregate and form colloid-sized particles. If these water particles coalesce to form adequately large water drops of liquid water or crystals of solid water, they settle from the sky as rain, sleet, or snow. Many condensation methods involve chemical reactions. We can prepare a red colloidal suspension of iron(III) hydroxide by mixing a concentrated solution of iron(III) chloride with hot water:

$$Fe^{3+}(aq) + 3Cl^-(aq) + 6H_2O(l) \longrightarrow Fe(OH)_3(s) + H_3O^+(aq) + 3Cl^-(aq).$$

A colloidal gold sol results from the reduction of a very dilute solution of gold(III) chloride by a reducing agent such as formaldehyde, tin(II) chloride, or iron(II) sulfate:

$$Au^{3+} + 3e^- \longrightarrow Au$$

Some gold sols prepared in 1857 are still intact (the particles have not coalesced and settled), illustrating the long-term stability of many colloids.

Soaps and Detergents

Pioneers made soap by boiling fats with a strongly basic solution made by leaching potassium carbonate, K_2CO_3, from wood ashes with hot water. Animal fats contain polyesters of fatty acids (long-chain carboxylic acids). When animal fats are treated with a base like potassium carbonate or sodium hydroxide, glycerol and salts of fatty acids such as palmitic, oleic, and stearic acid are formed. The salts of fatty acids are called *soaps*. The sodium salt of stearic acid, sodium stearate, has the formula $C_{17}H_{35}CO_2Na$ and contains an uncharged nonpolar hydrocarbon chain, the $C_{17}H_{35}$— unit, and an ionic carboxylate group, the — CO_2^- unit (**Figure 11.32**).

Hydrocarbon chain

Ionic end

$$CH_3-CH_2-CH_2-CH_2-CH_2-CH_2-CH_2-CH_2-CH_2-CH_2-CH_2-CH_2-CH_2-CH_2-CH_2-CH_2-CH_2-CO_2^-Na^+$$

sodium stearate (soap)

Figure 11.32 Soaps contain a nonpolar hydrocarbon end (blue) and an ionic end (red). The ionic end is a carboxylate group. The length of the hydrocarbon end can vary from soap to soap.

Detergents (soap substitutes) also contain nonpolar hydrocarbon chains, such as $C_{12}H_{25}$—, and an ionic group, such as a sulfate— OSO_3^-, or a sulfonate— SO_3^- (**Figure 11.33**). Soaps form insoluble calcium and magnesium compounds in hard water; detergents form water-soluble products—a definite advantage for detergents.

$$CH_3-CH_2-CH_2-CH_2-CH_2-CH_2-CH_2-CH_2-CH_2-CH_2-CH_2-CH_2-OSO_3^-Na^+$$

sodium lauryl sulfate (detergent)

Figure 11.33 Detergents contain a nonpolar hydrocarbon end (blue) and an ionic end (red). The ionic end can be either a sulfate or a sulfonate. The length of the hydrocarbon end can vary from detergent to detergent.

The cleaning action of soaps and detergents can be explained in terms of the structures of the molecules involved. The hydrocarbon (nonpolar) end of a soap or detergent molecule dissolves in, or is attracted to, nonpolar substances such as oil, grease, or dirt particles. The ionic end is attracted by water (polar), illustrated in **Figure 11.34**. As a result, the soap or detergent molecules become oriented at the interface between the dirt particles and the water so they act as a kind of bridge between two different kinds of matter, nonpolar and polar. Molecules such as this are termed **amphiphilic** since they have both a hydrophobic ("water-fearing") part and a hydrophilic ("water-loving") part. As a consequence, dirt particles become suspended as colloidal particles and are readily washed away.

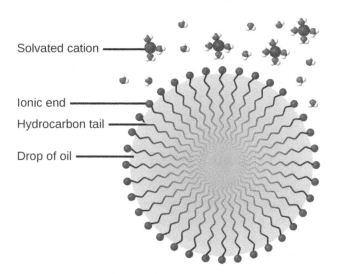

Solvated cation

Ionic end

Hydrocarbon tail

Drop of oil

Figure 11.34 This diagrammatic cross section of an emulsified drop of oil in water shows how soap or detergent acts as an emulsifier.

Chemistry in Everyday Life

Deepwater Horizon Oil Spill

The blowout of the Deepwater Horizon oil drilling rig on April 20, 2010, in the Gulf of Mexico near Mississippi began the largest marine oil spill in the history of the petroleum. In the 87 days following the blowout, an estimated 4.9 million barrels (210 million gallons) of oil flowed from the ruptured well 5000 feet below the water's surface. The well was finally declared sealed on September 19, 2010.

Crude oil is immiscible with and less dense than water, so the spilled oil rose to the surface of the water. Floating booms, skimmer ships, and controlled burns were used to remove oil from the water's surface in an attempt to protect beaches and wetlands along the Gulf coast. In addition to removal of the oil, attempts were also made to lessen its environmental impact by rendering it "soluble" (in the loose sense of the term) and thus allowing it to be diluted to hopefully less harmful levels by the vast volume of ocean water. This approach used 1.84 million gallons of the oil dispersant Corexit 9527, most of which was injected underwater at the site of the leak, with small amounts being sprayed on top of the spill. Corexit 9527 contains 2-butoxyethanol ($C_6H_{14}O_2$), an amphiphilic molecule whose polar and nonpolar ends are useful for emulsifying oil into small droplets, increasing the surface area of the oil and making it more available to marine bacteria for digestion (Figure 11.35). While this approach avoids many of the immediate hazards that bulk oil poses to marine and coastal ecosystems, it introduces the possibility of long-term effects resulting from the introduction of the complex and potential toxic components of petroleum into the ocean's food chain. A number of organizations are involved in monitoring the extended impact of this oil spill, including the National Oceanic and Atmospheric Administration (visit this website (http://openstaxcollege.org/l/16gulfspill) for additional details).

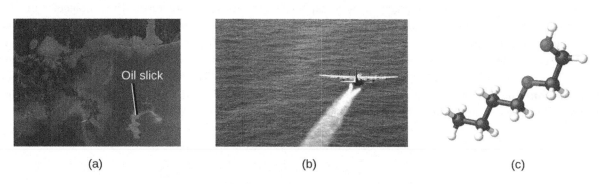

(a)   (b)   (c)

Figure 11.35   (a) This NASA satellite image shows the oil slick from the Deepwater Horizon spill. (b) A US Air Force plane sprays Corexit, a dispersant. (c) The molecular structure of 2-butoxyethanol is shown. (credit a: modification of work by "NASA, FT2, demis.nl"/Wikimedia Commons; credit b: modification of work by "NASA/MODIS Rapid Response Team"/Wikimedia Commons)

Electrical Properties of Colloidal Particles

Dispersed colloidal particles are often electrically charged. A colloidal particle of iron(III) hydroxide, for example, does not contain enough hydroxide ions to compensate exactly for the positive charges on the iron(III) ions. Thus, each individual colloidal particle bears a positive charge, and the colloidal dispersion consists of charged colloidal particles and some free hydroxide ions, which keep the dispersion electrically neutral. Most metal hydroxide colloids have positive charges, whereas most metals and metal sulfides form negatively charged dispersions. All colloidal particles in any one system have charges of the same sign. This helps keep them dispersed because particles containing like charges repel each other.

We can take advantage of the charge on colloidal particles to remove them from a variety of mixtures. If we place a colloidal dispersion in a container with charged electrodes, positively charged particles, such as iron(III) hydroxide particles, would move to the negative electrode. There, the colloidal particles lose their charge and coagulate as a precipitate.

The carbon and dust particles in smoke are often colloidally dispersed and electrically charged. Frederick Cottrell, an American chemist, developed a process to remove these particles.

Portrait of a Chemist

Frederick Gardner Cottrell

(a)   (b)

Figure 11.36   (a) Frederick Cottrell developed (b) the electrostatic precipitator, a device designed to curb air pollution by removing colloidal particles from air. (credit b: modification of work by "SpLot"/Wikimedia Commons)

Born in Oakland, CA in 1877, Frederick Cottrell devoured textbooks as if they were novels and graduated from high school at the age of 16. He then entered the University of California (UC), Berkeley, completing a Bachelor's degree in three years. He saved money from his $1200 annual salary as a chemistry teacher at Oakland High School to fund his studies in chemistry in Berlin with Nobel prize winner Jacobus Henricus van't Hoff, and in Leipzig with Wilhelm Ostwald, another Nobel awardee. After earning his PhD in physical chemistry, he returned to the United States to teach at UC Berkeley. He also consulted for the DuPont Company, where he developed the electrostatic precipitator, a device designed to curb air pollution by removing colloidal particles from air. Cottrell used the proceeds from his invention to fund a nonprofit research corporation to finance scientific research.

The charged particles are attracted to highly charged electrodes, where they are neutralized and deposited as dust (Figure 11.37). This is one of the important methods used to clean up the smoke from a variety of industrial processes. The process is also important in the recovery of valuable products from the smoke and flue dust of smelters, furnaces, and kilns. There are also ionic air filters designed for home use to improve indoor air quality.

Figure 11.37 In a Cottrell precipitator, positively and negatively charged particles are attracted to highly charged electrodes, where they are neutralized and deposited as dust.

Gels

When we make gelatin, such as Jell-O, we are making a type of colloid (**Figure 11.38**). Gelatin sets on cooling because the hot aqueous mixture of gelatin coagulates as it cools and the whole mass, including the liquid, sets to an extremely viscous body known as a **gel**, a colloid in which the dispersing medium is a solid and the dispersed phase is a liquid. It appears that the fibers of the dispersing medium form a complex three-dimensional network, the interstices being filled with the liquid medium or a dilute solution of the dispersing medium. Because the formation of a gel is accompanied by the taking up of water or some other solvent, the gel is said to be hydrated or solvated.

Figure 11.38 Gelatin desserts are colloids in which an aqueous solution of sweeteners and flavors is dispersed throughout a medium of solid proteins. (credit photo: modification of work by Steven Depolo)

Pectin, a carbohydrate from fruit juices, is a gel-forming substance important in jelly making. Silica gel, a colloidal dispersion of hydrated silicon dioxide, is formed when dilute hydrochloric acid is added to a dilute solution of sodium silicate. Canned Heat is a gel made by mixing alcohol and a saturated aqueous solution of calcium acetate.

Key Terms

alloy solid mixture of a metallic element and one or more additional elements

amphiphilic molecules possessing both hydrophobic (nonpolar) and a hydrophilic (polar) parts

boiling point elevation elevation of the boiling point of a liquid by addition of a solute

boiling point elevation constant the proportionality constant in the equation relating boiling point elevation to solute molality; also known as the ebullioscopic constant

colligative property property of a solution that depends only on the concentration of a solute species

colloid (also, colloidal dispersion) mixture in which relatively large solid or liquid particles are dispersed uniformly throughout a gas, liquid, or solid

crenation process whereby biological cells become shriveled due to loss of water by osmosis

dispersed phase substance present as relatively large solid or liquid particles in a colloid

dispersion medium solid, liquid, or gas in which colloidal particles are dispersed

dissociation physical process accompanying the dissolution of an ionic compound in which the compound's constituent ions are solvated and dispersed throughout the solution

electrolyte substance that produces ions when dissolved in water

emulsifying agent amphiphilic substance used to stabilize the particles of some emulsions

emulsion colloid formed from immiscible liquids

freezing point depression lowering of the freezing point of a liquid by addition of a solute

freezing point depression constant (also, cryoscopic constant) proportionality constant in the equation relating freezing point depression to solute molality

gel colloidal dispersion of a liquid in a solid

hemolysis rupture of red blood cells due to the accumulation of excess water by osmosis

Henry's law law stating the proportional relationship between the concentration of dissolved gas in a solution and the partial pressure of the gas in contact with the solution

hypertonic of greater osmotic pressure

hypotonic of less osmotic pressure

ideal solution solution that forms with no accompanying energy change

immiscible of negligible mutual solubility; typically refers to liquid substances

ion pair solvated anion/cation pair held together by moderate electrostatic attraction

ion-dipole attraction electrostatic attraction between an ion and a polar molecule

isotonic of equal osmotic pressure

miscible mutually soluble in all proportions; typically refers to liquid substances

molality (*m*) a concentration unit defined as the ratio of the numbers of moles of solute to the mass of the solvent in kilograms

nonelectrolyte substance that does not produce ions when dissolved in water

osmosis diffusion of solvent molecules through a semipermeable membrane

osmotic pressure (*Π*) opposing pressure required to prevent bulk transfer of solvent molecules through a semipermeable membrane

partially miscible of moderate mutual solubility; typically refers to liquid substances

Raoult's law the partial pressure exerted by a solution component is equal to the product of the component's mole fraction in the solution and its equilibrium vapor pressure in the pure state

saturated of concentration equal to solubility; containing the maximum concentration of solute possible for a given temperature and pressure

semipermeable membrane a membrane that selectively permits passage of certain ions or molecules

solubility extent to which a solute may be dissolved in water, or any solvent

solvation exothermic process in which intermolecular attractive forces between the solute and solvent in a solution are established

spontaneous process physical or chemical change that occurs without the addition of energy from an external source

strong electrolyte substance that dissociates or ionizes completely when dissolved in water

supersaturated of concentration that exceeds solubility; a nonequilibrium state

Tyndall effect scattering of visible light by a colloidal dispersion

unsaturated of concentration less than solubility

van't Hoff factor (*i*) the ratio of the number of moles of particles in a solution to the number of moles of formula units dissolved in the solution

weak electrolyte substance that ionizes only partially when dissolved in water

Key Equations

- $C_g = kP_g$

- $\left(P_A = X_A P_A^\circ\right)$

- $P_{solution} = \sum_i P_i = \sum_i X_i P_i^\circ$

- $P_{solution} = X_{solvent} P_{solvent}^\circ$

- $\Delta T_b = K_b m$

- $\Delta T_f = K_f m$

- $\Pi = MRT$

Summary

11.1 The Dissolution Process

A solution forms when two or more substances combine physically to yield a mixture that is homogeneous at the molecular level. The solvent is the most concentrated component and determines the physical state of the solution. The solutes are the other components typically present at concentrations less than that of the solvent. Solutions may form endothermically or exothermically, depending upon the relative magnitudes of solute and solvent intermolecular attractive forces. Ideal solutions form with no appreciable change in energy.

11.2 Electrolytes

Substances that dissolve in water to yield ions are called electrolytes. Electrolytes may be covalent compounds that chemically react with water to produce ions (for example, acids and bases), or they may be ionic compounds that dissociate to yield their constituent cations and anions, when dissolved. Dissolution of an ionic compound is facilitated by ion-dipole attractions between the ions of the compound and the polar water molecules. Soluble ionic substances and strong acids ionize completely and are strong electrolytes, while weak acids and bases ionize to only a small extent and are weak electrolytes. Nonelectrolytes are substances that do not produce ions when dissolved in water.

11.3 Solubility

The extent to which one substance will dissolve in another is determined by several factors, including the types and relative strengths of intermolecular attractive forces that may exist between the substances' atoms, ions, or molecules. This tendency to dissolve is quantified as substance's solubility, its maximum concentration in a solution at equilibrium under specified conditions. A saturated solution contains solute at a concentration equal to its solubility. A supersaturated solution is one in which a solute's concentration exceeds its solubility—a nonequilibrium (unstable) condition that will result in solute precipitation when the solution is appropriately perturbed. Miscible liquids are soluble in all proportions, and immiscible liquids exhibit very low mutual solubility. Solubilities for gaseous solutes decrease with increasing temperature, while those for most, but not all, solid solutes increase with temperature. The concentration of a gaseous solute in a solution is proportional to the partial pressure of the gas to which the solution is exposed, a relation known as Henry's law.

11.4 Colligative Properties

Properties of a solution that depend only on the concentration of solute particles are called colligative properties. They include changes in the vapor pressure, boiling point, and freezing point of the solvent in the solution. The magnitudes of these properties depend only on the total concentration of solute particles in solution, not on the type of particles. The total concentration of solute particles in a solution also determines its osmotic pressure. This is the pressure that must be applied to the solution to prevent diffusion of molecules of pure solvent through a semipermeable membrane into the solution. Ionic compounds may not completely dissociate in solution due to activity effects, in which case observed colligative effects may be less than predicted.

11.5 Colloids

Colloids are mixtures in which one or more substances are dispersed as relatively large solid particles or liquid droplets throughout a solid, liquid, or gaseous medium. The particles of a colloid remain dispersed and do not settle due to gravity, and they are often electrically charged. Colloids are widespread in nature and are involved in many technological applications.

Exercises

11.1 The Dissolution Process

1. How do solutions differ from compounds? From other mixtures?

2. Which of the principal characteristics of solutions can we see in the solutions of $K_2Cr_2O_7$ shown in **Figure 11.2**?

3. When KNO_3 is dissolved in water, the resulting solution is significantly colder than the water was originally.

(a) Is the dissolution of KNO_3 an endothermic or an exothermic process?

(b) What conclusions can you draw about the intermolecular attractions involved in the process?

(c) Is the resulting solution an ideal solution?

4. Give an example of each of the following types of solutions:

(a) a gas in a liquid

(b) a gas in a gas

(c) a solid in a solid

5. Indicate the most important types of intermolecular attractions in each of the following solutions:

(a) The solution in **Figure 11.2**.

(b) $NO(l)$ in $CO(l)$

(c) $Cl_2(g)$ in $Br_2(l)$

(d) $HCl(aq)$ in benzene $C_6H_6(l)$

(e) Methanol $CH_3OH(l)$ in $H_2O(l)$

6. Predict whether each of the following substances would be more soluble in water (polar solvent) or in a hydrocarbon such as heptane (C_7H_{16}, nonpolar solvent):

(a) vegetable oil (nonpolar)

(b) isopropyl alcohol (polar)

(c) potassium bromide (ionic)

7. Heat is released when some solutions form; heat is absorbed when other solutions form. Provide a molecular explanation for the difference between these two types of spontaneous processes.

8. Solutions of hydrogen in palladium may be formed by exposing Pd metal to H_2 gas. The concentration of hydrogen in the palladium depends on the pressure of H_2 gas applied, but in a more complex fashion than can be described by Henry's law. Under certain conditions, 0.94 g of hydrogen gas is dissolved in 215 g of palladium metal.

(a) Determine the molarity of this solution (solution density = 10.8 g/cm^3).

(b) Determine the molality of this solution (solution density = 10.8 g/cm^3).

(c) Determine the percent by mass of hydrogen atoms in this solution (solution density = 10.8 g/cm^3).

11.2 Electrolytes

9. Explain why the ions Na^+ and Cl^- are strongly solvated in water but not in hexane, a solvent composed of nonpolar molecules.

10. Explain why solutions of HBr in benzene (a nonpolar solvent) are nonconductive, while solutions in water (a polar solvent) are conductive.

11. Consider the solutions presented:

(a) Which of the following sketches best represents the ions in a solution of $Fe(NO_3)_3(aq)$?

(x)   (y)   (z)

(b) Write a balanced chemical equation showing the products of the dissolution of $Fe(NO_3)_3$.

12. Compare the processes that occur when methanol (CH_3OH), hydrogen chloride (HCl), and sodium hydroxide (NaOH) dissolve in water. Write equations and prepare sketches showing the form in which each of these compounds is present in its respective solution.

13. What is the expected electrical conductivity of the following solutions?

(a) $NaOH(aq)$

(b) $HCl(aq)$

(c) $C_6H_{12}O_6(aq)$ (glucose)

(d) $NH_3(l)$

14. Why are most *solid* ionic compounds electrically nonconductive, whereas aqueous solutions of ionic compounds are good conductors? Would you expect a *liquid* (molten) ionic compound to be electrically conductive or nonconductive? Explain.

15. Indicate the most important type of intermolecular attraction responsible for solvation in each of the following solutions:

(a) the solutions in Figure 11.8

(b) methanol, CH_3OH, dissolved in ethanol, C_2H_5OH

(c) methane, CH_4, dissolved in benzene, C_6H_6

(d) the polar halocarbon CF_2Cl_2 dissolved in the polar halocarbon $CF_2ClCFCl_2$

(e) $O_2(l)$ in $N_2(l)$

11.3 Solubility

16. Suppose you are presented with a clear solution of sodium thiosulfate, $Na_2S_2O_3$. How could you determine whether the solution is unsaturated, saturated, or supersaturated?

17. Supersaturated solutions of most solids in water are prepared by cooling saturated solutions. Supersaturated solutions of most gases in water are prepared by heating saturated solutions. Explain the reasons for the difference in the two procedures.

18. Suggest an explanation for the observations that ethanol, C_2H_5OH, is completely miscible with water and that ethanethiol, C_2H_5SH, is soluble only to the extent of 1.5 g per 100 mL of water.

19. Calculate the percent by mass of KBr in a saturated solution of KBr in water at 10 °C. See Figure 11.17 for useful data, and report the computed percentage to one significant digit.

20. Which of the following gases is expected to be most soluble in water? Explain your reasoning.

(a) CH_4

(b) CCl_4

(c) $CHCl_3$

21. At 0 °C and 1.00 atm, as much as 0.70 g of O_2 can dissolve in 1 L of water. At 0 °C and 4.00 atm, how many grams of O_2 dissolve in 1 L of water?

22. Refer to Figure 11.11.

(a) How did the concentration of dissolved CO_2 in the beverage change when the bottle was opened?

(b) What caused this change?

(c) Is the beverage unsaturated, saturated, or supersaturated with CO_2?

23. The Henry's law constant for CO_2 is 3.4×10^{-2} M/atm at 25 °C. What pressure of carbon dioxide is needed to maintain a CO_2 concentration of 0.10 M in a can of lemon-lime soda?

24. The Henry's law constant for O_2 is 1.3×10^{-3} M/atm at 25 °C. What mass of oxygen would be dissolved in a 40-L aquarium at 25 °C, assuming an atmospheric pressure of 1.00 atm, and that the partial pressure of O_2 is 0.21 atm?

25. How many liters of HCl gas, measured at 30.0 °C and 745 torr, are required to prepare 1.25 L of a 3.20-M solution of hydrochloric acid?

11.4 Colligative Properties

26. Which is/are part of the macroscopic domain of solutions and which is/are part of the microscopic domain: boiling point elevation, Henry's law, hydrogen bond, ion-dipole attraction, molarity, nonelectrolyte, nonstoichiometric compound, osmosis, solvated ion?

27. What is the microscopic explanation for the macroscopic behavior illustrated in Figure 11.15?

28. Sketch a qualitative graph of the pressure versus time for water vapor above a sample of pure water and a sugar solution, as the liquids evaporate to half their original volume.

29. A solution of potassium nitrate, an electrolyte, and a solution of glycerin ($C_3H_5(OH)_3$), a nonelectrolyte, both boil at 100.3 °C. What other physical properties of the two solutions are identical?

30. What are the mole fractions of H_3PO_4 and water in a solution of 14.5 g of H_3PO_4 in 125 g of water?

(a) Outline the steps necessary to answer the question.

(b) Answer the question.

31. What are the mole fractions of HNO_3 and water in a concentrated solution of nitric acid (68.0% HNO_3 by mass)?

(a) Outline the steps necessary to answer the question.

(b) Answer the question.

32. Calculate the mole fraction of each solute and solvent:

(a) 583 g of H_2SO_4 in 1.50 kg of water—the acid solution used in an automobile battery

(b) 0.86 g of NaCl in 1.00×10^2 g of water—a solution of sodium chloride for intravenous injection

(c) 46.85 g of codeine, $C_{18}H_{21}NO_3$, in 125.5 g of ethanol, C_2H_5OH

(d) 25 g of I_2 in 125 g of ethanol, C_2H_5OH

33. Calculate the mole fraction of each solute and solvent:

(a) 0.710 kg of sodium carbonate (washing soda), Na_2CO_3, in 10.0 kg of water—a saturated solution at 0 °C

(b) 125 g of NH_4NO_3 in 275 g of water—a mixture used to make an instant ice pack

(c) 25 g of Cl_2 in 125 g of dichloromethane, CH_2Cl_2

(d) 0.372 g of histamine, C_5H_9N, in 125 g of chloroform, $CHCl_3$

34. Calculate the mole fractions of methanol, CH_3OH; ethanol, C_2H_5OH; and water in a solution that is 40% methanol, 40% ethanol, and 20% water by mass. (Assume the data are good to two significant figures.)

35. What is the difference between a 1 M solution and a 1 m solution?

36. What is the molality of phosphoric acid, H_3PO_4, in a solution of 14.5 g of H_3PO_4 in 125 g of water?

(a) Outline the steps necessary to answer the question.

(b) Answer the question.

37. What is the molality of nitric acid in a concentrated solution of nitric acid (68.0% HNO_3 by mass)?

(a) Outline the steps necessary to answer the question.

(b) Answer the question.

38. Calculate the molality of each of the following solutions:

(a) 583 g of H_2SO_4 in 1.50 kg of water—the acid solution used in an automobile battery

(b) 0.86 g of NaCl in 1.00×10^2 g of water—a solution of sodium chloride for intravenous injection

(c) 46.85 g of codeine, $C_{18}H_{21}NO_3$, in 125.5 g of ethanol, C_2H_5OH

(d) 25 g of I_2 in 125 g of ethanol, C_2H_5OH

39. Calculate the molality of each of the following solutions:

(a) 0.710 kg of sodium carbonate (washing soda), Na_2CO_3, in 10.0 kg of water—a saturated solution at 0°C

(b) 125 g of NH_4NO_3 in 275 g of water—a mixture used to make an instant ice pack

(c) 25 g of Cl_2 in 125 g of dichloromethane, CH_2Cl_2

(d) 0.372 g of histamine, C_5H_9N, in 125 g of chloroform, $CHCl_3$

40. The concentration of glucose, $C_6H_{12}O_6$, in normal spinal fluid is $\dfrac{75\ mg}{100\ g}$. What is the molality of the solution?

41. A 13.0% solution of K_2CO_3 by mass has a density of 1.09 g/cm^3. Calculate the molality of the solution.

42. Why does 1 mol of sodium chloride depress the freezing point of 1 kg of water almost twice as much as 1 mol of glycerin?

43. What is the boiling point of a solution of 115.0 g of sucrose, $C_{12}H_{22}O_{11}$, in 350.0 g of water?

(a) Outline the steps necessary to answer the question

(b) Answer the question

44. What is the boiling point of a solution of 9.04 g of I_2 in 75.5 g of benzene, assuming the I_2 is nonvolatile?

(a) Outline the steps necessary to answer the question.

(b) Answer the question.

45. What is the freezing temperature of a solution of 115.0 g of sucrose, $C_{12}H_{22}O_{11}$, in 350.0 g of water, which freezes at 0.0 °C when pure?

(a) Outline the steps necessary to answer the question.

(b) Answer the question.

46. What is the freezing point of a solution of 9.04 g of I_2 in 75.5 g of benzene?

(a) Outline the steps necessary to answer the following question.

(b) Answer the question.

47. What is the osmotic pressure of an aqueous solution of 1.64 g of $Ca(NO_3)_2$ in water at 25 °C? The volume of the solution is 275 mL.

(a) Outline the steps necessary to answer the question.

(b) Answer the question.

48. What is osmotic pressure of a solution of bovine insulin (molar mass, 5700 g mol^{-1}) at 18 °C if 100.0 mL of the solution contains 0.103 g of the insulin?

(a) Outline the steps necessary to answer the question.

(b) Answer the question.

49. What is the molar mass of a solution of 5.00 g of a compound in 25.00 g of carbon tetrachloride (bp 76.8 °C; $K_b = 5.02$ °C/m) that boils at 81.5 °C at 1 atm?

(a) Outline the steps necessary to answer the question.

(b) Solve the problem.

50. A sample of an organic compound (a nonelectrolyte) weighing 1.35 g lowered the freezing point of 10.0 g of benzene by 3.66 °C. Calculate the molar mass of the compound.

51. A 1.0 m solution of HCl in benzene has a freezing point of 0.4 °C. Is HCl an electrolyte in benzene? Explain.

52. A solution contains 5.00 g of urea, $CO(NH_2)_2$, a nonvolatile compound, dissolved in 0.100 kg of water. If the vapor pressure of pure water at 25 °C is 23.7 torr, what is the vapor pressure of the solution?

53. A 12.0-g sample of a nonelectrolyte is dissolved in 80.0 g of water. The solution freezes at −1.94 °C. Calculate the molar mass of the substance.

54. Arrange the following solutions in order by their decreasing freezing points: 0.1 m Na_3PO_4, 0.1 m C_2H_5OH, 0.01 m CO_2, 0.15 m NaCl, and 0.2 m $CaCl_2$.

55. Calculate the boiling point elevation of 0.100 kg of water containing 0.010 mol of NaCl, 0.020 mol of Na_2SO_4, and 0.030 mol of $MgCl_2$, assuming complete dissociation of these electrolytes.

56. How could you prepare a 3.08 m aqueous solution of glycerin, $C_3H_8O_3$? What is the freezing point of this solution?

57. A sample of sulfur weighing 0.210 g was dissolved in 17.8 g of carbon disulfide, CS_2 ($K_b = 2.43$ °C/m). If the boiling point elevation was 0.107 °C, what is the formula of a sulfur molecule in carbon disulfide?

58. In a significant experiment performed many years ago, 5.6977 g of cadmium iodide in 44.69 g of water raised the boiling point 0.181 °C. What does this suggest about the nature of a solution of CdI_2?

59. Lysozyme is an enzyme that cleaves cell walls. A 0.100-L sample of a solution of lysozyme that contains 0.0750 g of the enzyme exhibits an osmotic pressure of 1.32×10^{-3} atm at 25 °C. What is the molar mass of lysozyme?

60. The osmotic pressure of a solution containing 7.0 g of insulin per liter is 23 torr at 25 °C. What is the molar mass of insulin?

61. The osmotic pressure of human blood is 7.6 atm at 37 °C. What mass of glucose, $C_6H_{12}O_6$, is required to make 1.00 L of aqueous solution for intravenous feeding if the solution must have the same osmotic pressure as blood at body temperature, 37 °C?

62. What is the freezing point of a solution of dibromobenzene, $C_6H_4Br_2$, in 0.250 kg of benzene, if the solution boils at 83.5 °C?

63. What is the boiling point of a solution of NaCl in water if the solution freezes at −0.93 °C?

64. The sugar fructose contains 40.0% C, 6.7% H, and 53.3% O by mass. A solution of 11.7 g of fructose in 325 g of ethanol has a boiling point of 78.59 °C. The boiling point of ethanol is 78.35 °C, and K_b for ethanol is 1.20 °C/m. What is the molecular formula of fructose?

65. The vapor pressure of methanol, CH_3OH, is 94 torr at 20 °C. The vapor pressure of ethanol, C_2H_5OH, is 44 torr at the same temperature.

(a) Calculate the mole fraction of methanol and of ethanol in a solution of 50.0 g of methanol and 50.0 g of ethanol.

(b) Ethanol and methanol form a solution that behaves like an ideal solution. Calculate the vapor pressure of methanol and of ethanol above the solution at 20 °C.

(c) Calculate the mole fraction of methanol and of ethanol in the vapor above the solution.

66. The triple point of air-free water is defined as 273.15 K. Why is it important that the water be free of air?

67. Meat can be classified as fresh (not frozen) even though it is stored at −1 °C. Why wouldn't meat freeze at this temperature?

68. An organic compound has a composition of 93.46% C and 6.54% H by mass. A solution of 0.090 g of this compound in 1.10 g of camphor melts at 158.4 °C. The melting point of pure camphor is 178.4 °C. K_f for camphor is 37.7 °C/m. What is the molecular formula of the solute? Show your calculations.

69. A sample of $HgCl_2$ weighing 9.41 g is dissolved in 32.75 g of ethanol, C_2H_5OH (K_b = 1.20 °C/m). The boiling point elevation of the solution is 1.27 °C. Is $HgCl_2$ an electrolyte in ethanol? Show your calculations.

70. A salt is known to be an alkali metal fluoride. A quick approximate determination of freezing point indicates that 4 g of the salt dissolved in 100 g of water produces a solution that freezes at about −1.4 °C. What is the formula of the salt? Show your calculations.

11.5 Colloids

71. Identify the dispersed phase and the dispersion medium in each of the following colloidal systems: starch dispersion, smoke, fog, pearl, whipped cream, floating soap, jelly, milk, and ruby.

72. Distinguish between dispersion methods and condensation methods for preparing colloidal systems.

73. How do colloids differ from solutions with regard to dispersed particle size and homogeneity?

74. Explain the cleansing action of soap.

75. How can it be demonstrated that colloidal particles are electrically charged?

Answer Key For Chapters 1–11

Chapter 1

1. Place a glass of water outside. It will freeze if the temperature is below 0 °C.

3. (a) law (states a consistently observed phenomenon, can be used for prediction); (b) theory (a widely accepted explanation of the behavior of matter); (c) hypothesis (a tentative explanation, can be investigated by experimentation)

5. (a) symbolic, microscopic; (b) macroscopic; (c) symbolic, macroscopic; (d) microscopic

7. Macroscopic. The heat required is determined from macroscopic properties.

9. Liquids can change their shape (flow); solids can't. Gases can undergo large volume changes as pressure changes; liquids do not. Gases flow and change volume; solids do not.

11. The mixture can have a variety of compositions; a pure substance has a definite composition. Both have the same composition from point to point.

13. Molecules of elements contain only one type of atom; molecules of compounds contain two or more types of atoms. They are similar in that both are comprised of two or more atoms chemically bonded together.

15. Answers will vary. Sample answer: Gatorade contains water, sugar, dextrose, citric acid, salt, sodium chloride, monopotassium phosphate, and sucrose acetate isobutyrate.

17. (a) element; (b) element; (c) compound; (d) mixture, (e) compound; (f) compound; (g) compound; (h) mixture

19. In each case, a molecule consists of two or more combined atoms. They differ in that the types of atoms change from one substance to the next.

21. Gasoline (a mixture of compounds), oxygen, and to a lesser extent, nitrogen are consumed. Carbon dioxide and water are the principal products. Carbon monoxide and nitrogen oxides are produced in lesser amounts.

23. (a) Increased as it would have combined with oxygen in the air thus increasing the amount of matter and therefore the mass. (b) 0.9 g

25. (a) 200.0 g; (b) The mass of the container and contents would decrease as carbon dioxide is a gaseous product and would leave the container. (c) 102.3 g

27. (a) physical; (b) chemical; (c) chemical; (d) physical; (e) physical

29. physical

31. The value of an extensive property depends upon the amount of matter being considered, whereas the value of an intensive property is the same regardless of the amount of matter being considered.

33. Being extensive properties, both mass and volume are directly proportional to the amount of substance under study. Dividing one extensive property by another will in effect "cancel" this dependence on amount, yielding a ratio that is independent of amount (an intensive property).

35. about a yard

37. (a) kilograms; (b) meters; (c) kilometers/second; (d) kilograms/cubic meter; (e) kelvin; (f) square meters; (g) cubic meters

39. (a) centi-, $\times\ 10^{-2}$; (b) deci-, $\times\ 10^{-1}$; (c) Giga-, $\times\ 10^{9}$; (d) kilo-, $\times\ 10^{3}$; (e) milli-, $\times\ 10^{-3}$; (f) nano-, $\times\ 10^{-9}$; (g) pico-, $\times\ 10^{-12}$; (h) tera-, $\times\ 10^{12}$

41. (a) 8.00 kg, 5.00 L, 1.60 kg/L; (b) 2.00 kg, 5.00 L, 0.400 kg/L; (c) red < green < blue < yellow; (d) If the volumes are the same, then the density is directly proportional to the mass.

43. (a) (b) Answer is one of the following. A/yellow: mass = 65.14 kg, volume = 3.38 L, density = 19.3 kg/L, likely identity = gold. B/blue: mass = 0.64 kg, volume = 1.00 L, density = 0.64 kg/L, likely identity = apple. C/green: mass = 4.08 kg, volume = 5.83 L, density = 0.700 kg/L, likely identity = gasoline. D/red: mass = 3.10 kg, volume = 3.38 L, density = 0.920 kg/L, likely identity = ice; and E/purple: mass = 3.53 kg, volume = 1.00 L, density = 3.53 kg/L, likely identity = diamond. (c) B/blue/apple (0.64 kg/L) < C/green/gasoline (0.700 kg/L) < D/red/ice (0.920 kg/L) < E/purple/diamond (3.53 kg/L) < A/yellow/gold (19.3 kg/L)

45. (a) 7.04×10^2; (b) 3.344×10^{-2}; (c) 5.479×10^2; (d) 2.2086×10^4; (e) 1.00000×10^3; (f) 6.51×10^{-8}; (g) 7.157×10^{-3}

47. (a) exact; (b) exact; (c) uncertain; (d) exact; (e) uncertain; (f) uncertain

49. (a) two; (b) three; (c) five; (d) four; (e) six; (f) two; (g) five

51. (a) 0.44; (b) 9.0; (c) 27; (d) 140; (e) 1.5×10^{-3}; (f) 0.44

53. (a) 2.15×10^5; (b) 4.2×10^6; (c) 2.08; (d) 0.19; (e) 27,440; (f) 43.0

55. (a) Archer X; (b) Archer W; (c) Archer Y

57. (a) $\dfrac{1.0936 \text{ yd}}{1 \text{ m}}$; (b) $\dfrac{0.94635 \text{ L}}{1 \text{ qt}}$; (c) $\dfrac{2.2046 \text{ lb}}{1 \text{ kg}}$

59. $\dfrac{2.0 \text{ L}}{67.6 \text{ fl oz}} = \dfrac{0.030 \text{ L}}{1 \text{ fl oz}}$

Only two significant figures are justified.

61. 68–71 cm; 400–450 g

63. 355 mL

65. 8×10^{-4} cm

67. yes; weight = 89.4 kg

69. 5.0×10^{-3} mL

71. (a) 1.3×10^{-4} kg; (b) 2.32×10^8 kg; (c) 5.23×10^{-12} m; (d) 8.63×10^{-5} kg; (e) 3.76×10^{-1} m; (f) 5.4×10^{-5} m; (g) 1×10^{12} s; (h) 2.7×10^{-11} s; (i) 1.5×10^{-4} K

73. 45.4 L

75. 1.0160×10^3 kg

77. (a) 394 ft
(b) 5.9634 km
(c) 6.0×10^2
(d) 2.64 L
(e) 5.1×10^{18} kg
(f) 14.5 kg
(g) 324 mg

79. 0.46 m; 1.5 ft/cubit

81. Yes, the acid's volume is 123 mL.

83. 62.6 in (about 5 ft 3 in.) and 101 lb

85. (a) 3.81 cm $\times$ 8.89 cm $\times$ 2.44 m; (b) 40.6 cm

87. 2.70 g/cm^3

89. (a) 81.6 g; (b) 17.6 g

91. (a) 5.1 mL; (b) 37 L

93. 5371 °F, 3239 K

95. −23 °C, 250 K

97. −33.4 °C, 239.8 K

99. 113 °F

Chapter 2

1. The starting materials consist of one green sphere and two purple spheres. The products consist of two green spheres and two purple spheres. This violates Dalton's postulate that that atoms are not created during a chemical change, but are merely redistributed.

3. This statement violates Dalton's fourth postulate: In a given compound, the numbers of atoms of each type (and thus also the percentage) always have the same ratio.

5. Dalton originally thought that all atoms of a particular element had identical properties, including mass. Thus, the concept of isotopes, in which an element has different masses, was a violation of the original idea. To account for the existence of isotopes, the second postulate of his atomic theory was modified to state that atoms of the same element must have identical chemical properties.

7. Both are subatomic particles that reside in an atom's nucleus. Both have approximately the same mass. Protons are positively charged, whereas neutrons are uncharged.

9. (a) The Rutherford atom has a small, positively charged nucleus, so most α particles will pass through empty space far from the nucleus and be undeflected. Those α particles that pass near the nucleus will be deflected from their paths due to positive-positive repulsion. The more directly toward the nucleus the α particles are headed, the larger the deflection angle will be. (b) Higher-energy α particles that pass near the nucleus will still undergo deflection, but the faster they travel, the less the expected angle of deflection. (c) If the nucleus is smaller, the positive charge is smaller and the expected deflections are smaller—both in terms of how closely the α particles pass by the nucleus undeflected and the angle of deflection. If the nucleus is larger, the positive charge is larger and the expected deflections are larger—more α particles will be deflected, and the deflection angles will be larger. (d) The paths followed by the α particles match the predictions from (a), (b), and (c).

11. (a) $^{133}Cs^+$; (b) $^{127}I^-$; (c) $^{31}P^{3-}$; (d) $^{57}Co^{3+}$

13. (a) Carbon-12, ^{12}C; (b) This atom contains six protons and six neutrons. There are six electrons in a neutral ^{12}C atom. The net charge of such a neutral atom is zero, and the mass number is 12. (c) The preceding answers are correct. (d) The atom will be stable since C-12 is a stable isotope of carbon. (e) The preceding answer is correct. Other answers for this exercise are possible if a different element of isotope is chosen.

15. (a) Lithium-6 contains three protons, three neutrons, and three electrons. The isotope symbol is ^6Li or ^6_3Li. (b) $^6Li^+$ or $^6_3Li^+$

17. (a) Iron, 26 protons, 24 electrons, and 32 neutrons; (b) iodine, 53 protons, 54 electrons, and 74 neutrons

19. (a) 3 protons, 3 electrons, 4 neutrons; (b) 52 protons, 52 electrons, 73 neutrons; (c) 47 protons, 47 electrons, 62 neutrons; (d) 7 protons, 7 electrons, 8 neutrons; (e) 15 protons, 15 electrons, 16 neutrons

21. Let us use neon as an example. Since there are three isotopes, there is no way to be sure to accurately predict the abundances to make the total of 20.18 amu average atomic mass. Let us guess that the abundances are 9% Ne-22, 91% Ne-20, and only a trace of Ne-21. The average mass would be 20.18 amu. Checking the nature's mix of isotopes shows that the abundances are 90.48% Ne-20, 9.25% Ne-22, and 0.27% Ne-21, so our guessed amounts have to be slightly adjusted.

23. 79.904 amu

25. Turkey source: 0.2649 (of 10.0129 amu isotope); US source: 0.2537 (of 10.0129 amu isotope)

27. The symbol for the element oxygen, O, represents both the element and one atom of oxygen. A molecule of oxygen, O_2, contains two oxygen atoms; the subscript 2 in the formula must be used to distinguish the diatomic molecule from two single oxygen atoms.

29. (a) molecular CO_2, empirical CO_2; (b) molecular C_2H_2, empirical CH; (c) molecular C_2H_4, empirical CH_2; (d) molecular H_2SO_4, empirical H_2SO_4

31. (a) $C_4H_5N_2O$; (b) $C_{12}H_{22}O_{11}$; (c) HO; (d) CH_2O; (e) $C_3H_4O_3$

33. (a) CH_2O; (b) C_2H_4O

35. (a) ethanol

(b) methoxymethane, more commonly known as dimethyl ether

$$\begin{array}{ccc} & H & & & H \\ & | & & & | \\ H- & C & -O- & C & -H \\ & | & & & | \\ & H & & & H \end{array}$$

(c) These molecules have the same chemical composition (types and number of atoms) but different chemical structures. They are structural isomers.

37. Use the molecular formula to find the molar mass; to obtain the number of moles, divide the mass of compound by the molar mass of the compound expressed in grams.

39. Formic acid. Its formula has twice as many oxygen atoms as the other two compounds (one each). Therefore, 0.60 mol of formic acid would be equivalent to 1.20 mol of a compound containing a single oxygen atom.

41. The two masses have the same numerical value, but the units are different: The molecular mass is the mass of 1 molecule while the molar mass is the mass of 6.022×10^{23} molecules.

43. (a) 256.528 g/mol; (b) 72.150 g mol^{-1}; (c) 378.103 g mol^{-1}; (d) 58.080 g mol^{-1}; (e) 180.158 g mol^{-1}

45. (a) 197.382 g mol^{-1}; (b) 257.163 g mol^{-1}; (c) 194.193 g mol^{-1}; (d) 60.056 g mol^{-1}; (e) 306.464 g mol^{-1}

47. (a) 0.819 g;
(b) 307 g;
(c) 0.23 g;
(d) 1.235×10^6 g (1235 kg);
(e) 765 g

49. (a) 99.41 g;
(b) 2.27 g;
(c) 3.5 g;
(d) 222 kg;
(e) 160.1 g

51. (a) 9.60 g; (b) 19.2 g; (c) 28.8 g

53. zirconium: 2.038×10^{23} atoms; 30.87 g; silicon: 2.038×10^{23} atoms; 9.504 g; oxygen: 8.151×10^{23} atoms; 21.66 g

55. AlPO$_4$: 1.000 mol
Al$_2$Cl$_6$: 1.994 mol
Al$_2$S$_3$: 3.00 mol

57. 3.113×10^{25} C atoms

59. 0.865 servings, or about 1 serving.

61. 20.0 g H$_2$O represents the least number of molecules since it has the least number of moles.

Chapter 3

1. The spectrum consists of colored lines, at least one of which (probably the brightest) is red.

3. 3.15 m

5. 3.233×10^{-19} J; 2.018 eV

7. $v = 4.568 \times 10^{14}$ s; $\lambda = 656.3$ nm; Energy mol^{-1} = 1.823×10^5 J mol^{-1}; red

9. (a) $\lambda = 8.69 \times 10^{-7}$ m; $E = 2.29 \times 10^{-19}$ J; (b) $\lambda = 4.59 \times 10^{-7}$ m; $E = 4.33 \times 10^{-19}$ J; The color of (a) is red; (b) is blue.

11. $E = 9.502 \times 10^{-15}$ J; $v = 1.434 \times 10^{19}$ s^{-1}

13. Red: 660 nm; 4.54×10^{14} Hz; 3.01×10^{-19} J. Green: 520 nm; 5.77×10^{14} Hz; 3.82×10^{-19} J. Blue: 440 nm; 6.81×10^{14} Hz; 4.51×10^{-19} J. Somewhat different numbers are also possible.

15. 5.49×10^{14} s^{-1}; no

17. Quantized energy means that the electrons can possess only certain discrete energy values; values between those quantized values are not permitted.

19.

$$E = E_2 - E_5 = 2.179 \times 10^{-18} \left(\frac{1}{n_2^2} - \frac{1}{n_5^2} \right) J$$

$$= 2.179 \times 10^{-18} \left(\frac{1}{2^2} - \frac{1}{5^2} \right) = 4.576 \times 10^{-19} \, J$$

$$= \frac{4.576 \times 10^{-19} \, \cancel{J}}{1.602 \times 10^{-19} \, \cancel{J} \, eV^{-1}} = 2.856 \, eV$$

21. -8.716×10^{-18} J

23. -3.405×10^{-20} J

25. 33.9 Å

27. 1.471×10^{-17} J

29. Both involve a relatively heavy nucleus with electrons moving around it, although strictly speaking, the Bohr model works only for one-electron atoms or ions. According to classical mechanics, the Rutherford model predicts a miniature "solar system" with electrons moving about the nucleus in circular or elliptical orbits that are confined to planes. If the requirements of classical electromagnetic theory that electrons in such orbits would emit electromagnetic radiation are ignored, such atoms would be stable, having constant energy and angular momentum, but would not emit any visible light (contrary to observation). If classical electromagnetic theory is applied, then the Rutherford atom would emit electromagnetic radiation of continually increasing frequency (contrary to the observed discrete spectra), thereby losing energy until the atom collapsed in an absurdly short time (contrary to the observed long-term stability of atoms). The Bohr model retains the classical mechanics view of circular orbits confined to planes having constant energy and angular momentum, but restricts these to quantized values dependent on a single quantum number, n. The orbiting electron in Bohr's model is assumed not to emit any electromagnetic radiation while moving about the nucleus in its stationary orbits, but the atom can emit or absorb electromagnetic radiation when the electron changes from one orbit to another. Because of the quantized orbits, such "quantum jumps" will produce discrete spectra, in agreement with observations.

31. Both models have a central positively charged nucleus with electrons moving about the nucleus in accordance with the Coulomb electrostatic potential. The Bohr model *assumes* that the electrons move in circular orbits that have quantized energies, angular momentum, and radii that are specified by a single quantum number, $n = 1, 2, 3,$ ..., but this quantization is an ad hoc assumption made by Bohr to incorporate quantization into an essentially classical mechanics description of the atom. Bohr also assumed that electrons orbiting the nucleus normally do not emit or absorb electromagnetic radiation, but do so when the electron switches to a different orbit. In the quantum mechanical model, the electrons do not move in precise orbits (such orbits violate the Heisenberg uncertainty principle) and, instead, a probabilistic interpretation of the electron's position at any given instant is used, with a mathematical function ψ called a wavefunction that can be used to determine the electron's spatial probability distribution. These wavefunctions, or orbitals, are three-dimensional stationary waves that can be specified by three quantum numbers that arise naturally from their underlying mathematics (no ad hoc assumptions required): the principal quantum number, n (the same one used by Bohr), which specifies shells such that orbitals having the same n all have the same energy and approximately the same spatial extent; the angular momentum quantum number l, which is a measure of the orbital's angular momentum and corresponds to the orbitals' general shapes, as well as specifying subshells such that orbitals having the same l (and n) all have the same energy; and the orientation quantum number m, which is a measure of the z component of the angular momentum and corresponds to the orientations of the orbitals. The Bohr model gives the same expression for the energy as the quantum mechanical expression and, hence, both properly account for hydrogen's discrete spectrum (an example of getting the right answers for the wrong reasons, something that many chemistry students can sympathize with), but gives the wrong expression for the angular momentum (Bohr orbits necessarily all have non-zero angular momentum, but some quantum orbitals [s orbitals] can have zero angular momentum).

33. n determines the general range for the value of energy and the probable distances that the electron can be from the nucleus. l determines the shape of the orbital. m_l determines the orientation of the orbitals of the same l value with respect to one another. m_s determines the spin of an electron.

35. (a) $2p$; (b) $4d$; (c) $6s$

37. (a) $3d$; (b) $1s$; (c) $4f$

39.

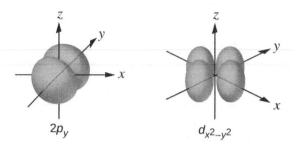

$2p_y$ $d_{x^2-y^2}$

41. (a) x. 2, y. 2, z. 2; (b) x. 1, y. 3, z. 0; (c) x. 4 0 0 $\frac{1}{2}$, y. 2 1 0 $\frac{1}{2}$, z. 3 2 0 $\frac{1}{2}$; (d) x. 1, y. 2, z. 3; (e) x. $l = 0$, $m_l = 0$, y. $l = 1$, $m_l = -1$, 0, or +1, z. $l = 2$, $m_l = -2, -1, 0, +1, +2$

43. 12

45.

n	l	m_l	s
4	0	0	$+\frac{1}{2}$
4	0	0	$-\frac{1}{2}$
4	1	−1	$+\frac{1}{2}$
4	1	0	$+\frac{1}{2}$
4	1	+1	$+\frac{1}{2}$
4	1	−1	$-\frac{1}{2}$

47. For example, Na^+: $1s^2 2s^2 2p^6$; Ca^{2+}: $1s^2 2s^2 2p^6$; Sn^{2+}: $1s^2 2s^2 2p^6 3s^2 3p^6 3d^{10} 4s^2 4p^6 4d^{10} 5s^2$; F^-: $1s^2 2s^2 2p^6$; O^{2-}: $1s^2 2s^2 2p^6$; Cl^-: $1s^2 2s^2 2p^6 3s^2 3p^6$.

49. (a) $1s^2 2s^2 2p^3$; (b) $1s^2 2s^2 2p^6 3s^2 3p^2$; (c) $1s^2 2s^2 2p^6 3s^2 3p^6 4s^2 3d^6$; (d) $1s^2 2s^2 2p^6 3s^2 3p^6 4s^2 3d^{10} 4p^6 5s^2 4d^{10} 5p^4$; (e) $1s^2 2s^2 2p^6 3s^2 3p^6 4s^2 3d^{10} 4p^6 5s^2 4d^{10} 5p^6 6s^2 4f^9$

51. The charge on the ion.

53. (a)

2s   2p

(b)

3s   3p

(c)

(d)

(e)

55. Zr

57. Rb^+, Se^{2-}

59. Although both (b) and (c) are correct, (e) encompasses both and is the best answer.

61. K

63. $1s^2 2s^2 2p^6 3s^2 3p^6 3d^{10} 4s^2 4p^6 4d^{10} 5s^2 5p^6 6s^2 4f^{14} 5d^{10}$

65. Co has 27 protons, 27 electrons, and 33 neutrons: $1s^2 2s^2 2p^6 3s^2 3p^6 4s^2 3d^7$.
I has 53 protons, 53 electrons, and 78 neutrons: $1s^2 2s^2 2p^6 3s^2 3p^6 3d^{10} 4s^2 4p^6 4d^{10} 5s^2 5p^5$.

67. Cl

69. O

71. Rb < Li < N < F

73. 15 (5A)

75. Mg < Ca < Rb < Cs

77. $Si^{4+} < Al^{3+} < Ca^{2+} < K^+$

79. Se, As^-

81. $Mg^{2+} < K^+ < Br^- < As^{3-}$

83. O, IE_1

85. Ra

87. (a) metal, inner transition metal; (b) nonmetal, representative element; (c) metal, representative element; (d) nonmetal, representative element; (e) metal, transition metal; (f) metal, inner transition metal; (g) metal, transition metal; (h) nonmetal, representative element; (i) nonmetal, representative element; (j) metal, representative element

89. (a) He; (b) Be; (c) Li; (d) O

91. (a) krypton, Kr; (b) calcium, Ca; (c) fluorine, F; (d) tellurium, Te

93. (a) $^{23}_{11}Na$; (b) $^{129}_{54}Xe$; (c) $^{73}_{33}As$; (d) $^{226}_{88}Ra$

95. Ionic: KCl, $MgCl_2$; Covalent: NCl_3, ICl, PCl_5, CCl_4

97. (a) covalent; (b) ionic, Ba^{2+}, O^{2-}; (c) ionic, NH_4^+, CO_3^{2-}; (d) ionic, Sr^{2+}, $H_2PO_4^-$; (e) covalent; (f) ionic, Na^+, O^{2-}

99. (a) CaS; (b) $(NH_4)_2SO_4$; (c) $AlBr_3$; (d) Na_2HPO_4; (e) $Mg_3(PO_4)_2$

Chapter 4

1. The protons in the nucleus do not change during normal chemical reactions. Only the outer electrons move. Positive charges form when electrons are lost.

3. P, I, Cl, and O would form anions because they are nonmetals. Mg, In, Cs, Pb, and Co would form cations because they are metals.

5. (a) P^{3-}; (b) Mg^{2+}; (c) Al^{3+}; (d) O^{2-}; (e) Cl^-; (f) Cs^+

7. (a) $[Ar]4s^23d^{10}4p^6$; (b) $[Kr]4d^{10}5s^25p^6$ (c) $1s^2$ (d) $[Kr]4d^{10}$; (e) $[He]2s^22p^6$; (f) $[Ar]3d^{10}$; (g) $1s^2$ (h) $[He]2s^22p^6$ (i) $[Kr]4d^{10}5s^2$ (j) $[Ar]3d^7$ (k) $[Ar]3d^6$, (l) $[Ar]3d^{10}4s^2$

9. (a) $1s^22s^22p^63s^23p^1$; Al^{3+}: $1s^22s^22p^6$; (b) $1s^22s^22p^63s^23p^63d^{10}4s^24p^5$; $1s^22s^22p^63s^23p^63d^{10}4s^24p^6$; (c) $1s^22s^22p^63s^23p^63d^{10}4s^24p^65s^2$; Sr^{2+}: $1s^22s^22p^63s^23p^63d^{10}4s^24p^6$; (d) $1s^22s^1$; Li^+: $1s^2$; (e) $1s^22s^22p^63s^23p^63d^{10}4s^24p^3$; $1s^22s^22p^63s^23p^63d^{10}4s^24p^6$; (f) $1s^22s^22p^63s^23p^4$; $1s^22s^22p^63s^23p^6$

11. NaCl consists of discrete ions arranged in a crystal lattice, not covalently bonded molecules.

13. ionic: (b), (d), (e), (g), and (i); covalent: (a), (c), (f), (h), (j), and (k)

15. (a) Cl; (b) O; (c) O; (d) S; (e) N; (f) P; (g) N

17. (a) H, C, N, O, F; (b) H, I, Br, Cl, F; (c) H, P, S, O, F; (d) Na, Al, H, P, O; (e) Ba, H, As, N, O

19. N, O, F, and Cl

21. (a) HF; (b) CO; (c) OH; (d) PCl; (e) NH; (f) PO; (g) CN

23. (a) cesium chloride; (b) barium oxide; (c) potassium sulfide; (d) beryllium chloride; (e) hydrogen bromide; (f) aluminum fluoride

25. (a) RbBr; (b) MgSe; (c) Na_2O; (d) $CaCl_2$; (e) HF; (f) GaP; (g) $AlBr_3$; (h) $(NH_4)_2SO_4$

27. (a) ClO_2; (b) N_2O_4; (c) K_3P; (d) Ag_2S; (e) AlN; (f) SiO_2

29. (a) chromium(III) oxide; (b) iron(II) chloride; (c) chromium(VI) oxide; (d) titanium(IV) chloride; (e) cobalt(II) oxide; (f) molybdenum(IV) sulfide

31. (a) K_3PO_4; (b) $CuSO_4$; (c) $CaCl_2$; (d) TiO_2; (e) NH_4NO_3; (f) $NaHSO_4$

33. (a) manganese(IV) oxide; (b) mercury(I) chloride; (c) iron(III) nitrate; (d) titanium(IV) chloride; (e) copper(II) bromide

34. (a) eight electrons:

;

(b) eight electrons:

;

(c) no electrons
Be^{2+};
(d) eight electrons:

;

(e) no electrons
Ga^{3+};
(f) no electrons
Li^+;
(g) eight electrons:

$:\overset{..}{\underset{..}{N}}:^{3-}$

36. (a)

Mg²⁺ $:\overset{..}{\underset{..}{S}}:^{2-}$

;

(b)

Al³⁺ $:\overset{..}{\underset{..}{O}}:^{2-}$

;

(c)

Ga³⁺ $:\overset{..}{\underset{..}{Cl}}:^{-}$

;

(d)

K⁺ $:\overset{..}{\underset{..}{O}}:^{2-}$

;

(e)

Li⁺ $:\overset{..}{\underset{..}{N}}:^{3-}$

;

(f)

K⁺ $:\overset{..}{\underset{..}{F}}:^{-}$

38.

$:P\equiv P:$

40. (a)

$:\overset{..}{\underset{..}{O}}=\overset{..}{\underset{..}{O}}:$

In this case, the Lewis structure is inadequate to depict the fact that experimental studies have shown two unpaired electrons in each oxygen molecule.

(b)

H—C═O with H above C

;

(c)

F—As—F with F above As

;

(d)

$$\ddot{\underset{..}{Cl}}-\overset{}{N}=\ddot{\underset{}{O}}$$

;

(e)

$$\underset{..}{\overset{..}{Cl}} \quad$$

$$:\overset{..}{\underset{..}{Cl}}-\overset{:\overset{..}{Cl}:}{\underset{:\overset{..}{Cl}:}{Si}}-\overset{..}{\underset{..}{Cl}}:$$

;

(f)

$$\left[H-\overset{H}{\underset{..}{O}}-H \right]^{+}$$

;

(g)

$$\left[H-\overset{H}{\underset{H}{N}}-H \right]^{+}$$

;

(h)

$$\left[:\overset{..}{\underset{..}{F}}-\overset{:\overset{..}{F}:}{\underset{:\overset{..}{F}:}{B}}-\overset{..}{\underset{..}{F}}: \right]^{-}$$

;

(i)

$$H-C\equiv C-H$$

;

(j)

$$:\overset{..}{\underset{..}{Cl}}-C\equiv N:$$

;

(k)

$$C\equiv C^{2+}$$

42. (a) SeF_6:

(b) XeF_4:

(c) $SeCl_3{}^+$:

(d) Cl_2BBCl_2:

44. Two valence electrons per Pb atom are transferred to Cl atoms; the resulting Pb^{2+} ion has a $6s^2$ valence shell configuration. Two of the valence electrons in the HCl molecule are shared, and the other six are located on the Cl atom as lone pairs of electrons.

46.

48.

50. (a)

(b)

(c)

(d)

(e)

52.

54. Each bond includes a sharing of electrons between atoms. Two electrons are shared in a single bond; four electrons are shared in a double bond; and six electrons are shared in a triple bond.

56. (a)

(b)

;

(c)

;

(d)

;

(e)

58.

For NO$_2^-$

For O$_3$

60. (a)

(b)

CO has the strongest carbon-oxygen bond because there is a triple bond joining C and O. CO$_2$ has double bonds.

62. (a) H: 0, Cl: 0; (b) C: 0, F: 0; (c) P: 0, Cl 0; (d) P: 0, F: 0

64. Cl in Cl$_2$: 0; Cl in BeCl$_2$: 0; Cl in ClF$_5$: 0

66. (a)

$$O=\overset{..}{O}-\overset{..}{\underset{..}{O}}: \longleftrightarrow :\overset{..}{\underset{..}{O}}-\overset{..}{O}=O$$

Formal charge: 0 +1 −1   −1 +1 0

;

(b)

$$:\overset{..}{\underset{..}{O}}-\overset{..}{S}=\overset{..}{O} \longleftrightarrow \overset{..}{O}=\overset{..}{S}-\overset{..}{\underset{..}{O}}:$$

Formal charge: −1 +1 0   0 +1 −1

;

(c)

$$\left[:\overset{..}{\underset{..}{O}}=N-\overset{..}{\underset{.}{O}}: \right]^{-} \longleftrightarrow \left[:\overset{..}{\underset{.}{O}}-N=\overset{..}{\underset{..}{O}}: \right]^{-}$$

Formal charge: 0 0 −1   −1 0 0

;

(d)

$$\left[\begin{array}{c} :\overset{..}{O}:_{-1} \\ | \\ :\overset{..}{O}=N^{+1}-\overset{..}{\underset{..}{O}}: \end{array} \right]^{-} \longleftrightarrow \left[\begin{array}{c} :\overset{..}{O}:_{0} \\ || \\ :\overset{..}{\underset{.}{O}}-N^{+1}-\overset{..}{\underset{.}{O}}: \end{array} \right]^{-} \longleftrightarrow \left[\begin{array}{c} :\overset{..}{O}:_{-1} \\ | \\ :\overset{..}{\underset{.}{O}}-N^{+1}=\overset{..}{O}: \end{array} \right]^{-}$$

Formal charge: 0   −1   −1   −1   −1   0

68. HOCl

70. The structure that gives zero formal charges is consistent with the actual structure:

72. NF$_3$;

74.

75. The placement of the two sets of unpaired electrons in water forces the bonds to assume a tetrahedral arrangement, and the resulting HOH molecule is bent. The HBeH molecule (in which Be has only two electrons to bond with the two electrons from the hydrogens) must have the electron pairs as far from one another as possible and is therefore linear.

77. Space must be provided for each pair of electrons whether they are in a bond or are present as lone pairs. Electron-pair geometry considers the placement of all electrons. Molecular structure considers only the bonding-pair geometry.

79. As long as the polar bonds are compensated (for example. two identical atoms are found directly across the central atom from one another), the molecule can be nonpolar.

81. (a) Both the electron geometry and the molecular structure are octahedral.
(b) Both the electron geometry and the molecular structure are trigonal bipyramid.
(c) Both the electron geometry and the molecular structure are linear.
(d) Both the electron geometry and the molecular structure are trigonal planar.

83. (a) electron-pair geometry: octahedral, molecular structure: square pyramidal; (b) electron-pair geometry: tetrahedral, molecular structure: bent; (c) electron-pair geometry: octahedral, molecular structure: square planar; (d) electron-pair geometry: tetrahedral, molecular structure: trigonal pyramidal; (e) electron-pair geometry: trigonal bypyramidal, molecular structure: seesaw; (f) electron-pair geometry: tetrahedral, molecular structure: bent (109°)

85. (a) electron-pair geometry: trigonal planar, molecular structure: bent (120°); (b) electron-pair geometry: linear, molecular structure: linear; (c) electron-pair geometry: trigonal planar, molecular structure: trigonal planar; (d) electron-pair geometry: tetrahedral, molecular structure: trigonal pyramidal; (e) electron-pair geometry: tetrahedral, molecular structure: tetrahedral; (f) electron-pair geometry: trigonal bipyramidal, molecular structure: seesaw; (g) electron-pair geometry: tetrahedral, molecular structure: trigonal pyramidal

87. All of these molecules and ions contain polar bonds. Only ClF_5, ClO_2^-, PCl_3, SeF_4, and PH_2^- have dipole moments.

89. SeS_2, CCl_2F_2, PCl_3, and $ClNO$ all have dipole moments.

91. P

93. nonpolar

95. (a) tetrahedral; (b) trigonal pyramidal; (c) bent (109°); (d) trigonal planar; (e) bent (109°); (f) bent (109°); (g) $\underline{C}H_3CCH$ tetrahedral, $CH_3\underline{CC}H$ linear; (h) tetrahedral; (i) $H_2\underline{CC}CH_2$ linear; $H_2C\underline{CC}H_2$ trigonal planar

97.

B—A—B CO_2, linear

H_2O, bent with an approximately 109° angle

SO_2, bent with an approximately 120° angle

99. (a)

(b)

(c)

:C≡S:

;

(d) $CS_3{}^{2-}$ includes three regions of electron density (all are bonds with no lone pairs); the shape is trigonal planar; CS_2 has only two regions of electron density (all bonds with no lone pairs); the shape is linear

101. The Lewis structure is made from three units, but the atoms must be rearranged:

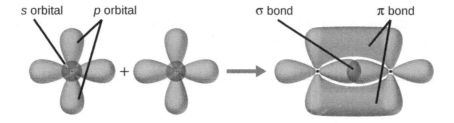

103. The molecular dipole points away from the hydrogen atoms.

105. The structures are very similar. In the model mode, each electron group occupies the same amount of space, so the bond angle is shown as 109.5°. In the "real" mode, the lone pairs are larger, causing the hydrogens to be compressed. This leads to the smaller angle of 104.5°.

Chapter 5

1. Similarities: Both types of bonds result from overlap of atomic orbitals on adjacent atoms and contain a maximum of two electrons. Differences: σ bonds are stronger and result from end-to-end overlap and all single bonds are σ bonds; π bonds between the same two atoms are weaker because they result from side-by-side overlap, and multiple bonds contain one or more π bonds (in addition to a σ bond).

3. Bonding: One σ bond and one π bond. The *s* orbitals are filled and do not overlap. The *p* orbitals overlap along the axis to form a σ bond and side-by-side to form the π bond.

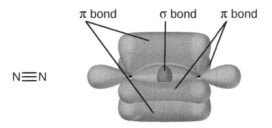

5. No, two of the *p* orbitals (one on each N) will be oriented end-to-end and will form a σ bond.

N≡N

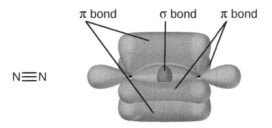

7. Hybridization is introduced to explain the geometry of bonding orbitals in valance bond theory.

9. There are no *d* orbitals in the valence shell of carbon.

11. trigonal planar, sp^2; trigonal pyramidal (one lone pair on A) sp^3; T-shaped (two lone pairs on A sp^3d, or (three lone pairs on A) sp^3d^2

13. (a) Each S has a bent (109°) geometry, sp^3

(b) Bent (120°), sp^2

$$:\ddot{O}=\ddot{S}-\ddot{O}: \longleftrightarrow :\ddot{O}-\ddot{S}=\ddot{O}:$$

(c) Trigonal planar, sp^2

(d) Tetrahedral, sp^3

15. (a) XeF_2
(b)

(c) linear (d) sp^3d

17. (a)

(b) P atoms, trigonal pyramidal; S atoms, bent, with two lone pairs; Cl atoms, trigonal pyramidal; (c) Hybridization about P, S, and Cl is, in all cases, sp^3; (d) Oxidation states P +1, S $-1\frac{1}{3}$, Cl +5, O –2. Formal charges: P 0; S 0; Cl +2: O –1

19.

Phosphorus and nitrogen can form sp^3 hybrids to form three bonds and hold one lone pair in PF_3 and NF_3, respectively. However, nitrogen has no valence d orbitals, so it cannot form a set of sp^3d hybrid orbitals to bind five fluorine atoms in NF_5. Phosphorus has d orbitals and can bind five fluorine atoms with sp^3d hybrid orbitals in PF_5.

21. A triple bond consists of one σ bond and two π bonds. A σ bond is stronger than a π bond due to greater overlap.

23. (a)

(b) The terminal carbon atom uses sp^3 hybrid orbitals, while the central carbon atom is sp hybridized. (c) Each of the two π bonds is formed by overlap of a $2p$ orbital on carbon and a nitrogen $2p$ orbital.

25. (a) sp^2; (b) sp; (c) sp^2; (d) sp^3; (e) sp^3; (f) sp^3d; (g) sp^3

27. (a) sp^2, delocalized; (b) sp, localized; (c) sp^2, delocalized; (d) sp^3, delocalized

29.

Orbitals in an isolated C atom

$2p$

$2s$

Hybridization

Orbitals in the sp hybridized C in CO_2

$2p$ $2p$

sp sp

E

Each of the four electrons is in a separate orbital and overlaps with an electron on an oxygen atom.

31. (a) Similarities: Both are bonding orbitals that can contain a maximum of two electrons. Differences: σ orbitals are end-to-end combinations of atomic orbitals, whereas π orbitals are formed by side-by-side overlap of orbitals. (b) Similarities: Both are quantum-mechanical constructs that represent the probability of finding the electron about the atom or the molecule. Differences: ψ for an atomic orbital describes the behavior of only one electron at a time based on the atom. For a molecule, ψ represents a mathematical combination of atomic orbitals. (c) Similarities: Both are orbitals that can contain two electrons. Differences: Bonding orbitals result in holding two or more atoms together. Antibonding orbitals have the effect of destabilizing any bonding that has occurred.

33. An odd number of electrons can never be paired, regardless of the arrangement of the molecular orbitals. It will always be paramagnetic.

35. Bonding orbitals have electron density in close proximity to more than one nucleus. The interaction between the bonding positively charged nuclei and negatively charged electrons stabilizes the system.

37. The pairing of the two bonding electrons lowers the energy of the system relative to the energy of the nonbonded electrons.

39. (a) H_2 bond order = 1, H_2^+ bond order = 0.5, H_2^- bond order = 0.5, strongest bond is H_2; (b) O_2 bond order = 2, O_2^{2+} bond order = 3; O_2^{2-} bond order = 1, strongest bond is O_2^{2+}; (c) Li_2 bond order = 1, Be_2^+ bond order = 0.5, Be_2 bond order = 0, strongest bond is Li_2; (d) F_2 bond order = 1, F_2^+ bond order = 1.5, F_2^- bond order = 0.5, strongest bond is F_2^+; (e) N_2 bond order = 3, N_2^+ bond order = 2.5, N_2^- bond order = 2.5, strongest bond is N_2

41. (a) H_2; (b) N_2; (c) O; (d) C_2; (e) B_2

43. Yes, fluorine is a smaller atom than Li, so atoms in the 2s orbital are closer to the nucleus and more stable.

45. 2+

47. N_2 has s-p mixing, so the π orbitals are the last filled in $N_2{}^{2+}$. O_2 does not have s-p mixing, so the σ_p orbital fills before the π orbitals.

Chapter 6

1. (a) 12.01 amu; (b) 12.01 amu; (c) 144.12 amu; (d) 60.05 amu

3. (a) 123.896 amu; (b) 18.015 amu; (c) 164.086 amu; (d) 60.052 amu; (e) 342.297 amu

5. (a) 56.107 amu;
(b) 54.091 amu;
(c) 199.9976 amu;
(d) 97.9950 amu

8. (a) % N = 82.24%
% H = 17.76%;
(b) % Na = 29.08%
% S = 40.56%
% O = 30.36%;
(c) % Ca^{2+} = 38.76%

10. % NH_3 = 38.2%

12. (a) CS_2
(b) CH_2O

14. C_6H_6

16. $Mg_3Si_2H_3O_8$ (empirical formula), $Mg_6Si_4H_6O_{16}$ (molecular formula)

18. $C_{15}H_{15}N_3$

20. We need to know the number of moles of sulfuric acid dissolved in the solution and the volume of the solution.

22. (a) 0.679 M;
(b) 1.00 M;
(c) 0.06998 M;
(d) 1.75 M;
(e) 0.070 M;
(f) 6.6 M

24. (a) determine the number of moles of glucose in 0.500 L of solution; determine the molar mass of glucose; determine the mass of glucose from the number of moles and its molar mass; (b) 27 g

26. (a) 37.0 mol H_2SO_4;
3.63×10^3 g H_2SO_4;
(b) 3.8×10^{-6} mol NaCN;
1.9×10^{-4} g NaCN;
(c) 73.2 mol H_2CO;
2.20 kg H_2CO;
(d) 5.9×10^{-7} mol $FeSO_4$;
8.9×10^{-5} g $FeSO_4$

28. (a) Determine the molar mass of $KMnO_4$; determine the number of moles of $KMnO_4$ in the solution; from the number of moles and the volume of solution, determine the molarity; (b) 1.15×10^{-3} M

30. (a) 5.04×10^{-3} M;
(b) 0.499 M;
(c) 9.92 M;
(d) 1.1×10^{-3} M

32. 0.025 M

34. 0.5000 L

36. 1.9 mL

38. (a) 0.125 M;
(b) 0.04888 M;
(c) 0.206 M;
(e) 0.0056 M

40. 11.9 M

42. 1.6 L

44. (a) The dilution equation can be used, appropriately modified to accommodate mass-based concentration units:
$\%mass_1 \times mass_1 = \%mass_2 \times mass_2$
This equation can be rearranged to isolate $mass_1$ and the given quantities substituted into this equation.
(b) 58.8 g

46. 114 g

48. $1.75 \times 10^{-3} M$

50. 95 mg/dL

52. 2.38×10^{-4} mol

54. 0.29 mol

Chapter 7

1. An equation is balanced when the same number of each element is represented on the reactant and product sides. Equations must be balanced to accurately reflect the law of conservation of matter.

3. (a) $PCl_5(s) + H_2O(l) \longrightarrow POCl_3(l) + 2HCl(aq)$; (b)
$3Cu(s) + 8HNO_3(aq) \longrightarrow 3Cu(NO_3)_2(aq) + 4H_2O(l) + 2NO(g)$; (c) $H_2(g) + I_2(s) \longrightarrow 2HI(s)$; (d)
$4Fe(s) + 3O_2(g) \longrightarrow 2Fe_2O_3(s)$; (e) $2Na(s) + 2H_2O(l) \longrightarrow 2NaOH(aq) + H_2(g)$; (f)
$(NH_4)_2Cr_2O_7(s) \longrightarrow Cr_2O_3(s) + N_2(g) + 4H_2O(g)$; (g) $P_4(s) + 6Cl_2(g) \longrightarrow 4PCl_3(l)$; (h)
$PtCl_4(s) \longrightarrow Pt(s) + 2Cl_2(g)$

5. (a) $CaCO_3(s) \longrightarrow CaO(s) + CO_2(g)$; (b) $2C_4H_{10}(g) + 13O_2(g) \longrightarrow 8CO_2(g) + 10H_2O(g)$; (c)
$MgCl_2(aq) + 2NaOH(aq) \longrightarrow Mg(OH)_2(s) + 2NaCl(aq)$; (d) $2H_2O(g) + 2Na(s) \longrightarrow 2NaOH(s) + H_2(g)$

7. (a) $Ba(NO_3)_2$, $KClO_3$; (b) $2KClO_3(s) \longrightarrow 2KCl(s) + 3O_2(g)$; (c)
$2Ba(NO_3)_2(s) \longrightarrow 2BaO(s) + 2N_2(g) + 5O_2(g)$; (d) $2Mg(s) + O_2(g) \longrightarrow 2MgO(s)$;
$4Al(s) + 3O_2(g) \longrightarrow 2Al_2O_3(s)$; $4Fe(s) + 3O_2(g) \longrightarrow 2Fe_2O_3(s)$

9. (a) $4HF(aq) + SiO_2(s) \longrightarrow SiF_4(g) + 2H_2O(l)$; (b) complete ionic equation:
$2Na^+(aq) + 2F^-(aq) + Ca^{2+}(aq) + 2Cl^-(aq) \longrightarrow CaF_2(s) + 2Na^+(aq) + 2Cl^-(aq)$, net ionic equation:
$2F^-(aq) + Ca^{2+}(aq) \longrightarrow CaF_2(s)$

11. (a)
$2K^+(aq) + C_2O_4{}^{2-}(aq) + Ba^{2+}(aq) + 2OH^-(aq) \longrightarrow 2K^+(aq) + 2OH^-(aq) + BaC_2O_4(s)$ (complete)

$Ba^{2+}(aq) + C_2O_4{}^{2-}(aq) \longrightarrow BaC_2O_4(s)$ (net)

(b)
$Pb^{2+}(aq) + 2NO_3{}^-(aq) + 2H^+(aq) + SO_4{}^{2-}(aq) \longrightarrow PbSO_4(s) + 2H^+(aq) + 2NO_3{}^-(aq)$ (complete)

$Pb^{2+}(aq) + SO_4{}^{2-}(aq) \longrightarrow PbSO_4(s)$ (net)

(c)
$CaCO_3(s) + 2H^+(aq) + SO_4{}^{2-}(aq) \longrightarrow CaSO_4(s) + CO_2(g) + H_2O(l)$ (complete)

$CaCO_3(s) + 2H^+(aq) + SO_4{}^{2-}(aq) \longrightarrow CaSO_4(s) + CO_2(g) + H_2O(l)$ (net)

13. (a) oxidation-reduction (addition); (b) acid-base (neutralization); (c) oxidation-reduction (combustion)

15. It is an oxidation-reduction reaction because the oxidation state of the silver changes during the reaction.

17. (a) H +1, P +5, O −2; (b) Al +3, H +1, O −2; (c) Se +4, O −2; (d) K +1, N +3, O −2; (e) In +3, S −2; (f) P +3, O −2

19. (a) acid-base; (b) oxidation-reduction: Na is oxidized, H^+ is reduced; (c) oxidation-reduction: Mg is oxidized, Cl_2 is reduced; (d) acid-base; (e) oxidation-reduction: P^{3-} is oxidized, O_2 is reduced; (f) acid-base

21. (a) $2HCl(g) + Ca(OH)_2(s) \longrightarrow CaCl_2(s) + 2H_2O(l)$; (b) $Sr(OH)_2(aq) + 2HNO_3(aq) \longrightarrow Sr(NO_3)_2(aq) + 2H_2O(l)$

23. (a) $2Al(s) + 3F_2(g) \longrightarrow 2AlF_3(s)$; (b) $2Al(s) + 3CuBr_2(aq) \longrightarrow 3Cu(s) + 2AlBr_3(aq)$; (c) $P_4(s) + 5O_2(g) \longrightarrow P_4O_{10}(s)$; (d) $Ca(s) + 2H_2O(l) \longrightarrow Ca(OH)_2(aq) + H_2(g)$

25. (a) $Mg(OH)_2(s) + 2HClO_4(aq) \longrightarrow Mg^{2+}(aq) + 2ClO_4{}^-(aq) + 2H_2O(l)$; (b) $SO_3(g) + 2H_2O(l) \longrightarrow H_3O^+(aq) + HSO_4{}^-(aq)$, (a solution of H_2SO_4); (c) $SrO(s) + H_2SO_4(l) \longrightarrow SrSO_4(s) + H_2O$

27. $H_2(g) + F_2(g) \longrightarrow 2HF(g)$

29. $2NaBr(aq) + Cl_2(g) \longrightarrow 2NaCl(aq) + Br_2(l)$

31. $2LiOH(aq) + CO_2(g) \longrightarrow Li_2CO_3(aq) + H_2O(l)$

33. (a) $Ca(OH)_2(s) + H_2S(g) \longrightarrow CaS(s) + 2H_2O(l)$; (b) $Na_2CO_3(aq) + H_2S(g) \longrightarrow Na_2S(aq) + CO_2(g) + H_2O(l)$

35. (a) step 1: $N_2(g) + 3H_2(g) \longrightarrow 2NH_3(g)$, step 2: $NH_3(g) + HNO_3(aq) \longrightarrow NH_4NO_3(aq) \longrightarrow NH_4NO_3(s)$ (after drying); (b) $H_2(g) + Br_2(l) \longrightarrow 2HBr(g)$; (c) $Zn(s) + S(s) \longrightarrow ZnS(s)$ and $ZnS(s) + 2HCl(aq) \longrightarrow ZnCl_2(aq) + H_2S(g)$

37. (a) $Sn^{4+}(aq) + 2e^- \longrightarrow Sn^{2+}(aq)$, (b) $[Ag(NH_3)_2]^+(aq) + e^- \longrightarrow Ag(s) + 2NH_3(aq)$; (c) $Hg_2Cl_2(s) + 2e^- \longrightarrow 2Hg(l) + 2Cl^-(aq)$; (d) $2H_2O(l) \longrightarrow O_2(g) + 4H^+(aq) + 4e^-$; (e) $6H_2O(l) + 2IO_3{}^-(aq) + 10e^- \longrightarrow I_2(s) + 12OH^-(aq)$; (f) $H_2O(l) + SO_3{}^{2-}(aq) \longrightarrow SO_4{}^{2-}(aq) + 2H^+(aq) + 2e^-$; (g) $8H^+(aq) + MnO_4{}^-(aq) + 5e^- \longrightarrow Mn^{2+}(aq) + 4H_2O(l)$; (h) $Cl^-(aq) + 6OH^-(aq) \longrightarrow ClO_3{}^-(aq) + 3H_2O(l) + 6e^-$

39. (a) $Sn^{2+}(aq) + 2Cu^{2+}(aq) \longrightarrow Sn^{4+}(aq) + 2Cu^+(aq)$; (b) $H_2S(g) + Hg_2{}^{2+}(aq) + 2H_2O(l) \longrightarrow 2Hg(l) + S(s) + 2H_3O^+(aq)$; (c) $5CN^-(aq) + 2ClO_2(aq) + 3H_2O(l) \longrightarrow 5CNO^-(aq) + 2Cl^-(aq) + 2H_3O^+(aq)$; (d) $Fe^{2+}(aq) + Ce^{4+}(aq) \longrightarrow Fe^{3+}(aq) + Ce^{3+}(aq)$; (e) $2HBrO(aq) + 2H_2O(l) \longrightarrow 2H_3O^+(aq) + 2Br^-(aq) + O_2(g)$

41. (a) $2MnO_4{}^-(aq) + 3NO_2{}^-(aq) + H_2O(l) \longrightarrow 2MnO_2(s) + 3NO_3{}^-(aq) + 2OH^-(aq)$; (b) $3MnO_4{}^{2-}(aq) + 2H_2O(l) \longrightarrow 2MnO_4{}^-(aq) + 4OH^-(aq) + MnO_2(s)$ (in base); (c) $Br_2(l) + SO_2(g) + 2H_2O(l) \longrightarrow 4H^+(aq) + 2Br^-(aq) + SO_4{}^{2-}(aq)$

43. (a) 0.435 mol Na, 0.217 mol Cl_2, 15.4 g Cl_2; (b) 0.005780 mol HgO, 2.890×10^{-3} mol O_2, 9.248×10^{-2} g O_2; (c) 8.00 mol $NaNO_3$, 6.8×10^2 g $NaNO_3$; (d) 1665 mol CO_2, 73.3 kg CO_2; (e) 18.86 mol CuO, 2.330 kg $CuCO_3$; (f) 0.4580 mol $C_2H_4Br_2$, 86.05 g $C_2H_4Br_2$

45. (a) 0.0686 mol Mg, 1.67 g Mg; (b) 2.701×10^{-3} mol O_2, 0.08644 g O_2; (c) 6.43 mol $MgCO_3$, 542 g $MgCO_3$ (d) 713 mol H_2O, 12.8 kg H_2O; (e) 16.31 mol BaO_2, 2762 g BaO_2; (f) 0.207 mol C_2H_4, 5.81 g C_2H_4

47. (a) volume HCl solution $\longrightarrow$ mol HCl $\longrightarrow$ mol $GaCl_3$; (b) 1.25 mol $GaCl_3$, 2.2×10^2 g $GaCl_3$

49. (a) 5.337×10^{22} molecules; (b) 10.41 g $Zn(CN)_2$

51. $SiO_2 + 3C \longrightarrow SiC + 2CO$, 4.50 kg SiO_2

53. 5.00×10^3 kg

55. 1.28×10^5 g CO_2

57. 161.40 mL KI solution

59. 176 g TiO_2

61. The limiting reactant is Cl2.

63. Percent yield = 31%

65. g $CCl_4 \longrightarrow$ mol $CCl_4 \longrightarrow$ mol $CCl_2F_2 \longrightarrow$ g CCl_2F_2, percent yield = 48.3%

67. percent yield = 91.3%

69. Convert mass of ethanol to moles of ethanol; relate the moles of ethanol to the moles of ether produced using the stoichiometry of the balanced equation. Convert moles of ether to grams; divide the actual grams of ether (determined through the density) by the theoretical mass to determine the percent yield; 87.6%

71. The conversion needed is mol Cr $\longrightarrow$ mol H_3PO_4. Then compare the amount of Cr to the amount of acid present. Cr is the limiting reactant.

73. $Na_2C_2O_4$ is the limiting reactant. percent yield = 86.6%

75. Only four molecules can be made.

77. This amount cannot be weighted by ordinary balances and is worthless.

79. 3.4×10^{-3} M H_2SO_4

81. 9.6×10^{-3} M Cl^-

83. 22.4%

85. The empirical formula is BH_3. The molecular formula is B_2H_6.

87. 49.6 mL

89. 13.64 mL

91. 1.22 M

93. 34.99 mL KOH

95. The empirical formula is WCl_4.

Chapter 8

1. The cutting edge of a knife that has been sharpened has a smaller surface area than a dull knife. Since pressure is force per unit area, a sharp knife will exert a higher pressure with the same amount of force and cut through material more effectively.

3. Lying down distributes your weight over a larger surface area, exerting less pressure on the ice compared to standing up. If you exert less pressure, you are less likely to break through thin ice.

5. 0.809 atm; 82.0 kPa

7. 2.2×10^2 kPa

9. Earth: 14.7 lb in^{-2}; Venus: 13.1×10^3 lb in^{-2}

11. (a) 101.5 kPa; (b) 51 torr drop

13. (a) 264 torr; (b) 35,200 Pa; (c) 0.352 bar

15. (a) 623 mm Hg; (b) 0.820 atm; (c) 83.1 kPa

17. With a closed-end manometer, no change would be observed, since the vaporized liquid would contribute equal, opposing pressures in both arms of the manometer tube. However, with an open-ended manometer, a higher pressure reading of the gas would be obtained than expected, since $P_{gas} = P_{atm} + P_{vol\ liquid}$.

19. As the bubbles rise, the pressure decreases, so their volume increases as suggested by Boyle's law.

21. (a) The number of particles in the gas increases as the volume increases. (b) temperature, pressure

23. The curve would be farther to the right and higher up, but the same basic shape.

25. About 12.2 L

27. 3.40×10^3 torr

29. 12.1 L

31. 217 L

33. 8.190×10^{-2} mol; 5.553 g

35. (a) 7.24×10^{-2} g; (b) 23.1 g; (c) 1.5×10^{-4} g

37. 5561 L

39. 46.4 g

41. For a gas exhibiting ideal behavior:

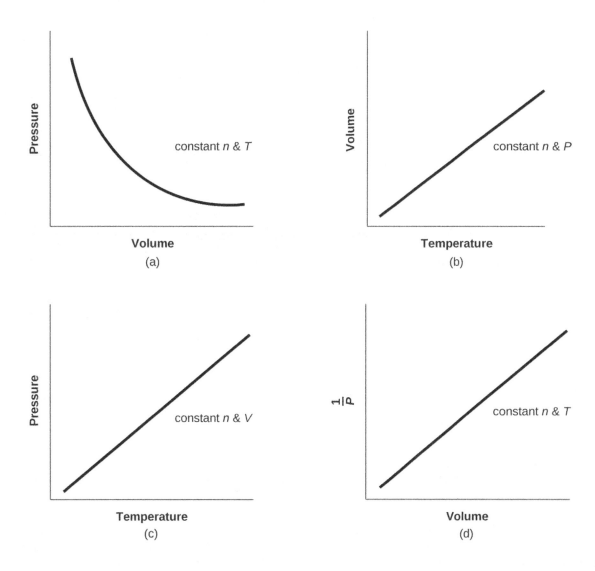

43. (a) 1.85 L CCl_2F_2; (b) 4.66 L CH_3CH_2F

45. 0.644 atm

47. The pressure decreases by a factor of 3.

49. 4.64 g L^{-1}

51. 38.8 g

53. 72.0 g mol^{-1}

55. 88.1 g mol^{-1}; PF_3

57. 141 atm

59. CH_4: 276 kPa; C_2H_6: 27 kPa; C_3H_8: 3.4 kPa

61. Yes

63. 740 torr

65. (a) Determine the moles of HgO that decompose; using the chemical equation, determine the moles of O_2 produced by decomposition of this amount of HgO; and determine the volume of O_2 from the moles of O_2, temperature, and pressure. (b) 0.308 L

67. (a) Determine the molar mass of CCl_2F_2. From the balanced equation, calculate the moles of H_2 needed for the complete reaction. From the ideal gas law, convert moles of H_2 into volume. (b) 3.72×10^3 L

69. (a) Balance the equation. Determine the grams of CO_2 produced and the number of moles. From the ideal gas law, determine the volume of gas. (b) 7.43×10^5 L

71. 42.00 L

73. (a) 18.0 L; (b) 0.533 atm

75. 10.57 L O_2

77. 5.40×10^5 L

79. XeF_2

81. 4.2 hours

83. Effusion can be defined as the process by which a gas escapes through a pinhole into a vacuum. Graham's law states that with a mixture of two gases A and B: $\left(\dfrac{\text{rate A}}{\text{rate B}}\right) = \left(\dfrac{\text{molar mass of B}}{\text{molar mass of A}}\right)^{1/2}$. Both A and B are in the same container at the same temperature, and therefore will have the same kinetic energy:

$KE_A = KE_B \quad KE = \frac{1}{2}mv^2$

Therefore, $\frac{1}{2}m_A v_A^2 = \frac{1}{2}m_B v_B^2$

$\dfrac{v_A^2}{v_B^2} = \dfrac{m_B}{m_A}$

$\left(\dfrac{v_A^2}{v_B^2}\right)^{1/2} = \left(\dfrac{m_B}{m_A}\right)^{1/2}$

$\dfrac{v_A}{v_B} = \left(\dfrac{m_B}{m_A}\right)^{1/2}$

85. F_2, N_2O, Cl_2, H_2S

87. 1.4; 1.2

89. 51.7 cm

91. Yes. At any given instant, there are a range of values of molecular speeds in a sample of gas. Any single molecule can speed up or slow down as it collides with other molecules. The average velocity of all the molecules is constant at constant temperature.

93. H_2O. Cooling slows the velocities of the He atoms, causing them to behave as though they were heavier.

95. (a) The number of collisions per unit area of the container wall is constant. (b) The average kinetic energy doubles. (c) The root mean square speed increases to $\sqrt{2}$ times its initial value; u_{rms} is proportional to $\sqrt{KE_{avg}}$.

97. (a) equal; (b) less than; (c) 29.48 g mol^{-1}; (d) 1.0966 g L^{-1}; (e) 0.129 g/L; (f) 4.01 × 10^5 g; net lifting capacity = 384 lb; (g) 270 L; (h) 39.1 kJ min^{-1}

99. Gases C, E, and F

101. The gas behavior most like an ideal gas will occur under the conditions in (b). Molecules have high speeds and move through greater distances between collision; they also have shorter contact times and interactions are less likely. Deviations occur with the conditions described in (a) and (c). Under conditions of (a), some gases may liquefy. Under conditions of (c), most gases will liquefy.

103. SF$_6$

105. (a) A straight horizontal line at 1.0; (b) When real gases are at low pressures and high temperatures they behave close enough to ideal gases that they are approximated as such, however, in some cases, we see that at a high pressure and temperature, the ideal gas approximation breaks down and is significantly different from the pressure calculated by the ideal gas equation (c) The greater the compressibility, the more the volume matters. At low pressures, the correction factor for intermolecular attractions is more significant, and the effect of the volume of the gas molecules on Z would be a small lowering compressibility. At higher pressures, the effect of the volume of the gas molecules themselves on Z would increase compressibility (see Figure 8.35) (d) Once again, at low pressures, the effect of intermolecular attractions on Z would be more important than the correction factor for the volume of the gas molecules themselves, though perhaps still small. At higher pressures and low temperatures, the effect of intermolecular attractions would be larger. See Figure 8.35 . (e) low temperatures

Chapter 9

1. The temperature of 1 gram of burning wood is approximately the same for both a match and a bonfire. This is an intensive property and depends on the material (wood). However, the overall amount of produced heat depends on the amount of material; this is an extensive property. The amount of wood in a bonfire is much greater than that in a match; the total amount of produced heat is also much greater, which is why we can sit around a bonfire to stay warm, but a match would not provide enough heat to keep us from getting cold.

3. Heat capacity refers to the heat required to raise the temperature of the mass of the substance 1 degree; specific heat refers to the heat required to raise the temperature of 1 gram of the substance 1 degree. Thus, heat capacity is an extensive property, and specific heat is an intensive one.

5. (a) 47.6 J/°C; 11.38 cal °C^{-1}; (b) 407 J/°C; 97.3 cal °C^{-1}

7. 1310; 313 cal

9. 7.15 °C

11. (a) 0.390 J/g °C; (b) Copper is a likely candidate.

13. We assume that the density of water is 1.0 g/cm^3(1 g/mL) and that it takes as much energy to keep the water at 85 °F as to heat it from 72 °F to 85 °F. We also assume that only the water is going to be heated. Energy required = 7.47 kWh

15. lesser; more heat would be lost to the coffee cup and the environment and so ΔT for the water would be lesser and the calculated q would be lesser

17. greater, since taking the calorimeter's heat capacity into account will compensate for the thermal energy transferred to the solution from the calorimeter; this approach includes the calorimeter itself, along with the solution, as "surroundings": $q_{rxn} = -(q_{solution} + q_{calorimeter})$; since both $q_{solution}$ and $q_{calorimeter}$ are negative, including the latter term (q_{rxn}) will yield a greater value for the heat of the dissolution

19. The temperature of the coffee will drop 1 degree.

21. 5.7 × 10^2 kJ

23. 38.5 °C

25. 2.2 kJ; The heat produced shows that the reaction is exothermic.

27. 1.4 kJ

29. 22.6. Since the mass and the heat capacity of the solution is approximately equal to that of the water, the two-fold increase in the amount of water leads to a two-fold decrease of the temperature change.

31. 11.7 kJ

33. 30%

35. 0.24 g

37. 1.4×10^2 Calories

39. The enthalpy change of the indicated reaction is for exactly 1 mol HCL and 1 mol NaOH; the heat in the example is produced by 0.0500 mol HCl and 0.0500 mol NaOH.

41. 25 kJ mol^{-1}

43. 81 kJ mol^{-1}

45. 5204.4 kJ

47. 1.83×10^{-2} mol

49. −802 kJ mol^{-1}

51. 15.5 kJ/°C

53. 7.43 g

55. No.

57. 459.6 kJ

59. −495 kJ/mol

61. 44.01 kJ/mol

63. −394 kJ

65. 265 kJ

67. 90.3 mol^{-1} of NO

69. (a) −1615.0 kJ mol^{-1}; (b) −484.3 kJ mol^{-1}; (c) 164.2 kJ; (d) −232.1 kJ

71. −54.04 kJ mol^{-1}

73. −2660 kJ mol^{-1}

75. 67.1 kJ

77. −122.8 kJ

79. 3.7 kg

81. On the assumption that the best rocket fuel is the one that gives off the most heat, B_2H_6 is the prime candidate.

83. −88.2 kJ

85. (a) $C_3H_8(g) + 5O_2(g) \longrightarrow 3CO_2(g) + 4H_2O(l)$; (b) 330 L; (c) −104.5 kJ mol^{-1}; (d) 75.4 °C

88. (a) −114 kJ;
(b) 30 kJ;
(c) −1055 kJ

91. The specific average bond distance is the distance with the lowest energy. At distances less than the bond distance, the positive charges on the two nuclei repel each other, and the overall energy increases.

92. The greater bond energy is in the figure on the left. It is the more stable form.

94.

$$HCl(g) \longrightarrow \frac{1}{2} H_2(g) + \frac{1}{2} Cl_2(g) \qquad \Delta H_1^\circ = -\Delta H_{f[HCl(g)]}^\circ$$

$$\frac{1}{2} H_2(g) \longrightarrow H(g) \qquad \Delta H_2^\circ = \Delta H_{f[H(g)]}^\circ$$

$$\frac{1}{2} Cl_2(g) \longrightarrow Cl(g) \qquad \Delta H_3^\circ = \Delta H_{f[Cl(g)]}^\circ$$

$$HCl(g) \longrightarrow H(g) + Cl(g) \qquad \Delta H_{298}^\circ = \Delta H_1^\circ + \Delta H_2^\circ + \Delta H_3^\circ$$

$$D_{HCl} = \Delta H_{298}^\circ = \Delta H_{f[HCl(g)]}^\circ + \Delta H_{f[H(g)]}^\circ + \Delta H_{f[Cl(g)]}^\circ$$

$$= -(-92.307 \text{ kJ}) + 217.97 \text{ kJ} + 121.3 \text{ kJ}$$

$$= 431.6 \text{ kJ}$$

96. The S–F bond in SF_4 is stronger.

98.

The C–C single bonds are longest.

100. (a) When two electrons are removed from the valence shell, the Ca radius loses the outermost energy level and reverts to the lower $n = 3$ level, which is much smaller in radius. (b) The +2 charge on calcium pulls the oxygen much closer compared with K, thereby increasing the lattice energy relative to a less charged ion. (c) Removal of the 4s electron in Ca requires more energy than removal of the 4s electron in K because of the stronger attraction of the nucleus and the extra energy required to break the pairing of the electrons. The second ionization energy for K requires that an electron be removed from a lower energy level, where the attraction is much stronger from the nucleus for the electron. In addition, energy is required to unpair two electrons in a full orbital. For Ca, the second ionization potential requires removing only a lone electron in the exposed outer energy level. (d) In Al, the removed electron is relatively unprotected and unpaired in a p orbital. The higher energy for Mg mainly reflects the unpairing of the 2s electron.

102. (d)

104. 4008 kJ/mol; both ions in MgO have twice the charge of the ions in LiF; the bond length is very similar and both have the same structure; a quadrupling of the energy is expected based on the equation for lattice energy

106. (a) Na_2O; Na^+ has a smaller radius than K^+; (b) BaS; Ba has a larger charge than K; (c) BaS; Ba and S have larger charges; (d) BaS; S has a larger charge

108. (e)

Chapter 10

1. Liquids and solids are similar in that they are matter composed of atoms, ions, or molecules. They are incompressible and have similar densities that are both much larger than those of gases. They are different in that liquids have no fixed shape, and solids are rigid.

3. They are similar in that the atoms or molecules are free to move from one position to another. They differ in that the particles of a liquid are confined to the shape of the vessel in which they are placed. In contrast, a gas will expand without limit to fill the space into which it is placed.

5. All atoms and molecules will condense into a liquid or solid in which the attractive forces exceed the kinetic energy of the molecules, at sufficiently low temperature.

7. (a) Dispersion forces occur as an atom develops a temporary dipole moment when its electrons are distributed asymmetrically about the nucleus. This structure is more prevalent in large atoms such as argon or radon. A second atom can then be distorted by the appearance of the dipole in the first atom. The electrons of the second atom are attracted toward the positive end of the first atom, which sets up a dipole in the second atom. The net result is rapidly fluctuating, temporary dipoles that attract one another (example: Ar). (b) A dipole-dipole attraction is a force that results from an electrostatic attraction of the positive end of one polar molecule for the negative end of another polar molecule (example: ICI molecules attract one another by dipole-dipole interaction). (c) Hydrogen bonds form whenever a hydrogen atom is bonded to one of the more electronegative atoms, such as a fluorine, oxygen, or nitrogen atom. The electrostatic attraction between the partially positive hydrogen atom in one molecule and the partially negative atom in another molecule gives rise to a strong dipole-dipole interaction called a hydrogen bond (example: $HF \cdots HF$).

9. The London forces typically increase as the number of electrons increase.

11. (a) $SiH_4 < HCl < H_2O$; (b) $F_2 < Cl_2 < Br_2$; (c) $CH_4 < C_2H_6 < C_3H_8$; (d) $N_2 < O_2 < NO$

13. Only rather small dipole-dipole interactions from C-H bonds are available to hold *n*-butane in the liquid state. Chloroethane, however, has rather large dipole interactions because of the Cl-C bond; the interaction is therefore stronger, leading to a higher boiling point.

15. −85 °C. Water has stronger hydrogen bonds so it melts at a higher temperature.

17. The hydrogen bond between two hydrogen fluoride molecules is stronger than that between two water molecules because the electronegativity of F is greater than that of O. Consequently, the partial negative charge on F is greater than that on O. The hydrogen bond between the partially positive H and the larger partially negative F will be stronger than that formed between H and O.

19. H-bonding is the principle IMF holding the DNA strands together. The H-bonding is between the $N - H$ and $C = O$.

21. (a) hydrogen bonding and dispersion forces; (b) dispersion forces; (c) dipole-dipole attraction and dispersion forces

23. The water molecules have strong intermolecular forces of hydrogen bonding. The water molecules are thus attracted strongly to one another and exhibit a relatively large surface tension, forming a type of "skin" at its surface. This skin can support a bug or paper clip if gently placed on the water.

25. Temperature has an effect on intermolecular forces: the higher the temperature, the greater the kinetic energies of the molecules and the greater the extent to which their intermolecular forces are overcome, and so the more fluid (less viscous) the liquid; the lower the temperature, the lesser the intermolecular forces are overcome, and so the less viscous the liquid.

27. (a) As the water reaches higher temperatures, the increased kinetic energies of its molecules are more effective in overcoming hydrogen bonding, and so its surface tension decreases. Surface tension and intermolecular forces are directly related. (b) The same trend in viscosity is seen as in surface tension, and for the same reason.

29. 1.9×10^{-4} m

31. The heat is absorbed by the ice, providing the energy required to partially overcome intermolecular attractive forces in the solid and causing a phase transition to liquid water. The solution remains at 0 °C until all the ice is melted. Only the amount of water existing as ice changes until the ice disappears. Then the temperature of the water can rise.

33. We can see the amount of liquid in an open container decrease and we can smell the vapor of some liquids.

35. The vapor pressure of a liquid decreases as the strength of its intermolecular forces increases.

37. As the temperature increases, the average kinetic energy of the molecules of gasoline increases and so a greater fraction of molecules have sufficient energy to escape from the liquid than at lower temperatures.

39. When the pressure of gas above the liquid is exactly 1 atm

41. approximately 95 °C

43. (a) At 5000 feet, the atmospheric pressure is lower than at sea level, and water will therefore boil at a lower temperature. This lower temperature will cause the physical and chemical changes involved in cooking the egg to proceed more slowly, and a longer time is required to fully cook the egg. (b) As long as the air surrounding the body contains less water vapor than the maximum that air can hold at that temperature, perspiration will evaporate, thereby cooling the body by removing the heat of vaporization required to vaporize the water.

45. Dispersion forces increase with molecular mass or size. As the number of atoms composing the molecules in this homologous series increases, so does the extent of intermolecular attraction via dispersion forces and, consequently, the energy required to overcome these forces and vaporize the liquids.

47. The boiling point of CS_2 is higher than that of CO_2 partially because of the higher molecular weight of CS_2; consequently, the attractive forces are stronger in CS_2. It would be expected, therefore, that the heat of vaporization would be greater than that of 9.8 kJ/mol for CO_2. A value of 28 kJ/mol would seem reasonable. A value of −8.4 kJ/mol would indicate a release of energy upon vaporization, which is clearly implausible.

49. The thermal energy (heat) needed to evaporate the liquid is removed from the skin.

51. 1130 kJ

53. (a) 13.0 kJ; (b) It is likely that the heat of vaporization will have a larger magnitude since in the case of vaporization the intermolecular interactions have to be completely overcome, while melting weakens or destroys only some of them.

55. At low pressures and 0.005 °C, the water is a gas. As the pressure increases to 4.6 torr, the water becomes a solid; as the pressure increases still more, it becomes a liquid. At 40 °C, water at low pressure is a vapor; at pressures higher than about 75 torr, it converts into a liquid. At −40 °C, water goes from a gas to a solid as the pressure increases above very low values.

57. (a) liquid; (b) solid; (c) gas; (d) gas; (e) gas; (f) gas

59.

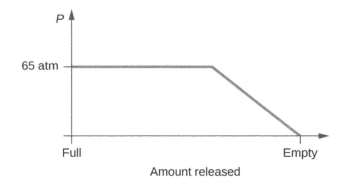

61. Yes, ice will sublime, although it may take it several days. Ice has a small vapor pressure, and some ice molecules form gas and escape from the ice crystals. As time passes, more and more solid converts to gas until eventually the clothes are dry.

63. (a)

(b)

(c)

(d)

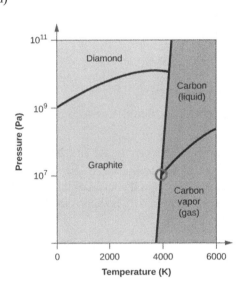

(e) liquid phase (f) sublimation

65. (e) molecular crystals

67. Ice has a crystalline structure stabilized by hydrogen bonding. These intermolecular forces are of comparable strength and thus require the same amount of energy to overcome. As a result, ice melts at a single temperature and not over a range of temperatures. The various, very large molecules that compose butter experience varied van der Waals attractions of various strengths that are overcome at various temperatures, and so the melting process occurs over a wide temperature range.

69. (a) ionic; (b) covalent network; (c) molecular; (d) metallic; (e) covalent network; (f) molecular; (g) molecular; (h) ionic; (i) ionic

71. X = ionic; Y = metallic; Z = covalent network

73. (b) metallic solid

75. The structure of this low-temperature form of iron (below 910 °C) is body-centered cubic. There is one-eighth atom at each of the eight corners of the cube and one atom in the center of the cube.

77. eight

79. 12

81. (a) 1.370 Å; (b) 19.26 g/cm

83. (a) 2.176 Å; (b) 3.595 g/cm^3

85. The crystal structure of Si shows that it is less tightly packed (coordination number 4) in the solid than Al (coordination number 12).

87. In a closest-packed array, two tetrahedral holes exist for each anion. If only half the tetrahedral holes are occupied, the numbers of anions and cations are equal. The formula for cadmium sulfide is CdS.

89. Co_3O_4

91. In a simple cubic array, only one cubic hole can be occupied be a cation for each anion in the array. The ratio of thallium to iodide must be 1:1; therefore, the formula for thallium is TlI.

93. 59.95%; The oxidation number of titanium is +4.

95. Both ions are close in size: Mg, 0.65; Li, 0.60. This similarity allows the two to interchange rather easily. The difference in charge is generally compensated by the switch of Si^{4+} for Al^{3+}.

97. Mn_2O_3

99. 1.48 Å

101. 2.874 Å

103. 20.2°

105. 1.74×10^4 eV

Chapter 11

1. A solution can vary in composition, while a compound cannot vary in composition. Solutions are homogeneous at the molecular level, while other mixtures are heterogeneous.

3. (a) The process is endothermic as the solution is consuming heat. (b) Attraction between the K^+ and NO_3^- ions is stronger than between the ions and water molecules (the ion-ion interactions have a lower, more negative energy). Therefore, the dissolution process increases the energy of the molecular interactions, and it consumes the thermal energy of the solution to make up for the difference. (c) No, an ideal solution is formed with no appreciable heat release or consumption.

5. (a) ion-dipole forces; (b) dipole-dipole forces; (c) dispersion forces; (d) dispersion forces; (e) hydrogen bonding

7. Heat is released when the total intermolecular forces (IMFs) between the solute and solvent molecules are stronger than the total IMFs in the pure solute and in the pure solvent: Breaking weaker IMFs and forming stronger IMFs releases heat. Heat is absorbed when the total IMFs in the solution are weaker than the total of those in the pure solute and in the pure solvent: Breaking stronger IMFs and forming weaker IMFs absorbs heat.

9. Crystals of NaCl dissolve in water, a polar liquid with a very large dipole moment, and the individual ions become strongly solvated. Hexane is a nonpolar liquid with a dipole moment of zero and, therefore, does not significantly interact with the ions of the NaCl crystals.

11. (a) $Fe(NO_3)_3$ is a strong electrolyte, thus it should completely dissociate into Fe^{3+} and (NO_3^-) ions. Therefore, (z) best represents the solution. (b) $Fe(NO_3)_3(s) \longrightarrow Fe^{3+}(aq) + 3NO_3^-(aq)$

13. (a) high conductivity (solute is an ionic compound that will dissociate when dissolved); (b) high conductivity (solute is a strong acid and will ionize completely when dissolved); (c) nonconductive (solute is a covalent compound, neither acid nor base, unreactive towards water); (d) low conductivity (solute is a weak base and will partially ionize when dissolved)

15. (a) ion-dipole; (b) hydrogen bonds; (c) dispersion forces; (d) dipole-dipole attractions; (e) dispersion forces

17. The solubility of solids usually decreases upon cooling a solution, while the solubility of gases usually decreases upon heating.

19. 40%

21. 2.80 g

23. 2.9 atm

25. 102 L HCl

27. The strength of the bonds between like molecules is stronger than the strength between unlike molecules. Therefore, some regions will exist in which the water molecules will exclude oil molecules and other regions will exist in which oil molecules will exclude water molecules, forming a heterogeneous region.

29. Both form homogeneous solutions; their boiling point elevations are the same, as are their lowering of vapor pressures. Osmotic pressure and the lowering of the freezing point are also the same for both solutions.

31. (a) Find number of moles of HNO_3 and H_2O in 100 g of the solution. Find the mole fractions for the components.
(b) The mole fraction of HNO_3 is 0.378. The mole fraction of H_2O is 0.622.

33. (a) $X_{Na_2CO_3} = 0.0119$; $X_{H_2O} = 0.988$; (b) $X_{NH_4NO_3} = 0.0928$; $X_{H_2O} = 0.907$; (c) $X_{Cl_2} = 0.192$; $X_{CH_2Cl_2} = 0.808$; (d) $X_{C_5H_9N} = 0.00426$; $X_{CHCl_3} = 0.997$

35. In a 1 M solution, the mole is contained in exactly 1 L of solution. In a 1 m solution, the mole is contained in exactly 1 kg of solvent.

37. (a) Determine the molar mass of HNO_3. Determine the number of moles of acid in the solution. From the number of moles and the mass of solvent, determine the molality. (b) 33.7 m

39. (a) 6.70×10^{-1} m; (b) 5.67 m; (c) 2.8 m; (d) 0.0358 m

41. 1.08 m

43. (a) Determine the molar mass of sucrose; determine the number of moles of sucrose in the solution; convert the mass of solvent to units of kilograms; from the number of moles and the mass of solvent, determine the molality; determine the difference between the boiling point of water and the boiling point of the solution; determine the new boiling point. (b) 100.5 °C

45. (a) Determine the molar mass of sucrose; determine the number of moles of sucrose in the solution; convert the mass of solvent to units of kilograms; from the number of moles and the mass of solvent, determine the molality; determine the difference between the freezing temperature of water and the freezing temperature of the solution; determine the new freezing temperature. (b) −1.8 °C

47. (a) Determine the molar mass of $Ca(NO_3)_2$; determine the number of moles of $Ca(NO_3)_2$ in the solution; determine the number of moles of ions in the solution; determine the molarity of ions, then the osmotic pressure. (b) 2.67 atm

49. (a) Determine the molal concentration from the change in boiling point and K_b; determine the moles of solute in the solution from the molal concentration and mass of solvent; determine the molar mass from the number of moles and the mass of solute. (b) 2.1×10^2 g mol^{-1}

51. No. Pure benzene freezes at 5.5 °C, and so the observed freezing point of this solution is depressed by $\Delta T_f = 5.5 - 0.4 = 5.1$ °C. The value computed, assuming no ionization of HCl, is $\Delta T_f = (1.0$ m$)(5.14$ °C/m$) = 5.1$ °C. Agreement of these values supports the assumption that HCl is not ionized.

53. 144 g mol^{-1}

55. 0.870 °C

57. S_8

59. 1.39×10^4 g mol^{-1}

61. 54 g

63. 100.26 °C

65. (a) $X_{CH_3OH} = 0.590$; $X_{C_2H_5OH} = 0.410$; (b) Vapor pressures are: CH_3OH: 55 torr; C_2H_5OH: 18 torr; (c) CH_3OH: 0.75; C_2H_5OH: 0.25

67. The ions and compounds present in the water in the beef lower the freezing point of the beef below −1 °C.

69. $\Delta bp = K_b m = (1.20\ °C/m)\left(\dfrac{9.41\text{g} \times \frac{1\,\text{mol Hg Cl}_2}{271.496\,\text{g}}}{0.03275\,\text{kg}} \right) = 1.27\ °C$

The observed change equals the theoretical change; therefore, no dissociation occurs.

71.

Colloidal System	Dispersed Phase	Dispersion Medium
starch dispersion	starch	water
smoke	solid particles	air
fog	water	air
pearl	water	calcium carbonate ($CaCO_3$)
whipped cream	air	cream
floating soap	air	soap
jelly	fruit juice	pectin gel
milk	butterfat	water
ruby	chromium(III) oxide (Cr_2O_3)	aluminum oxide (Al_2O_3)

73. Colloidal dispersions consist of particles that are much bigger than the solutes of typical solutions. Colloidal particles are either very large molecules or aggregates of smaller species that usually are big enough to scatter light. Colloids are homogeneous on a macroscopic (visual) scale, while solutions are homogeneous on a microscopic (molecular) scale.

75. If they are placed in an electrolytic cell, dispersed particles will move toward the electrode that carries a charge opposite to their own charge. At this electrode, the charged particles will be neutralized and will coagulate as a precipitate.

Index